Africa

Africa
Geography and Development

ALAN B. MOUNTJOY
Emeritus Reader in Geography in the University of
London, Royal Holloway and Bedford New College

DAVID HILLING
Senior Lecturer in Geography in the University of
London, Royal Holloway and Bedford New College
Formerly Lecturer in Geography at the University of Ghana, Accra

Hutchinson
London Melbourne Sydney Auckland Johannesburg

Barnes & Noble Books
Totowa, New Jersey

Hutchinson Education

An imprint of Century Hutchinson Ltd

62–65 Chandos Place, London WC2N 4NW

Century Hutchinson Australia Pty Ltd
PO Box 496, 16–22 Church Street, Hawthorn,
Victoria 3122, Australia

Century Hutchinson New Zealand Limited
PO Box 40–086, Glenfield, Auckland 10,
New Zealand

Century Hutchinson South Africa (Pty) Ltd
PO Box 337, Berglvei 2012, South Africa

First published 1988

First published in the USA 1988 by
Barnes & Noble Books
81 Adams Drive,
Totowa, New Jersey, 07512

Set in 10/12 point Linotron Melior

Printed and bound in Great Britain by
Richard Clay Ltd, Chichester

British Library Cataloguing-in-Publication Data

Mountjoy, Alan B.
Africa : geography and development.
1. Africa—Economic conditions—1960–
2. Africa—Description and travel—1977–
I. Title II. Hilling, David
330.96'0328 HC800

Library of Congress Cataloging-in-Publication Data

Mountjoy, Alan B.
Africa, Geography and Development.

Bibliography: p.
Includes index
1. Africa—economic conditions—1960–
2. Africa—description and travel—1977–
I. Hilling, David. II. Title
HC800.M68 1987 330.96'0328 87-1306

ISBN (UK) 0 09 170321 2 (paper)
ISBN (USA) 0–389–20722–5 (cloth)
ISBN (USA) 0–389–20723–3 (paper)

Contents

Part Nine The Zambezi and Limpopo Lands

Part Ten East Africa and the Islands

List of Figures

List of Tables

Preface

Africa has undergone great changes during the last thirty years and all too frequently its problems have come to command world attention. In presenting an up-to-date geography of Africa, the present authors feel that a mere revision of an earlier text of twenty years ago (Mountjoy and Embleton, *Africa, a Geographical Study*) would be inadequate. While some of the physical geography and regional divisions have been retained, the present book gives a new focus to the human geography with an emphasis upon economic and social development.

The preoccupation of African states today is with economic and social betterment, and this is now reflected in the human geography. We hold the view that any modern text of African geography should proceed from an analysis of physical and human resources to show their planned interactions, and make understandable the diversity of attempts at economic and social betterment that have been taking place over the last thirty years. The regional approach has been adopted as a logical scheme of analysis, but the treatment is not stereotyped and is adjusted to suit the varying character of different countries and the reliability and availability of information. We attempt not merely to cover the basic geography of Africa's fifty states, but to show that geography's relevance to the development problems with which each of these states now grapple. So far there have been but few success stories in African development planning, but the variety of reasons for failure must be grasped and current planning assessed with new realism.

We thus hope to offer a new and more relevant approach to Africa's geography, which will be of value in schools and universities and also to those with a broader interest in the continent's development progress and potential.

The spelling of African place and tribal names varies between different authorities. Here, those generally used in Britain have been adopted, following the spelling in *The Times World Atlas*. Metric units are used throughout the book, but conversion tables have been added for those more familiar with imperial units. Statistics are important in the book, but it is worth remembering that many African statistics lack the developed world's accuracy, indeed, many may be little more than 'guesstimates' even though they may appear under the World Bank or United Nations' imprint. Nevertheless we record our grateful thanks to these two bodies and affiliated organizations for the tremendous flow of statistical material they now publish. In most of the more general tables the order of countries follows the divisions given in the World Bank's *World Development Report 1985*, this order being based upon each country's GDP per capita within groupings that distinguish economies at different stages of development.

We record our thanks to Professor Embleton for permission to use some of his material in Mountjoy and Embleton, *Africa, a Geographical Study*; to Mr Ron Halfhide and Mrs Gilly Sharp for their dedicated work on the maps; to Mr Roy Davies for help with the photographs; to Mr Donald May and Bilfinger + Berger, Bauaktiengesellschaft, Wiesbaden, for assistance in obtaining illustrations; and to Mrs Liz Carey and Kathy Roberts for their typing.

A. B. M., D. H. January 1987

1

Introduction: geography and development

During the forty years since the ending of the Second World War Africa has commanded world attention, foremost for being the scene of the greatest acts of decolonization the world has known. Unlike the other continents, almost the whole of Africa was in the hands of colonial powers – Britain, France, Belgium, Spain and Portugal (Italy had lost her possessions during the war). These and other developed countries entered the post-war period with an enhanced perception of the poverty and backwardness of so much of the world and with the realization that the scientific and technological advances made in the war years could be employed in their eradication. In their own cases European economic development was spread over almost two centuries and in its progress nurtured both technological and social revolutions. In the last century the mainstream of economic development passed Africa by: now she is a continent in a hurry and the post-war years have seen Africa struggling to emerge into the modern world of which it had known so little.

Contemporary Africa is a continent of change: economies are being transformed, social structures and ideologies modified and aspirations lifted. Dynamic forces are at play as African peoples pass through agricultural, industrial, technological, social and political revolutions all at once. Peoples recently self-sufficient and living in relative isolation are being pulled into the complexities of Western commercial and urban ways of life, into close contact with other tribes and faiths and into new social and political groupings. Not surprisingly, the development road is rarely smooth: civil wars, harsh repression, crippling blows from an adverse environment, the inadequacies of leaders, the warpings of political ideologies – all are part of what, on balance, is a disappointing account of development over the last forty years.

The winds of change blew through Africa during the 1950s and 1960s, spearheaded by decolonization and the withdrawal of the 'Colonial masters'. In the period 1954–64 the number of independent African states more than quintupled. In most cases independence was negotiated peacefully, but in others bloody uprisings, sometimes lasting years, became necessary and set back development by years.

It is tempting to attribute the low level of African development to its history of colonial subjugation, but this is too simplistic. After all, except for half a dozen years under the Italian flag, Ethiopia was never colonized, yet it is the poorest of African states. Historical factors undoubtedly have played a part but geographical factors must also be cited. First, the size and shape of Africa must be appreciated. It is a compact land mass second only in size to Asia. Its area of 30,300,000 km^2 (11,700,000 square miles) is four times the size of the United States and, being almost bisected by the equator, it is the most tropical of continents with 23,400,000 km^2 (9,000,000 square miles) lying within the tropics, and is

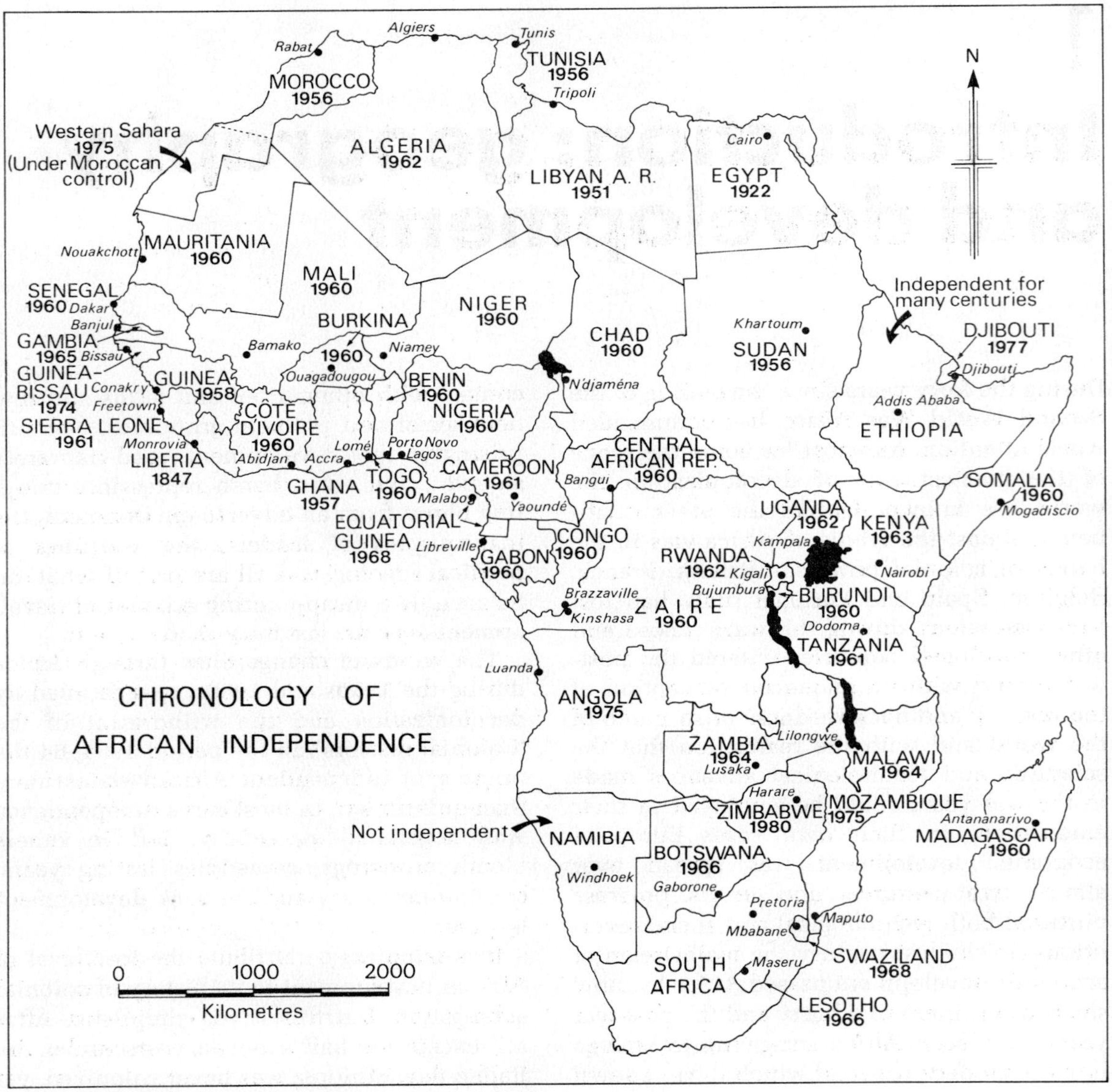

Figure 1 The chronology of African independence

thus subjected to a range of torrid climates. The compact shape offers little articulation of the coastline; there are few good harbours and penetration of the interior involves tremendous distances. For example, from the Copper Belt of Zaire and Zambia as the crow flies it is 1600 km to the west coast (1000 miles); by train to the copper ports is almost 2000 km (1250 miles).

The lack of major inlets in the coastline, a shallow sea for some little distance offshore, especially in parts of West Africa, and strong currents are further contributing factors that delayed discovery and retarded economic development. Much of the coastline is uninviting: there are long stretches of desert coastline and in West Africa the sea is bordered by swamp and mangrove forests. Other physical features discouraged penetration inland. Much of Africa consists of old, hard rocks forming plateau country; rivers fall in rapids over the plateau edge to a (usually) narrow coastplain but they may often have delta mouths. Thus the economic value of the larger rivers for transport is much impaired, although there is a good potential for hydroelectric power.

The slow opening up of Africa is also a reflection of the fact that explorers and merchants were more enticed by the Indies. The conquest and penetration of the uninviting deserts and coasts of Africa seemed to offer little; no great civilizations with riches of gold and silver were encountered as in Latin America. Slaves and tropical commodities eventually heralded settlement and penetration and then serious colonization with the 'Scramble for Africa' after the Congress of Berlin in 1884. Even so, the great heat and humidity of Africa's tropical lowlands were conducive to serious diseases – sleeping sickness, malaria, yellow fever – which took great toll of the early white administrators, merchants and missionaries. Only now in the post-war period are these diseases becoming tamed.

Africa's great size is reflected in the areas of African states. Even with the present fifty independent states the average area is quite high at 738,000 km^2 (285,000 square miles), but populations are low (average 10 million). Here lies the root of many economic difficulties – an excess of area and a deficiency of population. The weaker a state, the greater its need of friends and assistance. One consequence of this excessive political fragmentation is in attempts to play off Western democracies against Eastern communist states in the seeking of aid. Another consequence of the large number of political units lies in great lengths of boundaries and their division among many neighbours: Sudan has eight neighbours, Zaire has nine. Long boundaries and many neighbours add to defence costs and the danger of strife. Also, small populations limit the size of the market and increase the per capita cost of government and defence. In addition, small states often find it difficult to attract investment and loans from overseas.

Economic progress was retarded by sparseness of population in Africa, its tribal divisions and the subsistence nature of society. The mines, plantations and commercial farms that the colonists established drew in the African peoples, as did the new towns and ports. Law and order and a basic infrastructure came into being but little manufacturing industry, for manufactures became imported in exchange for the exported primary products. In terms of economic development colonist sights were set low: government incomes, mainly derived from taxation of subsistence peasantry, were small and both social and business infrastructure were rudimentary and progressed slowly. Before 1945 there was no pattern of international aid-giving and worldwide financial assistance. Development economics was in its infancy and planned economic development was a new concept whose implementation became delayed first by the depression years of the 1930s and then by the Second World War.

Purposed and planned development measures in Africa really did not begin until after the war, and they were soon to be overtaken by the great movement for decolonization. Generally – and often generously – helped by former 'mother' countries and such new bodies as the World Bank and the Development Assistance Committee of the OECD, the newly independent states grappled with development among a host of problems. Progress has been disappointing and results limited: although over thirty years significant advances have been made, to many they scarcely seem commensurate with the billions of pounds invested and the long period of endeavour. What is beyond doubt as we approach the last decade of the twentieth century is the serious under-development of Africa, no matter what criteria are applied. The average per capita income figures usually quoted beg a number of questions regarding the accuracy of the population and financial

Table 1 *Basic statistics*

Country	GNP per capita (US$, 1983)	Population (Total, 1983 (millions)	Av. Ann. growth, 1973–83 (%)	Life expectancy) (years)	Energy consumption per cap., 1983 (kg oil equiv.)	Illiteracy* (% for over-15s)
Chad	110	4.8	2.1	43	—	92
Ethiopia	120	41.0	2.7	43	19	96
Mali	160	7.2	2.5	45	22	90
Zaire	170	30.0	2.5	51	77	43
Equatorial Guinea	180	0.3	2.4	44	—	—
Guinea Bissau	180	0.8	1.8	38	—	80
Burkina Faso	180	6.5	1.9	44	22	91
Malawi	210	6.6	3.0	44	45	37
Uganda	220	14.0	2.8	49	23	48
Mozambique	230	13.1	2.6	46	95	73
Burundi	240	4.5	2.2	47	17	73
Niger	240	6.1	3.0	45	43	92
Tanzania	240	21.0	3.3	51	38	27
Somalia	250	5.1	2.8	45	84	98
Rwanda	270	5.7	3.4	47	35	51
Central African Republic	280	2.5	2.3	48	35	93
Togo	280	2.8	2.6	49	88	84
The Gambia	290	0.7	2.8	36	—	80
Benin	290	3.8	2.8	48	39	75
Guinea	300	5.8	2.0	37	54	92
São Tome and Principe	310	0.1	1.2	65	—	—
Ghana	310	12.8	3.1	59	111	70
Madagascar	310	9.5	2.6	49	59	50
Comoros	320	0.3	3.3	48	—	42
Cape Verde	320	0.3	—	64	—	63
Sierra Leone	330	3.6	2.1	38	102	85
Djibouti	340	0.4	7.1	50	—	—
Kenya	340	19.0	4.0	57	109	53
Sudan	400	20.8	3.2	48	66	85
Senegal	440	6.2	2.8	46	151	94
Lesotho	460	1.5	2.5	53	—	41
Angola	470	8.2	2.6	43	226	97
Liberia	480	2.1	3.3	49	357	75
Mauritania	480	1.6	2.2	46	130	83
Zambia	580	6.3	3.2	51	432	53
Egypt	700	45.2	2.5	58	532	61
Côte d'Ivoire	710	9.5	4.6	52	186	80
Zimbabwe	740	8.0	3.2	56	491	32
Morocco	760	20.8	2.6	52	258	79
Nigeria	770	93.6	2.7	49	150	66
Cameroon	820	9.6	3.1	54	128	59
Swaziland	870	0.7	2.3	55	—	45
Botswana	920	1.0	3.6	61	—	59
Mauritius	1160	1.0	1.6	67	—	39
Congo	1230	1.8	3.1	63	216	83
Tunisia	1290	6.9	2.5	62	473	48
Algeria	2320	20.6	3.1	57	982	74
South Africa	2490	31.5	2.4	64	2278	43
Gabon	3950	0.7	1.3	50	—	87
Libya	8480	3.4	4.3	58	2769	61

Note:
* Illiteracy figures are mainly for 1975–80.

Sources: World Development Report 1985 (OUP, 1985), Tables 1 and 8; *Geographical Digest 1984 (Philip, 1984); UNESCO Statistical Yearbook 1980.*

statistics, and the quality of national statistics for most African countries is open to doubt. Nevertheless, per capita income does provide a basis for comparison, and more than twenty African states – about two-thirds of the world total – have less than $400 and come in the World Bank's 'low income' group. Only Libya, in consequence of its oil revenue and relatively small population, has lifted itself into the World Bank's 'high income' group. Table 1 reveals that the mass of Africans live in poverty, the Gross National Product (GNP) per head is low, levels of life expectancy are low, rates of population increase are high, and relatively few Africans can read or write. African economies show a high proportion of subsistence agriculture with very limited investment and appreciation of technology. Manufacturing industry is minimal owing to a lack of capital, and unfamiliarity with machinery and its maintenance places a heavy reliance upon expatriate managers and technocrats. Levels of living are low, whether judged by possession of consumer goods, of vehicles or of telephones. Africa is very much a Third World continent.

Much of Africa is hostile to measures for development owing to its climate, vegetation and terrain. By hard work over the last century the infrastructure – roads, railways, power supplies, telephone, banks, settlements – in better endowed locations allowed limited and local spurts of economic advancement, generally based upon mineral income or commercial agriculture: the Copper Belt in interior Zambia or the nodes of development scattered along the railway and its branches in Kenya come to mind. Spatially these centres of economic activity are like oases amid a desert of subsistence agriculture and widespread, little-controlled pastoralism. It is in these centres that the modern world rubs shoulders with the African world of tradition.

DUALISM

The introduction of money and cash-crop economies and modern manufacturing industry in such favoured areas, paralleling the traditional subsistence way of life, exemplifies *dualism*. Within these countries two differing types of economy with differing technologies are demonstrated. The traditional sector operates usually in small family units, is labour-intensive, with little invested capital; it is concerned mainly with agriculture and principally is aimed at subsistence. The modern sector of the economy operates in large units, uses hired labour, is supported by capital investment and uses advanced (or relatively advanced) technologies; it is concerned mainly with plantations, mines, manufacturing industry and utilities.

The two types of economy nurture two very different types of society, the one being an imported social system from the West and the other indigenous and traditional. In these two societies there will be differing values, attitudes and aspirations. Thus there is more to dualism than the mere differences between subsistence and exchange sectors, for dualism is manifested in a money economy and financial services; in economic organization; in technological advances; in new habits and ways of life; and it exhibits a marked spatial aspect by bringing about regional inequalities of centre and periphery character. Other factors that need emphasis are the inbuilt features of the modern sector, the lack of which retards change in the traditional sector. These features include access to capital, finance and credit; to economic organization and division of labour; to foreign markets and firms – facilities denied or generally inaccessible to the small economic units in the traditional sector. Industrial policies furthering import-substitute industries discriminate heavily in favour of the modern sector at the expense of agriculture and artisanal industry. They even protect the larger-scale modern factories from the competition of the village workshop. Consequently such policies further regional inequalities that are already in being and which, from a national point of view, should be reduced. The dual economy is not a passive institutional element, but is dynamic and divisive in its economic, social and spatial effects. It is the quickening dynamism inherent in the fusion of the dual economy elements that carries forward the economic development of Third World economies, and with their social and spatial extensions makes the term 'modernization' appropriate. Development – in the widest sense of the term – is proving to be a difficult and uncomfortable process, mainly because of the evident divisive nature of the growing modern sector of whichever African economy one chooses to examine.

Development measures are accompanied by growing dualism and growing spatial inequalities, for favoured areas act as cores pulling in labour and resources from the surrounding areas. The settlement hierarchy and income distribution become imbalanced and population mobility brings increasing social and political pressures. Regional imbalances are likely to deepen rather than lessen, and there becomes a need for government planning measures to give support to the periphery. Unless such corrective policies are applied the forces of dualism encourage large-scale enterprise and neglect the small-scale operator in his rural setting. Agriculture thus remains backward, being denied capital and modern resources, and soon is inadequate to feed the growing urban masses. These trends are enhanced by practically every poor African country seeing its development in terms of major capital works and the development of manufacturing industry. All over the continent successive development plans channelled vast sums, given or loaned, into the industrial sector and its supports. Few were prepared to accept that their poverty, which restricted development, stemmed mainly from their inadequate and inefficient agriculture sectors. The vicious circle of poverty ('you are poor because you are poor') is no longer absolute in its restriction on capital formation; foreign aid, development and commercial loans can break the circle and start the upward spiral with new investment, theoretically to give a forward move in the economy.

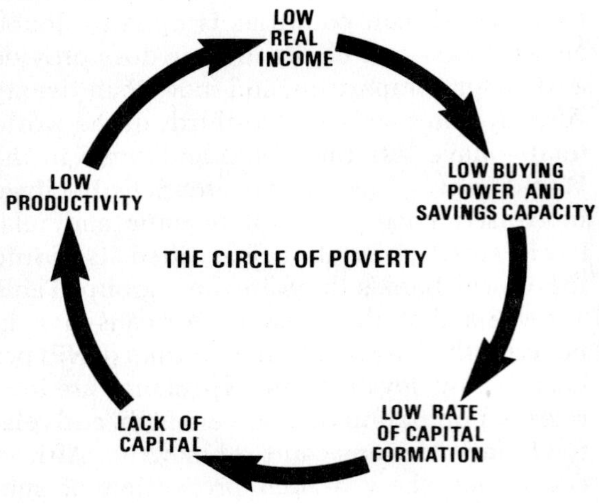

Figure 2 The circle of poverty

It is apparent that there is now a substantial understanding of development theory and of interrelationships invoked by development planning. It is therefore all the more disappointing that efforts at development in Africa over the past thirty years have been so limited in their results. There is much to go wrong and every state has been confronted by development problems unique to its own conditions. Aspects of these problems and the related geography are now to be examined.

PART ONE: PHYSICAL GEOGRAPHY

2 Geology, structure and landforms

The larger part of Africa consists of a vast continental shield, stretching between the Atlas Mountains in the north and the Cape Ranges in the extreme south, and comparable in form and origin to the Brazilian or Laurentian shields. Since the end of the Pre-Cambrian era this relatively rigid block has been subjected to vertical displacement and fracturing, but it has suffered only comparatively slight folding. It is now apparent that the shield's structure is by no means simple, and certainly in the Pre-Cambrian era it was subjected to several periods of earth movement, the surface expressions of which have been removed by long, unimpeded periods of denudation. Only in the extreme north-western and southern extremities of the continent – the Atlas and Cape Ranges – do the present landforms relate directly to orogenic structures.

THE GEOLOGICAL RECORD

The broad outlines of Africa's geology are represented in Figure 3. It is well to remind ourselves that for many parts of Africa the geology is only known in outline and detailed geological surveys have still to be undertaken. However, even in outline some knowledge of the geology is an essential background to an understanding of the continent's structure and relief, and of the development potential. Crystalline rocks of the Pre-Cambrian basement shield underlie most of the continent and outcrop at the surface over approximately one-third of the total, being particularly important in much of West Africa, the Sudan, East Africa, Zimbabwe and as an aureole around younger rocks in the Zaire basin. Pre-Cambrian formations in places consist of thick, unfossilized sediments which, more importantly, have been subjected to metamorphic and igneous activity; this is often associated with considerable mineralization and forms the basis of significant mining industries in West Africa (iron ore, gold, diamonds, manganese) and Central Africa (copper, cobalt, uranium, chrome). It has been said of the Pre-Cambrian era that 'its geographic importance is equalled by its economic importance'.[1*]

Except in small areas of the Sahara and northern Africa, Cambrian strata are conspicuous mainly by their absence. Much of southern Africa is covered with Palaeozoic sedimentaries, sandstones and shales of Silurian/Devonian age and in the Cape Ranges these have been folded against the margins of the basement block. In northern Africa, the record of the Lower Palaeozoic is rather more complete and in parts of West Africa and the Sahara is represented by shallow-water limestones, sandstones and shales.

In terms of geographical extent the most significant rocks of southern Africa are the

* Superior figures refer to the References at the end of chapters.

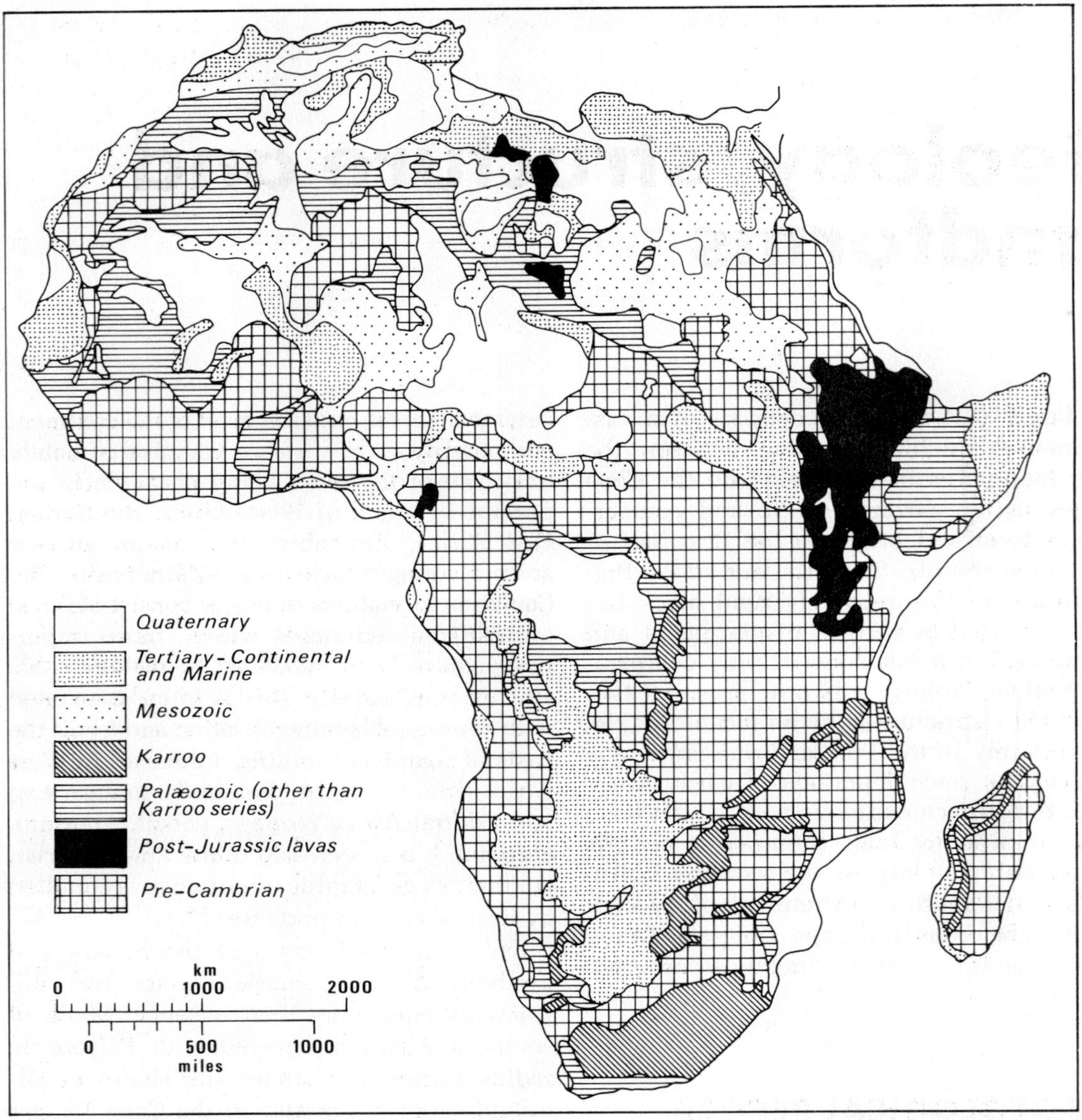

Figure 3 The geology of Africa

so-called Karroo series. These vary in age from Carboniferous to Lower Jurassic, sit unconformably on the older rocks and, apart from some volcanics, consist mainly of great thicknesses (as much as 2000 m in places) of sediment accumulated under continental conditions varying from swamp/lacustrine to glacial or arid and representing the products of prolonged erosion of the Pre-Cambrian basement. The economic importance of the Karroo series rests in the fact that they contain Africa's only significant coal deposits and are the basis for the coal mining industry in South Africa and Zimbabwe.

Broadly comparable in age with the Karroo series of southern Africa are certain continental formations of the Sahara. First, there are the series of Nubian sandstones of Libya and parts of the Sudan, accumulations in broad basins from Carboniferous to early Cretaceous. Second, in the western Sahara, are the sandstones, conglomerates and clays of the Continental Intercalaire dated to the Jurassic and Cretaceous. In general these rocks have little significance for their minerals but do form the major water-bearing strata below the surface of the desert.

During the Cretaceous period, sagging of the northern part of the continent allowed marine transgression which brought sediments, now represented by limestones and sandstones, to a belt stretching discontinuously from the Gulf of Guinea to the Mediterranean. During this time southern Africa remained essentially continental, with marine formations found only on the coastal margins where downwarping allowed great thicknesses to accumulate locally.

It is in the sedimentaries of this period, especially in northern and western Africa, that the continent's main oil reserves are to be found; but it is a measure of their recent identification that a major textbook of 1961 could claim that 'Apart from the fields along the shores of the Gulf of Suez in Egypt, and a small yield from three tiny fields in Algeria and four in Morocco, Africa has no oil'[2].

The Tertiary period saw the gradual withdrawal of the marine conditions from northern Africa, and the bulk of the continent was once again exposed to the agents of sub-aerial denudation and continental weathering, and deposition in interior basins often to considerable thicknesses – as much as 150 m in the Kalahari. Over much of the continent the present surface deposits reflect these weathering processes: for example, the extensive areas of laterite and alumina/ferruginous accumulation in the humid areas, and the superficial sands of the arid areas. Indeed, there are large areas where it is difficult to find bedrock near the surface that could be used for road or building stone, railway ballast or breakwater and dam construction, and suitable rock has sometimes to be transported to construction sites over considerable distances and at great cost.

Several important points emerge from this brief review. First, it is necessary to emphasize that at the local level knowledge of African geology is often imprecise and much money and effort has still to be put into geological exploration if African countries are to capitalize on their mineral resources. Second, in geographical and economic terms it is impossible to over-estimate the importance of the Pre-Cambrian basement – it provides the foundation of the continent and contains a wealth of mineral resources. Third, while not as extensive as the Pre-Cambrian, the Karroo series are vital for the coal that they contain in the southern parts of the continent and for their aquifers in the north. Fourth, the distribution of the Cretaceous marine sediments provides a valuable guide to the existence of oil and has provided several northern and western, coastal states with considerable oil wealth. In some measure, the oil found most abundantly in the northern part of the continent is complemented by the coal that is found almost entirely in the south.

THE STRUCTURAL EVOLUTION OF THE CONTINENT

There is increasing evidence from plate tectonics to support the view that the African block was once part of a larger land mass, Gondwanaland, which gradually drifted apart to give the now separate southern continents and India. There are similarities in the geological record, and in particular there is evidence from India, South America, Australia and South Africa of tillites and fossil boulder clays indicative of a shared ice age in the Carboniferous period. Similarities of rock type and magnetic evidence also suggest a common origin.

However, while the causes of the break-up of Gondwanaland in the Mesozoic period are not our concern, the results most definitely are. Much of Africa is characterized by extensive, rather monotonous planation surfaces, generally at altitudes of over 1200 m, and it has been suggested by L.C. King[3] that these represent the old Gondwanaland surface. King also argues that Africa's coastline took on approximately its present form at the time of the break-up and that subsequent modifications have been mainly by deposition at the margins. Because the Gondwanaland interior was much higher than its original distant margins there was considerable fracturing as the blocks moved apart, with the creation of escarpments towards the centre. Africa, being near the centre of Gondwanaland, therefore emerged as a continent with a high interior

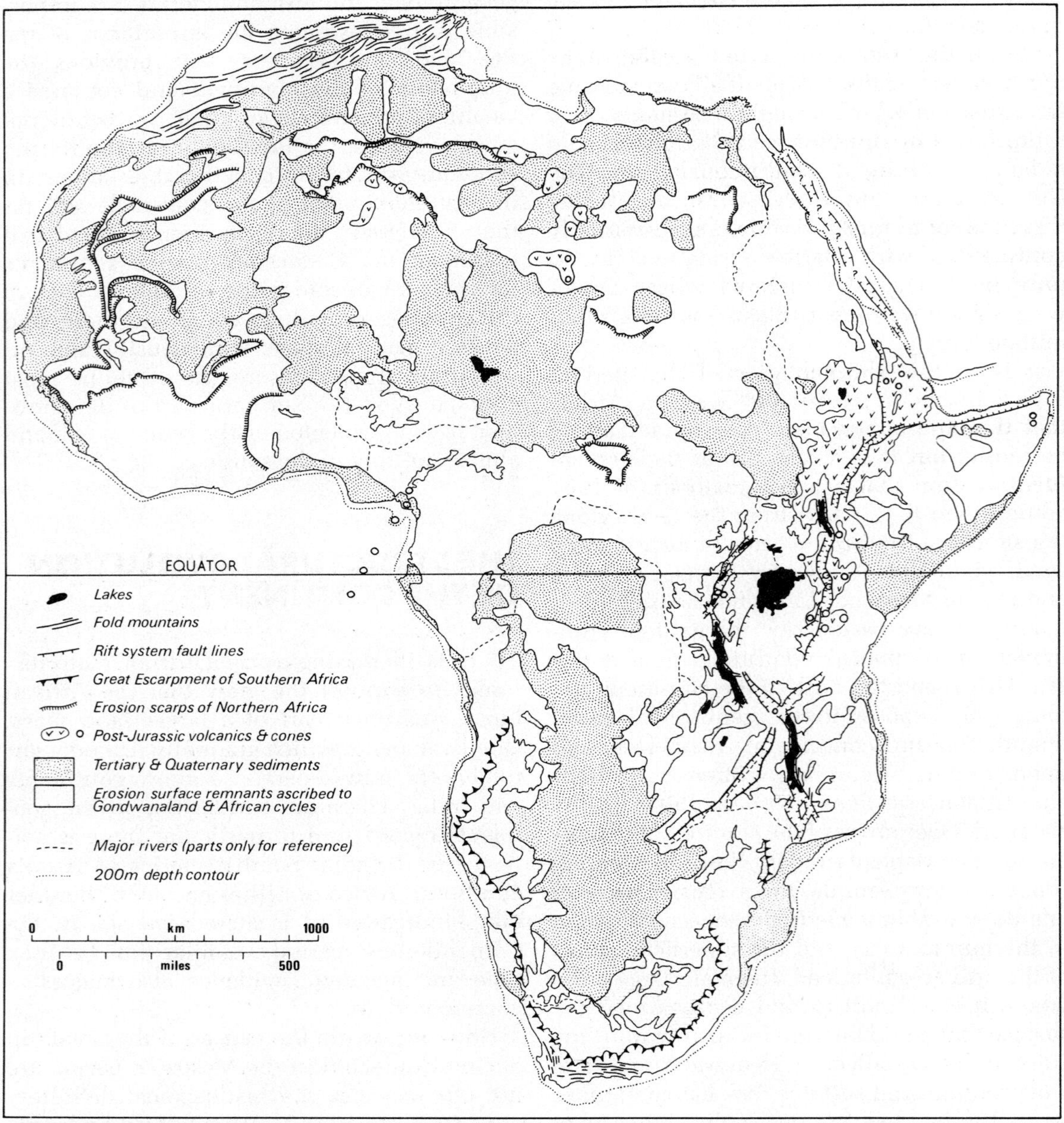

Figure 4 The geomorphology of Africa

plateau and steeply rising sides. Subsequent erosion has pushed back these escarpments from their original coastal positions, but later uplift has if anything increased their magnitude (Figure 4). The impressive Natal Drakensberg, rising to over 3000 m, provides an example of this.

Another major result of the fracturing of Gondwanaland was the dismemberment of the existing river system. Many of the African rivers were deprived of their lower courses, which even now have not in all cases fully readjusted to the new base levels, a process that has been hindered by subsequent continental uplift. Thus many of Africa's major rivers possess gorge sections, waterfalls or cataracts of considerable size in their lower or middle courses, while the upper courses in the continental interior, not yet reached by the rejuvenation process, exhibit the features of maturity. As will be seen later, this feature of many African rivers had important implications for the early exploration and later economic development of the continent.

Since the supposed separation of Africa from Gondwanaland the continent has continued to be subject to earth movements, and except in the fold mountains of the extreme north-west these have been mainly epeirogenic in nature and involving uplift. However, such uplift has not been uniform, and the result is a series of great basins separated by areas of upland, both being characterized by general monotony and lack of local relief. The basins vary in age as can be seen from their sedimentary infilling. The Zaire Basin, filled as it is with sediments of Karroo age, must have been initiated as a downwarp of the Pre-Cambrian floor during the Palaeozoic period. The presence of the softer Karroo or similar sediments in some basins has allowed the river systems to expand easily within the basins and still maintain an outlet to the sea despite further uplift of the basin rim. The Zaire and Zambezi provide examples of this. The Chad Basin is of more recent origin, being a downwarp of Quaternary age, and Lake Victoria occupies a gentle crustal sag associated with the later phases of the evolution of the Rift Valley.

Uplift has been greatest in the southern and eastern parts of the continent, and in consequence the whole has a general tilt towards the north-west. Additionally there has been the tendency, especially in southern Africa, for the rim to rise in relation to the interior, a fact which explains why a number of the rivers cut through and are superimposed across the rim. This process of coastal uplift has possibly been exaggerated in the south-east by a major and still active monoclinal flexure running parallel with the coast of Natal and possibly extending around the Cape and into Namibia. Maximum elevation has been along the line of the Drakensberg Zimbabwean highlands and to a lesser extent along the Namibian highlands, but the interior Kalahari Basin has risen more slowly than the surrounding uplands.

THE EAST AFRICA RIFT SYSTEM

Evidence for the immense scale of the epeirogenic forces operating in Africa comes from the spectacular rift valley system of the eastern part of the continent. From the Mozambique coast at its southern end to the northern Red Sea the African section of the rift stretches over 5500 km but demonstrates a remarkably consistent width of 40–50 km. In East Africa the sides rise steeply to heights of as much as 1900 m, while the floor of Lake Tanganyika is at 670 m below sea level. Between Lakes Albert and Edward the Ruwenzori horst rises to over 5100 m and provides a snowfield and glacier-capped block within the rift itself. In parts the rift is associated with vulcanicity, as evidenced by extinct volcanoes in the Mount Kenya–Kilimanjaro area and in Ethiopia, while present-day geothermal activity in the same areas, which has already been tapped on a small scale, could be of even greater value in the future as an energy source.

THE FOLD MOUNTAIN SYSTEM

Most of Africa is characterized by features derived from differential uplift on a large scale and extensive warping and faulting. Only in the extreme north-west and south of the continent are there fold mountains comparable to those found in the Alps, Andes, Rockies or Himalayas.

In South Africa the Cape Ranges derive from late Tertiary orogenic activity resulting possibly from pressure exerted by the part of Gondwanaland still to the south. They attain heights of 2400 m and two principal trends can be identified: north–south in western Cape Province and east–west along the south coast. The Cape Ranges are relatively simple fold structures, except in the Hex River Mountains where the two fold trends meet.

The more extensive fold mountains of the Atlas stretch for 2400 km from southern Morocco to Tunisia and rise in places to heights of 4000 m. Between the African shield and a land mass to the north (now represented fragmentally by Corsica, Sardinia, etc.) there developed during the Jurassic period a geosyncline in which great thicknesses of sediments (including massive limestones) accumulated. During the mid-Tertiary, these Tethys Sea sediments were subjected to complex pressures from the two land masses, and particularly from the north, which resulted in uplift and folding along a west-south-west/east-north-east axis. This was particularly intense in what is now the Rif, flanking the Mediterranean, but more open farther south in the High and Saharan Atlas where the sedimentaries rest on the African basement rocks.

THE GENERAL MORPHOLOGY

Some of the basic elements in the structure of Africa have already been commented upon. In particular, much of the continent is of plateau character, with marked uniformity over large areas. Indeed, over 62 per cent of the surface is above 360 m, while for Africa south of the equator the equivalent figure is 80 per cent, with no less than 47 per cent over 900 m. In eastern South Africa are the highest plateaux at 1200 to 1900 m, while much of Zimbabwe, Zambia and East Africa is at heights of 1000 to 1500 m. In Angola the plateau is between 900 and 1500 m. Through north-central Africa levels of 500 to 1000 m are usual, but in West Africa the common levels are between 300 and 500 m. Most of the Sahara does not rise above 300 m. These variations in general altitude obviously reflect the continental tilting to which reference has been made. While little of Africa can be classed as lowland, most of it is certainly not mountainous.

A principal landscape element of Africa is the extensive area of very subdued relief. These are in fact planation surfaces – the end product of individual cycles of erosion of long duration – and they rarely bear any direct relation to the underlying rocks across which they are indiscriminately bevelled. Undoubtedly their development has been helped by the general stability of the Pre-Cambrian basement, which was fractured but not greatly folded, and by the general lack of recent marine transgression. Some of the surfaces certainly date from the Jurassic era and have not been extensively covered since that time. Some even older surfaces are in the process of being exhumed as later deposits are stripped from them. The precise age of many of these surfaces is open to dispute because even where they are overlain by datable deposits there is no knowing how long the surface existed before being covered. Differential fracturing and warping also makes correlation difficult between fragments of surface. A possible chronology has been provided by Buckle (Table 2).

Another landscape element associated with the surfaces is the scarp that separates them. Like the surfaces themselves, these scarps are often fragmentary, quite complex in character and have gorge-like re-entrants, the deepening

Table 2 *African surfaces*

Surface	*Age*	*Type areas*	*Height (m)*
Gondwana	Jurassic (pre-break up of Gondwanaland)	Drakensberg (Lesotho)	3000–3300
		Cherangani Mts (Kenya)	2700+
		Jos (Nigeria)	1400–1500
African	Cretaceous/early Miocene	Muchinga (Zambia)	1350–1450
		High Veldt (S Africa)	1000–1500
		High Veldt (Zimbabwe)	1200–1500
		High Plains (Nigeria)	600–700
End Tertiary	Late Miocene/Pliocene (greatest extent)	Zambian Plateau	
		Tanzania Central Plateau	
		Northern Uganda	
		North-west Ghana	
Quaternary	Pleistocene/recent	Coastal areas	
		Valleys of rivers such as Niger, Benue, Orange, Zambezi, Volta	

Source: After Buckle (1978)

and widening of which is an important element in their retreat. The Great Escarpment of South Africa and the Bandiagara Escarpment of Mali in West Africa, while different in scale, are similar in type and equally impressive in their own way.

Rather different in origin but not dissimilar in the landscape that results are the fault-determined scarp features that characterize the sides of the East African Rift, South Africa's Table Mountain, and the Isalo Massif of Madagascar.

While the precise nature of their origins is open to debate, there are often residual hill features (inselbergs, bornhardts or kopje, depending on the area) standing above the general level of the surrounding surface. At least in part, these are probably the result of the recession of scarps, although it is likely that the processes themselves vary with the rock type. Certainly their physical characteristics do. Thus in horizontally bedded sandstones they are likely to take the form of flat-topped, scarp-bounded features, while in areas of more massive metamorphic or igneous rocks they are often in the form of rounded domes.

Sunk into the plateau surfaces are the large structural basins – El Juf in the western Sahara, the Middle Niger, the Chad Basin, the Zaire Basin and the Kalahari Basin. The significance of these basins in terms of the drainage patterns of Africa will be described later; but the general landscapes that they provide, apart from the obvious differences of altitude, are not markedly different from those of the plateaux, with similar uniformity and general lack of major relief features.

The point has already been made that Africa's fold mountain scenery is restricted to the Atlas and Cape ranges. However, in some other parts of Africa past and present vulcanicity is an important determinant of local landscapes and often serves to provide mountain features. Associated with the rift in East Africa are the volcanic cones of Kilimanjaro (5800 m), Mount Kenya (5200 m) and Elgon (4300 m), and there are the active volcanoes of Meru (Eastern Rift) and Nyamlagira and Nyiragongo (Western Rift). The Hoggar, Tibesti and Jebel Marra provide mountainous 'islands' of volcanic origin in the Sahara, and active Mount Cameroon (4070 m) sits astride a major fault zone separating the main east–west structural trend of West Africa and the north–south structures that characterize western equatorial Africa, The Afar Triangle and the islands of Cape Verde, the Canaries, Reunion and Comoro also owe their landscapes to volcanic activity.

RIVERS AND DRAINAGE

So important are the river and drainage systems for the human geography and development potential of the continent that rather more attention must now be devoted to them.

The structural elements of the continent already outlined are clearly reflected in the overall drainage pattern. Each of the five major rivers (Nile, Niger, Zaire, Zambezi and Orange), for at least a part of its course, flows through and receives drainage from one or more of the structural basins. Originally drainage lines would have been towards the centres of the basins, and the present river outlets are of subsequent (and in cases relatively recent) date (Figure 5).

The original source of the Nile was probably at about latitude 18–20°N, from where it flowed northwards across the various planation surfaces. The present River Atbara may have been one of its head streams, but the Sudd region would then have been a separate enclosed drainage basin taking waters from the northern rift valley (Lakes Albert and Edward). Possibly as recently as 25,000 years ago, Lake Victoria, as a result of tilting of the East African plateau, found a new outlet northwards to the Sudd, the great enlargement of which forced an overflow into the Nile–Atbara system in the region of Sabaloka, about 80 km north of Khartoum.

Plate 1 Seasonal river, northern Ghana

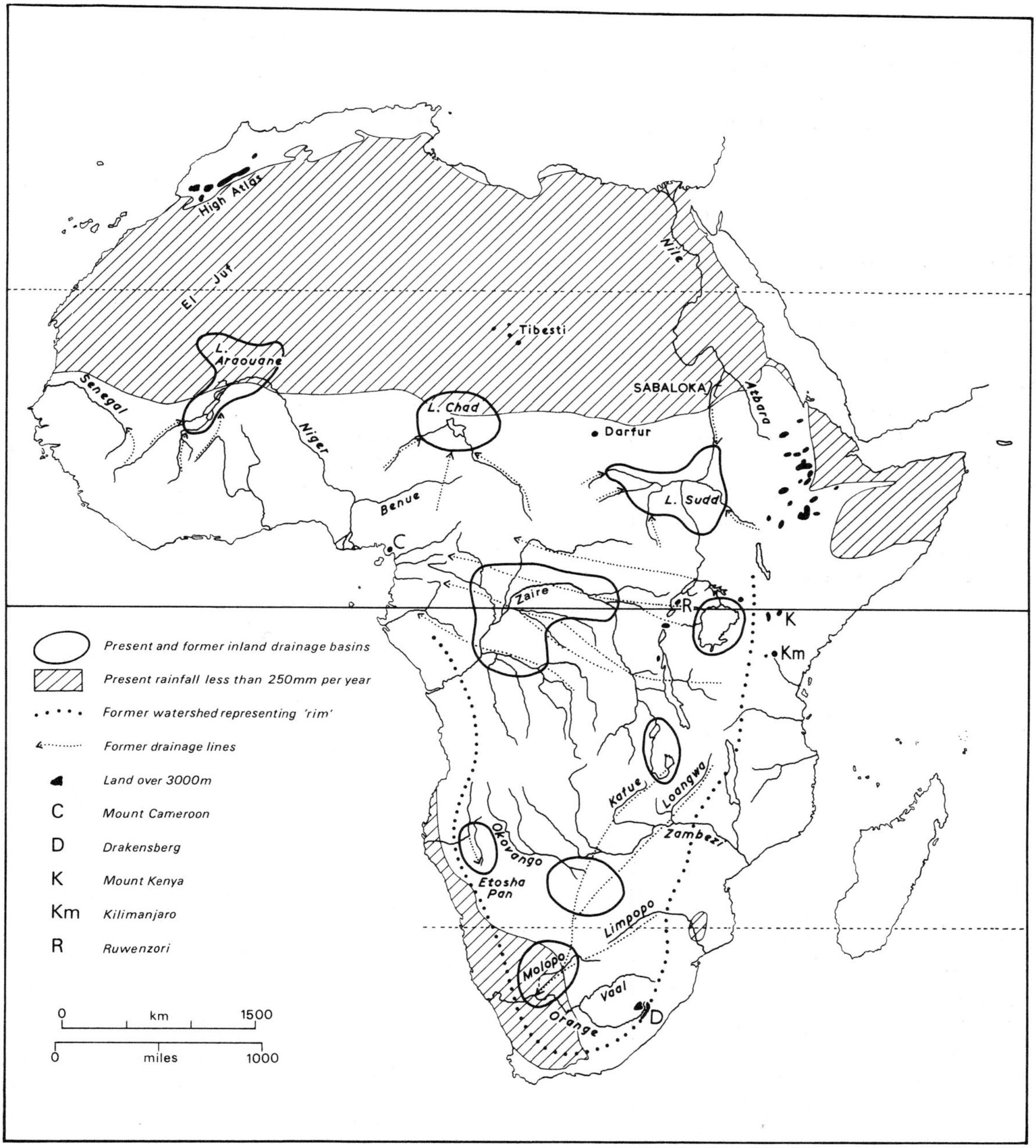

Figure 5 Evolution of African drainage systems

In the mid-Tertiary era the upper Niger was a headstream of what is now the Senegal river, until increasing accumulations of sand and gravel in the region north of Bamako forced the river to flow north-eastwards into the Timbuktu basin. In this area a large Lake formed (named Lake Araouane after a village north of Timbuktu), but the inflow exceeded evaporation and after considerable infilling the waters found an escape south-eastwards in the direction of what is now the lower Niger. Cutting back of the lower Niger probably assisted this breakthrough. Likewise, initial outlets of the Zaire into Lake Chad, and possibly later through what is now Cameroon, became blocked, possibly by earth movements, with the resultant formation of an ever larger lake (so recent that there is archaeological evidence of settlement retreat as the waters rose), until it spilled over westwards of Kinshasa and cut the great Inga gorge now found betwen there and the sea.

It is possible that in South Africa, too, the headwaters of present rivers such as the Zambezi, Orange, Limpopo, Okovango and Vaal originally flowed inland towards a depression centred on the Kalahari. The basin structure would have been emphasized as the rim rose during the early Tertiary period, but eventually the floor level of this basin, too, must have risen and enabled excess water to find an outlet through the channel now marked by the lower Orange river. On the east coast, trough faulting along the lines of the lower Limpopo and Zambezi, associated with the splitting of Madagascar from the mainland, created powerful, steeply graded rivers that extended headwards to capture rivers such as the Loangwa, Kafue and upper Zambezi, and to reverse the Limpopo drainage. Thus, the Kalahari was deprived of much of its drainage and the Orange–Vaal system ceased to receive water from the north. The presence of several dry gorges on the southern margins of the Kalahari, and the great width of the Orange gorge below Aughrabies, attest to the much greater volume of water once carried by the lower Orange – in excessively dry periods the Orange river may now fail to flow continuously to the sea.

Given the continent's history of uplift and the rather similar origins of the main river systems, it is perhaps not surprising that these rivers should at the present time possess certain similarities of profile. The Zaire drops nearly 300 m in its last 400 km; the Niger has falls above Jebba (now covered by Lake Kainji) 700 km from the sea; the Aughrabies Falls (146 m in height) on the Orange river are 550 km from the sea; the lower Zambezi has several interruptions in its lower-middle course, including the 110 m Victoria Falls. The first cataracts on the Nile at Aswan are some 800 km from the delta head but still very much in the lower part of the river.

Successive uplifts and the initiation of new erosion cycles has meant that these main rivers have profiles marked by knick-points represented by waterfalls and rapids of varying size. The gradual northward tilting of the continent has, however, meant that the knick-points on the Nile are smaller than those on the southern rivers. Local geological conditions (e.g. more resistant rock outcrops) and the phasing of the uplift will also influence the size and spacing of the individual knick-points. Between the higher-gradient river sections, where erosion is the dominant process, will be better graded stretches in places related to old lake floors. For example, between Kinshasa and Kisangani the Zaire has an average gradient of only 63.3 cm per 10 km, and the White Nile in the Sudd between Juba and Khartoum falls only 7.9 cm every 10 km. These areas of low gradient are often marked by considerable deposition and indeterminate drainage patterns – the 'inland delta' of the Niger upstream from Timbuktu provides an excellent example.

From this brief outline of the evolution of Africa's drainage it is not difficult to appreciate why some 12 per cent is endoreic (to inland basins with no outlet to the sea), a further 40 per cent is areic (having no organized surface drainage, and often the residual areas of former interior lakes, e.g. in the Niger inland delta or central Zaire basin), and only about 48 per cent has direct drainage to the oceans. It is also of interest to note that a considerable part of this exoreic drainage is accounted for by the main river systems just described, with only a small part accounted for by a number of relatively short rivers on the continental margins where rainfall is adequate.

The climates of Africa will be dealt with in the next chapter, but it will be clear from the great length of the main rivers (Nile, 6500 km; Niger, 4186 km; Zaire, 4375 km; Zambezi, 3540 km; Orange, 2100 km) and the directional changes brought about by their evolution that they will not be restricted to any one uniform climatic region. The river flow patterns or regimes will therefore be a possibly complex reflection of the climates of areas through which they pass.

The discharge of the Nile in its lowest course is the sum of waters from several sources. Accounting for 56 per cent of the flow is water from the Blue Nile, with its headwaters in the Ethiopian Highlands and summer rains which bring a rapid increase in flow from June to September. The Atbara river, accounting for 22 per cent of the Nile waters, also has its origins in the Ethiopian Highlands and its flow follows a similar pattern. The White Nile, with its origins in Lake Victoria, has a much more even flow reflecting the rainfall of the East African plateau and the moderating affect of the lakes. The April maximum on the Zambezi reflects the summer rain of the upper Zambezi basin.

The season of high water on the Orange is from November to April, reflecting in the first month or so the melting snows of the Lesotho mountains and subsequently the summer rainfall of the high Veldt. The regime of the lower Zaire is more complex and tends to display double maxima, in May and December, reflecting tributaries with origins both north and south of the equator and therefore receiving their rainfall in different seasons. This also accounts for the fact that the Zaire has the most uniform flow of the major African rivers. The ratio between the mean and maximum discharges is only 3 for the Zaire, but is 13 for the Nile, 11 for the Zambezi and 14 for the Orange. The ratio between maximum and minimum flow may be far in excess of these figures.

The Niger river has its headwaters in the Guinea Highlands where there is high rainfall in the summer, but runoff from the upper basin takes 4–6 months to reach the lower parts of the river and the flood is flattened as it makes its way through the inland delta. The August–November peak in the middle-lower course is mainly from direct runoff as a result of high rainfall during the summer months. The discharges of the Niger and Benue are not quite in phase, and this leads to a smoothing of the discharge curve in the lower Niger.

THE IMPORTANCE OF THE RIVERS

From the historical and development potential points of view it would be impossible to over-estimate the significance of Africa's rivers. We have seen that the courses of many of the rivers are interrupted by rapids or falls, and this was undoubtedly a factor which delayed exploration and development of the continental interior. Continuous inland penetration was possible on only a few of the rivers, and the variable flow added to the problems of navigation. The difficulties of navigation on the Niger are illustrated in Figure 6, which shows that navigation is restricted to certain sections and is variable from one time of the year to another. River transport was very important on the Niger until the 1950s when a decline set in, but there have been signs of a revival in the last few years. The Zaire and Nile, despite the difficulties associated with variable flow and discontinuity of navigation, are nevertheless important transport arteries over sections of their middle and lower courses.

With such a large part of Africa to be classed as arid or semi-arid (see Chapter 3), the rivers have a particular importance for irrigation, particularly as four of the largest have their origins in areas of high rainfall and then flow through areas where the rainfall is inadequate. Storm rainfall on dry ground produces rapid runoff into rivers, but high temperatures result in great evaporation losses both from ground and water surfaces. The great variations in discharge also make river regulation and control an expensive process.

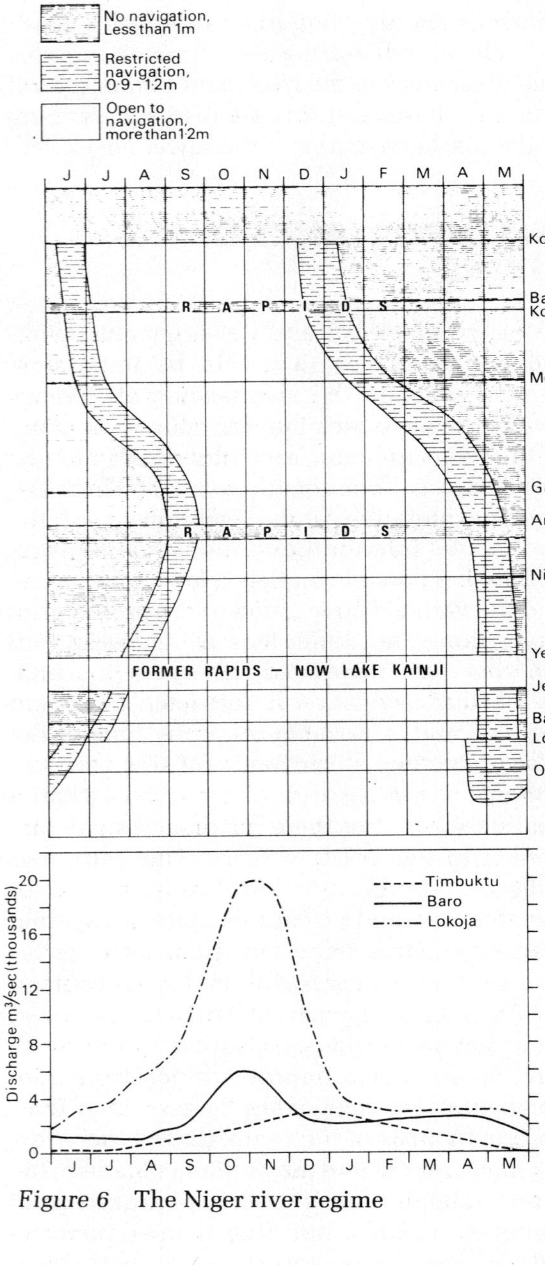

Figure 6 The Niger river regime

Plate 2 Collecting water in dried-up river bed, Bathia river, Chad

However, the tectonic history we have outlined and the falls, rapids and gorges which typify the rivers as they flow from surface to surface give Africa the greatest hydroelectric power potential of any continent, variably estimated at between 27 and 40 per cent of the world total. The resistance and relative impermeability of much of the Pre-Cambrian basement and the high rainfalls in many river source areas are added advantages against which must be balanced the high evaporation rates (as much as 1875 mm a year from a lake surface), the variability of flow and the possibility of earth movement in zones of crustal instability at the margins of the tectonic blocks. The choice of a rock-fill rather than concrete wall design for the Akosombo Dam in Ghana was in part determined by the possibility of earth movement. However, the distribution of HEP potential within Africa is far from even, and areas with less than 1300 mm of rain a year are unlikely to produce rivers with suitable flow characteristics. North and West Africa respectively account for only 5 and 10 per cent of the continental HEP potential; southern Africa has 17 per cent, with Angola and Madagascar particularly well endowed; East Africa has 22 per cent, largely located along the line of the rift valley; and Central Africa accounts for as much as 46 per cent of the total, with Zaire alone possibly having as much as 10 per cent of the total world potential. In the Inga rapids where the Zaire river cuts through the continental rim, the estimated generating capacity is 30,000 MW, or the equivalent of 40 per cent of Britain's total installed capacity. While no other African river can compare with the Zaire, rivers such as the Kafue-Zambezi, Niger and Nile provide considerable potential, particularly in their upper reaches, and rivers such as the Volta (Ghana), Sanaga (Cameroon), Kouilou (Congo), Tana (Kenya), Pangani (Tanzania), Shire (Malawi) and Awash (Ethiopia) have great importance locally.

While the potential is great, the actual exploitation of hydroelectric power is still relatively limited despite the number of well-known schemes (Aswan, Owen Falls, Kariba, Akosombo, Kainji, Inga). This is partly explained by the great cost of developing the sites which are often distant from the markets (the Inga scheme in Zaire is 1800 km from the Shaba copper processing area where the power is really needed) and the markets are still too small to justify the development of many of the sites.

AFRICA'S COASTS

Because of the general plateau nature of the continent, coastal lowlands are not extensive. Nowhere have the great rivers built up wide alluvial plains in their lower course, since these courses are either entrenched or ungraded. Africa's largest delta is that of the Niger (41,600 km^2), while the Nile delta, although supporting nearly 60 per cent of Egypt's population, in fact occupies less than 26,000 km^2. True coastal plains occupying areas larger than this are limited to the Mozambique plain, Somalia–Kenya and Mauritania–Senegal.

It has been said of Africa's coasts that they act as barriers rather than zones of contact. Much of the 27,000 km of coast is certainly inhospitable, linear with few sheltering inlets and often with heavy surf. Many of the river mouths are either blocked by sand bars or deltaic in character – only the Zaire has a true deep-water estuary and that is not easily navigated. A classification of coastal types reveals that only 8 per cent of Africa's coastline is made up of 'riverine interface' (compared with 14 per cent for South America), while 15 per cent is classed as 'barrier interface' (compared with only 3 per cent for South America) in which there is some offshore obstruction (reef, islands). Africa has a low percentage of mud-flat coast (3 per cent), mainly in West Africa, but a very high percentage of sand coast (38 per cent), reflecting the desert conditions of the Saharan, Namibian and Somali coastal areas. Only 6 per cent comprises swamp delta, although this possibly ranks high as the popular perception of Africa's coasts.

It follows that with few coastal indentations, either riverine or resulting from rock headlands, Africa has a limited number of naturally protected deep-water port sites. A number of West Africa's ports (Monrovia, Buchanan, Takoradi, Tema, Lomé, Cotonou) are completely artificial harbours built at great cost. The port of Beira (Mozambique) is costly to maintain, and ports such as Douala (Cameroon), Lagos and the delta ports (Nigeria) require considerable dredging for access depths to be maintained. Undoubtedly, the character of the coast has impeded port construction and added greatly to the cost of port provision.

Africa's continental shelf, as defined by the 100-fathom line, is relatively narrow. Rarely is it more than 20–32 km in width, and is sometimes as narrow as 5 km (Angola, Somalia, Southern Natal) and is in places virtually non-existent. The only areas of more extensive shelf are off Cape Agulhas in South Africa (where it reaches a maximum width of 200 km) and off the coasts of Guinea and Guinea–Bissau in West Africa (where it reaches 190 km). A main effect of this lack of shelf development is that feeding grounds for fish are limited.

REFERENCES

1 Furon, R., *The Geology of Africa*, London, Oliver and Boyd, 1963, p. 3.
2 Stamp, L.D., *Africa: A Study in Tropical Development*, New York, Wiley, 1961, p. 53.
3 King, L.C., 'The study of the world's plainlands', *Quart. Jnl. Geol. Soc.*, **106** (1959), pp. 101–31.

3 Climatology

It is not without justification that Africa has been described as 'the most tropical of the continents'. It has a relatively symmetrical disposition about the equator, extending from 37°21'N at Cape Blanc in Tunisia to almost 35°S at Cape Agulhas. The greatest width of the continent, about 7400 km from Guinea to Somalia, is at 12°N and roughly two-thirds of the continental area lies within the tropics. Only the extreme northern and southern parts of Africa are affected by the mid-latitude westerly airstreams and their associated disturbances, and Africa is unique in being strongly influenced by the sub-tropical high-pressure belt in both hemispheres.

Comparisons with South America are instructive. Africa tends to lie farther north and attains its greatest width in latitudes where the Americas dwindle to a narrow isthmus. The Atlas lands are equivalent in latitude to the Cotton Belt of the United States, and no part of Africa extends farther south than the latitude of Buenos Aires. South Africa is separated from Antarctica by over 3200 km of open ocean, whereas South America is separated by only the narrow Drake Strait. The absence in Africa of lengthy, continuous north–south mountain chains comparable with the Andes in South America means that general zonal circulation is stronger and not interrupted, the sub-tropical high-pressure areas have greater continuity, and this serves to check the northward advance of cold polar air – a common feature of South America. The absence of sharp interruptions to circulation also means that gradual change is a feature of African patterns of climate and climatic boundaries are not defined with precision.

However, much of east, central and southern Africa is high plateau, and this inevitably has a modifying influence on local temperatures; this is certainly one of the main reasons why permanent white settlement was attracted to these areas. In coastal areas the climate may be modified by the existence of colder water offshore. Large stretches of the Atlantic coast are washed by relatively cool water; the Canaries current (16–21°C) affects the coast between Morocco and Cape Verde, and in the southern hemisphere the Benguela current (13–18°C) affects the coast from Cape Town to Cap Lopez (Gabon). With the exception of the Ghana–Benin coastal area (sometimes referred to as the 'Dahomey Gap'), where there is also cold offshore water, the rest of the West African coast from Gabon to Senegal is in contact with relatively warm water (usually about 27°C). These lower water temperatures are the result partly of mass transfer from higher to lower latitudes, and of coastal up-welling of cold water from great depths brought about by the angular set of the surface currents in relation to the coast. The colder offshore water has the effect not only of reducing coastal temperatures, but also of stabilizing the air and reducing the possibility of precipitation. Thus the areas washed by the Canaries and Benguela currents are backed in part by desert, and the Dahomey Gap is an area of anomalously low rainfall in comparison with the rest of West Africa.

On the eastern seaboard only relatively small areas are affected by cooler offshore waters, and then only in the northern solstice season when the south-westerly airstream over Somalia pushes warm surface water to the east, its place being taken by cooler waters from below (21°C). The rest of the coast of eastern Africa from Natal to the Red Sea is in contact with relatively warm waters all the year, varying from 18°C in the south to 29°C near Aden, and sometimes as high as 35°C in the Red Sea in July.

Along the north coast, the Mediterranean is relatively warm for its latitude, being maintained generally above 13°C in February and possibly above 24°C in August. Continual evaporation in excess of the inflow of fresh river water results in high salinity, and the outflow of this more saline water over the shallow Gibraltar 'sill' reduces the depth of warmer Atlantic water that is able to enter the Mediterranean.

TEMPERATURES OVER AFRICA

Africa is the only continent in which the 10°C sea-level isotherm never appears and it might therefore be classed as the hottest of the continents. Cape Town, at the southern extremity, records a July mean temperature of 13°C, while Algiers, in the north, has a January mean of 12°C. There is, of course, the altitudinal modification to which reference has already been made, but even at Johannesburg at 1670 m the June mean is 10°C. In parts of the continent very high temperatures are recorded, with a claimed world record for Tripolitania of 57.8°C. Insalah in Algeria (latitude 27°N) has a July mean of 37.2°C and for the same month an average daily maximum of 47.2°C. Southern Africa with its smaller land area and greater oceanic influences does not normally record such high temperatures, although in the Kalahari, below 900 m, temperatures in excess of 38°C may be experienced.

The equatorial parts of the continent do not have such high temperatures as those parts nearer the tropics, nor do they experience great seasonal variations. Thus in Zaire, along the equatorial and Guinea coast and on the East Africa plateaux, the seasonal range is usually less than 6°C. Moving to higher latitudes, the annual range of temperature increases steadily to 8–11°C in South Africa and as much as 20°C in the Sahara. Except in the northern and southern extremes of the continental mass, the diurnal temperature range tends to be greater than the seasonal range. At night in the Sahara temperatures may drop below freezing, and frost is certainly not unknown in higher parts of southern Africa.

PRESSURE AND CIRCULATION

Africa's latitudinal extent brings it under the principal influence of the sub-tropical high-pressure belts separated by the equatorial low. It follows that the main airstreams involved will be the north-east trades of the northern hemisphere and the south-east trades of the southern hemisphere, converging as these do in the equatorial region. As these belts move with the overhead sun there are times when the trades of one hemisphere cross over into the other, and the operation of the Coriolis force induces a westerly component into the airstream. Thus the south-westerly 'monsoon' of West Africa is in fact the re-curving south-east trades after they have crossed the equator.

It is as well at this point to introduce the idea of the Inter-Tropical Convergence (ITC), a term that is preferable to Inter-Tropical Front by which the feature is sometimes known. This is the zone where the converging trades meet and is a fundamental element of the circulation patterns. Although the converging air masses may have very different characteristics (e.g. the dry continental tropical air of the Sahara meeting the moist re-curving south-east trades from the Atlantic), the differences tend to be in terms of humidity rather than temperature and the convergence itself is not a rain zone – in this sense it is not a front comparable with the mid-latitude disturbances. Figure 7 shows a section across

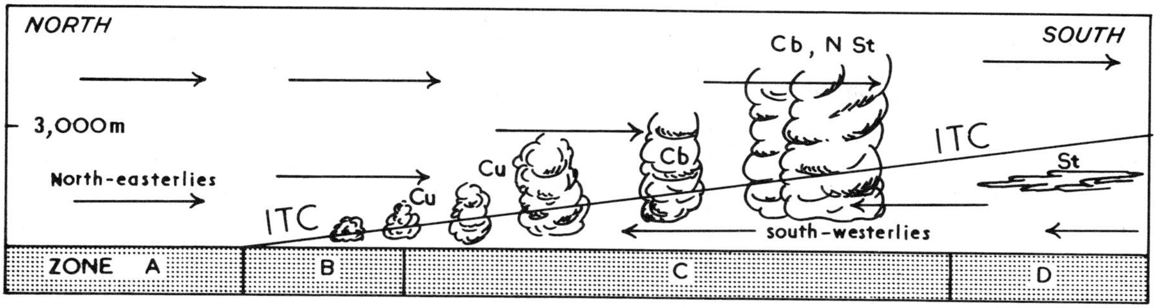

Figure 7 A section through the Intertropical Convergence: *A* Dry, haze; *B* Moist air, little rain; *C* Deeper, moist air, convection, line squalls; *D* Less intense more continuous rain

the ITC, from which it will be seen that the belt immediately behind the ITC on the ground (zone B), a distance of possibly 320 km, is not characterized by rain, the moist air being of insufficient depth to generate precipitation. Rain is more characteristic of the thicker, moist air in zone C, where convective activity will be considerable and rainstorms sharp and heavy, possibly related to disturbances within the moist air stream, and zone D, some 1120–1440 km behind the ITC, where rain will be less intense but more continuous.

The general patterns of pressure and the resultant changes in the distribution of the air masses that influence the different parts of the continent are best considered on a seasonal basis.

In the northern hemisphere in winter, the high-pressure belt is continuous from the Azores, across northern Africa and into Arabia (Figure 8A). At the same time over southern Africa a relative low pressure develops. During this season continental polar air from eastern Europe and Asia may bring relatively low temperatures into north-east Africa, and moisture acquired in the passage over the Mediterranean has even been known to bring snow to Cairo (Figure 8B). More normally, much of coastal northern Africa will at this time come under the influence of maritime polar air from the Atlantic and mid-latitude rain-bringing depressions. This is therefore an area of winter rain.

To the south of the high-pressure zone there is a broad belt subject to continental tropical air, and for much of northern Africa this will be very dry air off the desert. Weather is characterized by stability, very low humidities, no rainfall, and considerable dust haze, conditions known as 'Harmattan' in West Africa. This continental air may penetrate southwards as far as the West African coast for short periods, but with increasing distance inland the length of the dry season becomes ever longer, until in the central Sahara it is continuous throughout the year. While the position of the ITC is clearly defined in West Africa there is less certainty about its location further east. The general consensus favours a southwards sweep of the ITC through central southern Africa and then eastwards through Mozambique. The eastern coastlands from Somalia to Mozambique will be under the influence of the north-east trades and modified continental tropical air in the north and maritime tropical air further south. Particularly in the north these produce very little rain.

To the south of the ITC the predominant influence will be the south-east trades which re-curve into Gabon and Zaire from the Atlantic. As a result of subsidence associated with the South Atlantic high-pressure zone and stability imparted by passage over the colder waters of the Benguela current, the coastal zones of southern Africa receive little rain. Inland, plateau Angola receives considerable rain from this airstream and the onshore maritime tropical air brings high rainfall to Madagascar, Mozambique and South Africa.

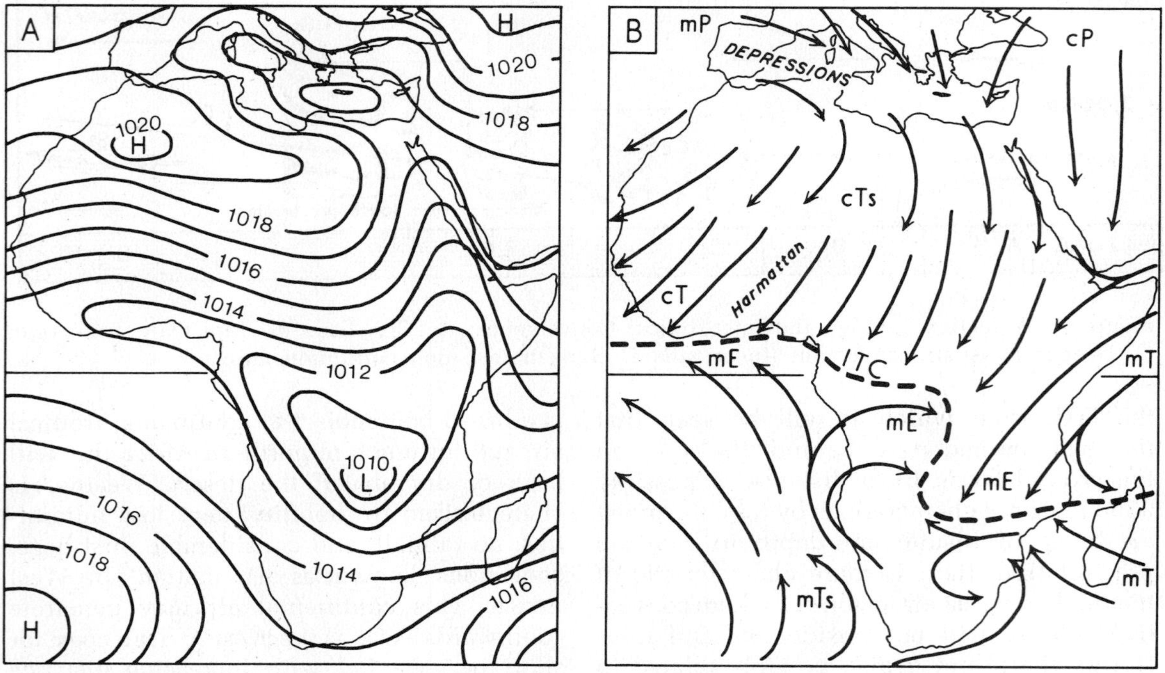

Figure 8 Mean pressure and circulation, January

In the northern hemisphere in summer the main airstreams are unchanged but their spatial impact is very different. At this time the Sahara has become a vast thermal low-pressure area, while southern Africa takes on its rightful role as a part of the southern sub-tropical high-pressure belt. These thermal pressure changes superimposed on the normal zonal circulation tend to intensify the resultant circulation patterns. The ITC moves to its most northerly position at approximately 20°N in August, when the Saharan low pressure has the effect of drawing moist, south-westerly maritime equatorial air into the continental interior (Figure 9B). Some climatologists argue that this monsoon effect is different only in degree and not in kind from that of the Indian Ocean, but others feel that the mechanism is sufficiently different for the term pseudo-monsoon to be more appropriate. This is the rain season in West Africa and its start can be quite abrupt, although its duration decreases as one moves into the interior. The southern part of the continent comes mainly under the south-east trades at this time, but these bring less rain than might be expected because the temperatures are lower and the air has greater stability.

It will be appreciated that over the year the position of the ITC and the associated distribution of the different air masses will oscillate with the overhead sun, the northward movement of the ITC being at a rate of about 160 km a month while the southward movement is at roughly twice that speed.

Much of the African rainfall is convective in character and thunderstorms are frequent, especially over the higher plateau areas. It follows that with much of the rainfall occurring in relatively short but very heavy storms its effectiveness is diminished. Runoff will be very rapid, ground percolation reduced, and the erosional impact of the rainfall and the possibility of flash flooding will be considerable. Tropical revolving storms are of limited influence in Africa, being confined largely

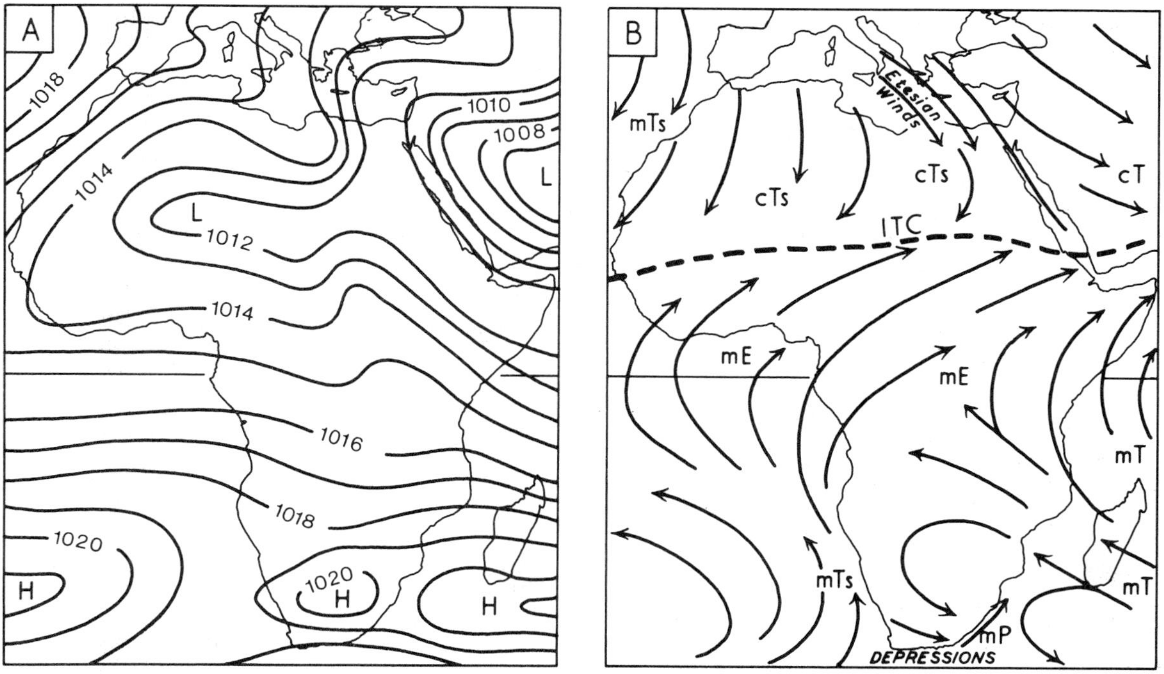

Figure 9 Mean pressure and circulation, July

to the Madagascan and Mozambique coasts between November and April. Even here, however, the frequency is only 0.9 per year compared with 7.3 in the Caribbean. In West Africa a feature once known as a tornado is now known not to be of the same mechanism as the true revolving storm and is a disturbance line or line-squall which usually moves rapidly from east to west, brings a sudden change in wind direction from normal westerly to easterly, a marked increase in wind force and brief torrential rain. It is estimated that in West Africa as much as 90 per cent of the rain results from such line-squalls.

THE PATTERN OF CLIMATES

Having briefly considered the mechanisms involved, we can now describe the climatic patterns that result. In Africa the temperature is rarely critical, and although there are large areas where it is modified by altitude there are few areas where the temperatures are such as to restrict plant growth except for the shortest periods of time. Rainfall therefore provides the main differentiating factor, but it is as well to bear in mind that the divisions that follow are not sharply defined in practice and the boundaries on the maps represent broad zones of transition.

Figures 10 A–D indicate the regional pattern of rainfall and serve to emphasize its markedly seasonal characteristics. The equatorial belt is characterized by adequate rainfall in all months but with double maxima associated with the equinoxes. Northwards and southwards the amount of rainfall tends to decrease and the duration of the rain season shortens. As the rainfall decreases the greater its variability becomes, both in total amount and timing. There are large parts of Africa where the variability exceeds 40 per cent and relatively small areas where it is less than 20

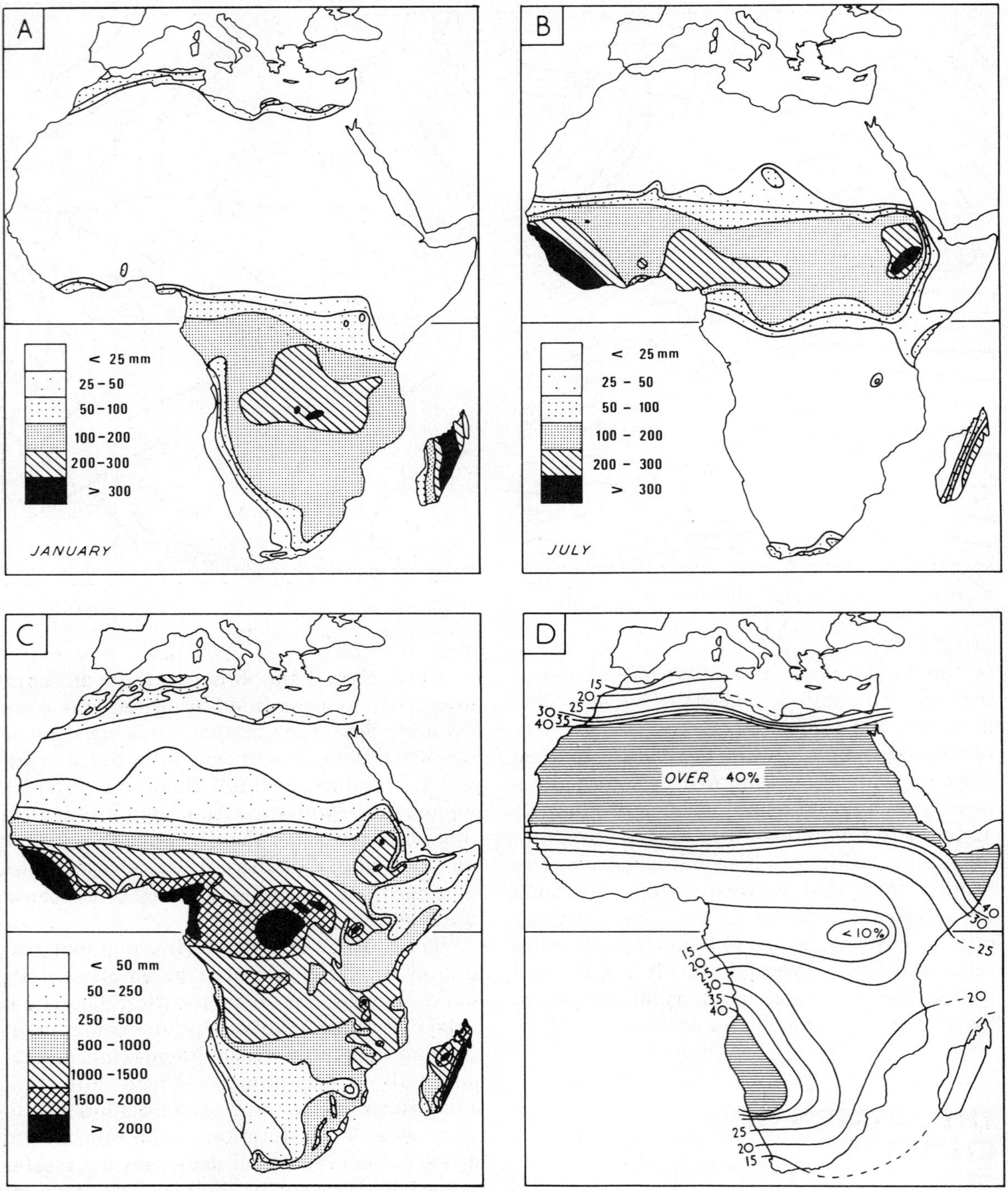

Figure 10 Mean monthly precipitation in January (*A*) and July (*B*), mean annual precipitation (C) and rainfall variability (*D*)

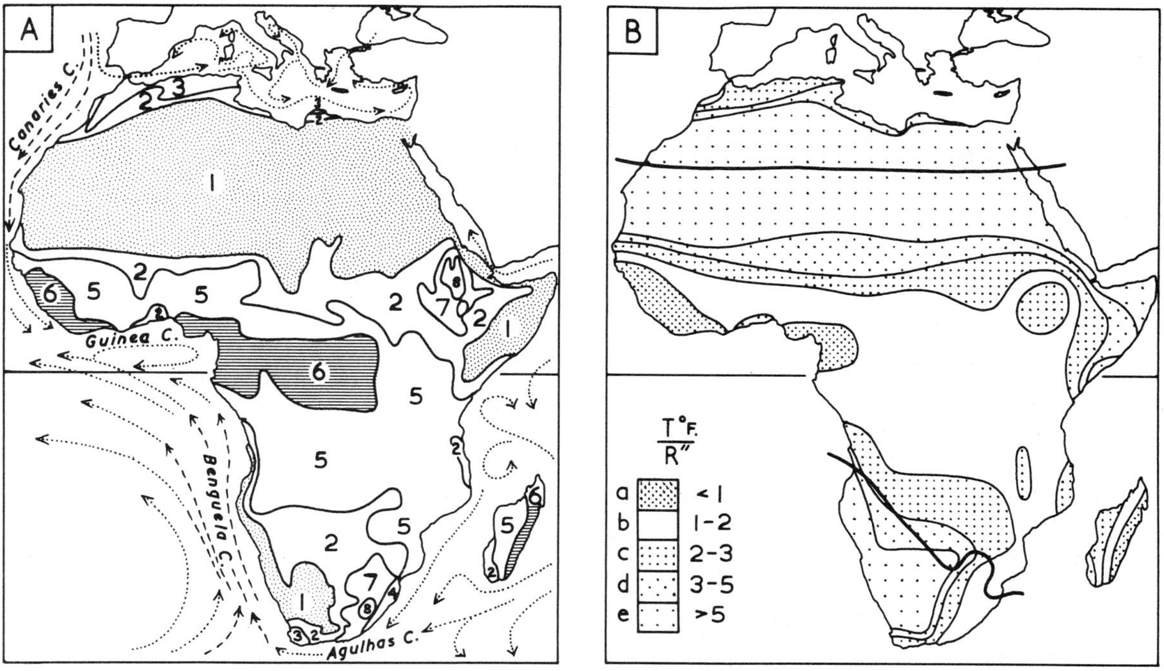

Figure 11 A Climatic regions of Africa
1 Arid; 2 Semi-arid; 3 Dry summer sub-tropical; 4 Humid sub-tropical marine; 5 Tropical wet and dry; 6 Tropical humid; 7 Warm temperate upland, summer rain; 8 Cool temperate highland. Ocean currents for January

B Moisture regions of Africa
a Perhumid; b Humid; c Sub-humid; d Semi-arid; e Arid. Part of Africa between heavy lines has no month with mean temperature below 18°C except restricted highland areas
Source: After Miller, 1951.

per cent. It follows that much of Africa has uncertain rainfall and this will be a critical factor where development strategies are concerned. The early 1970s' Sahel drought and its repetition over even wider areas of Africa in the 1980s emphasize the vulnerability of much of the continent in climatic terms.

Figures 11 A and B define the broad climatic regions. A critical consideration is the relationship between the precipitation and evaporation. Given the high temperatures that prevail over much of the continent the normal evaporation rates are high. Over the year, an open water surface loses as much as 1520–1780 mm, a fact that has serious implications for water storage reservoirs and hydro-electric power development. It is estimated that precipitation exceeds evaporation over only 10–15 per cent of the continental area, that the two are more or less in balance for the period of the main rain season over 20–25 per cent of Africa, and that a further 30–35 per cent is characterized by short periods just after the rains in which precipitation equals evaporation and for long periods when there is moisture deficiency. For 25–30 per cent of Africa the precipitation is negligible in relation to potential evaporation and there is serious moisture deficiency. On this basis evaporation exceeds precipitation except for very short periods over 65 per cent of the continent. Much of the continent is therefore to be classed as *arid* or *semi-arid*, and this will have important consequences for natural vegetation, agricultural practice and development potential.

4
Vegetation and soils

VEGETATION

For the most part the vegetation of Africa (Figure 12) is not natural in the strict sense of the term because there are few areas where it has not been modified by human activities, especially cultivation based on burning and clearing, and grazing of animals. Nevertheless, there is a broad relationship between the vegetation type and the pattern of climates described in Chapter 3, although there will be local variations dependent on soil, terrain, and hydrological and microclimatic conditions. As with the climatic regions, the boundaries between vegetation types are not as precise as the map suggests, and the changes over short distances, for example, in the highland areas, will not be apparent.

It is important to realize that the present vegetation pattern is neither static nor stable. In terms of centuries or longer periods, slow climatic change has its effects. Since the last pluvial period of the Quaternary (more or less contemporaneous with the last Glacial period of higher latitudes) African rainfall has diminished considerably, while there have also been less-pronounced shorter-term fluctuations. Neolithic man was able to cross the Sahara and inhabit parts of it that have since become desiccated. Then it must be remembered that the vegetation of much of Africa, particularly between the tropical rain forest and the desert, changes remarkably from season to season. Where the grass has been burnt off and the majority of the trees are leafless, the savanna may appear as a semi-desert waste; but seen after the rains, with tall lush grass and trees in full leaf, it resembles an open forest with rich undergrowth.

With these points in mind, the vegetation regions depicted on the map will be described. One distinction between *savanna* and *steppe* possibly needs explanation. The term savanna has on occasions been used for a supposed climatic climax vegetation zone and is here used simply for areas where perennial grasses exceed 1 m in average height and are subject to burning at intervals. Steppe refers to the shorter grasses associated with drier conditions and less affected by burning.

Tropical rain forest

This is the climax vegetation of those humid tropical areas possessing no pronounced or lengthy dry season, but in areas of higher population the species may well be secondary as a result of intermittent clearance and cultivation.

The mature rain forest consists of tall evergreen or partly evergreen trees, an abundance of other woody plants and little undergrowth except along river banks. The trees may attain great heights: 50 m is common, and some specimens of 100 m have been recorded. The forest contains a great many species, so that commonly each tree differs from its neighbour. The dense canopies supported by the trees, often at two or more distinct levels, permit only a little sunlight to filter through to the ground, so that undergrowth is not dense except where clearings or rivers break up the forest. As a result of the continuous heat and heavy rain there are no obvious seasonal

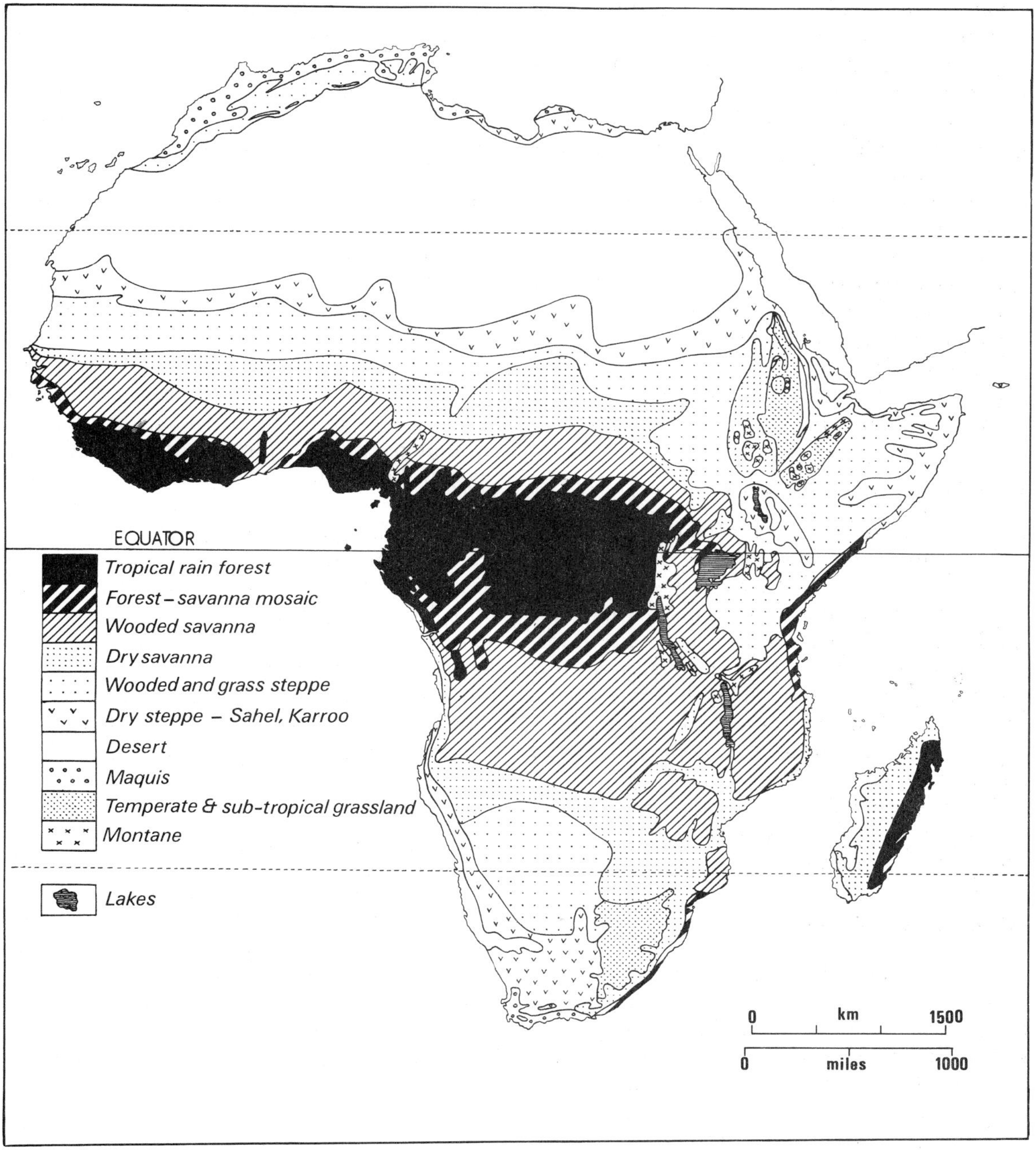

Figure 12 The vegetation of Africa

changes, except in some areas where a well-marked dry season occurs; flowering and fruiting can and do occur all year round. It is often claimed that the rain forest is impenetrable, but this notion of dense jungle areas arose mainly because the forest was viewed from a river traversing it. The forest is obviously more difficult to pass through than, say, savanna country, but it is the moist underfoot conditions and fallen logs and branches that make progress in the forest slow and laborious, rather than the thickness of the vegetation.

The extent of the true rain forest has often been exaggerated. Even within those regions shown on the map there are areas of lighter tropical forest and patches of wooded savanna often associated with highly laterized soils, of swamp and of land cleared for cultivation.

Forest covers no more than about 18 per cent of the continent but in these areas may be a valuable resource. However, the variety of species, the low density of particular trees of economic value and the problems of transport provision often make exploitation difficult.

Forest–savanna mosaic

Largely forming a fringe on the north or south of the rain forest, this consists of patches of rain forest surrounded by tall-grass savanna. The distribution of the forest or savanna bears no direct relationship to physical conditions. It is generally agreed that the savanna in this mosaic has been derived by burning of the rain forest. Most parts of the savanna are fired annually, so that only fire-tolerant trees and shrubs survive.

Trees may reach 30 m and where a denser canopy forms the grass growth is restricted. In the open area grasses may reach 4 m.

Wooded savanna

Within the tropical regions of Africa subject to a long and severe dry season in winter and a rainy season in summer, the larger part is occupied by various forms of vegetation collectively included in the conventional term 'savanna'. The climax vegetation is thought to be closed woodland with little grass, though on level, poorly drained areas, or on lateritic soils possessing a ferruginous hardpan, tree growth has naturally been inhibited. Tree growth also becomes more restricted towards the bordering dry savanna and semi-arid regions, principally because of the lengthening of the dry season. The latter in the wooded savanna zone varies from three to seven months in most cases.

Grassland is dominant mainly because of fire. The 'bush' is burned regularly in the dry season, to clear the land for cultivation, or perhaps to hunt out animals. The trees remaining today in the savanna are fire-tolerant to a greater or lesser extent. The density of tree cover therefore depends not only on physical conditions but on the frequency and severity of human interference, and thus indirectly on population density. In parts of West Africa, for instance, alteration of the vegetation has been particularly rapid and radical owing to repeated clearing for cultivation. In sparsely populated country, on the other hand, the trees of the savanna may form a light canopy and grow in height to 20 m, and if there is both sufficient moisture and protection from fire, shrubby undergrowth may develop. The grasses of the savanna are adapted to the annual climatic rhythm, presenting a varied picture throughout the year. When the rains are plentiful they grow rapidly to heights of 2–4 m, but in periods of drought they are either burned off or die right down to their roots, remaining in this dormant condition until the next rains.

Dry savanna

With increasing aridity and higher summer temperatures there is a gradual transition from tall-grass savanna to short-grass steppe, with scattered deciduous or drought-resistant trees and shrubs. Much of the 'bushveld' of the northern Transvaal and Limpopo valley falls in this category, as well as areas around the Angola–Namibia border and from Senegal to the southern Sudan.

Wooded and grass steppe

A further stage in the transition to semi-desert is provided by areas of short grass, acacia scrub and thickets of thorn trees. This is characteristic of the Kalahari from the Okovango towards the Orange river, of the southern edge of the Sahara and the drier parts of Kenya and eastern Ethiopia. All species are adapted to withstand prolonged drought. Occasional thorn trees may reach 3–6 m. Grasses are generally sparse and wiry, growing in tussocks, and provide only meagre grazing for nomadic pastoralists. On the upper parts of the Namibian highlands, however, the slightly cooler and moister conditions produce rather better pasture.

Dry steppe, sahel and karroo

The plant cover becomes discontinuous, with many bare patches of ground. There are a few low perennial shrubs; annuals, including grasses, flourish for only a few weeks after rain. Tree growth is generally found along water-courses.

Desert

Vegetation is very sparse, though not entirely absent – except in some areas of rock or mobile dunes. Plants have either adapted themselves in some way to the lack of water, or consist of varieties which, when a shower of rain falls, are able to grow, flower, set fruits and seeds, and then die down when all moisture has evaporated, the seeds only remaining until the next rain. A rainfall of as little as 30 mm after 14 years without rain has been known to produce vegetation adequate for camel grazing, an indication that changes in vegetation over time do not necessarily imply large changes in rainfall and that relatively small amounts of water may be significant from the point of view of development potential. Occasional perennial low herbs, or shrubs such as tamarisk, may appear. In the oases the familiar date-palms are cultivated, often providing shade for other crops.

Maquis

This is the well-known Mediterranean sclerophyllous flora composed of evergreen species. The long summer drought promotes the development of plants protecting themselves by various devices (shiny leaves, spines, etc.) against loss of moisture by evaporation. In parts of north-west Africa, where the rainfall is above average, more substantial tree growth may occur; this consists of evergreen species of cork oak, cedar, pine, olive, juniper and many others according to the nature of the locality. Cedars are mostly found on the slopes of the Tell Atlas above 900–1200 m where conditions are cooler. In the south-west Cape region various forms of scrub vegetation, rarely attaining heights of more than 3–4 m, are most characteristic. There are now, in fact, few trees here compared with north-west Africa, except on some of the higher Cape ranges such as the Cedarberg, where the trees are less accessible and the rainfall greater. Further inland the maquis scrub degenerates still further into the dry steppe and karroo vegetation.

In both these areas of Mediterranean climate the vegetation has frequently been removed or altered. Goats in particular have proved very destructive, especially in the hilly parts, where erosion is all too easily provoked by removing the cover of vegetation. Excessive cutting of the cork oak and other forests in north-west Africa, of the cedars and cypresses of the Cape, and the pasturing of too large flocks of sheep and goats, have resulted in great depletion and alteration of the natural flora.

Temperate and sub-tropical grassland

At altitudes from about 1000 to 2700 m in South Africa there is almost pure grassland. Apart from the occasional acacias it extends monotonously for hundreds of miles on the High Veld. The grasses vary considerably: in the better areas, as regards climate and soil, grass may reach 0.6–1.0 m in height, but it never attains the luxuriance of some of the savanna grasses. Since the rainfall in summer is subject to heavy evaporation losses, and as it also falls in sporadic downpours, the veld often presents a parched appearance at this time of the year. The spring, before the temperatures rise too high, is the only season of growth, when the landscape appears green. Winter frost is a factor in restricting tree growth to a minimum.

On the Ethiopian plateaux and highlands, at altitudes from about 1800 to 3000 m, various forms of grassland predominate. Trees are abundant up to 2400 m in the better parts, but as a result of lower temperatures they disappear rapidly at higher altitudes. Above 3000 m, as in Lesotho, the grassland bears some resemblance to Alpine pasture.

Montane communities

These are very diverse. Above certain altitudes, dependent on height, location and slope conditions, distinctive montane species and associations appear. Evergreen forest, bamboo thicket, Alpine grassland and woodland consisting of tree-ferns and giant heathers are just some of a great range of peculiar floristic communities to be found. Tundra-like vegetation appears in the highest areas in Lesotho and Ethiopia and also below the snow-line on the East African mountains.

SOILS

In Africa the majority of the population is still dependent on agriculture. The soils are therefore an important determinant of present farming practice and of development potential. Indeed, there are many areas where detailed soil surveys have still to be undertaken, and soil maps of Africa are frequently generalized from classifications based on different criteria – climate, parent material, relief, drainage, vegetation, age, human activity – or produced for different purposes. Given the variety of factors influencing pedogenesis, the variations of soil type are almost infinite. However, the map of soil types (Figure 13) does bear a relationship with the broad climatic zones.

Some experts have thought that soil humidity is a critical regulator of the various soil-forming processes. Thus, rock weathering will in general be more rapid and upper layers of soil may be deprived of certain mineral constituents by leaching in areas of higher humidity. Conversely, in drier areas the predominant direction of movement of soil moisture will be upwards as a result of evaporation and capillary action. This will result in the deposition of soluble salts at or near the surface.

Another consideration is the permeability of the soil, for if rainfall is in excess of the amount of water that can be absorbed by the soil, surface runoff will develop and may cause erosion of the soil. In this connection the character of the rainfall is of great importance, for heavy downpours not only encourage leaching but also apply water to the soil in excess of its percolation capacity, so that surface runoff and erosion are promoted. Heavy rain may also beat down the surface of the soil, reducing its percolation capacity even further. All these conditions are frequently encountered in most parts of Africa; concentrated downpours of rain, rather than prolonged light rain, are the general rule. The seasonal distribution of the rain, too, has a great influence on soil development. In the rainy season downward leaching of minerals and organic compounds will be paramount; in the dry season some compounds may be returned to the surface layers by capillary action, possibly forming 'crusts' or 'hardpans' which will in turn affect the movement of soil water. According to the relative lengths of dry and wet seasons, a range of different soil types will be produced. Africa, with climates ranging from arid to very humid through all the intermediate zones of seasonal rain, may be expected to produce many contrasting varieties of soils on these considerations alone.

Although soil moisture and its movement are important, the effects of temperature must not be forgotten. In this connection soil tem-

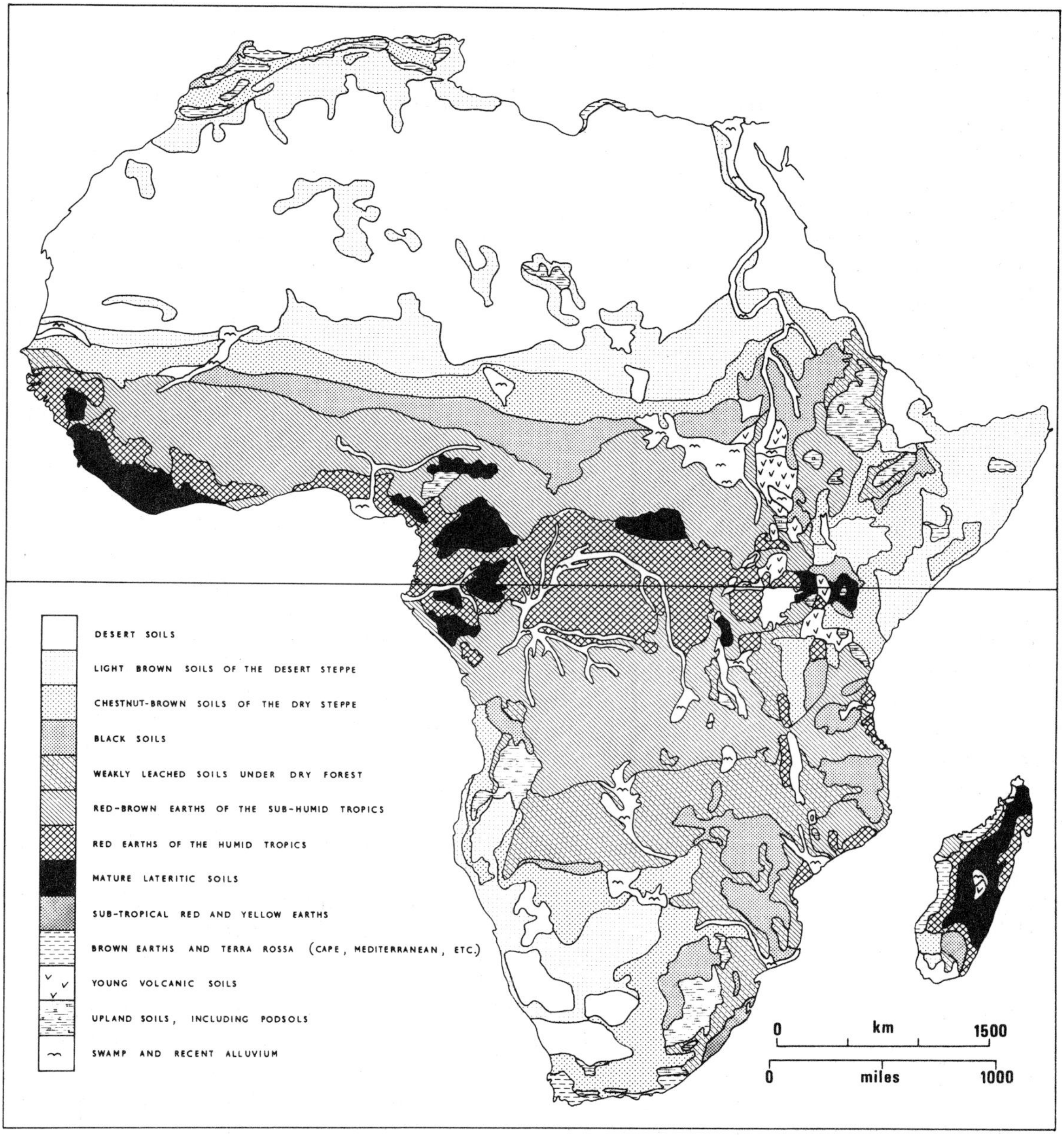

Figure 13 The soils of Africa

perature will be more significant than air temperature, but the latter will provide a useful guide. It is well known that, in general, the higher the temperature, the more rapidly chemical reactions proceed. In the humid tropics, which occupy much of central Africa, both rock weathering and soil formation therefore take place relatively quickly and efficiently. Even in the arid tropical regions the general lack of soil moisture is to some extent offset by the intensity of chemical reactions in high temperatures. In general, soil forms most rapidly and reaches maturity sooner in hot, wet conditions; while, on the other hand, cold, dry conditions (almost unknown in Africa) discourage the soil-forming processes.

However, there are other factors affecting soil development. Geology must not be ignored, relief and drainage also affect soil character and vegetation has a considerable influence. The influence of rock type on soils is most easily seen in areas where soil development is slow or has been retarded. Given sufficient time, and conditions of stability such that the soil is not affected by erosion, movement or surface deposition, the soil character will, with one exception, come to be independent of the underlying rock. It is well known that the chemical composition of all rock types, save only limestone, is basically very similar, consisting of 60–70 per cent silica, 5–20 per cent oxides of iron and aluminium, and numerous less-important minerals. The products of rock weathering are therefore very similar also; only in the case of limestone is the material on which the soil-forming processes set to work very different, and limestone formations are not extensive in Africa south of the Sahara.

The major part of Africa has been a region of stability since early geological times, and over large areas soil formation has gone on for long periods of time. In such areas the relatively minor differences in parent rock have become completely disguised by soil formation, provided only that there have been sufficient supplies of moisture to enable the soil-forming processes to work efficiently. It is common to find in Africa that the same rock in different climatic regions will give rise to different soils. Examples of areas in Africa where rock-type has more influence on soils are the deserts (where soil formation is retarded by lack of moisture) and regions of recent deposition (where soil-forming processes have not had time to operate).

The part played by relief and drainage in the development of various soil types has already been hinted at. Areas of free drainage help the movement of moisture through the soil; in extreme conditions of free drainage the soil may dry out, or if there is much rainfall the soil will be readily leached. On the other hand, in areas of impeded drainage, such as swamps or even some irrigated lowlands, the continuous evaporation often leads to the soil becoming excessively saline or alkaline. Relief is also of decisive importance in determining the local character of the soil. On flat areas, such as the widespread planation surfaces in Africa, soil development may proceed uninterrupted by superficial movement or significant erosion, and a soil may be able to reach full maturity (i.e. it becomes completely adapted to the local climate and hydrography irrespective of rock type). But in areas of strong relief, or wherever erosion is actively at work, the soil will always be immature, and reflect the parent rock more closely. On hillsides a whole series of different minor soil types will be found, according to degree of slope, drainage and rate of supply of weathered material from above. In Africa the great planation surfaces are all up-lifted; in consequence, their margins are areas of considerable dissection where no mature soils are likely to be found.

It is often thought that climate and soil largely determine the vegetation. Yet the latter has important effects on the soil in turn. It supplies the humus or organic matter to a soil; desert areas without vegetation possess only accumulations of weathered rock, which are not strictly soils. One must beware, however, of thinking that the vegetation can be used as an indicator of soil fertility. That this is a fallacy is easily shown by reference to the tropical rain forest, which, if cleared, exposes relatively poor soil. In this case it is the warm climate that encourages such luxuriant growth, the growth in turn providing its own organic nourishment. Clearing of rain forest, too, often leads to excessive leaching and surface erosion as a result of the high rainfall. One of the principal influences of all types of vegetation on the soil is to protect it. Vegetation will not only protect the surface from erosion (except under extreme conditions), it also shades the ground from temperature changes and protects it from excessive evaporation. The roots of plants serve not only to break up the soil, and therefore aid percolation, but also to hold it in position so that it has a better chance of mature development.

It has been pointed out that the decay of vegetable matter provides humus to enrich the soil. Humus is able to retain surprisingly large amounts of moisture, but can, of course, be removed by leaching if there is an excess of percolating water. Furthermore, humus may itself decompose, a process encouraged by high temperatures; over 25°C the decomposition of humus tends to outpace its formation. Many tropical soils are therefore poor in organic content.

Soils of generally reddish colour occur widely throughout tropical Africa and in South Africa even beyond the Tropic. This group of soils thus covers about one-third of the continent. The common characteristic of these soils is that they have been affected by a process known as 'laterization'. In a few areas this process has been carried virtually to completion, producing in the soil a material termed laterite, but over much larger areas the soils are only partly laterized. These immature tropical soils are often called 'red earths' or 'yellow earths', depending on their colour.

The formation of lateritic soils is complex and not fully understood, but the essential points are these. Under conditions of high temperature and abundant moisture in the soil, silica is leached downwards to accumulate in the lower layers. The oxides of iron and aluminium remain behind in the surface layers, but also appear to be greatly enriched by the same compounds moving upwards from the lower layers during dry periods. Thus, Fe_2O_3 and Al_2O_3 are precipitated in the form of a crust. The upward movement of these iron and aluminium compounds can only take place in dry periods and in conditions where the water table is not far below the ground surface. It is thus essential for the formation of mature lateritic soils that there should be an alternation of wet and dry seasons.

Other conditions linked with the process of laterization are that temperatures should be sufficiently high to promote leaching of the silica, and also to prevent any significant accumulation of humus in the soil; and that the area should not be liable to erosion. The second is most effectively maintained on areas of subdued relief such as planation surfaces, and under some form of vegetative cover in the initial stages at least. The mature lateritic soil may later become so infertile that vegetation degenerates into poor scrub. Then surface erosion may expose the iron crust to transform the surface layers into a purely mineral formation.

It should be emphasized again that the final product of laterization is relatively restricted in its extent in Africa. Over vast areas reddish soils representing early stages of laterization are to be found, but they have many characteristics in common with the mature lateritic soil. Low humus content leads to rapid soil exhaustion if lateritic soils are employed for any form of intensive agriculture. The high rainfall of the wet season leaches out many elements valuable for plant growth, such as potash, nitrogen or phosphorus. The great depth of weathered material associated with humid tropical conditions provides many opportunities for soil erosion once the vegetation is cleared on even moderate slopes; and the incipient iron crust makes it very difficult to arrest gullying once started, for the gullies rapidly enlarge by undercutting the crust.

Finally, brief mention at least must be made of man's potent influence on soil formation. Clearing of vegetation, cultivation of crops, the grazing of animals, all affect the soil. The practice of bush-fallowing affects the soil, and is in turn adapted to it, for incomplete clearance helps to prevent widespread soil erosion, and temporary abandonment of a patch of land helps it to regain a little of the fertility extracted by cultivation. More

Plate 3 Soil erosion as a result of overgrazing and overcultivation in northern Ghana

modern methods of cultivation usually involve ploughing the soil; this not only breaks up and mixes the surface soil, but also compacts the lower layers, thus hindering percolation and encouraging surface runoff. Removing vegetation before ploughing also leads to increased evaporation from the soil surface and exposes the soil to rainwash and erosion. In tropical areas of heavy rainfall it is essential that the land be cleared in small patches, that a temporary cover crop be employed and that ploughing should be done along the contour. Even such precautions may not be successful in preventing erosion. Intensive agriculture – repeated cash crops, for instance – quickly exhausts the natural fertility of the soil. Examples of this can be seen over many parts of Africa. All too often there is no attempt at crop rotation; in many cases manure or artificial fertilizers are not available or are too expensive. It is important to bear in mind how easily and quickly a soil, built up over thousands of years, can be impoverished or destroyed by unsuitable methods of cultivation, and that once destroyed, little can be done to replace it. Given the environmental conditions in many parts of Africa the soils are relatively fragile in a physical and chemical sense, and this has to be considered in the planning of agricultural development.

PART TWO: HUMAN GEOGRAPHY

5
Political evolution

From the fifteenth century onwards various European countries established settlements around the coasts of Africa. The earliest European settlements were in general of two sorts. There were 'ports of call', serving the trade routes with India and the East, such as those established in southern Africa by the Portuguese and later by the Dutch. Second there were the trading posts, also located on the coast, which dealt in the several commodities that Africa itself produced. Since the eastern side of the continent was far less accessible, and because most of it was already in the hands of the Arabs, these trading posts were located mainly along the Atlantic coast, and particularly along the shores of the Gulf of Guinea, where they could tap the resources of the area south of the Sahara.

The early traders were interested in a limited range of valuable products that could be obtained by barter without any need to penetrate inland. Ivory, gold and spices were in great demand, and names such as the Ivory Coast and Gold Coast date from this period. The most lucrative and extensive form of commerce, however, was the slave trade. In this case, too, the trade was carried on along or near to the coasts, where forts were built. In the interior the slave trade had long been under the control of the Arabs, whose influence and power extended right across the Sahara to the grasslands beyond the desert in West Africa, and who were jealous of any European attempts to penetrate from the coast and seek slaves for themselves. Largely because of the slave trade, the Africans were hostile to any Europeans, and it was due to these and other difficulties that the exploration of interior Africa was so long delayed.

As late as the year 1860 a map of Africa (Figure 14) shows only very limited European settlements and colonies, with the exception of the south, where the Dutch had been established since 1652 and the British since 1806. Throughout the whole of tropical Africa, European settlement was confined to the coastlands. The only settlement with non-European connections was Liberia. The founding of Liberia was linked with the freeing of slaves by several countries in the early nineteenth century. American desire to help ex-slaves led to the establishment of a colony for them in 1822 on Providence Island (Monrovia), and in 1847 the state of Liberia was founded. Earlier the British had also undertaken the resettlement of slaves in parts of Sierra Leone, and it was at this time (1792) that Freetown, the present capital, received its name.

In the two decades between 1880 and the close of the century the greater part of the continent of Africa was divided up among six European powers. Before taking a look at the manner in which the partition was effected, let us consider briefly why there should have been such a scramble for territory in Africa in these years. The second half of the nineteenth century showed a growing appreciation by European nations of the resources of Africa. It was soon realized that the most accessible source of tropical and sub-tropical products was West Africa. It was also realized that tropical Africa had considerable potentialities for the production of crops such as cotton, coffee, cocoa and sugar. With the progress of the Industrial Revolution, and the other

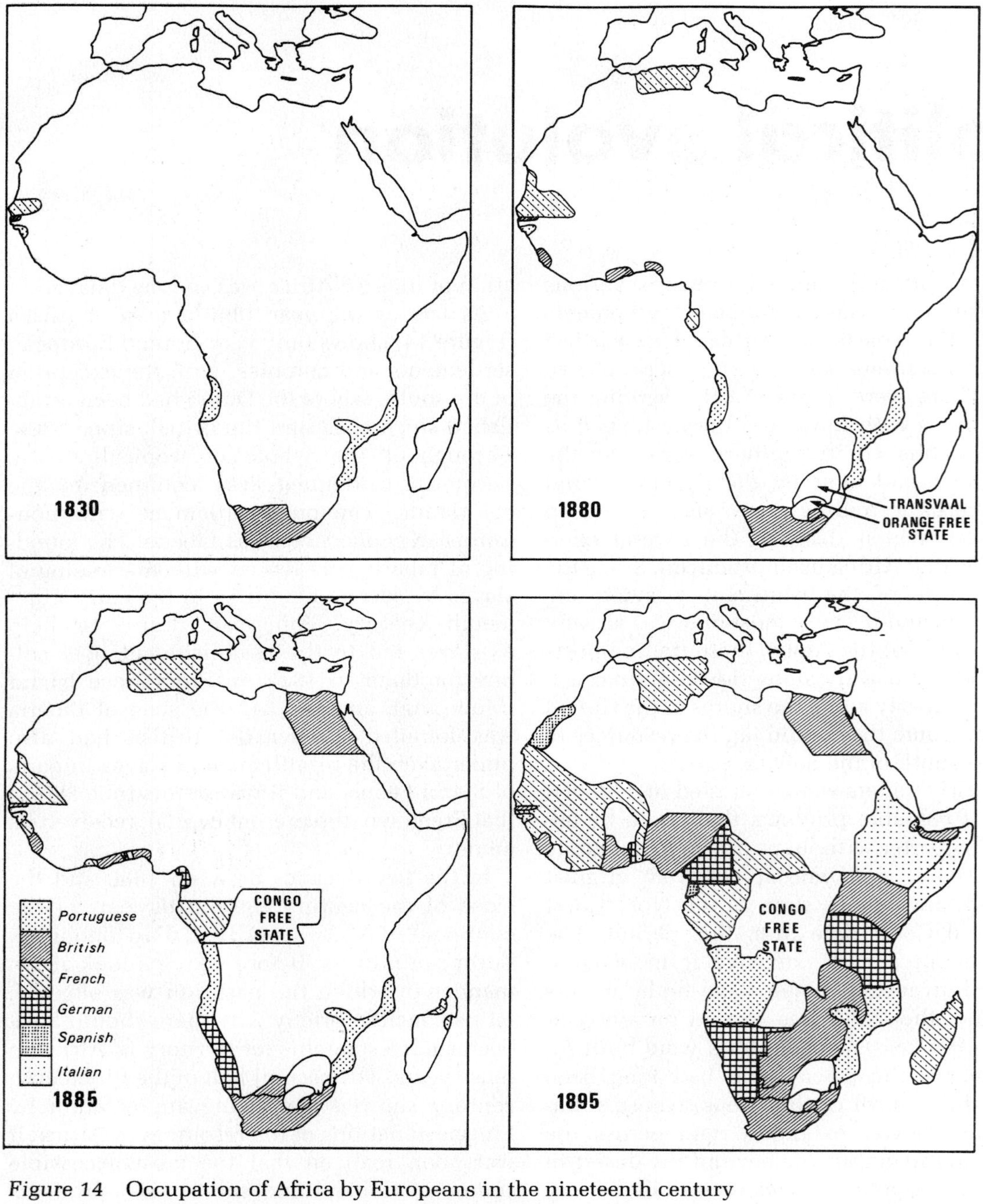

Figure 14 Occupation of Africa by Europeans in the nineteenth century

advances of the nineteenth century, raw materials and products such as these were in great demand. No longer were coastal trading posts in tropical Africa sufficient to cater for this demand; it was becoming essential to reach the sources of the raw materials in order to develop their production.

There was also a growing awareness among

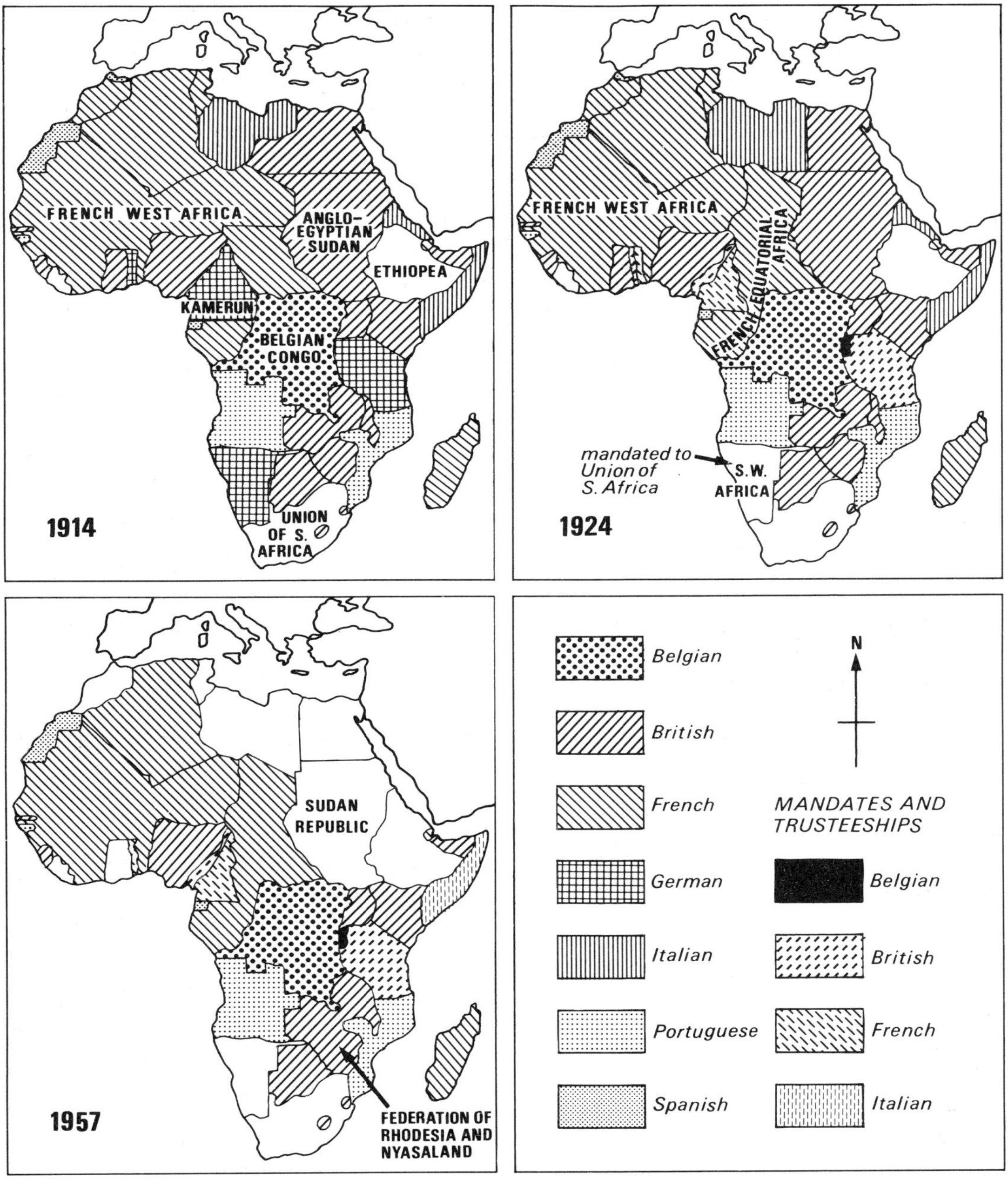

Figure 15 Occupation of Africa by Europeans in the twentieth century

industrialists of the period that the considerable population of Africa, particularly West Africa, represented an important market for the cheaper products of the Industrial Revolution; and, furthermore, the local population would provide the necessary cheap labour for the extraction of raw materials and the development of the resources.

These, briefly, were the main economic reasons why it was desirable to 'open up' Africa. But there were also political motives. Overseas colonies served to raise the prestige of the country possessing them, and there were already several successful examples of colonies in Africa. The French had established themselves in the north since the 1830s, and the British in the Cape since 1806. Explorers of various nationalities had demonstrated the main outlines of African physiography by 1880, and had revealed the existence of resources and lands merely awaiting acquisition and exploitation.

One other event in the second half of the nineteenth century must be mentioned: the opening of the Suez Canal in 1869. At last a direct route to eastern Africa was available, and at last Arab domination of eastern Africa and the Red Sea was broken. A new route to India was created, and as the Cape region of Africa declined in importance strategically, so the lands bordering the Red Sea and the Indian Ocean acquired a new significance.

In 1884 the first international convention to discuss the claims of various European nations to parts of Africa was held in Berlin, when it was agreed that claims to any territory must be upheld by effective occupancy. The Berlin Conference was followed by a rush on the part of the six major European nations interested in Africa to extend their territorial claims inland from their original coastal footholds. A spate of treaties between various nations and with the African chiefs ensued; tracts of land changed hands for loops of beads, and boundaries were laid down rapidly and arbitrarily as each power sought to obtain the largest possible slice of territory in Africa. By 1914 most of the present political boundaries in Africa were in existence and the process of partition was virtually complete.

The boundaries agreed between the colonizing powers brought arbitrary divisions where none had been before. Some followed watersheds, others used rivers (thereby disrupting the essential unity of a river basin), some were based on parallels, meridians or other mathematically defined lines. Very few paid heed to the convenience or customs of local tribes or peoples, for some cut across tribal lands or the regularly used routes of nomads (e.g. Kenya – Somalia). Rival tribes found themselves in the same country and hostility between them continues despite independence (e.g. the Shona and Ndebele and Zimbabwe). Rivers and ports were severed from their hinterlands (e.g. Gambia) and a number of territories had no direct access to the coast and ports. The artificial character of the boundaries reflects the speed with which they were drawn up and a general ignorance of inland Africa and its inhabitants.

Thus the present countries of Africa owe their shape, size and independence to the disintegration of imperial systems quite unrelated to local conditions. Adjustment of unsatisfactory boundaries upon the attainment of independence did not take place. The imposed political pattern was accepted: it was felt that the existence of the new state depended upon assertion of the validity of the inherited boundaries, and within those boundaries an awareness of a national identity needed to be inculcated.

RECENT POLITICAL CHANGES IN AFRICA

The story of the partition of Africa between approximately 1880 and 1920 is a complex one and has been summarized in Figures 14 and 15. Developments in Africa since 1920, and more especially since 1945, have been proceeding at a rapid pace. The progress of settlement, the improvements in communications, the expansion of agriculture, mining and industry, and general attempts at economic development, will be dealt with in the regional chapters; at the moment it is the major political changes that command attention.

The period since the Second World War has seen the growth and emergence of African nationalism, which (except in the Republic of South Africa) has established self-government by Africans throughout the continent. In 1950 the only independent states in the continent were the Union of South Africa, Egypt, Ethiopia and Liberia. By 1980 all the countries of Africa (except Namibia) had attained independence, even though many still retained economic or defence links with the former colonial power.

Independent Africa has cut a sorry figure during the last twenty-five years. It remains the poorest of the continents, it has the lowest levels of life expectancy, the lowest rates of economic growth. Vast areas suffer from famine; several million refugees exist in misery beyond their own frontiers; civil wars rage with inhuman ferocity, wasting scarce resources; democratic government has been swept from nearly every African state as dictators, or the military with their generals, stifle opposition and seize power. (In 1985 nearly 20 African states had military governments.) In the last 25 years over 50 leaders in nearly 30 African countries have been swept from power by assassination, purges or *coups*.

In general the handover of power and withdrawal of the colonial powers was too hurried and ill-prepared. Among the indigenes there was a dearth of experienced administrators and civil servants and a lack of managers, accountants, clerks and technicians to keep the fabric of a modern state in repair. This was particularly so where, as in Algeria, there was an almost complete exodus of the French who ran the businesses, banks, industries and farms. Many Africans who were little more than just literate found themselves in managerial positions.

For much of the period aid in the form of grants, loans and food was generously available from ex-colonial powers, the World Bank and other developed countries: a reaction to conscience expected as their due by the ex-colonies. This meant that they remained dependent – economic colonialism became recognized. Aid and investment necessarily became channelled into the newly independent states via their governments and the burgeoning bureaucracies that fed upon it and politicized every aspect. This easily obtained wealth was dissipated on costly prestigious projects, into grandiose schemes never completed and enormous amounts became siphoned off to private purses, for bribery and corruption became a way of life. Avarice and lust for power brought out rivalries and strife and the enlisting of support, and the obtaining of arms from either East or West. Ideology fashioned policies, from the use of Cuban troops (e.g. in Angola) to Marxist socialist programmes among the mainly left-wing governments. What is clear is that the mass of African peoples received independence but little liberty; they have benefited little for there has been a general neglect of agriculture and the countryside in favour of the urban centres. Too often they have a vote, but it can only be cast for one man. With this background it is, perhaps, not astonishing that African rulers in their scramble to gain and hold power have paid so little attention to the immediate problems of starvation and massive debt and indulged too much in anti-colonial rhetoric. In this last decade of the century, faced by massive debts and in places by famine, a new realism among African governments is becoming apparent. Disciplined public spending policies to restore faith in agriculture, to boost private initiatives and to follow Western rather than discredited Marxist policies are now becoming accepted.

6
Population and society

Population data for Africa slowly increase in volume, scope and reliability, but there are nevertheless still large deficiencies in our demographic knowledge of the continent and a considerable awareness of the tentative character of the statistics that are published. The UN estimate for the total population of the continent for 1985 was 550 million, and this figure is probably several million too much or too little. It will be several more decades before reasonably accurate figures derived from comprehensive census-taking become available.

Much of tropical Africa so far has had no more than one census, and in these censuses techniques are rudimentary in comparison with the sophisticated operation in most European countries. The high levels of illiteracy necessitate enumerators visiting, questioning and recording each household; the scarcity of literate persons makes it difficult to secure sufficient enumerators and necessitates carrying out the census over a lengthy period. In some cases censuses of sample areas are taken and estimates of total population are made from them, but as techniques improve the enumeration increasingly becomes extended to whole countries. Also the scope of the information sought widens from a simple counting of heads to include such data as race, age, sex, place of birth, marital status, polygamy, number of sons born and occupation. Where elements of the population are suspicious or hostile, inaccuracies are bound to occur, and since almost everywhere in Africa there is no registration of birth, age data are very unreliable. Nevertheless much progress has been made since the end of the Second World War in response to the urgent need for more population data in a host of former colonies where franchise is becoming extended and where it is necessary to have population data as an aid to economic and social planning.

The racial composition of Africa's population is a factor of great importance. Here the Sahara is something of a divide. The Sahara is often held to separate Africa from Europe, rather than the Mediterranean, for the countries of North Africa are Mediterranean countries and closer to Greece, southern Spain and Turkey than to the countries of *Afrique Noire* to the south of the great desert. These countries of northern Africa contain some 105 million people, while 'black Africa' holds some 445 million. An important fact is that, of this vast total, little more than 4 million are of European descent. These relatively few white people have a far greater importance than their puny numbers suggest. They have been the energetic leaders and innovators responsible for the economic development of the continent by bringing in ideas, techniques, capital, enterprise and organization, and imposing law, order and stability in the process. Of these 4 million about 3 million are in the Republic of South Africa and about half a million in former French North Africa. Thus the white population over the rest of Africa numbers less than 1 million. Other notable components of the population are Asians, probably less than 1 million and mainly Indian, but also including Syrians and Lebanese. The Indians are to be found along the east coast, particularly in Natal and East Africa, where at the turn of the century they entered as indentured labour to help on sugar plantations or in railway construction, afterwards settling, many to become traders, shopkeepers and small business people.

DENSITY AND DISTRIBUTION OF POPULATION

Of considerable economic significance is the fact that Africa is a continent with a low density of population (17 per km^2 in 1985); but this is a considerable increase on the 9 per km^2 in 1960 and 11 per km^2 in 1970 and reflects the fact that, whereas Africa lagged behind the other continents in the 'population explosion', it is now overtaking them in the rates of increase to its population.

The low density of population emphasizes the fact that many African countries are held back in their economic development by a lack of population and, paradoxically, many are also being held back by the recent increases in their people's fertility which change the structure of their populations.

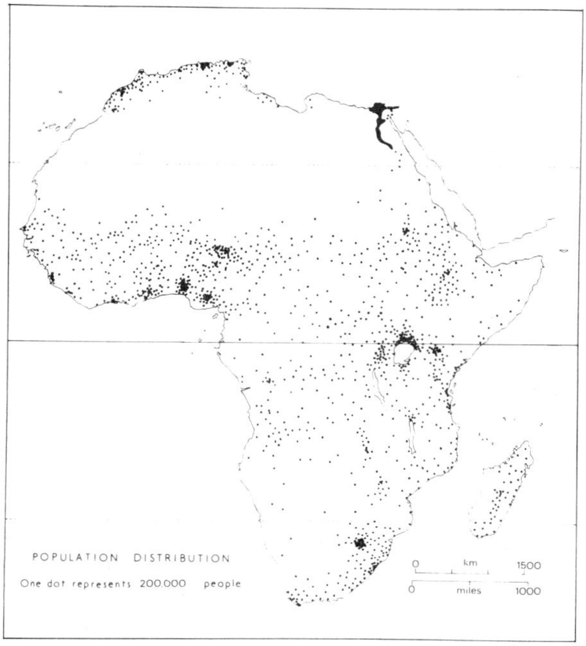

Figure 16 Population distribution

The distribution of the population over the continent (Figure 16) is quite uneven and in some areas very high densities prevail. The Nile valley supports in places over 1000 people per km^2, adjacent to the uninhabited wastes of the Sahara which cover more than a quarter of the continent. Except for the Nile valley in Egypt, the valleys of the major rivers of Africa are not densely settled, the physical conditions generally being unfavourable. If one excepts the few developed industrial and mining areas of southern Africa, it will be perceived that water supply is the paramount geographical influence upon the pattern of African settlement, for most livelihood is dependent on farming or pastoral activities.

Much of Africa offers too much or too little rainfall, but aridity is the principal limiting factor. A number of favoured areas support heavy populations, and in certain places over-population imposes increasing problems, as in parts of West Africa, the lake region of the East African highland and the Egyptian Nile valley. The sparseness of population over wide areas has far-reaching social and economic implications and is particularly noticeable in many cases where foreign (usually European) commercial and mining ventures need to overcome labour shortage by fostering labour migrations on a considerable scale. In a sense this eases the problems of many of the over-populated areas which supply the migrant labour, but raises a number of other serious social and economic problems. Local over-population leads to over-stocking and over-cropping of the soil, resulting in lowered soil fertility and the alteration of both the chemical and physical properties of the soil; steep slopes progressively come under cultivation with the ever-attendant danger of soil erosion. This, if in the hills near watersheds, is particularly serious, for the continent is short of water and cannot afford the destruction of catchment areas.

POPULATION STRUCTURES

Our knowledge of the structure of African populations (i.e. proportions between the sexes and between the age groups) is remarkably slender. Some African countries have not yet carried out censuses in sufficient detail, and for those that have a considerable degree of error must be accepted. In any case it is rare for a previous census to exist which would permit comparisons.

From the data that have been collected it is clear that the population is now increasing markedly after a period when it was probably static or increasing but slowly. This is due principally to the effects of the 'medical revolution', whereby growing medical knowledge, new drugs and instruction in hygiene are preserving and lengthening lives, especially those of babies and young children. The population pyramids (or bar graphs of age and sex distribution) of African countries where data are available bear this out (Figure 17). The very broad base where each succeeding cohort is larger than its predecessor is typical. Thus the very high proportion of young children is a notable factor that will have increasing social and economic impact in future years.

Each new member of society adds to demands on education, health and other public services and ultimately requires employment. These needs can only be met by increased capital investment in expanding existing facilities (e.g. extra housing, schools, hospitals) instead of increasing capital investment per worker to enlarge productivity. Thus heavy increases of numbers creating populations of substantial juvenility (where over 40 to almost 50 per cent of the population are under 15 years of age, as in Kenya, Zimbabwe, Côte d'Ivoire and Ghana) may be expected to retard economic development and even to reduce output per head unless vast capital resources are available. The increasing number of old folk (e.g. over 65) added to the mass of young gives a dependent status to a very high proportion of these populations.

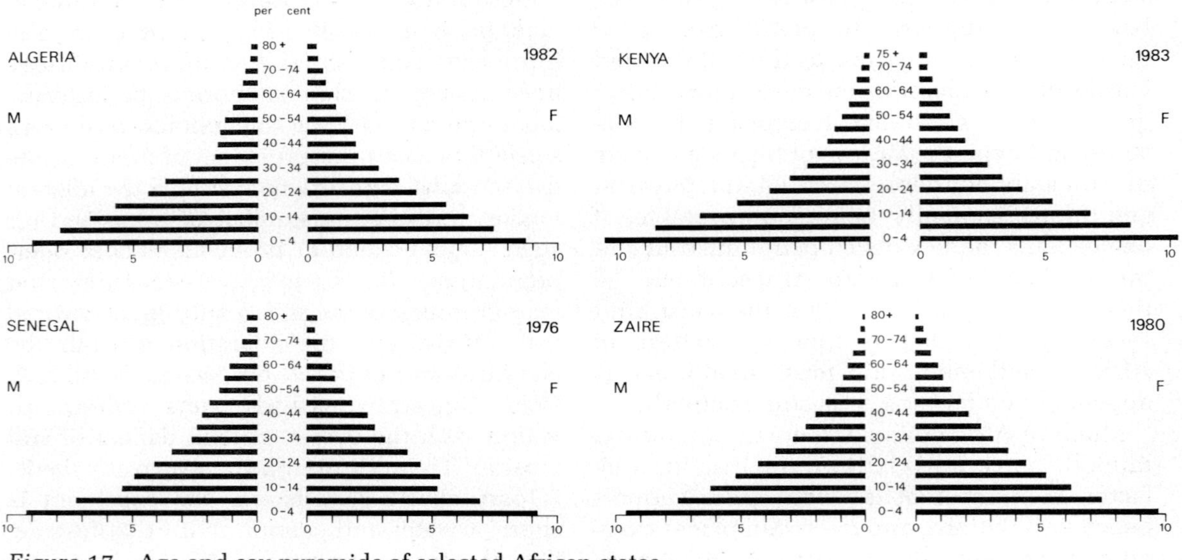

Figure 17 Age and sex pyramids of selected African states

Africa now contains countries with some of the highest rates of population increase in the world (see Table 1). If present rates continue Kenya, for example, will double its 22 million in the next 18 years and Côte d'Ivoire's 10 million will double in 20 years. This emphasizes the geometric character of population increase: the present growing number of children with the passing of years will enter the reproductive period and unless their fertility reduces will create a population of unprecedented fecundity. In Africa the level of fertility is very high, birth rates generally being between 40 or 50 per thousand. Death rates (from about 15 to 25 per 1000) are still moderately high, but as they continue to reduce the excess of births over deaths will grow unless birth rates lessen. Experience shows that the latter usually occurs with economic and social development and the spread of education, situations not yet widely experienced over most of Africa.

Although there is little to indicate a slowing down of the rate of population increase in the near future, the attitudes of governments to family planning are changing. In 1974 only seven African countries had family planning programmes, but by 1980 fifty-one countries went so far as to acknowledge a relationship between their population difficulties and implementing their development programmes. Over most of Africa no more than 1–2 per cent of married women were using contraceptives in 1982, although in a few countries the percentages were much higher (e.g. Egypt 24, Morocco 26, Zimbabwe 22, Tunisia 41). Africa is now beginning to experience the 'population explosion' formerly experienced by Asia and South America.

Plate 4 Family planning clinic, Basse, The Gambia

THE PEOPLES OF AFRICA

Racial composition

The 550 million African people are not homogeneous. They are divided into innumerable tribal groupings, speak about 700 different languages and reveal a variety of physical types.

Archaeological and anthropological evidence suggests that Africa has been peopled by a succession of invasions from the east and north-east, particularly by way of the Horn of Africa. Each increment of newcomers has tended to push the established peoples fanwise from East Africa, and we now find some of the earliest people still at a most primitive level pushed off the southern savanna grazing and hunting lands to the semi-arid Kalahari. In all cases, over long periods, inter-marrying must have occurred: this fusion has blurred the physical characteristics of the different stocks, so that today ethnic classification relies more on language and culture. The peoples of Africa have been derived from the following stocks or an admixture of two of them: Negritos (or Pygmies), Bushmen, Negro, Hamites and Semites and, mainly in South Africa, Caucasians. The intermixing of Hamites with the Negroes has produced such subtypes as Nilotes and Nilo-Hamites.

The major classification of African people is according to their Negroid or non-Negroid characteristics. The Sahara, the North African littoral and the Horn of Africa are principally peopled by the Semitic and Hamitic ethnic groups: people akin to Jews and Arabs. There has been much mixing, but Hamitic people of Caucasoid descent occupy the Horn of Africa, the western Sahara and parts of Algeria and Tunisia. They represent the older peoples, many of whom were overcome and absorbed by the Semitic–Mohammedan invasions of the seventh and eleventh and twelfth centuries which led to the immigration of some 400,000 Arabs and the spread of Islam and the Arab language. Inter-marriage has frequently made it difficult to distinguish between these peoples. The name Berber is pplied to the Hamitic people of North Africa (from the Latin *Barbari*). Anthropologists recognize a number of Berber types, but generally they are fairly tall, light-brown or fair skinned, with brown hair, straight thin noses and non-everted lips. The thinly populated Sahara is the home of the Hamitic Tuareg, Tibu and Fulani. The last show much evidence of dilution with West African Negroid peoples on the southern edge of the desert. In the eastern Sahara the earliest Egyptians were of Hamitic stock and their present descendants, despite much Semitic infusion, still bear many resemblances to their predynastic forerunners. To the south, Hamitic and Semitic peoples extend to the Somali coast. Ethiopian people are mainly Hamitic but Semitic influence in culture and language is strong. In parts of the upper Nile Basin and of the East African plateau, probably as a result of a southward move of Hamites, distinctive hybrid types have developed, partly Hamitic and partly Negroid. These people are darker than the Hamites, but they retain the finer non-Negroid facial features with the woolly hair of the Negro. The term Nilotes has been given to these peoples in the Sudanese parts of the Nile valley, particularly the pastoral Shilluk and Dinka. Farther south, on the East African plateaux, small groups of Hamito-Negro people exist in a mainly Bantu Negroid area. Examples are the virile pastoral Nandi and Masai people of Kenya and northern Tanzania.

South of the Sahara and the Horn of Africa, Africans are members of the Negro race but show considerable variations in stature, pigmentation, hair-form and facial characteristics. Over the centuries, in Central and East Africa, migrations – generally south-westward from the lakes and southward down the eastern part – have brought about a great mixing of Negroid peoples, usually classed as Bantu-speaking, and have pushed into the equatorial forest the Negroid pygmies and to the Kalahari desert and its fringes the interesting remnants of the Bushmen and Hottentots. The Pygmies average 1.35 m in height and are hunters, trappers and collectors. They shun outside contacts and have thus preserved their identity. There are probably about 150,000 of them living in small communities in forest clearings in Zaire and Congo. The Bushmen have been reduced to a few surviving bands. Their way of life – among the world's simplest – has continued to be based on hunting and they are hard put to survive in their inhospitable semi-desert environment. The Hottentots, once herding peoples, have now become servants and labourers of the incoming white peoples and are a major element in the coloured population of the Cape.

The Bantu-speaking peoples of southern, Central and East Africa occupy nearly one-third of the continent. They speak various dialects of a common language. In the eastern part of Africa, south of the Sahara, on the drier upland plains (except where the tsetse fly is prevalent), pastoral economies are paramount. Cattle are the principal animals reared, and in some areas (such as East Africa) a prestige system based upon numbers of cattle possessed irrespective of quality lends a social rather than economic aspect to such a system. The system generally includes agricultural self-sufficiency based on family gardens, but for long there was little exchange of goods (apart from beasts during ceremonial occasions). Thus the market is a feature fairly new to eastern Africa, and there has been little stimulation of native crafts. An exception to this general pattern is seen in the densely peopled area around Lake Victoria, especially in Uganda. Farther south the settlement of the white man on the better land and introduction of new ways of living have led to considerable disruption of tribal life. For example, the once great Zulu people, living east and south of the Drakensberg Escarpment, have suffered considerable disintegration by the spread of white settlement, which brought with it opportunities for work in farm, mine and factory.

In the lower-lying forested basins and plains of the Zaire river, the heavier rainfall and the prevalence of tsetse fly and other pests and diseases have helped to make agriculture the prime activity, rather than pastoralism. Some Bantu peoples, such as the Fang inhabiting parts of equatorial Africa, practice shifting cultivation in forest clearings, rarely staying more than two or three years in one place. Others, such as the Bakuba, occupying a more open part of the Kasai Basin, engage in more settled agriculture. Trade plays a part in the economic and social life and regular markets are maintained.

Some of the purest Negro types are found across the northern savanna lands from the western Sudan into West Africa and these comprise the Sudanese Negro type. These Negroes are tall, with black or very dark-brown skin, woolly hair, broad nose and thick, everted lips. Almost all are cultivators. This concentration on agriculture allows the support of a denser population and has facilitated a degree of specialization and division of labour. Metal-working, textiles and pottery of a high quality exemplify this tradition and have fostered trade, the market and the town of the Guinea coast and western Sudan. Indeed, the passion for trading seems inherent in west-African people, from the enterprising Hausa of northern Nigeria to the bustling tribes of the coast where the Yoruba market women – the 'mammies' – with their high, gaily coloured head-dress are a familiar sight. This part of Africa leads in having a well-established middle class: merchants who handle goods rather than produce them and who may well trace back their affluence to ancestors who became 'trade-boys', supplying visiting European vessels with much-prized gold and slaves from the hinterland.

THE DECLINE OF THE TRIBAL SYSTEM

The closing years of the twentieth century are witnessing a rapid decline of the tribal system in Africa. The pace of change varies in different parts of the continent, but the process seems inevitable as social and economic values change, as Western technology finds application and as political power becomes a real, desirable and attainable thing. The tribal system has become outmoded. With the principal exception of the more urban West Africa, until recent years there was little division of labour, no notable wealthy class, nor dominant aristocracy among the majority of African people; ideas of class and caste have been alien to the African mind. The common links between members of a group or tribe are symbols in the form of myths, dogmas, rituals, sacred places and persons. Sacred values contribute to a cohesive social system where there are duties and obligations to elders and position within a tribe only advances with age. The self-sufficient organization of such communities has offered little opportunity for innovation or individualism. Problems are decided by communal decision, central authority generally is absent. The system has not fostered inter-tribal links, but rather has tended to emphasize differences and rivalry. It has also tended to keep women in a position of inferior status and, by its system of communal land working and annually changing allotment of land, gives the cultivator no incentive to improve the plot he crops. On the whole this system has hindered progress.

The undermining and weakening of the tribal system has been the most notable result of the introduction of a money economy, leading to the growth of desire for manufactured novelties and goods impossible to attain under a communal subsistence system. These desires have been fanned by the return of men from their migration to work in mines, industry and towns, bringing with them knowledge of new social and economic values.

A major but unexpected result of the white man's occupation of Africa is to be seen in the growing numbers of Africans travelling often hundreds of miles in search of employment. Fiscal measures requiring the payment of money taxes, the overcrowding of reserves and tribal lands, and no doubt the desire to be a man and see the world, all contribute to these labour movements where mines of Zambia, the growing industries of Zimbabwe, the mines and industries of the Republic of South Africa and the plantations of the Côte d'Ivoire are the main magnets. The movements are no longer haphazard; quotas are imposed by the receiving countries, and the proportion of families accompanying their menfolk slowly increases. All this has had unfortunate effects upon traditional life styles.

The tribal African entering urban society is confronted by entirely different social and economic values, where individualism is not merely unchecked but often encouraged, where personal responsibility is the rule, where conduct is no longer controlled by tradition and enforced by elders, where he is expected to labour all the time for a set period and often beside men of different tribal origins and habits. He finds himself subjected to all manner of social and moral innovations and temptations. He has entered a new world and returns to his tribal home a changed man, wearing an air of sophistication, possibly sceptical of tribal observances and less impressed by the elders. This continuing process results in growing numbers breaking with the tribe and drifting to permanent employment in the towns – the landless, wage-earning, detribalized natives.

Other forces are also at work. The waning of subsistence economies and growth of cash and exchange economies lead to changes in forms of land tenure which strengthen the individual at the expense of the tribe. Improvements in agricultural efficiency require the consolidation of fragmented holdings into a lesser number of larger plots, and the long-term identification of these plots with particular individuals who will then have incentive to improve the husbandry. From this arises the need for the issuing of title deeds and registering of the land, which give security value for the raising of loans and mortgages and thus make it possible for the peasant cultivator to raise the capital for improvements. All this weakens the tribal system which suffers further when state nationalism, which to be effective must override tribal boundaries, brings into power those dedicated to a new order. The period of uneasy transition and readjustment will be lengthy, while modern administrative and technical services, government and a new ordering of society gradually evolve as traditional influences slowly wane.

7
Settlement patterns, health and education

URBAN EXPANSION

Before the coming of the white man, over most of the continent the African people had not developed towns. The exceptions were in West Africa and in the Arab north. Over most of the continent the pattern, only now becoming disturbed, has been for settlement in family groups within the tribe. In Bantu Africa this takes the form of dispersed nucleations of beehive-type, mud-walled, conical thatch-roofed huts, usually with attendant cattle-pens and adjacent gardens or fields. In Negroid Africa the housing form is often clay-walled, thatch-roofed rectangular buildings around a central compound. Thick thorn hedges enclose and protect the human and animal population. This pattern reflects the subsistence character of the economy, is often related to water supply and shaped for defence and mutual protection. Sometimes the grouping may be no more than a hamlet comprising the half-dozen huts of a family group, but in other cases a young 'town' of scores of huts may surround the kraal of the tribal chief.

Among the settled population of North Africa the tribal influence is far less prevalent, but the agglomeration of the agricultural population into villages remains typical. In the Nile valley and delta the mud-walled huts, their flat roofs thatched with millet or maize stalks, cluster in tight nuclei. In the Algerian Tell dense cactus and prickly-pear hedges surround similar hamlets, while in the less accessible Atlas Mountains houses of mud, stone and date-palm timber cluster, almost precariously, on precipitous crags and ridges.

The lure of the town is now strong throughout Africa. Nevertheless Africa is still the least urbanized of the continents, for barely 25 per cent of the population lives in communities of more than 5000 people. There are only 180 towns with populations of over 100,000, and the continent can boast only 12 or 13 'million' cities. In many countries the rural population exceeds 80 per cent of the total. The small number of long-established African towns founded by the indigenous peoples is mainly restricted to Arab Africa in the north. Cairo, Algiers, Tunis, Marrakech and Omdurman are examples where administrative and commercial functions burgeoning from favourable locations pre-dated European influence. In parts of West Africa an urban way of life is found chiefly among the Yoruba of western Nigeria (where about 50 per cent of the population lives in settlements of 5000 or more inhabitants) and the centres of the Moslem emirates of northern Nigeria. Examples of these towns are Ibadan, Ife, Sokoto and Katsina. Elsewhere in Africa, apart from towns of the white man's creation, grouping in villages is predominant.

The modern phase in Africa results from contacts with Europeans; the towns and cities of southern Africa in particular are the creations of white man at port, mine or mart. Already in the Republic of South Africa some 25 per cent of Africans are living in towns. The significance of urbanization to the African

Plate 5 Shanty settlement, Freetown, Sierra Leone

in terms of mental, social, economic and political effect must not be under-estimated. Urbanized Africans increasingly become Westernized Africans; the town is the door to Western culture and society. The urban setting is attractive to a variety of industries: the agglomeration of people makes possible the provision of pure water, sewerage, gas and electricity supplies, law and order, education, health facilities and so on. All are part of the infrastructure necessary for the establishment of modern manufacturing industry. Thus towns and their rates of growth become something of an index of economic development. Equally, these services and facilities are coming to be appreciated by the Africans, the demand for schools and hospitals is increasing sharply, and it is the towns that generally have first call on these expanding services. Also, a far greater range of employment opportunities and a higher standard of living are offered by the town than by the country. New and exciting wage-earning ways of living far different from the ill-rewarded communal toil of agriculture are now drawing the tribesman to the town and in time into the modern world, for the town's businesses require clerks, shop assistants, domestic servants, drivers, mechanics, factory operatives and labourers. Thus, particularly in the last two decades, the pace of urbanization has increased in Africa and a new range of problems has come into being. The influx of new population now bears little relation to the growth in the town's economy and the creation of new jobs.

The growing drift from the countryside gathers speed, but it is also selective: it is the capital cities and largest towns that attract most migrants, enhancing an already high degree of primacy. For example, in the decade 1962–72 Kinshasa quadrupled its population (from 400,000 to 1.6 million), a rate of growth far exceeding the rate of house building and the provision of health, education and other social services. This has meant that, along with many other major African cities, its character is changing. There is a core area of solidly built European-style buildings surrounded by spacious residential suburbs; but the whole is now almost submerged by the shanty towns of squatters mushrooming on vacant plots within the cities, but the majority necessarily being peripheral. These accretions have had insufficient time to become assimilated into the urban milieu; instead of the urbanization of rural migrants we are witnessing the ruralization of the towns, for the expanding shanty towns are becoming village appendages attached to the town. Their inhabitants coagulate into family and tribal groupings, in the city but not of the city. Under-employment in the countryside becomes transferred as unemployment in the towns, often creating unrest, discontent and delinquency.

Africa's expanding large towns have had an increasing influence upon development policies and measures. Political Africans are generally urban Africans, for it is in the towns that much of the political life is to be found. Meetings, newspapers, speakers bring new ideas and stir opinions. Discussion in the social and economic fields may well be affected by the presence and influence of discontented

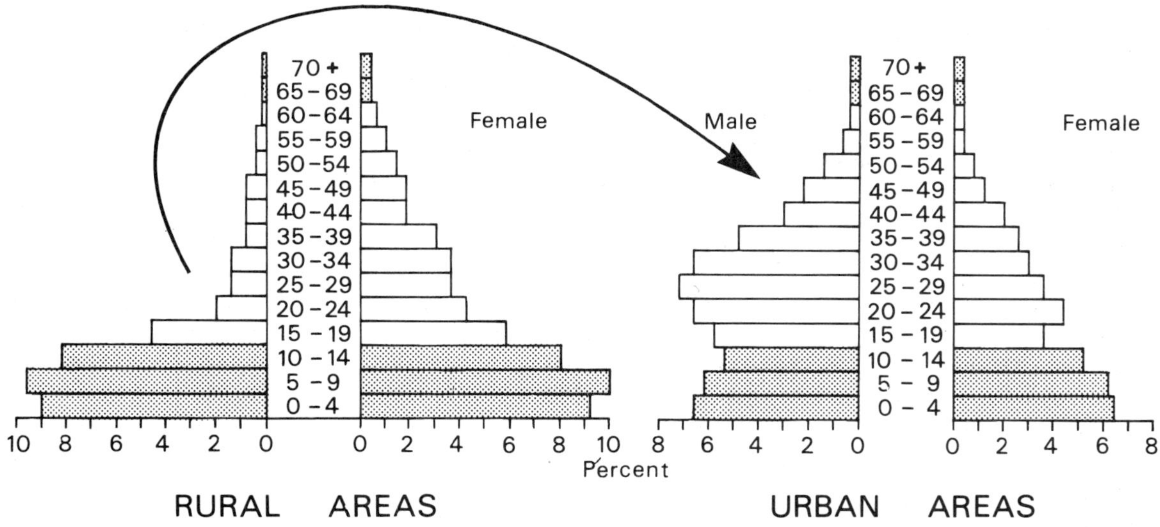

Figure 18 A typical rural–urban migration
Source: J. Hanks, *Rhodesian Science News*, **7** (1973)

urban masses. Planners and administrators are townsmen, often now with little understanding of the countryside. An urban bias in planning and in the disbursement of development and aid capital has been common; pricing measures whereby the urbanite gets cheap food, generally at the expense of the rural producer, is also widespread. Family incomes in towns are generally two to three times those of the countryside.

The rural areas suffer further for, as we have seen, the substantial migration to work and to the town leads to a shortage of men in farming. The countryside loses its most active workers – the more ambitious and better educated – and farming becomes left in the hands of less capable people. Production diminishes and increasingly concentrates upon subsistence needs. The needs of the growing urban masses have to be met by massive food imports, while at the same time reduced exports of primary products bring in less foreign exchange, and make it difficult to pay for the growing food imports.

The actual pace of African urbanization is becoming clearer as more data become available. The amazing rate of growth of the major African cities is shown in Table 3. In many cases the totals are under-estimated, for squatters are difficult to enumerate and many may be uncounted because the official town boundaries have not moved out to include them. It is possible that by the mid-1980s Greater Cairo held a population of 10 million, Tunis and Dakar over 1 million and Nairobi almost a million. Northern Africa has the highest proportion of urban population to total population, currently between 35 and 40 per cent; East Africa, from Kenya south to Mozambique, has the least urban population (7–10 per cent), but current rates of increase are high (8–10 per cent a year).

These figures reflect considerable in-migration in addition to a high rate of natural increase. Estimates are of town growth at 6–9 per cent a year (two or three times the average rate of African national increase), and the growth of squatter settlements reaching to 12 per cent a year. While it remains true that the large towns provide centres of modernization and instruments of change in people's outlooks, values and ways of life, these functions are becoming impeded with excessive growth, swamping the provision of basic services and amenities and with mushrooming shanty towns retaining village characteristics. Over-

Table 3 *Growth of major African cities, 1940–80*

	1940	*1950*	*1960*	*1970*	*1980*
Cairo	1,307,000	2,100,000	3,348,000	4,961,000	6,900,000*
Alexandria	682,000	925,000	1,516,000	2,032,000	2,318,000
Kinshasa		208,000	402,500	1,323,000	2,700,000
Casablanca	268,000	551,000	965,300	1,371,000	2,400,000
Algiers	252,000	315,000	883,900	1,000,000	1,740,000
Lagos		250,000	675,000	1,477,000	3,000,000
Johannesburg	286,000	880,000	1,111,000	1,433,000	1,726,000
Addis Ababa	150,000	300,000	444,000	799,000	1,277,000
Khartoum, Greater	190,000	240,000	350,000	648,000	1,264,000
Cape Town	187,000	594,000	745,800	1,096,000	1,500,000
Tunis	220,000	365,000	680,000	700,000	944,000
Durban	115,000	496,000	660,000	850,000	960,000
Abidjan		80,000	220,000	510,000	1,200,000
Ibadan	387,000	335,000	600,000	728,000	1,100,000
Nairobi	100,000	112,000	267,000	535,000	850,000
Dakar	165,000	230,000	374,000	590,000	979,000
Dar-es-Salaam		80,000	170,000	344,000	760,000
Accra	73,000	140,000	388,000	738,000	1,100,000
Harare	51,000	120,000	270,000	480,000	686,000
Lusaka			122,300	270,000	641,000
Pretoria	257,000	245,000	422,000	562,000	740,000
Oran	195,000	260,000	330,000	350,000	543,000
Port Elizabeth	125,000	148,000	274,000	469,000	585,000

Note: *1975 estimate.
Source: Demographic Yearbooks (New York, various years).

rapid urbanization associated with the neglect of agriculture and soaring food bills is the most serious problem facing most African states in the last decade of the twentieth century.

POPULATION MOBILITY

While African populations as a whole are reasonably static, considerable elements within them are highly mobile. Much of this mobility has been made possible by the enabling work of the white man, and then made necessary by his policies of taxation and his labour-needing commercial exploitation of mines, farms and plantations. The colonial governments stamped out tribal warfare and created peaceful conditions. They created and improved roads and railways, making cheap movement possible and furthering a growing pattern of labour migration, which is now one of the major forms of mobility in the continent. In comparison with the other continents the degree of mobility of African population is outstanding. Virtually every type of mobility is exemplified somewhere in Africa and a simplified typology is shown in Figure 19.

Some population movements are traditional and functioned long before the coming of the colonists. Principal among these are the old-established movements of pastoralists and some agriculturalists who still make their annual movements, ignoring modern bound-

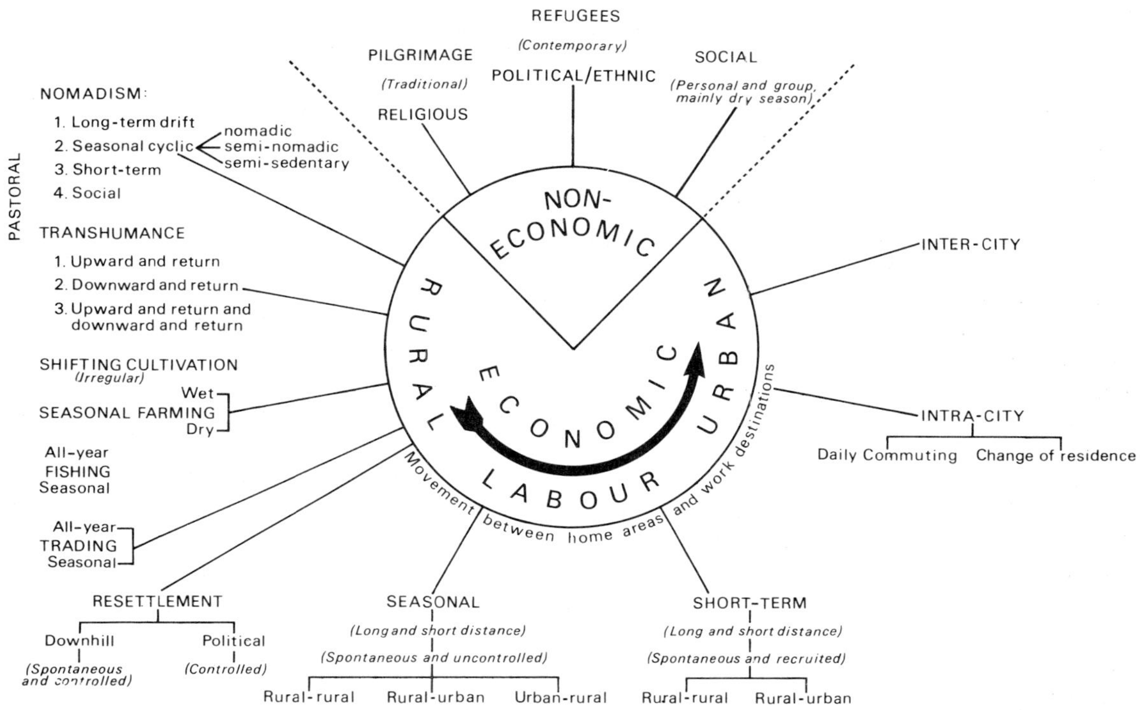

Figure 19 Simplified typology of African mobility
Source: After Prothero.

aries. The Somali pastoralists who move with their flocks and herds over the Haud in Ethiopia are a major example. Another traditional movement, made at least once in a lifetime, is the Moslem pilgrimage to Mecca. Northern Africa as far south as the Sahelian zone and the coastal parts of East Africa acknowledge Islam, and land and sea routes followed by the pilgrims are long-established. A major line of movement follows the Sudanic/ Sahelian belt from West Africa across to Sudan and the Red Sea. Some may take years to accomplish the pilgrimage, but with better roads and modern means of transport for many the process is now speedier.

However, the major modern population movements in Africa are migrations to work (Figure 20) which have arisen as a result of economic developments pushed by the European colonists. The mine, the large commercial farm and the plantation function with African labour and European management. Some 60 per cent of the African labour in the mines of the Republic of South Africa (particularly gold and coal mines) come from outside the Republic, mainly from Mozambique, Malawi and Lesotho. The mines and industries of Zambia and Zimbabwe attract labour from Malawi and Mozambique; the commercial farms of Kenya (and formerly Uganda and Tanzania), particularly at harvest time, used considerable labour from Rwanda and Burundi. In West Africa it is employment at the ports that attracts workers from inland. All this reflects the wide-ranging economic developments under European colonial rule, including the setting up of plantations and the alienation of land for European farms, the growth of administrative and market towns and urban population, the opening up of mines and factories and, with the expansion of trade, the flocking of labour to the ports.

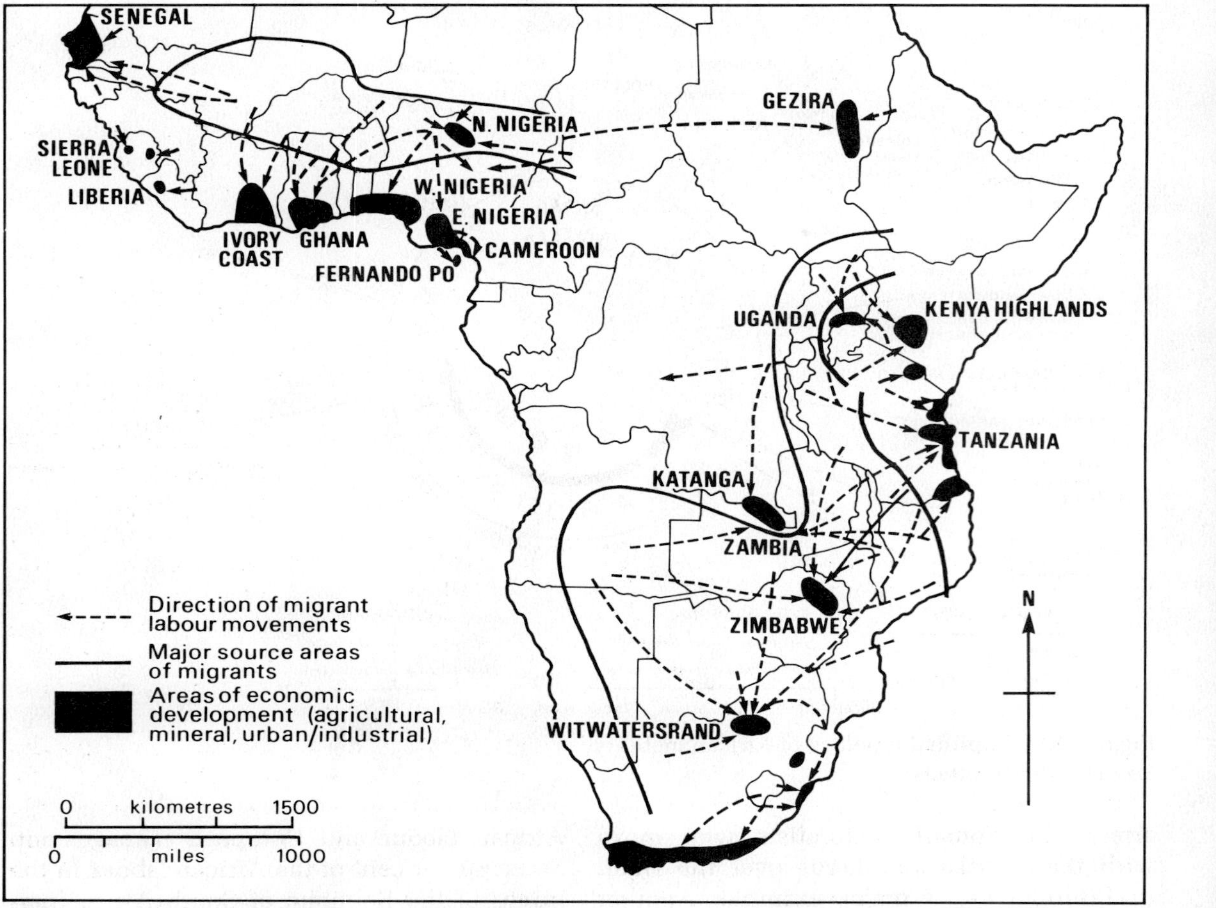

Figure 20 Migration to work in sub-Saharan Africa *Source*: After Prothero

Generally the colonial towns were founded mainly for Europeans, and most of the Africans were temporary residents whose stay was controlled. This was particularly so in the Republic of South Africa, which depends for much of its economic development upon migrant African labour. Recruitment, transport, employment and repatriation are still closely controlled. The migrant labourers usually work on contract for between eighteen and twenty-four months. Wives and families rarely accompany them, but remain and farm in the tribal area. Men return to their families at the end of the contract period but usually go back again and again for further contracts of paid employment.

It will be recognized that this is a very inefficient system. Workers who are temporary are given only the minimum of training and so remain virtually unskilled. Skilled, permanent wage-earners are still small in numbers and this is inimical to African development. Manpower is wasted in the long and arduous journeys, and progress in farming is held back by the lack of adult males. Despite the attractions of the towns most workers return to the countryside, usually when they have earned and saved enough money for a particular aim; hence they are given the name 'target workers'. Another reason for the continuation of the system relates to land tenure customs. In many parts of Africa, if the family accom-

Plate 6 Migrant worker settlement in the Gezira, Sudan.

panies the worker to the town or mine there would be no compensation for vacating the land and the right to return to the farm would be lost: hence the norm that the farm, offering subsistence, is fixed and cash employment away from home is temporary.

Finally, mention needs to be made of the large number (several millions) of refugees in Africa. The majority of these are victims of African independence, involving the clash of ideologies and civil wars. Sudan, for example, despite its own problems, shelters within its borders scores of thousands of refugees who have fled from Ethiopian resettlement and famine, from the disruption of recent years in Uganda, from the Central African Republic and from Zaire. Zaire in turn shelters many thousands who have fled from civil war in Angola and others from Uganda. Tanzania has thousands who have fled from Rwanda and Burundi and Mozambique. Senegal has been a refuge for thousands from Guinea (Bissau).

HEALTH

Malnutrition, disease and poverty (and the lack of a formal education) are the lot of the majority of black Africans. The full extent of these afflictions has only become appreciated and documented within the last thirty or forty years. Upon improvements in health and nutrition depend most plans for African economic development. Great advances have been made, particularly since the Second World War, but in return they have brought further problems.

The generally poor health of the African population is related mainly to nutritional diseases such as pellagra, beri-beri and rickets, and to a host of endemic and infectious diseases such as malaria, yellow fever, yaws, tuberculosis and intestinal worm diseases. Not only are diets inadequate in amount (leading to under-nutrition), but they are also usually ill-balanced (leading to malnutrition), with serious protein and fat deficiencies and over-emphasis on starch. Kwashiorkor, or protein malnutrition of young children, is another result of these conditions where the period of lactation is reduced and weaning is upon starchy diets such as banana and maize. Many of these children die, and the prevalence of cancer of the liver in later life has been noticed among those who survive. The nutritional diseases themselves are not heavily fatal but they so debilitate and sap the resistance that endemic and infectious diseases are able to take an immense toll.

Deaths from famine are limited to specific areas and specific events. In the savanna zones life relates to rainfall. If the rains fail, then starvation looms nearer. If they fail year after year, as across the Sahelian zones during the 1970s and in the early 1980s, then no amount of relief work and aid can save thousands from death. It is a marginal environment over-grazed in the high rainfall years of the 1960s, when numbers of both humans and cattle expanded, and a disaster area by the 1980s.

Malaria is widespread throughout Africa, except in the highland areas and the most southerly part of the continent. This is a most debilitating disease, and in that sense rather than the fatalities it causes it has been a major retarding factor in African development.

Since the Second World War, vigorous measures with modern insecticides such as DDT have done a great deal to check this disease, and other mosquito-borne diseases such as yellow fever which is particularly prevalent in West Africa. Cholera, too, has largely been conquered and its spread held. The great increases in the incidence of tuberculosis stem from industrialization and urban life and are associated with poverty and overcrowding. Africans seem poorly resistant to the disease, and measures such as hut taxes which aggravate overcrowding and the lack of timber which prevents traditional burning of the hut of a dead person help to spread this disease.

It is likely that the most widespread diseases of Africa are the helminthic or intestinal worm diseases. There are many kinds of parasitic worms infecting the population, but the most prevalent are hookworm (causing ankylostomiasis) and bilharzia (schistosomiasis), which produce anaemia, a lowering of vitality and may impair the functions of certain organs. Physical and mental activity is seriously reduced in infected persons. Some 50 per cent of the rural Egyptian population suffers from these diseases, as does a high percentage of the rural East African population. These diseases are not new (they have been identified in mummies of 1000 BC); they are carried and transmitted by water snails. Thus development in irrigation may spread the disease, for washing and bathing in canals and rivers allow the snail-carried bacteria to enter the human bloodstream through the skin. Eradication of this group of diseases is proving very lengthy.

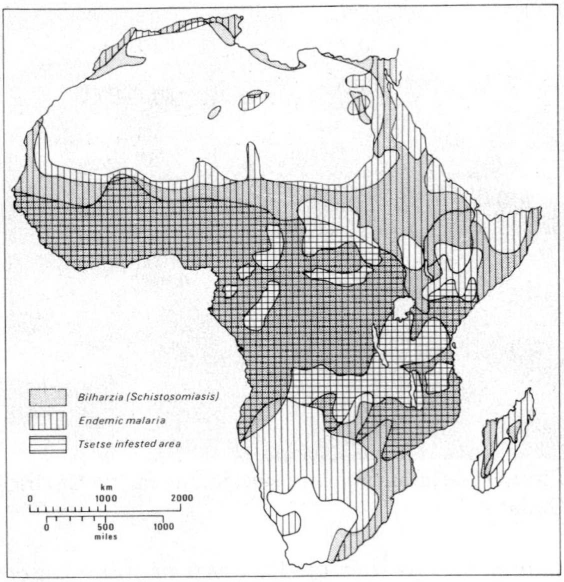

Figure 21 Africa: major diseases

Even more serious for the future is the incidence of Aids in Africa; there is now growing information abouts its heavy scale. By the middle 1980s it was realized that the disease was sweeping across Africa and that probably several millions were already infected. The World Health Organization has estimated that 50,000 Africans are suffering from Aids, but specialists believe this to be a gross underestimate. Even so, that figure is twice the number of cases recorded in the USA and Europe and for each such case it is thought that up to 100 others may be infected. The countries of Africa are helpless against this disease and the situation is worsened by the fact that in Africa Aids is a heterosexually transmitted disease and levels of health education aimed at reducing sexual promiscuity are minimal. The spread of the disease is aided by the frequent use of unsterilized equipment and the lack of adequate screening of blood donors. Thus its spread is likely to be rapid and increasingly Africa will depend on international help to fight it.

Whereas in the West it is usual to suffer at any one time from a single illness or disease, in Africa it is very common to find several different diseases or illnesses in the same person: 'From the waters the people get their food, also their cholera, their dysentery, their typhoid fevers, their malaria; from the earth they get their hookworm; from the crowded villages they get their tuberculosis and their yaws ... and from the food which earth, temperature and rain produce [they get] their protein deficiencies, their beri-beri'.[1†]

Great advances are being made in the eradication of these conditions, thanks to the greater use of DDT and antibiotic drugs such as penicillin, and improvements in hygiene and sanitation. Nutritional improvements depend upon greater productivity (linked with improving health), and especially on success in the struggle against trypanosomiasis and the tsetse fly, for the deficiency in animal protein is marked practically all over the continent, where the pot-bellied child (a sign of excess cereal consumption) is symptomatic. The task is enormous, but many different agencies make their contributions. The beneficial influence on African health and physique of good regular food and medical attention during a contract for work on the Rand mines has long been noted.

In order to grasp the magnitude of Africa's task we may note that the developed world averages 500–800 people per doctor, but for nearly all tropical Africa there are over 15,000 people per doctor, and in at least five countries there are over 40,000 people per doctor (Table 4).

These figures underline the poor provision of health care over most of the continent. If one realizes that it is in the cities and towns that

Table 4 *Health-related indicators*

	Population per physician		*Daily calorie supply per cap.*		*Infant mortality rate* (aged under 1)*	
	1965	*1980*	*Total 1982*	*As % of reqmt, 1982*	*1965*	*1983*
Ethiopia	70,190	69,390	2,162	93	166	—
Mali	49,010	22,130	1,731	74	184	148
Zaire	39,050	13,940	2,169	98	142	106
Burkina Faso	74,110	48,510	1,879	79	193	148
Malawi	46,900	41,460	2,242	97	201	164
Niger	71,440	38,790	2,456	105	181	139
Tanzania	21,840	17,740	2,331	101	138	97
Somalia	35,060	15,630	2,102	91	166	142
Togo	24,980	18,100	2,167	94	158	112
Guinea	54,610	17,110	1,987	86	197	158
Ghana	12,040	7,160	1,573	68	132	97
Sierra Leone	18,400	17,520	2,049	85	230	198
Kenya	12,840	7,890	2,056	88	124	81
Sudan	23,500	8,930	2,250	96	161	117
Chad	73,040	47,640	1,620	68	184	142
Mozambique	18,700	39,140	1,844	79	148	109
Zambia	11,390	7,670	2,054	89	137	100
Egypt	2,260	970	3,210	128	123	102
Zimbabwe	5,190	5,900	2,119	89	106	69
Morocco	12,120	10,750	2,671	110	149	98
Cameroon	29,720	13,990	2,102	91	155	116
Tunisia	8,040	3,690	2,656	111	145	83
Algeria	8,400	2,630	2,639	110	155	107

Note: * The infant mortality rate is the number of infants who die before reaching 1 year, per thousand live births in a given year.
Source: World Development Report, 1985 (New York, 1985).

† References for chapters 7, 8 and 9 appear on page 80.

most doctors are to be found, then it is clear that the scattered populations of the rural areas are almost devoid of qualified medical assistance. Travelling doctors and nurses are a possible response to this and the wider presence of clinics in rural areas seems a necessity.

Table 4 also reveals a considerable improvement in the infant mortality rates since 1965. Nevertheless, without exception current rates are depressingly high, only 6 out of the 23 countries having rates of less than 100. Rates for developed countries of Western Europe vary between 8 and 12 deaths under 1 year to 1000 live births. Finally, the table reveals that only six African states had enough food daily to meet (or surpass) their World Health Organization prescribed minimum levels of calorie intake. These figures are for 1982 and therefore are before the vast areas of famine that required enormous efforts of international aid in 1985–6.

EDUCATION

Advances in education are of paramount importance to the general social, political and economic advances of African peoples. Much investment in education and other social services was made by most of the colonial powers in Africa after 1945 and was continued after independence by the new governments, many of whom were keen to create universities rather than bush schools. Levels of literacy give a rough measure of education levels and they are still abysmally low over most of tropical Africa; in most countries less than 20 per cent of the population can read and write (Table 1) and the availability of schooling for all children is still a long way off. The problems associated with the building and equipping of schools can be overcome, but finding and training teachers for them is a longer task.

Plate 7 Graduation day in an African university – the right education for the right people?

Table 5 *School enrolment for selected countries, 1965 and 1982**

	Number enrolled in primary school as percentage of age group						*Number enrolled in secondary school as percentage of age group*	
	Total		*Male*		*Female*			
	1965	*1982*	*1965*	*1982*	*1965*	*1982*	*1965*	*1982*
Ethiopia	11	46	16	60	6	33	2	12
Mali	24	27	32	35	16	20	4	9
Zaire	70	90	95	104	45	75	5	23
Burkina Faso	12	28	16	28	8	16	1	3
Malawi	44	62	55	73	32	51	2	4
Niger	11	23	15	29	7	17	1	5
Tanzania	32	98	40	101	25	95	1	5
Somalia	10	30	16	38	4	21	2	11
Togo	55	106	78	129	32	84	5	27
Guinea	31	33	44	44	19	22	5	16
Ghana	69	76	82	85	57	66	13	34
Kenya	54	104	69	114	40	94	4	20
Sudan	29	52	37	61	21	43	4	18
Senegal	40	48	52	58	29	38	7	12
Liberia	41	66	59	82	23	50	5	20
Mauritania	13	33	19	43	6	23	1	10
Zambia	53	96	59	102	46	90	7	16
Egypt	75	78	90	90	60	65	26	54
Côte d'Ivoire	60	76	80	92	41	60	6	17
Zimbabwe	110	130	128	134	92	125	6	23
Morocco	57	80	78	98	35	62	11	28
Cameroon	94	107	114	117	75	97	5	19
Tunisia	91	111	116	123	65	98	16	32
Algeria	68	93	81	105	53	81	7	36

Note: *The data refer to estimates of students of all ages in primary and secondary schools. They are expressed as percentages of the total population of primary and secondary school age; these are generally 6–11 years and 12–17 years. For some countries gross enrolment may exceed 100% because some pupils are above or below a country's stated school ages.
Source: World Development Report 1985, (New York, 1985), Table 25.

It may be seen from Table 5 that advances in education – measured by improvements in school enrolment – are extremely patchy. Mali, Burkina Faso and Niger still have fewer than 30 per cent of their children enrolled, but others (such as Tanzania, Togo, Kenya and Zambia) have made great strides and almost all their children now attend school. It is the education of girls that is usually neglected, or limited to primary school, and this contributes to the appallingly inferior position of women in so many African societies. The World Bank has stressed the seriousness of the situation: 'Most girls become mothers, and their influence – much more than the father's – on their children is crucial'.[2]

The fact that African languages were unwritten raises the problem as to what languages Africans should be taught to read and write. It is uneconomic to print language books for language communities of fewer than 100,000, and many African languages and dialects have far fewer adherents. Attempts to impose a common African tongue over wide areas (as in Nigeria) have proved unsuccessful. It would seem that both for inter-tribal communication and for administration and commerce the European languages of the former colonial powers must remain.

8
Farming and industry

The character of much of African farming has altered during this century as a result of the impact of the settlement of the white man. Whereas subsistence farming had been practically universal, white settlers opened up new areas (as in the East African highlands), introduced new export crops (such as sisal, coffee and tobacco) or, in response to world demand, organized and expanded Africa's production of existing crops (such as cocoa and oil palm) and brought to Africa the two far-reaching alien concepts of private ownership of land and a money economy. These innovations, reinforced by the imposition of taxation to pay for essential services, and the introduction of attractive and desirable manufactured goods (bicycles, sewing machines, coloured cloth, umbrellas and so on), have had notable effects upon African economies.

INDIGENOUS FARMING

A restricted form of shifting cultivation is still the usual method of farming in the forest areas and wetter savannas, and represents an adjustment of traditional farming practice to the character of the soils. A virgin plot is cleared of trees and brushwood by cutting and burning and is then cultivated for the two or three years that the soil remains fertile. A long period of fallow follows while fresh plots are cleared and cropped. The whole process is known as bush fallowing: land that was formerly under cultivation is allowed to lapse to a fallow of secondary bush or forest for a few years and then re-used. This method of farming is in effect a rotation of land rather than a rotation of crops.

The humus content of tropical soils is low; various pests and diseases preclude the keeping of animals and the development of mixed farming, and thus no manure can be added. The burning of the cleared vegetation adds phosphate and potash and the first crop of millet or yams sown in the ash is often good, but the effect soon wears off. Many regard this system as an admirable adaptation to the environment; but the fact remains that it is prodigal in the use of land, and in some areas (e.g. in Nigeria) population increase and denser settlement patterns limit the area of land available and necessitate the re-use of land before it has had time to regenerate.

Pastoralism is restricted in many parts of the continent by the prevalence of trypanosomiasis and numerous other pests and diseases such as ticks and rinderpest. Trypanosomiasis is caused by the tsetse fly (which conveys sleeping sickness to humans) and is widely distributed throughout Central Africa (Figure 21). The fly sucks the blood of men and animals and acts as a carrier of the disease organisms which lurk in the blood of game and cattle. Animals bitten by the fly usually die after a few days and humans after a longer period of increasing lethargy and weakness. Thus over considerable areas of Central and West Africa no animals can be kept for meat, milk, manure or transport, and this has repercussions upon diet, soil fertility and farming practice. Much research is being done on this disease and innoculation campaigns for men and animals have had some limited success. The fact that wild game as well as cattle form the blood bank containing the disease makes its control difficult and has led to emphasis on practical measures to eradicate the carrier fly. The fly needs high temperatures, high humidities and shade, and thus lives and breeds in the thick bush at altitudes below 1600 m. Belts of bush are cleared to isolate blocks of land, where the fly is then exterminated. The clearing of vegetation has to be done with care to prevent soil erosion, and the Africans need to be instructed in mixed farming techniques in order to preserve the fertility of the soil. This is no easy matter for it cuts across the traditions of pastoral tribes who generally spurn agriculture as menial, dislike permanent settlement and measure wealth in quantity rather than quality of livestock. It is an uphill fight for the stock breeder and veterinary officer promoting ideas of selective breeding and laying stress on quality rather than quantity, for social custom and habit is against them.

Climate and soils also conspire against the pastoralist over most of Africa. The marked seasonal character of the rainfall over the savannas is inimical to the development of good pastures. The grass grows rapidly during and immediately after the rains and is then nutritious; but as the dry season progresses the grass coarsens, becomes more fibrous and loses in both protein and water content. If these difficulties are added to the scourges of disease and underscored by the African's lack of interest in quality of animal, we may understand why their herds are such a sorry sight.

The pastoral way of life is essentially one of movement, whereby the animals and their owners annually cover considerable areas in search of sustenance. A century ago, for example, the Masai had 650,000 km^2 of East African highland to roam over: today they have only 8000 km^2 and can no longer trample on the rights and lands of their agricultural neighbours. The growing restrictions of pastoralism in the face of expanding agriculture in much of East, Central and southern Africa increase risks of over-grazing with the attendant dangers of soil exhaustion, erosion, and lowering water tables. Less restriction has occurred on the nomads of the steppe pastures fringing both north and south of the Sahara, where sheep and camels are the dominant stock; but the series of drought years in the 1970s and 1980s across the Sahel exacerbated this situation, when millions of animals died and the desert edge extended southwards.

Much subsistence cultivation in the more settled areas is on a bush-fallowing basis, where deficiencies of soil fertility, possibilities of soil erosion and actual expenditure of labour are minimized. The tools of agriculture are primitive: a digging stick to make holes for the seeds or cuttings and sometimes to break clods, a hoe to loosen the surface soil, and a knife or axe. The simple form of plough which spread across North Africa early in the Christian era did not penetrate into black Africa, perhaps in part owing to the lack of draught animals. These ploughs, often made entirely of wood, do little more than score the surface of the soil. Europeans in Africa have learned to their cost that the deep ploughing of temperate lands is unsuitable under African conditions of leaching and laterization.

The principal crops grown are starch foods with little protein value: millet, maize, yams, cassava, plantain in tropical Africa, with wheat and barley assuming importance in the Atlas lands. Yields are invariably poor, and malnutrition and under-nutrition are all too prevalent. Throughout the tropics crops are grown in untidy-looking gardens rather than in fields in the European sense: the larger tree-stumps remain uncleared and several crops are inter-sown. In this way traditional practice retains some roots to hold the soil and supplies a varied vegetative cover, both reducing risks of soil erosion.

All over Africa women take a large share in the cultivation and harvesting of crops. Over most of tropical Africa it is their main duty, the men reserving themselves for the heavier clearing work, for fishing, for arguing matters

Plate 8 Traditional cultivation by hoe or digging stick is usually undertaken by women

of high policy, and stock-rearing where possible; but many now migrate to seek jobs in the towns and leave farming to their womenfolk and the older men.

Cash crops

The expansion of the agrarian population and the gradual adoption of cash crops have both helped to bring about change in certain parts of the continent. Cash crop growing by black Africans has developed since the end of the Second World War. It has been aided by an expanding world market for certain tropical products and by governmental policies reducing or restricting white settlement or plantation development in certain areas. The principal export crops are cocoa (Ghana, Nigeria, Cameroon, Côte d'Ivoire), ground nuts (Gambia, Senegal, Mali, Niger), palm products (Nigeria, Sierra Leone, Côte d'Ivoire), cotton (Egypt, Sudan, Uganda, Mali), coffee (Côte d'Ivoire, Angola, Uganda, Congo, Madagascar, Cameroon, Kenya). In the growing urban area markets are expanding for more basic foodstuffs such as maize, millet, sugarcane and fruit, and for tobacco.

The cash crops are not necessarily new crops and require virtually no extra effort to produce; many fit into the bush-fallowing system of agriculture and others are tree crops easily grown among the profusion of crops and trees in the African's 'garden'. The introduction of cash-crop growing has proved a lever by which to force in land-tenure systems – assured occupation is required if tree crops are to be grown – and to consolidate fragmented holdings; it is leading to one-crop specialism, an idea new to the African agriculturist. Such specialism is generally remunerative to the farmer; but beside having the disadvantage of tying his well-being to distant and often incomprehensible world markets, it leads to monoculture – all too often the preface to soil exhaustion: 'One-crop farming has been rewarding but is self-destroying rather than self-perpetuating and certainly not feasible in a rapidly expanding society. Subsistence crop farming was self-perpetuating, but not rewarding, nor is it any longer feasible'.[3] The adoption of rotation farming, and where possible mixed farming, would seem to be a desirable solution, but this does not commend itself for it means more arduous farming for those who stay to work the farm.

EUROPEAN FARMING

For a long time European interest in African agriculture was confined to tropical parts and to the establishment of plantations. The alienation of land and prodigal use of (often forced) labour were the means whereby an economy of exploitation was furthered. Few of the early plantations were successful. However, useful lessons were learnt, and in this century the more restricted development of plantations has been where land alienation can do least harm and where capital is available to infuse technology into this form of tropical agriculture.

Cocoa has become more and more a peasant-produced crop, and coffee plantations in East Africa lose ground to expanding peasant production. Only in the low latitudes, where an equatorial regime allows all-the-year production, and thus fixed labour requirements, or where, as in East African sisal and tea production, expensive processing machinery is necessary, are modern plantations holding their own. Firms such as Lever Brothers in Zaire (palm oil) and the Firestone Plantation company in Liberia (rubber) lead in enlightened development, including fringe benefits of housing, medical services and education for their African employees and their families.

The most developed European agriculture in Africa is to be found in the extreme north and the extreme south – in north-west Africa, especially Morocco, and in the Republic of South Africa. Here, several generations of settlers have put a Mediterranean European impress upon the landscape, with their emphasis on tree crops such as olive and citrus fruits and on vine and cereal cultivation. Elsewhere in Africa European settlers are in the uplands: the High Veld, the Kivu highlands of Zaire, the East African highlands. Ranching is possible in the tsetse-free higher lands and progress is slowly being made in cross-breeding European dairy and beef breeds with native cattle, or in some cases acclimatizing them. There is a constant struggle with a host of diseases and the sequences of tropical climate make the improvement of pastures difficult. The importance of the European farmer in tropical Africa must not be under-estimated. Although there are few European farms it is their produce that sustains the economies of several African states.

AFRICA'S FOOD CRISIS

Recent years have seen an increasing number of sub-Saharan states affected by a serious food crisis. Not enough food is being produced and balance of payments problems frequently make commercial imports difficult. This situation is jeopardizing many development programmes. About 22 sub-Saharan states have been particularly affected in recent years, and they include 40 per cent of the region's population. The cereal production of these states in 1983 was 13.9 million tonnes, or 1.2 million less than the 1982 harvest and 3 million tonnes below the good 1981 harvest. The gap between needs and normal supply was 3.2 million tonnes.[4]

There are a number of reasons why this has come about. First there are environmental factors: Africa is a mainly tropical continent with large arid or semi-arid areas and with a high variability of rainfall. This is a serious factor, and if droughts are frequent over a short period it can be a major factor. Parts of the Sahel were drought-striken throughout many of the years of the 1970s and again in 1983 and 1984. The droughts affect crop yields and reduce the volume of exports; terms of trade may also be adverse. Thus foreign exchange may be reduced at a time when it is needed most to pay for food imports. Its lack also leads to transport problems, lack of spare parts and fuel, and makes even the local movement of food difficult. Civil wars and insurgency seem to have been the lot of many African states since their 'colonial masters' withdrew. This has meant disruption of services, destroyed crops, movement of refugees and a deterioration of the rural economy. There are probably over 4 million refugees who can produce little but who require feeding: a serious burden for such countries as Sudan, Somalia and Ethiopia who hold large numbers of them and who must rely heavily upon international food aid.

The demographic situation is an important longer-term factor: African rates of population increase have been accelerating over the last 15–20 years. The total population in sub-Saharan Africa in 1960 was 213 million, in 1970 it was 275 million, in 1980 369 million. The African population now grows at the high rate of 2.7 per cent, whereby it will double within the next 20 years. Similar increases in food production have not been attained; with the accelerating drift to the towns the numbers of farmers have not increased proportionately and their effectiveness has diminished, for most of the urban migrants are young men. In Botswana 40 per cent of rural households are without men, in Cameroon almost 50 per cent. Thus a weaker farm population is failing to feed an urban population that is growing at 6–12 per cent a year. Past government policies, favouring the industrial and urban sector and neglecting the

Table 6 *Occupational structures, 1965 and 1981*

	Percentage of pop. of working age (15–64)		*Percentage of labour force** *Agriculture*		*Industry*		*Services*	
	1965	*1983*	*1965*	*1981*	*1965*	*1981*	*1965*	*1981*
Ethiopia	53	52	86	80	6	7	8	13
Mali	53	50	93	73	4	12	3	15
Zaire	53	51	81	75	10	13	9	12
Burkina Faso	54	52	90	82	6	13	4	5
Malawi	51	49	91	86	4	5	5	9
Uganda	53	50	88	83	5	6	7	11
Niger	51	51	94	91	1	3	5	6
Tanzania	53	50	88	83	4	6	8	11
Somalia	49	53	87	82	5	8	8	10
Central African Republic	57	55	93	88	3	4	4	8
Togo	53	50	81	67	10	15	9	18
Guinea	55	53	87	82	7	11	6	7
Ghana	52	49	61	53	16	20	23	27
Madagascar	54	50	92	87	3	4	5	9
Sierra Leone	54	55	75	65	14	19	11	16
Kenya	49	46	84	78	6	10	10	12
Sudan	53	53	84	78	7	10	9	12
Chad	56	56	93	85	3	7	4	8
Mozambique	56	52	77	66	10	18	13	16
Senegal	54	53	82	77	6	10	12	13
Lesotho	56	54	92	60	3	15	5	25
Liberia	51	53	78	70	11	14	11	16
Mauritania	52	53	90	69	4	8	6	23
Zambia	52	49	76	67	8	11	16	22
Egypt	55	57	56	50	15	30	29	20
Côte d'Ivoire	55	53	87	79	3	4	10	17
Zimbabwe	51	46	67	60	12	15	21	25
Morocco	51	52	60	52	15	21	25	27
Nigeria	52	50	67	54	12	19	21	27
Cameroon	56	51	86	83	6	7	8	10
Congo	55	51	47	34	19	26	34	40
Tunisia	50	56	34	35	25	18	41	47
Angola	55	52	67	59	13	16	35	53
Algeria	50	50	59	25	14	25	27	50
South Africa	54	56	32	30	30	29	38	41
Libya	53	52	42	19	20	28	38	53

Note: *The *agricultural sector* includes agriculture, forestry, hunting and fishing. The *industrial sector* includes mining, manufacturing, construction and utilities (electricity, water and gas). All other branches of economic activity are categorized as *services*.
Source: World Development Report 1985 (New York, 1985).

countryside, have much to answer for.

By the mid-1980s many African governments were realizing the need for rural rehabilitation and were framing policies to improve rural conditions and stimulate agricultural production. This will take time to accomplish. The occupational structures of African populations show the overwhelming importance of agriculture in most states (Table 6). Modest advances in the size of the small industrial sectors are revealed, but for the majority of African states rarely more than 10 – 12 per cent of the occupied population work in the industrial sector.

INDUSTRY

Although the majority of Africa's peoples are concerned with agriculture, since independence there has been considerable emphasis upon industrial development, all too often to the neglect of agriculture. However, despite promising beginnings, industrial development in Africa has shown disappointing progress over the last 20 years. The average manufacturing value added (MVA) per head was lower in real terms in the early 1980s than it was 20 years earlier: population has increased faster than the MVA. Progress generally has been disappointing, and Africa's share in world-wide manufacturing remains minimal and the proportion of workers employed in industry is smaller than in other parts of the developing world. The share of manufacturing in the Gross Domestic Product (GDP) is shown in Table 7.

The lack of success may be attributed to a number of reasons. A major one is the low level of education and technical skills held by the mass of the population, generally resulting in low levels of efficiency. To some extent this offsets a much-stressed advantage – cheapness of labour. Another reason for poor progress often lies in unfortunate decisions on development strategies. Strategies for industrialization have frequently stressed import substitution industries, but lack of skills, of capital, inadequate infrastructure and limited size of the home market have hampered progress and led to high-cost and poor-quality production, maintained only by costly tariffs to keep out competing imports.

The choice of technology to be adopted may

Table 7 *Share of manufacturing in gross domestic product*

	1965 (%)	*1983* (%)		*1965* (%)	*1983* (%)
Ethiopia	7	11	Lesotho	1	6
Zaire	17	2	Liberia	3	7
Uganda	8	—	Mauritania	4	—
Tanzania	8	9	Zambia	7	19
Somalia	3	6	Côte d'Ivoire	10	13
Rwanda	2	—	Zimbabwe	20	21
Central African Republic	4	8	Morocco	16	17
Togo	10	6	Nigeria	7	5
Guinea	—	2	Cameroon	10	11
Ghana	10	4	Congo	—	6
Sierra Leone	6	5	Tunisia	9	14
Kenya	11	12	Algeria	11	13
Sudan	4	8	South Africa	23	—
Senegal	—	17	Libya	3	4

Source: World Development Report 1985 (New York, 1985), Table 3.

Plate 9 Small-scale intermediate technology, concrete block production, Khartoum

Plate 10 Car assembly plant, Nigeria

also be critical. Labour-intensive manufacturing provides more jobs and a greater spread of wage money among the population than do capital intensive plants, but capital accumulation for continuing investment is usually small. Capital-intensive industries substitute machines for human labour. There are fewer jobs and a smaller dissemination of wage money, but there is a high rate of capital accumulation which, ideally, should be reinvested for rapid growth. Most African states have surplus labour, with large numbers migrating to the towns in search of work. Despite such a situation all too often scarce capital is used to establish highly sophisticated plants that offer few jobs and generally require expensive expatriate managers and technicians to operate them. They generally suffer from inadequate maintenance and often there are difficulties in obtaining spare parts, usually because of the scarcity of foreign exchange. The land-locked states of Africa suffer greatly from the disadvantage of the high cost of importing parts and machinery great distances inland.

Many of the sophisticated capital-intensive projects have little relationship to local resource bases. The Overseas Development Institute in London cites a number of such cases, including a loss-making automated bakery in Tanzania that uses imported machinery, replacing traditional bakers and leading to high transport costs for raw materials and final distribution. Another example is Nigeria which set up six vehicle-assembly plants that required subsidies and tariff protection. Mainly imported materials were needed and the plants operated at low capacity. In some cases the economic cost of production greatly exceeded the cost of directly importing the vehicles.[5]

An inadequate infrastructure often reduces economic efficiency, and here spatial spread of manufacturing plants may play a part. Early industries were usually set up singly and thus lacked the advantages and economies accruing from a number of industrial plants sharing the same location. When that occurs costs of services and infrastructure become shared among the plants, and often there are linkages between plants that can bring further economies.

The small size of the market is a problem common to nearly all African states. It reflects the poverty of the masses and is a significant cause of high-cost production; economies of scale are difficult to achieve with factories and plants either below optimum size or operating well below capacity. Regional integration would enlarge markets, but earlier attempts at this were unsuccessful in both East and Central Africa; this was mainly because of disagreement as to which industrial plants should be located in particular states, and because the more advanced and better infrastructured states tended to benefit most. Examples here were Southern Rhodesia in the Federation and Kenya in the East African Economic Community.

Most African countries show a limited diversification of production; they generally concern themselves with the processing of agricultural commodities, textiles and clothing and footwear. Exports are limited and import-substitute manufactures of greater sophistication have often failed for reasons mentioned above.

What is so often missing is an integration of industry with the other sectors of the economy and a widening of the industrial base. For example, only a few African states attempt to manufacture the diversity of inputs required (and imported) by their agricultural sectors. Nevertheless, a few African states can show some diversification in their industrial sector. Egypt, Algeria, Côte d'Ivoire, Nigeria and Zimbabwe have sophisticated capital goods sectors, including metals, machinery, electronic products and chemicals.

From the foregoing it may be deduced that the level of industrial product imports into Africa is very high. In fact, only in food products and textiles is the import to consumption ratio below 25 per cent for most countries. Conversely the record of exports of manufactured goods from African states is poor, but in a few cases there has been moderate success. Early in the 1980s about twelve African countries were each exporting annually over £30 million of manufactured goods; they included Algeria, Côte d'Ivoire, Kenya, Senegal and Zimbabwe. However, for the continent as a whole industrial exports are small in quantity and limited in range.

State involvement in manufacturing is all too frequent and rarely seems to be beneficial, and this has proved particularly so in Africa where most countries at independence favoured a socialist approach to their development. Operations of state enterprises are often affected by ideologies and industrial aims become ambivalent. Social benefits may be stressed and profitability may be disregarded, so that chronic losses eventually have a serious effect on the national exchequer. Sometimes politicians have interfered directly with factory operations; nepotism is pressed and bribery and corruption spring up where licences and permits to manufacture are made necessary. Adverse government influence also comes to bear where shortages and inflation cause it to apply price controls. These reduce both profitability and incentive. Indeed, they encourage entrepreneurs to forsake manufacturing for trading. By the early 1980s over much of Africa state-directed development had become discredited; particularly it stifles innovation and personal initiative.

Disappointment at the slow pace of development has caused views on the place of industrialization to change. The need for a firm agricultural base – to feed the population, to provide exports and foreign exchange and to supply raw materials for home industries – is once more acknowledged, and investment has now swung to rural rehabilitation and the improvement of agriculture. It is becoming accepted that greater integration between agriculture and industry is desirable and that industry should become more resource-based and rely less upon imported inputs. Small-scale industry is seen to have an important part to play, and rigid structures erected to protect state enterprises are likely to go in favour of freer economies with energetic private sectors. The future will require tighter and more effective economic planning that really will integrate the varied sectors of the economy into one entity. Rapid industrialization no longer has priority; for sustained industrialization a slower and more deliberate approach seems likely.

9 Minerals, power and transport

MINERALS

The output of minerals from Africa is now prodigious in quantity and value and manifold in character (Figure 22). It seems reasonable to suppose that for a very long time to come the continent's mineral output will expand as new discoveries are made and as increasing investment and development of transport make possible the working of already known but unexploited deposits. The shield character of the continent's structure, comprising a variety of ancient crystalline and metamorphosed rocks, has been particularly favourable to mineralization. Many parts of the continent still await even reconnaissance mineral surveys; substantial new discoveries are likely.

Minerals have played a notable role in the history of the continent, particularly in influencing exploration and shaping economic development. Long before Europeans came to Africa the gold of Ethiopia was known to seafarers of the Indian Ocean, and old workings and diggings, for example in Zimbabwe, have been valuable guides to modern prospectors. Tin and gold have been worked for centuries in West Africa. By the fifteenth century the Guinea lands were providing the gold necessary for the coinage of Portugal, Spain and Italy. The lure of gold as well as of slaves and ivory brought the traders and merchants to Africa's shores.

It was the discovery, in 1886, of the enormously rich goldfield of the Rand, less than 20 years after the opening up of the diamond working at Kimberley, that unlocked European capital and spurred on mineral exploration and exploitation throughout the continent. Interest is always centred first upon the precious metals giving assured returns, but this century has seen increasing investment in exploration and exploitation of base metals for which there is a growing range of industrial uses. The great copper deposits of the Katanga (Shaba) were discovered in 1892, and working began in 1910 when the railway from Beira reached Elizabethville (Lubumbashi). In 1902 copper was discovered in Northern Rhodesia and lead, zinc and vanadium at Broken Hill; tin became mined in Nigeria (1910), and in North Africa phosphates became worked in Algeria in 1896. In 1910 the first oil discoveries were made on the Red Sea coast of Egypt and manganese deposits were discovered in Sinai. The years up to the Second World War saw big advances in mineral exploitation all over the continent and some, such as copper, benefited by increased wartime demand. However, the between-wars period was one of capital shortage and economic depression and advances were but moderate.

Since the Second World War major developments in Africa's mineral industry have occurred. Of first importance have been the discoveries of oil and gas fields beneath the Sahara in Libya, Algeria and Egypt and

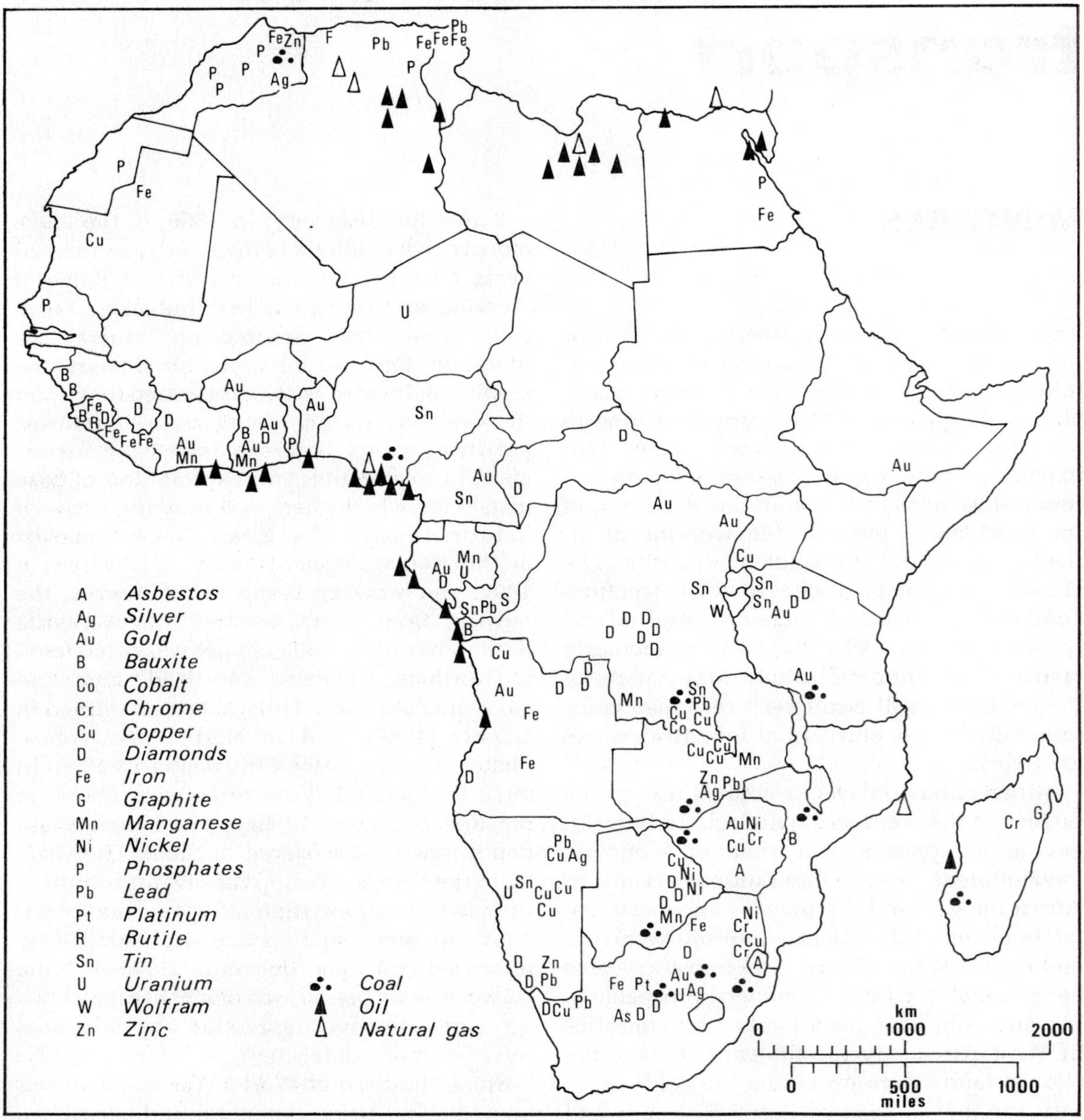

Figure 22 Mining in Africa in the 1980s

beneath the equatorial vegetation and offshore of Nigeria, Gabon and Angola. New iron-ore workings in the Mauritania Sahara (1963) and the expansion of phosphate quarrying in North Africa found ready markets with European consumers. At the same time existing mines have increased production of such minerals as asbestos, chrome, coal, vanadium and diamonds – the continent produces over half the world's gold and diamonds. In a number of African countries (e.g. Liberia, Sierra Leone, Mauritania, Zambia) mining dominates the economy, and in many mineral exports are a major source of foreign exchange.

Mineral exploitation is rarely easy in Africa: 'Tropical Africa is no place for the sourdough equipped with a hammer and a hunch'.[6] African conditions militate against the pioneer prospector; mining in Africa, as a rule, is big business. Two major problems must frequently be overcome by mining concerns in Africa. The first is the provision of adequate labour to operate the mines, the second is in the provision of transport to reduction plants and the coast. Much of Africa is sparsely populated and recruitment of labour for the major mines extends over enormous areas. The Rand gold mines draw upon labour mainly from Lesotho, Botswana, Malawi and Mozambique; Mozambique, with Angola and Malawi, supplies much labour to the Copperbelt and Zambian mines. To attract the many thousands of Africans needed from so far away requires inducements such as free housing, medical facilities, free or subsidized food as well as good wages. Actual wages for unskilled labour may be cheaper than in European mines, but in terms of work accomplished and allowing for the extra inducements costs are not markedly different. The days of 'cheap labour' for mine and plantation in Africa are over. The skilled engineers and technicians, almost invariably white men, also require high salaries and high-quality accommodation and living conditions to attract them to the discomforts of tropical mining sites.

Few mines are close to the sea, and efficient transport to and from the coast is essential, both for sending out the ore and to import all the supplies, machinery and equipment. Railways, roads and power supplies have to be made available at the outset. It is the lack of these facilities that prevents many known deposits from being worked – the iron-ore deposits of Wologisi in Liberia, are an example. The construction of transcontinental lines to serve the Shaba–Zambia Copperbelt is one of the greatest examples of the power of minerals. The ore travels on a single-track line for almost 2400 km, either to Beira, Lobito, Dar-es-Salaam or Maputo (practically the distance from Paris to Moscow).

Plate 11 Mineral exploration at Ghelb El Rhein, Mauritania

To stand these freight costs, plus ocean shipment, mining must be highly efficient. The expense of long hauls makes it necessary to concentrate or refine ores as near to the mines as possible, and this introduces problems of fuel and power and has necessitated the development of numerous hydroelectric and thermal–electric power schemes.

It will be appreciated that mineral exploitation has provided much of the basis of the growing industrial and commercial infrastructure of Africa. Minerals and transport go together, and except for a few strategic railways, such as the Mombasa–Lake Victoria line, most of the lengthy rail lines have grown up in response to mineral exploitation; for minerals can pay for long hauls all the year round and subsidize the less remunerative and more seasonal agricultural freight. Diamonds and gold laid the foundation of South Africa's railway network. Gold, coal and copper drew the railways into the Rhodesias and extended links to Angola and Mozambique. Mineral exports have been valuable in spurring on the development of port facilities in many countries (railway sidings, wharfs, deep-water berths and heavy equipment), all of which serve to attract other industries and commercial enterprises. Further, the mines have been foremost in power utilization and have formulated and speeded numerous power development projects to the benefit of a wider economy.

For some time yet mining will be controlled and operated by non-African capital and technicians, although Africans are now taking increasingly skilled mining jobs. This is because large capital sums, mining expertise with advanced technical knowledge and international connections are needed, conditions met by the great multinational mining companies. The minerals of Africa that seem likely to remain important in world trade for a long time to come are gold, copper, uranium, diamonds, cobalt, tin, asbestos, chromite, bauxite, iron ore and oil.

POWER

Economic development, whether by agriculture, mining or industry, demands increasing quantities of energy. Most African states today, among the poorest in the world, are vitally concerned with the provision of energy in one form or another to further economic development and raise living standards. Large parts of Africa are deficient in mineral fuels and still use wood, charcoal and dung, but the post-war period has also seen the great Saharan oil and gas discoveries. The formation of oil requires long periods of marine sedimentary conditions, rarely found over the vast mass of Africa, and although coal seams occur in the Karroo series the quality is generally poor. This general scarcity of coal and oil deposits renders the few areas that do possess them of particular importance to local economies.

The only large coalfield in Africa lies in the Republic of South Africa, and it has been the most important single factor in furthering the development of that country's great mining and manufacturing industries. The annual output of bituminous coal is about 135 million tonnes. The next largest output is from the Wankie colliery in Zimbabwe (3 million tonnes). Other African coal mines in Nigeria, Morocco, Algeria, Zambia, Mozambique and the Congo, are very small producers, each of only a few hundred thousand tonnes of rather poor-quality coal. Only in Zimbabwe and Natal are reasonably good metallurgical coking coals found.

Africa's mineral oil resources are substantial but restricted in location. The greatest resources lie under the northern Sahara and under the Niger delta. Lesser fields are in Gabon, Angola and the Congo (Table 8), while offshore discoveries are now being worked off the Sinai peninsula, off Tanzania and in Madagascan waters. The great international oil companies continue to explore for oil in nearly every African state. The consumption of oil in all Africa is only 150 kg per head (cf. Latin America's 620 kg per head), which may be taken as an index of under-development. African states without their own oil wells suffered severely after 1975 when OPEC trebled and then quadrupled the price of oil. High proportions of hard-won foreign exchange had to be used to pay for oil imports. As a result many development programmes suffered, until oil prices fell in the early 1980s.

The relative scarcity of mineral sources of energy focuses attention upon hydro resources. Here Africa has a tremendous potential, the greatest among all the continents; however, little of this is yet realized and much

Figure 23 Per capita energy consumption

Table 8 *Output of crude petroleum, 1950–84*

	Output (000 tonnes)		
	1950	*1973*	*1984*
Algeria	80	49,050	46,100
Angola	—	—	12,250
Cameroon	—	—	7,890
Congo	—	—	6,210
Egypt	2,370	13,720	42,500
Gabon	—	9,080	7,600
Côte d'Ivoire	—	—	1,120
Libya	—	104,370	53,000
Nigeria	—	101,790	68,600
Tunisia	—	3,950	5,840
Zaire	—	—	1,430

Source: Institute of Petroleum, London.

of it may never be so. Sites for hydroelectric power stations are generally limited by topography and climate. The greater part of Africa's potential lies in the equatorial zone, particularly in the Zaire Basin, remote from centres of industry and population.

Electricity becomes more costly the farther it is transmitted; the present economic limit is about 800 km. Unless some spectacular breakthrough in electricity transmission costs occurs it does not seem likely that any more than a fraction of equatorial Africa's potential water power will be used. A number of substantial schemes have been constructed during the past 30 years, some of the largest being outside the equatorial belt and relying upon water stored in great reservoirs to ensure even output throughout the year. The Aswan High dam on the Nile in Egypt has irrigation as its main purpose, but it also generates massive amounts of power. The Zambezi has been dammed for the Kariba scheme on the Zimbabwe–Zambia border and lower down for the Cabora Bassa scheme in Mozambique. The Volta scheme in Ghana and the Inga scheme in Zaire produce power for metallurgical and electrochemical industries, while the Kainji dam in Nigeria supplies the national grid.

It is clear that a marked increase in hydroelectric output will occur in the coming years, but much of it is likely to be from small plants favourably placed in areas of effective home demand. There may well be considerable scope in the future for employment of nuclear power, and in this connection it should be remembered that the mines of Shaba and the Rand are major uranium producers.

TRANSPORT

There is a clear relationship between levels of economic development and the provision of transport infrastructure, and the late start and slow pace of economic advance in Africa can be explained in part, and possibly a large part, by the problems of overcoming inaccessibility.

Although the camel in the north and the ox cart in the south have played major economic roles, the use of draught animals was proscribed over much of tropical Africa by the tsetse fly and associated endemic animal sleeping sickness. This delayed for a long time the use of wheeled vehicles and the need for improved tracks and roads and, of necessity, human porterage along bush paths prevailed over large areas and was the basis for indigenous exchange and European penetration. With one porter able to carry 30 kg over 30 km in one day, this was a form of transport which severely restricted the quantity and type of goods that could be moved and was both inefficient and costly – the cost of moving goods from the coast to Ghana's gold mines at Tarkwa dropped from £25.30 to £2 per ton when the railway replaced porterage in 1903.

The distinct advantage of the trade in slaves was that the 'commodity' was self-transporting and could be used for carrying other goods. As long as other goods were in small quantities or of high value (gold, ivory and spices) porterage was adequate, but as such goods were replaced in the nineteenth century by agricultural products (palm oil, rubber, groundnuts and cocoa) and minerals gained by modern mining techniques, so there developed the need for cheaper, bulk transport. Likewise, the need to demonstrate the 'effective control' required by the Congress of Berlin before a colony could be claimed also necessitated more efficient transport systems.

Rivers such as the Senegal, Gambia, Niger, Ogooué and Zaire (Congo) provided arteries for early exploration of the interior, but the rivers were not, in general, suitable for large-scale transport over long distances. Waterfalls near the coast prevent direct penetration from the sea, and others reduce the length of navigable sections inland. Regimes are highly seasonal, with flood discharges many times the average discharge and channel profiles extremely variable. Thus, while sections of the Nile, Niger and Zaire are significant commercially and are used by self-propelled and even by push tow units, railways have had to be provided in places to bypass rapids (e.g. Matadi–Kinshasa and Kisangani–Ubundu in the Zaire).

The restricted possibilities for river transport (Figure 24) meant that cheap, bulk transport had to be provided by railways, and so the penetration, annexation and opening up of Africa by Europeans coincided with the full flush of the railway era in the late nineteenth century. Most of the African railways were built between 1885 and 1930 and facilitated administration and the imposition of colonial rule; and in many places they served to stimulate economic development. The rapid expansion of cocoa cultivation in Ghana and Nigeria, groundnut production in Senegal and Nigeria and cotton in Uganda were directly related to the provision of rail transport, and the concentration of economic activity along 'the line of rail' in East, Central and southern Africa has persisted to this day. Not without justification the early railways have been described as 'long, weak lines of strong faith'.

The range of relief and climate in Africa is considerable. In East Africa railways operate at altitudes from sea level to 2700 m, in a temperature range of 1–43°C, and in torrential rain and dusty deserts. Track ballast, water and fuel may all be difficult to obtain, the distances are great and the traffic-generating potential negligible over long stretches. As a result, the construction and operating costs are high and lines were built only where stra-

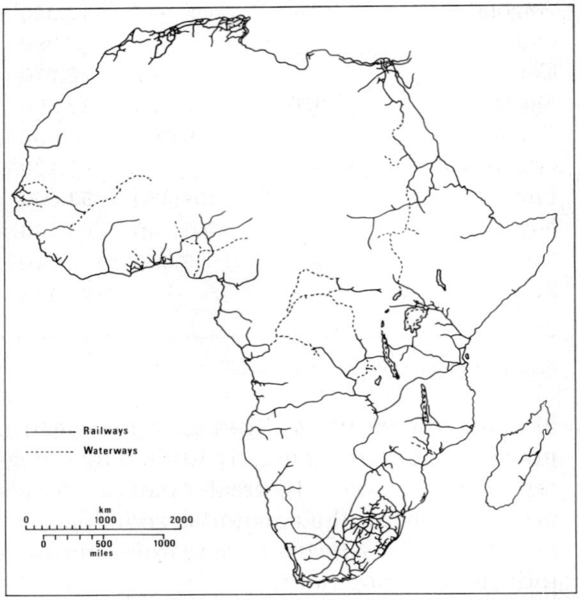

Figure 24 African railways and navigable waterways

tegic military considerations made them essential or where freight seemed assured. Only in South Africa, with two-thirds of Africa's railway mileage, can a network be said to exist, and elsewhere the map is one of disconnected lines (Figure 24) of variable and often narrow gauge. Narrow gauge, steep gradients, sharp bends and minimal design standards were often adopted to reduce costs, but the result is that running speeds are low and capacity restricted. In countries such as Algeria, Tunisia and Zaire the variety of railway gauges creates problems of internal integration, while the tendency for British territories to have 1.07 m gauge, French to have 1.00 m gauge and for some modern mineral lines (Mauritania, Liberia) to have 1.45 m gauge greatly reduces the possibility of establishing international network connections.

Mechanized road transport developed originally as 'feeders' to the railway lines, and while there is still an element of complementarity there has also been growing competition. In contrast with the rail networks which provide limited connectivity and access, roads from unimproved paths and tracks to motorways provide for denser networks, far greater penetration and, possibly, the only transport mode by which the extensive rural areas can be opened up. The different levels of construction technology allow road development to be phased in relation to growing demand, and road vehicles (bicycles, carts, mopeds, cars and lorries) can also reflect local conditions of geography and demand. In Africa the distinction between passenger and freight transport is far from clear, and road vehicles are adaptable in use as between the two – the 'mammy' lorry of West Africa is ideally designed for variable proportions of people and goods.

Only a fraction of Africa's road network is of the all-weather, motorable category and the more normal unsurfaced, dirt roads (laterite – 'swish' in West Africa and 'murram' in East Africa) are often impassable in the rains and very dusty in the dry season. The surface corrugates very rapidly, vehicle life is reduced and transport operating costs are high.

The great distances and difficult terrain favour the use of air transport and it plays a vital pioneer role in development. Initial surveys, establishment of 'base' camps and access for project equipment often depend on helicopters and short-take-off aircraft. Operational contact with diamond dredges in Sierra Leone, iron-ore mines in Mauritania and oil wells in many countries is by air. The cost of air transport is, however, high, and except for high-value goods can be prohibitive other than in exceptional circumstances – thus, Chad's frozen-meat exports have to be by air because of deficiencies of surface transport, Zambia's copper was air-freighted out when rail transport stopped after Rhodesia's declaration of independence in 1965, and much of the relief aid for drought-stricken areas has of necessity been by air.

Air transport is increasingly important in providing links within countries, between countries (Addis Ababa as the headquarters of the Organization for African Unity and the UN Economic Commission for Africa has emerged as a major focus of air routes) and between African and overseas countries. There are few African countries that do not now have their own airline for domestic (and in many cases long-haul) services despite the heavy financial

Plate 12 Chari river ferry crossing on Chad's main route to Nigeria

burden; justification is possibly in prestige rather than economic terms.

Sea transport provided the means whereby northern Africa was incorporated into the Mediterranean cultural and economic realm, brought the Europeans to western, southern and eastern Africa, and allowed Arab and Asian influences to affect East Africa. During the colonial period port facilities were improved at many points (Dakar, Freetown, Abidjan, Takoradi, Lagos, Lobito, Cape Town, Dar-es-Salaam and Mombasa to name but a few), and the ports often assumed the role of territorial capital and main focal point for external cultural, political and economic influence.

As much as 95 per cent of African trade is with overseas countries. The port therefore assumes a critical role in the development process – it will determine the quantity and nature of the goods that can be traded, and not surprisingly the post-independence era has brought massive investment in additional port facilities.

Transport has had high priority in many development plans, massive investment has not been restricted to ports, and recent years have brought considerable expansion and improvement of road networks, many new airports and some new railway lines. However, the need to get relief aid to Ethiopia, Sudan and Sahel West Africa demonstrated the still serious inadequacy of the transport infrastructure. Ports became congested, the capacity of the railways proved inadequate and roads and road vehicles were unfit for the task.

REFERENCES

1 May, J. M. quoted by A. L. Banks, 'Trends in the geographical pattern of disease', *Geog. Jnl.*, **122** (1956), pp. 172.
2 World Bank, *World Development Report, 1980*, New York, 1980, p. 50.
3 Kimble, G. H. T. *Tropical Africa*, New York, 1960, I, p. 139.
4 Overseas Development Inst., *Africa's food crisis*, London, 1984.
5 Overseas Development Institute., *Industrialisation in sub-Saharan Africa*, London, 1986.
6 Kimble, G. H. T. *Tropical Africa*, p. 293.

PART THREE: NORTH-WEST AFRICA AND THE SAHARA

10
The physical background

Northern Africa has a distinctive and un-African personality, as in many respects has the Sahara, which effectively separates the northern states from tropical Africa, or *Afrique Noire* as the French have termed it. For centuries the mass of Africa was regarded as the Dark Continent, but the Northern lands have been well known since classical antiquity: their history and development have been bound up with the Mediterranean world, to which their geography also belongs. This sweep of territory of more than 3000 km is divided between Morocco, Algeria and Tunisia and was under French control until the granting of independence in 1956, 1962 and 1956 respectively. The insular character of this part of Africa – surrounded by sea and sand – is emphasized by the Arabs calling it Gezira-el-Maghreb (Island of the West) and the term Maghreb for north-west Africa remains in use.

The native population of the Maghreb includes Berbers, Arabs and Jews. The two main Arab invasions of the Maghreb brought in about 150,000 men in the seventh century AD and a further 250,000 in the eleventh and twelfth centuries. Ever since the seventh century, Berbers and Arabs have inter-married and it is no longer possible to distinguish clearly between them. The proportion of Berber-speaking increases from east to west, as one might expect from the course of the Arab invasions. In Tunisia barely 1 per cent of the population is Berber-speaking; in Algeria 20 per cent; but in Morocco the proportion is thought to be as high as 40 per cent – much of it spoken in the highland areas and in the south of the kingdom. Most of the half-million Jews in northern Africa also speak Arabic; nearly half of them are to be found in Morocco.

Throughout the Maghreb there is a repetitive pattern of mountain, plain, steppe and desert and a related pattern of economic activity is to be discerned throughout the region. The valleys and coastal plains are devoted to peasant farming. Wheat and olives are the predominant crops; sometimes a few sheep and goats are kept. The fellaheen or peasant population live in hamlets or small villages, and these days there is a growing attraction to the towns and cities. In the mountain areas livestock-rearing, arboriculture and agriculture are important, in that order. The raising of sheep and goats, with seasonal up-and-down migrations in search of pasture, is the prime interest. Fig and olive tree cultivation and, finally, limited cultivation of cereals (often with irrigation) are secondary. The mountains have limited supporting power and many mountain people seek work in farms and towns on the plains. In some cases, as in Kabylia, emigration to work farther afield – in France – has become an established pattern.

In the steppe country of the plateaux which skirt the Saharan Atlas, sheep are reared by semi-nomadic peoples. They move northwards with the summer, usually in small family groups, their movements forming a regular annual pattern. However, gradually summer transhumance is diminishing throughout the Maghreb as tribal ties loosen and permanent settlement, cultivation and the towns appear more attractive.

Agricultural output in the Maghreb states has increased since the Second World War, but production per head has declined. This is one result of the population explosions which all the Maghreb states are experiencing as a result of the marked reduction of death rates and the maintenance of high birth rates.

Since attainment of independence the three states have striven hard to develop their economies and improve the standard of living. This they have done by a series of development plans principally aimed at the nurturing and the growth of industry, even at the expense of agriculture. The character of the regimes and ideologies embraced have led to interesting differences in the development planning and application and in the fortunes of the 50 million who now inhabit the Maghreb.

The Maghreb is one of the most urban regions of Africa and probably has been so since the founding of Carthage. Tunisian urban life is of long standing and Morocco, in Fez, Rabat and Marrakech, has cities dating back to the ninth century. Urban life is more recent in Algeria, much expansion being related to European occupation. Despite early urbanism the Maghreb has never had a single capital. Geography has much to answer for here, for the elongated shape of the area, the east–west trend of physical features, the lack of a natural focus, the clannish character of the mountain people, their antagonism to the plainsmen, all have militated against unity.

GEOLOGY AND STRUCTURE

The Atlas lands present a complicated, corrugated area derived essentially from folding and uplifting during the Alpine earth movements of the Tertiary period. During the Mesozoic and Tertiary eras various marine transgressions alternated with continental conditions over the present Atlas lands and parts of the Sahara. The limestones and sandstones and geosynclinal sediments to the north became heaved up by great pressure mainly from a northward movement of the Saharan shield. The earliest movements, the Pyrenean (Cretaceous – Eocene), were severe. The Rif Atlas were thrust up and at the same time the forerunner of the Tell Atlas of northern Algeria was created. Farther south the Saharan platform resisted the fold-waves which were diminished in strength and mostly only affected the surface veneer of younger rocks. Faulting and fracturing occurred and local vulcanicity followed. In the Miocene period, when the main Alpine folding took place in Europe, renewed folding occurred, especially of the Tell Atlas of Algeria.

In several ways the pattern of the more recently built mountains has been influenced by the earlier structural movements. The Alpine folds trend east-north-east to west-south-west, but the discontinuity of the ranges, the frequent intermingling of basins and valleys, owe much to the earlier underlying north–south Hercynian trend. The resistance of the Saharan platform permitted only open folding of the overlying sediments in the Middle Atlas and Saharan Atlas ranges, while marginal blocs, such as those known as the Moroccan and Oran Meseta, withstood the pressures.

In Algeria the resistant High Plateaux – a prolongation of the Oran Meseta – did much to confine the later violent Alpine movement to reviving the young Tell Atlas and including in them the shallow-sea limestones and sandstones of early Tertiary age. Thus the Tell Atlas and the Saharan Atlas encompass in the High Plateaux a distinctive area with few positive relief features. The rigid basement resisted the folding and shows only fractures and gentle undulations to mark the struggle; even these are considerably masked by a great mantle of debris. The two Atlas chains encircling the High Plateaux draw together in the high tumbled mass of the Aurès Mountains, and in eastern Algeria and Tunisia they cease to be distinct entities. Here Pyrenean folds were uplifted and rejuvenated by the later earth movements, and the eastern Tell and northern Tunisia is a tangled upland country with deep gorges penetrating and dissecting the mountain chains.

RELIEF

The series of mountain-building operations has resulted in a sequence of generally parallel relief features trending south-west to north-east and roughly paralleling the coast. The Atlas system is best developed in Morocco. Here the greatest elevations are attained, the widest geological diversity demonstrated and the greatest scenic grandeur revealed. The great snow-capped buttresses in Morocco have a very different personality from the more lowly broken ridges in Algeria.

The oldest of the fold mountains, the Rif Atlas, lie in the north in former Spanish Morocco and stretch from Tangier to the River Moulouya. Between them and the northern end of the Middle Atlas is a fertile lowland drained eastward through a narrow pass at Taza to the Moulouya and westward by the Sebou and its tributaries. South-west of this lowland for some 300 km down the coast and up to 160 km inland extends the plateau called the Moroccan Meseta, which rises gently from the coast to meet inland the half-encircling High and Middle Atlas Ranges. Its surface rocks are young, horizontal strata, mainly limestones, resting on the old crystalline platform, which is exposed in river gorges and in small areas inland. Nearer the Middle and High Atlas extend great plains of alluvial deposits washed down from the mountains. The resistance of the Archaean Meseta to the Alpine earth movements served to swing the fold-chains around it on the south and east. It is this positioning of these great fold mountains that has helped to make the Meseta into the home of nearly half the Moroccan population. The mountain slopes facing west or north-west receive the rain-bearing winds from the Atlantic. Seven hundred and fifty to a thousand millimetres is experienced over much of the upland and snow is usual from December to March. This precipitation nourishes numerous streams which flow across the Meseta to the sea all through the year.

The highest land in north-west Africa is in the High Atlas (Toubkal, 4080 m), which stretch with some majesty east-north-east from the Atlantic coast just south of Essaouira, subsequently passing into Algeria as the more subdued Saharan Atlas. In south-western Morocco many peaks exceed 3900 m, but very few surpass 1500 m in Algeria. Some of the highest country lies inland from Marrakech, where the ancient pre-Hercynian rocks have

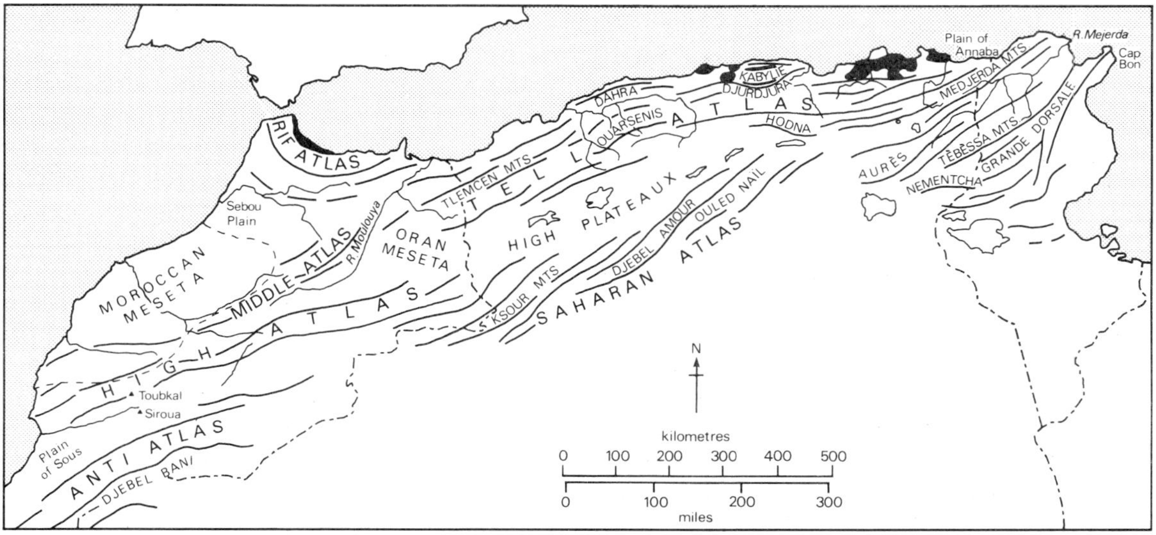

Figure 25 Principal fold trends in north-west Africa

been elevated to create mountain forms with sharp-crested peaks and displaying much evidence of glacial conditions in the recent geological past. From the centre of the High Atlas the ranges of the Middle Atlas swing northwards. Both ranges act as the Moroccan watershed; their Atlantic sides are well watered, but their east and south-east slopes fall under a Saharan regime. These slopes are scrub-covered and the streams are both fewer and mainly seasonal. The principal rocks in the broad folds of the Middle Atlas are limestones of varying ages. The heavy rain and snowfall has caused severe dissection, creating a wild plateau country interlaced with steep river gorges. This was one of the last parts of Morocco to be pacified after the French occupation. The eastern angle between the Middle and High Atlas constitutes a rather featureless stony plateau, the start of the old resistant Oran Meseta, itself the westernmost portion of the High Plateaux of Algeria. Here the River Moulouya, which receives water from both Atlas ranges, flows north with irregular discharge to the Mediterranean. In the south of Morocco the Sous Plain, a triangular structural depression opening on the Atlantic, separates the ranges of the High and Anti-Atlas. The Anti-Atlas shows evidence of folding but broadly represents a disturbed and elevated portion of the Saharan shield, comprising schists, quartzite and dolomitic limestone.

In Algeria the mountain system shows three major divisions. In the north the Tell Atlas, sometimes called the Maritime Atlas, parallels the coastal hills and the higher uplands inland which mark the northern edge of the second major physical division, the High Plateaux. These mountains differ from the more formidable ranges of Morocco in being lower, generally of younger rocks and far more interrupted. There is no single major range, but rather they comprise discontinuous hills, plateaux and massifs separated from one another by depressions, valleys and plains. The range of rock type is very great; limestones of varying ages predominate but sandstones and marls offer varied upland scenery. The result is a mosaic of individual topographic and economic sub-regions.

East of Algiers the Grande Kabylie is one of the most striking regions in the whole of the Atlas. It owes much of its personality to the core of Archaean and Pre-Cambrian rocks, once part of Tyrrhenia and now surrounding the limestone nucleus of the Djurdjura, the heart of the Grande Kabylie. Rising to 2272 m in the limestone peak of Lalla Kredidja and with flanking mountains of younger sandstones, limestones and flysch beds, it presents a heavily dissected country of steep gorges and narrow ridges. Difficult to penetrate, it remains a centre of Berber language and culture.

Between the Tell Atlas and the third mountain division, the Saharan Atlas and from the basin of the Moulouya river to the foothills of the Aurès extends a vast steppe region known as the High Plateaux. This undulating arid country lies mainly at altitudes between 750 and 1000 m, diminishing in height from west to east. The relief is subdued, and amid blunted ridges and escarpments extensive flats are provided by numerous shallow depressions known as 'chotts'. These form a chain of muddy salt basins, occupied by brackish waters during the brief rains. Farther to the east the country is drained by an ephemeral headstream of the River Cheliff, but for most of the year its course is dry and marked only by springs and wells. Further smaller chotts extend eastwards towards the second largest, the Chott El Hodna at 390 m.

The Saharan Atlas Mountains which bound the High Plateaux on their southern side extend from eastern Morocco to Tunisia. They are a lower and more open extension of the High Atlas. From the High Plateaux they appear disappointingly low – no more than hills; but from the Saharan side they emerge from an accumulation of debris to heights of 1500 m, and sometimes over 1800 m. The range is somewhat broken and falls into a number of distinct groups such as the Monts des Ksour, Djebel Amour and the Monts des

Ouled Naïl. The sandstone tabular mountains contrast with broken limestones ridges and gorges. Between the Monts des Ouled Naïl and the Aurès the Saharan Atlas lose height and merge with the High Plateaux. This provides a Saharan embayment immediately south of the Chott El Hodna, once the route of the Arab invaders and today a focus of roads to the desert from Constantine, Sétif, Bou Saada and Algiers. The higher hills receive annually a moderate 300–380 mm of rainfall, insufficient to nourish permanent streams across thirsty rock under the great heat. The streams flowing northwards across the High Plateaux and those flowing southwards towards the Sahara are all seasonal, their courses being dry for the greater part of the year.

The Aurès Mountains of eastern Algeria consist of folded Jurassic and Lower Tertiary sediments that have weathered into great ridges containing peaks and needles. Several of these peaks are over 2100 m high and they include the highest mountain in Algeria, Djebel Chelia (2291 m). This has proved another virtually impregnable highland where Berber ways persist. To the north are a number of inland basins, some such as the Plain of Sétif being the beds of former lakes. East and south-east a number of salt-marsh chotts occupy numerous smaller basins (the Constantine Chotts), relics of a great lake that once stretched over this whole region.

In the north a mass of folds, tightly packed ridges and valleys trend south-west to north-east into Tunisia, passing out to sea in headlands and promontories. They help to create good natural harbours, one of which became the French naval base of Bizerta. The principal river, the Medjerda, collects its waters from the upland mass of eastern Algeria and, flowing through the Plain of Tunis, joins the sea through a marshy delta (unique in north-west Africa) between Tunis and Bizerta. South of the Medjerda the Tunisian High Tell forms a succession of ridges, domes and basins of limestone or sandstone and trends north-eastwards to the Cap Bon Peninsula. The term Tunisian Dorsale is applied to the line of upland which serves as a climatic divide; to the north more pluvial Mediterranean conditions, to the south semi-desert.

CLIMATE

Only a small part of the Maghreb experiences a truly Mediterranean type of climate, for the parallel-trending relief features, themselves parallel with the coast, help to restrict this climate to a limited coastal area. Elsewhere elevation, distance from the sea and proximity to the Sahara are responsible for marked modification of the Mediterranean characteristics. Fundamentally the climate of the Barbary lands results from the interplay of air masses of diverse origins; the summer is dominated by tropical air and the winter season by modified Polar air and associated depressions.

In winter westerly winds are dominant over the Atlas lands. These are the winds moving around the series of depressions travelling north-eastwards along the line of the Mediterranean; generally they are rain-bearing winds, most having crossed the Atlantic. These depressions, and in the summer local depressions over the western Sahara, are responsible for the fierce off-desert local winds of northern Africa, possessing local names but of which the Sirocco is best known. These occur throughout the year but particularly in spring and are drawn to the advancing front of the depressions just as the Mistral and Bora of the northern Mediterranean coastlands are sucked into the rear. Coming from the desert these winds are excessively hot and dry, often dust-laden; they bring considerable bodily and mental discomfort and wither vegetation. Their duration varies greatly; sometimes they blow for less than an hour, sometimes for several days.

The climate of western Morocco differs from that of the rest of Barbary in that it owes much more to Atlantic than to Mediterranean influences. The Atlas ranges shelter western

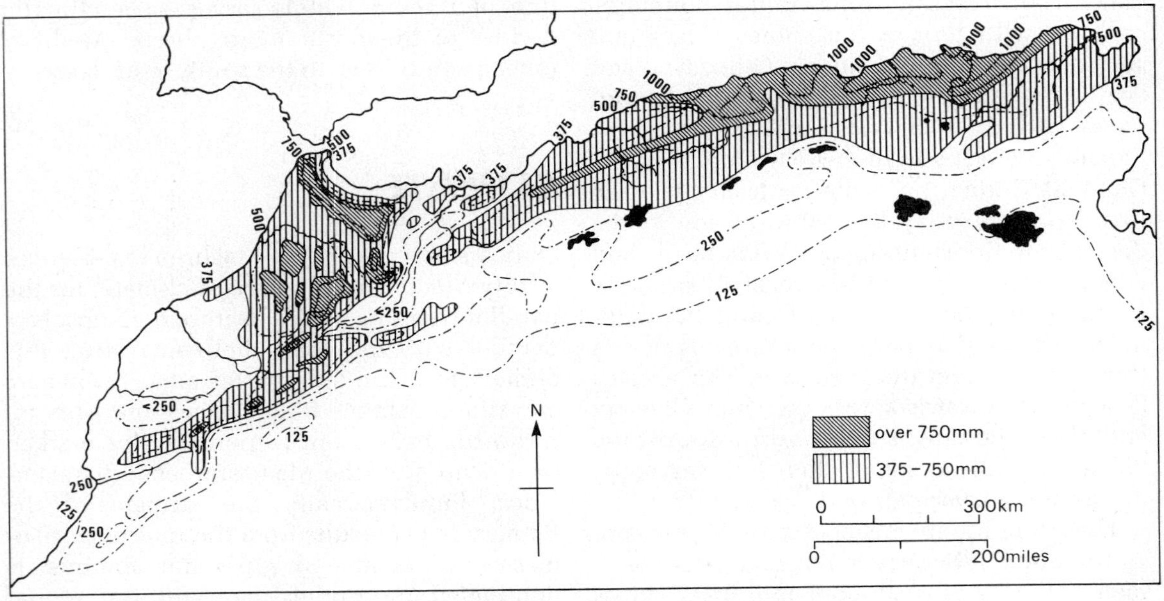

Figure 26 Mean annual rainfall in north-west Africa

Morocco from both the Sahara and the Mediterranean, while the cool Canary current flows offshore and serves both to reduce summer temperatures and rainfall along the coast. The Azores summer high-pressure centre (nearer the Canaries in winter) is responsible for north-easterly winds being dominant over Morocco. The winter winds bring rain to the Atlantic coastal regions and to the High and Middle Atlas ranges athwart their course. Summer is the dry season, for winds blow from the Mediterranean across warmer land and bring no rain except to the higher mountains. In the period May to September, Marrakech receives only 32 mm and in the rest of the year 200 mm (see Table 9). No stations exist in the High Atlas behind Marrakech, but rainfall there is probably over 750 mm.

On the Atlantic coast, land and sea breezes are a marked feature, the cold offshore current gives a cold, damp character to these breezes, and mist and fog are frequent. The Meseta experiences 250–400 mm annually and the Sebou lowlands to the north and the Taza gap enjoy about 600 mm. Like the Atlas, the Rif Mountains receive over 750 mm, but screen the lowlands to their east, and along the Mediterranean coast into Algeria no more than 250 mm is received. Similarly the lee side of the Atlas is in a rain shadow and Saharan conditions become apparent.

The proximity of the Atlantic and the cool offshore current modify temperatures and reduce the annual range. Temperatures in July are below 21°C along the coast. Farther from the coast on the Meseta the range of temperature increases and mean July temperatures reach over 26°C as sea influences become weakened. In the High and Middle Atlas winter temperatures below freezing point persist for several weeks; blizzards are frequent, passes become blocked by snow, which over considerable areas may lie over 1 m deep, thus providing a substantial reservoir for the west-flowing streams and rivers.

The climate of the rest of the Maghreb ranges between true Mediterranean in the north and Saharan in the south. Three more-or-less parallel east–west climatic regions are recognized: the Mediterranean coastlands and inner depressions and hills of the Tell, the

Table 9 *North-west Africa: temperature and rainfall of selected stations*

Station	*Altitude (m)*		*J*	*F*	*M*	*A*	*M*	*J*	*J*	*A*	*S*	*O*	*N*	*D*	*Year*
Essaouira	10	T	13.7	14.8	15.6	17.0	18.2	19.9	19.9	19.9	20.5	19.2	17.0	14.8	17.7
		R	54	38	54	18	16	1	—	—	3	30	60	60	334
Marrakech	463	T	11.1	12.7	14.8	19.2	21.0	26.0	27.7	29.3	24.4	21.0	17.0	12.1	19.2
		R	20	22	43	33	12	12	—	3	5	22	38	16	226
Algiers	22	T	9.3	10.5	11.7	13.2	16.1	19.9	23.3	23.8	21.0	17.7	13.7	11.1	16.1
		R	102	65	83	51	41	15	2	2	29	86	106	102	684
Biskra	123	T	11.6	16.1	16.1	19.9	25.0	29.3	33.3	32.7	29.3	22.7	16.1	11.6	21.6
		R	13	18	19	30	14	11	5	2	14	18	10	14	168
Tunis	42	T	9.3	10.5	12.1	14.3	18.2	22.2	25.5	26.1	23.9	19.3	14.9	11.1	17.1
		R	53	51	50	38	23	13	2	5	25	49	53	61	423

Notes: T = Temperature (°C); R = rainfall (mm).

High Plateaux and Saharan Atlas, and the Sahara. The coastal zone experiences a maritime Mediterranean climate (see Algiers, Table 9), the Inner Tell a Mediterranean climate but with rather more extremes. The whole of the northern part receives winter rains from the winds associated with the succession of cyclones passing along the Mediterranean. In the west on the coastal Plain of Oran this rainfall is as low as 380 mm owing to the screening effect of the Rif Mountains, but the hill ranges of the Tell Atlas receive 500 – 750 mm. Rainfall increases eastwards (as does the general relief), and east of the Mitidja (Algiers, 750 mm) the Kabylie Mountains and the Monts de Medjerda in Tunisia receive over 1000 mm. The high mass of the Djurdjura receives over 1500 mm, and this includes a considerable winter snowfall, the distant snow-capped peaks offering a seasonal backcloth to the groves of golden oranges and tangerines on the Algiers Plain. A sharp contrast always exists between the exposed and rainy north and west mountain slopes and the sheltered southern slopes.

The Mediterranean moderates summer temperatures which, along the coast, average 24 – 27°C in August, the hottest month. In winter coastal conditions are cool and rainy and in both seasons the daily range of temperature is small. Winter conditions are cloudier but the proximity of the Mediterranean mitigates temperatures and the mean for January, usually the coldest month, is 10–12°C. Frost is rare and the sheltered valleys and plains adjacent to the sea, such as the Mitidja, are suited to orange- and olive-growing.

The effect of the Mediterranean is not felt far inland and the sheltered valleys of the Inner Tell and Medjerda valley in Tunisia, cut off from the sea, show more continental conditions. Winters are colder, snow often falling on the ranges of the Tell Atlas, and summers

Plate 13 Snow capped High Allas southeast of Marrakech

are hotter, with July and August day temperatures of 38°C or more not uncommon in the more sheltered valleys such as that of the Cheliff. Away from the sea a greater range of temperature is apparent: at Bizerta it is 15°C (11°C in January and 26°C in August), whereas at Souk el Arba, in the Medjerda valley, it is 19°C (9°C–28°C). In southern Tunisia on the coast at Gabes it is 18°C (10°C–28°C), but inland at Gafsa it is 23°C (8°C–31°C).

The Tell Atlas reduces the precipitation reaching the High Plateaux, and since these plateaux at 750–1050 m are lower than the surrounding mountains, Mediterranean influences are excluded and continental conditions with marked seasonal contrasts are experienced. The greater distance from the sea and the rain shadow effect result in a precipitation of only 200 – 300 mm. Most of this falls in the spring, filling the temporary lakes or chotts which dry up during the summer. The contrast with the Mediterranean coastlands is heightened by cold winters, with mean January temperatures of 4°C and cold, dry north winds which sweep across the open country, often bringing snow and temperatures frequently below freezing-point. Frosts are common in December and January, and one must travel as far south as Biskra (240 km inland) before meeting temperatures as high as those of the coast (10°C). In summer this contrast between the High Plateaux and the Tell is less marked, the plateaux temperatures averaging 27°C in July, and when the sirocco blows (for about 40 days a year) absolute maxima of over 38°C are usual. Skies are cloudless, the air dry and a considerable diurnal range of temperature is experienced.

The ranges of the Saharan Atlas form a marked climatic divide between the steppe climate of the High Plateaux and that of the desert (Figure 26). With their greater elevation they receive more rainfall than the plateaux proper, and this rain is the source of much of the underground water supplying the chain of oases along the piedmont zone on the edge of the desert. Biskra stands at the junction of the two climatic types (Table 9). Its rainfall is of the Mediterranean winter type, but the small amount (170 mm) and the great seasonal (and also diurnal) range of temperature is more akin to Saharan conditions which extend across southern Tunisia into Libya.

In Tunisia the seasonal contrasts of climate are as marked as in the rest of North Africa and devolve from similar causes. Modifications of the general pattern are, however, brought about by the extended influence of the sea (for the coastline encompasses two sides of the roughly rectangular state) and by the confinement of a great deal of the highland to the west with broad plains to the east. The influence of the Mediterranean in reducing the range of temperature along the coast is striking. The northern Tunisian lowland has summer temperatures averaging 26°C, but southern and central Tunisia south of the Dorsale and away from the coast lies south of the 28° isotherm. Winters reveal mean January coastal temperatures around 11°C, but much of the interior is distinctly colder (the January mean around 5.5°C); and although temperatures are not as low as on the Algerian High Plateaux, frosts are common. The highest rainfall of over 890 mm is experienced in the mountains to the north-west. The annual rainfall diminishes to as little as 100 mm in the extreme south.

SOILS AND VEGETATION

The distribution of plant life depends upon the complex interaction of three factors: climatic, edaphic (soils) and biotic (plants and animals, especially man). Of these climate usually exerts the most powerful influence, and in northern Africa the amount and incidence of rainfall are of paramount importance. These in turn influence soil formation. The moderate to low rainfall of the Atlas lands retards rock-weathering, causing much of the soil to be immature, and restricts vegetative growth, affording little humus. With the wide variations of relief and geology the soils are very mixed and show close relationship with parent rock. Brown soils predominate, but the soils derived from limestones (rendzinas) are red. The amount of lime in the soil exerts some influence on the character of the vegetation. On the High Plateaux and steppe land of Tunisia, soils formed by aeolian (windborne) materials are important.

Most of this region of Africa is subject to two main types of climate, the Mediterranean in the north and the Saharan in the south, separated by a transitional steppe region. The mild, wet winters of the Mediterranean favour plant growth, whereas the summer droughts with their high rates of evaporation hinder growth. The greatest vegetative growth occurs in the spring when temperatures rise before the onset of the summer drought, and in the autumn when rainfall occurs before temperatures reach their minimum. This marked seasonal variation of rain and drought produces a rhythm of plant growth and structural adaptation to withstand the rainless period. The vegetation is characteristically xerophytic and demonstrates a range of adaptations for reducing transpiration: the bearing of spiny leaves and thorns, waxy coverings and thickened cuticles. Much of the region once bore woodland. Biotic influences in particular have reduced a good deal of this to evergreen thickets or maquis. The maquis consists of evergreen hard-leaved shrubs and low trees from 1 to 6 metres high. These include laurel, arbutus, myrtle, lentisk, rosemary, broom, buckthorns and aromatic shrubs such as lavender and thyme. They form dense tangles and thickets: well-developed maquis is impenetrable without mechanical aid. On the permeable limestone the maquis itself degenerates into heath and poor scrub known as 'garigue', where the vegetation is of patches of low-growing shrubs interspersed among bare rocks and soil. These include gorse, lavender and sage. The largest areas modified by man are the low platform of the Meseta and the lowlands of the Sebou to the north. Groups of degenerate cork oaks remain here and there, and are useful both for their bark and charcoal.

In the well-watered regions where there has been least interference, evergreen woodland predominates. This clothes the seaward-facing slopes of the Atlas and Rif of Morocco and the coastal hills and Tell Atlas of Algeria and Tunisia. Oaks and conifers are the dominant species. At the lower levels where destruction by man and animal has been greatest, brushwood and maquis prevail; from 900 m evergreen oaks and junipers predominate with cork oak on the more siliceous soils in eastern Algeria and Tunisia. From 1500 m cedars and thurifers form open forests and a valuable source of good timber. On the coastal mountains of eastern Algeria and north-western Tunisia deciduous trees such as Portuguese Oak, elm and ash grow in the deeper soils. The timberline is surpassed only in the High Atlas, where it is at about 3500 m. Above this height stony scrubland with spiny plants is the nearest approach to the Alpine vegetation of the north side of the Mediterranean.

Generally the vegetation of North Africa becomes progressively poorer from north to south with diminishing rainfall. The central zone of upland from eastern Morocco through Algeria into Tunisia (the High Plateaux) averaging 900 m in height has a long, dry season of 6–7 months and a lower rainfall of between 200 and 300 mm. Summers are hot and winters cold. Forests here give way to steppe vegetation composed of tufts of herbs and dwarf plants interspersed with patches of bare soil. The clay basins around the chotts, rich in mineral salts, provide a habitat for salt-steppe plants (halophytic), including sea lavenders, sea rushes and rice grass. They remain green throughout the dry season and provide food for flocks and herds in all seasons. The Anti-Atlas of Morocco and the Saharan Atlas mark a clear limit between Mediterranean and Saharan conditions. These ranges receive more rainfall than the High Plateaux and they support forest growth – in the west mainly Aleppo pine and holm oak and in the east cedar and thurifer on the higher parts (e.g. of the Aurès) with Aleppo pine and red juniper at lower levels.

11 Morocco

The kingdom of Morocco is separated from Europe by the 18 km-wide Straits of Gibraltar. It has strong religious and cultural ties with the Arab world, but it also forms a link with Europe whose capital and technical help it welcomes in its struggle for economic betterment. The kingdom (including former Spanish Sahara) has an area of 703,000 km^2. The population – mainly of Berbers and Arabs, but including some Europeans, Jews and Negroes – was 21 million in 1982. Europeans, mainly French, numbered about 100,000. The common language is Arabic and Islam is the common religion, both adopted in the eighth century. There is a deep national consciousness and pride in the country's long history and cultural inheritance.

Since 1956 the country has been a sovereign independent monarchy. Previously, from 1912 it was divided into two protectorates by France and Spain. The Spanish protectorate was the smaller and consisted of the strip of

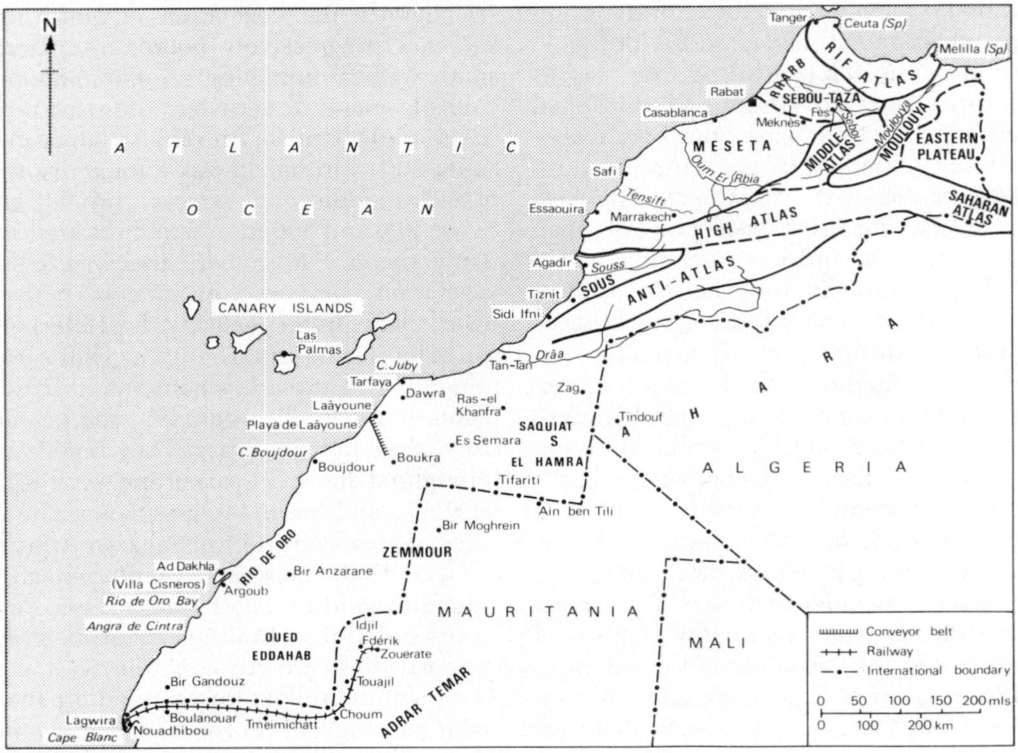

Figure 27 Geographical regions of Morocco

territory flanking the Straits of Gibraltar, mainly comprising the Rif Atlas. While ceding the bulk of the territory in 1956, Spain retained sovereignty over several coastal towns. The port of Tangier, declared an international zone in 1923, reverted to the kingdom of Morocco in 1956. Spain returned the small coastal enclave of Ifni to Morocco in 1969 and in 1976 withdrew from Western Sahara, handing the northern part to Morocco and the southern to Mauritania. The northern part contains valuable phosphate deposits and is vigorously held by Morocco against the Polisario guerrillas who want an independent state. Morocco also took over the southern part when Mauritania, seeing little benefit from its war with the Polisario, withdrew in 1979.

GEOGRAPHICAL REGIONS

On the basis of relief, climate and way of life Morocco may be divided into four distinctive parts (Figure 27): Atlantic Morocco, comprising the three lowland regions of Sebou-Taza, the Meseta and the Sous Plain; Western Sahara, part of the great desert; the Atlas Mountains with their series of distinctive ranges; and the plateau land to the east which may be regarded as an extension of the High Plateaux of Algeria.

The Atlantic lowlands

The bulk of the Moroccan population lives and works on the plains and plateaux facing the Atlantic. Here are the major cities, ports, industries and agriculture. In the north is the rich alluvial lowland of the **Sebou Basin and Rharb**, prolonged eastward in the Taza corridor. Atlantic influences penetrate far inland, tending to reduce temperature ranges; water is adequate and agriculture flourishes. The plains around Fez and Meknes through which a number of tributaries of the River Sebou now pass are particularly fertile, being derived from the floor of an old freshwater lake. Rainfall is only 500 mm, which is adequate for the predominant cereal cultivation; but the whole Sebou Basin is well watered by the springs and streams from the Rif and Middle Atlas, facilitating the widespread development of orchards, orange groves and vineyards, mainly as a result of the earlier French colonization. The Sebou is subjected to considerable spring flooding with the snow-melt off the Atlas. For the last 80 km to the sea, in the Rharb, its meandering course is raised above the general level of the plain and its flooding causes serious inundation.

South of Rabat between the Atlas and the Atlantic is the gently sloping platform of the **Moroccan Meseta**, rising from sea-level to more than 900 m. The higher inland portion is a dissected peneplain with the ancient rocks levelled down and thinly covered with Upper Cretaceous and Lower Eocene deposits. Several snow-fed rivers cross this plain to the coast, and although their volume is reduced in summer they make a valuable contribution to the agricultural economy. Chief among the rivers are the Tensift and the Oum er R'bia. In places these rivers have cut gorges through the Quaternary limestones, and occasionally the old Palaeozoic rocks are exposed. Land use varies considerably, with the best agricultural land stretching along the coast south from Casablanca. Here the coastal plain is up to 80 km wide and of fertile black soils. Traditional cultivation of wheat, barley and maize vies with expanding acreage devoted to sugar-beet, early vegetables and market gardening. The coast is inhospitable; there are few natural inlets to protect shipping from the strong Atlantic swell and most river mouths are obstructed by sand-bars. Farther from the sea, steppe vegetation offers sheep-grazing until cultivation recurs on a series of plains nearer the foot of the mountains. A large number of small oueds descend from the mountains and water this immediate piedmont zone, supplying oases and garden-type settlements and gradually losing their water in canals and small irrigation channels. Marrakech is in this zone. The drier climate renders irrigation necessary, and this city, white and red-brown from Saharan dust, stands at the foot of the mountains amid the fertile irrigated Haouz plain where palms, the vine, citrus fruit and market gardening flourish.

The remaining lowland, south of the Meseta and separated from it by the High Atlas, is the triangular downfold **Sous Plain** extending some 125 km inland from Agadir. The southerly position and enclosed character of the plain are responsible for a near Saharan climate. Agriculture and settlement are related to the irrigation from the River Sous and its tributaries, although these are irregular in flow and almost dry up in summer. Palms, itrus fruits and cereals are produced in these irrigated gardens; elsewhere the landscape is bare except for clumps of coarse grasses, fleshy spurge and argan trees which provide some grazing for sheep and the black Moroccan goats. The only other lowland of significance in Morocco is the valley of the River Moulouya which gathers its waters from both the High and Middle Atlas. The upper and middle valley is remote and inhospitable, lying in the rain shadow of the Middle Atlas (150–160 mm a year), but nearer the coast cereals and vines are grown.

Western Sahara

This was formerly Spanish Sahara: the northern part (Saquiat el Hamra) reverted to Morocco in 1975 and the smaller southern part (Ouedi Eddahab) when Mauritania renounced its claim to it in 1979. Here the desert comes down to the dune-fringed coast, where strong onshore mT winds from the Atlantic mitigate the heat, although they rarely bring rain (Dakhla:45 mm). Inland stretch great hammadas and table lands, much dissected by former water-courses and offering sparse grazing to camel- and sheep-owning nomads. This Moroccan part of the Sahara covers 266,000 kms; most of its light population of 75,000 are nomadic pastoralists. The large phosphate quarries at Bou Kraa provide practically the only other inland commercial activity, while there is some fishing along the coast. The former capital, Laayoune, has developed port facilities for the export of phosphate while, farther down the coast, Dakhla is the main fishing port. To strengthen its hold upon this desert area Morocco is doing much to improve living conditions. Numerous underground supplies of water have been found, wells have been dug and a desalinization plant to treat seawater has been set up at Boujour. A railway to link Laayoune with Marrakech has been surveyed and vigorous education, health and housing programmes have started. Nevertheless, Morocco's hold is challenged and is subjected to frequent Polisario guerilla raids in support of the declared Sahrawi Arab Democratic Republic (SADR).

The Atlas mountains

The great mountain chains of Morocco cover almost one-third of the country and support nearly two-fifths of the population. The **High Atlas**, at their widest here and attaining over 4400 m south of Marrakech, form a great physical and climatic barrier. The contrast between the Saharan and Atlantic side is remarkable. The north- and west-facing slopes are well watered and forested and the Berber peoples from their defensively sited and nucleated villages cultivate olives, tree fruits and cereals on terraced slopes. These days the mountain villages provide a reservoir of seasonal manpower for the farms and towns of the plains. The Saharan-facing slopes are dry, sunbaked and support only poor scrub. Here the tribes are more pastoral than agricultural. Settled life and cultivation is in oases, dependent on irrigation from the small streams, many seasonal, that flow southwards to lose themselves in the desert. Otherwise this is the domain of nomads with their flocks and herds.

The massive northerly spur of the Middle Atlas comprises mainly Jurassic limestone (giving a karstic landscape in the east). The western slopes are well forested and the relatively heavy rainfall and snowfall has made this area the main reservoir of the country. Much of the precipitation sinks into the fissured limestone and issues out as springs around the base of the mountains. The largest rivers of Morocco rise in the Middle Atlas and include the Oum er R'bia, the Sebou and the Moulouya. Here mountain pastures are the main resource and stock rearing is of greater importance than in the High Atlas.

THE ECONOMY AND WAY OF LIFE

As with the rest of Africa, the Moroccan economy has two distinct and unequal parts, which may be termed the traditional and the modern. The basis of the *traditional* economy is the agriculture that has evolved to satisfy the subsistence wants of more-or-less self-contained rural communities. Commerce is unorganized and local, depending upon incidental marketable surpluses. These activities are complemented by the traditional handicraft industries. The *modern* economy results from the French occupation, investment and settlement. Much is due to their first and outstanding Resident-General, Marshal Lyautey (1912–25) who, after his successful subjugation, devoted himself to Moroccan development.

The desire that the impact of modern civilization should not cause the speedy disintegration of the traditional urban and tribal society led to the housing of European and Moorish communities in separate towns and suburbs. Today's monument to this policy is the phenomenal growth of the port-city of Casablanca. The French made a fine artificial harbour at Casablanca for the export of minerals and vegetables, and in 70 years it has grown from a small town of 20,000 to 1.75 million inhabitants. It is now a city of huge modern offices and flats, the geographical centre and mainspring of the modern economy, which owes a great deal to European investment, enterprise, technology and skill. Moroccan participation is still mainly as semi-skilled and unskilled labour.

The modern economy accounts for over two-thirds of the country's total production, although it employs only about 30 per cent of the total population. If the subsistence element in the traditional economy is discounted, its share in the money economy is less than 15 per cent of total production. In other words, only a small proportion of Moroccans are involved in the money economy; the mass of the population, existing mainly on a subsistence basis, has very little purchasing power and no resources for investment. The traditional economy is generally one of stagnation. This underlines the difference between the two economies, for the modern economy in the long term demonstrates cumulative growth and is expanding.

Agriculture

The farming sector is crucial to the economy. It employs about 50 per cent of the working population, produces four-fifths of the nation's food requirements and contributes nearly one-third of total exports, coming second in importance to phosphates. There are two types of farming: the large traditional subsistence sector and the smaller modern sector derived from the European settlement and concerned with cash and export crops.

Over much of the country traditional methods of agriculture are only slowly changing: animal power is used and much hand labour is employed; fertilizers are little used, rotations are rare, yields are poor and there is an overwhelming emphasis on cereals. The climate, particularly rainfall, influences the pattern of agriculture and leads to considerable fluctuations in yields from year to year. The relatively well-watered Atlantic seaboard and mountain valleys are the scenes of cultivation and settled ways of life, but as the rainfall diminishes from north to south and from east to west the emphasis on stock rearing increases under semi-nomadic or nomadic regimes.

The traditional subsistence farming sector covers some 4 million hectares and most of the holdings are small. Earlier European land settlement had been restricted and amounted to about 1 million hectares in 6000 large holdings. The farming was modern and efficient and crop yields were markedly higher than those of the Moroccan small farmers. The higher returns also reflect the emphasis on more remunerative crops such as tree crops and garden vegetables. It was not in the Moroccan government's interest to break up the large commercial (mainly French) farms following independence, for they provided valuable revenue from exports; so they remained, gradually being bought out by Moroccan interests, and it was not until the 1970s that the remainder of these large farms were expropriated under land reform laws and some 400,000 ha were redistributed. Before this there was a marked imbalance in land ownership: some 87 per cent of farmers owned less than 2½ ha each, whereas 3 per cent owned more than 10 ha each and these holdings constituted one-third of all productive land.

The traditional agriculture is concerned with producing basic foods, and some 80 per cent of the cultivated land is under cereals (mainly wheat and barley). Nevertheless, in recent years increasing quantities of food have had to be imported.

Arable agriculture with permanent settlements lies mainly in the better-watered northern half of the Atlantic Plain, southwards along the coast and inland, with irrigation, at the foot of the mountains. In the semi-arid steppe areas the ground is scratched rather than ploughed and cereals planted: the bulk of the population then seeks summer pasture for the sheep and goats. There are also similar movements within the mountains, especially in the Middle Atlas. Here in November sheep and goats move down to the steppe of the Moulouya and the plains around Fez and Meknes and the Tadla Plain of the upper Oum er R'bia. In spring beasts and men return to the Atlas valley villages and the cultivation of maize, barley and wheat is put in hand. In June a proportion of the animals is taken higher up to the mountain pastures, but the bulk of the people remains in the valleys with their arable crops and fruit trees. Thus, one of Morocco's oldest occupations, stock-raising, is a natural response to a climate frequently unfavourable to arable agriculture. Stock can withstand the seasonal character and the variability of the rainfall better than crops and can take advantage of the pastures that range of altitude offers. Little care is lavished on the beasts, mainly sheep and goats, who furnish all the essentials for nourishment and clothing and are also mobile and hardy. This mobile element in the lives of a high proportion of Moroccans is further shown in a seasonal movement of labour, principally from the poorer south mainly to the farms of the coast and around Marrakech.

Just under one-quarter of Morocco receives annually more than 600 mm of rain; another quarter (with 300 – 600 mm) is semi-arid; and the remaining half is occupied by desert and steppe. In such a country the strengthening and development of the agricultural economy must give high place to irrigation. By the year 2000 Morocco hopes to have 20 reservoirs which will supply a million hectares of irrigated land. However, despite efforts under each development plan progress is slow and no more than 400,000 ha are currently under perennial irrigation. In general, surface flow is utilized in the north, but underground supplies in the south and east. Some progress has been made in improving the indigenous wells and foggaras, and small reservoirs have been built in the mountains to the south to store water for the summer. Major irrigation schemes involving large dam and canal construction have been, and are being, carried out on the Sebou tributaries, Oum er R'bia and its tributaries and the N'fis tributary of the Oued Tensift.

The problems to be overcome include the violent seasonal variability of the rivers, the permeable character of the limestones and the silting up of reservoirs. There is a need to educate Moroccan farmers in irrigation farming with its new crops and new techniques. The Beni Amir–Beni Mussa scheme, begun 40 years ago, is a major scheme that has shown success. It is situated in the Tadla Plain, a 350 mm rainfall steppe zone in the Meseta at the foot of the High Atlas. Previously the population was semi-nomadic, taking poor crops from plots along the Oum er R'bia and then ranging over the steppe to the mountain grazing. The scheme has trained the peasantry in a new mode of life, with a health service, schooling and public works. Fragmented holdings have been consolidated and cotton growing is included in the rotations. Another large irrigation scheme is being developed farther downstream at Abda Doukkala, where there is emphasis on sugar production.

Fishing

There are rich reserves of fish in the cold water of the Canary current off Morocco's coast, but these are mainly exploited by foreign fleets. The principal varieties caught are the sardine, bonito and tunny. The total annual catch is about 1.5 million tonnes, of which Morocco lands about 450,000 tonnes. Efforts are being made to modernize the fishing ports, to expand the home fleet and to obtain a share of the catch of the foreign fleets (especially from Spain and Portugal) that fish Moroccan waters. Exports of sardines meet severe competition from Portugal, Spain and Italy.

Mining and energy

Mining is an important industry in Morocco. It is efficiently organized for an export market and minerals account for 16 per cent of total exports by value. The principal mineral is phosphate of lime and Morocco is the world's leading exporter and third producer after the USA and USSR and holds about three-quarters of the world's reserves.

The main deposits occur in a band of limestone roughly paralleling the coast inland of Casablanca, Mazagan and Safi. The limestone is soft, easily mined and rich in phosphate. The main centres of mining are at Khouribga, Youssoufia, Ben Guerir and Bou Kraa. The latter, in Western Sahara, reopened in 1982 after seven years of inactivity following the Spanish withdrawal; it has an annual capacity of 10 million tonnes. With this augmentation Morocco planned to increase production to about 34 million tonnes by 1985. However, declining demand prevented this. Further expansion will occur near the end of the decade when a new mine at Meskala (inland of Essaouira) will be developed with Russian investment. Efforts are being made to expand phosphate processing plants to increase the value of the exported material: four plants are operating (based on Casablanca and Safi), producing phosphoric acid and superphosphate.

Other minerals produced and exported, albeit mainly in small quantities, are included in Table 10. Iron ore is mined at Uixan and Ait Amir and coal production from Djerada in eastern Morocco has increased in recent years to a million tonnes. Phosphates are shipped to most countries of western Europe, while manganese, lead and zinc are exported mainly to France. Moroccan domestic energy resources satisfy only one-fifth of her needs, which are increasing with the growth of the industrial sector. Emphasis is being placed on expanding hydroelectric power and intensifying oil and gas exploration. Little oil has yet been found, but a substantial gas field near Meskala has been discovered.

Table 10 *Morocco: mineral production*

	Production (000 tonnes)				
	1965	*1970*	*1975*	*1980*	*1982*
Phosphate	9,824	11,420	14,119	18,824	17,700
Coal	430	433	652	710	—
Iron-ore	900	522	336	36	—
Lead and zinc	78	85	68	119	105
Manganese	136	60	67	68	49

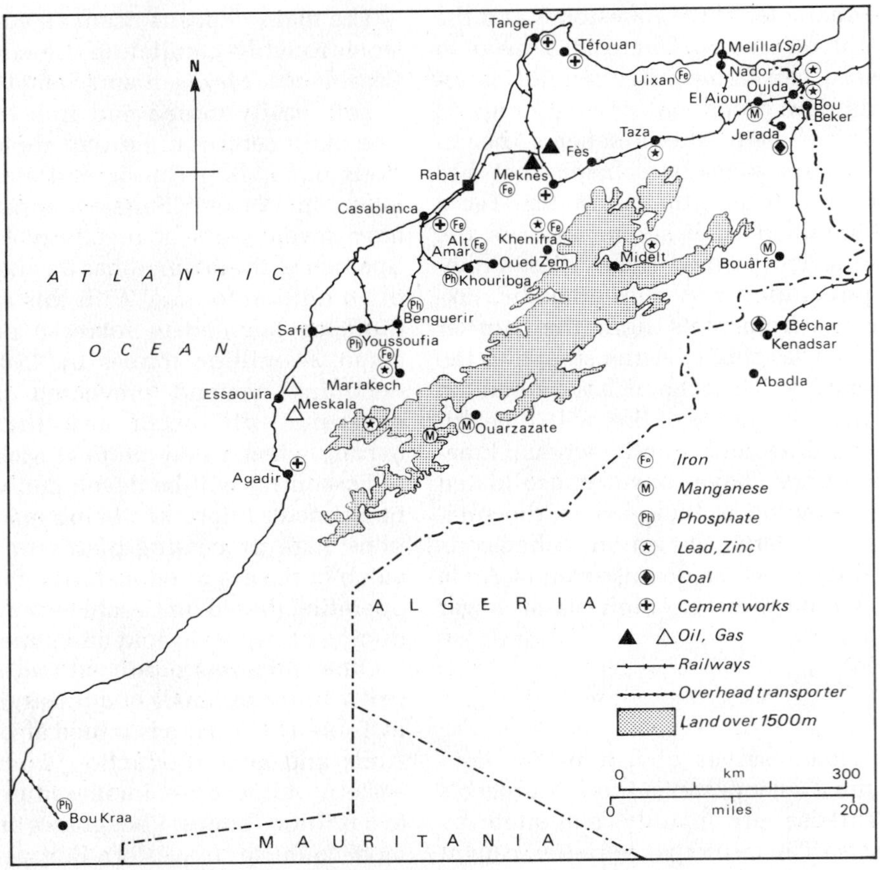

Figure 28 Mining and railways in Morocco

MANUFACTURING INDUSTRY AND PLANNED DEVELOPMENT

Since independence was attained in 1956 there has been a substantial and increasing development of manufacturing industry, which now accounts for about 17 per cent of the GNP. Again a division between traditional artisanal industry and the larger modern factory establishments is notable. Rather more than 300,000 people are employed in secondary industry, and over half of them are artisans in the traditional sector where textiles, ceramics and leatherwork are manufactured widely throughout the country.

The principal modern industrial region is the Chaouia and centres on Casablanca. Almost 70 per cent of industrial establishments are in and around this city, the core area of the country. Many manufactures are associated with the country's primary production and for the most part serve a home market. They include milling, brewing, sugar refining, vegetable oilseed pressing, tobacco manufacture, soap and candle manufacture. The government has encouraged other industries that substitute for imports. They include textiles, car assembly, plastics, cement manufacture, chemicals, paper. However, with the limited home market their fortunes have been indifferent, and recent years have seen some success in finding modest export markets for textiles, rubber tyres and fertilizers in addition to long-established exports of tinned fish and vegetables.

Traditional Moroccan industries have declined during this century, mainly as a result of imported manufactured goods. Carpet manufacture is centred upon Fez, Rabat and Casablanca and the traditional leather industry is centred upon Marrakech, Safi and Fez. The artisan industries are strongest in the old towns such as Fez, Meknes and Marrakech, noted for embroidery, textiles, leatherware, pottery and jewellery. These interest tourists, and Morocco now makes great efforts to attract the tourist trade. Almost 2 million tourists now visit the country annually.

Industrial development in Morocco has been hampered by constraints that are typical in most developing countries: a mainly illiterate population, a lack of skilled labour, limited capital and limited fuel and energy resources. Since independence Morocco has attempted to guide its development by a series of economic plans. However, the first decade of independence saw little progress for it was a period of political struggle between the king and a mainly left-wing parliament. King Hassan II, who ascended the throne in 1961, quickly gained power and popularity, became his own prime minister and laid down the goals of planning. The major aims of the series of plans have been to create economic independence of foreign countries and to reduce the regional inequality that had become most marked with the growing economic and social importance of the Casablanca region. Neither aims have yet been attained. The Three Year Plan 1965–7, which laid stress on agriculture, tourism and education, was inadequately financed and then ruined by severe drought in 1966 and 1967. Economic growth was small and nullified by the greater rate of population growth. The Five Year Plan that followed (1968–72) allotted nearly one-third of the total planned investment of £920 million to modernizing agriculture, particularly in expanding irrigation and export crops such as citrus fruits, tomatoes and early vegetables. Investment was also made in building hotels and creating tourist facilities. The priorities were right but the results disappointing, for the bulk of the farmers were loath to change from the traditional cereal cultivation.

The Fourth Plan (1973–7) was very different. The total investment was £2700 million, three times that of its predecessor. This vast sum came mainly from phosphate revenues: Morocco followed the example of the OPEC states and, relying upon its overwhelming share of the world phosphate market, tripled (and by 1975 had quintupled) the price of its phosphate exports. This worked well at first, but consumer resistance in more recent years has led to falling sales despite modest price reductions. The Fourth Plan allotted two-fifths of its resources to industrial development and, in an endeavour to spread development away from Casablanca, declared the towns of Fez, Marrakech, Meknes, Oujda and Agadir to be growth poles. A phased programme of Moroccanization of the factors of production was included; and to render this more palatable to overseas investors new and more liberal investment codes were introduced, offering incentives such as exemption from custom duties and product tax and between 50 and 100 per cent exemption from profits tax for the first ten years of a factory's operation. New sugar mills were built to accompany an expansion of sugar-beet cultivation, a car assembly plant was established at Casablanca (with the aid of Fiat and Simca), and considerable expansion was made to the textile industry with new mills at Fez and Beni Mellal in the cotton growing area. In all 95,000 new industrial jobs were planned for; but since 150,000 extra workers joined the labour force annually at that time, the majority of them still had to be absorbed into the agriculture section.

Poor harvests led to some disarray and three annual contingency plans followed before the Fifth Plan (1981–5). After two years this ambitious plan had to be revised in the light of lower phosphate prices, further droughts that necessitated increased food imports and mounting deficits in the balance of payments. Nevertheless it gave priority to food production (especially to the expansion of irrigation facilities), exploiting national energy resources (more hydroelectric power, offshore oil exploration and proving the gas field at Meskala), the expansion of the chemical industry, the completion of steel rolling mills at Nador, a cement plant at Oujda, and support for labour-intensive small and medium-sized enterprises: in all nearly a million new jobs were envisaged, the majority (optimistically) to be in the secondary and tertiary sectors. The plan also continued the emphasis upon education, particularly at the primary level. Some 21,000 new school rooms were planned, and by 1985 primary school enrolment was expected to rise from 69 per cent to 82 per cent of eligible children.

While none of the plans has been outstandingly successful, considerable social and economic advance has occurred, the per capita GNP more than doubled in the decade 1970–80 (US$300 to US$670). The government now focuses attention upon a full utilization of the country's natural resources, and to this end it is establishing a chemical industry based upon oil refining and the development of by-products from phosphates. The Nador steel rolling mill (using imported ingots) completed in 1984 is intended as the first stage in the development of an integrated iron and steel complex, based upon the local ores. National energy supplies (hydro power, coal mining at Djerada and the gas resources near Essaouira) are all being developed, for lack of power has limited industrial expansion. A part of the industrial expansion is particularly hampered by the lack of skilled workers for what are high-technology projects; the agricultural sector – the mainstay of the economy – suffers from periodic and often devastating droughts, and all sections are retarded by the slow progress of education and literacy.

POPULATION AND SETTLEMENT

In recent years the rate of population growth in Morocco – at over 3.0 per cent – has been one of the highest in Africa. If this rate persists population will double in just over 20 years with improving medical services. The rapid fall in mortality rates (to 14 per 1000) over the last 20 years accounts for this high rate of population increase, for birth rates have remained very high (45 per 1000). One result of this is that the population is 'young' – 45 per cent are under 15 years of age and, being non-productive, take an over-large share of current output that otherwise might be invested. The current rapid urbanization in Morocco is not overwhelmingly due to rural–urban migration, but also to a higher rate of natural increase in the large towns than in the country, because the death rates are lower in the towns.

As in most developing countries recent years have seen a surge to the towns in Morocco, particularly to Casablanca which now surpasses a 2 million population. Some 40 per cent of Moroccan population is now urban and there are now 15 towns each with more than 100,000 population. The drift from the countryside accentuates the regional imbalance and sees the core region, around Casablanca, attracting more and more population, investment, manufacturing and business. Current planning designating provincial growth poles offers inducements to attract industry to them, but so far with little success.

Most of the Moroccan population is to the north and west of the Atlas ranges, the most favoured areas being the Sebou Plain, the south-facing Rif foothills, the Atlantic face of the Meseta and the irrigated western foothill zone of the Atlas ranges. In all those areas, which favour agriculture, densities exceed 50 per km^2; they contrast severely with the few inhabitants living on the desert fringe south of the High Atlas. Moroccans have not traditionally been town dwellers, and it is only in recent years that the disdain for town life among the country and mountain folk has diminished as the greater opportunities for better living, for wide-ranging employment possibilities and for education have been perceived.

The dispersed character of the population has brought into prominence the *souk* or weekly market, an individual feature of rural Moroccan life. These markets are held in the open at predetermined sites which are deserted for the rest of the week. *Souks* are so located within tribal areas that tribesmen may visit them and return home within a single day; thus they may be 30–50 km apart. They are generally named according to the regular day of the week on which they are held. Moroccans are great walkers, but travel by bus is increasing and merchants also arrive by bus or car with their bales of cloth, imported groceries (tea, coffee, etc.); artisans such as blacksmiths, barbers, cobblers, makers of pots and pans and the travelling medicine man are all part of the pattern. These gatherings are social and political as well as commercial: news and gossip are exchanged, problems resolved and legal transactions discussed. The markets facilitate the exchange of rural surplus commodities for urban goods and further the exchange of local products, playing a large part in the life of the countryside. In the towns there may be a number of *souks* housed in narrow streets each specializing in particular merchandise.

The usual dwelling of the sedentary Berber or Arab is a one-roomed abode made of sun-dried clay with a clay-tiled roof. In mountainous areas these houses are often so huddled on the slopes that they rise in tiers, one man's roof being another man's roadway. In the Atlas of southern Morocco, in addition, gigantic 'kasbas' or strongholds of the Berber chieftains provide relics of a departed military power. The towns are little more than such groupings on a larger scale with ramparts and a mosque. The four elements discernible in the larger towns today are the huddle of Moroccan houses making up the 'medina', the Ghetto quarter ('mellah') of the Jews who have played an important part in commercial life, the kasba of the governor, and the European quarter, usually somewhat detached from the congested older agglomeration and much more spaciously planned (Figure 29). The separate European quarter was an outcome of Marshall Lyautey's attempt to preserve and protect the main Moroccan cities from modernization and European penetration. This has meant that the historic Moroccan cities have become museum pieces, for the modern sector of the dual economy burgeoned in the modern (European) sector of the city and as the Europeans withdrew after 1956 so middle-class Moslems moved out of the medina to new houses and a take-over of the European quarter. Migrants from the country crowded into the deteriorating medinas, filling sub-divided mansions and over-spilling into shanty towns (bidonvilles).

Plate 14 Phospate plant, Khouribga, Morocco

Casablanca (pop. 2,400,000 in 1981), the largest city, major port and economic capital of the kingdom, is essentially a modern creation. In 1907, after some assassinations of Europeans, the French occupied the port and made it the base for their subsequent subjugation of the kingdom. Today the well-planned European-type city, with spacious boulevards, banks, department stores and gleaming slabs of modern air-conditioned office blocks, reminds one of Los Angeles rather than an

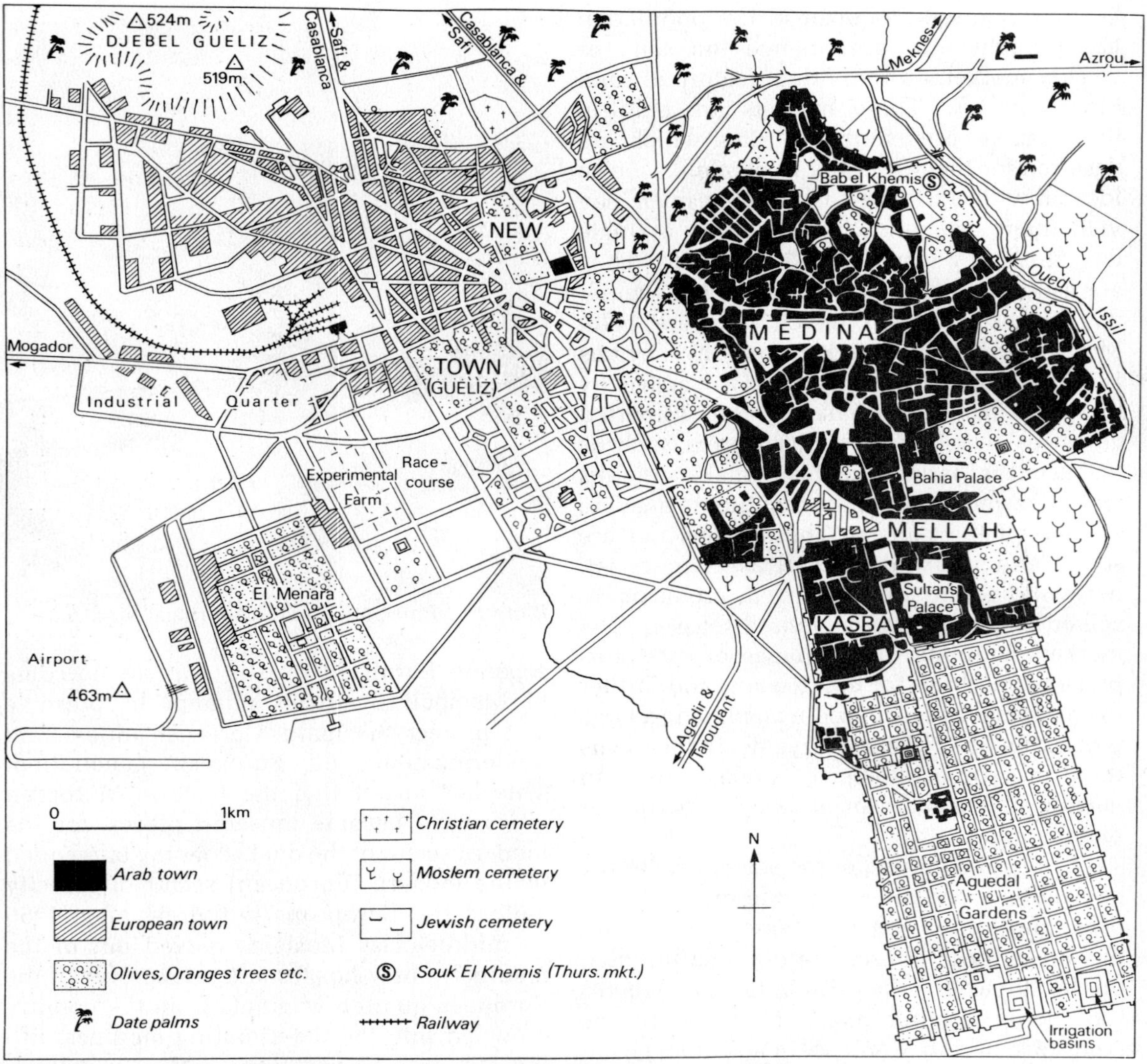

Figure 29 Marrakech showing customary components of the larger Arab towns in the Maghreb

African town. The original small roadstead has been transformed into a deep-water port with two great concrete moles giving shelter from the Atlantic swell. This port handles about 70 per cent of Morocco's foreign trade. The industries of the port include fish canning and curing, flour milling, cereal processing, ship repairing, sugar refining, oil refining, car assembly, cement and fertilizer manufacture. Excellent road and rail communications link Casablanca with its important hinterland of northern Morocco, with the coastal plain to the south and Marrakech.

Rabat-Sale (pop. 841,200). Rabat is the administrative capital of Morocco and with its twin town of Sale, on the north side, straddles the estuary of the small river, Bou Regreg. A large European town surrounds the medina and includes the king's palace and government offices. The port, with a maximum harbour depth of 5 m, has diminished in importance with the rise of the deep-water port of Casablanca.

Fez (pop. 562,900) has grown up at the crossing of two ancient and important routes. These are the great east–west trade route linking Algeria and the eastern Maghreb with the Atlantic cities via the Taza corridor, and the north–south caravan route from the Mediterranean coast at Tangier to the Sahara via the passes in the Atlas. It sprawls its jungle of narrow lanes and alleys on both sides of the Oued Fez, near its confluence with the Sebou. The town dates from AD 801 and for much of its history has been a capital city. It remains a great centre of Arab life, religious and cultural; and it is the foremost native industrial and commercial centre, enjoying a great reputation for its carpets and leatherwork.

Marrakech (pop. 548,700) is the largest native city in Morocco (Figure 29). It was established in AD 1062 and has grown up on the Haouz Plain in the valley of the Oued Tensift about 64 km from the foothills of the snow-capped High Atlas. It is at the meeting of two natural routes through the mountains from the south-west and the south-east. The old city is walled and bastioned and throughout its history has vied with Fez as capital. It is the great mart for the tribesmen of the High Atlas and much of the north-west Sahara. It has spread over a well-irrigated plain and represents a vast oasis settlement in a semi-arid region (average rainfall: 225 mm), being surrounded by date-palms, vineyards, groves of oranges and olives and other fruit trees. Native industries include carpet, pottery and jewellery manufacture.

COMMUNICATIONS AND TRADE

Part of the French legacy to Morocco is a relatively good network of communications. There are 1900 km of railway, mostly of standard gauge, linking the Atlantic coast with Algeria, Tangier and Marrakech (Figures 28 and 31). The railways do not form a net, but reflect economic development in linking the rich Fez–Meknes area with the coast, and the phosphate workings and Marrakech area with the ports of Safi and Casablanca. Another line through the Taza corridor links Morocco with Algeria and a spur from it serves the Bou Arfa mining district. There are 15,000 km of surfaced roads, many of them of first quality and constructed during the great period of infrastructure development early in the 1950s. The road network mainly serves the modern economy and is closest in the Sebou Plain and in Atlantic Morocco. All-weather surfaced roads have been made over the passes of the Middle and High Atlas.

The bulk of Morocco's trade is with Europe, mainly France. The chief exports are the minerals: phosphates and phosphate by-products; iron-ore, lead and manganese, but others of importance are barley, fruits and early vegetables. The principal imports are petroleum products, vehicles, tractors and certain foodstuffs.

Morocco's attempts at orderly planned development since independence have not been very successful, partly because of a number of severe droughts, because of inadequate investment resources and, when they were increased by large receipts from phosphate exports, because of the mounting pressure of population upon the resources the plans were to utilize. The great mass of young in the population necessitates large expenditure on education, health and housing and creates an annual problem of some 200,000 new workers requiring jobs. Nevertheless there have been both economic and social advances in recent years.

12 Algeria

Algeria, under French dominion from 1830, became an independent republic in 1962. Its area of 2,382,000 km^2 includes a very large part of the Sahara, but the habitable portion, northern Algeria, is quite small, being about 200,000 km^2. Thanks to over a century of vigorous French colonization, Algeria is the most developed of the three Barbary states. This progress has been aided by physical conditions less extreme than in Morocco. Sheltered plains and valleys benefit from their proximity to the Mediterranean and mountains are much restricted. However, the area of steppe, encouraging transhumance from the desert border, is much greater.

Algeria is a country displaying the great diversity that a varying distance from sea, variation of altitude, of geology and aspect would lead one to expect. One consequence has been the lack of a natural centre and a history of numerous and varied capital cities looking either eastwards to Tunisia or westwards to Morocco. The French tended to continue an earlier Turkish tripartite division, for long administering through three *departements* based upon Constantine, Algiers and Oran.

GEOGRAPHICAL REGIONS

The Tell

This region, which stretches from the boundary with Morocco to the district around the port of Bejaia, comprises the coastal plains and hills, the series of elongated massifs and inland plateaux forming the Tell Atlas, and the intermediate river valleys and basins. There is a considerable diversity of relief, geology and soils, and numerous sub-regions may be recognized; only two will be detailed here, the Mitidja Plain and the Grande Kabylie or Djurdjura Mountains. The climate is characteristically Mediterranean and the climatic and geological affinities with southern France, the proximity of the coast and ports, the relative ease of movement along the valleys, coupled with harsher environment and poorer facilities elsewhere, made this region the principal area of French settlement and the most productive part of Algeria.

Except for the great mass of the Grande Kabylie, the coastal hills and Tell Atlas are of folded rocks and display great variety of character and age. It is their tectonic history that helps to explain the broken character of these folded hills and mountains, creating discontinuous hill-masses and plateau formations. Aridity increases as one goes westwards and this, allied to the character of the soil, shows a marked effect on localizing settlement and cultivation. From the Cheliff valley westwards increasing preference is shown for the alluvial fans and terraces of the valley sides, whereas the compacted alkaline alluvium of the centre of the valleys and plains bears thin crops and provides sparse pasture for sheep. Numerous small streams, many seasonal, water the lowland. The Cheliff can trace some of its seasonal headstreams to the Saharan Atlas, but the others rise in the Tell Atlas and have shorter courses to the coast.

The Sahel of Algiers and Mitidja. This is the most populous and developed part of the Tell. It was the scene of early French colonization and over a century immense changes have been wrought. The Sahel is a region of low hills lying between the sea and the Mitidja Plain, mainly to the west of Algiers. The hills are of soft Pliocene limestones and rest on marly clays, so giving rise to springs and helping to form an attractive undulating green

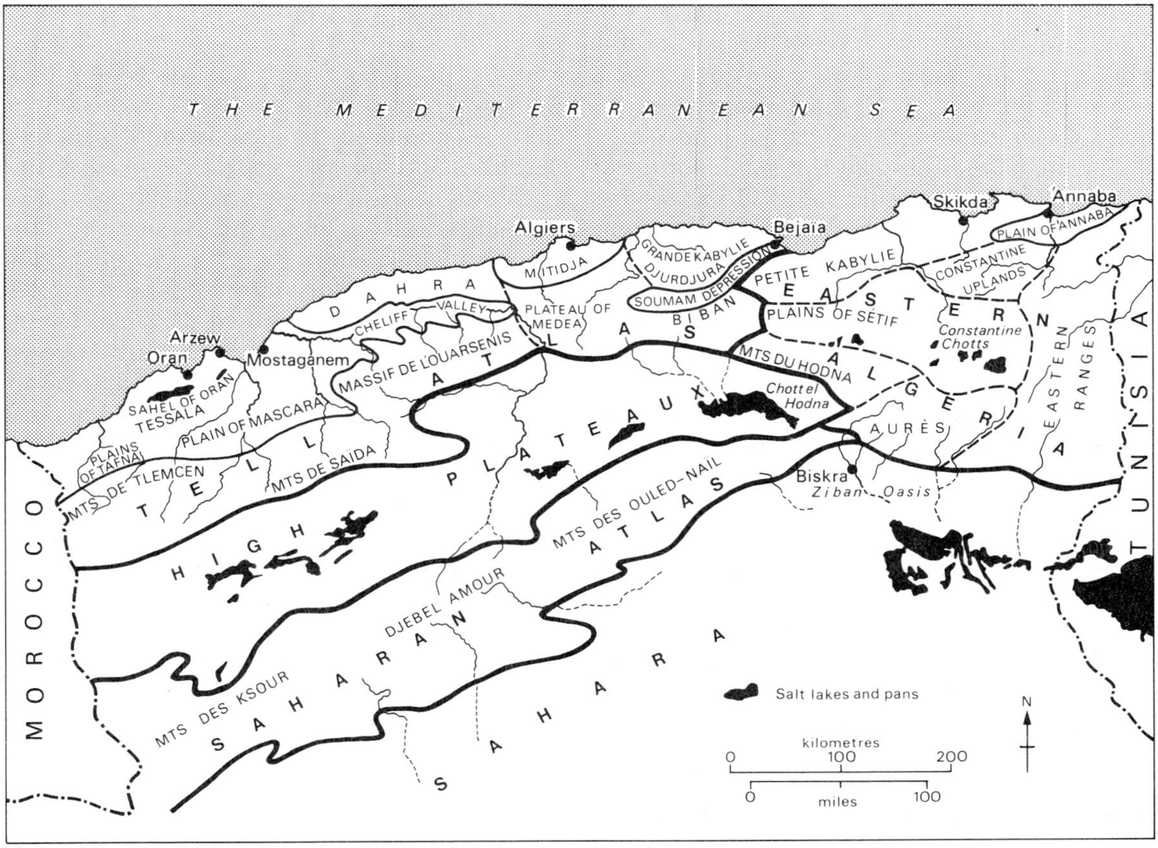

Figure 30 Geographical regions of Algeria

countryside. The Mitidja Plain, some 100 km long by about 20 km broad, slopes gently from the El Boulaida mountains of the Tell Atlas down to the Sahel and the sea. The plain is fairly level, although in fact it comprises an integration of many alluvial cones created by the swift seasonal Atlas streams infilling a local syncline. Originally much of the Mitidja was marshy and malarial, but nearly all has now been reclaimed and converted into fertile vineyards, orange groves, orchards and fields of tobacco, early vegetables, and flowers for scent making. The area became the showpiece of French colonization. The whole Algiers Plain is densely peopled; in addition to the capital and chief port it includes a number of local market and manufacturing towns such as El Boulaida, Boufarik and El Harrach, where the French imprint of rectangular street plan, solid buff-coloured houses with painted wooden shutters and iron balconies created a European quarter distinct from the poorer and more closely knit Arab sector. These towns contain pre-independence industries such as brick and tile works, flour mills, sugar refineries, tanneries and scent distilleries, and now a growing range of consumer goods industries, and petrochemical industries based upon oil refining.

Grande Kabylie. East of the Algiers Plain lies another most distinctive sub-region of the Tell. This is the highland region known as the Grande Kabylie and from some points of view might equally be included in eastern Algeria. On the north it is bounded by the Mediterranean and on the south and east by the easternmost part of the Oran–Bejaia depression. The core of the upland is of Archaean and Pre-Cambrian rocks (mainly schists and gneisses) flanked on the north-east and south by younger limestone, sandstone and clays. The young limestones to the south form the Djurdjura, the most imposing and impressive range in Algeria. It extends some 64 km from east to west in a double chain of serrated crests, mostly over 1800 m high. The landscape is harsh, with scree-girt ridges scored by the deep gorges of swirling streams. The higher areas receive over 1500 mm of rainfall and snow lies on these parts from November to the end of May. Much of this heavy precipitation drains northwards into the Oued Sebaou, creating a series of deep gorge-like valleys separated by narrow ridges which carry roads, tracks and villages. Central Kabylie, consisting of the older rocks, carries a high population. In contrast to the many bare slopes of the younger limestones, here slopes are clothed with oaks, ash, olives and figs (up to about 800 m), the ground beneath being worked in small plots by hand tools and primitive ploughs. Numerous villages cluster tightly on the ridge-tops at altitudes between 600 and 1200 m. Surprisingly the Grande Kabylie is one of the most densely peopled areas in Algeria, much of it carrying over 250 people per km^2, generally living in great poverty. Such a population cannot be supported solely by the primitive farming, and most families have one or two members away in city or town employment or in France, who send remittances home. Here in this mountain fastness, sheltered from external influences, Berber race, language and customs survive in their purest forms. The mountain strongholds have proved difficult to subdue; they have withstood Romans, Arabs and Turks. The French only pacified Kabylie after a full campaign and the establishment of Fort National to control it in 1857. In the 1954–62 rebellion, in order to control the area which harboured nationalist rebels, there were wholesale removals of population by the French to newly sited villages in the foothills.

The High Plateaux

South of the Tell Atlas, and extending from the Moulouya river in the west to the saline Chott el Hodna in the east, is the distinctive region of upland steppes usually called the High Plateaux. Their southern boundary is formed by the Saharan Atlas which separate them from the Sahara.

The High Plateaux offer abrupt contrasts with the fertile and populous Tell. Averaging rather more than 1000 m in height, the undulating landscape is open and, for most of the year, drab. The low rainfall (200–300 mm) is insufficient for trees and shrubs and has a highly seasonal incidence. It supports *sparte* and alfa grasses, tufted herbs and dwarf plants which develop with the scanty winter rainfall and remain green for no more than the first month of the seven-month dry season. Sheep roam widely over the steppe, grazing on the dried-up grasses and woody, salty plants. As summer advances, accompanied by their nomadic masters, they move northwards along recognized sheep walks to the greener pastures of the Tell Atlas.

An important activity of many members of the tribes engaged in this seasonal migration across the steppes with their flocks and camel herds is the collection of alfa leaves (esparto grass), which forms an important export of Algeria and is used for making high-quality paper. Locally it is of importance for the manufacture of rope, mats and baskets. The grass is extremely resistant to drought and grows in large tufts up to a metre high. Since the alfa grass is a defence against soil erosion, the amount to be harvested each year is determined by the authorities, and the grass rights are sold to companies who establish posts where camel loads can be weighed, stacked and dried before large lorries and trailers start the journey to the coast. Ruins of old irrigation works and buildings around the Chott el Hodna are a reminder that in the more pluvial past, and perhaps up to the Middle Ages, much of this land was more productive; grain crops and olives certainly were grown in

Roman times. Today wells and small irrigation works here and at the Chott Chergui provide water for stock.

The Saharan Atlas

These ranges, attaining over 2000 m, are slightly better watered than the High Plateaux and offer woodland, thickets and pasture on their slopes. Probably of greater significance are the water-courses on the southern side which lose themselves in the desert fringe, but supply the wells of numerous oases stretching along the desert edge. Notable in this piedmont zone are the 59 Ziban oases of which Biskra, with its 25,000 population and 150,000 palms, is the chief. This group of oases, extending 50 km west and 100 km east of Biskra, contains more than a million palm trees and over half a million other fruit trees. Farther west are the oasis towns of Laghouat, Figuig and Bechar, each with several thousand palms. Other fruit trees, vines, vegetables and cereals are grown beneath the palms.

The Sahara

South of the Saharan Atlas, except for the few oases and mining camps, is the desert realm of pastoral nomads and semi-nomads. More than four-fifths of Algeria is desert, but in fact only limited areas are of soft sand; traditional seasonal movements take place in spring over the gravelly rock surfaces to move flocks from the desert water points and oases to utilize the sparse pastures of the High Plateaux and Constantine Chotts until the autumn. The rapid development of the oil and gas industry has had a powerful impact upon the nomads, many of whom have found work in the desert mining centres.

The revival of many of the oases, thanks to the supply of deep-drilled artesian waters, has also aided this sedentarization trend. Until the middle of this century most of the oases were stagnant or contracting as the water level in the wells became lower, but the discovery of the artesian waters in the Albienne Nappe has brought renewal and expansion. At Ouargla, once a dying oasis, these waters were tapped at 1200 m and have given a new lease of life to an oasis now populated by 50,000 people (Figure 37). The artesian supplies have also made possible the creation of substantial oilfield towns, such as Hassi Messaoud with its 50,000 trees and 30,000 inhabitants. There is knowledge of a number of mineral ores in the Algerian Sahara, but remoteness, the cost of establishing transport facilities and uncertainty over the size of the ore bodies delays exploitation.

Eastern Algeria

Eastern Algeria differs from the western two-thirds of the country in being a complex upland displaying deeply dissected mountain knots and chains interspersed with limited plateaux and basins, some the beds of former lakes. Greater precipitation on the mountains, especially near the coast, allows considerable forest cover, mainly cork oak and cedar. Farther inland in the enclosed plains, such as the Constantine Chotts, it is enough to permit some cereal cultivation and the sustenance of thousands of sheep. The rainfall is marginal for cereals and in poor years wheat may be only 200 mm high; nevertheless, by sickle and by hand every ear is harvested by the Arabs.

French colonization has transformed favoured parts of the coast, such as the Plain of Annaba (about the size of the Mitidja), where malarial marshes and lakes have been coñained and reduced, and in the fertile soils the vine, tobacco, vegetables and citrus fruits are grown. Inland the population is more sparse and the way of life harder. Cereals are the principal arable crops, mainly native grown with emphasis on olive, figs, and other tree fruits on the higher land. The salt marshes around the Constantine Chotts offer good rough grazing over which there are seasonal migrations from spring to autumn of the flocks and herds of Arab tribes from the desert. From the chotts many of the younger Arabs temporarily leave their families for harvest work

Plate 15 Socialist re-settlement village in Algeria

(formerly on European farms) and use their camels to convey grain to market.

These migrations skirt the Aurès Massif, mainly the home of the Chaouia people. This deeply ravined mountain mass with peaks over 2100 m is a formidable and virtually impregnable region where, like the Djurdjura, Berber ways and language have been preserved. The mountains have proved a refuge and bulwark against both Arab and French invaders. Even today communication within the mountain mass is very difficult and only one indifferent road passes through it (mules have a longer expectation of life than cars in the Aurès). But despite their elevation, and because of the southerly position of the mountains, rainfall is nowhere abundant: it is probably over 500 mm in the north but only half that on the Saharan fringe. Climate and physique prevent a purely sedentary way of life. In the deep valleys vines, fruit trees, water melons and cereals are grown, sometimes on small irrigated terraces, and on the hillside small irregularly shaped fields are sown to oats, barley and beans; while olives, apricots and figs are valuable tree crops. By the end of July figs and apricots have been gathered and dried in the sun and cereals harvested, local pasture has become exhausted and a wholesale northerly movement of communities to high mountain pastures or across the Chott plateaux begins. By October the return south commences, followed in November by a lesser southerly movement to the oases belt around Biskra to gather dates from the few palms that each family likes to possess.

Defence plays a large part in the character and siting of the Berber mountain villages. Tightly knit, these perch on scarcely accessible slopes or ridges, the houses built of mud, stone or palm timber and rising in tiers as in the High Atlas. Deep conservatism met French attempts to improve conditions and progress has been slow.

THE ECONOMY

Agriculture

Most of Algeria is of limited value for agriculture, and except for oil and gas is but moderately endowed with mineral wealth. Most of the agricultural wealth of the republic is derived from the limited area of fertile valleys and basins near the coast that have been developed by Europeans throughout the past century. Elsewhere, the mountains and steppes offer forests and grazing rather than agricultural opportunity, and with subsistence cultivation and herding the majority of the Arabs and Berber population is poor. The dual division of the economy into modern and traditional sectors, discussed in the chapter on Morocco, is thus also apparent in Algeria. From 1954 to 1962 armed rebellion of Moslems against the French gradually brought the economy to a standstill. In coping with the rebellion, especially in the mountainous areas, the French military resorted to wholesale re-siting of village populations, moving them to 'safe' areas on lower ground. Some 2–3 million were compulsorily moved and a further 1–2 million moved voluntarily: in all, half Algeria's entire rural population was moved. Many never went back to the mountain villages and many drifted to the towns; all were exposed to new values, attitudes and consumption patterns.

With the granting of independence tremendous problems faced the new administration. Not only had physical damage to be made good, but the emigration, at a great loss to themselves, of almost all the Europeans dealt a crippling blow to the newly created republic. The thousands who departed, mostly to France, were farmers, engineers, industrialists, managers, accountants and teachers: the sort of people that no young developing country can afford to lose. Land abandoned by Europeans totalled almost 1,000,000 ha or nearly 40 per cent of European holdings; subsequently the remainder of these holdings was expropriated by the state. Also abandoned were several hundred industrial undertakings. Instead of a million Europeans, fewer than 100,000 remain. Attempts to continue large-scale capitalized commercial production were made by taking over some abandoned and expropriated farms as state farms and not dividing them into peasant plots. They were run by workers' committees; similarly workers' committees took over abandoned factories. Committees composed of illiterate peasants without technical or managerial training found it very difficult to keep farms running smoothly and levels of husbandry and agricultural production have fallen.

Much that has been said about the character of European and Moroccan agriculture also applies to Algeria, except that restrictions on European land-holding were lighter than in Morocco and a third of land under cultivation was formerly owned by Europeans. Prior to the rebellion in 1954, 22,000 European farmers owned 2.5 million hectares, whereas 6.3 million Moslem farmers shared 5 million hectares, many of their holdings being fragmented and too small to be viable. Some 600,000 peasants were landless and over 40 per cent of the rural population was unemployed or underemployed. Most agricultural exports were derived from the European holdings. Cereals are the chief crop of Algeria (wheat, barley and oats), the best coming from the Tell and the high plains of Constantine around Sétif, Constantine and Guelma. The vine is the principal commercial fruit grown and is generally confined to within 80 km of the coast. The olive is widespread, and among the principal fruits grown are oranges, figs, apricots and dates. The mildness of the winter along the coast has led to the growing of early vegetables and their export to Europe. Tobacco is another important crop especially in the east of Algeria, and is mainly in the hands of native Algerian farmers. The area under irrigated crops is just under 170,000 ha and is unlikely to expand by any marked amount owing to the paucity of the water resources.

Stock rearing is an important occupation suited to the considerable areas of steppe and seasonal pasture. There are over 5 million sheep spread widely between the sea and the semi-arid desert edge. There is a movement northwards with the pasture from the desert edge in early summer, and many of these sheep are sold in the autumn to farmers (formerly European) in the Tell for fattening before export. Algerian wool is coarse and uneven in length; the clip is small and is mainly used within Algeria. Both meat and wool could be improved with the betterment of breeds and greater care of the stock.

The bulk of Algerian cattle is found in the Tell, where water and grass are available. Pastures, however, are generally poor during the summer and few fodder crops are available. Eastern Algeria, where the rainfall is better, carries most stock and the chief cattle-breeding areas are the plains of Constantine and Guelma. Algerian cattle are hardy and strong and are much used for draught purposes as well as for meat and milk. Another most useful animal in Algeria, and one needing little attention, is the goat: there are 2 million in the country. The hair, milk, meat and skin are all used, the skins being exported to France, many for glove making.

Minerals

Algeria possesses valuable mineral resources,

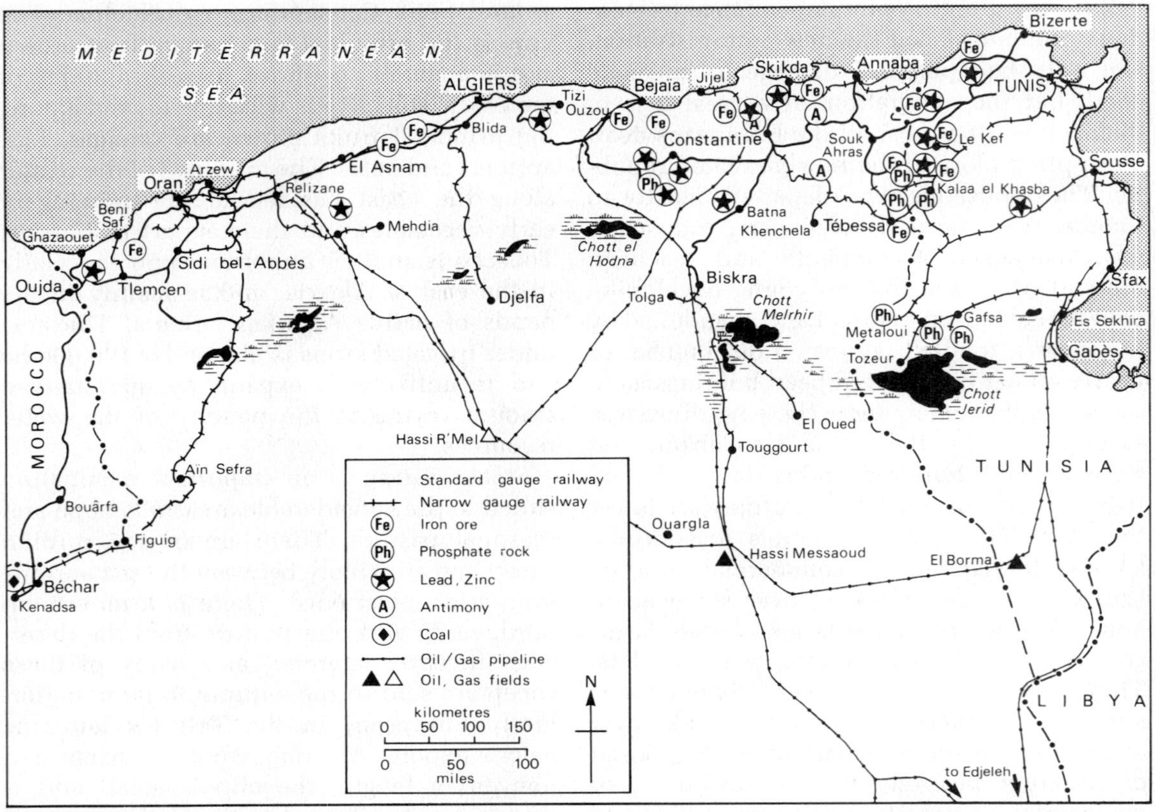

Figure 31 Algeria and Tunisia: mining and railways

the most important being iron-ore, phosphate, mineral oil and gas. The iron-ore is phosphorus-free, with a high iron content and suitable for high-grade steel making. It is mined beside the Tebessa–Souk Ahras railway near the Tunisian border and in the Cheliff valley of the Tell. Production is being increased, for much is being used in the Annaba iron and steel plant. Phosphates are mainly worked at Kouif, near Tebessa; production is annually over 1 million tonnes and most is used in the chemical fertilizer industry.

Among oil producers Algeria has only a moderate position. Oil production peaked in 1978 (78.5 million tonnes) and has since declined. In 1980 reserves were down to 20 years' supply, and Western oil companies (most of whom had left when Algeria nationalized its oil industry in 1971) were persuaded back to resume exploration. Oil was first discovered in the Algerian Sahara in 1956 at Hassi Messaoud, 320 km south of Biskra. Oil was struck at 3700 m, artesian water being reached at 1300 m, thus making the opening up of an oilfield possible. Other producing oilfields are at El Gessi and Edjele, and an enormous natural gas field is worked at Hassi R'Mel. Algeria is better supplied with natural gas than oil and is the world's largest gas exporter. Pipelines carrying oil and natural gas connect the main Saharan fields with Oran, Arzew, Algiers and Skikda. Arzew and Skikda are major gas ports with plants to liquefy the gas for export in special tankers.

The discovery of oil and gas in the Algerian Sahara has been of great economic significance. The revenues from these exports were the salvation of the State in the years immediately following independence and went on to provide a substantial part of the investment needed by the economic plans and to supply burgeoning industry both with cheap power and raw materials. Algerian planners, realizing the limited and finite character of these resources, have determined to develop petrochemical industries and to market more highly priced chemicals and derivatives as well as crude oil and gas.

MANUFACTURING INDUSTRY

Manufacturing industry to 1962

Up to the Second World War little industrial development was encouraged in Algeria, for France monopolized 90 per cent of the trade in manufactured goods and regarded Algeria as a market and outlet for French products. In return, Algerian agricultural products and minerals were sent to France. This policy channelled most capital and skill into agriculture and mining. In the war the isolation of North Africa from France gave an impetus to the rise of varied industries, many of which have since continued. They are concerned with food processing: flour milling, fish caning, wine and olive-oil manufacture, the preserving of fruit and vegetables, tobacco and leather manufacture. Other industries produce soaps, matches, glass and textiles. Not unexpectedly most of these industries are located within the Tell and particularly in the three major port areas, Algiers, Oran and Annaba.

Plans for industrial development were formulated in the Constantine Plan of 1958, but the war for independence prevented their early implementation. However, the iron and steel plant, proposed for the port of Annaba, was put in hand after independence, with Russian help, and was completed in 1969.

Post-independence economic development

In the years immediately following independence both agriculture and industrial output declined drastically. Agriculture suffered because of the dislocation and resettlement during the rebellion, the hasty exodus of the French farmers (whose farms were the most productive), the reduced demand for Algerian wine by the French, and severe drought. Industrial production collapsed as French managers, teachers, clerks and accountants left the country to be replaced by inexperienced workers' committees; investment tailed off and much French capital was withdrawn; unemployment soared, exacerbated by growing numbers drifting to the major towns from the impoverished countryside. During this period it was only the revenues from oil exports that kept Algeria from bankruptcy. These revenues increased and sales of natural gas began, France gave help and Russia made credits available, so that the early difficulties were surmounted and tentative economic planning began in the late 1960s.

The overall aim of creating a socialist pattern of society was to be attained by establishing industry as the leading sector of the economy, and the plans (that effectively began in 1967) laid much emphasis upon heavy capital-intensive industrial development requiring high technology. Such ventures may require long gestation periods and offer little employment, but once firmly established they should then nourish a wide spectrum of manufactures. This policy ignored a host of disabilities, including the lack of skilled and semi-skilled labour, the high rate of illiteracy, the lack of technological know-how and the limited size of the home market. Except in their constructive phases, the new iron and steel works, oil refineries and gas liquefaction plants have offered only limited employment to Algerians, and there has had to be much reliance upon costly foreign technocrats. Thus the development plans throughout the 1970s paid little attention to agriculture (which at

Plate 16 Processing for export – Algerian gas liquefaction plant

independence employed 70 per cent of the working population), nor to the unemployment problem. Living conditions remained depressed, particularly in the rural areas; but the government, thanks to oil and gas revenues, persisted with and carried out its centralized planning.

The early plans (1967–79) allotted 60% of investment to industrial and hydrocarbon development, notably into steel, mechanical and electrical engineering, oil refining and petrochemicals, gas liquefaction and cement. Cheap power for industrial development has been supplied by establishing thermal electric plants using Saharan oil and gas. State power was extended to control all basic industries including oil and gas distribution and banking. Agriculture, the mainstay of the bulk of the population, received little investment and so lacked modernization. Food production has declined by 25% since independence, and with a heavy rate of population increase Algeria now produces barely one-third of her food needs. Agrarian reform was introduced after 1972, but with the lack of resources for modernization wider land ownership has had little effect upon productivity.

It was not until the Third Plan (1980–4) that the proportion of investment in industry was decreased (to 39 per cent) and increased resources were allotted to agriculture, housing and education. By then Algeria was practically self-sufficient in iron and steel, chemicals, plastics, fertilizers and cement. This plan laid more emphasis upon fostering light industry, mainly based upon the heavy industry already established. It was hoped that a wide dissemination of new light industry would reduce the heavy concentration in the three main centres, that it would give more employment in rural areas and reduce imports of many consumer goods. Over the span of thirteen years (1967–80) the plans have been reasonably successful in changing the whole thrust of the Algerian economy, although little benefit has yet accrued to the mass of the population. A shortage of qualified personnel has been a constant constraint on industrial progress and many plants operate well below capacity, making for high-cost production.

Government policies have increased the concentration on the port areas of Algiers, Oran and Annaba, creating an imbalance that worsens as more and more flock to these centres from the rural areas. These three urban areas contain over 70 per cent of establishments having over 50 employees, and they generate 69 per cent of total industrial and commercial income. This process of growing concentration and intensification of the primacy of Algiers exemplifies the core bleeding dry the periphery and encourages the flight from the land. Consequently, after 1980 the government began measures to reduce regional imbalances and to accentuate 'spread' or trickling down effects to the periphery. Thus the recent plan (1980–4) attempted to redress this imbalance by spreading manufacturing industry into rural areas. Nevertheless momentum continues to carry forward the growth centres of Oran–Arzew–Mostaganem, Algiers and Annaba–Skikda, the major centres of industry. The 400,000 tonne capacity of the iron and steel complex at Annaba, making constructional steel and pipes, has been increased to 1.8 million tonnes, while other industries now include machinery construction, cement, phosphates, fertilizers, constructional materials, food and drink. Skikda has a gas liquefaction complex and also produces petrochemicals, plastics, PVC and caustic soda. To the west Arzew now has two gas liquefaction plants, a refinery and factories producing nitrogenous fertilizers and synthetic resin. Algiers, the capital, has a wide range of chemical, constructional and consumer goods industries which push out into suburbs and the surrounding Mitidja plain. Attempts are now being made to restrict the growth of Greater Algiers in order to facilitate spread effects in less favoured areas. Thus new industries of brick, tile and glass making, tanning, food processing and textiles are being promoted in provincial towns such as Batna, Saida and Tlemçen. More interesting, priority is to be given to opening up parts of the High Plateaux by new road, rail and air links, and to water programmes and new town development to accommodate 2 million Algerians by the year 2000 and so ease pressure on the overburdened northern cities.

Algeria's pattern of economic development through 'heavy' industries, firmly pursued throughout the 1970s, led to rapid rates of economic growth but at the expense of employment, food supplies, consumer goods, housing and other social services. The diversification of her oil and gas industry whereby chemicals and refined product exports are surpassing crude oil have helped to cushion the effects of the fall in oil prices and supplied much of the investment for industry. Algeria is now the world's largest exporter of natural gas and has the fourth largest gas reserves in the world. It exports liquefied gas to Britain, France, USA, Spain and Belgium and gas directly to Italy through the Trans-Med pipeline, completed in 1981. A further pipeline to Spain may be laid. Algeria's oil production has been falling since 1978 and oil exploration by the major Western oil companies has been resumed. Dwindling oil income has made more serious the heavy development debts incurred and Western oil companies have been attracted back to resume exploration. There are high hopes of discoveries in the central and southern areas, although here teams are hampered by lack of roads.

Algeria's centralized planning has led to considerable state bureaucracy, to limited scope for individual entrepreneurs and little immediate amelioration of the poverty of the masses. Lack of management skills and the need for expensive expatriate technocrats has led to unmet schedules, under-capacity operations and high-cost production. Nevertheless, after fifteen years of sacrifice, an industrial base has been made and a growth in manufacturing industry, in agriculture and in social measures may now follow.

POPULATION AND SETTLEMENT

The number of indigenous peoples increased rapidly under French rule, from about 2 million in 1830 to 9.2 million in 1958. European settlers (mainly French) totalled about 1 million in 1954, but after that the number diminished as armed rebellion flared up. Since 1964 the European population has numbered less than 100,000. The total population was estimated at 22 million in 1982. In the past high mortality rates nullified high fertility and moderated population growth, but over the last 40 years new drugs, better hygiene and European methods of disease control have cut crude death rates from 27.4 to 8 per thousand, but crude birth rates at 41 per thousand remain among the highest in Africa. Algerian population at the current rate of increase (3.4 per cent) will double within 20 years. The government has shown little interest in furthering birth control and family planning against traditional attitudes which favour early marriage and large families. Change here will be slow and may be brought about by the bettering of economic circumstances, but the rapidly increasing population and the fact that over half are under 20 years creates serious social and economic problems.

Four-fifths of the population live in the coastal cities and the Tell plains and cities. The most densely peopled parts of the Tell coincide with areas of heavy rainfall, mainly mountainous and in the east – Grande Kabylie and Petite Kabylie; and those parts most easy of access from the coast – the Mitidja, the Plains of Annaba and Skikda. Native Algerians, whether of Arab or Berber stock, have been slow to become town dwellers; but the opening up of new horizons by resettlement during the rebellion and the post-independence stagnation of agriculture have speeded the movement to town. The population is now about 30 per cent urban and Algeria now has 10 cities of over 100,000 population.

The way of life influences the styles of housing. In the Sahara and High Plateaux, the scantily populated districts used by pastoral nomads, the tent made of material woven from wool, goats' hair and esparto grass is used. In the Tell the semi-nomad owns fields as well as herds, and the stone or clay hut (or gourbi) is common. It stands alone near the fields and is used only while crops are sown or reaped. More permanent native dwellings are of mud-clay plastered sticks, flat-topped, huddled together with ragged vegetable gardens alongside, the whole often enclosed by a thick hedge of prickly pear. In the hills the clay- and stone-walled houses occupy defensive sites, often terraced. Houses of European style have increased greatly in number, but generally are still confined to the principal towns.

TOWNS AND COMMUNICATIONS

Algiers (pop. 1,740,000 in 1977) is the capital, seat of government and principal port of the republic. The original Turkish town with its kasba grew up on an easily defended rocky area at the northern end of an east-facing bay; for long it harboured the Barbary corsairs. The town now extends for 10 km around the bay. Long concrete jetties and moles protect the harbour in which large wharfs, quays and basins have been developed as the port has expanded. The city is the republic's leading industrial centre, with factories making chemicals, soaps, cigarettes, electrical goods and tin cans for the preserving industry, and a range of other consumer goods. There are flour mills, breweries, cement works, an oil refinery and a fertilizer factory.

Oran (pop. 543,000). The long, narrow and discontinuous character of the Tell helps to account for the growth of a number of ports each with a fairly restricted hinterland; among them is Oran, the second port and second city of Algeria. Its harbour is entirely artificial, being sheltered by concrete jetties. Oran is second to Algiers as an industrial centre (having large fish canneries, flour mills, brick works, cement and lime works, chemical and tobacco factories) and as part of a planned axial belt of industry is becoming linked with Arzew and Mostaganem to its east. The latter small ports have major petrochemical complexes, gas liquefaction plants and fertilizer factories.

Constantine (pop. 430,000), the third largest city, is 60 km from the coast at Skikda. The town has grown up on a rocky calcareous plateau, with gorges on three sides carved by the great loop of the River Rummel. It is a natural fortress. Lacking major industrial development, it has grown more slowly than other towns and shortly will be eclipsed by the port of **Annaba** (pop.313,000), which since independence has mushroomed as a major industrial growth pole. At Annaba are iron and steel works, refineries and petrochemical industries, cement works, fertilizer units, machinery construction and a growing range of consumer goods industries.

The east–west trend of the relief and the favourable character of the coastal lowlands for settlement and agriculture are clearly revealed in the pattern of communications. There are 4300 km of railway, almost equally divided between standard and narrow gauge, and a rudimentary network is discernible (Figure 31). The main line (of standard gauge) traverses the Tell from the Moroccan boundary via Algiers into Tunisia. All the other main ports are on branches from this main line. A number of lines (mainly narrow gauge) cross the High Plateaux to the edge of the Sahara. A good road network also exists in the Tell and metalled roads now extend to the principal north Saharan oases and oilfields. In its railways, roads and ports the republic inherited a better infrastructure for economic development than most new African states.

13
Tunisia

Tunisia, the smallest of the three political divisions of the Maghreb (164,150 km^2), has the longest history. Her position on the threshold of the western basin of the Mediterranean and but 145 km from Sicily led to early colonization, first by the Phoenicians, who founded Carthage near the site of modern Tunis, and then by the Romans who gave it the name of Africa, and held it with some interruptions until the Arab invasions of the seventh century. Arab and Berber dynasties held the country until the conquest by the Turks in the sixteenth century. During the nineteenth century the French tended to regard Tunisia as a natural extension of Algeria, and in 1881 entered Tunisia and forced the bey to accept the French Protectorate. Independence was granted Tunisia in 1956.

GEOGRAPHICAL REGIONS

Broadly speaking western Tunisia is high, with the highest land in the north-west, and eastern (or maritime) Tunisia is low. The annual rainfall, here the most significant element in the climate, is highest in the north (over 1000 mm) but diminishes to as little as 125 mm in the south. The interplay of these factors permits a division of Tunisia into three major parts: northern, central and southern (or Sahara), each including a number of subdivisions (Figure 32).

Northern Tunisia

This comprises a sequence of ridges and valleys generally trending to the north-north-east. The valley of the River Medjerda provides a series of closed basins separating the steep sandstone ranges of the north coast from the domes and basins of the sandstone and limestone High Tell and Dorsale. The northern coaŝal hills, the Monts de la Medjerda, with their sandstone-derived soils and heavy winter rain, support dense forests of cork and Portuguese oaks. Debarked cork oak trees and stacks of cork awaiting collection are often the only evidence of man for many miles. Outside the forests in clearings and depressions the reliable rainfall

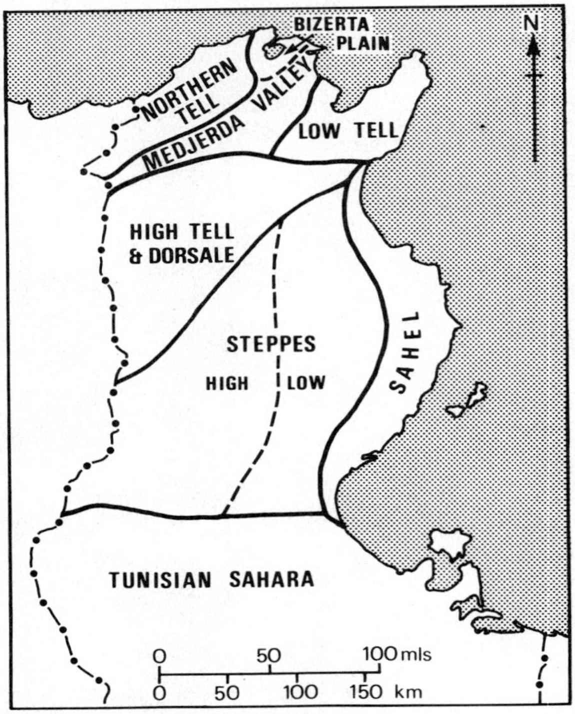

Figure 32 Geographical regions of Tunisia

favours cultivation and a sedentary way of life. Cereals, particularly barley, are the main crops; some cattle and goats are kept. The population is sparse: hamlets and villages, many on cleared slopes encircled by brushwood and prickly pear hedges, are few and far between.

The Valley of the River Medjerda which drains much of the High Plains of Constantine in Algeria is divided by rocky narrows into a succession of enclosed plains, formerly old lake basins now infilled and offering rich alluvial soil to the agriculturist. These well-watered dark soils yield heavy cereal crops, and formerly much of the middle Medjerda valley was farmed by European colonists. These farms have been relinquished or expropriated and are now run as cooperatives. The strongly seasonal character of the rainfall renders the Medjerda liable to dangerous flooding, occasionally submerging the whole flood plain between Tebourba and the coast and limiting settlement sites to higher ground. Stock rearing supplements grain growing and a number of small towns such as Souk el Arba ('market four', i.e. Wednesday), Beja and Medjez-el-Bab have become local market and administrative centres. North-west of the delta is the low-lying Plain of Bizerta. Well farmed by the French, this forms good agricultural land surrounding the lakes of Bizerta and Garait Achkel. These constituted a basin of internal drainage but have since been flooded by the sea giving a good harbour to the naval base at Bizerta.

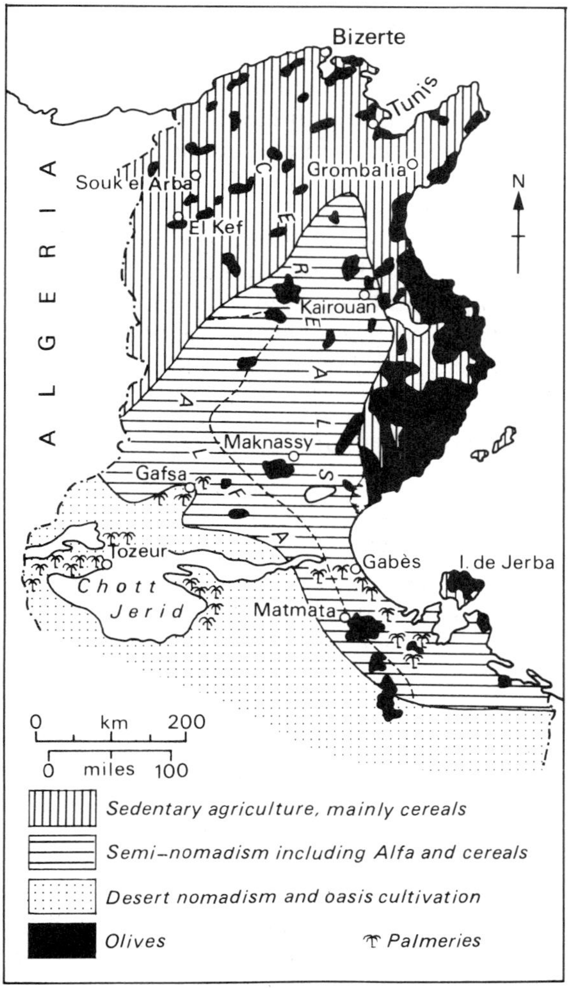

Figure 33 Tunisia: ways of life and land use

The High Tell and Dorsale represent the easternmost extension of the Saharan Atlas, of which the prevailing structure of domes and basins is reminiscent. Most of the area is above 600 m, and among the chain of heights forming the Zeugitane Mountains or Dorsale is Djebel Chambi (1519 m), the highest peak in Tunisia. The south-west to north-east trend is dominant and complex structures give broken relief of mountain masses separated by valleys and basins, many the sites of former lakes. The better-watered northern parts support a sedentary farming population: nowadays in the drier south the tent is slowly giving way to the hut. To the north-east the low Tell and Plain of Tunis are climatically somewhat distinctive. The rainfall (Tunis 423 mm) is akin to that of the Sahel to the south and considerably less than on the north coast (Bizerta 625 mm). Evaporation is high and the region is open to southerly winds and subjected to the sirocco. The enclosed lowland and Cap Bon Peninsula is little affected by the sea's proximity. Here cereals play a lesser part in the farming but the vine is characteristic; olives also are of some importance and other crops are vegetables, citrus fruits and tobacco.

Plate 17 Pressing olive oil at Mat'mata, Tunisia

Central Tunisia

South of the Dorsale in the Tunisian steppes the relief is more subdued. The pattern of north-east trending discontinuous upland plains persists but the lowland is more extensive. The steppe character of the natural vegetation results from the dry climate. Rainfall decreases rapidly from north to south, ranging from about 375 to 200 mm, and alfa grass and scrub of jujube trees become dominant; but to the south the terrain becomes increasingly barren. The High Steppe in the west varies from 770 m to 300 m, and this area contrasts with the Low Steppe to the east, hummocky distributary plains that descend to the coast plain. Camel- and sheep-owning nomads traditionally occupy these steppes, but here and there meagre harvests of cereals are produced in the depressions, while nearer the coast olives are grown. The phosphate deposits in the hills around Gafsa provide the only real wealth of the region.

The Sahel is no more than the coastal termination of the steppes where the solid rock is masked by young and recent deposits, generally of a sandy character. The sandy soil retains moisture and subsoil water is available. The low rainfall is also supplemented by copious dew and it is possible for cereals to be grown without irrigation. In the main, however, it is the olive that has transformed this region. The Sahel extends from Hammamet to just south of Sfax and inland some 40 km to the zone of sebkhas (or saltmarshes) into which the intermittent drainage of the Steppes occasionally finds its way. The Sahel contrasts with the Steppes in that it contains a large population, including a number of ancient towns such as Sousse, Sfax, Monastir and Moknine, where gardens and cornfields have been tilled since the days of Carthage. The real development of this coastal plain came with the granting of large areas to French Land Companies near the end of the last century. Viticulture was less successful than in the north, but the olive, able to resist moderate drought, proved eminently suitable without irrigation and thousands of acres were planted. Today there are over 8 million trees in the Sahel of Sousse and over 6 million in the Sahel of Sfax: thousands of acres of semi-arid land under widely spaced, evenly planted olive trees. Off this east coast the sea is very shallow and fishing is a major activity.

Southern Tunisia

The southern termination of the Tunisian Steppes is in the east–west trending Djebel Cherb. At their foot on the southern side are a number of extensive muddy, saline depressions, part of the group of chotts extending from near Biskra in Algeria to Gabes. On the higher land between these chotts and around their shores are valuable groves of date-palms, the irrigation wells depending upon the water received by the limestone hills to the north. In the Kriz-Tozeur district between the Chotts Rharsa and Djerid are a number of oasis settlements and nearly a million date-palms. Both here and in the Kebili district south-east of the Chott el Djerid, where there are 500,000 palms, screens are erected to halt encroaching sand dunes of the Grand Erg. South of the chotts, desert conditions increase and the relief and structure are Saharan: no longer are there folded strata, but plateaux and table-lands here and there eroded and fretted into isolated hills. Rainfall over most of the area is scanty and unreliable, averaging 150 – 200 mm along the coastal margin and rising to 250 mm on the Monts des Ksour (600 m) some 48 km inland, but elsewhere being below 125 mm. Much of the land provides scrubby pasture for the camels and goats of nomads. The coast is fringed with lagoons and sebkhas and the gravelly coastal plain, the Jeffara – throughout the centuries a major highway into the Maghreb – is sparsely settled, mainly along the coast itself.

POPULATION AND SETTLEMENT

The estimated population of Tunisia in 1985 was 7.1 million, including about 150,000 French and Italians. Following the granting of independence in 1956 some 100,000 Europeans left Tunisia, a serious blow to the new state since many were key officials, technicians and entrepreneurs. The birth rate has remained high since independence and is now 35 per 1000 of the population. With improving medical facilities the death rate has dropped to as low as 8 per 1000 of the population, accounting for the fact that over half the population is now under 20 years of age. Thus the rate of population increase at 2.7 per cent is very high and if continued will double the total population in 23 years. The provision of 70–80 thousand new jobs each year has proved too much for the series of economic plans and unemployment is a serious problem. Berber and Arab are inextricably mixed in Tunisia – indeed it is now said to be virtually impossible to distinguish between Arabized-Berber and Berberized-Arab. All profess Islam, which is recognized as the state religion.

Four-fifths of Tunisia's population live in the northern half of the country and a general relationship between density of settlement and annual rainfall can be discerned, with rural densities of more than 250 per km^2 where the annual rainfall exceeds 625 mm and below 125 per km^2 where the annual rainfall is below 250 mm. South of the chotts the population density is probably less than 12 per km^2. The most densely peopled areas are in the plains around Tunis and Bizerta, in the coastal bulge Sousse–Monastir–Moknine, around Sfax and the Isle of Djerba.

Tunis, the capital, is the only real city in the republic and now has a population of a million. The next largest towns are **Sfax** (pop. 475,000) and **Sousse** (pop. 255,000). Tunis is the natural market and outlet for much of the Tell, the Medjerda valley and the northern Sahel. It is built on a hilly isthmus separating the marshy Sebkret es Sedjoumi and the shallow Lac de Tunis, a lagoon which by separating the town from the sea preserved it from such a fate as that of Carthage and from the later attacks of Christian fleets. There are distinct native and European-style towns, the old native town being on the higher land; the modern town, regularly laid out, has developed on the flat ground between Tunis and its lake. It is the republic's major port, handling annually over 2 million tonnes of cargo, more than half being exports – mainly phosphates, iron-ore, olive oil, chemicals, textiles, fruit and vegetables. The major imports are foodstuffs, manufactured goods and machinery.

THE ECONOMY AND ITS DEVELOPMENT

Tunisia is a small country with modest physical resources, and these were poorly developed up to 1956 because of the dependence on France. At that time 70 per cent of the population made a precarious living in agriculture and fishing, consuming most of what they produced and bartering rather than engaging in monetary transactions. Per capita income, as low as US$100 in 1956, had increased to US$1300 twenty five years later – an indication of immense changes and reorientation in ways of life.

Until they were expropriated in 1964 the majority of large modern farms had been created by, and were in the hands of, Europeans. As these farmers left Tunisia some of their farms were broken up for the peasants but others, sometimes consolidated with adjacent peasant holdings, were worked collectively in units of about 500 ha. The early 1960s saw this programme of land reform by collectivization being imposed over the rich farmland of northern Tunisia, despite fierce opposition by both the larger Tunisian farmers and peasant proprietors. The policy was combined with crop diversification, irrigation and mechanization and initially there was some success. However, a succession of drought years, the excessive nature of the collectivization, lack of effort among the country people and the growing opposition, led to the policy being abandoned in 1969.

Now three divisions co-exist in the agriculture sector: public, cooperative and private, and among the latter there are particularly a large number of small holdings. Surplus production in some sectors – olive, vegetable, citrus fruits – contrasts with shortfalls in cereals and stock farming, for these are at the mercy of marginal land and fluctuating, barely adequate, rainfall. Agriculture now occupies about a half of the population and is responsible for one-fifth of the GDP. Much of the country is agriculturally unproductive, especially in the arid south. The area under irrigation is small (*c.* 120,000 ha), and thus rainfall can be a critical factor over much of central and southern Tunisia and accounts for fluctuations from year to year, particularly in cereal production. Relief and rainfall help to determine crop distribution: the vine and citrus fruit predominate around Tunis and Cap Bon, the olive in the Sahel and Low Steppes and the date in the south. Wheat and barley are cultivated widely throughout the country but yields are poor and imports are necessary. Tunisia, with one-quarter of the world's exports, is the second largest exporter of olive oil.

Tunisia's series of development plans have given prime place to industry and its infrastructure and only more recently has investment in agriculture increased. Unlike in Algeria, much industrial development in Tunisia has been of a labour-intensive kind and the provision of jobs (reflecting continuing population pressure) has high priority. Tunisia's natural resources are limited: she has sizable deposits of phosphates, iron-ore and lead and small but useful supplies of crude oil and natural gas. Her series of development plans seek to make the most of these resources. Much investment has gone into mineral exploration, particularly in the search for oil and gas resources. Annual oil production at 5 million tonnes is small but allows of some exports, and recent modest gas discoveries were planned to supply half the domestic needs by the early 1980s. Offshore prospecting for more oil and gas in the Gulf of Gabes continues. Phosphates production has almost doubled in the last 15 years, although other mineral production (iron-ore, lead and zinc) has decreased (Table 11).

Table 11 *Tunisia: mineral production*

	Production (000 tonnes)				
	1975	*1978*	*1980*	*1982*	*1984*
Phosphate	3512	3712	4502	4729	5600
Iron-ore	326	185	211	276	—
Lead	11	8	9	5	—
Zinc	6	7	9	8	—
Crude oil	4300	5400	5500	5800	5800

The locations of the principal mining areas are shown in Figure 31. French policy and the lack of fuel resources limited the range of manufacturing industry before independence mainly to the processing of agricultural produce. Since independence planned development of the economy has seen a considerable expansion of the mining–energy manufacturing sector and it now accounts for two-fifths of the GDP. The first three 4-year plans gave priority to infrastructure provision (roads, railways and port development) and basic industry (oil exploration, production and refining and metallurgy). The ensuing three plans (1973–86) place more emphasis upon manufacturing industry and job provision. The principal industries are food products, textiles, chemicals, building materials, paper and electrical equipment. The growing chemical industry is based upon the petrochemicals from the Bizerta oil refinery and local phosphate deposits.

The government is well aware of the narrow base to the Tunisian economy, where over 50 per cent of exports are from only three commodities – crude oil, phosphates and olive oil. Hence the early emphasis upon energy provision and the widening of manufacturing, generally at the expense of investment in agriculture. The growing need for food imports led to enhanced investment in agriculture, particularly in expanding irrigation, in the Sixth Plan (1982–6). A growing income is also obtained from the tourist industry, and by the mid-1980s there were some 2 million visitors a year. Royalties are also obtained on the oil for export sent by pipeline from the Algerian oilfield at Edjele to La Skhirra. Nevertheless, financial constraints shaped the Seventh plan (1987–91) to be one of consolidation and infrastructure improvement.

Tunisia is a small state with limited resources and a rapid rate of population increase. Nevertheless, by careful planning it has achieved substantial economic growth and now ranks as a 'middle income' country. However, a disequilibrium between population increase and economic growth continues; there is a high external debt and the small but important oil reserves are becoming depleted. In the coming years much will depend upon enlarging the tourist industry and increasing exports of minerals, specialist foodstuffs and chemicals.

14 Libya

Libya came into being as a kingdom in December 1951, when the three distinct territories of Tripolitania, Cyrenaica and the Fezzan under United Nations auspices were united under one king. In many ways the union was an act of faith for it brought together diverse territories and peoples of very different viewpoints and histories: so much so that in 1969 the monarchy was overthrown and a republic was declared.

This state, midway along the Mediterranean where the sea laps the Sahara, has never had individuality or entity. Between Cyrenaica and Tripolitania is a waste of bleached desert and scrub. Cyrenaica looks eastwards towards Egypt and the Middle East; Tripolitania looks westwards to the Maghreb, a situation the Romans recognized by incorporating Tripolitania in the province of Africa, under Carthage, and Cyrenaica within the province of Crete.

Like the rest of northern Africa the territory came under Turkish suzerainty until Italy, seeking African colonies, occupied Tripoli in 1911 and became recognized as the sovereign power by Turkey in the following year. These territories were wrested from Italy in the Second World War, by which time many millions of lire had been poured into them and over 100,000 Italians had settled there. Very few of these settlers now remain. At first the differences of outlook and interest between the mainly agricultural Tripolitania and the mainly pastoralist Cyrenaica were acknowledged by a federal constitution with a dual capital – at Tripoli in winter and Banghazi in summer. After the overthrow of the monarchy in 1969, Tripoli became the capital.

Libya is a desert country of 1,750,000 km^2; maritime influences touch only a small northern fringe, giving some mitigation from the fierce heat. Temperatures of over 40°C are recorded regularly at Tripoli during the summer. The rainfall reaches only a narrow coastal strip and diminishes in amount from west to east: Tripoli averages 335 mm a year, but Banghazi farther east only 250 mm. Except for a short distance from the coast, desert conditions pertain. It is in discontinuous stretches along the coast that the bulk of Libya's population is to be found. Two-thirds of the population live in Tripolitania, mainly between Zuara and Misurata, in a series of coastal oases where about 250 mm of rain falls in the average year. The triangle Garian–Tripoli–Homs is the best watered, with 325 mm, and was a major scene of Italian colonization. This area marks the eastern end of the Jeffara, the steppe land extending eastwards from Tunisia and rising gently from the coast to the Tripolitania Jebel, this being a series of fault scarps attaining over 800 m which begin the African plateau and mark off the coastal zone from the interior.

The Libyan landscape is of tabular formation, the product of faulting and differential erosion, and is very different from the folded ranges of the Maghreb (Figure 34). Here the crystalline basement downwarps towards the north, creating fault scarps in the overlying deposits at or near the coast. Shallow folding in these north-dipping sedimentary beds has facilitated accumulation of oil and water in this area. Inland are stony plateaux of limestone and sandstone such as the Hamada el Hamra (or red, stony desert) with sparse scrub scattered here and there. To the south-east are

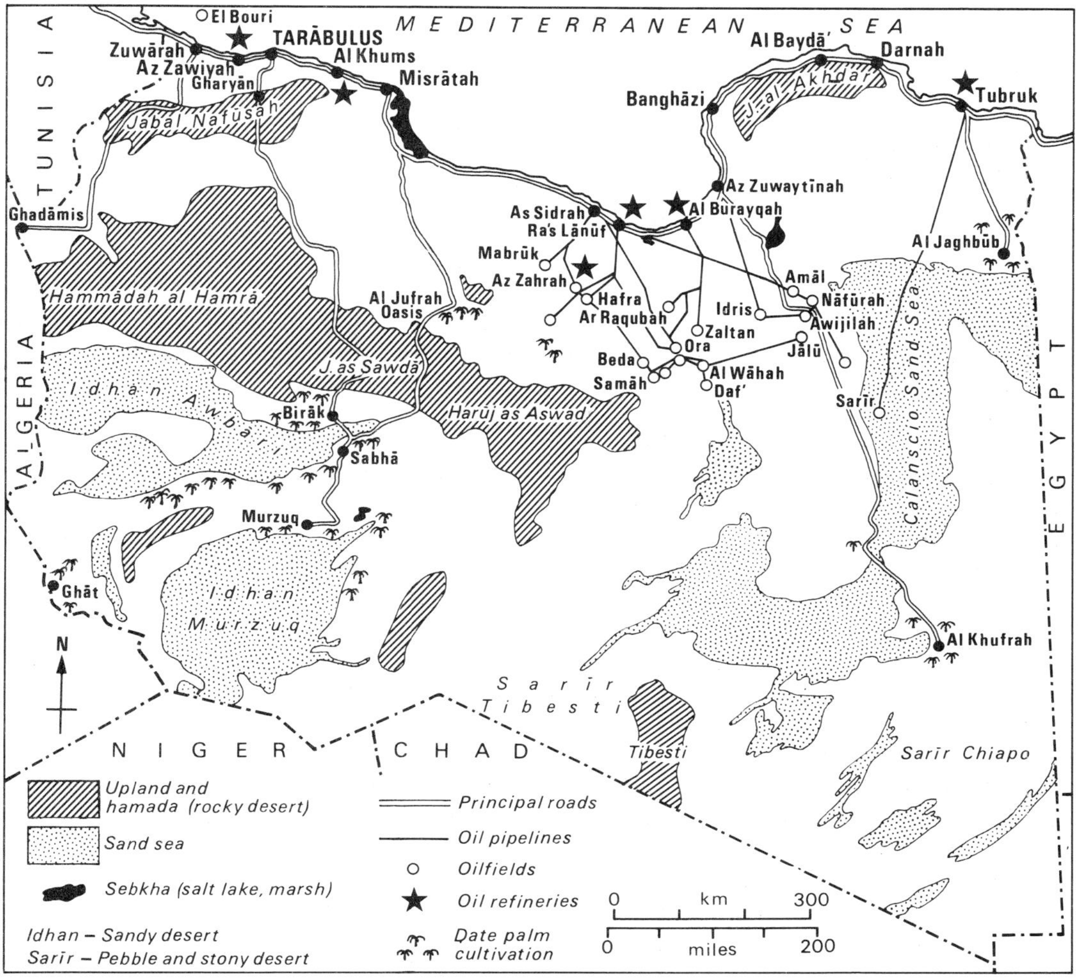

Figure 34 Libya: aspects of economic development

gaunt lava areas, and the purplish-black hills of the Jebel el Sauda. In the south-west, comprising much of the Fezzan, are great sand seas. There are wide depressions between the sandy areas in which occur a surprising number of oases, some very large (such as Ghat, Sabha and Brac). The Fezzan is virtually rainless and settlement is sharply confined to these favoured patches; yet in total the Fezzan has nearly 3000 ha of irrigated gardens and nearly 120,000 ha are planted with date-palms.

Cyrenaica bulges northwards into the Mediterranean, and its hills, the Jebel el Akhdar (800 m), in places drop steeply to the sea. Coastal plains are confined to the neighbourhood of Banghazi and Agedabia; round to the Egyptian frontier the coast is rugged. The greater rainfall (*c.* 570 mm) on this hilly limestone area allows woods of cypress and junipers and some slopes clothed with open maquis, but little settlement. Much of the settlement is near the foot of the hills along the coast, where springs create oasis conditions and the terraced slopes with glimpses of the sea are more akin to Greece than the Sahara.

POPULATION AND SETTLEMENT

The population of Libya is estimated at about 3.2 million, of whom 2,100,000 live in Tripolitania, 1,000,000 in Cyrenaica and only 100,000 in the Fezzan. Over the last 20 years the crude death rate has fallen from 19 to 12 per thousand, but the crude birth rate is still over 40 per thousand and the population increases at over 3 per cent a year. Population distribution reflects the wide expanses of arid land and the few better watered areas. There is a marked concentration of settlement along the coast and almost 75 per cent of the population lives within 30 km of the sea. The three areas of dense settlement are the coastal area in Tripolitania from Zuara to Misurata and behind the hilly areas of Jebel Nefousa and Jebel Akhdar in Cyrenaica. To the south in Fezzan Sabha the provincial capital is no more than a large village, but it is important as the centre of numerous other oases settlements. A proportion of the population (possibly about 15 per cent) is nomadic and semi-nomadic. True nomads are small in numbers and the majority who are semi-nomads make their seasonal migrations from the settled areas in the North. As in the Maghreb there is a slow reduction in the numbers of nomads as the economy develops and the openings for paid employment increase.

Plate 18 Drilling for water in the Libyan desert, El Khidama

The three principal towns, **Tripoli** [Tarabulus] (pop. 550,000), **Banghazi** (pop. 300,000) and **Misurata** (pop. 103,000), hold almost one-third of the total population and their dominance increases with a considerable movement of population to them from the inland oases and marginal areas. Forty-five per cent of the population is now classed as urban.

THE ECONOMY AND ITS DEVELOPMENT

Agriculture

High summer temperatures, desiccating desert winds, lack of rainfall and poor soils all contribute to the scantiness and poverty of Libyan agriculture. Less than 1 per cent of Libyan land is productive and three-quarters of this is suitable only for grazing. Much of the agriculture is carried on extensively after the rains on semi-arid or marginal land and yields are low.

The historical division of the country into Tripolitania, Cyrenaica and Fezzan also relates to agricultural regions. Tripolitania is the most productive area and agriculture here owes much to the earlier Italian colonization. The coastal zone from the western border to Homs receives about 250 mm of rain annually and locally this is supplemented by irrigation. The Jeffara is the most favoured area and the major producer of barley, wheat and vegetables. Tree crops, olives, almonds, citrus fruit and vines increase in importance, the olive being the chief crop on the Jebel behind Tripoli. Cyrenaica has a third of the arable land but the largest area for pastoralism. The Bedouin move south in winter to graze steppe pastures and return to the grazing of the Jebel in late spring; they then harvest the cereal patches planted the previous autumn. Barley is again the major cereal, while fruit and vegetables, mainly in irrigated gardens, grow along the coast and benefit from springs emerging from the base of the limestone Jebel. Agriculture in the Fezzan is confined to the oases which contain many million date-palms. In addition to dates, millet and vegetables are the other staples of diet. In recent years increasing demand from oil camps and northern towns has stimulated the production of fruit and vegetables, but the pull of these centres is also attracting manpower away from the oases. The dispersion of these agriculturally favoured regions as well as their limited area impedes the modernization and expansion of Libyan agriculture.

The dualism between the traditional and modern sectors becomes more pronounced as increasing investment flows into agriculture. Large numbers are able to remain in the traditional sector by receiving cash from social security benefits for children and their education and remittances from relatives working in the modern sector. Thus new farms created under the development plans have no great attraction to the mass of traditional farmers, and this limits modernization and increases in productivity.

The state now operates some of the farms previously owned by Italian companies (expropriated in 1970) and some have become cooperatives. Since the revolution agriculture has received the largest share of development investment (average 18 per cent a year) for a high degree of self-sufficiency is aimed at, the eventual depletion of the oil revenues being accepted. Thus the 'Ten Year Plan for agriculture development 1973 – 82' put in motion a green revolution aimed at expanding and modernizing farming. Among its measures were the provision of grants and loans to small farmers for seeds, machinery and farm buildings; the organization of cooperatives; the purchase of local produce at favourable prices; the promotion of agricultural research and establishment of certain major projects. Over a hundred agricultural projects have been started; one aim being that eventually every farmer in the traditional sector will be given a new modern farm.

The most spectacular of these projects is at Wadi Kufra oasis in the desert south-east of Libya. Early in the 1960s oil exploration here discovered fresh water aquifers in the Nubian sandstone at depths of 200 m. The sandy soil lacks humus, but with the application of water and fertilizer it can become quite productive. The oil company began an experimental agriculture project, since taken over and expanded by the government. From the Kufra production project some 10,000 ha of irrigated fodder is being produced for sheep breeding and fattening, and nearby the 5000 ha Kufra settlement project of nearly 900 small irrigated farms grouped into sixteen hamlets is well established. Such a project in the heart of the desert presents innumerable difficulties and is accomplished only at vast cost. The remoteness of the area deters new settlers, and with improving education active members of local populations tend to migrate to the more agreeable environment offered by the developing coastland. It is difficult to hire skilled workers for the projects and the remoteness also creates marketing problems; sheep are air-freighted to Tripoli. Finally, the fact that fossil water is being used (i.e there is no replenishment) limits the expansion and the life of the project. This water will also be drawn upon for a multi-million-pound 'Great Man-made River' project in which the water is to be piped from underground reservoirs in the interior to the heavily populated coastal regions. Preliminary work has begun despite the economic difficulties arising from reduced oil income.

Manufacturing and service activities

The whole economy of Libya was enlarged after 1960 with the exploitation of its oil wealth. Previously non-agricultural activities were mainly limited to the processing of agriculture products, flour milling, oil pressing, fish canning and artisanal work in leather and textiles.

With the great wealth from the sale of oil a reconstruction and expansion of towns has taken place, so enlarging the construction industry, and the manufacture of consumer goods has been encouraged (e.g. clothing, footwear, paper making, metal working). But, with limited raw materials and a tiny home market no great enlargement of secondary activities is likely, and the emphasis on import substitution was abandoned in the 1981–5 development plan. Instead, increasing investment in industry is now directed to metallurgy (iron, steel and aluminium products), petrochemicals and plastics. Six coastal centres (Zuara, Misurata, Sirte, Marsa Brega, Ras Lanouf and Abu Kammash) are to develop these industries.

However, it is the service sector that has increased markedly in recent years. Imports have expanded to the benefit of commerce, transport and banking. Along the coast the growing hotel and tourist industries have offered new jobs and numbers in government service have increased. There has been a growing number of jobs in the northern towns – Tripoli, Banghazi, Misurata and Homs – and a considerable exodus from agricultural areas to them and to the oil camps.

Oil

Oil in commercial quantities was discovered in 1959 in Zelten, about 300 km south of Banghazi. These discoveries were the first of a series in the Sirte basin. Pipelines connect the many fields with newly created coastal terminals at Ras Sidra, Ras Lanouf, Marsa Brega, Zuetina and Tubruk. Six refineries are in operation and four more are being constructed under the 1981–5 plan. Oil operations have been restricted to the Sirtica basin, but oil exploration is now extending to western Libya, the offshore areas and to the south. After Nigeria, Libya is Africa's second largest producer. Crude-oil exports account for 99 per cent of Libyan total exports. Since 1969 liquid gas has been exported to Spain and Italy. However, the oil industry is capital- rather than labour-intensive, and the numbers employed at the oilfields and coastal installations are only a few thousand.

Nevertheless the growth and spread of the oil industry provides hosts of new well-paid ancillary jobs and the circulation of much money. Drivers, contractors, builders, farmers and hoteliers all benefit, and so does the nomad, drawn in by the increasing demand for labour.

THE FUTURE

Libya is a country of great distances, poor communications, small population and great wealth. In a series of development plans the revolutionary government has endeavoured, since 1969, to use oil revenues to lift Libya from the traditional into the modern world and to organize an economy that can survive the dwindling oil revenues, possibly in 40–50 years' time. There has been some measure of success in diversification of the economy and in expanding irrigated agriculture. New roads are being constructed and town rebuilding and slum eradication are well advanced.

But the problems, are formidable. The Arab socialist philosophy, now pertaining, leads to increasing government control over a wide range of economic activity. Foreign banks, some oil companies, all firms with more than five employees and retail trade have been nationalized. Property holding and personal money holdings are restricted. The aim is to allow a more equal distribution of the country's wealth, but it also leads to bureaucracy, corruption and the stifling of entrepreneurship. Most serious is the lack of educated and skilled labour: more than one-third of the total workforce and two-thirds of managerial and skilled staff come from abroad, mainly from other Arab countries (particularly Egypt). One most difficult task facing Libya is likely to be the training of artisans and professional men to take over from the foreign engineers, doctors and administrators. It is in human rather than economic fields that major problems are being faced, such as staying a drift to the towns from the thinly populated countryside and goading traditional peasantry into new and more productive husbandry.

15
The Sahara

The Sahara is the world's largest desert and gets its name from the Arab word *Sahra* (wilderness). It extends from the Atlantic to the Red Sea, at its maximum almost 5000 km; from north to south it varies between 1300 and 1600 km. Its total area, approximately 7.5 million km^2, is nearly one quarter of the continent. This great width of desert is only breached in the east by the Nile passing waters from the equatorial highland northwards to the Mediterranean.

Politically the Sahara is much divided, originally by the major powers who occupied and pacified it from their colonial territories to north and south, now by their independent successors: Morocco, Algeria, Libya, Chad, Niger, Mali, Mauritania and, in the east, Egypt and the Sudan.

The Sahara is underlain by the crystalline Basement Complex which in places outcrops at the surface. It comprises a broad platform of Archaean granites and gneisses, once folded and then denuded to peneplain form. Unevenly distributed upon this platform is a series of younger deposits, many accumulated under long periods of continental conditions. During the Cretaceous era much of the Sahara was submerged, the sea depositing wide expanses of limestone. This was followed in Tertiary times by continental conditions alternating with a number of lesser marine transgressions, particularly in the north. The vast quantities of sand in the Sahara are not of marine origin, for there has been no major marine transgression since the Eocene period. The sands are more recent and represent the weathered material and river deposits of the later Tertiary and Quaternary periods; recent wind action has been responsible for a limited amount of re-sorting and the creation of dunes. Volcanic rocks, many dating from the dislocations associated with the period of Alpine mountain building to the north, appear in the Anti-Atlas Mountains of Morocco and in the Red Sea hills of Egypt. They help to form the high mountains across the central Sahara, notably the Ahaggar, Tibesti and the Marra Mountains of Darfur in the Sudan.

RELIEF AND LANDSCAPE

The upstanding and mountainous character of the volcanic rocks is in striking contrast with the wide plains and plateaux of strata such as the almost horizontally bedded Cretaceous limestone, here and there fretted into vales and escarpments by former river channels or containing broad basins etched out by the wind. These forms related to the structure give but the bony frame of the landscape: the character of the covering is the result of the interaction of three weathering agents: insolation, wind action and the effect of water (much of it in the past rather than now). The surface rock, unprotected by soil and vegetation, is exposed to immense variation of temperature between the burning sun by day and great heat loss through radiation by night, a range of temperature at times amounting to 75°C. The expansion and contraction of the surface layers may lead to their disintegration if the rocks are sufficiently weak, but most cases of crumbling and 'exfoliation' are now thought to represent chemical weathering in the presence of minute quantities of moisture.

The processes of rock weathering give rise to three types of scenery and surface (Figure 35). The first is the erg or sandy desert of shifting dunes, difficult to traverse and avoided by travellers. Contrary to popular belief these soft-sand deserts form a relatively small proportion of the Saharan surface and their positions, if not their precise bounds, are mapped. Two of the largest sand deserts are the Grands Ergs Occidental and Oriental in the Algerian Sahara, separated by a stony and rocky desert that permits relatively easy travel south to the Ahaggar Mountains. Other notable erg deserts lie in south-western Algeria, in Mauritania and in Libya, with barchans and various forms of sand ridges. Very different is the second type of desert, the windswept *hamada* or rock waste of boulders and bare rocky platforms, such as those that practically surround the Ahaggar and Tibesti Mountains. The third type, the reg desert, is intermediate between the other two and consists of gravel and pebble spreads, sometimes of even surface for scores of miles as in the Tanezrouft, where camel and car can travel without difficulty. In the mountains of the central Sahara evidence of desert sculpturing processes is abundantly manifest in the mountain flanks seamed with gorges and wadis of intermittent and irregular torrents, the heavy screes of shattered rock and the bizarre forms of wind-eroded and undercut rock pillars and blocks.

From north-west to south-east across the central Sahara, sandstone and crystalline plateaux – part of the Saharan shield – form the plinths for the volcanic mountains of Ahaggar, Tassili, Aïr, Tibesti and Darfur. Here

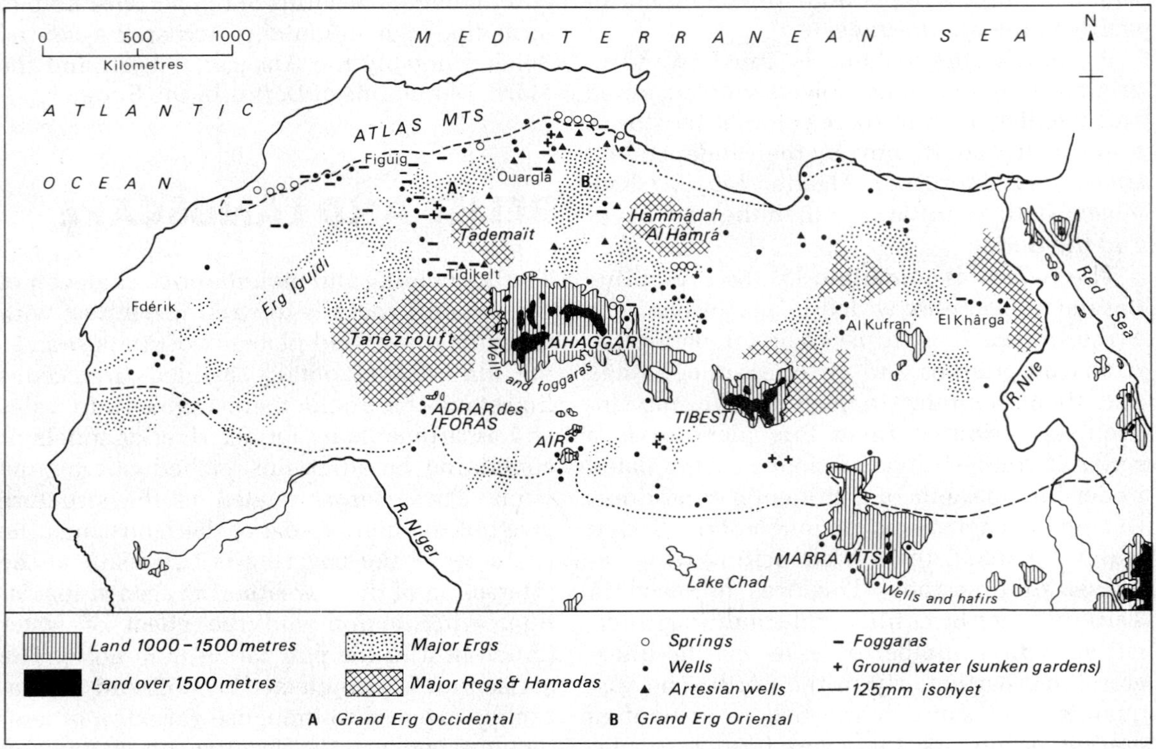

Figure 35 The Sahara: relief, surface features and water supply

lava outpourings from the Pliocene era onwards are mainly responsible for abruptly rising mountain masses up to and sometimes above 3000 m in height. The Ahaggar Mountains are the size of England and attain 2950 m; 1100 km to the south-east the Tibesti Mountains of similar character attain, in the extinct volcano of Emi-koussi, 3360 km. These mountains are stark and inhospitable. The uplift of the old planation surface, and the outpourings of lava, related to the folding of the Atlas, gave new vigour to erosion which bears the stamp of fluvial processes. Networks of valleys dissect and splay out from the main mountain masses, but there is no longer running water; they are the fossil river systems of the Pleistocene period. Then, when Europe was ice-covered, the Sahara was an inhabited steppe traversed by great rivers. The form of the valleys suggests a cycle of erosion arrested at the youthful stage, for they radiate in a simple pattern as consequents, with steep ungraded profiles. Here and there the deep and narrow canyons, formerly containing rapids, open upon level expanses that might have been lakes and marshes (often a dampness here now supports pasture), giving the typical ungraded profile of the youthful stream.

The great height of these central Saharan mountains favours some precipitation, usually in the form of short storms. Of more lasting value is a persistent cloud cover sufficient to nourish pasture. The highest parts of the Ahaggar are snow-covered for a few days each year, but farther inland in the Tibesti Mountains the humidity is very low. While freezing temperatures are common during winter nights, the absence of water reduces the effectiveness of frost as an agent of weathering, though it was undoubtedly more active in the Quaternary period.

CLIMATE

The climate of the desert is characterized by aridity, a considerable temperature range (both seasonal and diurnal), a dry atmosphere, clear skies and a maximum amount of sunshine throughout the year. The weather is remarkably stable.

During winter the pressure falls towards a tongue of low pressure just south of the Guinea coast from a fairly constant high-pressure system over the Moroccan Atlas and High Plateaux of Algeria. Thus the greater part of the Sahara receives northerly cT winds which for a time carry Saharan conditions to West Africa and which are slowly filling up Chad Basin with desert dust from the north-east. In West Africa this dry dusty wind is known as the *Harmattan*. In summer, with the land mass warmer than the surrounding oceans, the Inter-Tropical Convergence Zone of low pressure moves north over the southern Sahara. Thus winds blow towards the southern part of the desert from all directions. Over the northern part of the desert northerly winds continue to blow strongly almost every day. In the southern Sahara mE winds from the south-west are common: monsoonal indraughts bringing rain from the Gulf of Guinea are experienced as far north as Ardrar Des Iforas, the Aïr, and some years may even reach the Ahaggar, but by then these airstreams are almost dry. There is across the central Sahara a gap between the southern limit of the Mediterranean front rains and the northern limit of the tropical monsoon rains. The cold current off the Atlantic coast is responsible for the aridity there, for the mT air is cooled and stabilized, giving no rain.

Rainfall is irregular and usually in the form of short and often violent storms. In some parts of the desert (e.g. the Libyan desert) years may pass between such storms. The term 'mean annual rainfall' has little significance under such conditions. It is probable that, except for the mountain masses, the greater part of the central Sahara annually receives under 25 mm, while it is estimated that of the mountainous areas the Ahaggar and Aïr may receive up to 250 mm and Tibesti 125 mm (see Table 12). The aridity of the air is due to the character of the prevailing northerly and north-easterly winds, mainly descending from the upper atmosphere in the sub-tropical high-pressure zone and becoming warmed by compression. The farther south they blow, the greater the diminution in their relative humidity. The soil also receives some water in the form of dew. This is difficult to measure but is appreciable along the Atlantic littoral, in the beds of wadis and in dune areas. It is doubtful if this penetrates far enough into the soil to affect the water table.

The Sahara is one of the hottest parts of the earth's surface (see Table 12). The clear skies favour unbroken sunshine and the world's highest summer temperature has been recorded here (59°C at Azizia in Tripolitania on 13 September 1922). Large areas experience mean July temperatures of over 40°C, and in many years mean temperatures of over 50°C have been recorded. The annual range of temperature (about 17°C) is of less significance than the great diurnal range. By midday the desert surface is oven hot, but immediately the sun falls there is a rapid loss of heat from the bare ground, for the air is clean and dry and the sky generally cloudless. The nocturnal fall of temperature is remarkable, in summer dropping to around 16°C and in winter nearly to, and occasionally below, freezing-point, creating in general a diurnal range of 17–22°C throughout the year.

Frost occurs regularly each year in a number of the oases: Biskra, Touggourt and Ouargla have more days with frost than Algiers. These great extremes are counteracted by the wearing of heavy clothing, both to give protection against chilly nights and from the heat, glare and dust of the day. It is the dryness of the air the traveller from more humid parts notices most. Nails soon become brittle, lips crack and the skin becomes roughened; the fierce heat, often burning the sand surface to 70°C or more, militates against plant life and evaporates body moisture from the pores at an astounding rate. There is a constant feeling of thirst but no visible perspiration. In the summer manual workers at Hassi Messaoud oil wells lose (and drink) over three gallons of water a day.

Strong convection currents often associated with shallow depressions give rise to powerful winds that whip up dust and sand and blow locally as the sirocco of Algeria, the simoon of Libya and the Khamsin of Egypt. There are numerous types of these winds: some are purely local 'dust devils', but others are on a larger scale and may last two or three days.

VEGETATION

Saharan vegetation is related to the character of the surface rock and the presence of surface or subsoil water. Large areas are devoid of all

Table 12 *Saharan temperatures and rainfalls*

Station	*Altitude (m)*		*J*	*F*	*M*	*A*	*M*	*J*	*J*	*A*	*S*	*O*	*N*	*D*	*Year*
Tripoli	17	T	12.1	13.2	15.6	18.2	20.4	23.3	26.1	26.8	25.5	23.3	18.2	14.3	18.8
		R	84	45	23	13	7	2	—	—	13	45	62	120	414
In Salah	276	T	12.6	15.6	19.9	24.4	29.9	34.4	37.1	40.0	33.3	26.8	19.9	14.3	25.5
		R	—	—	—	—	—	—	—	—	—	—	—	—	—
Aswan	120	T	14.9	17.1	21.0	25.5	29.3	32.1	32.7	32.1	31.0	27.7	22.2	16.6	22.7
		R	—	—	—	—	—	—	—	—	—	—	—	—	—

Notes: T = Temperature (°C); R = rainfall (mm).

vegetation, but the sudden irregular rainstorm often has surprising results, particularly on the *hammada*, being followed for a short period by rapidly growing grass and shrubs that have the power of remaining dormant over months or even years. The gravel and pebble reg and the sandy *erg* sustain least vegetation. The southern and northern desert edges support more regular vegetation. Streams from the Atlas that lose themselves in the desert still support tufted bushes and grass, predominantly tamarisk and the purple-and-white flowered broom (*Retama Raetam*), along the line of their beds after their waters have seeped below the surface, while at intervals depressions facilitating well digging support date-palms, gardens and population. The Tuat oases of southern Algeria are a good example. They extend along the seasonally watered channel of the Saoura Messaoued from the Saharan Atlas at Figuig for nearly 650 km into the desert at Tidikelt (Figure 35).

The highlands within the Sahara have proved disappointing to botanists in that their bare sheets and faces of rock permit little vegetation. In the fissures and ravines and on the beds of the wadis debouching on to the surrounding plateaux, stunted acacia species, dry tufted herbs with woody root stocks and pasture such as the *Panicum* grass and tufted grasses survive and support sheep, goats and camels. Thus, contrary to popular ideas, a large part of the Sahara has a permanent vegetation of trees, shrubs and bushes. Distribution is confined to the general drainage lines, but is to be found right across the continent.

The vegetation of the oases, including date-palms, Mediterranean fruit trees and cereals, is introduced by man and continues only so long as man remains in control. Where oases have been deserted the vegetation introduced (much of course, entering as seed with the crops or with merchandise) rapidly dies out, and even date-palms become tufted, ragged and soon degenerate. Wind and detritus choke the water supply and soon, once man has withdrawn, the character of an 'oasis' no longer applies.

HUMAN AND ECONOMIC GEOGRAPHY

Agriculture in the Sahara is necessarily confined to the oases and in scale is akin to gardening. The plots are usually small and rectangular, being no more than 3 m long and bounded by small earth ramparts, permitting a flooding every few days. Two crops a year are possible; the principal ones are barley, millet, beans, wheat, vegetables and, in addition to the date-palm, citrus fruit, peaches and apricots are usual. There are, in fact, several levels of vegetation: vegetables at ground level, fruit trees above them and date-palms towering above all. Cereals are usually sown separately out of the shade of the trees.

Permanent settlement in the central Sahara consists of hamlets of stone or hardened-clay huts situated at the debouchments of the principal oueds around the upland periphery. Wells in the beds of the dry oueds provide irrigation water for the gardens worked for the Berber owners by the servile, bronze-complexioned half-castes known as *Haratin*. The Tuareg of the Ahaggar and Aïr and the Tibu of Tibesti do not engage in cultivation but herd camels, sheep and goats. The harshness of the environment obliges them to live in a state of continual movement between oueds and wells and over sparse mountain pasture. They move in small groups and use quickly erected grass and matting huts for shelter, although stone shelters and huts are used in the rocky Tibesti. The Tuareg formerly levied tribute from trans-Saharan caravans. They are the 'people of the veil', so called because the males constantly wear a long strip of cloth wound round the head to form a hood and covering the mouth and nose, only the eyes being visible. The Sahelian droughts of the 1970s decimated the Tuareg's herds and caused many to turn to a settled way of life along the southern margins of the desert.

The true nomads of the Sahara are a dwindling force. Tent dwellers move with their camels from well to well, the animals subsisting on sparse acacia and salt bush grazing; a hard but mainly self-sufficient way of life out of tune with modern living. Attempts are increasing in Algeria and Libya to settle the nomads in order to facilitate administration, education and the raising of their standard of living. New possibilities of lucrative employment in the new mining and oil-well settlements (once the rudiments of Western living have been absorbed) are a further lure that may help to break down their proud tradition.

Water supply developments

The successful exploitation of underground wealth in the Algerian and Libyan Sahara since the Second World War is having far-reaching effects on traditional nomadic and oasis economies. Success has attended searches for water, oil, natural gas and minerals. Great deep-seated basins in the north Sahara, Tanezrouft and Fezzan contain bountiful artesian aquifers, the most celebrated being the great nodular sandstone bed of Cretaceous–Jurassic age known as the *nappe albienne* or Continental Intercalaire extending under the northern Sahara and, in the Egyptian Sahara, the Nubian sandstone. Much of the water must have been accumulating over several thousands of years, in fact, but there is some annual replenishment from the rainfall in the upland marginal areas where these beds are exposed. It is the tapping of these subterranean waters 1000–1250 m deep in the northern Sahara that is reviving dying oases and permitting the establishment of permanent settlements for mining and oil exploration.

In many oases the water supply is obtained from wells or waterholes penetrating into seepage layers below the dry oueds, the water being hauled up in a skin by a camel, donkey or bullock. In other cases *foggaras* are constructed. These are subterranean channels dug to tap seepage areas and to lead the water by gravity to the cultivated plots (Figure 36). In a few cases, as at Ouargla in Algeria (Figure 37), artesian waters are used; over 1000 wells

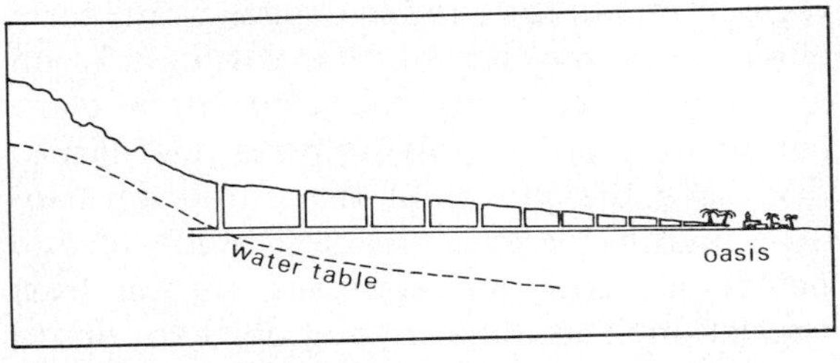

Figure 36 Section through a foggara

irrigating nearly 2 million date-palms. Over the years the level of the water table has fallen, but since the Second World War deep boring has reached water under great pressure in the Continental Intercalaire at 1125 m, and this has led to a resuscitation of these oases, where the population is now 40,000.

Communications

Transport across the great desert has always been difficult, but nevertheless possible thanks to the camel. For centuries considerable trade between the summer-rain Sudan and the cool-season-rain Maghreb has been carried across the desert by caravan. The trade moving south included silk and woollen textiles from Morocco, olive oils and sponges from Tunisia, brass, pottery and Venetian glass through Algeria. The trade moving north included slaves, gold, spices, ivory, ebony, skins and leather. Caravans from Kano in northern Nigeria to Morocco took from 90 to 150 days on the journey. Camel traffic is still important for the nomad calling at the oases to trade animals, wool, leather and salt for grain and fruits. Oases such as Ghardaia, Biskra, Kufra, Agades and Atar are still busy centres for local camel caravans.

Modern means of communication, notably the motor-car and the aeroplane, are doing much to open up the desert and to lessen its hazards. The first car crossed the desert in 1924. Regular bus and lorry services (taking about six days) now cross the Sahara, except during the hottest months. There are a number of roads available to cars and lorries, but the two main trans-Saharan roads used by

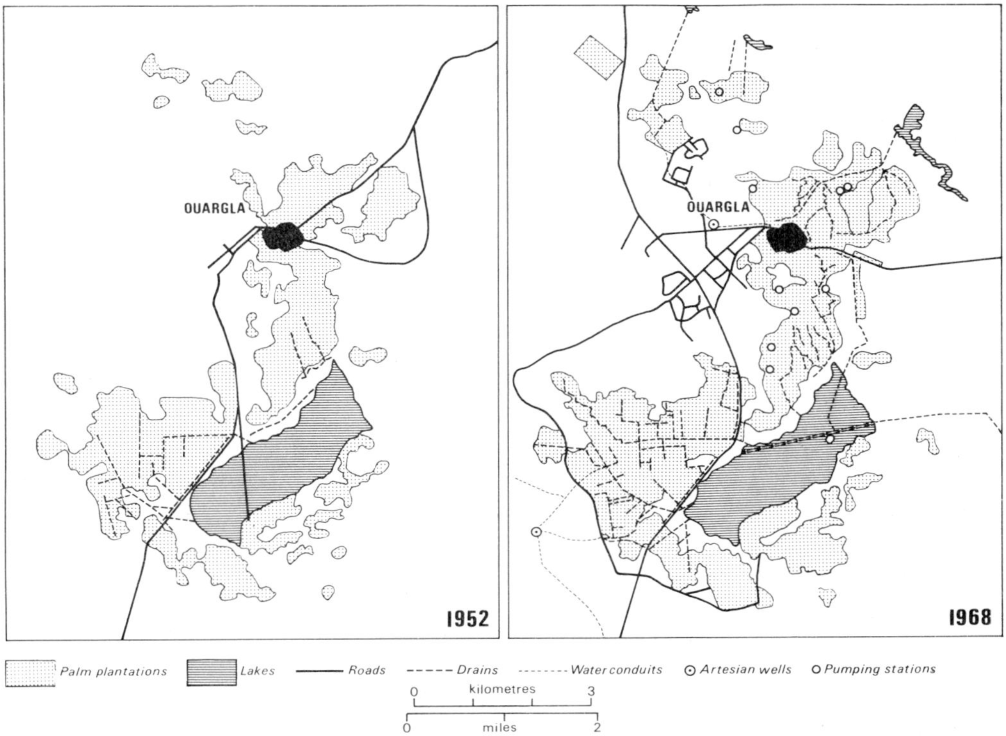

Figure 37 Ouargla Oasis: artesian water and development

buses are from Algiers, El Golea, In Salah, Tamanrasset to Agades and Kano, and another from Colomb Bechar to Gao on the Niger. For the most part the roads are the natural desert floor, but from northern Algeria bitumen-surfaced roads are gradually being extended to the oases and oilfields in the north of the desert. Already 1800 km of surfaced roads reach southwards to Colomb Bechar, El Golea and Hassi Messaoud.

First mooted in 1876, several projects to construct north–south trans-Saharan railways have been examined and surveys carried out. The project is technically feasible, but only at very great expense, and it is doubtful whether the quantity of freight available would merit such expenditure. The most recent railway construction in the Sahara has been the 650 km line from F'Derik to Nouadhibou, built specifically for the movement of iron-ore.

All these developments are indicative of the great changes now occurring in the human geography of the Sahara. The feudal system of the oases is becoming disrupted. Slavery, abolished in name, has persisted in fact, for the Negro slaves and their descendants have remained bound to their masters in the isolation of the oases through lack of alternative employment. Now paid employment is becoming available, a road network extended and the Negroes are discovering a new mobility which permits them to move to new work and become better off financially than their camel-owning former masters. These changes are timely, for previously, with a lowering water level in the oasis wells and a growing rate of population increase as new medical knowledge was applied the plight of the oasis cultivators and share croppers was becoming acute. Much still needs to be done, but the impact of new people, new ideas and ways of life, new spending power and new accessibility are beginning to change the outlook of the Saharan peoples.

PART FOUR: THE NILE BASIN AND HORN OF AFRICA

16
Physical geography

The Sahara stretches its barren waste across northern Africa to the Red Sea, but its pattern is broken near its eastern periphery by the basin of the River Nile and by the mountains flanking the Red Sea, which extend south towards the great mass of the Ethiopian highlands. Here there is a diversity of terrain that has provided a home for man since the earliest recorded times.

Today the peoples of this part of Africa are a mixture of Caucasian stock with the black or Negro race. Here was the threshold across which Hamitic and later Semitic peoples entered the continent from Arabia to displace the Negro peoples, the purest of whom are now to be found in West Africa. Ancient Egyptians were probably a fusion of the Hamite and Semite, later becoming diluted with Negro elements from the south. In the seventh century AD, Semitic Arabs conquered Egypt and spread up the Nile valley, while others crossed the Red Sea into Ethiopia and the Sudan. Gradually these became merged with the indigenous peoples, but Arab culture, language and religion now extend firmly from the Mediterranean to the northern limits of the Sudd and from the Indian Ocean into the foothills of the Ethiopian highlands.

STRUCTURE AND GEOLOGY

Structurally and geologically this part of Africa includes three distinctive major elements. Much of the area, particularly in the Sudan, is floored by the Crystalline Basement Complex; to the north of the Sudan and into Egypt increasingly younger sedimentary rocks bear witness to succeeding incursions and withdrawals of the sea; south and east of the Sudan the highland masses represent a period of disturbance and uplift with rifting and much vulcanicity.

Rocks of the Archaean Basement are exposed at the surface over more than 50 per cent of the Sudan and 10 per cent of Egypt. Outcrops of these igneous and metamorphic rocks in the Nile valley account for the cataracts. In the Sudan they are partly masked by recent deposits, some of continental origin arising from weathering under arid conditions and others of alluvial character mainly from the vast semi-inland-drainage centre of the Sudd. The Crystalline Basement rocks extend in a long tongue from Ethiopia and the Sudan northwards along the Red Sea coast as far as the Gulf of Suez, and form the highest mountains in the south of the Sinai Peninsula; they are continued across the Red Sea in Arabia. West of the Nile they are less prominent, but form a basement for the Tertiary lavas, mainly basalts, which make up the Jebel Marra and are responsible for Mount 'Uweinat in south-west Egypt.

The Nubian sandstone is the product of very long periods of continental weathering and denudation of the Archaean Basement rocks. The great thicknesses of sandstones (in places of more than 500 m) also contain occasional beds of clays, marls and conglomerates. These unfossiliferous rocks range in age from the Carboniferous to the Cretaceous and cover about 25 per cent of the Sudan and 30 per cent of Egypt. They derive their name from the district of Nubia in the northern Sudan and extend widely across the Sahara. They possess the valuable property of being aquiferous and convey northwards much of the precipitation falling on the Darfur–Ennedi–Tibesti highland. Following the Archaean rocks they dip gently to the north and provide water for wells at a number of oases in the Western and Libyan deserts.

From the Cretaceous period oscillation in the land level to the north allowed a number of sea incursions which were responsible for extensive Cretaceous, and later Eocene, limestones. These are the most widespread of marine deposits in Egypt, extending over the central section of the Western desert and the northern part of the Eastern desert. It is the massive thicknesses of these limestones that have provided most of the building stone used in the valley and delta.

The crustal movements of the Alpine mountain-building period began near the close of the Oligocene era with the formation of the Red Sea Basin and uplift of its bordering mountains. However, the real shaping of the Horn of Africa as we know it occurred with the great displacements and fracturings of the Oligocene–Miocene period, when the creation of the Red Sea trough and Gulf of Aden severed Africa from Arabia. This period of crustal disturbance had much influence upon the evolution of the River Nile and led to the cutting of the great trench of the Nile valley in a broad syncline paralleling the anticline of the Red Sea highlands.

The incursion of the Pliocene sea was more local, mainly affecting the Nile syncline and the Red Sea trough, where fluviatile conglomerates, gravels and sands were deposited. The deposits of the Quaternary period include the oolitic limestones of the coastal strip west of Alexandria; the gravels, sands and Nile mud of the delta and Nile valley; and the drifted sands of the Western desert formed by aeolian action upon disintegrating bedrock. In the Pleistocene period, contemporaneous with the Ice Ages in Europe, Egypt experienced pluvial periods. Torrential river flow of these times accounts for sands, gravels and large pebbles which form the basement of the present cultivated alluvium of the delta. This alluvium is very recent (probably deposited during the last 16,000 years) and is derived mainly from the weathering and erosion of the volcanic rocks of the Ethiopian highlands.

Much detailed work has yet to be done on the geology and geomorphology of the Ethiopian highlands, but the general pattern is understood and its structural relationship with the East African highlands appreciated. Much of the lofty plateau of the Ethiopian highlands has been built up on massive lava sheets, which issued from both fissures and volcanoes that accompanied the series of tectonic adjustments affecting this zone of instability. Towards the end of the Eocene period, but before the main Alpine movements, considerable uplift took place. The uplift was accompanied by the up-welling of magma and the ejection throughout the rest of the Tertiary period of vast quantities of lava, mainly basalts and trachytes sometimes many hundreds of metres thick, upon the underlying Mesozoic surface or the Crystalline Basement.

The great crustal adjustments accompanying the Alpine orogenesis produced the striking series of rifts from Syria through Ethiopia to south-east Africa (see Chapter 2). Colossal fracturing and displacement occurred (often of up to 2000 m) which, by the creation of a major rift valley aligned south-south-west towards Lake Turkana (Rudolph), here splits the highland mass into two unequal parts: the Ethiopian plateau to the north-west and the Somali plateau (sometimes called the Central plateau) to the south-east. Renewed vulcanicity accompanied these great movements, producing not only great lava sheets, but also a large number of volcanoes. The Crystalline Basement extends through Danakil to the Red Sea and in the east through Ogaden into Somalia. Less disturbed, and without lava cappings, the gneisses and schists are here responsible for sandy plateau country descending from 1700 m to 380 m above sea-level.

RELIEF AND DRAINAGE

The great mass of the Ethiopian highlands, rising abruptly from surrounding deserts, dominates the geography of north-east Africa. This highland mass averages 2300–2700 m in height, but its rolling upland tracts are deeply scarred by fissures (often of fault origin) and overlooked by lofty bastions 4300–5000 m in elevation. The main ranges flank the rift valley and then bifurcate, the Harrar highlands swinging to the east through northern Somalia to constitute the 'horn' of Africa, while the major range on the northern side swings due north, its 2700 m escarpment overlooking the Danakil scrub desert. Heavy rainfall and steep slopes produce powerful rivers which cut deeply into the volcanic rocks dividing the plateau into semi-isolated blocks. The highest peaks are in the Simen ranges in Amhara. These run north-east from Lake Tana and comprise a number of peaks, sometimes snow-covered, over 4000 m high, culminating in Ras Dashan (5050 m).

The rift valley from the neighbourhood of Lake Turkana is a clearly defined trench and contains a chain of lakes, some of considerable size (Lake Abaya is 80 km long). The northern third of the rift is drained by the River Awash issuing from the Shoan uplands west of Addis Ababa and then, 80 km from the coast, losing itself in the more arid funnel-shaped low plateau into which the rift has widened. Only a few short streams flow eastwards, in turn also to peter out in the Danakil desert or in salty marshes short of the coast. The effective drainage of the mountain limb south of the rift valley is by a number of streams which unite in Somalia to form the River Juba.

The principal drainage of the highlands, however, is to the Nile Basin by means of three principal rivers: the Sobat, the Blue Nile and the Atbara (Takkaze). These three rivers account for four-fifths of the entire drainage. The Sobat gathers its waters from a number of streams rising in the south-west corner of Ethiopia. The Blue Nile rises in the Gojjam highlands, flows north into the shallow Lake Tana (2000 m), and then out again by a series of rapids and falls, plunging into a deep gorge, in places 1300 m below the general level of the plateau. It flows first in a south-easterly direction and then swings round to flow west and then north-west through the Sudan to join the White Nile at Khartoum. Most of its water comes from its torrential tributary streams (rather than from Lake Tana), themselves the product of heavy seasonal rainfall. The Atbara's principal headstream, the Takkaze (the Terrible), rises among the high peaks of Amhara and flows north in a spectacular gorge to join the Atbara in the Sudan, which in turn flows into the Nile nearly 320 km below Khartoum.

In contrast to Ethiopia the relief of the Sudan is low and relatively uniform. Half the Sudan is below 500 m and constitutes the plain of the River Nile; only about 2 per cent is over 1200 m. Most of the republic is included in the Nile Basin and mainly comprises vast clay plains and extensive sandy areas of low undulations, emphasized in a few localities by isolated granite hill masses such as the Red Sea highlands, the Nuba Mountains of Kordofan in central Sudan and the Jebel Marra of Darfur province.

The Nuba Mountains comprise a number of relict granitic hill masses, most rising abruptly from a detritus-strewn pediment of rocks of the Archaean Basement Complex. Elevations of nearly 1700 m are attained, which is about 1000 m above the surrounding plain and sufficient for a rather heavier and more reliable rainfall, although not enough to nurture permanent streams. The Jebel Marra in western Darfur are volcanic masses mainly of basalt, also resting on the Archaean Basement. The range is not extensive, being about 110 km north to south and 48 km east to west. It attains a height of 3350 m. An upwarping of the basement along the Lake Chad–Nile divide here gives a general elevation of about 1000 m to the plain proper. The Red Sea highlands, also formed of Crystalline Basement rocks, are a northward continuation of the hills of northern Ethiopia and continue to flank the Red Sea in Egypt, presenting a tangled arid upland mass heavily faulted and dissected and exhibiting a wide range of rock types, with granites predominating. The ranges extend northwards over 800 km to the Gulf of Suez. A number of peaks rise to over 2000 m, the highest being Gebel Shayeb (2400 m). These hills constitute over a third of Egypt's Eastern desert, the remainder being the platform of sedimentary rocks sloping to the Nile: mainly Nubian sandstone to the great Nile bend and massive Eocene limestone farther north. It was the drainage from the Red Sea Mountains in more pluvial periods that accounts for the acute dissection of these sedimentary rocks, making the character of the Eastern desert very different from that of the Western desert. This Western desert is indeed the eastern part of the Sahara proper. It is a massive plateau of sedimentary rocks, mainly limestone, resting upon the Nubian sandstone and Archaean Basement. Few parts exceed 300 m and slopes are gentle except in a few deep basins, such as the Qattara Depression and the oasis depressions of Kharga, Dakhla, Baharyia, Farafra, Faiyum and Siwa.

The River Nile

The greater part of north-east Africa is drained by the Nile, the father of African rivers. By its anomalous behaviour the Nile long troubled the ancients, who advanced delightful theories to account for this great river flowing for 2400 km across a desert and rising to a flood in the summer, contrary to all experience in their Mediterranean world. Exploration up the Nile was much obstructed by cataracts and then the marshy Sudd, and it was not until 1862, at Gondokoro, that the origin and course of the river became verified when Speke and Grant penetrating north from East Africa met Sir Samuel Baker travelling south from Cairo.

The Nile is estimated to be over 6600 km long from its source at the head of the Luvironza river which flows into Lake Victoria. Its south-to-north flow, reaching the Mediterranean on almost the same meridian as its source, marks it off from other major African rivers which mainly trend east and west. In all, it flows through 35 degrees of latitude (3°50′S to 31°50′N) and consequently through the range of climates from equatorial to Mediterranean.

The long profile of the river shows four distinct sections and serves to emphasize other anomalous features. The first section is that within the Lake plateau of East Africa, comprising a number of headstreams and lakes that feed the White Nile. This issues from Lake Victoria by the Ripon Falls (now submerged by the lake formed behind the Owen Falls Dam just to the north) and passes through the swamp vegetation of the shallow Lake Kyoga into Lake Albert via the Murchison Falls. From Lake Albert the river, now called the Bahr el Jebel (river of the mountains), falls at first gently but later by a series of rapids from the plateau to the swampy Sudd Plains.

The second section as far as the Sabaloka (or Shabluka) gorge is one of very low gradient. The river passes through the Sudd, accepting the Bahr el Ghazal (river of gazelles) from the west, the Sobat to the north of the marshes and then the Blue Nile at Khartoum. The Sobat floods in summer as a result of the Ethiopian monsoon and causes widespread inundations over the 300 km of plains through which its middle and lower course passes before joining the White Nile.

From the sixth cataract at Sabaloka, 80 km north of Khartoum, for the next 2000 km as far as Aswan, the river bed alternates between gentle stretches and series of rapids where outcropping crystalline rocks provide the famous cataracts. Below Aswan the fourth section is of low uninterrupted gradient to the sea, with the river generally incised into the sandstone and limestone surface rocks. Just below Cairo, about 150 km from the Mediterranean, the river bifurcates and flows in two distributaries, the Rosetta and Damietta branches, across the level funnel-shaped delta to the sea. The alternation of graded and ungraded sections in the long profile suggests that the present river is relatively young and represents the amalgamation of a number of formerly independent systems. Tertiary earth-movements are thought to be the principal cause of adjustments in the drainage pattern.

CLIMATE AND VEGETATION

Since the basin of the River Nile extends for some 3200 km from the Mediterranean to the East African plateau, and we add for our present purpose also the whole highland mass of Ethiopia and the dry Horn of Africa, it is clear that a number of distinctive climates may be discerned.

Virtually the whole of the north-east quadrant of Africa experiences a tropical climate. Marine influences are remarkably limited, and it is relief that introduces variation into otherwise model climatic transitions related to changing latitude. Much of the region is part of the far larger desert belt of Africa and Arabia, dominated all the year round by cT air (see Figures 8 and 9). During the northern winter when the ITC is far to the south, dry north and north-easterly winds penetrate deep into Africa and almost the whole of the Nile Basin is rainless. In the northern summer the ITC usually moves as far north as the central Sudan; then the southern part of the Nile Basin, including the highland mass of Ethiopia, experiences air masses of mE type drawn from the south-west to the monsoonal centres of Ethiopia and India. These moist air masses behind the ITC are responsible for the characteristic summer rainfall alternating with winter drought in the Sudan. It is these moist airstreams impinging upon the mountain masses of East Africa and Ethiopia that release heavy rainfall (over 1500 mm) and nurture and sustain the Nile in its 2500 km sinuous traverse across the Sahara.

Nowhere within the Nile Basin is true equatorial or true Mediterranean climate experienced. The plateau character of Uganda and Tanzania modifies the equatorial climate; and the southern shores of the eastern basin of the Mediterranean, being 5° farther south than those of the western basin, are but little affected by the winter depressions which move eastwards along a more northerly course. The Mediterranean therefore has but limited effect; it cools the northern shores and grants a few millimetres of rain to a very narrow fringe of the Nile delta in winter. The Red Sea, almost entirely enclosed, is hot for all seasons and also has only local influence upon the surrounding even hotter shores.

Climatic regions (see Figure 38)

The Somalia coastlands and lower plateau. Somalia is hot and dry throughout the year. With the northward advance of the ITC, marine tropical air from the Indian Ocean impinges upon this part of Africa, having been deflected eastwards on crossing the equator. These airstreams flow parallel with the coast across the gently rolling low plateau of Ogaden and the Haud (300–1000 m), from the north-east in winter and south-west in summer. In the winter months no rain at all is recorded and the summer rainfall is light. In the summer off the east coast of Somalia the sea is several degrees cooler than in the open ocean because of the upswelling along the coast of water from the ocean depths. This leads to frequent fogs between June and August and is a further contributive cause of the aridity of the littoral. This east coast is much cooler than the north coast opposite the Gulf of Aden. Much of Somalia consists of the intermediate plateau country between the narrow coastal plains and the Ethiopian highlands. The light rainfall (about 400 mm) and average temperature at 1500 m of 16°C in January to 24°C in July make this a region of semi-arid thorn-bush grazing.

Thus Somalia, peripheral to the massive upland of Ethiopia, experiences desert and semi-desert conditions. Its highest rainfall in the Ogaden is only 450 mm. The prevailing vegetation is grass with thorn bush and numerous species of acacia. As is frequent in tropical latitudes the appearance of the

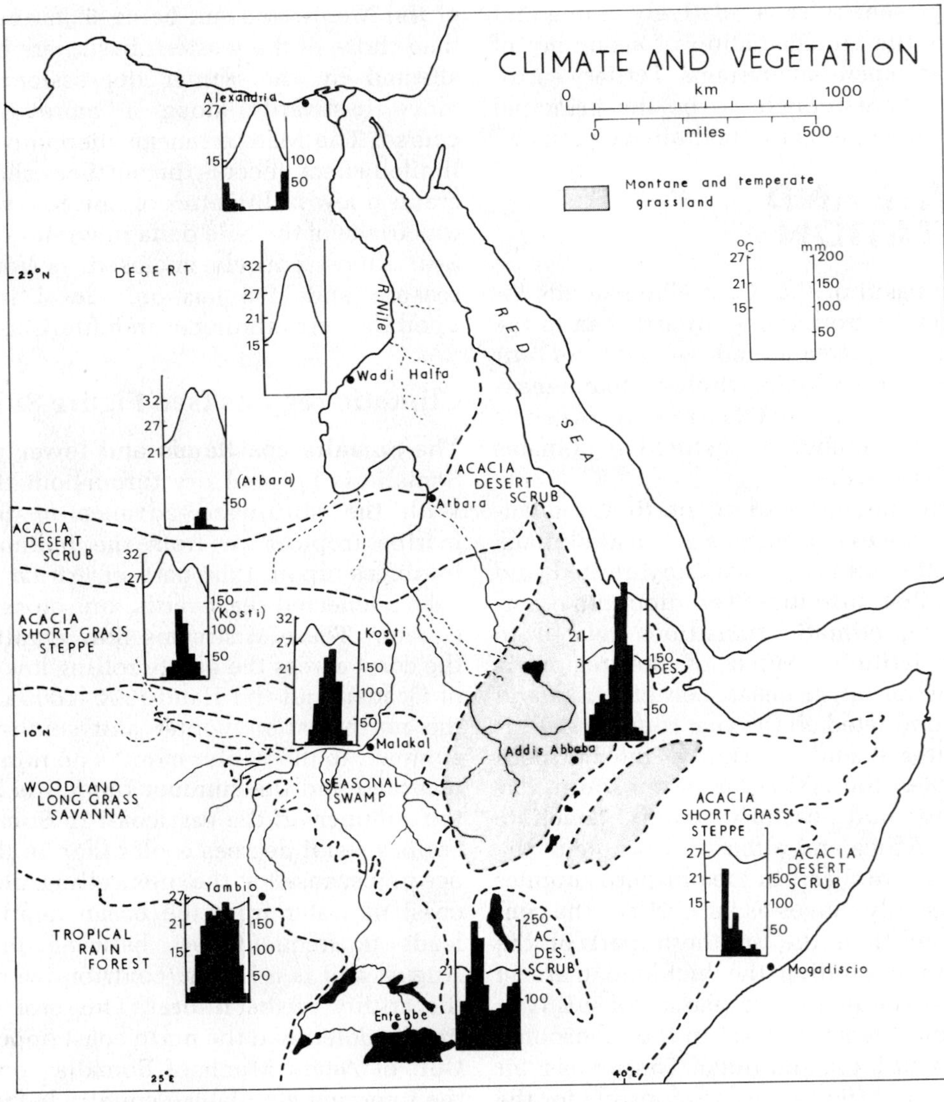

Figure 38 Nile Basin and Horn of Africa: climate and vegetation

countryside changes markedly with the seasons, dry brown grasses and leafless tree thickets during the dry season giving way to astonishing growth and verdure with the arrival of the rain.

The Red Sea hills and coastlands. The narrow strip of land flanking the Gulf of Aden and the Red Sea, frequently backed by fault scarps, is one of the hottest regions of the world. Rainfall is very scanty (75–125 mm) and differs from that of Somalia in being winter rain. This comes from the north-east winds which give mists and light rains on the hills behind the coast. Virtually no summer rain is experienced, for the ITC normally only just attains latitude 20°N and consequently summer temperatures are not mitigated by rainfall. Temperatures of over 38°C are recorded daily in August. At Berbera the mean temperature for the summer months exceeds 32°C.

Even the coolest month at Berbera has a mean temperature of 24.4°C (Table 13). Much of this is desert; at best vegetation is limited to sparse herbs and scrubby bushes from which gums and resins are collected and which offer frugal pasture for sheep and goats.

The Highlands of Ethiopia. Masses of mE air blowing from the south-west, and possibly supplemented by the indraught from the Indian Ocean, give heavy rainfall farther inland upon the Ethiopian highlands. This rain is heaviest in the south-west of the plateau, where in places it exceeds 1800 mm and gives at least 1000 mm over most of the plateau above 2000 m. Most of this part of the highlands is drained by tributaries of the Nile. The rains begin in early April but become heavy and consistent in July, August and September. The heavy downfalls run off the crystalline rocks with great rapidity and torrents of red-brown floodwater sweep down the deep gorges on their way to Egypt and the Mediterranean. The rift valley, being partially in the rain shadow, receives about 635 mm, but the Danakil plateau, fully in the rain shadow and receiving the descending winds, is hot and arid.

Ethiopians divide their country climatically and vegetationally into three altitude levels. The first is the *Kolla*, the lower land up to 1600 m: mainly valley bottoms which are hot, sticky and in parts still malarial. Second, there is the *woina dega* (wine highland), at 1000–3000 m and the most attractive part for settlement, with good pastures and well-cultivated, fertile volcanic soils. At Addis Ababa the warmest month has an average temperature of 19°C and the coolest (November) 15°C. The rainy season of May to September is regarded as winter; the dry season as the summer. The third zone is the *dega* (highland), comprising all above 3000 m where conditions of heavy rainfall and cold do not favour settlement. It will be seen that despite its tropical latitude the plateau enjoys a mild temperature throughout the year. With a mean annual temperature at Asmara of 18°C and at Addis Ababa of 17°C, this climate has been termed one of perennial spring.

The great range of climate with varying altitude means that almost all forms of African vegetation are found in the Ethiopian highlands. The deep valleys of the *Kolla* are forested with a range of tropical trees, including ebony, banana, rubber vines and bamboo, while the indigenous coffee shrub flourishes. The more open plateau tracts at 1600–2000 m in the interior provide open parkland with few trees, although in the moister south-west there is greater tree growth. In the cool middle highland, *woina dega* wooded or park savanna prevails, grassland with thorny trees but no extensive woodland – indeed, wide views over great distances are possible. In this zone species of fig and native juniper thrive, as do Mediterranean fruits and cereals. The higher and colder *dega* contains more grass but fewer trees and shrubs. Broadly these correspond to Alpine pastures but include great thistles and giant lobelias, some of which attain 6 m in height.

The Rainlands of the southern and central Sudan. Throughout the Sudan, climatic conditions reflect the lack of notable physical barriers obstructing the airstreams from the Mediterranean to the East African plateau; this means that climatic conditions can change gradually with the latitude. No rain falls during the period of these north-easterly winds (cT type) and vegetation is dominated by the two-season character of the year, one rainy the other dry. In the extreme south the dry season is short, lasting from December to February, and is the hottest period of the year. Being within 5° of the equator the annual range of temperature is low (Juba: March 29°C, August 25°C; rainfall: 965 mm). By the latitude of Khartoum the dry season lasts eight months and the mean annual rainfall is 125 mm. The rainfall totals in the south reflect both the increasing relief and proximity to the equator: over 1000–1250 mm, with two maxima, associated with the overhead passage of the ITC, are experienced annually

Table 13 *Nile Basin and Horn: temperature and rainfall of selected stations*

Station	*Altitude (m)*		*J*	*F*	*M*	*A*	*M*	*J*	*J*	*A*	*S*	*O*	*N*	*D*	*Year*
Mogadiscio	18	T	24.9	26.1	27.3	27.7	26.8	24.9	23.8	24.4	24.4	24.9	24.4	24.9	25.5
		R	—	—	—	178	55	89	51	15	13	18	12	—	431
Berbera	9	T	24.4	24.4	25.5	27.7	30.4	35.5	36.6	36.0	32.7	28.2	26.1	24.9	29.3
		R	2	7	18	13	12	—	2	2	—	2	—	2	58
Addis Ababa	2400	T	15.6	17.1	18.2	18.2	18.8	17.7	16.6	16.1	16.1	16.6	14.9	14.9	16.6
		R	12	33	76	120	127	89	129	160	94	34	15	12	901
Khartoum	384	T	21.0	23.3	26.1	29.9	32.7	33.3	31.5	30.4	31.0	31.0	26.8	22.2	29.2
		R	—	—	—	—	2	8	39	56	18	4	—	—	127
Cairo	29	T	12.6	13.7	17.1	21.0	24.4	26.8	27.7	27.7	25.5	23.3	18.2	14.3	21.0
		R	12	6	6	6	—	—	—	—	—	—	2	6	38
Alexandria	32	T	14.3	15.6	17.1	19.3	22.2	24.4	26.1	27.2	26.1	23.8	19.9	16.1	21.0
		R	55	22	13	4	—	—	—	—	—	8	36	65	203

Notes: T = Temperature (°C); R = rainfall (mm).

along the Sudan–Uganda border, but this amount diminishes steadily northwards. Conditions at Khartoum are semi-arid and true desert occurs immediately to the north.

In the central Sudan three seasons are generally recognized: the hot and very dry, early summer (March – June); the hot rainy period (July – October); and the cool dry winter. In June the daily temperature at Khartoum reaches 34.5°C, for the north wind (cT air) blows off the Sahara and dust storms are frequent. The rain comes with the south-west winds and temperatures fall perceptibly (Khartoum: August mean daily temp 30.5°C). The rainy season lasts from three to seven months according to latitude and the progress of the ITC. It is followed by the cooler and dry winter, when skies remain cloudless and temperatures vary between 21°C and 27°C.

The prevailing vegetation in its character, height and thickness can be correlated closely with the amount of rainfall, the major variable factor in the climate. Consequently, a series of zones changing from south to north may be observed (Figure 38). In the extreme south are a few limited areas of evergreen tropical forests; but with the gradual extension of the dry season as one moves north, the prevailing vegetation of the southern Sudan is rather open wooded savanna containing broad-leaved deciduous trees, with grasses attaining 1.5 m or more as the dominant ground herb. Nearly 260,000 km^2 of the south-central Sudan comprises the Sudd or Flood Region. This consists of numerous rivers with floating vegetation amid marshy, reedy swamp zones and slightly elevated interfluves supporting perennial grasses and herbs.

Farther north, as the dry season lengthens and the total annual rainfall diminishes, the grasses become shorter and the trees sparser and lower. Below 500 mm, thorny and more drought-resisting species appear. In general the grasses in the central Sudan are sweet and many of the shrubs are also browsed: the acacia short-grass steppe provides an important cattle rearing region. This vegetation degenerates to steppe or semi-desert below the 400 mm isohyet.

The desert of Egypt and the northern Sudan. North of the 125 mm isohyet is true desert which extends northwards almost as far as the Mediterranean coast. The principal characteristics are aridity, a considerable temperature range (both seasonal and diurnal), a dry atmosphere and a high amount of sunshine throughout the year. The desert is not entirely bereft of vegetation, for here and there sparse scrub vegetation and tussocks of coarse grass appear among wadi floors – especially in the east and on the flanks of the Red Sea highlands.

Within this Saharan zone summer temperatures surpass 38°C, the sun burning down from a cloudless sky. At night, a fall of 12–16°C takes place. Rainfall is meagre and very irregular. Years may pass without any precipitation, and then a sudden storm may give up to 50 mm.

In the spring, sporadic depressions from the Sahara traverse eastwards to the Delta of Egypt. These are responsible for excessively dry southerly winds which sometimes bring dust and sandstorms (khamsin), and which may persist for three or four days. During the winter, temperatures drop substantially (the January mean being 13–16°C) but frosts are unknown in the Nile valley and plant growth continues. The Egyptian year is therefore one of somewhat monotonous climatic conditions where two seasons only are clearly distinguishable: the hot summer from May to October heralded by the khamsin, and the cooler winter from November to April.

The Mediterranean coastlands. The climate of the Mediterranean coast for a few miles inland differs from that of the rest of Egypt since it experiences a small winter rainfall (100–200 mm), milder winters, but slightly lower summer temperatures (Alexandria: January 14°C, August 27°C, see Table 13) as a result of the tempering effect of the sea and a prevailing onshore wind from the north-west. Winter depressions along the Mediterranean bring to this limited area strong winds, cool weather and short but heavy rains. The Delta shares the characteristics of both Mediterranean and Saharan climates, having a small winter rainfall (Alexandria: 200 mm, diminishing southwards to 35 mm at Cairo), mild winter temperatures and hot dry summers (Cairo: January 12.5°C, July 27.7°C).

NILE HYDROLOGY

This century has seen the establishment of a series of large-scale irrigation works on the Nile that have radically transformed the Nile valley of Egypt and the Sudan to permit it to support nearly 60 million out of the 70 million living in the Nile Basin. Immense study of the whole river has had to be made; as a result, our knowledge of the character and regime of the Nile is probably greater than that of any other major river in the world, and already the Nile is controlled and harnessed to a very high degree for the benefit of humanity.

Comprehensive conservation schemes propounded soon after the Second World War might well have led to the establishment of a 'Nile Valley Authority' for the mutual benefit of all the riparian states; but lack of interest on the part of Ethiopia, suspicion and fear in Egypt and a general air of procrastination left the plans in abeyance. After 1952 the new revolutionary and nationalistic government in Egypt recognized the seriousness of mounting pressure of population and determined, at enormous expense, on the creation on Egyptian soil of the largest artificial dam in the world, the High Dam at Aswan.

The annual discharge curve of the river, showing the contributions of major tributaries, is demonstrated in Figure 39. The diagram makes clear the overwhelming part that the Blue Nile plays in bringing the river to its great flood in August, September and October, and demonstrates the small flooding capacity of the White Nile. This is because the White Nile headstreams lie in regions receiving rain all through the year; further, the sequence of lakes and the Sudd through which it flows

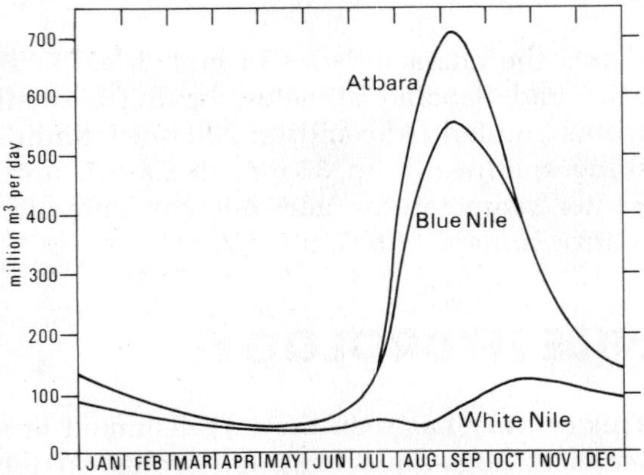

Figure 39 Components of Nile flow above the Aswan High Dam

serve as regulators and even out moderate fluctuations of discharge. There is a tremendous loss of water by evaporation in the Sudd; the greater the rains the more the loss, for greater inundation follows, so increasing the surface of water subject to evaporation. The White Nile (Bahr el Jebel) enters the Sudd at Mongalla with an average annual flow of 27 thousand million cubic metres, and leaves it at Malakal, where the average annual flow is only 14 thousand million cubic metres. In other words only half the water passing Mongalla reaches the junction with the Sobat, and one is also led to conclude that much of the summer rain of the southern Sudan never reaches the Nile at all. In southern Sudan the flood begins in April but it does not reach Aswan in Egypt until July; similarly in the south the flood wanes by November but in the north not until January.

The great flood of the Nile, so beneficial to Egypt, is the result of the torrential summer rains of the Ethiopian plateau, which sweep down through deep gorges to swell in chocolate-coloured flood the Blue Nile and Atbara. The Blue Nile is a perennial stream, but the Atbara shrinks to a series of pools in the dry season (January to June). An analysis of the Nile flow at Aswan before the High Dam reveals that, at maximum discharge in early September, the White Nile accounts for 10 per cent of the discharge, the Blue Nile for 68 per cent, the Atbara 22 per cent; the total daily discharge being about 700 million cubic metres. In early May when Nile discharge is at a minimum it is made up as follows: White Nile 83 per cent, Blue Nile 17 per cent; the total daily discharge being only 45 million cubic metres. In the average year 84 per cent of Nile water now flowing into Lake Nasser comes from Ethiopia and 16 per cent from the East African lake plateau.

NILE CONSERVATION AND IRRIGATION

Throughout much of the Sudan and practically the whole of Egypt agriculture necessarily relies upon irrigation. This reliance is partial in the Sudan but total in Egypt and is based almost entirely upon the waters of the Nile. The use of the Nile for irrigation in Egypt may be traced back to the dawn of history, when seed was sown in the mud left after the annual flood waters had subsided. With the passage of time this became refined, with the division of the land by earth banks into a series of large basins in which the silt-laden waters were allowed to stand for about 40 days before being permitted to drain back to the river. Seed was still sown in the fertile surface layer of mud; the crops grew throughout the winter and were reaped in April and May, when the land remained fallow and parched until the next August flood.

This form of irrigation, while fitting the annual regime of the river, is at the mercy of the year-to-year fluctuations in the size of the flood (hence the 'seven fat and seven lean years' of the Old Testament), and as numbers grew it became imperative to adopt a more sophisticated, albeit far more expensive, irrigation system. Perennial irrigation, now adopted, is much more complicated. It has required great storage reservoirs both in Egypt and in the Sudan, a system of barrages (or large weirs) across the river to raise the level of the water to feed a comprehensive system of distributory canals, and an intricate drainage system to carry the used water to the sea.

Perennial irrigation began in Egypt in about 1820, when Mohammed Ali attempted to extend the area under summer crops (and especially cotton) by creating a system of canals in the Delta. This was unsuccessful, for the Nile was too low at this season, and in 1834 Mohammed Ali agreed to the building of a barrage across the Nile at its bifurcation at the head of the Delta. This was intended to pond back the river to raise the level of water upstream for the supplying of the canals. Engineering techniques were then inadequate and full success did not attend this ingenious scheme until long after Mohammed Ali's death. It was not until 1890, when British engineers completed a major work of reconstruction, that the Delta Barrage functioned properly and made possible the spread of perennial irrigation throughout the Delta.

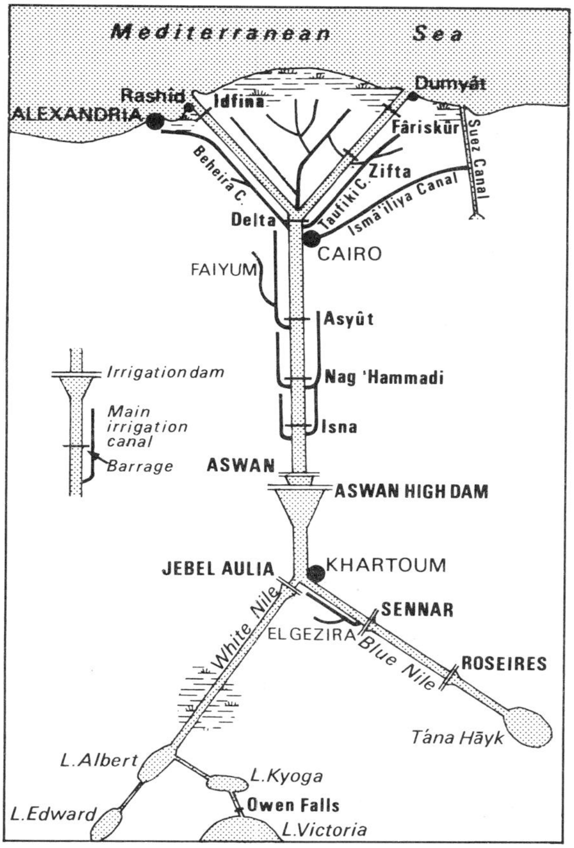

Figure 40 Nile Conservation works

The British occupied Egypt after 1882 and put in hand an ambitious irrigation programme (Figure 40). This led to the building of other barrages across the Nile and to the construction of two vast reservoirs at Aswan (completed in 1902 and enlarged in 1912 and 1934) and Jebel Aulia in the Sudan (1937), for it became clear that the only way to supply plentiful water during spring and early summer when the Nile was low would be by conserving surplus water from the previous flood. In this way the great annual fluctuation of the river could be reduced somewhat and early summer water guaranteed. Thus perennial irrigation relying upon large dams has been developed in Egypt only during this century. With this system there was always the danger of a year of very low flood which might not be able to fill the dams. This and a number of associated problems were solved by the construction of the vast Aswan High Dam during the 1960s. Now there is no flood season in Egypt, for the High Dam has capacity enough to allow a more even flow throughout the year. No longer is there a great summer flood (Figure 41).

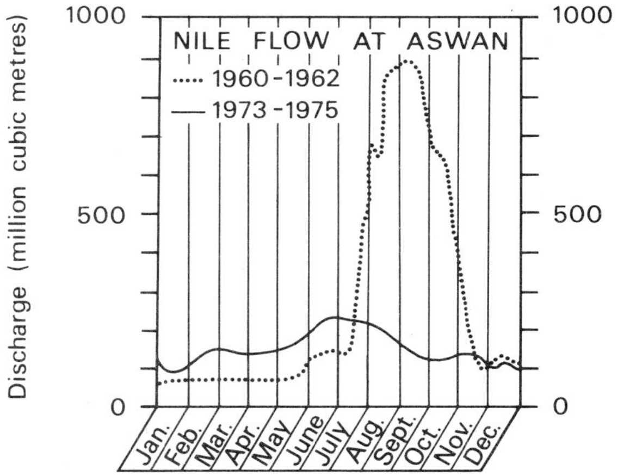

Figure 41 Nile flow from the Aswan High Dam

The Aswan High Dam

With the system based on seasonal storage dams there was the danger of the occasional high Nile which might burst the banks and flood large areas of densely populated land, and of the very low Nile when it might not be possible to fill the reservoirs completely. Further, every year a great amount of Nile flood water carrying rich silt from the Ethiopian highlands flowed out to the Mediterranean unused. It was to solve all these problems that one of the early acts of the revolutionary government of Egypt was to construct the Aswan High Dam. The site of the new dam is some 6 km above the old Aswan Dam. The new one is of colossal size: its capacity is 130 thousand million cubic metres (twenty-five times the capacity of the old Aswan Dam), retained by a dam wall over 3 km long. The lake formed behind the retaining wall (Lake Nasser) extends 145 km into the Sudan.

The enormous capacity of the Aswan High Dam allows it to fulfil several roles. The danger of slow accumulation of silt can be regarded with equanimity; a capacity of 30 thousand million cubic metres has been written-off to silting. The same amount is earmarked for flood protection, so that when the Nile flood is high and dangerous much of it can be held back in the reservoir. The dam capacity allotted to water for irrigation is 70 thousand million cubic metres. Here the dam differs from those already existing on the Nile: they are dams for seasonal storage, but the High Dam's capacity is so great that it provides over-year storage and surplus from good years no longer flows into the Mediterranean but is held back for use in low Nile years. The extra water available from the new dam is allowing up to 2 million more feddans of land to come under cultivation (one feddan is 1.038 acres or 0.42 ha).

The basin-irrigated lands in Upper Egypt have been converted to perennial irrigation, and an increase in rice cultivation in the Delta has been possible. Also, vast quantities of hydroelectric power are being generated; the total capacity of the power houses is 2100 megawatts, making this one of the biggest hydroelectric schemes in the world.

However, there is also a debit side. For example, the substantial flow of the river throughout the year has increased bank erosion. Formerly silt deposition and erosion were balanced, but now most of the silt accumulates at the bottom of the reservoir. Village brickmakers are becoming short of clay, and increasingly concrete bricks, tiles and prefabricated housing are being used. Soil fertility has also suffered with the silt loss and growing salinity as the water table has tended to rise. A greater use of artificial fertilizers and the installation of tile drainage has become necessary. The sardine fisheries off the Delta have dwindled, and there is erosion rather than deposition at the Delta – in a sense made up for by creating fisheries in Lake Nasser and reclaiming land around the lake's shore.

Irrigation in the Sudan

The Sudan also makes use of the Nile for irrigation, but on a much smaller scale. The total area under pump or gravity irrigation is about 2.4 million feddans, or approximately one million hectares. One reason for this is that the irrigable areas of fertile soil are much more limited and that summer rains are enjoyed; reliance upon the Nile is not absolute, therefore, and diminishes towards the south.

The principal area of perennial irrigation in the Sudan is the clay plain interfluve between the two Niles, south of Khartoum, called the Gezira. Here irrigated farming became possible in 1925 with the completion of the Sennar Dam on the Blue Nile, 200 km above Khartoum (Figure 40). Whereas the Jebel Aulia Dam in the Sudan on the White Nile reserves water for Egypt, the Sennar Dam was constructed for the Sudan's own use. It has a smaller capacity than the other two Nile dams (800 million cubic metres) but serves two purposes: it raises the river level to feed the Gezira canal system, and it stores water for late watering in the Gezira when the Nile is at its lowest.

The cultivation of the Gezira has been strikingly successful: the clay soils are less permeable than the silt-augmented soils of Egypt, and it is necessary to exercise a very close control over the amount of water released. Evaporation losses are high but are somewhat balanced by reduced loss from percolation.

Extension of the cultivated area in the Gezira proceeded slowly until the 1959 *Nile Waters Agreement* with Egypt was implemented, when further Nile works made more water available for the Sudan. The agreement was made between Egypt and the Sudan to replace one made in 1929 when Britain ruled or controlled most of the Nile Basin. The old agreement recognized Egypt's overwhelming reliance on the Nile by allotting her annually some 48 thousand million cubic metres, and only 4 thousand million to the Anglo-Egyptian Sudan. The new agreement became necessary with the attainment of independence by the Sudan – her increasing use of Nile water for expanding irrigation schemes having already reached the limit of her water allotment – and because the projected Aswan High Dam would conserve more water. Although the High Dam is located in Egypt it will permit extended irrigation in the Sudan, for whereas after the flood the Blue Nile waters had been entirely reserved for Egypt (while the Sudan relied on the Sennar Dam and certain pumps), now the Sudan can make use of the Blue Nile water in this season, Egypt making good this amount from the over-year storage in the new reservoir. Consequently the new agreement allotted Egypt 55.5 and the Sudan 18.5 thousand million cubic metres.

The Sudan has been enabled to proceed with further irrigation projects, which include a new storage dam at Roseires, to allow further perennial irrigation of the clay plains south of the present Gezira, and conversion to perennial irrigation of the basin areas in the Shendi and Dongola districts in the north. Irrigation from the Atbara is also being undertaken with the scheme at Kashm el Girba, where the peasants from Nubia whose homes were covered by the waters of the Aswan High Dam have been resettled. In addition to perennial irrigation, pump irrigation, is also practised on the Main and White Niles, both under government and private schemes (see Figure 50).

17 Egypt

Egypt, or the United Arab Republic, has a distinctive and un-African personality. Proud of its ancient heritage as one of the earliest cradles of civilization, conscious of its age-long ties with the Mediterranean world, nevertheless it keeps kindled the burning flame of the desert and in more recent years has come to regard itself as a leader in the Arab world.

Most of Egypt is desert. With the exception of a few oases in the Western desert the habitable part of Egypt is restricted to the Nile valley and delta – a mere 35,500 km^2 out of a total of 1,002,000 km^2. Habitable Egypt is, in fact, one 1100 km-long oasis made up of the triangular delta north of Cairo and the narrow ribbon of the Nile valley, rarely more than 16 km wide. Throughout, the contrast between the desert and the sown is abrupt and dramatic. In this continuous oasis live 97 per cent of Egypt's 50 million people. The basis of the modern state was laid by Mohammed Ali (1815–49), an Albanian who seized power after the expulsion of Napoleon, vigorously restored the country's economy and while still recognizing the suzerainty of Turkey established the dynasty that ended only with the expulsion of King Farouk and his son in 1952 and 1953.

Britain's communications with India and the Far East made use of Egypt even before the cutting of the Suez Canal. A river boat was used from the Mediterranean to Cairo, and then a desert caravan to the Red Sea, whence steamships completed the journey. Britain's purchase of the bankrupt Khedive's shares in the Suez Canal in 1874 made the link firmer, and in 1882 a revolt and massacre of Europeans at Alexandria led to Britain landing an army, effectively becoming the protecting power and doing much to restore the country's economy. The Protectorate was ended in 1922 when the Sultan of Egypt became hereditary ruler. Ineptitude and intrigue by a corrupt ruling class were ended in 1952 when a group of young army officers under General Neguib and Colonel Nasser seized power and, in 1953, declared a republic.

GEOGRAPHICAL REGIONS

An examination of the geography of Egypt is helped by the country's falling conveniently into four distinct physical divisions: the Western desert, the Eastern desert, the Sinai Peninsula and the Nile valley and delta.

The Western desert comprises nearly three-quarters of the republic. It forms the north-east corner of the great Libyan desert and stretches south from the Mediterranean to the Sudan border and from the Nile valley west to the borders of Libya. The greatest altitude is attained in the extreme south-west, where the Gilf Kebir plateau surpasses 1000 m and the outcropping Archaean rocks of Gebel 'Uweinat reach over 2000 m. From Gilf Kebir the sandstone tableland slopes gently north to depressions, probably due to aeolian action, in which lie the Kharga and Dakhla oases. On their northern side a marked escarpment indicates the southern edge of the great limestone plateau where, in more northerly depressions, lie the oases of Farafra and Bahariya and, nearer the Nile, the large oasis of El Faiyum

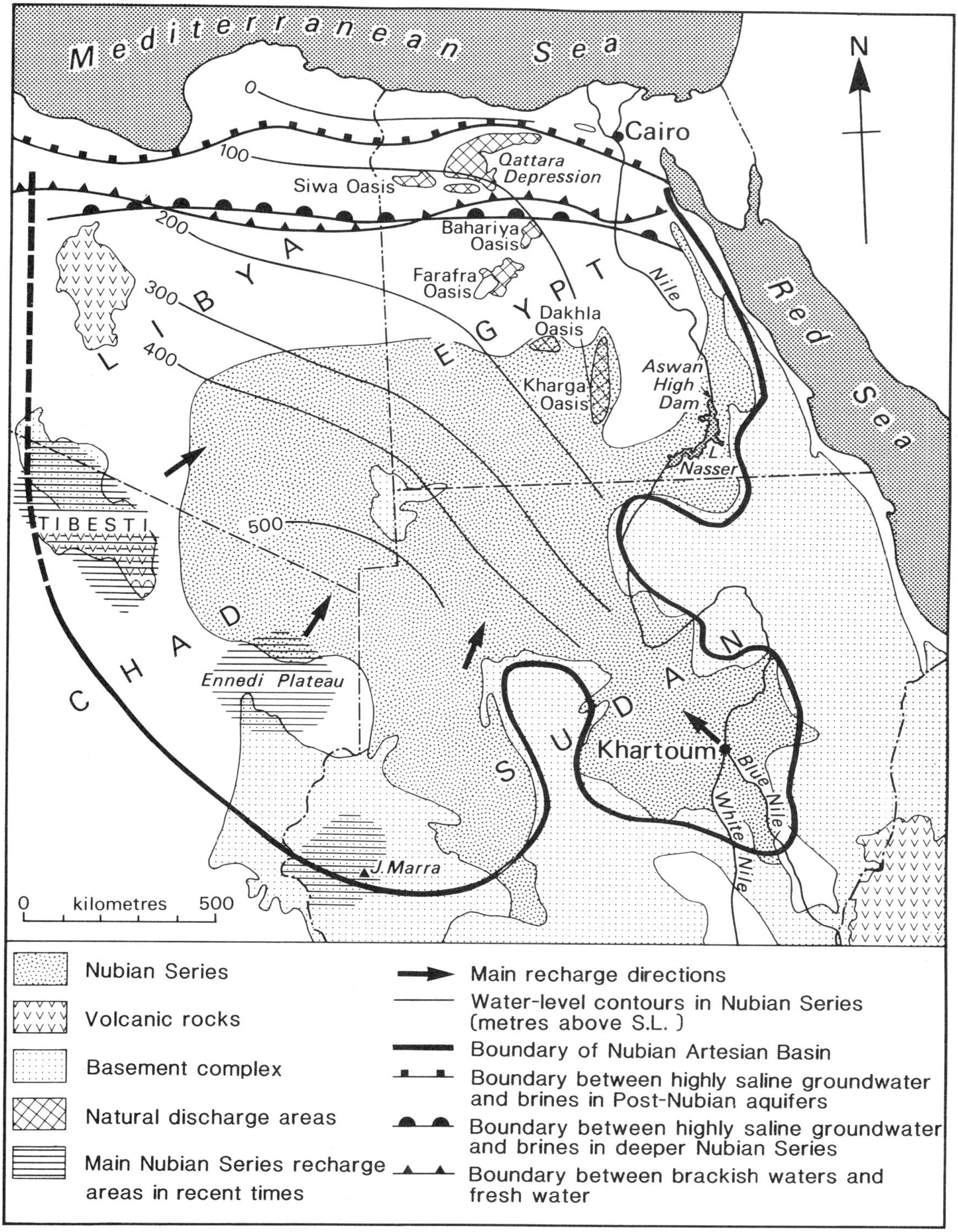

Figure 42 North-east Africa: water resources

which is below sea-level and irrigated from the Nile.

Nearer the Mediterranean, and in still younger limestones, lie the depressions of Siwa and Qattara. The Qattara is the largest depression, with a floor over 130 m below sea-level; it contains salt lakes and marshes. Oil has been discovered here and near El Alamein. The surface of the desert is stony or sandy in character, and fretted into scarps, ridges and mesas. The absence of drainage lines is notable, as is the great area of sand dunes forming the Great Sand Sea which extends from Siwa oasis to Gilf Kebir.

The gentle northward descent of the strata from the Ennedi–Tibesti divide and the wide mass of pervious rock resting on the impervious Basement series are conducive to the provision of underground water supplies. Aquifers in the sedimentary rocks are tapped by wells in the depressions and cultivation becomes possible (Figure 42).

Except in these favoured oasis areas and in a few small settlements along the Mediterranean coast, the wide sandy plains and occasional rocky outcrops are repellent to all but a few of Egypt's nomads, the majority of whom prefer to move with flocks and herds in the Eastern desert. The oasis communities are mainly self-sufficient, growing vegetables and cereals and usually selling dates (Siwa also sells olive oil) in exchange for manufactured goods. Experiments in extending the cultivable area are taking place near Kharga and Dakhla oases where artesian supplies are being tapped. These waters are being used to reclaim large areas of desert land in what is termed the New Valley project.

The Eastern desert extends from the Nile valley eastwards to the Gulf of Suez and the Red Sea. It consists essentially of an easterly chain of rugged mountains – the Red Sea highlands – flanked on the north-east and west by considerably dissected limestone and sandstone plateaux. This region of much scarred upland averages 600 m but includes some peaks over 2000 m high. Narrow and deep wadis trending both east to the Red Sea and west to the Nile carve the upland into detached blocks. The fractured and uptilted Crystalline Basement rocks in the northern third are overlain with sedimentary sandstones and limestones, but to the south Archaean rocks, mainly granites, are widely exposed in a wilderness of sharp peaked ranges. Here Gebel Shayeb attains 2300 m. The drainage from these mountains in more pluvial periods accounts for the complexity of wadis, emphasizing the great contrast with the easily traversed plateau land west of the Nile.

Water resources, although sparse, are more plentiful than in the Western desert, although structural dislocations prevent extensive artesian supplies. The greater elevation causes a small rainfall, and water can be found in sheltered hollows, beneath dry stream beds and from occasional springs. Nomadic shepherds roam these uplands and there are no permanent settlements. Settlement is confined to villages along the Red Sea coast and mining camps. Phosphates are worked near Safaga and Quseir, iron-ore near Aswan, and oil is obtained from wells in the sedimentary rocks at Ras Gharib and Hurghada.

The Sinai Peninsula is separated from Egypt proper by the isthmus of Suez. It is an irregular plateau, lofty in the south where the core of the peninsula is formed by a complex of old crystalline rocks, a continuation of the Red Sea hills. The northern two-thirds of the peninsula is a severely dissected limestone plateau. The gravel-covered central part known as the Wilderness of Tih ('the Wandering') averages 1000 m; its highest part in the south, the Egma plateau, attains 1600 m. The Sinai Mountains of the south, a mass of sharp peaks, gorges and ravines, are the highest in Egypt and culminate in Gebel Catherina (2637 m). They are composed of metamorphic and igneous rocks, predominantly red in colour, from which the Red Sea takes its name. A series of fault scarps on the south-west drop down to the Gulf of Suez and the coastal plain is very limited. To the south-east bold fault faces overlook the Gulf of Aqaba. To the north, however, the country is more open and drains by shallow wadis to a dune-covered plain and the Mediterranean.

Rainfall is scanty – about 150 mm a year in the north but less than 75 mm in the south – and this, coupled with inaccessibility, explains why the sparse population remains almost entirely in the north. The wadis here are broad, and pockets of cultivation surround wells and springs such as at el Arish and Nekhl, for the plateau is waterless for most of the year. Elsewhere nomadism prevails. A number of small oilfields are exploited at Sudr, Asl, Wadi Feirain and Bala'eem. Much has yet to be learned of the mineral resources of the peninsula, for both exploration and development are retarded by inaccessibility.

The Nile valley and delta. From the Sudanese frontier north to Cairo the Nile flows in a relatively flat-bottomed groove, sinuous in outline. It is cut deeply into the Nubian sandstone as far as the crystalline outcrop at Aswan; from near Isna the valley broadens between cliffs of white limestone. At Cairo the valley opens into the delta of the Nile, with the land surface sloping gently to the sea and falling some 16 m from Cairo in a very gentle gradient of 1 in 10,000.

The delta comprises an infilled gulf of the Pleistocene Mediterranean and is composed of silt brought mainly from the Ethiopian highlands. The average thickness of the silt is 20 m. In the north along the coast are shallow brackish lagoons and salt marshes: Lakes Mariut, Edku, Burullus and Menzaleh. Low sand belts separate the last three from the sea, but limestone ridges intervene between Lake Mariut and the Mediterranean and the lake level is kept at 3 m below sea-level by pumping. This allows a steeper gradient for the drainage channels carrying the used irrigation water seawards. This belt of 'Barari' or barren land is so near sea-level that drainage by free flow is impracticable, and considerable washing and pumping operations are necessary to reclaim it to agricultural land. In the first century AD, Strabo recorded the Nile as having seven delta distributaries; today these have become controlled and consolidated into two, known as the Rashid and Dumyat Branches from the small ports at their mouths.

Some 97 per cent of Egypt's population is located in the Nile valley and delta. From the earliest times this was the home of man, where the reliable flooding and automatic renewal of fertility contrasted with the enclosing desert. Today this narrow trench of fertility and the delta plain contain some of the most densely settled agricultural land in the world, with population densities averaging 1100 per km^2. It is not easy for those living under the highly artificial conditions of an industrial society removed from the land fully to comprehend what these numbers mean in terms of living conditions. Although there is a growing import of basic food grains, this is mostly required by the urban population; most fellaheen live substantially upon their own produce. With land scarce and too many desiring to farm it, land prices and rents (despite government attempts at control) are high; and with many labourers available, wages are low. The result is rural poverty, and the tendency for large numbers to migrate to major towns or seek work in other, richer, Arab states.

In Upper Egypt (i.e. south of Cairo) there are few towns other than the provincial capitals with their market and administrative functions, but within the delta are to be found nearly all the major towns and cities, the bulk of the country's industry and two-thirds of the total population. Alexandria, lying west of the mouth of the Rashid Branch (and thus avoiding silting up, for the longshore drift is from west to east), is the republic's principal port and formerly, owing to its more moderate summer temperature, was the summer seat of the administration. The only other large port, concerned mainly with canal transit trade, is Port Said at the Mediterranean end of the Suez Canal. The northern and eastern parts of the delta are marshy wastes being reclaimed slowly so that the narrow Canal Zone is still separated from the delta proper. Only limited areas of it are irrigated, for example around Ismailia, for fresh water is scarce and still largely depends upon the Ismailia or Sweetwater canal which carries water from the Nile to this sterile isthmus. This canal was enlarged in the 1980s to permit more land reclamation around Ismailia.

THE ECONOMY

The strictly limited amount of farmland in Egypt and the increasing millions who struggle to live off it are potent in the shaping of both social and economic conditions. Egypt is still essentially an agricultural country with nearly 50 per cent of its labour force engaged in farming; but the great strides taken in industrialization since the Second World War owe much to the spur of population pressure, as does the growing import of food grains and the small but growing export of manufactured goods.

The poverty of the mass of the fellahin is worsened by ill-health, generally the result of insanitary living conditions. Rural conditions have substantially improved since the revolution; for example, pure drinking water is now piped to all villages, and drinking from, and washing in, the water of the nearest canal or drain is no longer necessary. Water-borne diseases are a major scourge of the rural population, the two worst being the worm diseases bilharzia and ankylostoma (hookworm). Over 50 per cent of the rural population suffers from these debilitating diseases, which engender apathy and sap the vitality. Malaria, eye diseases and tuberculosis are also prevalent. Greater provision of health centres and the use of insecticides are slowly bringing improvements.

Egypt first moved along the path of economic planning with its Land Reform Act of 1952, extended in 1961 and 1969. The maldistribution of land ownership had for long created social unrest. Until 1952 two-thirds of the farmland was owned by 6 per cent of landowners, whereas 2 million peasants owned only 13 per cent in plots of less than a feddan (about one acre or 0.4 ha) each, and another 2 million were landless. The large estates were usually let and sublet in smaller plots on a share-cropping basis, and many of the big landowners were absentees living, often ostentatiously, in Cairo or Alexandria. When the revolutionary government came into power in 1952 it passed a Land Reform Act limiting family holdings to a maximum of 300 feddans. The surplus was expropriated and allotted in small plots to landless peasantry.

In 1961 and 1969 maximum holdings were further reduced to 100 and then 50 feddans. The practice of the landowners or their agents in directing and marketing the farming has been taken over by village cooperatives, and this has facilitated the spread of a triennial rotation. Generally the new holdings were given in three small plots, one in each of three large blocks of land. Each block is sown with one crop. This allows of collective treatment, ensures the rotation, simplifies watering, pest control and fertilizer application. Farmers carry out their cultivation on their own plots within the large fields. Higher yields are being secured under this system.

That such a large population can live on so small an area is due principally to the richness of the alluvial soils (now heavily supplemented with artificial fertilizers), the sunny climate, the reliable water supply derived from one of the world's most elaborate and efficient irrigation systems, and the unremitting toil of a population skilled at gardening rather than farming.

Agriculture

Agriculture supplies, either directly or processed, about 20 per cent of all exports by value and accounts for 35 per cent of the GDP. Agriculture's share of exports has diminished in recent years owing to oil exports taking an increasing share. Some 45 per cent of the country's labour force is employed in agriculture. In recent years productivity has lagged behind the population increase (2 per cent against 2.5 per cent) and food imports have increased. It is expected that yields will rise with the installation of tile drainage, now proceeding. From the irrigation system already outlined, Nile water is now conserved and so distributed that Egypt's farmland receives adequate water during the early summer months when the Nile is at its lowest and the land otherwise would be parched. Thanks to the Aswan High Dam the flow of the Nile in Egypt is now so controlled that it is much more regular throughout the year; perennial irrigation now covers the whole agricultural area. The provision of summer water enables cotton to be grown, and this has been Egypt's foremost export crop over the last 100 years.

Diversification of agricultural exports (cotton, onions, rice, citrus fruits) and growing domestic use had in 1982 reduced cotton's share of the export market (by value) to 25 per cent, whereas a decade earlier it was 80 per cent. Egypt's competitive advantages in the world market arise from her highly suitable soil and a sunny climate where the amount of water can be closely controlled. The average yield of cotton in Egypt is about 960 kg per hectare, against a world average yield of 460 kg/ha. Cotton growing demands a considerable labour supply, but in Egypt labour skilled in cotton growing and tending is plentiful and cheap. World prices of cotton are higher than those for grain crops and cotton is therefore a far more remunerative and 'safe' crop to grow. Egypt provides the bulk of the world's long staple cotton, but in recent years has been using more than half the production in her own textile mills. The fine, strong silky cotton has special uses: examples are typewriter ribbons, high-quality dress and shirt materials, book-binding materials and windproof clothing.

The other principal crops are maize (a summer crop mainly grown in Lower Egypt), wheat, bersim, rice (a summer crop of the central part of the delta), barley, lentils, beans and – in Upper Egypt – sugar cane. The rice acreage used to vary from year to year according to the size of the Nile flood; but with the regular flow from the Aswan High Dam rather more than a million feddans (420 thousand hectares) is now under rice each year. The yields of crops in Egypt are among the highest in the world and continue to improve. Dates are grown throughout the Nile valley, and in recent years grape and citrus growing in the delta has been encouraged.

The pressure on the land for human food production reduces fodder crops, and pastoralism plays a minor part. The apparently high cattle and water-buffalo population is kept principally for draught purposes; meat production is low. The animals, usually in poor condition, are kept on bersim, chopped straw and maize fodder. Lean sheep and goats are found in most villages and the keeping of poultry is widespread.

The contribution of fish to the Egyptian diet is small. There is some fishing in the delta lakes and Lake Moeris, but the sardine fisheries off the Nile delta have dwindled, probably because of the reduced silt load from the Aswan High Dam. To replace them substantial fisheries are being developed at Lake Nasser.

Minerals and energy

Mineral resources are still comparatively little exploited owing to an incomplete survey and problems of inaccessibility. Crude oil, phosphates, iron-ore, natron (natural soda) and salt are the principal minerals worked (Table 14). Egypt possesses no coal (coke is imported for the steel works), and this has helped to retard industrial development.

In recent years oil production has increased, and this is now the country's main fuel. Egypt's resources of crude oil appear to be modest, but exploration by major oil companies is actively under way. Considerable discoveries have been made during the last decade, and Egypt's tiny oil production of 7 million tonnes in 1965 has been increased sixfold – one-third of this provides a valuable export. Some 90 per cent of oil production comes from wells along the Sinai coast and offshore on the Gulf of Suez.

Table 14 *Egypt: industrial and mineral production*

	Production (000 tonnes)			
	1960	1970	1980	1984
Extractive industries				
Crude oil	3,319	18,945	30,000	43,300*
Phosphate	566	716	679	754
Iron-ore	239	451	1,776	2,236
Manufactures				
Cotton yarn	102	164	236	243
Cotton fabric	64	110	633†	583†
Refined sugar	338	547	616	746*
Alcohol (thousand litres)	17	32	26	27*
Superphosphate	188	411	488	588*
Nitrate of lime	257	285	2,584	4,038
Cement	1,903	3,684	3,038	3,798*
Paper and cardboard	49	125	191	153
Tyres and tubes (thousands)	485	1,566	2,344	2,882
Cotton-seed oil	104	118	196	222

Notes: *1983; †Million metres
Source: Federation of Egyptian Industries.

Lesser oil fields have been discovered near El Alamein and near the Libyan border in the Western desert. A promising gas field under Aboukir Bay, east of Alexandria, is now being developed. Oil and gas account for 40 per cent of Egypt's energy supplies, almost all of the remaining 60 per cent being hydroelectric power from the Aswan High Dam. Expanding industry and a rural electrification programme are increasing demand so rapidly that nuclear power plants are being planned to be in operation by the year 2000.

Phosphate rock is mined along the north-east of the Red Sea, but principally at Quseir. Some 2 million tonnes of iron-ore is now mined from the haematite deposits (*c*. 50 per cent iron) just east of Aswan. This ore supplies the iron and steel works established at Helwan near Cairo.

MANUFACTURING INDUSTRY

It is not generally realized that Egypt is the most industrialized country in Africa after the Republic of South Africa. Most industrial development has occurred within the last 30 years, although its beginnings go back to 1930 when tariffs were first imposed on manufactured imports. The spur of population pressure, the need to diversify the economy and so satisfy aspirations of nationalism, have contributed to these developments (see Table 14).

One reason for the slow expansion of manufacturing industry was the lack of capital, for it was far more profitable to invest money in land where a high return was assured. Other reasons were the small home market, for the mass of the people are too poor to satisfy more than minimal requirements of manufactured goods; the dearth of technical and managerial skills; and generally high-cost production by small units, whereby economies of scale did not accrue and better-quality imported goods maintained their market.

By 1952, when the revolution took place, manufacturing industry contributed no more than 10 per cent of the national income. The revolutionary government invested public money in utilities such as roads, railways and power supplies, upon which any growth of industry relies. After the seizure of the Suez Canal (1956) the government gradually took more and more industry into its grasp by seizing foreign business, banks and insurance, and then nationalizing or partly nationalizing first the large and then the smaller Egyptian industrial concerns. These measures, designed to give the government greater control over industry and investment and to reduce the power of wealthy industrialists, actually proved harmful to the economy since they included the confiscation of property and seizure of assets of many of Egypt's growing commercial middle class, which numbers Syrians, Italians, Greeks, Lebanese, etc., who provide the businessmen, managers and entrepreneurs so urgently needed if industrial expansion is to go on.

The need for a comprehensive development plan for the whole economy was clear, and the first Five Year Plan was eventually announced in 1960. Although there was some expansion in textile, cement and artificial fertilizer production, the plan did not meet its targets mainly because of poor coordination and the shortage of foreign exchange. A second plan was extended to 7 years and then abandoned: Egypt was at war with Israel, who occupied Sinai and closed the Suez Canal.

Thus, the 1960s saw a swing of government policy towards autarky and widespread nationalization, with the aim of enlarging the public sector of the economy and achieving greater control of development measures – to ensure the reinvestment of profits, to increase self-sufficiency by expanding Egyptian industry, and to continue to reduce the power of wealthy landowners and industrialists.

The second Ten Year Plan was announced by President Sadat in 1973. The previous plan had shown that import-substitute industrialization soon expended itself by increasing the burden on balance of payments instead of reducing it. Policies of autarky were dropped, and the new president swung Egypt from the Eastern bloc once more to the Western and linked the nationalized economy once more with capitalism. Foreign companies and capital were welcomed and wooed by tax and fiscal concessions, and private enterprise was encouraged. Nevertheless the legacy of the earlier plan is that the public sector still holds three-quarters of industrial establishments and blights Egyptian industry by bureaucracy, poor management, high manning levels, poor productivity and high cost production.

Textiles, which are by far the largest industry of Egypt, include the spinning, weaving, dying and printing of cottons, wool, silk and rayon. A wide variety of fabrics, knitwear and furnishings is produced; indeed, the entire home demand is now satisfied, and exports of yarn and fabrics are made to Sudan and other Arab states. Much of the output comes from large, modern factories situated in the two textile towns of the delta, Mehalla el Kubra and Kafr el Diawal. Other industries, based upon local agriculture, include sugar refining, oilseed crushing, vegetable preserving and the manufacture of boot, shoe and leather goods, alcohol, soaps, paints and varnishes. Egypt now manufactures a wide range of consumer goods, from lorries and cars to razor blades. The chemical industry has expanded with the growth of oil refining and petrochemicals – pharmaceuticals, cosmetics, medical supplies and fertilizers are produced. The Helwan iron and steel plant, just south of Cairo, leads the metallurgical industry: recently enlarged, it now has has an annual capacity of 1,500,000 tonnes of iron and steel. A further state plant is being constructed at El Dikheik, near Alexandria. Aluminium (from imported bauxite) is produced at Nag Hammadi in Upper Egypt. There are oil refineries at Suez and Alexandria, and the large cement works there now have a considerable export trade.

There is a high concentration of industry upon the two main cities, Cairo and Alexandria. These two centres and adjacent areas include nearly three-quarters of the total number of industrial establishments, employing 70 per cent of the industrial labour force. The agglomeration of industry in and around these cities reflects the disproportionate pull of the few locations in under-developed countries where public utilities such as electricity, gas, pure water and telephones are available and where there is a provision of labour and an effective market. On social and political grounds attempts are now being made to disperse some new industrial growth throughout the Nile delta. There is very little industrial development in Upper Egypt.

POPULATION AND SETTLEMENT

Egypt has a major population problem that has deep repercussions upon her economy. The population in 1986 was over 50 million and is increasing by a million annually. The annual rate of increase to Egyptian population has speeded up since the Second World War owing to a medical revolution which particularly reduces infant mortality and the crude death rate. Birth rates have remained high, and it was not until the beginning of the decade of the 1980s that a modest fall began to be recorded. The rate of population increase is 2.5 per cent, which could double the population in 25 years. In fact the population did double in the last 30 years, but the habitable area has altered very little and population pressure has become intense. Some 65 per cent of the population is in Lower Egypt (delta) and the Canal Zone, but some of the highest densities are in Upper Egypt where densities of more than 1000 per km^2 are common. As in other northern African states, recent demographic trends are expressed in a relatively young population: two-thirds of Egypt's peoples are under thirty.

Most Egyptian's live in hamlets and villages, but the proportion of town dwellers is increasing and now 45 per cent live in towns of over 25,000 inhabitants. The two major cities of Cairo and Alexandria overshadow all others and continue to grow at a faster rate. **Greater Cairo** has shown phenomenal growth in recent years, and with a population of around 10 million is the largest city in the Islamic World and its intellectual and cultural centre. **Alexandria**, the chief port, with its suburbs approaches 3 million. Cairo was founded in AD 960, located on high ground near the 200 m escarpment of the Mokattam hills. The Nile, then broader and uncontrolled, flowed farther east than now and here had islands that facilitated a crossing. With its famous Citadel, built in AD 1176 by Saladin, the city occupied a position ideal as a market and commanded both valley and delta. Modern Cairo really dates from Ismail's rule (1863–79). Railways were built, the Suez Canal constructed and a new Cairo laid out beside the Nile at the foot of the old. Fringing marshlands were reclaimed, wide avenues laid out and government offices moved to new buildings from the Citadel. This century has seen a northward and westward expansion, with satellite towns developing west of the river and connected by bridges to the main city. Giza is now a busy industrial suburb with over a million population. The dormitory towns of Helioplis, Ma'adi and Helwan are linked by electric railway. The city is the administrative, business and now industrial centre of Egypt. In its wide and busy main streets with their department stores and stylish shops, European dress mingles with the gown and turban of the East; but away from the tall ferro-concrete hotels, shops, offices and apartment houses, thousands live in tortuous alleys of old mud-brick houses.

Rural–urban migration flows are major factors in the tremendous growth of Cairo during recent decades, a rate of growth that has outstripped the provision of utilities and services: housing, traffic, sewers, water, electricity, telephones all break down frequently and the collapse of the city has seemed imminent. A new metropolitan railway system with an underground section is under construction. This is expected to reduce the congestion and traffic jams that cause some 30 million work hours to be lost each year. Also plans are at last being implemented to reduce the population influx into the Cairo metropolitan region

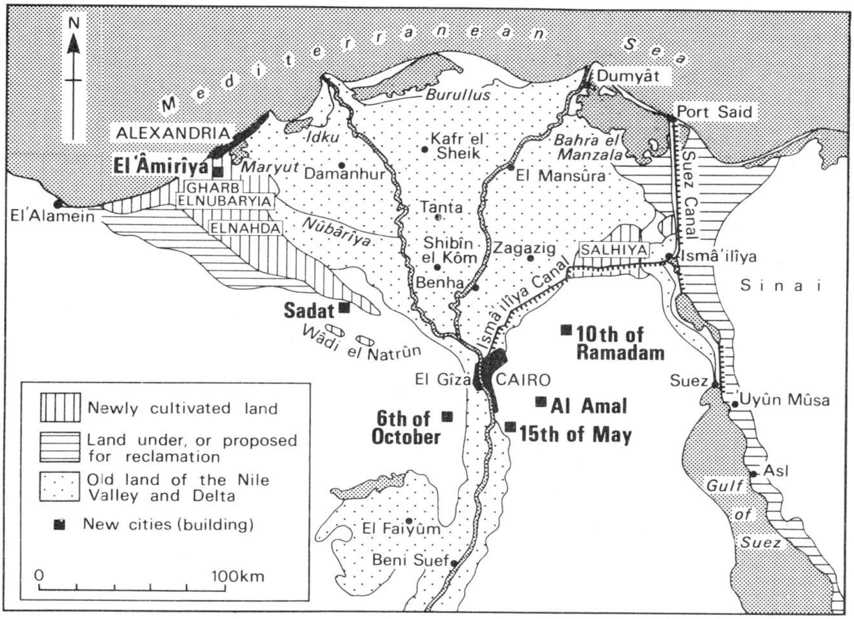

Figure 43 The Nile delta: land reclamation and new towns

and to channel it into a system of newly built satellite cities, mainly 30–50 km from Cairo and most holding one-half to one million inhabitants (see Figure 43). This may prove beneficial, but unless several hundred thousand jobs can be provided in the new cities the workers will merely commute to work in Cairo, worsening the congestion and disrupting their social life.

Alexandria is less of a market centre, having its hinterland limited by the brackish Lake Maryut; but it is Egypt's foremost port, handling 80 per cent of the total trade. The city was founded in 332 BC by Alexander the Great, mainly as a naval base, being clear of the Nile silt and protected by the Pharos island. The gradual silting of a mole across to the island has created an isthmus half a mile wide, now partly occupied by the modern city. This isthmus divides eastern and western harbours, the main port lying on the west side. Cotton ginning, rice milling and cement manufacture are important activities connected with the export trade. There is an oil refinery, textile factories, and cigarettes are manufactured from imported tobacco.

MODERN DEVELOPMENTS

Egypt's overriding problem – that of population pressure upon limited resources – has shaped social and economic policy and has had repercussions upon political affairs. Egypt is a desert state with limited agricultural land and great limitation on the expansion of that land. Reclamation, particularly of the marshy area to the north of the delta, has proceeded unevenly throughout this century. The revolutionary government selected suitable land for reclamation on the desert edges beside the delta, but all such work was restricted by lack of a guaranteed water supply. However, this problem was eased when the waters of the Aswan High Dam became available from 1971.

Areas planned for land reclamation and resettlement are shown in Figure 44. The most interesting are the desert reclamation schemes of Tahrir Province (Nubariya) and the New Valley. Tahrir (Liberation) Province is an area of desert adjacent to the delta, midway between Cairo and Alexandria. Taming this desert area and providing it with the Nile and

Plate 19 Improved piped water supplies in an Egyptian village

subsoil water has proved slow and expensive. The poverty of the soil slowed down developments, and targets have not been met. Nevertheless, in places high-value crops such as grapes, mangos, citrus fruits, plums and olives are proving successful, and as the land becomes productive carefully planned new settlements are established. It is probable that the resettled population so far numbers no more than 50,000.

The New Valley scheme is associated with the discontinuous oasis depressions in the Western desert, well away from the Nile valley. Within and around them are large expanses of level land having soils amenable to cultivation. Good water of artesian character has been discovered in the Nubian sandstone at a depth of 1000 m, and much work has been done to assess the water available, its source and rate of natural replacement. Successful pilot schemes were launched in Kharga and Dakhla oases, and there have followed 20 years of drilling, soil sampling and crop experimenting. The task is enormous, involving the establishment of planned irrigation and drainage systems, the building of roads and villages and devising cropping schemes to enrich the sandy soils. Plans are for irrigation units of 1000 feddans (420 ha), each 150–200 feddans being supplied from one well. Each

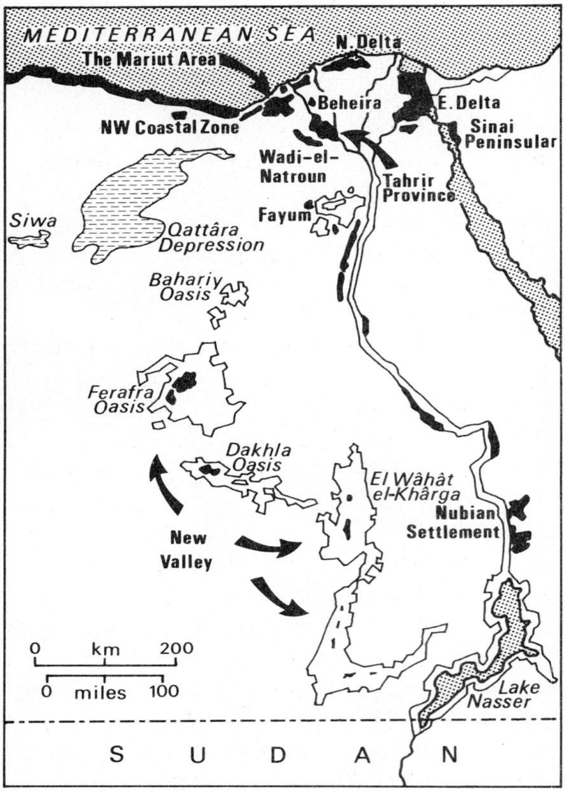

Figure 44 Egypt: Planned reclamation works

family is allotted about 5 feddans (2 ha) of land. It is proving economically expensive and progress is slow. In 20 years the original population of 50,000 has doubled.

The total 'new' land reclaimed for farming during the past 20 years is about 500,000 feddans. With the 'old' land the total area of farmland is now 6.3 million feddans. The rate of increase is below that of the population, and the man/land ratio has continued to diminish: it was 0.25 feddans in 1955 and 0.15 feddans in 1981. Theoretically each square kilometre of farmland now needs to support 1370 people, an impossible task. Thus imports of foodstuff have been necessary, and by 1980 these had increased to 50 per cent of Egypt's requirements. The future is sombre for, at present rates, by the year 2000 food production will total 11 million tonnes but the enlarged population will require 53 million tonnes. This situation is occurring because the rate of population increase exceeds that of agricultural production and because 45 per cent of that population is now urban. The improving standards of living in recent years are also reflected in a greater consumption of food per head. Exports (such as cotton, crude oil and certain manufactures) help to pay for food imports, but this may become more and more difficult if increase in demand continues at the current rate.

The major constraint on the productivity of Egyptian agriculture is recognized to be land, and planning in recent years has allotted 30 per cent of agricultural investment to land reclamation. Over the last 24 years 1.1 million reclaimed feddans have come into production, but it is now accepted that only one-third of it has proved profitable, another third is barely suitable and the final third quite unsuitable for cultivation. Meanwhile each year some 50,000 feddans of farmland are being lost to urban encroachment. Plans to reclaim as much as 2.8 million feddans by the year 2000 are now being re-appraised, and the World Bank urges improvement of the 'old' lands and has made substantial grants to install tile drains to overcome excessive use of High Dam water.

The war with Israel hindered Egypt's economic development, and the peace she finally made caused the rich Arab oil nations to cut off their financial assistance. However, new sources of finance and foreign currency came to her aid. With peace tourism returned to Egypt, and in 1985 contributed £300 million of foreign currency. The Suez Canal, deepened and widened, brought in £550 million in 1985. The modest but growing surplus of crude oil exports (21 million tonnes out of 44 million tonnes) and royalties on oil pumped from Suez to Alexandria in the SUMED pipeline contributed £1450 million to the economy in 1985.

Finally, between 2 and 3 million Egyptians (mainly professional and skilled workers) work abroad, mainly in other Arab states.

Plate 20 Land reclamation for irrigation in Egypt

Their remittances home in 1984 contributed a record £1700 million. These incomes and aid from the richer Arab states (resumed in 1984) have helped reverse external debt balances and give hope of success to current plans.

The greatest obstacle to economic growth in Egypt is the high rate of population growth set against its very limited and not easily enlarged habitable area. It is this serious and worsening demographic situation that has motivated and shaped economic policies over the past 30 years. These policies have sought to make agriculture more productive and currently spend enormously to transform desert and marsh into farmland. They have spurred on and expanded industry, to increase national income and to provide jobs for the tide of surplus labour leaving the land. They have made capital from resources such as oil and services such as the Suez Canal and SUMED pipeline; but until the last few years almost nothing was done to reduce the rate of increase to the population. Economic development in Egypt that brings real advances in the standard of living depends upon a continuing reduction in human fertility.

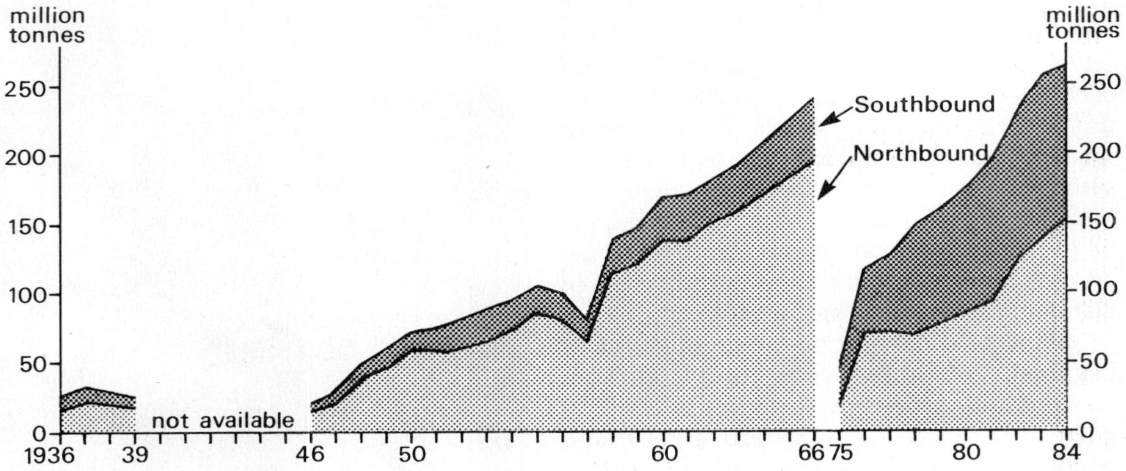

Figure 45 Suez Canal: goods tonnage

THE SUEZ CANAL

The canal breaches the isthmus between the Mediterranean and the Red Sea, and by shortening sea routes between Europe and the East has become the world's most important sea canal. Basically it is a ditch excavated in sandy soil, which makes use of the depressions of Lake Timsah and the Bitter Lakes. It was completed in 1869, is 160 km long and is at sea-level throughout.

When it was first opened, at certain points the depth of channel was only 6 m. A succession of improvement schemes has both deepened and widened the canal over the years, the present depth being 20 m.

The canal was owned and operated by an international company (in which the British Government was an important shareholder), and by a Convention of 1888 it should be open to vessels of all nations and free from blockade. The company's concession was due to expire in 1968, but Egypt seized and nationalized the canal in 1956 and its revenues are now an important element in the Egyptian economy.

Figure 45 shows a remarkable increase in traffic through the canal since 1945. There has been an increase in the number of vessels and in their size. Numbers of vessels using the canal and their cargo tonnage have almost quadrupled since 1950. Three-fifths of the 22,000 vessels travel northwards and among their cargoes they carry 85 million tonnes of oil. Only the very largest oil tankers cannot negotiate the canal, and they either take the long route around the Cape to Europe and the USA, or discharge their oil near Suez for it to be pumped through the SUMED pipeline to Alexandria, from where other tankers carry it to its final destination. The canal shortens the sailing distance to India from the United Kingdom by 7000 km; to Kuwait by 7680 km; to Singapore by 5760 km; and to Melbourne by 1440 km.

Port Said (with ***Port Fuad*** on the eastern side) has become the third largest town in Egypt. Most of its business is now with vessels in transit through the canal. Oil-bunkering services are available and ships are repaired. At the southern end, **Suez** and **Port Tewfig** have also grown: there are, for example, two oil refineries and fertilizer factories. These towns, with **Ismailia** on Lake Timsah, have been rebuilt and expanded following the peace with Israel.

18
Sudan

Sudan is the largest country in Africa, having an area of 2,505,805 km^2. The population was estimated in 1983 to be 20 million. Of these, nearly 70 per cent are Moslem Arabs and Nubians living in the north; the remainder in the south are Nilotic and Negro peoples. This draws attention to a most significant factor in the geography of the Sudan, its position and size, encompassing a number of climate and vegetation belts and including peoples of very different ways of life, language and religion. The republic extends south from the heart of the Sahara on the Egyptian border to the foothills of the East African highlands.

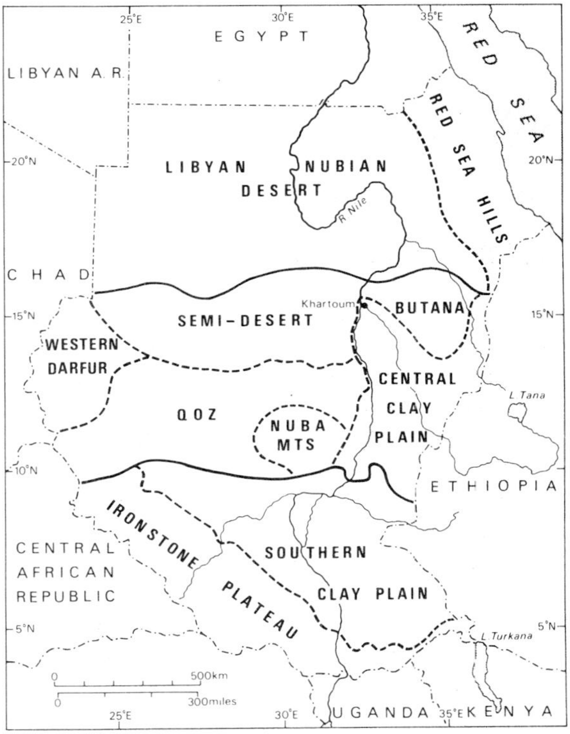

Figure 46 Sudan: geographical regions

GEOGRAPHICAL REGIONS

Northern Sudan

This is a part of the Sahara, an extension of the Libyan desert, and stretches from the boundary with Egypt (a straight line across the sand waste at about 22°N) to where steppe vegetation appears with the light summer rainfall at about latitude 16°N. Three sub-divisions are the desert, the Nile valley and the Red Sea hills.

West of the Nile the land surface consists of sandy or gravelly plains with occasionally well-dissected hills of the Nubian sandstone. Towards the north-west are areas of sand dunes, outliers of the Great Sand Sea of Egypt's Libyan desert. A few water-courses debouch to the river from the outcrops of the Archaean Basement rocks south of the great bend of the Nile; these are seasonally supplied by the light and variable summer rainfall (50–100 mm). East of the Nile and partially contained within its great bend is the Nubian desert. Most of it is developed on the igneous and metamorphic Archaean rocks of the Basement Complex. Outside the Nile valley, oases are few and seasonal water-courses, except near the Red Sea hills, are rare. These arid areas support small parties of Arab nomads with camels, sheep and goats; a settled way of life is impossible. Towards the Red Sea in the broken hill country rainfall is low and irregular and pastures are poor;

Hamitic people (the Beja) predominate and combine poor cultivation in seasonal stream beds with nomadic pasturing of camels and sheep, some of them descending to the narrow coastal plains in the winter.

A settled way of life is limited to discontinuous stretches of the palm-fringed Nile valley, particularly where the river has cut a broad trench in the Nubian sandstone. Between Khartoum and Wadi Halfa this is usually flanked by river terraces. Except locally this part of the Nile is not navigable, since it contains five of the six cataracts. Around Shendi and Dongola are irrigated basins beside the river that once were a part of its bed; many of these flood naturally and some by simple channels. In some cases pumps have been installed, converting them to perennial irrigation. Agriculture rarely extends as much as 3 km from the river and a number of settlements marks these more fertile stretches. They include Shendi, Atbara (at the confluence of that river with the Nile), Berber, Abu Hammad, Merowe and Dongola. In these villages nomads trade animals and goatskins for grain and pulses. On the border with Egypt is Wadi Halfa. This is the northern terminus of the Sudan railway and there is a river connection with the southern terminus of the Egyptian railway at Aswan. All this part of the Nile valley has been flooded with the filling of the Aswan High Dam.

Between latitudes 16°N and 10°N is an intermediate zone between the desert and the long-grass savanna and swamp of the better-watered Negroid south. The title Central Rainlands emphasizes the characteristics of this area, which is the most productive and most populous part of the republic. A number of subdivisions based on soil, climate and vegetation may be distinguished: in the north is semi-desert steppe land, in the west the higher western Darfur, in the centre the Qoz and the Nuba Mountains, and east of the White Nile the clay plains.

The semi-desert steppe, west of Khartoum and Butana to the east, offers sparse grazing to a number of nomadic camel and sheep-owning Arab tribes. The rainfall (100–200 mm) lasts only through three summer months and largely conditions the movement of the tribes who, for nomads, are reasonably well off. The rains are generally reliable, but if they are below average a more southerly pasture-seeking movement is possible by arrangement with neighbours.

Each tribe has a number of base areas with watering points where they will have concentrated by the end of the dry season and in which small areas of millet are sown. From these bases they move southwards with the onset of the rains, dividing into small family groups. With the rains a northerly circuit is followed between June and November, visiting known waterpoints and wells, until, finally, all other pasture used, they return to the winter grazing ground (Figure 47). Here gum is collected from small incisions in acacia bushes, skins are prepared, camel and goat hair and wool are spun and rugs made. Annual visits to market towns such as Omdurman, El Obeid, and En Nahud enable them to trade animals, gum arabic, rugs and saddlery for grain, cloth, sugar and tea.

Western Darfur. West of the Central Rainlands, the land rises to culminate in the volcanic range of the Jebel Marra (3088 m). Here in western Darfur rocks of the Basement Complex provide the plinth for these volcanic, mainly basaltic, rocks. The plateau of these old rocks, an undulating peneplain, varies between 700 and 1000 m and is emphasized here and there by isolated hills (inselberge) and ridges. Rainfall is more plentiful – up to 750 mm over a good deal of the uplands – and the vegetation varies from thorn bush on the thin soils of the uplands to denser woodland savanna in the south. Streams radiate from the upland; some are perennial for their first 8–15 km, but surface flow beyond these limits occurs only during the wet season (May to September).

Except in the drier north where nomads and semi-nomads move with sheep and goats (the

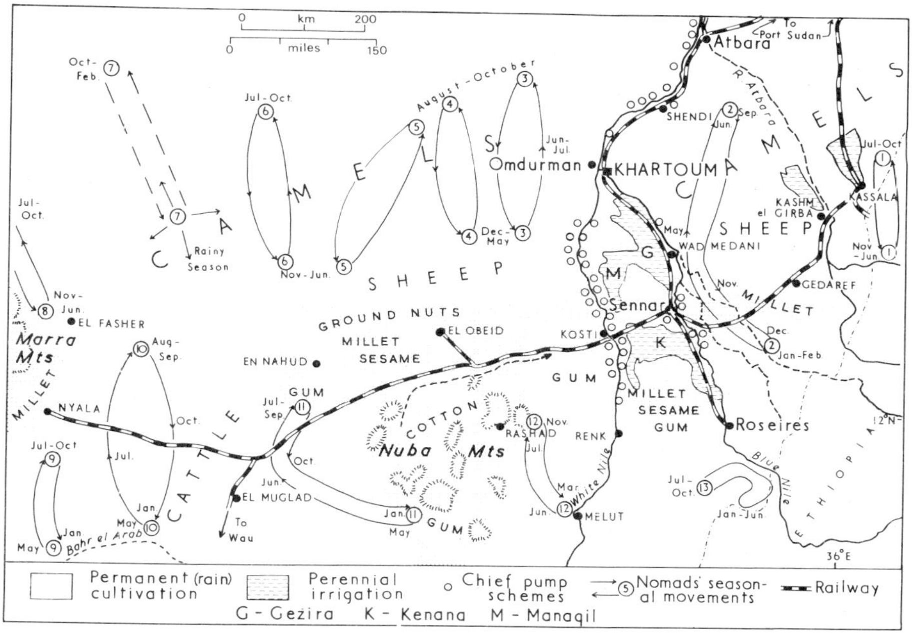

Figure 47 Economy of the Central Sudan

Note: Numbers refer to the following tribes: 1 Beni Emer; 2 Rufaa Es Sharq; 3 Hawawir; 4 Kababish; 5 Hammar; 6 Kawahla; 7 Meidob; 8 Zaghawa; 9 Habaniya; 10 Rizeiquat; 11 Mesirna Zurug; 12 Awlad Himeid; 13 Ingessana

Source: After K. M. Barbour.

stony country is unsuitable for camels), most of the population of western Darfur clusters round the upland and beside the stream beds, for even in the dry season the water table is not far below the stream beds. Silty alluvial fans and river terraces provide the principal areas of settlement and cultivation of the Fur. Millet, groundnuts, sesame and maize are the principal crops, and in some of the larger villages tree fruits – mangos, citrus and bananas – are grown. Rather poor-quality cotton is indigenous and is used locally for cloth making.

The Qoz. East of Darfur and stretching to the White Nile is the very different terrain of the Qoz: a great stretch of undulating sand, once a southward lobe of the Sahara and now fixed by short grass and acacia scrub vegetation. This has always been a zone of movement between desert and swamps and, particularly since the Moslem conversions, has become the pilgrim route from West Africa to Mecca.

The landscape is somewhat monotonous, the undulating surface being clothed with grasses, herbs (sweet veld) and scattered low trees. To the south, with increasing rainfall, the trees become larger and more numerous.

Semi-nomads move over the borders into the Qoz both in the north and the south and serve as a reminder that until this century agriculture here was subsidiary to pastoralism. The prevailing pattern of settled agriculture has developed during the last half-century and is still evolving. It has arisen as a result of firm government, improving communications and establishment of market towns, and a great programme of water reservoir development. The spine of the settled area has become the railway, extended from Sennar to El Obeid in 1911 and continued to Nyala in Darfur in 1960, supplemented by the road from El Obeid to El Fasher. The rail link from the Nile valley at Atbara to Port Sudan was completed in 1905. Deeper and more productive wells were bored in the railway zone with modern appliances; and people became encouraged to settle permanently, cultivating millet, sesame and groundnuts during the rainy season, sowing with the rains in July, and harvesting in December in the dry season. Sheep and goats are kept to provide milk, meat, skin, hair and wool. The railway, only a single-track line, has now become an important artery of trade. Lorries bring grain, groundnuts, sesame, cotton, gum arabic and melon seeds into the stations.

The improvement of rural water supplies is basic to further development of the Central Rainlands. Since 1945 a number of measures to create water storage facilities for the six-month dry season have been quite successful. Foremost among them has been the use of machinery to bore wells and of modern earth-moving machinery to excavate *hafirs.* The hafir was a small hand-excavated cistern or pond, usually related to seasonal streams, which could store some water for most, if not all, of the dry season. The new hafirs are much larger and with access roads have helped to open or consolidate settlements over considerable areas. Nearly a thousand hafirs have now been made, a large number being in the areas surrounding the Nuba Mountains and impounding runoff from the hills. The new wells have been created by deep bores being put down 120 – 200 m to reach aquifers in the Nubian sandstone. Many areas have thus come under cultivation and cotton has been successfully introduced as a cash crop.

In this most southerly section of the Qoz, around and among the Nuba hills, the nomadic Baggara tribes are found. They winter along the Bahr el Arab and move north to the sweeter grasses of the Qoz with the coming of the rains and floods. A growing number are gradually turning to agriculture, some attracted by high cotton prices.

The clay plain. From the junction of the White and Blue Niles and east from the Nuba Mountains to the Ethiopian border stretches a monotony of clay plain. Amazingly level, the deeply cracking clays in the north are well adapted to irrigation agriculture, necessary because of the limited rainfall. Numerous irrigation schemes here, from hafirs to the famous Gezira scheme, have completely altered the landscape and way of life of thousands.

Plate 21 Hafir excavation in the Sudan

The plain between the two Niles (Gezira = island or peninsula) slopes down to the north and west and thus facilitates the flow of irrigation water impounded in the Sennar Dam on the Blue Nile. The main irrigation canal is on the east side of the Gezira and its distributaries now serve about 400,000 ha, mainly in the east. It has been found that some of the soils nearer the White Nile are too poor to repay irrigation. The Gezira scheme was a successful venture in cooperation between European management and African cultivators and still continues, although few Europeans now remain. When the original concession lapsed in 1950 the Sudan Government established a Gezira Board to take over the function of the original private Gezira Syndicate.

The scheme operates as a triple partnership between government, who provide land and water and take 42 per cent of the net return, the Board which takes 10 per cent for its management (the syndicate took 20 per cent), and the tenant, who receives 44 per cent plus 4 per cent in social services. Land allocations have been on a princely scale in comparison with peasant holdings in Egypt, tenants holding approximately 40 feddans (17 ha) in four fields. An eight-year rotation is cotton, fallow, millet (dura), fallow or lubia (fodder legume), fallow, cotton, fallow, fallow; thus cotton is grown only one year in four. This whole system is lavish of land and underlies the light pressure of population in comparison with Egypt. In the more recent Manaqil extension of the irrigated area holdings are reduced to about 15 feddans. Of this 5 are under cotton within a three-year rotation: cotton, dura millet and lubia fodder (2½ feddans each) and fallow (5 feddans). Tenancies in the Gezira when they fall vacant are now being reduced to 20 feddans each. A prime object of the scheme was to produce an export crop and provide a source of revenue to aid the government in the development of the country. It has proved highly successful: medium-long staple cotton (over 35 mm) is grown and its export provides 50–60 per cent of all export receipts.

The Manaqil extension (completed in 1962) added 800,000 feddans under perennial irrigation in the middle of the Gezira. Other extensions of perennial irrigation are being developed using the greater share of Nile water (agreed with Egypt in 1959) which allowed the building of a new large storage dam on the Blue Nile just above Roseires. This supplied the later phases of the Manaqil extension and a further massive addition (the Rahad scheme) south of the Sennar Dam. The potential for extension of irrigation in the Sudan is very great and lies mainly in the clay lands beside the Blue Nile south of Khartoum and beside the Atbara farther east. An important development making use of the waters of the Atbara river in the early 1960s was the building of a dam at Kashm el Girba to supply irrigation water to the resettlement scheme for the 40,000 people displaced from Wadi Halfa. They lost their homes there when Egypt's Aswan High Dam flooded the Nile valley (creating Lake Nasser) beyond the border, into Sudan. Egypt paid for the resettlement in the semi-arid Butana where the town New Halfa and 22 villages were established. The dam, designed to hold 1300 million cubic metres of water, due to siltation now holds only 800 million cubic metres, enough for some 300,000 feddans instead of the 500,000 planned (average annual rainfall is 300–390 mm). Of this amount 125,000 feddans were used for resettlement, 25,000 feddans reserved for local people (most being semi-nomads), and 45,000 feddans devoted to sugar cane production. A sugar factory has been built.

Not all agriculture in the clay plain depends upon irrigation. This is a marginal rainfall area and in the 500–625 mm zone large-scale grain farming takes place headed by the Mechanized Crop Production Scheme near Gedaref. This covers a million feddans, of which 600,000 feddans are annually under cultivation. Tenants, often city businessmen, hold 1000 feddan (420 ha) blocks and most of the farming operations are mechanized. The principal crops are millet and sesame. East of the Nile are two small rivers – the Baraka and Gash – flowing from the Ethiopian Highlands. Their flood waters are used to irrigate the alluvial soils of their delta areas – the one at the coast and the Gash inland, near Kassala. Cotton, millet and castor are the main crops.

South of the irrigated Gezira are many villages whose inhabitants depend upon unirrigated cultivation supplemented by water from the Blue Nile: wells or hafirs allowing sesame, millet and maize to be grown. Nomadic tribes also move regularly across the southern clay plain. The Baggara astride the White Nile use the grasses that grow beside it after each summer's inundation and move a short distance from the river during the rains and flood period. Other nomads such as the Rufaa el Hoi in the southern Gezira traverse more than 300 km, wintering in the south as the marshes dry out and moving north with the onset of the rains to avoid the scourge of flies and mosquitoes in the southern marshy areas.

Southern Sudan

The southern clay plain. This comprises the southern part of the pear-shaped clay plains and the fringing uplands to the west and south. The southern clay plain is exceedingly flat. The gradient of the Nile passing through it is only 1:13,000; consequently the great volume of additional water during the rainy season cannot be accommodated by such level rivers and widespread flooding occurs. Thus during the rainy season almost the entire plain becomes a swamp, impassable except by boat along the main rivers. The waters recede and evaporate with the dry season, until permanent water is confined to the main rivers and some areas of permanent swamp supporting the tall reed-like papyrus (*Cyperus papyrus*), whose extent was overestimated before aerial reconnaissance revealed that it rarely extended more than 10 km from the permanent channels. The general term *sudd* (Arabic for barrier) applied to this area derives from the great masses of floating vegetation that occasionally block the navigable channels. Grass fires sweep much of the area in the dry season and this, with the clay soil, helps to account for the paucity of trees. The lack of shade and dryness do not favour the tsetse fly, and cattle rearing is the main occupation.

The Nilotic tribes – mainly Shilluk, Nuer and Dinka – adapt their mode of living to these conditions. As the floods rise they move their beasts and possessions to the few islets of interfluves, upon which they crowd, and to the surrounding unflooded land, particularly in the west on the edges of the laterite uplands called the Ironstone Plateau. Here, in fact, are their permanent conical thatch-roofed huts and cattle byres, the former often built on piles to allow fires underneath to smoke out flies and mosquitoes. Tiny patches of sorghum

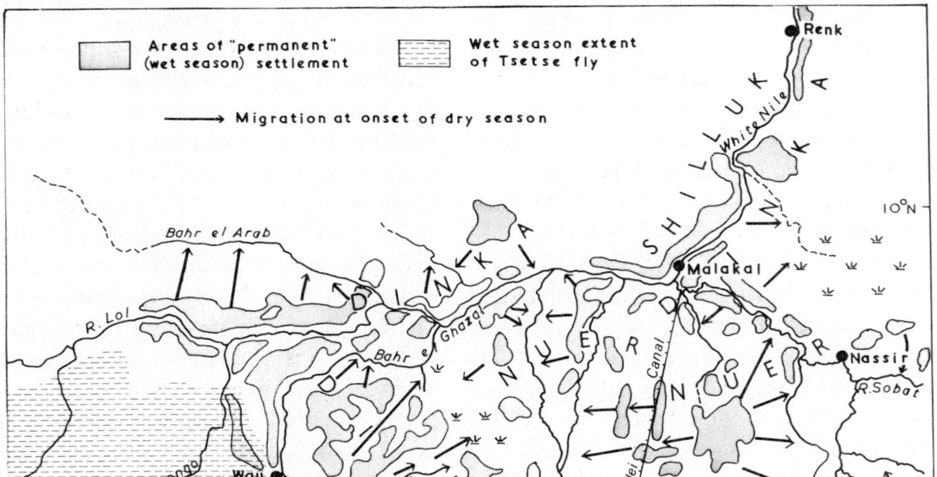

Figure 48 Seasonal movements in the Southern Sudan

millet, maize and vegetables are grown, often scarcely enough for subsistence. Fishing is an important pastime, but cattle are the real interest. They become lean on the very limited grazing during the wet season but fatten up as the young men move them back over the young grass as the waters recede. The families are reunited when the harvest has been reaped. Cattle camps close to the permanent channels or swamps are left with the onset of the first rains in April. Such migrations may be from 15 to 80 km.

The only town in the region is Malakal (pop. 10,000), a dry-point settlement east of the Nile, the centre of administration and a local market. Difficult and poverty-stricken though their way of life is, these Nilotic peoples have shown very little disposition to explore other ways of living. Some changes may come about in this area when the Jonglei Canal is completed. This is a waterway 360 km long, 55 m broad and 4–7 m deep which leaves the White Nile at Bor just above Jonglei and passes along east of the swamp to rejoin the river in Malakal. The canal (which will be navigable) will reduce the sudd swamps and preserve for use downstream much of the water at present lost by evaporation and percolation. An all-weather road along the canal will reduce by 300 km communication with Juba, the southern Sudan main town. More than half the canal has been excavated, but near-insurrection in the south brought the work to a standstill in 1984. Also brought to a standstill was oil exploration, after some encouraging finds that led to thoughts of an oil refinery to be established at Kosti.

The Ironstone Plateau and Southern Hills. South-west and south of the southern clay plains is the distinctive region of the Ironstone Plateau and Southern Hills. This higher area is mainly of red laterite soil with little humus and subject to severe erosion under the prevailing substantial rainfall (1000–1500 mm): it is lightly populated by subsistence agriculturists. The remoteness of the region, its poor soils and, for such crops, barely adequate rainfall deter attempts at commercial production of, for example, cocoa, coffee or rubber.

The south as a whole is a problem region for Sudan. The north has been unified by Islam, but the south with its swamps and forests has remained remote, backward and tribally divided. English, not Arabic, remains the *lingua franca* of the south and the Christian religion has many adherents. Attempts to arabicize the south have been resisted by civil war. There are few educated southerners, and the recent establishment of a university at Juba, the principal town at the edge of the Ironstone Plateau, is little more than a gesture while primary and secondary education throughout the region remains limited.

THE ECONOMY

Sudan is a country of great plains: about one-third of its total area is suitable for cultivation or grazing, mineral resources so far known are negligible, and industrial development is only just beginning. Thus the main activities and wealth of the country are agricultural and pastoral. The customary African dual division of the economy into subsistence and money sections prevails. The subsistence sector is based on rain-fed growth of food crops under primitive methods, the money economy on commercial growing of irrigated cotton and sugar. The areas of commercial production are in the Khartoum–Gezira area and along the river and rail lines, mainly in the north-eastern quadrant of the country. Subsistence production occupies more than half the population and uses 80 per cent of the cultivated area. Grazing is principally left to the nomadic tribes peripheral to the Central Rainlands.

Industrial development has made some progress since the Second World War; it is concerned mainly with the processing of agricultural products, thereby reducing imports. Khartoum North has emerged as the major industrial centre, but manufacturing industry is also important in Khartoum, Omdurman, Wad Medani, Atbara and Port Sudan. Goods made now include clothing, shoes, soap, sweets, beer, furniture, cigarettes, rubber tyres and plastics. A cement works was established at Atbara in 1949 and another at Rabak in Blue Nile Province in 1964; a meat-canning works at Kosti in 1952; textile mills at Nazara in 1950; two aluminium-working plants and a glass factory in Khartoum–Omdurman. Much foreign capital is invested in these enterprises, which for the most part are located in the east-central Sudan and underline its economic dominance.

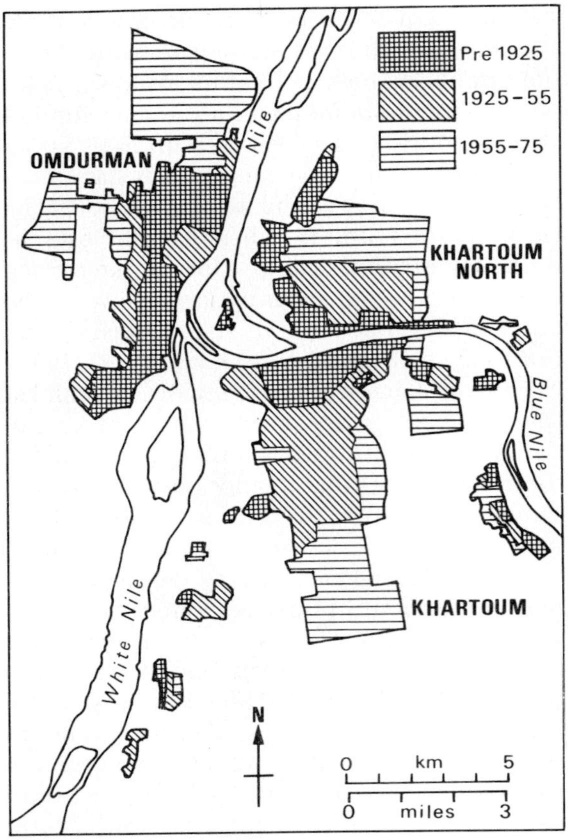

Figure 49 Stages in the growth of Greater Khartoum

POPULATION AND SETTLEMENT

The population of Sudan, in 1985 estimated to be 21 million, is increasing at a very high rate (probably at over 3 per cent a year), and nearly 50 per cent of the population is below 15 years of age. Some 80 per cent of the population is rural, but the few urban centres have an importance disproportionate to their size and numbers, for they provide the centres and mainsprings of administrative, political and economic activity.

In studying the modern economic geography of the Sudan one cannot but be aware of the dichotomy between the large traditional sector and the limited modern sector. As in so many other African states these differences encourage a high degree of mobility among the population. Each year over 300,000 fellahin from all parts of the country leave their holdings and villages for seasonal work in the big irrigated agricultural schemes such as the Gezira, Guneid, and Kashm el Girba. This movement also includes considerable numbers of West Africans, of whom there are between 2 and 3 million in the Sudan. Most are Moslem, crossing Africa on the pilgrimage to Mecca. This is usually a step-like movement and may take years; many never complete it but settle in the Sudan. The greatest need for labour is for cotton picking in the Gezira and its extensions during the first three to four months of the year, and over a quarter of a million seasonal workers move in for this each year. These movements feed back to the villages knowledge of town life and living standards and help to foster the growing movement of population from the countryside to the town and cities, especially to the largest urban area, the Khartoum conurbation.

This conurbation is by far the largest urban centre in the Sudan and consists of three towns. Khartoum itself, a European-style town but now much extended, faces the Blue Nile; on the White Nile is Omdurman, a much older Arab settlement; and across the river from these two settlements is Khartoum North, a new and mainly industrial foundation.

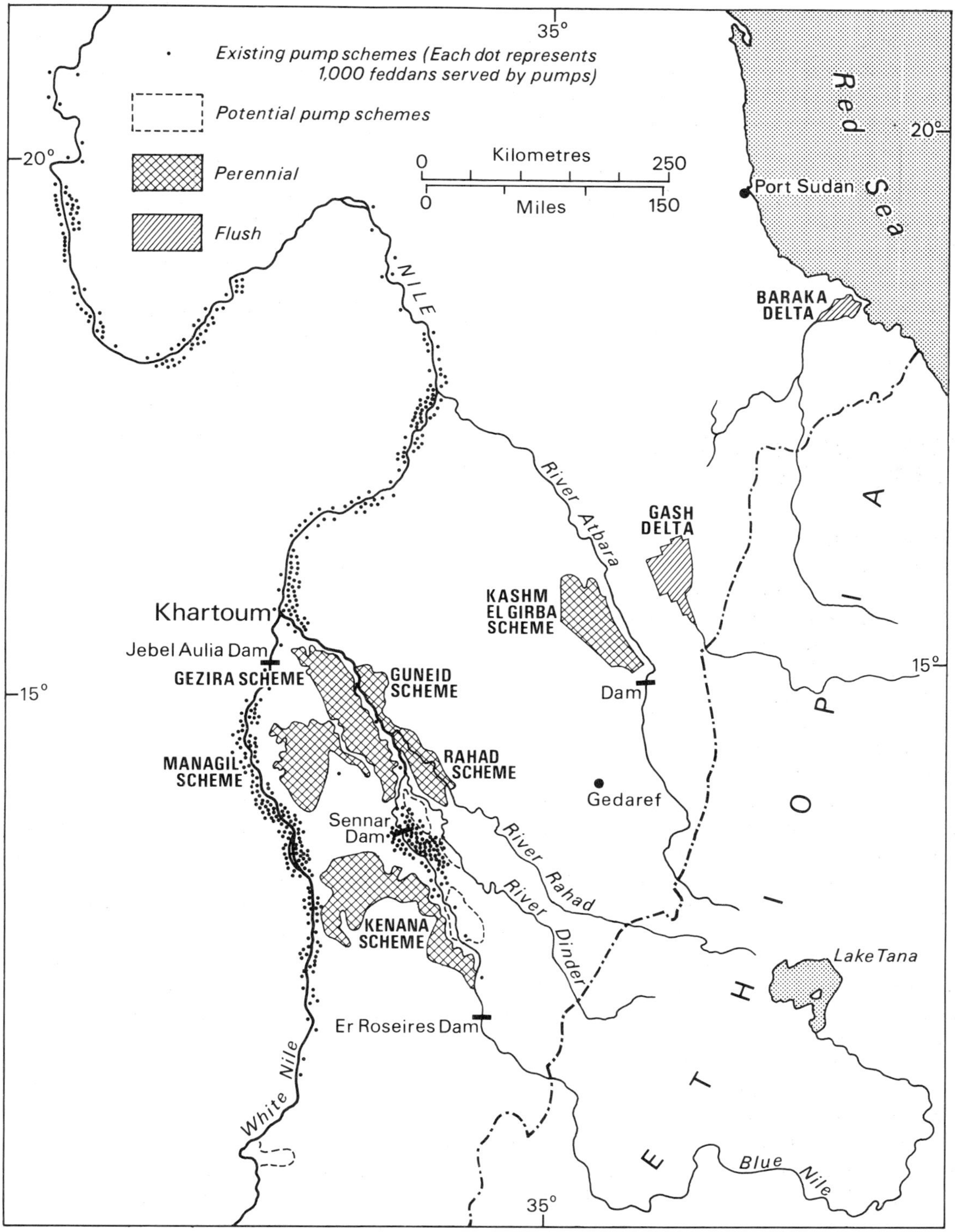

Figure 50 Irrigation schemes in the Sudan

There has been almost explosive growth of the three towns since the Second World War, and their population now approaches 1 million.

MODERN DEVELOPMENTS

The middle 1970s saw great incomes being received by the oil-rich Arab states whose territories were mainly desert. The great potential in Sudan for large arable farming seemed to complement their needs, and Arab investment for large-scale agricultural schemes was promised over a 20-year period. Sudan aimed at attaining self-sufficiency in sugar, wheat and coffee and then in producing surplus sugar and wheat for export so that it could become the breadbasket of the Arab world. The featureless central clay plains offered large areas for such development. The new schemes that were planned differed from their predecessors in that they were mainly capital-intensive, utilizing modern irrigation technology and offering only limited participation by the peasantry.

In the late 1970s large-scale mechanical schemes were put in hand. The Kenana scheme, south of Manaqil, covering 115,000 feddans, was to become the largest sugar estate in the world. Waters from the White Nile supplying 85,000 feddans are lifted 50 m to be pumped on to the fields, and a large factory was built. The Rahad scheme south-east of Gezira, covering 300,000 feddans, uses Roseires water for cotton and groundnut production. Farther south along the White Nile other areas for more sugar growing were delineated. Unfortunately the high hopes of the planners were not achieved, and the limited success of these large-scale projects highlights development problems that face many African states, in particular problems of infrastructure and finance. Kenana now produces sugar, but several years later than planned and a third of the crop is harvested by hand. The scheme cost six times the original estimate, proved difficult to finance, and in real terms the cost of production of early Kenana sugar was above world market prices.

Infrastructure problems were severe: Kenana lies 1000 km from Sudan's single congested port – Port Sudan – and relies upon a single-track railway system. Machinery and other imports take several months to arrive, and even sugar sacks are not made locally and have to be imported. Periodic diesel and petrol shortages and lack of adequate maintenance of the machinery slow up all operations. Sudan, with its vast area of 2,500,000 km^2, possesses only 5000 km of single-track railway and only 2500 km of all-weather roads, a transport infrastructure that is quite inadequate to sustain major developments and that limits advances to a few favoured localities. Future development projects are pointless unless these transport difficulties are removed.

The notion of becoming the Arab world breadbasket also has not worked out, mainly because of financial problems as well as inadequate transport infrastructure and rainfall variability. Sudan has great financial burdens, some arising from servicing debts incurred in earlier years of attempted development. There is a constant trade deficit (oil imports being

Plate 22 Gezira cotton provides Sudan with a principal export

very costly) and a shortage of foreign exchange. Terms of trade have been adverse and little progress is possible without international aid and investment. Indeed, Sudan's financial difficulties deterred other Arab states from investing. In all the schemes there is a heavy dependence on foreign technicians, while at the same time there is a 'brain drain' from Sudan of teachers, lawyers, doctors, engineers and technicians at all levels. They seek more certain careers and greater rewards in richer Arab states, but their absence retards Sudan's own future development.

With under 20 per cent of the population classified as urban, the Sudan is one of the least urbanized countries of Africa. However, the shift from rural to urban areas is now taking place at a remarkable speed, for the growing disparity in income between the large urban centres and the countryside is resulting in a large-scale exodus of rural people. Economic development has taken place in but a few limited locations. Here towns have emerged and expanded and with the main commercial agricultural areas these centres continue to grow, whereas the vast remainder of the country is left as a backward economic periphery.

Finally, it is fitting to draw attention to the importance of geography in influencing Sudan's pattern of development. The sheer size of the country – almost the size of Western Europe – and its light population mean that the per capita cost of supplying modern transport away from the country's centre becomes excessive. Yet adequate means of transport are essential for economic progress. Further, soil, water and position not only influence economic development in favour of agriculture, but also result in a pattern of enclaves and corridors of commercial activities set amid extensive areas of subsistence farming. It seems inevitable that the coming years will see the economic decline of the west, with a shift of population to the centre and east. The concentration of development capital into these areas of the greatest potential seems a logical response to geographical factors.

19
Ethiopia, Somalia and Djibouti

The Horn of Africa, shared between Ethiopia, Djibouti and Somalia, stands as a well-watered mountainous bastion between the Red Sea and the East African Highlands. This mountainous mass, where the bulk of the population is concentrated, is divided into two unequal portions by a northern extension of the East African Rift valley. In the highland population densities in places exceed 130 per km^2, but in the torrid lowland that severs Ethiopia from the East African Highlands and the arid Eritrean coastlands the population density falls to about 5 per km^2.

Ethiopia has a long history and an independent outlook that is intimately related to its mountain isolation. For sixteen centuries the greater part of the country has been Christian; and from the seventh century almost isolated by the conquests of Islam which closed the Red Sea and encircled the mountain mass. Except for a brief period in the sixteenth century when Portugal assisted in repelling the Moslems, the country remained cut off from the Western world until the nineteenth century when travellers, merchants and missionaries made gradual penetration, to be followed by treaties with the Great Powers. Italy, who possessed Eritrea in the north and Somalia to the south-east, invaded and annexed Ethiopia in 1935, but British forces restored the country to the Emperor Haile Selassie in 1941. The former Italian colony of Eritrea was transferred to Ethiopia by the United Nations in 1952 and became an autonomous unit within the new Federation of Ethiopia and Eritrea. The area of Ethiopia is 1.2 million km^2 and the population of 43 million increases annually at the high rate of 2.7 per cent.

A military coup overthrew the Emperor of Ethiopia in 1974 and abolished the monarchy in favour of a single-party socialist state. A great deal was made of social and economic equality: wholesale nationalization of banking, insurance and commercial and industrial companies took place and was followed by the nationalization of all urban and agricultural land and the replacement of land tenure by cooperative ownership. Resources have been wasted in fighting secessionist movements, particularly in Eritrea, and in war for a time with Somalia who claimed part of the Ogaden.

GEOGRAPHICAL REGIONS OF ETHIOPIA

The Highlands, split into two unequal portions by the rift valley, present a rolling upland area averaging 2400 m, but with many of the higher parts over 4000 m. Within part of the rift itself and on its eastern margins these highlands are bounded by spectacular escarpments. The mountain areas are particularly distinguished from the lower interior plateaux by the greater rainfall they enjoy and the milder summer temperatures. Many of the highest areas are snow-covered for a short time each year, and a rainy season – mainly

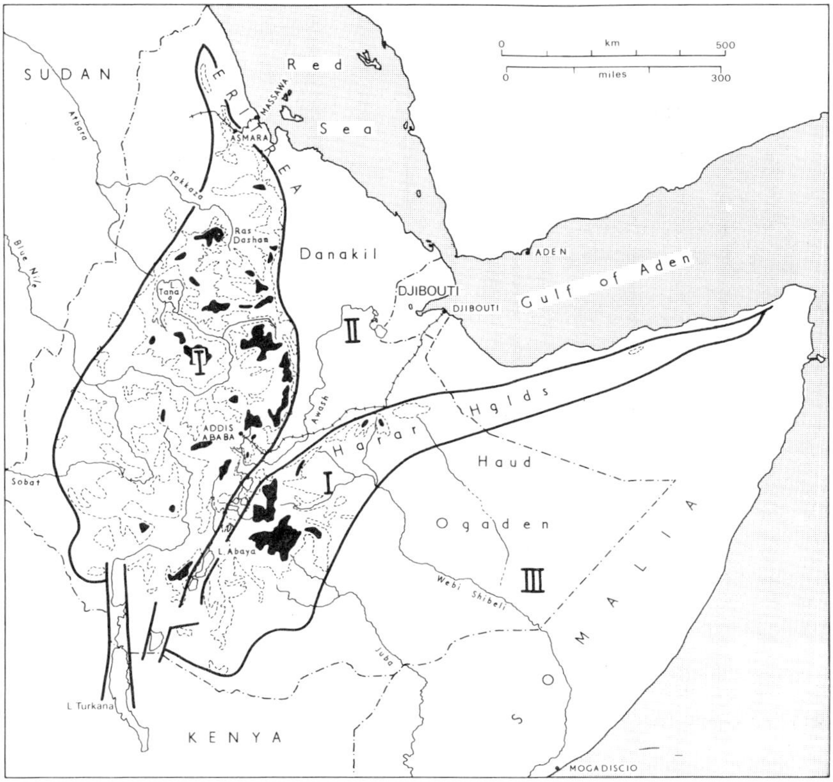

Figure 51 Ethiopia and adjacent regions: I Highlands; II The Red Sea littoral and Danakil lowlands; III Low plateaux and Somali coastlands. Land over 3000m shaded.

between June and October in sympathy with the Indian monsoon – gives over 1000 mm. The driest months, when only a few showers fall, are confined to November to January in the south, but the period becomes longer in the north. These highland areas extend from 5°N to 17°N, about 1250 km. The main mass flanks the rift valley for over 500 km but tapers to the north; the highest parts lie to the east, centre and north where considerable areas above 3600 m are common. South of the rift valley the Somali–Harar highlands drop down steeply to the south-west, the highest peaks (nearly 4300 m) overlooking the rift.

The heavy runoff feeds powerful rivers that cut deep gorges in the volcanic rocks, often being guided by rifts and fissures. These break up the uplands into a series of *ambas* or flat-topped mountains, sometimes their tops protected by resistant strata, which possess water, grass and arable land, and are natural strongholds. Eighty per cent of Ethiopians live in the highlands, mainly in tight little independent villages of round wattle huts beneath gum-tapped eucalyptus trees. They obtain their livelihood by agriculture and stock rearing. Frost is unknown, and tropical vegetation thrives in the *kolla*: the hot lower slopes of the highlands and the valleys below 1500 – 1800 m. Bananas and coffee are the more important products, coffee being an important export crop: *arabica* coffee is believed to have originated in Ethiopia. Most Ethiopian coffee grows wild and is found at altitudes between 1500 m and 2000 m in the south-west of the highlands in the provinces of Kaffa (whence the name 'coffee'), Gamu and Harar south of the rift. The output could be substantially expanded if cultivation and marketing became more systematic. Annual exports of coffee account for two-thirds of the country's export revenue. Most of the highland population lives in the *woina dega*, the middle highlands between 1800 and 2800 m. Here cereals are grown and tree fruits such as the orange, apricot and fig are produced. Sheep and cattle are kept.

Ethiopians in the highlands recognize two principal types of soil: black and red. Black soils occur in areas liable to waterlogging in the wet season – shallow valleys and basins, for example. Red soils are found on the better-drained slopes and are less fertile than black soils. Cereals (the tiny-seeded grass t'eff, wheat, barley, rye, sorghum and maize) and pulses (chick peas, green peas, beans and lentils) are the principal crops grown. Up to 2400 m, t'eff and wheat are most important; above this barley and wheat predominate. In the highlands two crops a year are frequently grown in succession in the same field, for the heavy rainfall makes certain the maturing of the second crop.

The ox-drawn plough was first introduced by the Amhara and is now used all over the highland area. The hoe, the digging stick and the sickle are the other principal implements, the first two being used more at lower altitudes where fields are cleared by slashing and burning and some shifting cultivation takes place. In the upland areas of settled farming, domestic animals – mainly sheep and cattle – graze the fallow fields, their droppings helping to restore fertility to the soil. The stock population is heavier in the drier north than in the south of the highlands.

Above 2500 m is the *dega* proper: here the hardier cereals will grow, but it consists mainly of open, short grassland offering abundant pasture for animals. There is very little bush except in sheltered places and few trees except introduced eucalyptus, grown beside almost every habitation. Here the population is sparse, but transhumance is less general than might be expected. Altitudinal movement of herds is local only; cattle may be sent upwards under the supervision of boys and young men during the rainy season to avoid mud and flies, a small seasonal fee being paid to the chief controlling the grazing areas. Goats and sheep are rarely moved. In the north the cattle are the humped zebu type, in the south a long-horned zebu type. Cattle are valued highly in Ethiopia and a man's wealth is often measured by the size of his herds. Hides and skins serve a variety of household and agricultural uses and also provide a substantial export.

The Interior Plateaux, including the rift valley, stand as independent features mainly to the south of the highland mass. Here they drop down through Ogaden to the Somalia littoral. The lower altitude of this *kolla* zone (900–1500 m) is responsible for the greater heat and marked diurnal range of temperature. Rainfall is also less, much of the area having under 500 mm. The great heat is somewhat mitigated by the fact that the valleys are broader here. In better-watered parts, such as the Awash valley in the rift, sugar cane and oil-seed crops are grown, including castor, sesame, groundnuts and sunflowers; but much of this area is pastoralist country.

Plate 23 An Oxfam garden-irrigation from borehole project, Wollo, Ethiopia

The Red Sea Littoral. In the east the highlands are girt by the arid lower land flanking the Red Sea. The parched, hot and treeless coastal plain is narrow (16–80 km) and backed by low hills in Eritrea and Djibouti and by the more substantial prolongation of the Harar highlands overlooking the Gulf of Aden. Between the Ethiopian highlands and the Eritrean coast lies the burning Danakil desert, in places below sea-level. There is little settled life in so arid an area: most of the population is nomadic, rearing animals and collecting gum arabic. Although the Red Sea is rich in fish, fishing is little developed.

POPULATION AND SETTLEMENT IN ETHIOPIA

With 43 million in 1985, Ethiopia has Africa's third largest population. At 2.7 per cent the annual rate of increase is high and may well increase as medicine and hygiene become more practised and as resettlement and overseas aid overcome deaths from famine in drought areas. Ethiopia has provided the meeting ground for many peoples, and in its mountain fastnesses many languages and cultures have been preserved. Some 70 different languages are spoken, but the official language is Amharic and at least one-third of the people are the Amhara, commonly called Ethiopians. They inhabit the central Ethiopian highlands, and to their north are related peoples, the Tigreans. These peoples are of mixed Semitic and Hamitic origin but Christians; the Emperor claimed descent from King Solomon and the Queen of Sheba, who herself was Ethiopian. They are proud and warlike and, although in numbers a minority, they have been the ruling people in Ethiopia for many hundreds of years. The coastal areas flanking the Red Sea, Gulf of Aden and Indian Ocean and the uplands of the Horn of Africa which they contain are the home of Hamitic peoples originally from southern Arabia. The Galla and Somali are the most important, the majority of them being Moslems.

Addis Ababa, the capital, now has well over 1 million inhabitants and excepting Asmara (the capital of Eritrea) is the only large town. Much of the capital's growth has been in recent years. It became the capital in 1889 and for the next 20 years consisted of little more than the royal palace and one or two African villages set in eucalyptus woodland on a broad but ravine-scarred bench, a fatiguing 2400 m above sea-level. The capital, with its unmade rutted roads and jumble of squalid buildings, was not far advanced from the African village stage when the Italians took over in 1935. The real advance has come during recent years when, with the spread of independence throughout Africa, the city was modernized to become a fitting capital for the doyen of Africa's independent rulers. Old streets were widened, and asphalted double-carriageway roads, new hotels and ministeries were constructed; a new international airport was completed and new facades attached to dilapidated shops and residences. In 1961 the Emperor inaugurated a magnificent building complex known as Africa Hall, erected especially to provide an Assembly Hall and Secretariat building for the United Nations Economic Commission for Africa. It provides a meeting place, and home of the permanent secretariat, of the independent states in Africa. The city's population is most diverse: there is a substantial body of several thousand Yemeni merchants as well as Greeks, Armenians, Syrians, Indians and some many thousand Europeans and Americans. The city is connected by railway with the coast at Djibouti (780 km).

Perched in the highlands on an outmoded defensive site, Addis Ababa gives one a feeling of isolation and remoteness out of keeping with the overwhelming tasks of bringing communications and economic development to the rest of the potentially rich upland country. The only other railway is that between Agordat and Massawa via Asmara (307 km) in Eritrea. This addition of Eritrea, although arid and poor, has a rather different personality, for it reflects 60 years of Italian occupation.

There are roads, towns and two ports, Massawa and Assab. In Ethiopia good roads total no more than 8000 km, and away from them transport is by pack animals: mules, donkeys, horses and camels. This paucity of modern means of communication retards economic development. The transport system is still that of a backward people engaged in subsistence farming, although the recent development of air transport linking Addis Ababa with foreign capitals and a number of internal towns must be noticed. Foreign trade is quite small; coffee, hides and skins are the only important exports.

MODERN DEVELOPMENTS IN ETHIOPIA

Since antiquity, in common with other parts of the Middle East and East Africa, Ethiopia has suffered the scourge of the desert locust. Periodically these descend to destroy crops in the arid areas and less frequently do great damage in the highlands. Ethiopia is free from the tsetse fly. Little mineral wealth has yet been proved: there is a small gold production, some potash salts are worked in the Danakil plains, and salt is also produced. Exploration for oil is being carried out in Ogaden. Industrial development is yet in its infancy – most is located at Addis Ababa. Textiles, cement, bricks and tiles, leather goods are made and sugar is milled. There is a tractor assembly plant and an oil refinery is located near Assab.

Over the last 30 years there has occurred both spontaneous and planned resettlement of scores of thousands of rural families. The general movement is from the arid and often drought-stricken north and north-east to the more southerly highlands and the rift valley. Growing imports of food in the early post-war years spurred greater productivity in agriculture, but the more fertile uplands to the south came under complex land tenure patterns that deterred new settlement and limited more productive peasant farming. Thus the government made land grants and gave support to commercial estate agriculture in the lowlands: planned resettlement of peasants was on a small scale. The neglect of the rural poor was a contributary cause of the fall of the Imperial regime. The Revolutionary Government nationalized all land and abolished the land tenure system. This facilitated resettlement schemes and saw increasing movement of the peasants from the drought-stricken north to the south, to man many of the commercial farms which were abandoned by owners and managers upon nationalization.

Over the years more and more coercion has been employed in forcing such movements, which also became caught up with the scorched earth policies in the secessionists' wars against the left-wing government. During the 1980s the speed of resettlement was quickened, aided by famine conditions particularly in the north. The government paid little attention to the food shortages, leaving them to be tackled by international action of the foreign aid agencies. The government had little interest in the peasantry but poured resources into the army and its operations, into attempts to develop industry and into the urban sector. The peasantry lacked cohesion and political organization and could be discriminated against by the government.

Thus the Marxist–Leninist government has continued with the villagization programme, aimed eventually at resettling 20 million peasants. It claims that the new planned villages facilitate the provision of services and allow better control of the rural population. It is regarded as a step towards communal farming aimed at producing export crops, for no real efforts were made to reverse the fall in food production, and even when famine became severe in the Northern Highlands in the 1984–5 period, much of the aid received is thought to have gone to the army and the towns. The forced character of some of the villagization in the 1980s with wholesale confiscation of possessions and crops by the state led to thousands of peasants fleeing to seek refuge in neighbouring Somalia and Sudan.

A 10-year development programme was announced in 1981, but the continuing war in Eritrea and the famine in the arid north rendered its fulfilment precarious. Much expenditure was allocated to infrastructure; it was hoped to start the mining of copper ore and planned to increase hydroelectric production as well as raise output in agriculture and industry. The sixth poorest country in the world, Ethiopia is held back by illiteracy, lack of skilled workers, poor managers, inadequate transport facilities, left-wing ideologies with rigid government controls, uncertain economic policies and costly military operations.

SOMALIA

The Somali peoples are dispersed over the Horn of Africa, throughout the new Somali Republic, in the south-east of Ethiopia and also in the north-east of Kenya. Their republic attained its independence in 1960 and comprises the peninsula of the former Italian and British Somali territories, the one facing the Indian Ocean, the other the Gulf of Aden. The small enclave of former French Somaliland is now independent as the Republic of Djibouti (1977).

In the north there is practically no coastal plain, for the prolongation of the Harar highlands brings 2000 m mountains close to the Gulf of Aden. On the Indian Ocean side the plateau descends from Ethiopia in a number of escarpments to a final one a few hundred metres high; this overlooks, between Mogadiscio and Kismayu, an alluvial plain watered by the seasonal Webi Shibeli which, in fact, does not reach the sea.

The population of the Somali Republic is estimated at between 2 and 3 million. The capital is Mogadiscio (pop. 400,000), and there are no other towns of any size. The area of the Republic is 638,000 km^2 and the whole of it is hot, semi-arid or outright desert. Some of the highest area in the north receives a little over 250 mm of rain annually, and a limited area along the south-east coast around Mogadiscio (a roadstead port) receives more than 375 mm; but otherwise sparse grazing and scrub desert prevail, the aridity enhanced by the permeability of the limestones and sands comprising much of the surface rock.

Pastoralism is the mode of livelihood of 70 per cent of the population, most of them being nomadic or semi-nomadic, paying little attention to boundaries and in the north moving up into Ethiopian Ogaden and the Haud in summer. Sheep and goats are their principal animals and the collection of gums and resins from the scrubby desert bushes brings in a small supplementary income. Agriculture is limited to a few better-watered areas such as the valleys of the Juba and Webi Shibeli, where former Italian estates produce sugar cane, bananas (the main export) and cereals. On the coast fishing and salt evaporating give some employment.

Since independence the objective of 'Greater Somalia', to include the Somali-inhabited areas of south-east Ethiopia, Djibouti and north-east Kenya, led to guerrilla warfare and skirmishes with Ethiopia whose Cuban-backed army won the day. The warfare and recurrent drought caused at least 700,000 refugees to move from the Ogaden into Somalia. Many have given up their pastoral way of life and have gone south to seek work in agricultural settlements and fishing villages. This situation has led to a continuing drain on resources and has retarded planned development measures.

DJIBOUTI

Djibouti, capital of the Republic of Djibouti (pop. 150,000), is of some importance, for it is the principal outlet and inlet for 60 per cent of Ethiopia's trade (the railway to Addis Ababa was completed in 1913) and a port of call for ocean shipping. It serves as an international transit port and refuelling centre. The port now has a deep-water container terminal, completed in 1985. Its airport has been improved and accepts air freight for re-export from several of Africa's landlocked countries. Generally, however, it depends on foreign aid to finance its development and sustain its balance of payments. It has virtually no merchandise exports of its own, but lives by its entrepot services.

PART FIVE: WEST AFRICA

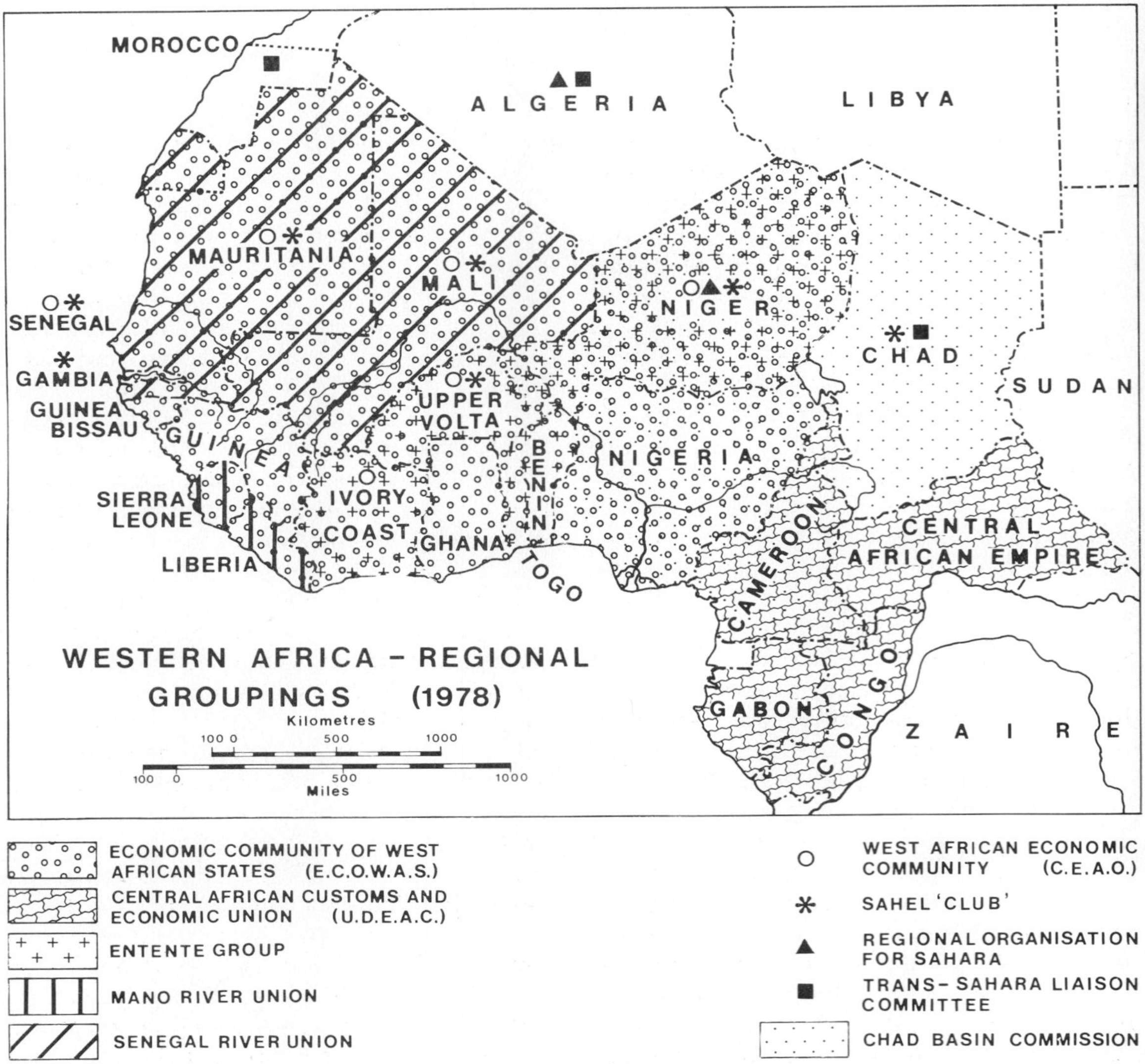

Figure 52 West Africa: supra-national groupings

20 Human and physical geography

There is about any regional sub-division a degree of arbitrariness and the divisions adopted here are no exception. However, the east–west zonal arrangement of relief, climates, vegetation and patterns of development does provide a reasonable basis for grouping together the countries from Mauritania and Senegal in the west to Nigeria and Chad in the east. Certainly the physical zones extend further eastwards, except where the higher north-east/south-west trending Adamawa massif on the Nigeria–Cameroon border provides more of a physical barrier and a zone of distinctive montane flora. Yet even this boundary is not ideal, and the Cross River, just to the west, is a significant faunal boundary and is also the western limit of the semi-Bantu group of African languages.

The only country not resting too easily in this division is Chad, which was part of the former French Equatorial Africa and still has close functional links with the Central African Republic and Congo but which from an environmental and development viewpoint has similarities with the other states on the Sahara's southern margins. It is also convenient to distinguish between the generally better watered coastal states from Senegal to Nigeria and the lower-rainfall Saharan margin or Sahelian states, including coastal Mauritania and land-locked Mali, Burkina Faso (Upper Volta until August 1984), Niger and Chad.

The coastal states provided the Europeans with many of their earliest African footholds, and sections of the coast took their names from the principal trade commodities; the Grain (grains of pepper), Ivory, Gold and Slave Coasts respectively from west to east. Yet these commodities were never wholly exclusive to particular parts of the Guinea Coast, and from the sixteenth to the nineteenth century as many as 15 million slaves were taken from the whole coast. After the early nineteenth century abolition of the slave trade, agricultural exports such as palm-oil, groundnuts, coffee, rubber, cocoa and cotton, gradually assumed greater importance and timber and mineral ores were later added to the list of exports.

Indeed, it could be claimed that it was the commercialization of such commodities, combined with the colonialism that gave the political control necessary to safeguard the trade, which provided West Africa with its distinguishing regional characteristics. With the exception of Liberia, developed as a 'home' for freed American slaves after the 1820s and an independent republic from 1847, all the now independent territories had their origins as colonies, principally of France and Britain, but also Germany (Togo), Portugal (Guinea Bissau), and Spain (Cape Verde Islands). The Canary Islands are still a part of Spain. Yet there were elements of a colonial situation even in Liberia, where for long the small number of Americo-Liberians, descendants of the freed slaves, effectively controlled the indigenous African population in whose territory they settled.

The overall political geography of West Africa is, then, a legacy of the colonial period. It is a highly fragmented region, the present state boundaries deriving from European power politics rather than the underlying physical or human geography or resource endowment. The countries vary in size from Mali, Niger and Chad, each approximately 1.25 million km^2, to the Gambia (11,000 km^2) and Guinea Bissau (36,000 km^2). In population they vary from Nigeria (89 million), Africa's most populous country, to its smallest, Guinea Bissau and The Gambia, both with about 0.5 million inhabitants.

So numerous would be the problems of readjustment that the Organisation of African Unity has agreed that the inherited political boundaries should be accepted as the basis for the independent states. Yet the boundaries and the states they delimit are far from satisfactory in a number of respects which, in many cases have influenced the course of economic development of the countries concerned. Size in relation to the total number and distribution of population and the geography of resources may be critical. Thus, it could be argued that for administrative convenience Chad's population (4.5 million) is too small and too widely and unevenly dispersed in relation to its size but too large in relation to its resources. The same would be the case for Mauritania, Mali and Niger. Nigeria's population is, arguably, too large in relation to its size and resources. Some countries have awkward shapes (The Gambia, Togo, Mali) which make administrative cohesion difficult, especially when associated with large size. Long boundaries (Mauritania, Mali, Niger, Chad) are difficult to control and the land-locked states (Mali, Burkina Faso, Niger, Chad) have severe transport problems and dangerous dependence on relations with neighbours. Chad shares borders with six other states.

West Africa has as many as 500 ethnolinguistic groups with varying degrees of homogeneity, and inevitably there are many places where the state boundaries cut through the tribal territories. The Ewe people divided by the Ghana–Togo boundary is just one of a large number of examples. It follows that the natural lines of movement, communication and trade may be severed, especially, but understandably, because the new states are hypersensitive on questions of sovereignty and territorial integrity and the boundaries have hardened since independence. It is also the case that most West African countries have considerable ethnolinguistic diversity. Guinea wished to reduce the status of French after independence and tried to develop six local languages at school level without being able to adopt a dominant national language. Educational standards are said to have suffered in consequence. Ghana, with a population of 12 million in 1984 and only 239,000 km^2 has over thirty reasonably distinct linguistic groups, and Radio Ghana broadcasts in five languages. In Chad, virtually the whole period since independence in 1960 has been marked by internal conflict deriving in large measure from ethnic divisions, while in Nigeria the late 1960s was a period of civil war as the central government crushed the Ibo-created secessionist state of Biafra in the east-central part of the country. At independence in 1960 Nigeria started as a federation of three states; but mainly in response to local, particularist tribal pressures, the number increased to four in 1962, twelve in 1967 and nineteen in 1976, with proposals for many more.

There can be no doubt that the progress of development has been hindered by the size (too small or too large), fragility and vulnerability of many of the states, both in terms of their internal cohesion and external relations. It is not surprising that West Africa, possibly more than any other world region, has been characterized by the multiplicity and the diversity of the supranational groupings that have been created (Figure 52). These vary in size from the nineteen-nation Economic Community of West African States (ECOWAS) to the three-nation Mano River Union (Liberia, Sierra Leone and Guinea) or two-nation confederation of Senegal and The Gambia. In some the ties are largely historical (e.g. the former French West African colonies grouped in the Entente), but in others more political in character (The Gambia with Senegal). There are cases where the initial stimulus came from the desire to regularize customs and economic affairs (ECOWAS, Mano River Union), others where coordinated development of resources provided the basis (Chad Basin Commission, Senegal River) and some where a common problem provided the bond (the 'Club' of the drought-affected Sahel states). The success of most of the unions has been restricted, but in many cases they are an understandable reaction to the lack of geographical logic in the inherited political map and the problems it creates.

This political map has been superimposed upon a physical geography which we can now consider in more detail.

GEOLOGY AND RELIEF

The broad outlines of the geology were sketched in Chapter 1. From Figure 3 it can be seen that as much as 40 per cent of West Africa is composed of granite, gneiss and schist of the Pre-Cambrian basement complex. There is a particularly large, almost continuous block of such rocks underlying Côte d'Ivoire, most of Liberia and Sierra Leone, parts of south-west Guinea, much of Ghana and Burkina Faso, Togo and Benin and large areas of south-western and north-eastern Nigeria. There are smaller, separate blocks of crystalline rocks in the western and central Sahara. West Africa does not have zones of concentrated mineralization comparable in scale with Shaba–Zambia or the Witwatersrand, but what minerals there are occur for the most part either in, or as a consequence of weathering of, the Pre-Cambrian crystallines just delimited. However, two zones of rather greater mineral concentration can be identified: in south-western Ghana and in the Liberia–Sierra Leone–Guinea region. In the former, gold (which gave Ghana its pre-independence name of Gold Coast), diamonds, manganese and bauxite are all important, while in the latter iron-ore is widespread and gold, diamonds and bauxite are also found. In the Jos Plateau of Nigeria tin has been exploited for many years, while in the Saharan Pre-Cambrian iron-ore and copper have been mined in Mauritania and tin and uranium in Niger. These minerals have been a variable, but in cases significant, basis for economic growth in the countries concerned. There are certainly numerous further deposits of these and other minerals still not fully surveyed and assessed but likely to be exploited as and when market conditions are suitable.

The Palaeozoic rocks, mainly sandstones, found in Ghana's Volta basin, and more extensively in a discontinuous zone from coastal Guinea (including the Fouta Jallon highland) through western Mali and into Mauritania, are not well-endowed with minerals.

The Cretaceous of eastern Nigeria and the Niger–Benin trough does contain some coal, exploited near Enugu, and also low-grade iron-ore near Ajaokouta where it is the basis of a new iron and steel complex. In southern Togo there is a large, worked deposit of phosphate of Cretaceous age, and in Senegal several worked deposits of either Cretaceous or Eocene age. There are other unworked deposits in the Senegal valley, Mali, Burkina Faso, Benin and Nigeria.

Tertiary rocks, mainly sandstones, are the main oil-bearing formation of the Niger delta and the basis of Nigeria's well-developed oil industry, and they also contain some lignite. Although small, Côte d'Ivoire's oil production from offshore wells is from strata of similar type and age as is Ghana's minute production. There could very well be more oil in such Tertiary rocks.

Nowhere in West Africa is there spectacular relief and scenery. The principal features are the relatively monotonous surfaces which are found at 180–300 m, 450–600 m and 900–1200 m. West Africa's coast line is generally smooth and lacking the indentations which would provide good natural harbours. However, it is possible to identify four distinct coastal types.

North of the Senegal mouth. There is a straight coast backed by sand dunes and an arid interior with no rivers. The only shelter on this exposed coast is provided by the southward-projecting Cap Blanc peninsula in northern Mauritania, where the port of Nouadhibou has been located.

Senegal to Sierra Leone (Cape St Anne). Here there is a much better watered hinterland in the Fouta Jallon and Guinea highlands, and numerous rivers – the lower courses of some having been drowned (e.g Freetown River) to give good natural harbours. Other rivers such as the Saloum, Casamance and Gambia also provide port sites and more numerous rocky headlands also provide shelter. The port of Dakar has been developed in the shelter of the Cape Verde peninsula. However, some of the rivers bring down considerable silt, so that their mouths often have variable sand bars and nearshore navigation can be difficult.

Sierra Leone to western Niger delta. Here is over 1800 km of coast with no indentation able to provide more than partial shelter for seagoing ships. Nevertheless, there is an alternation of two rather different coast forms. Parts of the coast are characterized by numerous small headlands and bays with sheltered beach landing places which provided early European fort (and later port) sites. This type of coast is known as 'Elmina' after the original Portuguese settlement on the Gold Coast. Separating stretches of Elmina coast are sections of 'Dahomey' type in eastern Côte d'Ivoire and Togo–Benin–western Nigeria. This is characteristically straight, backed by lagoons and with heavy surf. At Abidjan, an artificial cut – the Vridi Canal – allows ships to enter the sheltered lagoon waters, and at Lagos there is an improved natural break which gives ships similar access. Otherwise, all ports on this inhospitable coast have been built in the shelter of artificial breakwaters, and nearly everywhere there are problems of considerable west–east littoral sediment movement.

The Niger delta. The distributaries of the Niger delta and the rivers of south-eastern Nigeria provide riverine port sites, but rapid siltation makes access variable and sometimes difficult.

With its lack of shelter and heavy surf this coast acted more as a barrier than a zone of contact between land and sea. However, the early European settlements on the coast reflected the natural availability of port sites, and the character of more recent port development has been strongly influenced by the same physical geography.

The coast is generally backed by a fairly narrow coast plain, except in Senegambia where it is in effect a westward extension of the Senegal–Niger trough. Elsewhere, one rises fairly quickly to the usually well-dissected lower surface, and eventually to the middle surface which is the most extensive. Locally, these surfaces are broken by higher plateaux of restricted extent and residual inselbergs or extended scarp features (e.g. Mampong or Gambaga escarpments in Ghana, and Bandiagara and Hombori escarpments in Mali). In the Fouta Jallon and Guinea Highlands there are more extensive areas over 1200 m, and Mount Bintumani in Sierra Leone rises to 1947 m.

On the eastern margins of West Africa as we have defined it are the complex crystalline plateaux and mountains of the Adamawa massif, with areas rising to over 1800 m. Also markedly above the surrounding plains and separated from Adamawa by the Benue trough is the Jos Plateau of Nigeria.

Most of West Africa's drainage is to the Atlantic, but the main watershed lies relatively close to the coast, particularly in the Fouta Jallon – Guinea Highlands area which provides the headwaters of major rivers such as Senegal, Gambia and Niger. The Senegal and Gambia rivers flow north-westwards. The Niger initially flows north-eastwards towards the major trough which marks its middle course, and where formerly there was a large inland lake from which the river eventually broke out south-eastwards near Tosaye. There is still a large area of inland drainage west of Timbuktu.

Small ocean-going ships can penetrate only a short distance into the Niger delta, for some 240 km to Kuntaur on the Gambia and not at all on the Senegal. Some of the smaller rivers are able to take sea-going ships for short distances (the Casamance to Ziguinchor, the Saloum to Kaolack), and the Freetown river has been dredged for 23 km above Freetown to Pepel, the iron-ore loading port. It would be easy to under-estimate the role of inland waterways in West Africa because on most rivers and coastal lagoons there is some, and often considerable, use by local craft, and more sophisticated vessels are used over variable distances on a seasonal basis on rivers such as the Niger-Benue and Senegal.

THE CLIMATE

The general determinants of the pattern of climates in Africa were described in Chapter 3. In West Africa it is the seasonal movement of the *Inter Tropical Convergence* (ITC) which is the critical factor, determining as it does the distribution of the two principal air masses that affect the area, the amount and distribution of rain, the length of the dry season and other characteristics of the weather.

The two main circulatory systems involved are the *north-east Trades*, which are *continental tropical* (cT) air off the Sahara, and the *south-east Trades* which re-curve as they cross the equator to give a south-westerly flow of *maritime equatorial* (mE) air. Not surprisingly, the north-easterlies are associated with low relative humidities, little cloud formation, negligible rainfall, suspended dust which give haze and poor visibility, lower night temperatures and wide diurnal range of temperature. They have a desiccating effect on plants (which may cease to grow) and on humans, whose skin and mucous membranes dry up and in whom the serious cerebrospinal meningitis may develop. This is the 'harmattan' weather.

In contrast, the south-westerlies consist of moist air. As this wedge of moist air thickens southwards from the Convergence Zone deeper clouds are able to form. Much of the rain will be associated with these clouds and triggered by local convection, so that it will tend to be intermittent and in short sharp storms. Average maximum temperatures will tend to be lower and the minimum higher than in harmattan air, with resultant low diurnal and annual range of temperature.

The true equatorial climatic regime in which rainfall is high and evenly spread throughout the year is restricted in West Africa, and more usually the rainfall is peaked, either with a double or single maximum (Table 15). The former is found nearer the

Table 15 *West Africa: temperature and rainfall of selected stations*

Station	*Altitude (m)*		*J*	*F*	*M*	*A*	*M*	*J*	*J*	*A*	*S*	*O*	*N*	*D*	*Year*
Dakar	40	T	22.2	21.6	22.2	22.8	24.4	27.3	27.7	27.3	27.7	27.7	26.8	23.3	25.0
		R	—	—	—	—	—	17	89	254	131	38	2	8	539
Freetown	67	T	27.2	27.7	28.3	28.3	28.3	26.8	26.1	25.5	26.1	26.8	27.2	27.7	27.2
		R	11	8	30	104	292	508	904	930	724	319	130	36	3996
Accra	20	T	26.8	26.8	27.2	27.2	26.8	25.5	24.4	23.8	24.4	25.5	26.8	26.8	26.2
		R	15	25	45	93	144	178	42	15	25	49	38	18	673
Ibadan	224	T	26.8	27.7	28.3	27.7	26.8	25.5	24.4	24.4	25.0	25.5	26.8	26.8	26.8
		R	12	24	89	139	150	181	161	84	178	154	45	12	1236

Notes: T = Temperature (°C); R = rainfall (mm).

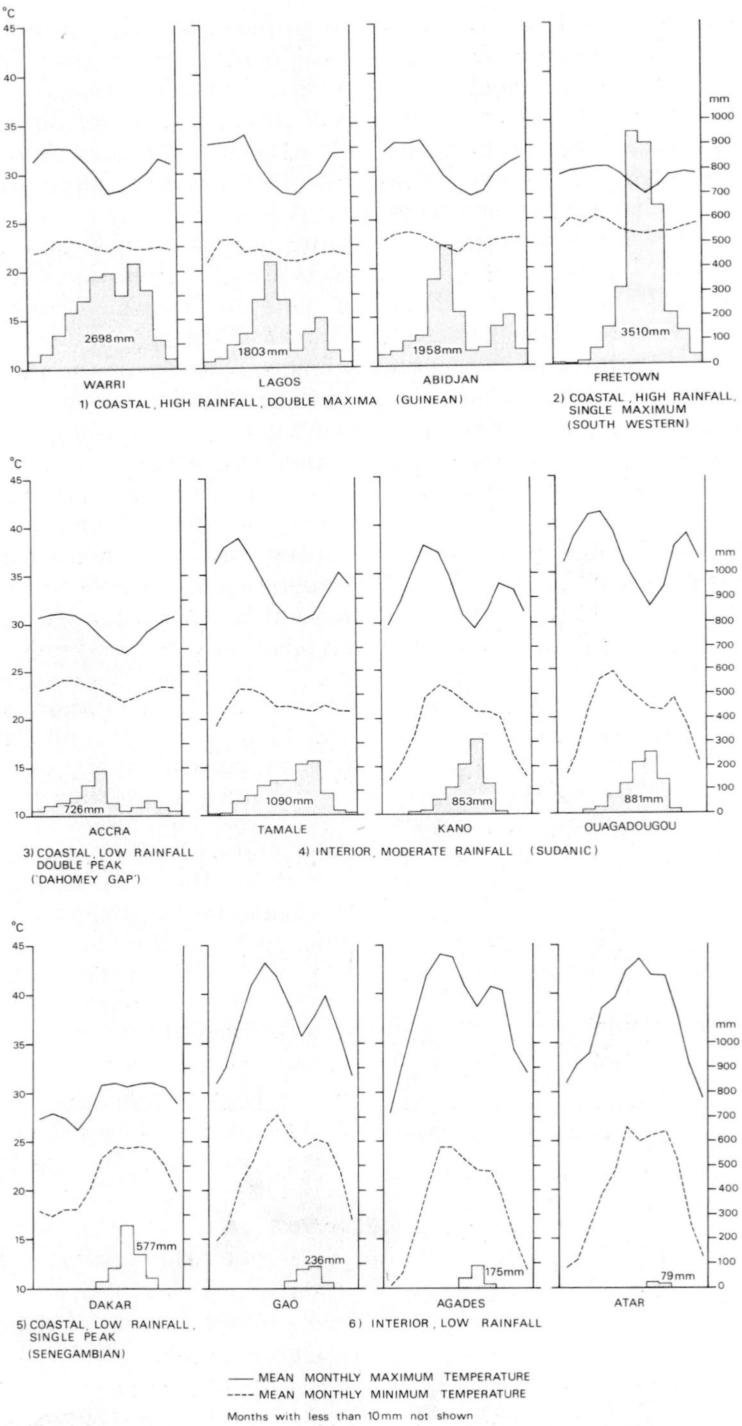

Figure 53 West Africa: climatic regions

coast (see Figure 53); and the first peak in the summer, as the ITC advances northwards, is usually more marked than the second, which comes in the autumn as the ITC retreats. As one moves inland the rain gradually increases to a single maximum in the summer as the ITC reaches its northward limit (see Chapter 3).

Except in a few higher areas and at night well inland under harmattan conditions, temperatures rarely drop below 6°C, and nowhere does the mean monthly temperature drop below 18°C. In general, the temperature range is least nearest the coast and increases inland, the greatest range usually being associated with harmattan conditions. Near the coast, heavy cloud during the rain season is also associated with lower ground temperatures. Thus, by any of the normal climatic classifications the whole of West Africa is tropical, and there is no period of the year when plant growth is inhibited by temperature. This is clearly important from an agricultural point of view because it means that moisture availability becomes the critical determinant of agricultural potential.

From Figure 53 it can be seen that rainfall totals tend to decrease inland from the coast and northwards along the coast. What might be classed as very high rainfall (2500 mm) is restricted to the Niger delta, parts of the highlands bordering Nigeria and Cameroon and the south-western coastal zone of Guinea, Sierra Leone, Liberia and western Côte d'Ivoire. Of note for its anomalous low rainfall is the coastal zone of eastern Ghana, Togo and Benin (the 'Dahomey Gap' of some books). Just east of Accra the average yearly rainfall is as low as 635 mm, a total which is only found as far north as southern Mali and Niger. This low rainfall has been explained in terms of the coastal alignment in relation to rain-bearing clouds and the stabilizing effect of cool offshore waters.

There is a dramatic increase in the length of the dry season as one moves inland and also northwards along the coast (Figure 54). As a generalization, 100 mm may be accepted as the minimum monthly rainfall to sustain agriculture. On this basis there is only a relatively limited southern area where this rainfall is exceeded for more than seven months, and for most of West Africa rainfall will be deficient for agriculture for at least half of the year.

While the popular perception of West Africa is of high rainfall and forest, the reality is very different. Potential evapo-transpiration rates for West Africa have been calculated at about 2000 mm for the Saharan fringes, decreasing to about 1000 mm near the coast. With such potential evapo-transpiration rates, and by virtue of the rainfall totals, the seasonal distribution, the stormy nature and rapid runoff and the increasing variability as the totals decline, much of West Africa has low effective rainfall and has a moisture deficit for the whole or considerable parts of the year. It is against this background that agricultural development has to be considered, and there are only relatively small areas where water is not a limiting factor.

THE SAHELIAN DROUGHT

The Sahel drought will now be considered in detail. The Arabic term 'Sahel' means shore – the shore or margin of the Sahara. It is the area approximately between 13°N and 17°N and marks the most northerly inland penetration of the deeper, rain-giving, south-westerly air. The actual limit of penetration and the depth of the moist air will vary from year to year, and at best this will be a marginal area for agriculture as there will be no guarantee of the 3–4 months with at least 100 mm, which might be considered minimal for grains. From 100 mm total, usually accepted as the desert boundary, the Sahel rainfall increases to about 760 mm on the southern margin. The rainfall at such low totals will be marked by extreme variability, as the figures in Table 16 illustrate.

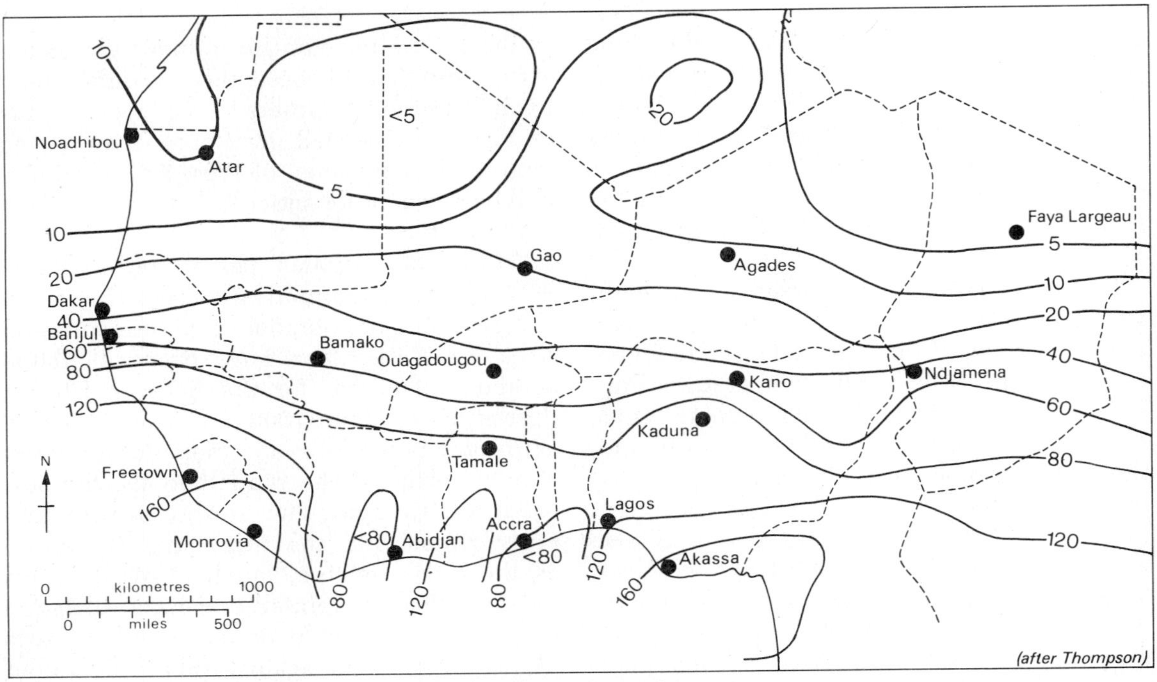

Figure 54 West Africa: mean annual rain days with more than 1 mm

Table 16 *Rainfall of selected Sahelian settlements*

	Mean (mm)	*Recorded extremes (mm)*
Nouakchott	126	15–259
Agades	142	37–285
Gao	245	88–429

With variations of this order there is a question regarding the extent to which any year's deviation from the mean may be considered abnormal. When it is remembered that a rainfall of 200–300 mm is needed to renew pasture and 150–200 mm will mean restrictions on grazing, the vulnerability of this zone for animal husbandry will be all too apparent. Indeed, the nomadic pastoralism which characterized the area was well adapted in a physical and social sense to the rainfall variability we have described.

There is considerable statistical and literary evidence to support the view that the rainfall has fluctuated over time, with, in the comparatively recent period, maxima centred on 1920, 1931 and 1957 and minima on 1913, 1942 and the early 1970s. However, there is also evidence of a longer-term southward movement of the isohyets (between 1960 and 1970 of about 78 km) and suggestions that this has continued into the 1980s. It is when lower than average rainfall is repeated year after year, as it has been in recent years, that the normal becomes abnormal. This is the 'desertification' process or the 'advance of the Sahara' which has captured attention, both popular and scientific.

There is no general agreement regarding the causes, nor indeed would this be the place to go into them. Suggestions include changes in the global circulation patterns, with gradual southward displacement of the tropical high-pressure zones. Some have tried to establish links with the strength of the so-called Walker cell in the Pacific, associated as this seems to be with up-draughts, storms and flooding in western South America (the El Nino) and down-draught, and drought in the western

Pacific and possibly backwash drought effects in Africa. This seems possible as an explanation of the recent widespread drought in southern Africa, but obviously the global circulatory systems are connected. Our concern is more for the results and implications.

Even if the scale is questioned in places the general results are not in doubt. There has undoubtedly been widespread reduction in pasturage, serious loss of livestock (20–40 per cent in Senegal, Mauritania, Mali, Niger and Chad) and drops in grain production. Over 95 per cent of the grain production in the Sahel is rain-fed and a 20–50 per cent below 'normal' rainfall in Senegal in 1983 left the country with a 250,000-tonne cereal deficit. In the early 1970s and again in the early 1980s there has been widespread increase in malnutrition and hunger, with localized deaths from famine, and formerly nomadic peoples have fallen back on the towns in large numbers.

Some understanding of the nature of the drought is clearly important as a basis for finding solutions to the problems it causes. The strategy for dealing with generalized, irreversible, long-term climatic change will have to be different from those for dealing with a cyclic phenomenon on different time scales. There is a school of thought which holds that, more than anything else, it is human activity that has turned the recent drought, for which the people of the region are customarily prepared, into a disaster.

The end of warfare and raiding, reductions in the death rate through improved medical services, increased population, extension of cultivation into ever more marginal areas which were once the preserve of the pastoralists, firewood extraction (estimated at 2.5–3.0 tonnes per family a year or over 50 million tonnes for the whole region) and increased livestock (more people keeping livestock, better veterinary services and a trend to keeping cattle and sheep which are more demanding on pasture than goats and camels) have resulted in ecological imbalance and environmental degradation. It is for these and some political reasons (e.g. pastoralists are not able to move so freely across frontiers) that it has been suggested that the Sahel disaster was caused only proximately by drought.

Since 1975 annual per capita aid to the Sahel has averaged $40, compared with $20 for the rest of Africa and $12 for other developing countries. Between 1975 and 1978, 72 projects for export crop production (e.g. cotton) received aid, compared with only 28 for food crops. The average annual increase in irrigated cropland has been a mere 5000 ha, and rain-fed agriculture, on which the bulk of the population depends, has received only 4 per cent of all aid. Not surprisingly, the renewed drought of 1983–4 found the region in no better position to cope with the problems.

A meeting of the 'Sahel Club' of countries late in 1983 confirmed that food production was growing less rapidly than population, that the land resources of the Sahel were becoming depleted, that deforestation continued despite some forestation projects, and animal husbandry had still to be modernized. It was felt that far more attention should be paid to irrigation of food crops, that the rural communities had to be more involved to ensure their cooperation, that range-land management was needed for cattle, and that forestry projects had to be vastly extended in scale if they were to have any impact. Too much aid has been directed (and often misdirected) towards relief and not enough has been devoted to effective agricultural production projects. There have been cases where well-intentioned provision of bore-holes and watering points has served to increase cattle population, extend trampling of vegetation around water points and so add to devastated pasturage.

It is well to remember that drought has also in recent years been a recurrent feature of Ethiopia and the Horn of Africa, parts of East Africa and parts of southern Africa, so widespread in fact that major climatic changes seem possible. Within West Africa the worst affected area (Figure 55) is a broad belt including central Chad, southern Niger, northern Nigeria, Burkina Faso, southern Mali and southern Mauritania, with Senegal and Gambia

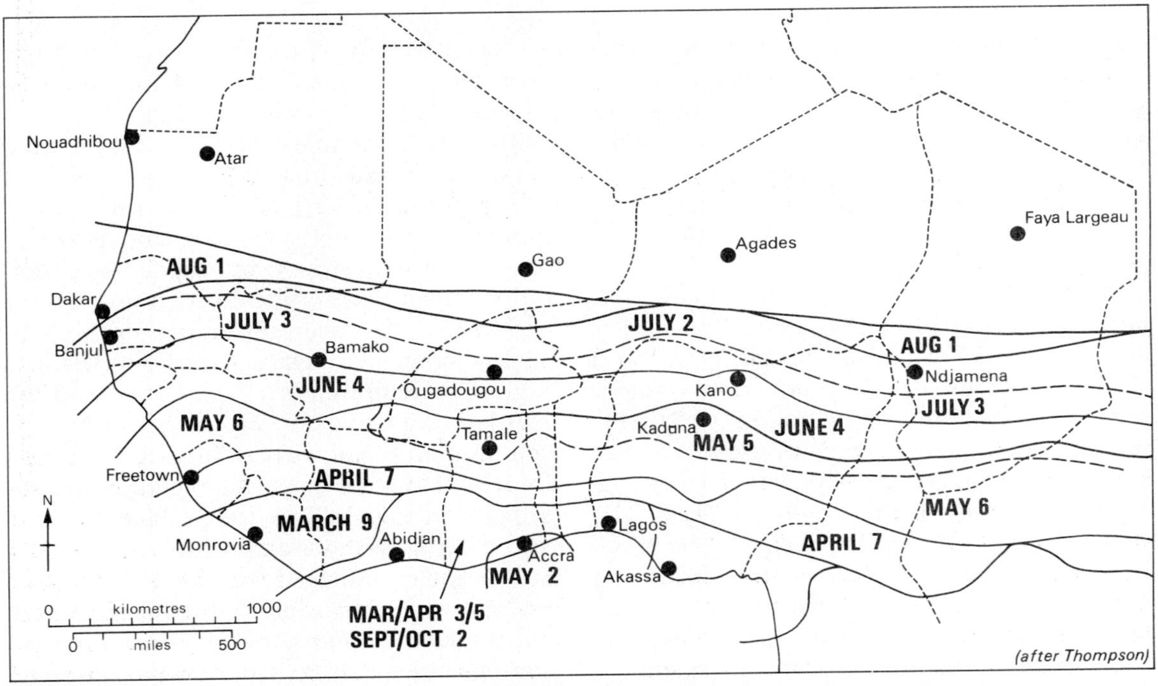

Figure 55 West Africa: first month and number of months with rainfall in excess of 100 mm

less severely affected. Even better-watered areas such as Ghana and Côte d'Ivoire in 1983 suffered extensive bush fires as a result of prolonged dry weather. Ghana's Volta River has its headwaters much further north in areas of much reduced rainfall, and the level of Lake Volta has fallen so much that hydroelectric power has been reduced, the aluminium smelter closed and other electricity users severely restricted. Côte d'Ivoire's Koussou HEP scheme has also been on reduced output as a result of low water levels.

21 The dry lands of West Africa

The arid and semi-arid countries of West Africa, Africa's 'crisis belt', were introduced in the discussion of the Sahel in Chapter 20. Mauritania, Mali, Niger and Chad have large parts of their territories that are truly Saharan, and all have strong links historically with Saharan and northern African culture. It was said of Mauritania by its first President, and it is as true of Mali, Niger and Chad, that 'by virtue of its geographical situation, its history and its economic conditions it is rather a hyphen (between West and North Africa)'. Although there are no clear boundaries between the ethnic groups, these countries display a dualism between peoples of North African stock – Caucasoid, Hamitic language and Islamic stock – and peoples of southern African stock – negroid and Negritic/Bantu language. In Mauritania and Chad these contrasts have certainly provided a basis for continuing conflict.

With Burkina Faso, these countries also share a common colonial heritage. Until 1960 they were French colonies, Mauritania, Mali, Niger and Burkina Faso being parts of the administratively integrated French West Africa, and Chad a part of French Equatorial Africa. With the exception of Mauritania they have the problems associated with being landlocked – long distances and high cost of transport to ports, political problems and the added disadvantage of rain-season disruptions to their poorly developed transport systems. The low rainfall, its variability and general marginality for agriculture, both cultivation and pastoral, provide a common basis for their development potential and problems. Chad, Burkina Faso and Mali with per capita Gross National Product of \$120, \$190 and \$190 respectively, are among the world's poorest nations, while Mauritania (\$320) and Niger (\$330) have moved slightly up the scale. The reasons for the generally low level of economic development can now be examined as we consider each country in more detail.

THE CAPE VERDE ISLANDS

The Cape Verde archipelago, which is separated from mainland Cape Verde by a sea passage of 500 km in width, obtained its independence from Portugal in 1975. The archipelago consists of ten larger and five small islands. With the exception of the low-lying Sal, Boavista and Maio, the islands are mountainous, highly dissected volcano remnants, Fogo rising to 2600 m and being still active.

In relation to the prevailing north-east trade winds the islands may be divided into two groups – the windward group comprising Santa Antao, Sao Vicente, Santa Lucia, Sao Nicolau, Boavista and Sal and the leeward group of Maio, Sao Tiago, Fogo and Brava. The total area of the islands is 4035 km^2 and only three exceed 600 km^2 – Sao Tiago (992), Santa Antao (754) and Boavista (622). The total population in 1983 was estimated to be 306,000, which gives an overall density of 76

Plate 24 Wind powered water pump on the semi-arid Cape Verde Islands

persons per km², but some 150,000 are concentrated on Sao Tiago – the next most populous island being Santa Antao (45,000). The capital Praia (49,000) is located on Sao Tiago, but Mindelo (30,000) on Sao Vicente is the economic capital and main port.

The islands are rightly considered as part of 'dry' West Africa, with a rainfall of only 125–250 mm, a normal water deficiency and periodic spells of longer, often devastating drought. The years since 1968 have been one such period, and Portugal had to launch relief programmes. Such droughts are often punctuated by short, very heavy storms which cause flash flooding and damage but provide little effective moisture.

The bulk of the population derives its livelihood from agriculture, but only 20 per cent of the food consumed comes from local farms. Over half of the farms are less than 1 hectare, and share-croppers make up half of the farming population. Beans, maize, cassava and sweet potatoes are the main food crops, with bananas and sugar on some larger estates. About 2000 ha are under irrigation, and there are plans to expand this to 6000 ha; but even with intensive use of terraced hillsides it is estimated that only 40 per cent of food needs can be satisfied by local production. In 1978, 45,000 tonnes of grain had to be imported, and at Praia special grain-storage facilities have been provided and have served to attract population to the capital. On the flat islands animal husbandry is more important and provides about 25 per cent of the value of exports. The fishing industry employs over 3000 people and provides 40 per cent of the export value. Tuna provide the main deep-water catch with lobster important in the near-shore zone. With over 600,000 km² of exclusive economic zone, Cape Verde is in a position to expand its fishing industry, and with Icelandic and Swedish aid improvements are taking place in the type of vessels used, storage and processing.

During the first 5- year plan, which ended in 1985, there was an emphasis on social and economic infrastructure, but a cement industry has been established and a shipyard at Mindelo. There is a canning factory for fish and cigarette and clothing industries have been set up. During the second plan it would seem that port improvements will be a priority and there will be attempts to make better use of locally produced pozzolana, a volcanic rock that could possibly be used in the cement industry, and salt produced on the island of Sal. The desalinization plant on Sao Vicente is to be modernized and there are plans for a tourist complex on Boavista.

The country is clearly disadvantaged by its small size, dispersed population and problems of inter-island communication (the international airport is on low-lying Sal which is not a main concentration of population), the lack of land for cultivation, the problems of water supply and the generally low level of Government income to finance development. Some income is generated by ship and aircraft refuelling services, but with as many Cape Verdeans living overseas as on the islands themselves, and with their remittances actually in excess of the island-generated GNP, it is this, more than anything, that enables the economy to survive even if it does not allow for growth.

MAURITANIA

With an area of 1.03 million km^2, Mauritania is larger than France and Spain combined and occupies the Atlantic façade of the Sahara from the Senegal River northwards to Cap Blanc. The coast is relatively smooth, with only a few promontories such as Arguin and Cap Blanc, and backed by dunes and salty mud-flats known as Sebkhas. Inland, the relief is generally of monotonous plains but with some residual scarp features trending north-east/south-west and facing westwards. East of Atar, one such feature rises to over 500 m and the highest point in the country is in the Kedia D'Idjil (915 m) in the north. Where these residual features have considerable linear extent they are called *kedia*, while smaller isolated inselbergs are known as *guelb*.

Much of the northern and western part of the country comprises Pre-Cambrian crystalline rocks, part of the Western Saharan shield. As in other areas these are mineralized, but the eastern parts of the country consist mainly of Palaeozoic sandstones and shales, the western edge of which is marked by the scarp feature near Atar already mentioned. As much as 40 per cent of the country is covered by superficial deposits, principally sand. In the south the linear north-east/south-west trending dunes tend to be 'fixed' with vegetation, but in the north – as for example along the western part of the railway line to Nouadhibou – the dunes are highly mobile 'barchans' which can cause considerable problems along lines of communications.

In a country in which two-thirds of the population is nomadic, census taking is not easy; but on the basis of a 1976 count the estimated population in 1982 was 1.73 million. This gives an overall density of 1.67 people per km^2, but large parts of the north and east of the country are virtually uninhabited – part of the 'empty quarter of the Western Sahara' – and the highest regional population density is only 7 people per km^2 in Gorgol. Some three-quarters of the population are of Arab–Berber stock, divided into a superior group (the Bidan) and a traditionally servile group (the Haratin), and in 1981 it was still being claimed that 10 per cent of the population were slaves. They are predominantly nomadic peoples. In a narrow zone along the Senegal river in the south are negro peoples who are mainly sedentary cultivators. The country's cultural ties with northern Africa are reflected in its official designation as an Islamic Republic.

Climate

The country may be divided into two main zones. Saharan conditions with annual rainfall of less than 100 mm prevail over some two-thirds of the country, mainly in the north and east. Nouadhibou has a mean annual rainfall of 32 mm, and at the northern iron-ore mining centre of Zouerate some years may go by without rain. Even here, the occasional rainstorm will produce some brief vegetation cover (R'bia) able to support camels. Very high daytime temperatures and low evening temperatures are typical. There is no permanent surface water, but depressions may hold some moisture and capillary action produces salt pans at the surface and a traditional Saharan trade commodity.

The rest of the country may be classed as Sahelian, with rainfall increasing towards the south to a maximum of just over 600 mm in the Selibaby region. All that has been said about rainfall variability applies here. In normal years this summer rain will be adequate to provide some temporary tributaries to, and flooding in, lower-lying clay areas along the Senegal river. This *Chemama* area is important for cultivation, and for fishing as the receding waters leave fish trapped. There is also a narrow zone in which the cold Canary Current has the affect of reducing temperatures, creating some fog but not producing any precipitation.

It has been calculated that the 250 mm isohyet has moved 200 km southwards in the last two decades, so that Mauritania is in effect becoming more Saharan in character.

The traditional economy

At the time of independence in 1960 the exports comprised livestock (86 per cent by value), fish (5.0 per cent), gum arabic (4.5 per cent), dates (3.5 per cent) and salt (1 per cent).

There are no reliable figures on animal husbandry, but it understandably provided the traditional economic base for the nomadic peoples in such a marginal area. Pasture able to support cattle is found only in the south in areas of rainfall in excess of 200 mm, and northwards sheep and goats increase in importance. In the centre of the country camels are dominant, but in the east and north there is a large area where even camel pasture is deficient. Most of the livestock export consisted of cattle 'on the hoof' to Senegal and Mali, but there is now an abattoir at Kaedi. However, in 1983 it was estimated that some 80 per cent of the pasture lands had in two decades been 'lost to the desert', and whereas in 1965 nomads comprised 83 per cent of the population, the proportion has now fallen to 25 per cent as people have been driven to the towns. The basis of the traditional pastoral economy is therefore in jeopardy.

The cool offshore waters provide valuable fishing grounds, traditionally fished by Canary Islanders, many of whom based their operations and landed their catch at what is now Nouadhibou (formerly Port Etienne) in the sheltered waters of the Baie du Levrier. The very low relative humidity and almost complete lack of rain made simple sun-drying an effective form of processing, and dried fish – as much as 15,000 tonnes in good years – was exported as far as Gabon and the Congo. Many other countries have started fishing Mauritania's waters and, while it is not easily controlled, there has been an attempt to persuade them to land and process the fish at Nouadhibou. Some half dozen new fishing companies have been set up for this purpose, and exports in some years have reached 80,000 tonnes. In addition there is fishing on the Senegal River and its tributaries.

The gum arabic was collected from acacia trees mainly in the southern part of the country and exports reached 5000 tonnes in 1968. However, the drought has reduced acacias by some two-thirds in a zone within 100 km of the Senegal River. Date production is confined to the oasis areas (principally those of Atar, Tidjikja and Kiffra), but it has never been more than a minor export. Some wheat, tobacco and vegetables are grown in the shade of the date-palms. Salt has traditionally been dug at a number of Saharan locations.

In addition to providing some exports these commodities were also consumed locally and there was a zone of more general cultivation along the Senegal River. The rainfall variability has always made this a marginal area, and 77 per cent of the cultivation was dependent on 'stored' water of the river depressions and wells, and seasonal flooding. Millet is the principal grain crop, providing over 80 per cent of the tonnage; but even before the drought the crop was barely adequate to satisfy demand and, from peaks of about 90,000 tonnes, production has dropped in some years to as little as 20,000 tonnes. In 1981, low water levels resulted in only 20 per cent of normal planting, and food aid has been essential in recent years. Crops of lesser importance in the chemama are rice, maize, yams, sugar and cotton, and vegetables are found in areas where groundwater can be tapped.

The traditional economy was, therefore, very limited in its scope. It was essentially subsistence, with 95 per cent of the population dependent on agriculture, with at most about 35 per cent of the livestock and 15 per cent of the crops exported. The trade, such as it was, was mainly just across the borders with near neighbours, especially Senegal and Mali; and apart from the salt and fish, the economic centre of gravity was in the south of the country. Indeed, the colonial territory of Mauritania was administered from St Louis in Senegal, and Dakar provided the main link with the world economy. There was no scope for capital accumulation and the economic system was incapable of generating growth. It was clear that any economic growth would be by way of an external influence (or 'impulsion exterieure' of the French writers).

Economic development

Since independence in 1960 there has been a major change in the economy – and this did in fact come about as the result of an external influence, namely, the demand for iron-ore. As long ago as the eleventh century there were references to the *djbel le hadid*, or iron mountains. During the Second World War aircraft compasses went badly astray when crossing parts of north-central Mauritania, and between 1952 and 1957 detailed prospecting identified the multiple ore bodies of the minerally enriched Kedia D'Idjil (Figure 56), and high-quality haematite iron reserves of over 200 million tonnes. Between April 1960 when work started and June 1963 when the first shipment of ore was made, a full industrial infrastructure had to be created in the northern desert. Mine installations at Zouerate and F'Derik were completed, 52 km of road constructed, airstrips provided, a 650 km railway built across difficult terrain of large barchans and moving sand dunes, two towns developed (each with full services for a population of over 5000), an ore-exporting port provided at Point Central near Nouadhibou, and electricity and water supplies ensured. The mining company started as a joint French, British, German, Italian and Mauritanian government enterprise, but it was nationalized in 1974 – in which year production reached a record 11.9 million tonnes. A slump in world demand, low prices and in the late 1970s disruption to transport resulting from Mauritania's war over Western Sahara, led to reduced export and income.

The Kedia D'Idjil deposits have been worked now for 20 years and their life expectancy is a further 10 years, in which time the higher-grade ores will have been exhausted. In the late 1970s work started on a new mine at Guelb El Rhein some 40 km from F'Derik, and production started in 1984. This will certainly extend the life of iron mining, but the lower-grade (37 per cent) ores have to be beneficiated to a saleable grade (around 65 per cent Fe). There are other reserves (e.g. at Oum Arwagen) that can be exploited.

There can be no doubting that the economic impact of the iron mining, now providing over 80 per cent of export earnings, has boosted per capita GDP to $320 (a figure which conceals a range from as low as $150 in the traditional

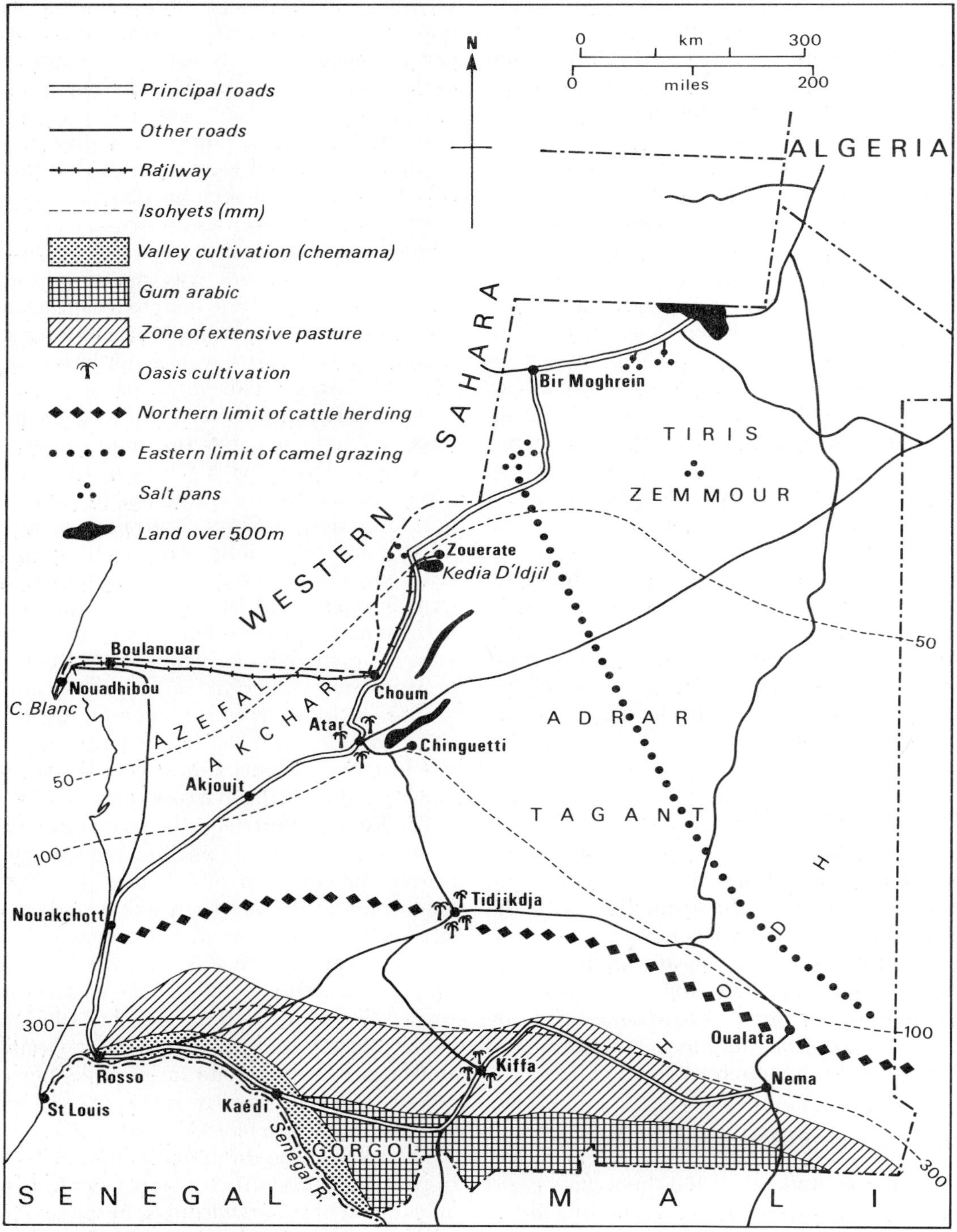

Figure 56 Mauritania: economic development

sector to $1300 in the modern), provided basic infrastructure and moved the economic centre of gravity to the north of the country. The availability of water and electricity at Nouadhibou has made possible the development of fishing and the fish processing industry, and general port facilities have been developed. A small oil refinery scheduled to open in 1978 has still to become operational.

Between 1971 and 1978 copper-ore was mined at Akjoujt. It was, however, refined by an expensive process which was plagued by operating problems, and the mine was eventually closed. Akjoujt was linked to Nouakchott by a surfaced road, and there are proposals to reactivate the mine and refinery with Arab money when world copper prices are right. It is thought that gold could also be obtained as a by-product of the copper mining. There are indications of uranium in the extreme north of the country and large deposits of gypsum, now mined in very small quantities for export to Senegal, not far from Nouakchott (where a new port was commissioned in 1987).

Mauritania is still a poor country, and although fiscal resources has been greatly increased, it is doubtful if the bulk of the population has yet benefited.

Development planning

If the income of the mining industry is to benefit the country, the revenue has rapidly to be channelled into self-sustaining economic development. Four-year plans between 1964 and 1971 tried to extend irrigated cultivation, especially rice and sugar, and saw the establishment of the Kaedi meat processing plant, a sugar refinery and a cement works. There were also improvements to the road system, especially on the east–west axis from Nouakchott to Nema through the agricultural south; further feeder roads to this are planned.

In recent years much of the effort has been devoted to the immediate problems created by the drought. Development emphasis has been shifted back to the rural sector, the extension of irrigation and the redevelopment and reorganization along modern lines of the livestock industry. Mauritania is a member of OMVS (Senegal River Authority) which in 1986 completed a saline exclusion barrage at Diama near the mouth of the Senegal River, and which is working on a water storage dam at Manantali. Eventually these should greatly increase the potential for irrigated agriculture and improve the river as a transport artery.

Meanwhile, the population is retreating from the rural areas. It is estimated that Nouakchott, the new capital designed in 1960 for a population of 25,000, has now reached 500,000, most of whom live in shanty and tent settlements devoid of facilities. Even the smaller towns have grown rapidly. In consequence there are pressures on the government to channel resources into job creation and urban improvement. The drought has clearly compounded the problems of an already fragile economy and postponed the day when the population at large will benefit from economic development.

MALI

In a number of respects the potential and problems of Mali are similar to those of

Plate 25 Dry scrubland in the Mali Sahel zone

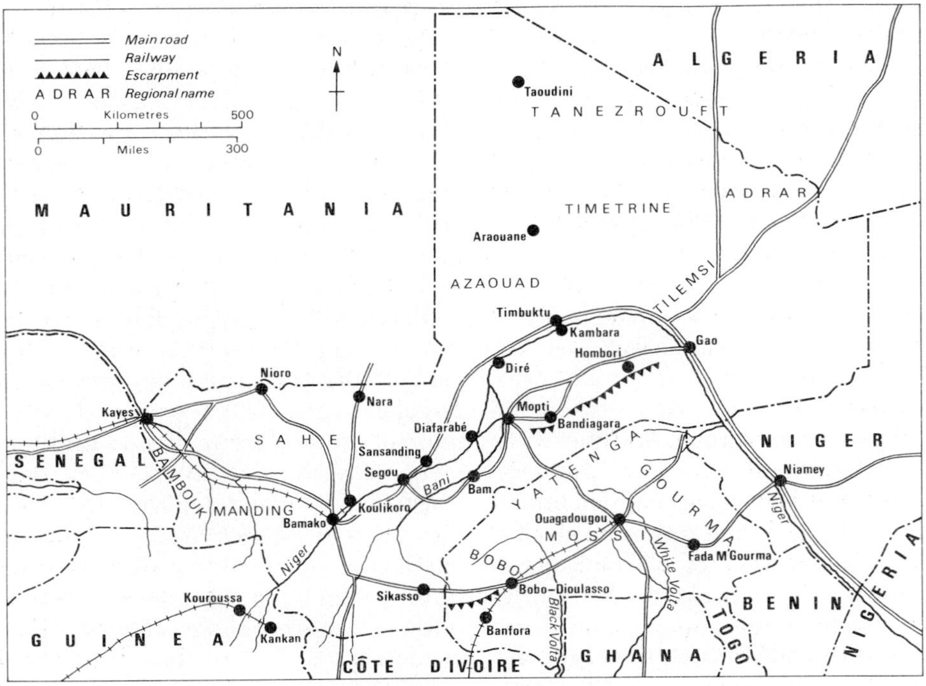

Figure 57 Mali and Burkina Faso

Mauritania, although the country is rather larger (1.14 million km^2) and has a greater population (estimated at 7.02 million in 1982). Yet this total gives an average of only 5.66 people per km^2 for the whole country, and as in Mauritania the highest densities are found in the better-watered south-western parts of the country (57 per cent of the population is to be found south and west of Bamako and only 14 per cent in the northern half of the country).

The country can be divided into five fairly distinct regions (Figure 57). In the extreme south-west is an area of higher relief with rocks of Ordovician–Silurian age – the Bambouk and Manding Mountains – which are the northern flanks of the Fouta Jallon extending into Mali as sandstone scarp features, one of which terminates south of the Niger just to the east of the capital, Bamako. These features also serve to provide breaks of slope on the Senegal River at Kayes and the Niger east of Bamako, and they disrupt navigation on both rivers.

The region south and east of the Bani River and extending into Burkina Faso comprises a series of plateau surfaces separated by eastward-facing sandstone scarps, the most impressive of which, with a 250 m scarp face, is that from Bandiagara to Hombori.

West of Segou and north of the Niger is a fairly monotonous sandy plain area extending into the Hodh region of south-eastern Mauritania.

The extensive area north of Timbuktu is varied geologically, with Palaeozoic limestones and sandstones and, in the Adrar, an area of Pre-Cambrian granites. Only in the Adrar (600 m plus) south-western extension of the Ahaggar is there any higher ground. Elsewhere the relief is fairly monotonous stony desert, as in Tanezrouft, or more sandy surfaces as in Azaouad. The Tilemsi depression marks a former pluvial period course of the middle Niger.

The Niger river provides the artery of the country and its course can be divided into several distinct sections. In the higher land south-west of Bamako is what is best termed the Upper Valley, with numerous smaller headwaters and fairly narrow main river valley. From Koulikoro to Sansanding the main river is much broader but the flood plain is restricted in width. East of Sansanding is the inland delta. The area of the former middle Niger inland lake is still marked by a braided main river and much indeterminate drainage. A distinction is sometimes made between the 'dead' delta from Sansanding to Diafarabe, where the Niger divides, and the 'live' part eastwards to Timbuktu with a complex network of water courses and seasonally flooded depressions. Below Kabara, port for Timbuktu, the Niger once again becomes a single river in a valley 12-15 km in width. The Niger's main tributary, the Bani, also provides a zone of better-watered land.

The importance of the Niger for the economic development of the country will be appreciated in relation to the climate; only in the extreme south of the country is a rainfall total in excess of 100 mm experienced for 5–7 months of the year. At Bamako the total is 1200 mm and only 3–5 months have in excess of 100 mm. North of Timbuktu the climate is Saharan with negligible rain (Araouane: 50 mm). Therefore, most of the country is moisture deficient for a large part of the year, and this determines agricultural practice.

The agricultural economy

Mali's land area is 60.3 per cent desert, 27 per cent sub-desert, 7 per cent grazing, 3.7 per cent woodland, and 1.5 per cent arable. Of Mali's 1.8 million ha of arable land (some 23 per cent of the total for all Saharan countries), 80 per cent is devoted to food crop production, 8.6 per cent for groundnuts and 3.2 per cent for cotton. The productivity of the traditional cultivation is low, as is the ratio of cultivated to cultivable land.

In view of the climatic regime it is not surprising that livestock husbandry (largely nomadic) is a main element of the economy, with, at a peak, some 4.5–5.0 million cattle, 10 million sheep and goats, and 165,000 camels. In the 1960s live animals invariably provided the leading export in terms of value, with cattle moving on the hoof and by road and rail – principally to Côte d'Ivoire and Senegal, but also to some other neighbours. Kayes is an important centre for this trade in the west and has a tannery, Bamako has an abattoir and Mopti a large cattle market. As a result of the drought there has been the tendency for greater southward movement of pastoralists, with over-grazing and conflict between herdsmen and cultivators. In 1984 it was reported that 1.6 million head of cattle had converged on the Mopti region where there was grazing for half that number. There is also evidence of people with greater income buying up cattle at very low prices from desperate herdsmen. Herds which had been greatly depleted at the height of the drought had by 1982 been restocked, only to be reduced again in 1983–4.

Millet and sorghum are the main crops where there is dependence on the rain; but where flood waters can be utilized and where there is more formal irrigation, rice is of greater importance. Groundnuts, often grown in rotation with cotton and millet, used to be an important crop especially westwards from Bamako to Kayes; this provided an export of declining importance after independence in 1960. There were certainly French visions of Mali as the 'bread basket' for its West African colonies, but the potential has never been realized and a normal small cereal deficit rose to a shortfall of over 300,000 tonnes in 1983–4 after two years of low rainfall.

Irrigation

Along the Niger and its tributaries the potential for irrigation is vast, yet less than a quarter of the land available for irrigation is so used and much of that not very effectively. What the Nile is to Egypt, the Niger could be to Mali.

In the Upper Valley the Niger and some of its tributaries, together with some small barrages and canals, are the basis for irrigating relatively small areas for rice, cotton and tobacco. Downstream the seasonal flooding is a traditional basis for cultivation, especially of millet, and there have been both small-scale projects to use water more effectively and large-scale perennial irrigation projects. In the early 1920s the French installed large, wood-fired steam pumps at Diré, the main impact of which was deforestation. This scheme was revived with diesel pumps in the 1940s and again with solar pumps in 1979 to irrigate a mere 150 ha.

On a grander scale was the Sansanding Barrage on which work started in 1934 under the Office du Niger. The barrage raises the water level in the Niger by over 4 m and allows water to be diverted into canals and some former dry courses of the river. Land has been levelled and a total of 45,000 ha is irrigated. The original plan was to grow cotton, but the emphasis gradually switched to rice. The Office du Niger has absorbed a large part of Mali's agricultural investment without producing commensurate returns. The reasons for this seem to be partly physical (the soils are not comparable with those along the Nile), but mainly administrative and social. There were constant changes of plans, inefficiency of organization and lack of experience and even reluctance on the part of the farmers. Even now only 4500 families are supported. Since 1975 the irrigated area has hardly increased, with new land often replacing that which has gone out of use. Despite suggestions that large dams are an expensive way of increasing productivity, one of the two main dams proposed by the Senegal River Authority (OMVS) is located on the Sofring tributary in Mali and this will serve as a main flow regulator for the main river. It is not clear how far Mali will benefit from this project in the isolated south-west of the country, unless it be from the hydroelectric power rather than from irrigation.

Evidence suggests that an emphasis on small schemes with the full cooperation of the peasant farmers will show better returns. For example, near Diré in the mid-1970s, simple but efficient water control on some 250 ha has provided a sedentarized Tuareg group of 140 families with a surplus of rice, and they are now upgrading some grazing areas for milk-giving goats. Community cooperation can clearly be effective where it is not politicized. A project is in progress at Sélimgué to provide HEP for Bamako, the capital, and some irrigation.

Planning

After independence Mali adopted a doctrinaire socialist approach to development, with widespread but largely ineffective state involvement in production and services. The 1960–5 Five-Year Plan emphasized peasant involvement, irrigation, improved stock-raising and a start on industrialization, but during the 1960s growth in production, especially in agriculture, was lower than population growth. Later, there was greater emphasis on industry (a groundnut oil-mill, a sugar refinery, cotton and textile mills, meat processing, fruit conservancy, tobacco, matches, footware, cement and metal-working), but only the textile factory at Segou and the cigarette and sugar works seem to have been successful, possible because they were financed and managed by the Chinese.

Since 1980 the government appears to have adopted a more realistic food production, storage and distribution strategy, with an overhaul of the cereal market and pricing system; but it is doubtful whether the farmers yet have the real incentive to improve their methods and increase their production, as undoubtedly is possible with better use of the available water. In 1984 a plan was initiated to provide 4.5 million people and 11,000 villages in the Sahel zone with adequate water over a 10–15 year period.

During the 1960s there was considerable investment in mineral exploration. There is some iron-ore near the Senegalese border possibly some gold and uranium, and phosphate in the Tilemsi depression. Salt is mined at Taoudini in the extreme north. However it does not appear that minerals provide any immediate prospect of raising Mali from the bottom five of the world's poorest nations.

Transport

As a landlocked country, Mali's development problems are exaggerated by the distance and cost of transport to external markets. The Niger river is seasonably navigable between Koulikoro and Gao (July–December), from Mopti to Gao (December–March), and from Bamako to Kourrousa (July–December). The Senegal river is navigable below Kayes from August to October, but this could be extended as water levels rise behind the Diama Barrage.

Mali's main traditional westward link was the railway from Koulikoro and Bamako to Kayes and the Senegalese port of Dakar. For political reasons this route was closed for a time in the early 1960s, and roads were improved from Bamako through Sikasso to the Côte d'Ivoire–Burkina Faso railway at Bobo Dioulasso. This provided an alternative route to the sea through Abidjan. The need to bring rapid food aid to Mali in the mid-1970s demonstrated the inadequacy of the transport, the Dakar Niger railway having a freight capacity of only 1500 tonnes a week. Only 6100 km of the country's 13,360 km of roads are classed as all-season, and a mere 1693 km are surfaced. Certainly, Mali can ill afford the intermittent conflict (which surfaced again at Christmas, 1985) over its southern boundary with Burkina Faso, a dispute inherited from the colonial era.

BURKINA FASO

Burkina Faso (Upper Volta until August 1984), with an area of 274,000 km^2, is the smallest of the Sahelian states but has the largest population (an estimated 7.29 million in 1982). With an average population density of 26.6 people per km^2 it compares with some of the coastal rather than Sahelian states; but this average conceals the fact that large areas have only a sparse population, and most of the population is concentrated in the country's middle belt, the region in which the Mossi people predominate.

There are several factors influencing this population distribution. There has been a retreat from the Volta River headwater valleys where river blindness is endemic. The Gourma region of the east is a somewhat negative area with considerable laterization of basement rocks and some superficial sand towards the north-east. In a narrow band along the south-east border and in the north-west are areas of permeable Palaeozoic sandstones which give an arid, infertile surface.

The bulk of the country comprises Pre-Cambrian crystallines which give rapid runoff and soils which are generally thin and easily eroded. An exception to this is the lower Pre-Cambrian Birrimian rocks in a band across the west-central part of the country, which give both more hilly relief and better soil. With the exception of the eastward-facing Banfora scarp, an extension of Mali's southern area of Palaeozoic sandstones, Burkina Faso is characterized by the monotony of its relief.

Burkina Faso's rainfall ranges from over 1200 mm south of Bobo-Dioulasso, with six months in excess of 100 mm; through about 900 mm in the Ouagadougou region, with only four months in excess of 100 mm; to less than 700 mm in the north. These totals are subject to some variability, and the effectiveness of the rainfall is further reduced by the rapid runoff in the crystalline rock areas and the extreme porosity of the sandstones. The country was adversely affected by the drought in the early 1970s which ended fragile growth prospects for a decade, and in 1982 the rainfall in the Yatenga region was reported 40 per cent down on normal, with serious grain deficits.

The economy

The economy is almost entirely based on agriculture, which supports 95 per cent of the population, and the traditional sector accounts for as much as 70 per cent of the GDP. Some 90 per cent of the crop area is taken up by the main food crops, guinea corn (especially in the south-west) and millet (the Mossi area) with smaller areas of maize, rice, yams and cassava. The main export crops are cotton, groundnuts, benniseed and shea nuts. The groundnut and shea nut oil is also used extensively in local cooking. At independence in 1960, Burkina Faso exported 2000 tonnes of cotton, but this had increased to over 20,000 tonnes by 1981 (probably much more if 'unrecorded' exports are included). Much of the development aid in the 1960s went into export crop production when arguably it would have been better devoted to food crops for which, in relation to population, there has been a negative growth of –2.8 per cent a year.

Traditionally, livestock has provided the principal export. The northern and eastern parts of the country are largely free of tsetse flies, and the more resistant Ndama breed of cattle are found in the south. Much of this trade was 'on the hoof' with the Côte d'Ivoire and Ghana, and Burkina Faso has been noted for the high proportion of its trade accounted for by near neighbours rather than overseas.

The general poverty of the country is reflected in the Burkinabe having the lowest life expectancy of any country (39 years), a very low per capita GDP ($190), a 5 per cent literacy level, only 10 per cent of population having access to reasonable water, and with only one doctor for every 55,000 people. Diseases such as sleeping sickness, malaria, bilharzia and river blindness are widespread. Large numbers have traditionally left, either seasonally or more permanently, the over-populated rural areas to seek employment in Côte d'Ivoire and Ghana. Yet with declining levels of economic activity these countries are increasingly reluctant to accept such migrants, and in 1979 Ghana actually repatriated many.

There has been no real industrial policy. Industrial activity is still rudimentary, with a total employment of about 4000 in the 26 largest enterprises, largely concentrated in the capital, Ouagadougou, and Bobo Dioulasso. The largest, and possibly most successful, of the industries is cotton textiles, and there are local cotton ginneries. Other resource-based industries include a tannery and shoe factory, a sugar refinery (operating well below capacity for most of the time), an abattoir, a rice mill, and groundnut, cotton-seed and shea nut oil mills, a soap factory and fruit conservery. Attempts at import substitution have involved soft-drinks, cigarettes, watches, tyres, batteries, bicycle and moped assembly. With the low local incomes, and high cost of energy and transport, the country does not provide a good market for industrial goods, and the modern sector has been largely stagnant for the last decade.

Small quantities of gold have been produced intermittently at Poura in the south-west, and there are small-scale workings of iron (with traditional simple smelting) at Banfora and Ouahigouya. In the extreme north-east near Tambao there are large manganese deposits and lime-calcium which could be the basis of a cement industry. However, it seems unlikely that minerals are going to provide an immediate solution to the country's development problems.

Transport problems

One factor which reduces the likelihood of mineral exploitation is the problem of transport. Land-locked Burkina Faso has a rail link to the Côte d'Ivoire port of Abidjan, but it is a costly haul over the 1144 km from Ouagadougou to the coast. There are plans to extend the railway for over 350 km as a preliminary to exploiting the Tambao manganese, and the rail bed has been prepared for a part of that distance. However, there is no immediate prospect of funding becoming available for completion for what some would consider to be a prestige rather than essential development project.

In the one year, 1981, over 350 aid missions supposedly visited Burkina Faso, which suggests a lack of coordination and possibly even contradictory aims. The country's agricultural resources base is not particularly rich, but with most of the population in the rural areas these at last seem to have become the focus of government attention. Local self-help projects to provide wells and water storage, combat soil erosion, plant trees and improve farming output seem to provide the best way forward.

NIGER

With a per capita GDP of £330, Niger can claim to be the richest of the interior Sahelian countries. More than anything else, this reflects the benefits that uranium mining has brought to the national economy, although most of the country's inhabitants may not have noticed any real change in their life style.

Niger is a large country of 1.267 million km^2, with an extreme north–south extent of 1200 km and an extreme east–west extent of 1400 km. With a 1982 total estimated population of 5.52 million it has an average population density of only 4.4 people per km^2. However, 10 per cent of the population comprises nomadic Fulani in the south and Tuareg in the Sahara, and the northern Agades Department, with 55 per cent of the national area, has only 2 per cent of the population. Over 32 per cent of the population is located in the extreme south-west close to the Niger river, and a further 56 per cent is dispersed along a fairly narrow zone including the towns of Tahoua, Maradi and Zinder close to the Nigerian border. Here the people are mainly sedentary Hausa.

Niger's climate is entirely Saharan and Sahelian, with rainfall exceeding 100 mm in only two or three months, even in Niamey (total 550 mm) in the better-watered south-west. Further north the rainfall drops to 350 mm in Tahoua, 150 mm in Agades where there are convectional storms, and north of Bilma it is negligible. This is a very inadequate basis for rain-fed agriculture.

Except to the west of the Niger river, around Zinder and in the Aïr massif of the Sahara where there are Pre-Cambrian basement crystallines, the bulk of the country is underlain by sandstones and limestones of Devonian, Jurassic, Cretaceous (the 'Continental Intercalaire') and post-Eocene age, but with a superficial sand cover over about 60 per cent of the country. The porosity of much of the bedrock and sand cover reduces the effectiveness of what little precipitation there is. The Aïr is a dissected massif of the Pre-Cambrian era with average levels of 1000–1500 m, a highest point of over 1800 m, and rises fairly abruptly from the monotonous plains which characterize most of the country. In the extreme north is the much eroded limestone and sandstone Djado plateau which links the Ahaggar and Tibesti. As evidence of previously higher rainfalls there are numerous, usually dry, relic river valleys both in the south-west and west of the Aïr. At times of higher rainfall some of these may still be temporary water-courses.

Several distinct regions may be identified. The lands adjacent to the Niger river in the south-west provide a region in which the river flood of January delayed by its progress through the inland delta comes in the dry season and provides the possibility of almost year-round cultivation. Here, cotton, rice, sugar and vegetables are grown in addition to the guinea corn and millet which provide the staple cereals. Niamey (pop. 150,000), the capital, provides the principal centre in this more favoured region. Second, there is the fairly narrow area of rain-fed cultivation close to the Nigerian border. Here there is a variable surface of laterite, clay and more sandy soils. Around Tahoua there is a drier, rather negative, area, but the sandy plains around Maradi provide one of the main groundnut-producing regions and also provide some cotton. Eastwards around Zinder, the territory's capital from 1911 to 1926, there is a clay plain with a shallower water table and rather more surface water, which is known for its gum-arabic producing acacias and some groundnut production. Eastwards from Zinder there is a dry sandy area, but with pasture on the margins of Lake Chad. It is in the same better-watered southern regions that livestock husbandry is important, and cattle, hides (cattle, sheep and goat) and camels have always been a principal export.

The vast Saharan region is from an agricultural point of view largely negative, except for some oasis cultivation (e.g. around Bilma) and some rather better pastures in the Aïr and its western margins.

The traditional economy

Agriculture supports 90 per cent of the population, and in 1980, alone among the Sahel states, Niger was virtually self-sufficient in food. In 1970 traditional cultivation and pastoralism accounted for two-thirds of the GDP, although in the case of the former occupied only 3 per cent of the national area, but by the late 1970s had dropped to about one-half. Groundnut production increased steadily during the 1960s and by 1969 accounted for 60 per cent of the value of exports; however, it was badly affected in the drought of the early 1970s and by a virus disease in the mid-1970s. Cotton cultivation was introduced in 1956 but production has increased only slowly. Considerable state effort was directed to agriculture in the 1979–83 Five-Year Plan, and targets have been established for extension of irrigation and production of main food and export crops.

Between 1938 and 1968 the cattle population increased from 750,000 to 4.5 million and sheep and goats from 3 to 9 million; but from 1968 to 1973 the drought reduced livestock by half. By 1984 herds were back to 75 per cent of their peak. Breeding centres were set up to increase reproduction rates and there have been attempts to regulate cattle numbers, grazing and slaughtering; export gradually increased again after 1975 but was controlled to ensure herd growth.

The modern sector

There can be no doubt that the comparatively healthy state of Niger's agriculture is related to investment of revenues derived from the modern sector of the economy. Uranium was discovered at Arlit in Aïr in 1966 and first exported in 1971. In the early 1970s world uranium prices were very high, so that in 1976 uranium provided 64 per cent of Niger's export revenue. In 1978 production increased by 40 per cent to 2100 tonnes with the opening of a second mine at Akouta, and Niger became the fifth largest world producer. Other deposits exist and these could well be exploited. However, much depends on the world market price for uranium, and in the 1980s there has been a slackening of demand, lower prices and much reduced income for development finance. Niger has been trying to diversify its uranium market. The costs of mining and processing are high, especially as the deposits are located in such a remote region of a land-locked country and all equipment and processing materials have to be imported. There is the advantage that the exported uranium concentrate is of very high value in relation to its weight.

Cassiterite and wolfram are also mined in small quantities in the same area,and mineral exploration has revealed large phosphate deposits of high quality at Tapoa, south of Niamey, some coal, iron-ore and even oil in the Lake Chad region. A surfaced, all-season road links Arlit with Parakou, the Benin rail terminal; but while the requirements of the uranium industry can be accommodated in this way, road transport would not be suitable for other low-value bulk minerals. There have been plans for the extension of the Benin railway northwards into Niger, and this could possibly materialize in the future. There has also been a proposal to take iron-ore by barge down the Niger to the steel industry now being developed in Nigeria.

The dual economy

It has been said of the Arlit mines that they are 'unreal – built from nothing in the middle of nowhere and populated by expatriates'. The road to Arlit does little but serve the mines,

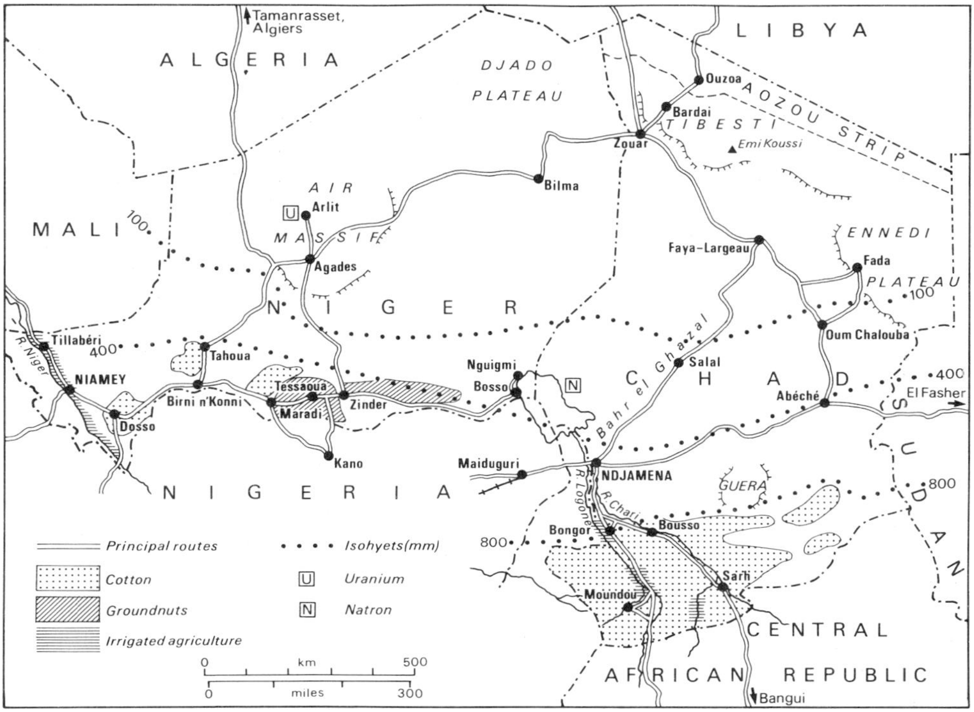

Figure 58 Niger and Chad: economic activities

although along the way there are several anti-desertification and irrigation schemes.

In view of the cost of establishing the industry, the arguments against proliferation of nuclear arms and energy and the vulnerability of dependence on fluctuating market prices, it does not seem an obvious base for economic development. Certainly, until 1980, when prices dropped, uranium had provided Niger with the means of improving its infrastructure, economic (e.g. the surfaced road Niamey to Zinder) and social (especially education and medical services), and allowed much needed improvements in agriculture which took one-third of all investment in the two development plans of 1976–8 and 1979–83. Yet even now only 30,000 km^2 is under systematic irrigation. Niger has done more than other Sahelian countries in experimenting with solar energy.

In the longer term much more emphasis needs to be placed on policies to counter deforestation and desert encroachment and to reduce isolation by improving road links to neighbouring states. There is little other industrialization apart from some local processing of agricultural products (oil mills, canning, tannery, ginneries, textile mills) and import substitution (flour milling, plastics, radio assembly, soft drinks, brewing), mainly located in Niamey, and hindered by high energy and transport costs. It is clear that for some time to come the development potential hinges on the way in which uranium income is diverted into other self-sustaining economic activities, both agricultural and industrial; but at least for Niger there would appear to be some hope of breaking out of the poverty trap.

CHAD

In 1983 an article in the *Sunday Times* in the UK said: '(Chad) was designed by a doubtless well intentioned set of nineteenth-century statesmen, none of whom had ever been there, and is divided by a somewhat arbitrary line into two halves, one occupied by brown people praying to Allah and the other by black persons professing allegiance either to Christianity or to an assortment of pagan deities.'[1]

Although once a part of French Equatorial Africa and still having strong functional links with the countries of that region, Chad has geographical similarities with some of the states being considered in this chapter. Like them it extends well into the Sahara and acts as a link between the ethno-cultural provinces of northern and western-central Africa. Like them it has been affected by the Sahelian drought. With a per capita GDP of only $110 it is possibly the third-poorest nation in the world. The life expectancy is 43 years and infant mortality is 20 per cent in the first few years. There are only four hospitals in the whole country and one doctor for every 42,000 of the population.

The resource base

The structural downwarp which creates the inland drainage basin of Lake Chad (250 m above sea-level), and which is the main feature of the centre of the country, comprises Quaternary sedimentaries. In the extreme north these give way to Palaeozoic sedimentaries and in the Tibesti to Pre-Cambrian crystallines and more recent volcanics. These also provide the country with its greatest relief, rising at Emi Koussi to 3400 m. From Lake Chad the land also rises north-eastwards to the Palaeozoic sandstone massif of the Ennedi Plateau which, with heights over 1500 km, forms the Chad–Nile watershed. Towards the Sudan border is the Quadai Plateau with its south-westward extension in the Guera Hills, the former reaching nearly 1500 m and the latter nearly 1700 m. Except in these higher areas, much of the north and central part of the country is rather monotonous, rocky desert terrain. The south-west of the country comprises a peneplain area, highly dissected by the rivers Logone and Chari and their tributaries.

Extending over 1600 km from 8°N to 23°N, Chad has four principal climatic zones. The northern third of the country (Figure 58) is pure desert with negligible rainfall (Faya Largeau: 23 mm), except in the Tibesti where some orographic precipitation supports sedentary population in small basins flanking the mountains. There is then a narrow zone of sub-desert (what some might call northern Sahel) with rainfall from 100 to 300 mm. Southwards there is a zone of Sahel-type climate with totals of 300–800 mm, with 2–4 months with in excess of 100 mm. In the extreme south the rainfall increases to over 1200 mm and the rain season extends to some 5–7 months. Except in this southern zone, the seasonability and variability of the rainfall creates serious problems of water availability for much of the year. A reflection of this rainfall variability is the area of Lake Chad itself, which varies from 1500 to 3800 km^2.

Only on the margins of some of the higher ground in the north and in depressions where springs support oases is pasture available, but in the better-watered south the numerous permanent water-courses often flood large areas during the rains, when swampland becomes extensive.

Economic activity

The distribution of population and economic activities reflects this physical background. The population was estimated at 3.6 million in 1982 but is very unevenly distributed. The three northern prefectures, comprising some 47 per cent of the national area, have only 2 per cent of the population, the central eight prefectures account for 43 per cent of the area and 51 per cent of the population, and the five south-western prefectures have only 10 per cent of the area but 47 per cent of the population. The average population densities for the three zones are respectively about 0.1, 4.1 and 16.3 people per km^2.

The northern half of the country is almost entirely negative economically, being able to support only a very sparse nomadic population except in a few favoured areas near Tibesti. In the central zone animal husbandry is of greater importance but is still based on nomadic search for better pastures, often with a northerly movement just ahead of the rains (to avoid tsetse fly infection) and a southerly movement after them. Animal products are Chad's second export in terms of value and comprise on-the-hoof movements to Nigeria and the Central African Republic (much of it unrecorded because of the impossible task of controlling such lengths of frontiers) and processed exports.

In peak years 250,000 cattle are slaughtered, and at N'Djamena and Sarh there are processing plants (controlled by SOTERA – Societé Tchadien pour L'Exploitation des Resources Animaux) for freezing, canning, tanning and leather production. From a peak of about 12,000 tonnes in 1970 exports declined to about 7000 tonnes in the later 1970s, a reflection of the impact of the drought on pasture availability and cattle numbers.

Cultivation is largely confined to the southern half of the country and increases in importance towards the south-west. It is mainly rain-fed, but there are small areas of modern irrigation along the Chari and Logone and larger areas of flood plain cultivation. The main traditional crops are millet and guinea corn, with some maize in areas of highest rainfall.

In 1928 cotton was introduced as a compulsory cash crop: it was gradually accepted by the peasants and became the country's main export in terms of value. The main area of cultivation is south-west of a line through Sarh and Bousso, where the rainfall is most reliable. Altogether about 140,000 ha are under cotton, and from the peak of 175,000 tonnes in 1975/6 production has declined dramatically (in 1985 it was 45,000 tonnes) and fluctuated widely. It is not clear if this is a reflection of climatic factors or, as seems more likely, is the result of political unrest. Cotton now accounts for 75–80 per cent of the value of exports and is controlled by a government organization (COTONTCHAD) which has 1200 buying points (a large number to reduce distances over which peasants have to 'head-load' the cotton) and 22 ginneries (also probably more than actual production justifies). There is some local spinning and weaving but most of the cotton is exported. Indeed, only a relatively high-value crop such as cotton can stand transport charges to the ports of neighbouring countries, and at the ports transport costs already account for 16 per cent of the value of the cotton.

Rice and sugar are grown in particular on irrigable land in valleys of the south and on Lake Chad 'polders'. There have been recent attempts to increase the area under these crops, and at Bourno an experimental rice station has been established. Groundnuts are often grown in association with millet but are mainly consumed locally, with very litle of the production being exported. Small amounts of gum arabic are also collected.

About 100,000 tonnes of fish are obtained annually from the Chari, Logone and Lake Chad and some dried and smoked fish is exported. A small amount of natron soda is mined in the Lake Chad region; and a modest oil find at Kanem, north of Lake Chad, has resulted in plans for a small (2000 barrels/day) oil refinery at N'Djamena – which would satisfy local demand.

Chad is one of the least industrialized of all African states, with a total industrial employment of only 4000 in some basic food-processing plants (meat, sugar, flour, rice, vegetable oils). Other industrial activity concerns a brewery, a cigarette factory, a textile mill, a tannery, radio and cycle assembly factories, watches and a soft drinks plant.

Development problems

The extremely low level of economic development is in part a reflection of the poverty of the resource base. The agriculture provides a fragile basis for development and there are few other resources. There are indications of uranium and manganese in the Tibesti area in the disputed Aozou strip to which Libya lays claim, and there could possibly be more oil in the Chad basin.

Chad's first development plan (1966–70) emphasized 'poles of development' at N'Djamena, Sarh and Moundou, diversification, and increased agricultural production – with efforts concentrated in a few south-western areas rather than dispersed. Very little was, in fact, achieved, and the second plan (1971–5) was adversely affected by the drought. As a result of the drought, the 1975 plan largely revolved around food-for-work schemes. In 1982 a Reconstruction Plan was designed largely to combat 'emergencies' in food and health, with emphasis on water resources in the pastoral areas. Chad is a member of the Chad Basin Commission; so far this has not brought great benefits but it could lead to more irrigation and fishing. Low levels of plan implementation are mainly the result of lack of income for investment.

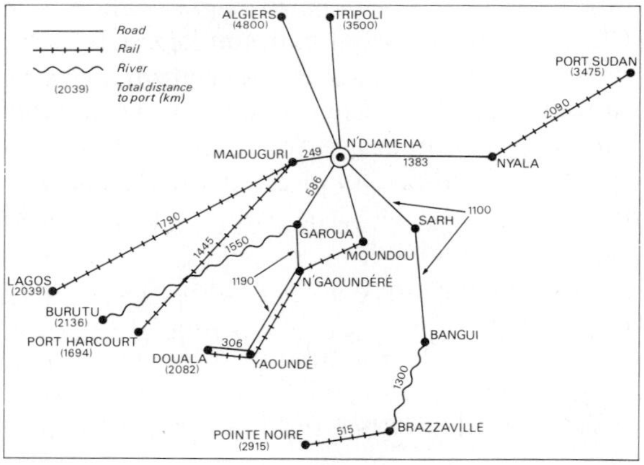

Figure 59 Chad: routes to sea

Any project development in Chad will be expensive in view of the distances from ports and increased cost of all imports. In the colonial era the 'route federale' was developed from N'Djamena (then Fort Lamy) by road through Sarh (Fort Archamboult) to Bangui, thence by river to Brazzaville and rail to Pointe Noire, a total distance of nearly 3000 km (Figure 59). The roads are not surfaced nor open all seasons, the Congo–Ocean railway is mainly single-track, and Chad has to compete with her neighbours for limited transport capacity. Attempts to retain inter-state control of the through route after independence were eventually abandoned, and political uncertainty has been added to the physical inadequacy of the route. Yet as Figure 59 indicates, the alternatives also involve considerable distances and numerous transhipments. There is a critical low-capacity ferry across the Chari (replaced by a temporary bridge financed by 'Band Aid' in 1985) on the road route to Maiduguri, and the river port of Garoua is open for only two months each year. Given the very low total tonnages involved a projected rail link to the Cameroun system seems unlikely to materialize.

The oil of Kanem is 300 km from N'Djamena, and for the small amount of oil involved the necessary pipeline will never be an economic proposition. Exploitation of any minerals in Tibesti would face similar problems. Such are the problems of surface transport that the processed meat has to be air-freighted, at great cost, to markets in Gabon, Congo and Zaire.

An additional complication is the civil war which has been waged intermittently for virtually the whole time since independence was gained in 1960. For five years after independence the northern three prefectures (nearly half the country) remained under French military administration, and there has been continuous opposition to the government from the Tibesti, northern and eastern parts of the country. In 1971 Libya annexed the Aozou strip and advanced plans for a Toubou state. For long the conflict was essentially between a government dominated by the negro peoples of the Sara tribe, supported by the French, and Islamic northerners supported by Libya. Yet in the 1980s the conflict continues, although the battle-lines have become increasingly confused as one of the northern factions has taken control of the government.

Not without justification it has been said of

Chad that the French 'stitched together a vast country (1.28 million km^2) whose boundaries are among the most artificial in the African continent'.[2] It lacks basic unity, and with its vast size, land-locked location and general poverty of resources it is one of the countries for which it is impossible to be optimistic about the development potential.

REFERENCES

1 *The Sunday Times*, 17 July 1983.
2 *The Guardian*, 5 September 1983.

22
The western coastal states

In contrast with the states of dry West Africa, the western coastal states from Senegal to Liberia tend to be much smaller in size, with higher population densities and generally higher per capita incomes. Further, in common with the other coastal states they have, for better or for worse, had much longer periods of contact with European culture, commercial enterprise (including the slave trade) and the money economy.

However, the countries concerned show considerable variations – based in part on physical geography but also related to differences in colonial experience. The dry-land states have a degree of uniformity based on the French colonial control that they shared, whereas the coastal states were administered by France (Senegal, Guinea), Britain (The Gambia, Sierra Leone) and Portugal (Guinea Bissau), with Liberia never under the political control of a European power.

SENEGAMBIA

In 1982 Senegal and The Gambia merged in a confederation, and while the functional linkages are still far from complete this does mark an important step in the elimination of one of Africa's more bizarre politico-geographical legacies from the colonial period. For the moment, however, the cricket square in Victoria Park, Banjul, and the 'Corniche' in Dakar represent fundamental differences of attitude and approach and as much mutual suspicion as has existed between Britain and France themselves over the years. The countries will, therefore, be treated separately in this chapter.

THE GAMBIA

In 1889 an agreement between Britain and France created the 'Gambian frankfurter in the Senegalese roll', a country 480 km in length but averaging only 30 km in width, surrounded by Senegal except at the coast, the boundary defined in places by arbitrarily defined 10 km arcs from the outer bends of a river which at that time had not even been surveyed! Within these completely artificial boundaries The Gambia became independent in 1965.

It has an area of only 11,000 km^2 and in 1982 an estimated population of 590,000, which gives an average density of 54 people per km^2. This average density conceals considerable variations, with Banjul–Kombo St Mary, the capital and main developed area, having a density of 890 people per km^2, and parts of the lower and middle river valley, especially where mangrove is well developed, having densities of fewer than 20 per km^2. The population is increasing at 2.8 per cent a year – certainly at a faster rate than production from limited resources – and there has been considerable migration into the Banjul area which has been growing at 8 per cent a year and now has 15 per cent of the country's population. This is not surprising when one considers that Banjul, the capital (45,000 in 1983), is the main centre for medical and education facilities (it has the only sixth-form in the country), is the principal focus of the tourist industry, is the country's main port and the only area where there has been substantial growth of modern sector employment.

Much of Senegambia consists of a low,

fairly level plateau of tertiary sandstone across which the Gambia river is incised. In The Gambia this provides the highest ground but never rises much above 60 m and accounts for 27 per cent of the country. The soils tend to be lateritic and of poor quality. The second terrain type is provided by the 'sandhills', transitional between the plateau and the riverside lands, and giving more varied relief of low hills and broad, shallow valleys. Accounting for 41 per cent of the country's area, the lighter, sandy soils of this region are ideally suited to groundnut cultivation. The remaining 32 per cent of the country comprises river flats consisting of saline-brackish water mangrove swamp, especially along the lower river, more restricted areas of freshwater swamp upstream, and the 'banto faros' or alluvial lowlands bordering the river along the middle and upper valley. The mangrove timber can be used for firewood, but this region is of no great agricultural potential unless completely reclaimed. In contrast, the occasionally but not necessarily regularly flooded banto faros are ideal for rice cultivation, are suitable for a wide range of food crops including vegetables, and have a considerable development potential.

Rain is markedly concentrated in the summer months and in total decreases from 1200 mm at Banjul to 870 mm inland. The rains arrive marginally earlier inland, but maritime influences near the coast increase humidities and reduce the desiccating impact of the 'harmattan'. However, the dry season lasts for seven months, rainfall totals are variable and the country has been adversely affected by recent droughts. Any intensification of agriculture will have to be related to the control and distribution of river water.

Economic activity

Over 80 per cent of the inhabitants depend on agriculture for their livelihood, but even in the best years food production satisfies only 70 per cent of the requirements. In 1983–4 food production fell by 50 per cent as a result of low rainfall, while in 1979 there was reduced output of cereals because of widespread pest infestation. The basic traditional food crops are millet, guinea corn, cassava and dry rice, although swamp rice has been increasing in importance. Animal husbandry is important in the drier areas, and The Gambia has started exporting Ndama breeding cattle to Gabon and Nigeria.

Plate 26 Market for 'tourist' goods; Bakau, The Gambia

By far the most important export is groundnuts, which are the cash crop for many of the peasant farmers, especially in the sandhills terrain, and The Gambia is a supreme example of a monoculture economy. In 1970 groundnuts provided 94 per cent of the export income, but during the 1970s drought adversely affected 90 per cent of the producing area. Such heavy dependence on a single crop, production of which fluctuated from as low as 45,000 to as high as 137,000 tonnes in the years from 1965 to 1983, places the economy in a very vulnerable position. It is clearly impossible to predict government income from year to year, and this makes forward planning very difficult. Groundnut oil mills operate at Banjul and Kaur and their output is likewise subject to wide fluctuation.

Not surprisingly there have been efforts to

diversify and increase agricultural production. Since the mid-1960s the area of irrigated rice has increased to about 1100 ha. Chinese technical assistance has been involved in this, and while the potential is considerable progress has been slow. This could be explained by the fact that traditional rain-fed rice cultivation has been largely by women, whereas the irrigation requires bund, channel, pump and equipment maintenance – which is the work of men and needs a fundamental change in the division of labour, with possibly serious social implications. The capital cost is also high, and even in its peak year (12,000 tonnes in 1981) irrigated rice was only one-third the output of rain-fed rice.

Cotton has been a traditional crop but there have been attempts to increase the area and output. Planting now accounts for about 1500 ha and production 1500 tonnes. A new ginnery has been built at Basse, and cotton, small as the output is, has become the second export crop.

The river has always provided fish in some quantity, and a fish farming pilot project is being undertaken near Georgetown. In 1984 an EEC-funded project provided a pier for trawlers at Banjul, with associated storage and processing facilities. While this is still in its infancy there seems to be great potential for the further development of both river and coastal fisheries.

Tourism

Tourism now provides The Gambia with its second most important source of income. Tourist arrivals increased from 300 in 1965, when the country boasted two hotels, to 44,829 in 1982–3 by which time there were 16 large hotels in the coastal region west of Banjul. The extended dry season, winter sun, attractive beaches, the river, the relative proximity to Europe, the improvement of Banjul's Yun Dun airport to accept large jets – and the fact that the well-known book and television series *Roots* were located in The Gambia – have all been contributory factors in the expansion of tourism beyond the dry season.

Yet the expansion of tourism is a mixed blessing. Many of the tourists are low-spending sun-seekers on package tour arrangements, and the financial benefits to The Gambia are limited. The tourism is still markedly seasonal, with implications for employment; and in such a small country tourism can have a 'negative demonstration effect' by introducing undesirable social behaviour (begging, drugs, gambling and prostitution). Many of the development materials and equipment and day-to-day needs of tourism (food, drink, vehicles) have to be imported, which greatly reduces, or even eliminates, any net benefit to the economy. However, the tourist industry has undoubtedly created much needed employment, either directly in hotels or indirectly in services (transport, guides) and industry. There has been an increase in craft industrial production – especially traditional batik and other textiles, and carving – to cater for tourist demand; but most of the employment tends to be urban-based, is mainly concentrated around Banjul and serves to exaggerate urban-rural contrasts.

The River Gambia

It has been said of The Gambia that 'it is the river'. Smaller ocean-going vessels can navigate to Kaur, 190 km from Banjul, and at Kuntaur, a further 55 km, they can load to a maximum draught of 4.6 m.

Over thirty wharves are served by regular ferry or by self-propelled or towed barges of the Gambia River Transport Company, which carries groundnuts, rice, cotton and imported fertilizer. In recent years thirteen of the wharves have been reconstructed.

The value of the river as a transport artery is limited because it is cut off from much of its natural hinterland by the proximity of the political boundary. As Senegambia moves towards greater integration the river could assume its rightful role. This will be encouraged by the proposed multi-purpose barrage at Yelitenda, 135 km upstream from Banjul. By

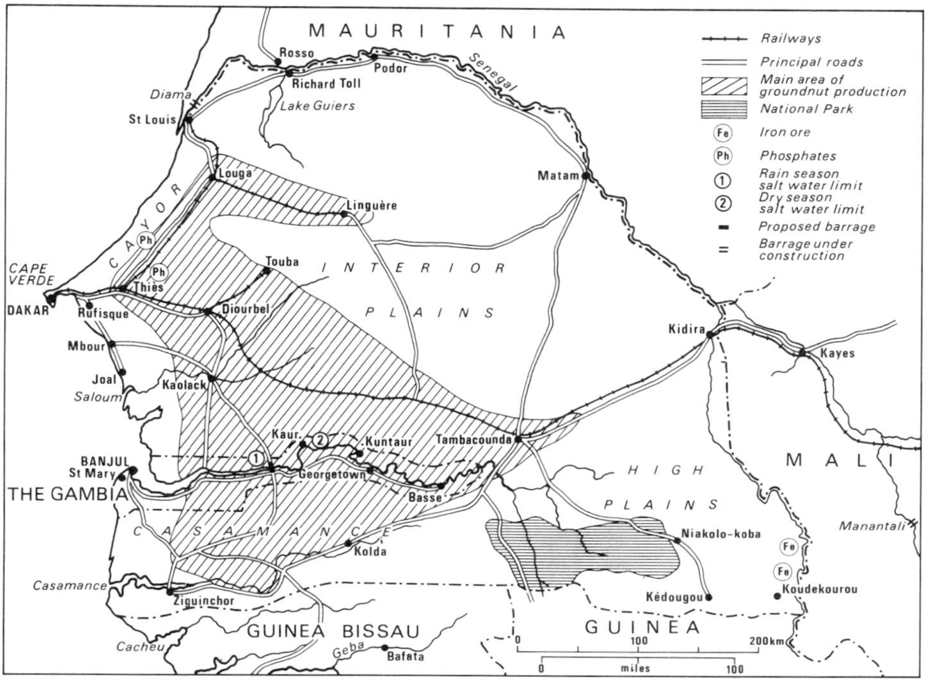

Figure 60 Senegambia

increasing water levels upstream navigation will be improved and the barrage will have locks to allow the passage of larger vessels. The barrage will provide a road crossing to replace the existing ferry, and this will link the Casamance region of Senegal more closely with The Gambia, particularly as a new river port, to be located near the barrage, could attract traffic from across the border. By excluding salt water from the middle reaches of the river the barrage will make available over 24,000 ha for irrigation. This scheme is certainly the main focus of attention in longer-term development planning.

SENEGAL

With an area of 196,000 km^2 and a population of 5.97 million in 1982, and with an average per capita income of $450, Senegal has a much more varied resource base and greater development potential than The Gambia which it surrounds. In Dakar it also has a far more sophisticated urban centre, with a seaport and an airport of international significance.

Regional divisions

Although having a narrow rim of Pre-Cambrian crystallines on its eastern margins, most of Senegal comprises Post-Cretaceous marine and continental sediments which produce little relief except where local faulting provides modest escarpments, as near Thiès. Volcanic activity has produced some localized higher ground in the Cape Verde region, including the plateau area of Dakar itself. A number of distinctive terrains may be identified.

The Senegal valley is broad and shallow and the river course in places divided. There is considerable seasonal flooding and good soils which, as across the river in Mauritania, provide a basis for millet cultivation, the post-harvest stubble providing cattle pasture for nomadic herders. Towards the coast the river forms a delta with abandoned courses, current distributaries and swamp land, but the river mouth itself has been diverted southwards by the ever-lengthening sand spit, the Langue de Barbaria. The river entrance is shallow and constantly changing and this prohibits access to ocean-going vessels. Small vessels can navigate to the island town and former capital, St Louis.

The coastlands. From St Louis to Rufisque the coast is smooth, except where the once separate volcanic cone of Cape Verde is now connected to the mainland by a sand accretion, providing Dakar with its naturally sheltered harbour. The coast is backed by dunes and marshy depressions. South of Rufisque the coast consists of alternating low sandstone cliffs and sandy embayments, more numerous drowned valleys and extensive areas that are seasonally inundated – these are too saline for cultivation and remain as mangrove.

The plains which make up most of the interior are undulating and consist of sandstones comparable with those of The Gambia, with local relict dunes and extensive laterization.

The High Plains of the south-east margins rise to over 400 m, are largely of Pre-Cambrian rocks and provide a more hilly terrain marking the Senegal–Mali border.

Climatic variations can be identified on both south–north and coast–interior bases. Along the coast – especially in the northern parts – the maritime influence reduces the diurnal and annual temperature range, lowers temperatures generally and increases humidity in the dry season. The annual rainfall at Ziguinchor, Casamance, is 1600 mm, with five months in excess of 100 mm; but at Dakar it is about 580 mm, with only two months having more than 100 mm. Inland at Tambacounda the rainfall is 1000 mm but declines northwards to 600 mm in the middle Senegal valley. Everywhere the rainfall is concentrated in a summer peak and subject to variations in amount and timing.

Traditional economy

Three-quarters of the economically active population are in the rural areas, although farming and fishing account for only 28 per cent of the GDP. The most widespread food crops are millet, guinea corn, cassava (especially on poorer soils) and maize, with rice in the moister areas of the Casamance or along valleys. Although very much a part of local traditional dishes, rice is not grown in adequate quantities, and in 1983 over 300,000 tonnes had to be imported – indeed, food imports overall make up 25 per cent of the import bill. Most of the cultivation is rain-fed, and it has been said that 'when the rains fail or are late, no-one can work or be productive in rural Senegal'. Nor indeed, since independence, has there been much attention devoted to getting away from this vulnerable situation.

Along the Senegal river valley in the north and some of the more numerous rivers of the Casamance there is flood-plain cultivation, but this too is dependent on the vagaries of river level and therefore rainfall.

Senegal has an estimated 2.7 million head of cattle, with concentrations in the Diourbel–Kaolack region where the Serere people practice a form of mixed farming, and in the Casamance. In the drier northern and eastern parts of the interior plains pastoralism is mainly practiced by semi-nomadic Fulani people. Sheep and goats number about 2.8 million and are found in most areas. There is only a limited commercial sale of livestock, and Senegal has to import – traditionally from Mauritania.

Some 50,000 people are dependent on traditional fishing methods, both along the rivers and coast, and there have been recent attempts to improve the equipment, fishing craft and productivity. Dakar has become one of West Africa's principal fishing ports.

Groundnuts provide the main cash income for many of the peasant farmers and the country's main export crop. The widespread sandy, low-clay-content soils are particularly suitable for groundnut cultivation but tend to become impoverished fairly rapidly. Rainfall variability gives wide fluctuations in annual production. Groundnuts have been a traditional local foodstuff for three centuries and exporting started in the mid-1800s. Initially, cultivation was in the immediate hinterlands of St Louis and Dakar, but it spread rapidly especially as the railways were pushed inland at the end of the last century. The importance of the railway in determining the pattern of cultivation is still evident (Figure 60).

About half of the crop is delivered to oil extraction mills at Dakar, Louga, Diourbel, Kaolack and Ziguinchor, and there is further refining of oil at Dakar, Diourbel, Ziguinchor and Lyndiana. In a normal year, groundnuts, groundnut oil and groundnut cake make up 50 per cent of the export value. Groundnuts account for 45 per cent of the cultivated area and arguably are a mixed blessing – they add to the trade balance but take away on the budget account. This is because the government heavily subsidizes the price paid to farmers to protect them from low world prices, and the concentration on groundnuts impoverishes the soil and increases food imports.

In the late 1960s production was over one million tonnes a year, but in 1977 it was down to 460,000 tonnes, the lowest since 1947. It has been even less in several recent years when world prices have been exceptionally low, and the national economy faces serious problems as a result of reduced government revenue.

The modern sector

The only real attempt to get away from rainfed farming dates back to the colonial era. The Richard Toll irrigation scheme of the late 1940s involved a barrage across a water-course connecting Lake Guiers with the Senegal river. The stored water is distributed by costly pumping to 6000 ha of rice cultivated by mechanical methods, and since the 1960s sugar cultivation has been added. It cannot be claimed that the scheme has been a great success, and higher hopes are now being expressed for the Diama dam (completed in 1986) for the purpose of excluding saline water from the delta and lower Senegal river so that irrigation can ultimately be extended to as much as 200,000 ha.

Partly because it served as the industrial base for the whole of French West Africa, and also because in Dakar it has an urban market of nearly one million with a large expatriate community (30,000 or more), Senegal has long had a wider range of industries than most West African states. At independence in 1960 it already had 30 factories each with more than 200 employees, and during the 1960s manufacturing grew at 7 per cent a year and now accounts for 19 per cent of the GDP and 40 per cent of local demand. Initially, industry was based on the processing of local commodities (vegetable oils, cereals, fish, sugar), but it has now diversified into textiles, clothing, tobacco, drinks, cement, plastics, chemicals, paints, engineering, vehicle assembly, ship construction and repairs and oil refining. A high proportion of this industry is concentrated in the Dakar area.

Until 1964 there was extraction of zircon and titanium from beach sands in the Saloum river area, but the principal mining activity is now for phosphates at Taïba and Thiès. At present the phosphate is exported in an unprocessed form, but there are plans for a fertilizer and phosphoric acid plant at Taïba. In 1983 a company was established to develop iron-ore mining at Koudakourou in the extreme south-east of the country. This will require a rail link from Tambacounda, the upgrading of the existing rail line and the construction of an ore exporting terminal on the coast at Bargny, south of Dakar. How rapidly this is implemented could well depend on the world demand for iron-ore. The country's first gold mine, at Sabodala, is scheduled to start operations in 1988.

The Senegal is navigable throughout the year for small craft between St Louis and Podor and from Podor to Kayes during the period July to December. There is 1113 km of railway, and the main line from Dakar to Kidira is extended to Bamko and Koulikoro, providing Mali with an important outlet to the sea. Senegal has over 3000 km of surfaced road, and Dakar's location at the extreme western point of Atlantic Africa has made it a vital tourist stop on air and sea routes. The port of Dakar has been greatly expanded for fishing, ship repairs, cargo handling and bunkering, but the high levels of bunkering which characterized periods of Suez Canal closure have now declined. In the late 1970s a Free Industrial Zone was established at the port but this was slow to develop. In 1982 a new promotion drive resulted in the creation of 1300 jobs.

The history and sophistication of Dakar, the winter dry season, numerous good beaches, possibilities for sport fishing and game hunting and existing level of infrastructure provision suggest a tourist potential which could be further developed. Senegal shares with The Gambia the advantages of being the part of 'black' Africa which is nearest to the European tourist market.

Although Senegal's agricultural base is still somewhat vulnerable, the prospects for future development are considerable if the Senegal river can be fully harnessed for irrigation. This can be linked with hydroelectric power provision and a reduction in energy costs, now an impediment to growth. There is the need at present to import all the oil refined at M'bao but there are hopes for offshore oil and gas as exploration proceeds. There is a real danger that too much of the expected growth will be focused on Dakar itself, and there is an urgent need to decentralize. The Gambia barrage river crossing will certainly allow more effective integration of the Casamance into the national economy.

GUINEA BISSAU

One of the smallest West African states (36,000 km^2), Guinea Bissau was a Portuguese colony until 1974. It became independent after a prolonged war of liberation which greatly disrupted the territory's economy and during which large numbers fled the country. The population was an estimated 800,000 in 1982, which means an overall density of 22.5 people per km^2. The capital, Bissau, has a population of about 70,000 and is the centre of a coastal zone of higher population density which extends into the north of the country. In general the offshore islands, the south and interior are less-densely peopled.

Geologically, the country is divided into a western area extending into Senegal and comprising Post-Eocene continental sedimentaries, and an eastern area with Palaeozoic sandstones and shales and Pre-Cambrian crystallines. In the south-east, close to the Guinea border, the land reaches 300 m in the Fouta Jallon foothills, but elsewhere comprises transitional plateaux surfaces such as the Planalto de Gabu, low plateaux such as the Planalto de Bafatá, and in the coastal region shallow, drowned valleys with low-lying, seasonally inundated margins. Offshore is an archipelago of low-lying islands. There is considerable offshore siltation; navigation is thus not easy as the islands, mud-flats and channels constantly change their outline and water depths vary.

The rain season extends over some five months, with totals being higher on the coast (about 2000 mm) than inland. Harmattan influences are also more marked inland. There is considerable mangrove development in the coastal regions, giving way to swamp forest on its margins and in the interior savanna woodland.

Even before the warfare which led to independence disrupted the country, the economy was at best fragile and wholly dependent on agriculture. Rice is the staple food crop and is either of the swamp variety in coastal and riverine marshes or the dry upland type inland. There have in the past been some years with a surplus for export, and attempts have been made in recent years to expand cultivation. Maize, cassava and beans are the other main food crops. On the islands and in the coastal regions the oil palm is important and provides oil for local use and export and kernels for export. Groundnuts are the main cash crop of the interior plains and the country's main export. Cattle, about 250,000 head, are important in the interior and provide some hides and skins for export. There is a small fishing industry.

On this limited resource base it is not perhaps surprising that the per capita income amounts to only $160. There is certainly some scope for expanding each of the agricultural sectors, the industries based on them and the fishing; but the market for industrial products is limited by the small population and low income level, and there is virtually no modern manufacturing industry. There are indications of bauxite, phosphates, zinc and oil, but no immediate prospect for exploitation. The numerous rivers – especially the Cacheu, Geba and Corubal – provide for transport; but they also serve to disrupt movement and increase distances on land. Only 70 km of the 2000 km road network is in fact surfaced, and attention will have to be devoted to the improvement of infrastructure before other developments can take place.

GUINEA

Guinea achieved independence in 1958. When, unlike the other French African colonies, it voted to sever links with the French community, this brought reprisals from France. Initial support came from the Soviet Union for a regime which adopted a 'socialist' approach, with almost complete state control of commercial activities – banking, imports, industry, farmers' collectives and even a state tax-in-kind on farmers. The agricultural sector supporting the bulk of the population declined, import substitution industries stagnated, and the economy was further distorted by an emphasis on mineral exploitation and the servicing of heavy foreign debts – problems shared with many African states, but exaggerated in Guinea's case.

Geology and terrain

In the west and north of the country are small areas of Pre-Cambrian and Primary intrusives (e.g. granites) surrounded by Palaeozoic sandstones and shales. The eastern half of the country consists almost entirely of Pre-Cambrian crystallines. Undoubtedly, Guinea includes some of the most highly mineralized areas in West Africa.

Coastal swamplands of low-lying, drowned shallow valleys with muddy estuaries and a mangrove fringe continue those of Guinea Bissau, with occasional interruptions by rocky headlands and metamorphic rocks in the Kaloum peninsular. The swamps are backed by a fairly narrow and still low-lying and sometimes inundated area of gravel material derived from the **Fouta Jallon**. The Fouta Jallon is one of West Africa's main mountain and river source regions, with extensive areas over 900 m and maximum heights of over 1500 m near the Senegal border. The fairly horizontal Palaeozoic sandstones have an abrupt, faulted western margin but drop more gradually towards the east. Locally the level plateau surface is deeply incised with more spectacular scenery as a result of faulting and intrusive sills. Soils are generally thin, extensively laterized and severely eroded as a result of heavy rain on steep slopes. A broad trough at about 300 m, the **Niger Plains**, is underlain by Pre-Cambrians and gives way southwards through foothills to the **Guinea Highlands**, the source area of the Niger river and an area of relatively good soils and mineralization – such as iron-ore on the Liberian border (Figure 61).

Climate

By virtue of its coastal location and areas of higher relief, Guinea has generally high rainfall. The highest totals are at Conakry (4300 mm), on the western flanks of the Fouta Jallon and in the Guinea Highlands (Macenta: 2850 mm). Eastwards of the Fouta Jallon and north of the Guinea Highlands the rainfall

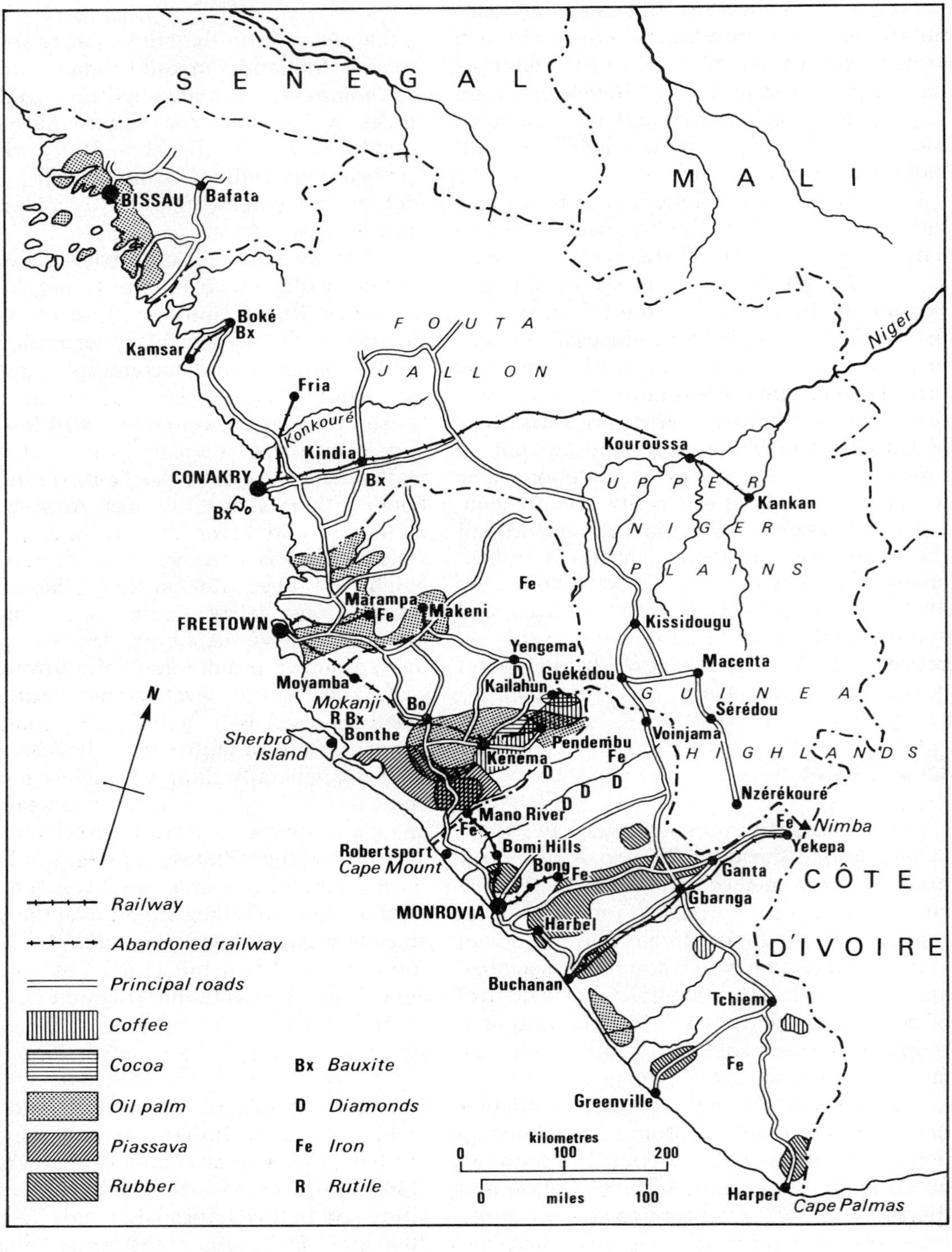

Figure 61 Western coastal states

averages 1500–1800 mm (e.g. Kouroussa: 1700 mm). In the coastal and northern interior there are 5–7 months with substantial rain, and in the Guinea Highlands this rises to nine months. In all areas the single peak is characteristic, being July–August on the coast and in the south and August–September inland. Large areas become flooded and inaccessible during the rain season.

Agriculture

With this pattern of climate a range of crops is possible, in places with several harvests a year. Cassava is widely grown, and swamp rice is important in the coastal areas (sometimes on reclaimed land) and on river flood plains in the Fouta Jallon, Niger Plains and Guinea Highlands. Upland rice, the original local form, and maize are also widely cultivated, and millet increases in importance to the north-east. Livestock husbandry, mainly by Fulani people, is especially important in the Labé area of the Fouta Jallon and has traditionally provided some export to Sierra Leone and Liberia. The main cash crops are bananas, largely from the coastal zone just north of Conakry to the Sierra Leone border; pineapples from the same area and from around Kindia and Mamou in the Fouta Jallon; kola and oil-palm from the coastal zone; and coffee from the Guinea Highlands.

However, Guinea's agricultural production has not kept pace with population growth: food imports have increased, and the total quantity and real value of agricultural exports has declined to about 5 per cent of the total exports. For products such as bananas and pineapples Guinea has found it increasingly difficult to compete with the quality of Côte d'Ivoire's production. Tax-in-kind, collectivization of livestock production, low producer prices and very poor distribution and marketing arrangements all combine to discourage farmers. Only since a *coup* in April 1984 has there been a start on dismantling inefficient parastatal organizations, and a new emphasis on agriculture, both peasant and agribusiness.

Mining

The neglect of agriculture was a by-product of the dynamic growth of the mining industry. In the early 1960s minerals made up 70 per cent of the exports but have since increased to around 95 per cent.

Guinea has some of the world's largest deposits of bauxite, mined on Kassa Island near Conakry from 1952 to 1967, on Tamara Island since 1968, at Fria (230 km from Canakry) since 1960 and at Sangaredi (Boké) since 1973. The Fria bauxite is processed into alumina at Sabenda for export via Conakry, while that of Boké is taken by a new 136 km railway to the processing plant for calcined bauxite at Kamsar, where a new port has been constructed to handle the exports. This latter mine has a capacity of 9 million tonnes a year and is now operating near that capacity. These are large, private enterprises drawing capital from American, Canadian, French, German and Italian sources – with Guinean participation – and at Kindia there is a Russian-financed bauxite mine.

Diamonds are mined in the Guinea Highland but the potential has been reduced by poor management, illicit mining and smuggling. In 1984 a new concession was granted for alluvial mining – the Areder scheme – which it is hoped will soon yield 250,000 carats a year, rising to one million at the end of the decade, with 90 per cent of gem quality. Gold mining was scheduled to start in the Koron-Diai region during 1986 and further exploration is taking place near Kouroussa.

Low-grade magnetite iron-ore was mined near, and exported from, Conakry between 1953 and 1966, but hopes now rest with the Mines de Fer de Guinea (MIFERGUI) Nimba project. This high-grade haematite is on the Guinean side of the border with Liberia, in the Nimba range, where Liberia has been mining since 1963. The start on mining on the Guinean side has been delayed by the world recession, the present need to use the Liberian railway to Buchanan for export, and Guinea's preference for an all-Guinea route which will require lengthy and costly rail links to be constructed.

Oil exploration is being held up by a dispute over the offshore boundary with Guinea Bissau, and when this is resolved there are hopes that oil will also be available. With the high rainfall and relief in the Fouta Jallon and Guinea Highlands, Guinea has considerable potential for hydroelectric power, and any further processing of bauxite-alumina will depend on cheap electricity being available. A scheme for the Konkouré river has been on the drawing board for decades but has yet to attract finance.

The future

Several decades of neglect have left agriculture, industry and infrastructure in a poor condition. The railway from Conakry to Kankan has been badly maintained, it is of low capacity and would have to be completely reconstructed if it were to take bulk minerals. Only a small part of the road network is surfaced and all-weather roads have not been properly maintained. Vehicles are scarce and road haulage is difficult at best and often impossible during the rains. This is a serious impediment to agricultural development, especially for crops such as bananas and pineapples where speed of handling is critical. A contract was signed in mid-1984 for the up-grading of the 127 km Guékédou–Sérédou section of the vital Conakry–Nzérékouré road, and improvement of the whole route was scheduled for completion in 1986.

Conakry, the capital (pop. 550,000), provides the only general cargo port facilities; these need extension and improvement. At present Guinea has little more than a few import substitution industries – cigarettes, matches, soap, paint, plastics, fruit canning and vehicle assembly at Conakry, a textile plant at Saviaga and sawmill at Kissidougou. This small industrial sector has been stagnant for years and existing industry needs rehabilitation before new enterprises are started.

Yet Guinea is blessed with a range of agricultural, forestry, mineral and power resources which, if properly developed and managed, should ensure economic growth and a base for industrialization. The population of 5.28 million (in 1982) provides a modest local market; but there seems no reason why the present $290 per capita income could not be greatly increased, and the geographical dispersion of the natural resources could ensure widespread regional benefit.

SIERRA LEONE

With an area of 72,000 km^2, Sierra Leone is a relatively small country; but with an estimated population of 3.7 million in 1985 it has a density of 51 people per km^2. Freetown, the capital, was adopted by the British as a base for suppressing the slave trade and, as its name suggests, was a settlement for freed slaves whose descendants have given the Freetown peninsula a considerable Creole population.

Relief regions

With the exception of a narrow zone of Tertiary and Quaternary sediments in the coastal region, the country is underlain by Pre-Cambrian strata. These are principally granites, but there are two north-west/south-east belts of sediments, metamorphozed in places to give gneisses and schists. Three regions can be identified.

The **coastal zone** is a generally low-lying but complex area of sands, gravels and clays with relict beaches and sand bars and evidence of a variety of lake, lagoon and marine environments. With an intricate pattern of water-courses, much of the area consists of swamp, mangrove or freshwater. On higher sandy areas a bush vegetation is found. Rising abruptly from this area is the 900 m Freetown peninsula of intrusive rocks. Viewed from the sea this appeared to early Portuguese mariners as a lion and so gave the peninsula and country a name which has persisted. In the shelter of the peninsula the estuary provides one of the world's largest natural harbours, and port facilities have been constructed relatively easily.

Inland there is a belt of undulating **plains**, remnants of old erosion surfaces, varying in height from about 50 to 120 m but with occasional hills rising to over 200 m. There are considerable areas of laterization and the soils are not in general very fertile. Much of the region is underlain by belts of metamorphic rocks to which reference has already been made, and these are responsible for some of the hill areas and are associated with mineralization. Iron-ore has been mined at Lunsar/Marampa since 1933, and there are other iron deposits at Tonkolili and in the Sula Hills. Near Mokanji are worked deposits of bauxite and rutile.

The interior of the country is the western part of the **Guinea Highlands** and comprises fairly level plateau surfaces of 400–600 m, with isolated hills and more extensive higher, dissected hill areas rising to over 1500 m. Kimberlite, a localized intrusion, has weathered to provide extensive areas of diamond-rich alluvium, especially around Yengema and Kenema. The soils are heavily leached and easily eroded on steeper slopes.

Climate and vegetation

Sierra Leone is characterized by generally high rainfall totals. Orographic influences in the Freetown peninsula give over 6000 mm in places, and Freetown itself has 3360 mm. In the coastal zone rainfall is 2500 – 3000 mm, but reduces in the interior to 1700 – 2500 mm. Over most of the country the rainfall is concentrated in the 'monsoon' season, from May to November near the coast and for a shorter period inland. However, towards the Liberian border the rainfall tends to be more evenly distributed throughout the year.

Despite the high rainfall, Sierra Leone does not have rich vegetation, and only in the south-east is there any 'high' forest. Almost certainly there was formerly more forest cover which has been removed by cultivation and subsequent degradation of the soil in physical and chemical terms. At present some 60–70 per cent of the country has only low bush and grassland vegetation.

Economic activity

Agriculture supports 75 per cent of the population and provides one-third of the GDP. Until the early 1950s, when there was rapid expansion of the mining industry, and again in the late 1970s with mining in depression, agriculture also provided the main exports.

The principal crop in terms of farmer involvement (81 per cent of them) and cultivated area (62 per cent of the total) is rice. Formerly this was mainly of the 'upland' variety but there has been considerable mangrove swamp reclamation for rice cultivation in the coastal zones, and along most river valleys rice is an important crop. Despite government attempts to encourage rice production the country still has to import when it could be self-sufficient. Cassava, millet, maize and groundnuts are the other crops grown largely for local consumption, the groundnuts mainly in drier areas of the north and east of the country.

The oil-palm is grown widely in the Scarcies river region, the area inland from Freetown and in the south-east and provides for home consumption and, in the past particularly, for export. Much of the production is from scattered palms, and undoubtedly output could be increased by expanding the area of better-managed plantations.

The other principal export crops are cocoa and coffee, both grown mainly in the forest areas of the south-east around Kailahun and Kenema. In 1977–8, coffee accounted for 37 per cent of the value of exports, but variations in both world prices and yields result in very variable contributions to the national economy. Minor agricultural exports include kola nuts from the Moyamba and Freetown areas, ginger from around Moyamba, piassava fibre from the coastal swamps and benniseed from the Bo area. The marketing of these crops is controlled by the Sierra Leone Produce Marketing Board, and it has been argued that its pricing policy has not always served to encourage the local farmers and may have stimulated smuggling.

Large-scale farming is still in its infancy. It is usually government controlled and confined to the crops favoured by mechanization and local processing. The government, with the help of multilateral agencies, is establishing several integrated agricultural development schemes in which farmers are provided with a 'package' of assistance, including extension services, credit, infrastructure and marketing facilities.

Cattle are important locally in the northeast, sheep and goats are widespread and there have been attempts to improve pig and poultry production. However, many agricultural improvement projects have been held back by lack of finance and poor organization. Certainly from an environmental point of view, Sierra Leone's agricultural output could be higher and more diverse than it is, and greater efforts could be directed this way to ensure local food self-sufficiency (25 per cent of the import bill is now for foodstuffs) and to provide a base for manufacturing.

Mining

It is now clear that mining does not necessarily provide an assured base for the country's development. Platinum was first mined from stream gravels near Freetown in 1929 but this activity has long since ceased. There was also a short-lived chrome mining scheme. Diamonds are found widely along the flood plain of rivers such as the Bafi, Sewa and Moa. Once providing over two-thirds of export earnings, they have declined in importance since the mid-1970s. The decline is partly accounted for by smuggling – mainly into Liberia; but some of the alluvial workings have become exhausted and the world market has been depressed. In 1982 initial arrangements were made to start underground mining in the Kimberlite source area of the diamonds in the Kono district. Such a deep mine would be easier to control than widely dispersed alluvial workings.

Smuggling is also thought to be adversely affecting gold exports. These have never been large, but they fell from 10,031 ounces in 1982 to only 2040 ounces in 1983, but then rose to 12,000 in 1984. Bauxite mining started in the Mokanji Hills in 1964; production rose to 442,000 tonnes in 1968 and 694,000 tonnes in 1981, after which low world prices reduced exports until 1983, when they rose again to 701,000 tonnes. The ore is taken by road to a stockpile at Nitti and then by barge down Bagni Creek to vessels at anchor off Bonthe – a costly means of handling ore. In the same region rutile is mined by suction dredging in man-made lakes, but this has suffered numerous technical problems and in 1982 the operation was threatened with closure. However, production has been maintained and in 1984 output reached 70,000 tonnes.

Iron-ore mining started at Marampa in 1933 and there was a big expansion of production in the late 1960s, with a peak of 3 million tonnes in 1969. In 1964 a new ore exporting terminal was built at Pepel, and an approach channel dredged to allow access by vessels of up to 65,000 tonnes. Mounting costs, particularly of fuel, and problems of spares for equipment led to a sudden closing of the mine in 1975. Several thousand lost their jobs, Marampa became a 'ghost' town and the rail link to Pepel ceased to be maintained. However, in 1982 a new company resumed production with a planned output of 1 million tonnes a year to be obtained by the beneficiation of specularite ore and waste from the former operations. The actual output was 64,000 tonnes in 1982/3 and 417,000 in 1983/4; but it was clear that the company is operating under difficulties, especially with the world demand for iron-ore in a depressed state – and production has stopped once again.

The future

Neither a relatively favoured climate nor diverse mineral resources have brought much economic progress, and the government has pressed for Sierra Leone to be added to the United Nations' list of 'least-developed' countries. Low world prices and lack of incentives have reduced agricultural production, and mining has been adversely affected by depressed markets, the extreme difficulty of controlling smuggling, and the high operating costs resulting from the need to import all equipment and fuel.

The Pepel–Marampa railway line has been retained, but the former 500 km of government railway, built early this century on a narrow gauge with steep gradients and sharp curves, was finally closed in 1969. Yet only the principal road routes are surfaced and all-season. The bulk of the electricity is generated from costly imported fuel oil, and there has been little development of industrial activity apart from a small oil refinery, brewing, flour-milling, and the manufacture of shoes, cement and matches.

In the 1950s Freetown was provided with its first deep-water port facilities, and these were extended in the 1960s; but the trade of the country is relatively small and attempts to attract trans-shipment traffic have not been very successful.

Possessing the sea, sand and sun that tourists find attractive, Sierra Leone has tried to build up a tourist industry by providing hotel accommodation at favoured locations such as Lumley Beach near Freetown. This has failed to attract more than a trickle of tourists, who are possibly deterred by the relative shortness of the dry season and a residual image of the 'white man's grave'. Perhaps of more importance, the government has not had the resources, financial and human, to put in the necessary concentrated promotion, nor has it been able, as in The Gambia, to persuade others to do so.

Clearly, Sierra Leone's development potential still hinges critically on the world mineral market, revitalizing and extending the mining industry, and channelling resources into agriculture to ensure food self-sufficiency and an industrial base.

LIBERIA

The coastal areas of what is now Liberia had intermittent contact with European traders after the fifteenth century and became known as the 'Grain Coast' after the guinea grains (peppers) which were its main export. It was never a primary slaving area because the population density was very low and the coast not favoured for port development and settlement. In the 1820s, Mesurado (later to be Monrovia) was selected by the American Colonization Society for the settlement of liberated slaves. In all some 10,000 of American origin were settled – mainly at Monrovia, but also at some other coastal locations – and an ethno-cultural and economic dualism was established; conflict with the local population has never been completely eliminated. In 1847 Liberia became an independent republic, thereby avoiding the colonialism that was to be the experience of its neighbours. One of the country's presidents was later to remark that this had been to Liberia's disadvantage since it did not acquire even the rudimentary infrastructure which had been provided in most colonies.

The territory had to develop an economic base, and in the nineteenth century attempts were made to cultivate coffee, sugar, cotton and palm produce, all with little success despite an almost insatiable demand for such produce in Europe after 1860. Liberia was unable to capitalize on its suitability for such crops because the Americo-Liberian settlers had no capital, and their conflict with the indigenous population deprived them of labour and made difficult attempts to open-up the interior of the country. In the late nineteenth century the British influence strengthened, but an attempt in 1904 by a British company to establish a rubber plantation on the Farmington River had been abandoned by 1920.

The regions

Liberia is composed almost entirely of rocks of Pre-Cambrian age. These are mainly granites, with some intrusive dykes providing some of the main coastal headlands (Cape Mesurado, Cape Palmas and Cape Mount – the sites respectively of Monrovia, Harper and Robertsport) and sills interrupting some of the river profiles. In the extreme south-west and along the northern border are areas of well-mineralized strata of Birrimian age comparable with those of south-west Ghana. The main regions are to be defined more in terms of relief than geology.

The coastline itself is generally inhospitable, with sand bars associated with promontories and river mouths, some lagoon development and mangrove swamps on lower-lying areas along rivers and creeks. Nowhere is there more than partial natural shelter for ocean-going ships, a factor contributing to the lack of early development. The coastal plain is some 20–50 km in width and does not rise above 100 m. The rainfall in this coastal region is heavy – over 4000 mm in the west and over 2500 mm in the east – with only 3–4 months (December to March) in which the rainfall is not substantial. A double peak is sometimes discernible. The rainfall is such that soils are well-leached and a forest-savanna mosaic is the typical natural vegetation, much of it now of secondary character.

Inland there is a zone of low hills and plateaux with heights of 120–350 m, but there are also some higher residual mountains such as the Puta and Bong ranges, both of which are zones of considerable mineralization. In the north-west there is a more extensive area of low mountains in the Wologisi range, a zone of known extensive iron-ore deposits, and on the extreme northern border at Nimba and around Voinjama are the southern flanks of the Guinea Highlands, rising at Mount Nimba to nearly 1400 m. The higher areas have low population densities; and although in general the rainfall is less than it is nearer the coast, they have high forest vegetation. While much of the country has forest of some sort it is mainly in the higher areas, away from the coast, over one-third of the total area, that the forest is best suited for timber extraction.

The boundaries between these relief regions are defined by scarp features and the courses of most rivers are interrupted by falls and rapids. These could provide sites for hydro-electric power development.

Agriculture

The staple crops are rice and cassava, with yams, maize, sweet potatoes and groundnuts of subsidiary importance. Tree crops such as plantain, oil-palm and citrus are also widespread. Some 90 per cent of the population (the total was 1.7 million in 1982) lives in the rural areas, and 75 per cent of the working population is employed on the land. Only 5 per cent of the cultivable land is actually cropped, but while there is no land shortage the relatively poor soils and bush-fallowing cultivation results in low productivity . The traditional agricultural sector accounts for only 17 per cent of the GDP.

An estimated 140,000 farmers, out of a total of 150,000, grow rice, with an average of 1 ha per farm; but output is well below the 200,000 tonnes a year that is needed. The deficit has to be imported and there have been considerable efforts since the 1960s to expand production. Over 85 per cent of the rice production is of the 'upland' type which is not suitable for large-scale or mechanized cultivation. Farmers have been encouraged to form co-operatives, advice and technical assistance have been made available, fertilizer and seed have been provided and more emphasis placed on the swamp varieties. The government has initiated mechanized rice projects (e.g. at Foya-Solumba, Zeleh Town and Kpartawee), large firms have been encouraged to start rice farming, and rice is often an element in some integrated agricultural

Table 17 *Liberia: sector contributions to exports (percentages of total value)*

	1958	*1968*	*1975*	*1980*
Rubber	48.5	12.8	11.7	17.0
Palm produce	2.0	1.0	0.8	0.9
Coffee	0.8	1.5	1.1	5.5
Cocoa	1.0	0.7	1.1	1.7
Logs/timber	—	0.7	3.7	12.1
Diamonds	5.6	20.0	4.7	5.6
Iron	19.9	58.2	74.4	51.7
Miscellaneous	22.2	5.1	2.5	5.5

Source: Economic Survey of Liberia, 1980.

development schemes. The promised self-sufficiency has yet to be achieved, and in 1979 rice shortages led to riots which were a contributory factor in a *coup* and change of government.

Also to the disadvantage of the traditional sector has been the emphasis on foreign concessions and commercial farming. Following the abandonment in 1920 of the attempt to develop a rubber plantation by a British company, Liberia suffered severe economic problems; it was rescued by a financial agreement with the American Firestone rubber company, which took a 99-year lease on 117,000 ha of land for rubber cultivation in the area east of Monrovia. The Second World War stimulated production, which reached 20,000 tonnes at the end of the war with peak employment of 36,000 people. Liberia has on occasion been called the Firestone Republic.

Firestone now has a second plantation at Cavalla and other companies have established plantations at Copopa (Liberia Company), Greenville (African Fruit Company), Tappita (Liberian Agricultural Company), Salala (Salala Rubber Corporation) and Klag and Gbarnga (Guthries, formerly Goodrich). These concessions now total over 946,500 ha, of which the actual planted area amounts to 60,000 ha.

In 1950 rubber accounted for 85 per cent of the value of exports. With the development of mining after 1951, however, its relative contribution declined dramatically, although total production has in recent years remained steady at 75–80 thousand tonnes. Table 17 shows the insignificance of other agricultural exports.

Liberians, mainly the Americo-Liberian urban dwellers, have also engaged widely in commercial agriculture. About 63,000 ha of rubber is cultivated by them, with 37 per cent of the 9,000 farms being under 4 ha and only 20 per cent being over 20 ha. Such farms tend to have lower yields of poorer-quality rubber than the plantations, and from a slightly larger area produce only 28 per cent of the total output. Many of the small rubber farms are located adjacent to plantations so that they can use their transport and processing facilities. Small-scale farms are also responsible for the bulk of the cocoa, coffee and palm produce.

Overall, government planning has neglected agriculture which, over four development plans, has averaged only 11 per cent of planned investment with actual expenditure often much below that. Yet clearly, the low overall population density favours large-scale concessionary arrangements, and there is considerable untapped agricultural potential.

Forestry

Closed forest accounts for 33 per cent of the national area, and there is another 6 per cent of 'broken' forest. These forests contain some 60 species in commercial quantities, of which 12 are already well established in trade. Yet for a country so well endowed with forest and with the advantage of a low population density to reduce land-use conflicts, Liberia has not developed its forests as might have been expected. No logs were exported before 1961, and in 1968 the value of timber exports was a modest $1.5 million. In the late 1960s and early 1970s a large number of concessions were granted, and timber production and contributions to exports increased greatly (Table 17).

In recent years timber production has averaged 250,000 m^3 a year, and although this production is modest there is still the danger of too rapid deforestation. In theory timber companies are required either to replant for each tree cut or pay into a Reafforestation Fund. In practice it would appear that reafforestation is not keeping pace with cutting and the forests are a wasting asset.

There were government plans to eliminate log exports by 1977 and to ship only sawn or processed timber but although some saw mills and a plywood factory have been set up, logs still account for the bulk of the trade. The growth of the timber industry has undoubtedly been hindered by the small local market (in contrast with Ghana, Côte d'Ivoire and Nigeria), and the general inadequacy of the transport system and developments that have taken place, especially in the eastern part of the country, have been associated with port improvement at Harper and Greenville and improved road access. The iron-ore port of Buchanan has become second timber port after Greenville and receives logs by rail.

Mining

As Table 17 showed, mining and iron-ore in particular came to dominate the economy in the 1960s. For many decades diamonds have been produced intermittently and in small quantities from alluvial workings on the Lofa river and in the Nimba region, but there is reason to believe that recent increased exports derive mainly from across the border in Sierra Leone.

Plate 27 The LAMCO railway for iron ore movement to the port of Buchanan, Liberia

The first iron-ore mine started production at Bomi Hills (by the Liberia Mining Company) in 1951 and was followed at Mano river (the National Iron Ore Company) in 1961, Mount Nimba (LAMCO) in 1963 and Bong Hills (DELIMCO) in 1966. From 1.3 million tonnes in 1953, exports increased to a peak of 25.3 million tonnes in 1974, since when stagnation in world steel markets and low prices for ore have reduced production (12.7 million tonnes in 1982) and its contribution to the national economy.

In 1958 the Bomi Hills mine had to resort to mining lower-grade itabirite ore and in 1975 ceased operations. The Mano river mine has had to be provided with improved concentration facilities and has sought aid for a rehabilitation programme. The LAMCO pelletizing plant at Buchanan closed in 1979 because of reduced demand, and mining of the lower-grade Tokadeh ores (51 per cent Fe) have been started to compensate for gradual exhaustion of the better grade (62 per cent Fe) Nimba ore. Plans for the mining of iron at Wologisi where there are large deposits of high grade have been postponed by the recession, as have plans for a local steel industry.

Iron-ore has become a main, but clearly vulnerable, support for the economy. The potential is vast but further developments will await improvement in world steel markets. Like the rubber companies, the mining companies have contributed greatly to the provision or improvement of roads, railways, ports, education, medical services, housing, amenities and welfare and provide employment for 10,000 (90 per cent of them Liberians). The LAMCO mine township of Yekepa (pop. 15,000) has become the country's second largest town, and their railway and port at Buchanan also enable other enterprises to export forest and agricultural commodities (114,000 tonnes in 1979). There is the real danger that if self-perpetuating growth is not initiated while there is income from mining, Liberia will have nothing to show for it at the end of the day apart from some large holes in the ground.

Development policy

The small home market for manufactured goods has not encouraged industrialization: manufacturing accounts for only 4.5 per cent of the GDP. Much of the industrial employment is in local food processing industries, but the modern sector includes an oil refinery, cement, explosives, detergents, hand tools, foam rubber, tobacco/cigarettes, fish conserving and brewing. In 1985 a ship-breaking industry was started. Some 63 per cent of the private sector employment is concentrated in the capital, Monrovia; and apart from the first-stage processing of local commodities such as rubber and timber and the concentration of ores, few industries have been attracted elsewhere despite incentives to do so. The transport problems probably contribute to this. The 1981 establishment of an industrial free zone in Monrovia will further exaggerate the regional imbalance in industrial employment: it has already attracted hand-tool, vegetable oil and ship repair industries.

It was in 1944 that the then President Tubman initiated his 'Open Door' policy which led to many of the rubber, mining and forestry concessions being granted and to the setting up of some of the industries. Liberia has continued with this policy and it has been extended to its shipping registry. Liberia is the leading 'flag of convenience' and has the world's largest fleet (62 million GRT), attracted by low registration fees and the relative lack of regulations. In the face of criticism the regulations with respect to safety, inspection and manning have become more demanding, but supervision costs money and would reduce the income, now about $15 million a year.

By virtue of its mining industries Liberia has one of the highest per capita GDPs in West Africa ($570), but this conceals a marked dualism between a small number (mainly Americo-Liberians) with active participation and high incomes derived from the modern sector and the bulk of the population not much removed from the subsistence level. There is also the spatial dualism already noted, with the overwhelming concentration of modern sector activities in the capital and port of Monrovia (200,000 people), a few other coastal settlements and the mining and large plantation centres, and the bulk of the country which has a low level of accessibility and infrastructure provision. Since 1980 there have been more obvious attempts by government to bridge these gaps by extending transport, communications, education and welfare services into the deprived area.

Liberia's economic difficulties would soon be solved by an improvement in world iron-ore markets. Basic studies have been undertaken so that the Wologisi deposits could be mined once the transport routes have been provided. For the mass of the population the best hope is probably the extension of commercialized farming on a small-scale basis, but possibly with functional linkages with large plantations.

The Mano River Union. In 1973 Sierra Leone and Liberia created The Mano River Union and in 1980 they were joined by Guinea. There have been slow moves towards harmonization of customs regimes and the establishment of common external tariffs. Fourteen joint industrial projects have been identified (food processing, pharmaceuticals, soap concentrates, salt and soda, vehicle parts, glass) and market studies initiated. A joint hydroelectric power development has been proposed. However, the most tangible changes to date have been the completion in 1976 of a bridge across the Mano river border and the start of work in 1984 on the first stage of the road improvement between Freetown and Monrovia. Perhaps the larger market so created will help the three countries and avoid the costly duplication of development projects.

23
Côte d'Ivoire and Ghana

Contrasts in the economic development of Côte d'Ivoire and Ghana are based on differences of colonial history, post-independence economic strategies and political factors, rather than differences of resource endowment.

As the 'Gold Coast', Ghana had a long history of contact with European trading interests, and there was fierce competition between European nations for footholds on the coast in an attempt to control the gold trade. During the nineteenth century Britain gained an ascendancy and complete control, and as early as 1919 the Gold Coast had its first 10-year development plan. Emphasizing transport, this must rank as one of the first attempts at development planning and was undoubtedly the basis of economic strength of the Gold Coast when it became independent in 1957. The country had a good deep-water port at Takoradi, a reasonable road and rail system, and had built up considerable financial reserves. However, economic growth has since been irregular or lacking, the reserves have been spent, a once favourable balance of trade has become unfavourable, and a massive external debt has accumulated.

Côte d'Ivoire with its sparsity of sheltered coastal landing places, little gold and lower population density, was less attractive to the Europeans than the adjacent Gold Coast; it received only spasmodic attention until the nineteenth century, when the French gradually extended their control and in 1893 declared it a colony. As a part of the vast French West Africa, Côte d'Ivoire was overshadowed by Senegal and Abidjan became the capital only in 1934. Economic development on any scale came only after the deep-water lagoon of Abidjan was opened to shipping on the completion in 1950 of the Vridi Canal linking sea and lagoon. Not without justification it has been claimed of Abidjan that 'le port est la porte'. Côte d'Ivoire became independent in 1960 and with political stability maintained an average economic growth rate of 8 per cent a year until the late 1970s, a rate achieved elsewhere in sub-Saharan Africa only by oil producers such as Gabon and Nigeria, and the more spectacular because it is based on agricultural rather than mineral production.

Larger than Ghana (Table 18), Côte d'Ivoire has a greater longitudinal range, more restricted latitudinal range and rather less diversity of relief. Nevertheless, the two countries display a similar range of climatic, natural vegetation and resource endowments.

Table 18 *Ghana and Côte d'Ivoire: basic statistics*

	Ghana	*Côte d'Ivoire*
Area	239,000m^2	322,000km^2
Population (1985 est.)	12.2 million	8.9 million
Population density	51.0 per km^2	28.0 per km^2
Population growth rate	3.1%	2.6%
Per capita	$1150	$420

PHYSICAL DIVISIONS

The coastal zone displays a contrast between stretches of low, rocky cliff and headlands with small, sandy embayments and smooth, unindented sections with sand bars and backing lagoons. The former, 'Elmina' type of coast, is found where Pre-Cambrian rocks form the coast west of Fresco in Côte d'Ivoire and between the Ankobra river and Saltpond in Ghana (Figure 62). In Ghana particularly it was the sheltered beach landing places which provided the sites for European forts, some of which (e.g. at Takoradi, Sekondi, Cape Coast and Accra) were to become the main ports of the colonial era. In Côte d'Ivoire, Sassandra was provided with a wharf in 1951 and San Pedro developed as the second port after Abidjan. The 'Dahomey' type of coast with younger rocks and recent sand deposits found in eastern Côte d'Ivoire and eastern Ghana provides no natural shelter for ships, and the development of the port of Abidjan was dependent on the artificial breaching of the sand bar to give access to the lagoon system. Only eastwards from Accra in the Lower Volta Plains does the coast plain widen to any extent.

The generally narrow coastal lowland gives way inland to low **interior plains**. The Pre-Cambrian rocks produce a rather monotonous rolling surface in Côte d'Ivoire, but in south-west Ghana there is a more hilly landscape with a general north-east/south-west grain and an average elevation of 250–300 m. Much of northern Côte d'Ivoire and north-western Ghana is also made up of Pre-Cambrian crystalline rocks and is best described as **plateau**, but the Guinea Highlands extend eastwards into the Man region and produce a more mountainous scenery rising to over 1200 m. Local residual relief features are characteristic of the interior plateaux surfaces. In Ghana the Palaeozoic sandstones of the Volta basin are bounded by a series of west- and north-facing scarp features (Kwahu, Mampong, Gambaga), rising in places to over 600 m, but the basin itself has a monotonous relief. In eastern Ghana the north-east/south-west trending Akwapim–Togo ranges provide the country's only mountainous landscape, rising to over 1200 m.

The undifferentiated Pre-Cambrian strata which underlie most of Côte d'Ivoire are not

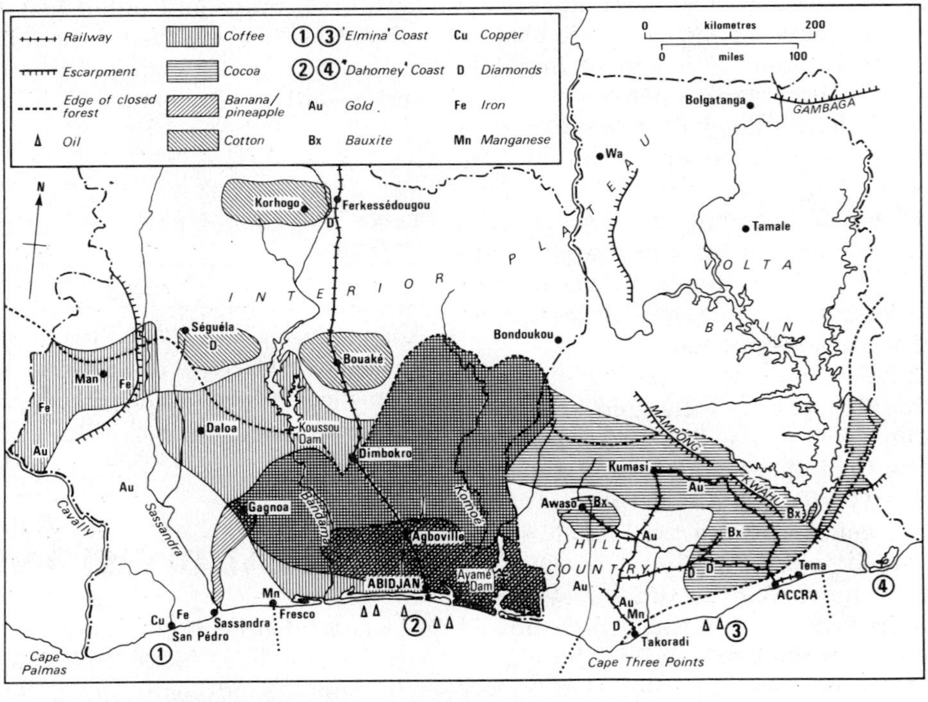

Figure 62 Côte d'Ivoire and Ghana: regions and development

highly mineralized, although there are small, localized deposits of gold, diamonds, iron and manganese (Figure 62). In south-west Ghana, the older Birrimian and younger Tarkwaian series of Pre-Cambrian rocks consist of metamorphic and intrusive strata, the former associated with gold, diamonds, manganese and bauxite and the latter gold. Bauxite is in places weathered from both series and is also found on the southern margins of the Volta basin. It was the gold which attracted the Europeans, gave the country its original name, provided a main reason for the initial development of the railway and continues to provide a source of income.

Near the coast in both Côte d'Ivoire and Ghana there are two rainfall peaks, but inland a single peak is characteristic. Where the coastal alignment crosses the path of the moist south-westerly airstream, in south-west Ghana, south-east Côte d'Ivoire and extreme south-west Côte d'Ivoire, the rainfall is between 1500 and 2000 mm. The central Côte d'Ivoire coastlands have less than 1500 mm, but nothing comparable with the anomalous low rainfall of less than 750 mm which characterizes the area east of Accra in Ghana. Higher areas inland (e.g. the Man Highlands) receive over 2000 mm, but over most of the interior rainfall is in the 1000–1300 mm range.

In consequence of this rainfall pattern, rain forest is well developed over much of the southern half of Côte d'Ivoire, the south-western part of Ghana and the Akwapim–Togo ranges. The forest zone narrows in the lower rainfall area of south-central Côte d'Ivoire, and this provided a convenient route for the railway northwards from Abidjan. North of the forest there is a belt of derived savanna with gallery forest, giving way to savanna grassland in the northern parts of each country. The low rainfall of the Accra Plains also has a scrub-grassland vegetation, and the coastlands have a generally narrow belt of strand and mangrove vegetation.

Broadly speaking, these physical conditions provide the basis for a contrast in each country between, on the one hand, a better-watered, forested south with a good root crop (yam, cassava) subsistence base and potential for crops such as cocoa, coffee, rubber, palms and tropical fruits, and on the other hand a lower-rainfall, savanna north where grain production depends critically on the rainfall and where animal husbandry assumes importance as tsetse infection declines in significance. There is then an inherent spatial dualism which in Ghana particularly is reinforced by the location of the main mineral resources in the forested south-west of the country.

With this general similarity of resource base in mind, the development of economic activity in each country will now be examined.

CÔTE D'IVOIRE

The lack of natural harbours and landing places in Côte d'Ivoire limited European contact and commerce and discouraged export production by local people. Grand Bassam was the first seat of administration and site of a lighterage pier after 1901. Until 1931 this was the territory's only port facility, but a second pier was then built at Port Bouët, more conveniently located to serve the new seat of government at Abidjan from where the railway link inland was started in 1904.

A dual production structure gradually emerged. With some encouragement from government, Africans started growing cash crops as an adjunct to their subsistence food crop cultivation. The first such crop was cocoa, followed in the 1930s by coffee. As the cultivated area expanded labour was increasingly imported, especially at harvest times, from Burkina Faso and there emerged a small group of relatively prosperous farmers who, as the Coffee Producers Association, became a powerful lobby. After the Second World War there emerged from their number Felix Houphouët Boigny who was to become the country's first president – a post he still held in 1987.

Simultaneously, and with some local

opposition, European firms were also establishing cocoa and coffee plantations, and by 1947 there were 17 cocoa and 19 coffee processing plants, 17 saw-mills, five cotton ginneries, two kapok factories, three sisal factories, four vegetable oil mills, three rice mills and one producer of banana flakes. These were dispersed among a number of small settlements, at Bassam, Lahou, Sassandra, Abidjan and Badikaha (near Korhogo). Indeed, until the 1950s the urban hierarchy was only weakly developed. Overall, production from these plantations and associated processing plants remained small until the 1950s, when they provided the foundation for rapid expansion of the agricultural sector and economic growth.

Agriculture

Although losing ground to cocoa in recent years, coffee is still the second export, accounting for 21 per cent of export earnings in 1982. Originally introduced in the lagoon area of the south-east, cultivation spread westwards and there are now important concentrations of production around Abidjan, Agboville, Daboa, Dimbokro, Gagnoa and Man (Figure 62). In the 20 years from 1960, annual production has been as low as 97,000 and as high as 305,000 tonnes, and in good years is well above the International Coffee Organisation's imposed quota of 190,000 tonnes. There are now over 280,000 farms amounting to 1.2 million hectares, and an estimated 2.4 million people owe their livelihood to coffee production and the guaranteed price paid by the government.

The general policy for coffee is to improve the quality rather than expand the quantity. To this end there is a need to replant large areas where 60 per cent of the trees are now older than 15 years. There are also experiments to improve the flavour of the robusta by crossing it with the higher quality arabica variety.

Cocoa was introduced from Ghana in the late nineteenth century as a forced cash crop, and the main producing area is still an extension of that in Ghana (Figure 62). Cocoa production increased gradually from 93,000 tonnes in 1960 to 505,000 tonnes in 1985; from being the fourth largest world producer in 1968, Côte d'Ivoire has surpassed Ghana to become leading producer. The bulk of the production is from 225,000 African farms: farmers receive guaranteed cash payments from the government, but these have never been reduced despite world market price fluctuations. Cocoa and its ancillary services now benefit about 650,000 people. The country has greatly increased its cocoa storage capacity to almost 200,000 tonnes as a means of regulating the supply, and it is hoped the world price, of cocoa. If Ghana's experience in 1965 is any guide, this is unlikely to work.

Bananas were first introduced in the early 1930s. Production expanded rapidly once suitable export facilities became available at Abidjan in the 1950s and as the road network improved. Production is now mainly from the immediate Abidjan hinterland and a secondary area exports through Sassandra. Although the number of African planters has increased, the bulk of the banana production is still from European plantations. Exports now average about 150,000 tonnes a year.

Plate 28 Co-operative banana picking station, Cote d'Ivoire

Pineapples, also mainly from the Abidjan area, now provide income for 15,000 farmers and are grown on company plantations. Production increased twelve-fold in the 15 years after independence, and much of the crop is now conserved as fruit or juice in local canneries. For that part of the crop exported fresh, speed and care in transport are essential, and this is now possible by means of one of West Africa's best transport networks.

A natural tree of the West African forest, the oil-palm has been greatly extended by the development of village and large-scale plantations – especially after the creation by the government in 1963 of the Société pour le Développement Palmiste (SODEPALM). Cultivation is mainly in the coastal regions and a good part of the vegetable oil produced is marketed locally.

There has been a purposeful policy of diversification, and this has involved crops such as rubber, cotton, sugar, citrus and rice. Established first in 1956, rubber cultivation expanded rapidly in the mid 1970s when higher oil prices made synthetics more expensive. From 6000 tonnes in 1968 production increased to 39,000 tonnes in 1985, and Côte d'Ivoire seems well on its way to overtaking Liberia as leading African producer by the end of the century. The bulk of the production is now from two large industrial producers (Société Africaine de Plantations d'Heveas, and Société des Caoutchoucs de Grand-Bereby); but there are monetary incentives for African farmers to produce rubber in the vicinity of the large plantations where they can take advantage of the processing facilities.

A temporary world shortage of sugar in the early 1970s prompted an Ivoirian sugar programme, with plans ultimately to produce 600,000 tonnes a year, mainly for export, from twelve complexes scattered over the northern region (e.g. Ferkessedougou, Bereton-Ko, Zenoula). The cost escalated, world prices dropped and hints of poor administration and possible fraud led to a reduced programme of six complexes. Output climbed from 33,000 tonnes in 1977/8 to 180,000 tonnes in 1982/3, of which local consumption accounted for 80,000 tonnes. Export started in 1980 but production costs are high and sales are subsidized by the government.

Far more successful has been the expansion of cotton cultivation, as with sugar an attempt to bring development to the less prosperous north. Main areas of cultivation are around Bouaké and Korhogo (Figure 62). After 1961 the Mono variety was gradually replaced by the higher-yielding Allan variety, and by 1972 122,000 ha of the latter was cultivated on an industrial basis. A research station has been established at Bouaké, and the country has become the second largest franc zone producer after Chad. A state-owned foreign-managed organization, SODERIZ, has been expanding rice production by starting paddy cultivation and then handing over to peasant farmers: output increased from 250,000 tonnes in 1965 to 514,000 tonnes in 1985.

The success of Ivoirian agriculture clearly hinges on the use of larger enterprises as 'growth points' and the use of financial incentives and price stabilization to encourage small-scale farming. A Stabilization Fund has ensured this and has made good overall profits for the government. Undoubtedly a good transport system, extension services and efficient marketing have also helped. Increasing peasant participation and the emergence of a 'kulak' group has generated a vested interest in agricultural growth.

Other economic development

Although the country provides one of the few examples where substantial economic growth has been based on agriculture, there have been impressive contributions to Ivoirian development from other sectors. Forest exploitation started early this century along rivers flowing into the lagoon system, but more recent expansion has been facilitated by improved road transport and by deep-water port facilities at Abidjan to serve the traditional producing area of the south-east. In the late 1960s the development of a second deep-water port at San Pedro made possible the opening up of extensive, previously untapped reserves in the south-west.

At a peak in the mid-1970s Côte d'Ivoire exported over 2.5 million tonnes of timber a year, and while in theory timber is a renewable resource, exploitation at this rate was dangerously excessive. It has been estimated that the forest will disappear by the end of the century. Removal of the forest cover hastens soil erosion and leads to speculative agriculture on cleared areas. There is the need to enforce existing regulations on illegal cutting, quotas on protected species and replanting. However, with forest-related industries and timber handling employing 40,000 people – accounting for one-third of Abidjan's port traffic, one-third of the country's road transport and valuable export earnings – there is reluctance to reduce production to levels at which the forest resources would be self-regenerative.

Minerals make only a small contribution to the economy. Alluvial diamonds are obtained from workings south of Korhogo and from near Seguel, and small amounts of manganese from near Fresco. Gold is mined at primitive workings along the Cavally river. There are plans, dependent on world gold prices, for a modern gold mining industry and a joint venture with state participation has been established. Numerous iron-ore deposits have been identified, the richest being that in the west, an extension of Liberia's Mount Nimba deposits. There has been a feasibility study for nickel–cobalt extraction near Man, and copper exploration continues.

Possibly of greater significance, oil was discovered offshore from Grand Bassam in 1975 in what is now known as the Bélier field, and in 1979, offshore west of Abidjan, the Espoir field proved productive. Original hopes for this field have not been upheld, but Côte d'Ivoire has at least attained self-sufficiency with the possibility of some small surplus for export as exploration continues. There are plans to exploit natural gas for use in electricity generation.

While agriculture and forestry have provided the basis for export-led growth they have also generated considerable industrial development, so that Côte d'Ivoire now has a well-diversified industrial sector and the number of industrial enterprises has grown from 60 to over 602 in the years since independence. Much of the development has been of local resource-based industries such as edible oils, fats, soaps, canning, textiles, instant coffee, milling, food processing, veneers and furniture. There has been diversification into fields such as metals and engineering, vehicle and bicycle assembly, radios, oil refining, chemicals, fertilizers and cement.

From Table 19 it is clear that the contribution of the secondary manufacturing sector has been growing steadily while that of the primary sector has been declining. The tertiary sector – including commerce, transport

Table 19 *Côte d'Ivoire: indicators of development*

	1960	*1965*	*1975*	*1980*
Per capita GDP (francs cfa)	38,183	55,718	81,138	121,036
Contribution to GDP				
primary	46.8%	39.4%	30.2%	31.8%
secondary	15.2%	19.0%	23.8%	24.7%
tertiary	36.0%	41.6%	46.0%	43.5%
Trade through Abidjan (tonnes)				
imports	757,112	1,412,278	2,335,100	3,442,976
exports	1,009,597	2,199,908	2,745,591	2,618,724

Note: £1.00 = 480 francs cfa
Source: after Penouil (1981).

and tourism – has also grown. The number of tourists rose from 44,864 in 1974 to 179,484 in 1978; Abidjan alone, which had 11 hotels in 1970 had 50 by 1980. Abidjan's 3229 hotel rooms compares with 589 in beach resorts (mainly in the Assinie area and including a Club Mediterranée) and 2152 in the interior, including a network of 'village hotels'. The tourist industry has benefited from political stability and a relatively sophisticated infrastructure but has been adversely affected by recession in the 1980s. There has been an attempt to diversify into conference and lower-priced package arrangements. Nearly 80 per cent of the hotels are Ivoirian-owned, which contrasts with the foreign domination noted in The Gambia.

Development policy

Until 1930 there was little positive development policy and the economy was still basically of a 'gathering' kind. However, land originally granted to Europeans was taken back, and this allowed the development of smaller-scale farming at a later stage. The construction of the railway and wharf at Grand Bassam provided openings for external trade. From 1930 to 1950 there was a period of 'balanced' growth, with regional administration encouraging agricultural development with European and African plantations in association with traditional subsistence cropping. Rising incomes from agriculture provided the basis for the development of other sectors, including industry.

With the opening of the port of Abidjan in 1950, the overall pace of economic development quickened markedly. However, whereas traditional regional inequality was based on the geographical contrasts between south and north, it was now Abidjan that became the economic growth pole and exerted a powerful attraction on capital, development and people. Its population expanded from 124,000 in 1955 to over 1.8 million in 1983, with 26 per cent of the inhabitants in 'shanty' towns. Abidjan accounts to 65 per cent of all the country's business dealings and concentrates a high proportion of the industrial investment and employment. It has served to exaggerate the regional inequalities.

A Ministry of Planning was created in 1966 and initiated a series of 5-year plans, which initially placed emphasis on infrastructure (roads, the Koussou HEP scheme) and industry (including a number of state enterprises – palm produce, mining, sugar, rice, rubber). In the 1975–80 and 1980–5 plans there has been greater emphasis on agricultural development, and in particular an attempt to replicate in the south-west and north the successful agricultural-based development of the south-east. In the south-west the new port of San Pedro has provided a focal point for the expansion of plantation agriculture (rubber, oil-palm), forestry exploitation and a pulp and paper industry. From a small village in 1965 San Pedro has grown to a town of over 40,000 inhabitants. In the centre and north of the country the emphasis has been on rice, cotton, sugar and animal husbandry, each with related processing industries. This is encouraging urban expansion at places such as Bouaké (pop. 175,000), Man, Korhogo and Daboa (all over 50,000). In 1983, a draft law was approved whereby the capital functions will ultimately be transferred from Abidjan to Yamoussoukro, the birthplace of Houphouët-Boigny. This move may be interpreted in political terms or as a part of a longer-term economic strategy to decentralize development effort and relieve congestion at Abidjan.

Until the late 1970s, the bulk of the investment in development projects came from private enterprise and capital, much of it from overseas. Some have argued that whilst this undoubtedly resulted in rapid growth it was at the expense of growing 'dependency' on external influences. In 1979, 61.5 per cent of the employers were non-African, 77 per cent of company directors were non-Ivoirian, and it is estimated that there were 2 million non-Ivoirian Africans, mainly from Burkina Faso, Guinea and Ghana, in the country and accounting for half of the agricultural labour force. There are now 50,000 French in Côte d'Ivoire, five times the number at independence.

Côte d'Ivoire has been cited as an example of 'development from above' and 'centre-down' but without direct participation by government. The impetus and political stability so necessary for outward orientation of the economy derives from a small, wealthy planter class, typified in Houphouët-Boigny himself, closely linked to France and attaching great importance to the potential of export-based agriculture.

In comparison with all its neighbours, Côte d'Ivoire has been successful; but 70 per cent of its export revenue still derives from the narrow and potentially vulnerable base provided by coffee, cocoa and timber. Although a wider spectrum of the population has undoubtedly benefited, the polarization of wealth in relatively few hands and spatially in Abidjan and the south-east creates problems that have still to be satisfactorily addressed. However, Côte d'Ivoire has demonstrated that growth can be led by agriculture, and given political stability and favourable market conditions there is reason to believe that this could be translated into real development and transmitted to the regions and the bulk of the population.

GHANA

The 'Gold Coast' became the independent Ghana in 1957 and provided the example soon to be followed by most of its neighbours. However, few of them had the same initial advantages of a relatively well-developed infrastructure, social and economic, and a sound economic base. Ghana started as a country of considerable potential and promise, but disappointingly, its post-independence performance has fallen far short of expectations.

The development of agriculture

The forest environment of southern Ghana (Figure 62) is well-suited to perennial tree crops such as rubber, oil-palm, coffee, cocoa, bananas, kola, citrus and mango. In the nineteenth century it was palm-oil that emerged as the main replacement for the lost slave trade. The main producing area was a fairly narrow belt along the southern margins of the forest zone, so that transport to ports was reduced to a minimum, and palm-oil was the leading export from 1853 to 1890 when for a brief period rubber assumed dominance. Like palm-oil, the bulk of the rubber came from the southern forest zone and was mainly 'gathered' rather than cultivated.

During the later nineteenth century, cotton, gum copal, kola and coffee were all exported in small quantities, and for a brief period there was a coffee processing plant. However, it was cocoa that came to assume the dominant role. Cocoa was first introduced successfully in 1878 by a Gold Coast African returning from Fernando Po where he had been working on cocoa plantations. He supplied neighbours with seeds, the government established an experimental farm from which cocoa seedlings were distributed, and the farmers of Akwapim, north-east of Accra, responded rapidly.

Having successfully established cocoa farming in their homeland they started to purchase land further north and west, and cocoa farming spread rapidly. The completion of the Sekondi–Kumasi railway in 1903 and the Accra–Kumasi line between 1908 and 1925 greatly facilitated transport and stimulated production away from the original areas. In 1905 cocoa exports amounted to 5070 tonnes and by 1916 had increased to 60,000 tonnes. Ghana became the leading world producer in 1913, a position it retained until overtaken by Côte d'Ivoire in 1978, since when it has slipped to fourth position. Cocoa cultivation accounts for 1.87 million hectares, about 50 per cent of the total cultivated area, and is still by far the country's most important export.

An important feature of cocoa cultivation in Ghana is that it is entirely by peasant farmers on small plots of 0.5–1.0 ha and gives work to

24 per cent of the active labour force. The cocoa is grown in the shade of forest trees; this reduces the risk of soil erosion and need for fertilizer but possibly increases the risk of plant disease and the problems of controlling it. Since the 1930s, a virus disease, swollen shoot, and the insect-spread capsid disease have devastated large areas of cocoa, especially in the earlier established areas of the south-east. The only real solution is to cut out all affected trees, and over 110 million – a small part of the total – have already been removed.

Annual cocoa production and exports fluctuate in response to weather, disease and prices, but the trend was upwards to a peak of nearly half a million tonnes in 1965, since when there has been a dramatic decline to 1920s levels (Table 20). With cocoa until recently providing 60–70 per cent of the value of exports this is obviously critical for the national economy – such overwhelming dependence on a single commodity inevitably makes for vulnerability.

A number of factors have contributed to this decline. Selective out-migration from rural areas has left cocoa farmers as an ageing group (average age more than 50), and the younger men are not attracted into cocoa farming. This is largely because the farmers have never been paid the market price for their cocoa by the government's Cocoa Board and were paid by 'chit' which could take a long time to redeem as cash. The income and status of cocoa farmers has declined. The cocoa trees themselves are ageing, and with 60 per cent over 25 years old and subject to disease, production has dropped. This could have been averted by proper incentives for cutting, replanting and spraying, but the subsidies given for insecticide, spraying machines and fertilizers have been inadequate and the spraying programme too erratic. The cocoa extension services have been poor and technical assistance lacking. Negligible road maintenance, lack of vehicles and shortages of spare parts, tyres, and fuel have made transport increasingly inadequate.

Table 20 *Ghanaian cocoa exports*

Year	*Exports (tonnes)*
1900	536
1920	125,000
1930	191,000
1940	224,000
1950	267,000
1960	303,000
1965	494,000
1969	303,000
1979	250,000
1984	158,000

In 1982 a cocoa rehabilitation programme was started by the then new military government, the strategy being to concentrate attention on the favoured western region – the only area not showing a decline in production and where over 60 per cent of the trees are less than 15 years old. The disease control programme is being stepped up and a buffer zone created between the areas worst affected by disease and the key areas in Ashanti and the west. Storage and transport facilities are to be improved and the Cocoa Board functions partly privatized. Given the right conditions, production could certainly be increased; but there were setbacks in 1983, and again in 1985, when drought and bush fires affected large areas and the rehabilitation programme could prove to be too little and too late.

Although of importance in the past, it is a long time since other agricultural products made more than a minor contribution to exports. However, kola nuts, palm-oil and rubber from the forest, coconut and sugar from the coastal zone and lower Volta region, and rice and cotton from the north are all important in domestic trade and as a basis for local industries, and rubber exports started again in 1986. The grasslands of the Accra plains and north support animal husbandry but are unable to provide for Ghana's meat needs. The country has been increasingly unable to feed itself and food imports have risen dramatically.

Ghana has had a series of agricultural development programmes, starting immediately after independence with state farms and large-scale cultivation of food and industrial crops, followed by the mid-1970s military government's Operation Feed Yourself and Operation Feed Your Industries, the 'New Deal' of the 1979 civilian government and the 'Green Revolution' of the last few years. Yet only a small proportion of planned investment has in fact been devoted to agriculture, and the overall impact has been negligible or even counter-productive. Basically, this is because schemes have been of the wrong type and management has been poor.

There has been a heavy emphasis on 'socialist' approaches – with government participation in the initiation and control of state farms, machinery stations, irrigation projects and plantation development. At a peak, state farms numbered over 100, but the 0.76 ha of land cultivated per employee was only marginally better than the 0.68 ha of the peasant farmer with his traditional hoe cultivation. This made nonsense of the mechanized methods, the efficiency of which was further eroded by lack of skilled labour and import restrictions. Output of sugar, vegetables, vegetable oils, meat, cotton and kenaf fibre has never been able to satisfy the needs of the industries established to process the commodities.

Much of Ghana is moisture-deficient, the north has been affected by drought and cultivation is still largely rain-fed. Well over 200 small water-storage schemes have been constructed in northern Ghana, mainly by self-help methods; but a large-scale irrigation scheme at Dawhenya on the Accra plains, initiated in the early 1960s, has still to become fully operational. In 1983 rice irrigation schemes on the lower Volta at Adidome and Akatsi were reactivated after abandonment in 1966. Further plans for extensive irrigation on the Accra plains, originally proposed as part of the Volta River Project, have as yet come to nothing; but in the north the Tono scheme near Navrongo has been completed and work is still in progress on the 94,000 ha Pwalugu scheme started in 1978. As a consequence of

Plate 29 'Self-help' construction of a water storage scheme, northern Ghana

such irrigation schemes the number of farmers growing cotton increased from 272 in 1967 to 38,000 in 1979, and rice production has been expanded.

The main approaches to agricultural development have largely ignored the peasant farmers, who still account for the bulk of the food and export crop production and on whom the socio-economic well-being of the rural areas depends. There is no reason to believe that the peasant farmers, given the proper technical support and financial incentives and freed from the coersive aspects of the larger projects, could not produce enough to feed themselves, provide exports in larger quantities and supply local industry.

Mining

Mining provides Ghana's second most important export sector (Table 21). Gold gave the country its original name and is found in enriched quartz veins in the Pre-Cambrians, and as alluvial deposits deriving from these rocks. Easily produced in large quantities by primitive surface 'grubbing', it was only late in the nineteenth and early twentieth century that modern mining was established. Gold output has declined from an annual average 900,000

Table 21 *Ghana: principal exports (percentage of total value)*

	1959 (%)	*1965 (%)*	*1969 (%)*	*1975 (%)*	*1982 (%)*
Cocoa	61.0	61.1	55.9	59.4	43.9
Cocoa products	0.9	5.5	7.0		2.6
Logs	7.1	5.9	6.2	8.3	4.9
Sawn timber	4.7	5.1	3.8		
Gold	9.9	8.5	7.6	8.9	13.3
Diamonds	7.7	6.1	3.5	1.4	2.0
Manganese	6.0	4.3	1.8	1.8	1.5
Bauxite	0.3	0.6	0.4	0.5	1.0
Others	1.7	2.6	13.0	19.7	30.8

Source: Ghana Economic Surveys.

ounces in the early 1960s to about 300,000 ounces at present. There have been no major new mining ventures since 1938, and since 1958 exploration has been inadequate, qualified personnel often lacking, spares and supplies difficult to obtain and ad hoc policies have discouraged investment. A gold refinery established in the early 1960s has not worked since 1966.

Diamonds were originally found in 1919 and occur either as 'pipes' in the Pre-Cambrians or as 'placer' deposits in the valleys of rivers originating on, or flowing across, these rocks. The main sources are the gravel terraces of the Birrim and Bonsa rivers near Tarkwa. Output at the Akwatia diamond mine fell from 2,400,000 carats a year in the mid-1970s to 700,000 in 1982, and the mine is thought to be near the end of its useful life. New prospecting was started by an American company in 1984.

Mining of manganese – derived from deep weathering of phyllites – by open-cast methods was started at Nsuta near Tarkwa in 1916 and from peaks of over 800,000 tonnes a year production has recently been around 200,000 tonnes. A higher-grade oxide deposit is nearing exhaustion, but in 1981 a plant was completed to convert lower-grade carbonate ore into manganese pellets. Expansion of output will, however, require up-grading of present old mining equipment and the rehabilitation of the now seriously inadequate rail link to Takoradi.

Numerous weathered summits have bauxite cappings. During the Second World War there was mining for a time at Mpraeso on the Kwahu Scarp, and there is still mining at Awaso which is connected by rail to Takoradi. Ore has recently been stockpiled at the mine because the railway has been unable to take it all, and this despite the fact that 250,000 tonnes a year production is well below peak levels.

Ghana's mining is small-scale so that competition is difficult with large, recently established producers of manganese such as Gabon or bauxite such as Guinea. Undoubtedly Ghana still has large untapped reserves of all her minerals, but the government has failed to produce the conditions that would allow for expansion.

Forestry

One-third of Ghana's area is forested, with more than 300 species, many of them valuable tropical woods. The industry has since 1960 been under general government control. Processing capacity has increased to 90 saw mills, 23 veneer slicers and 9 ply mills, but nearly all these operate far below capacity as a result of lack of equipment and spares and transport problems. There has been serious over-cutting of a limited range of species (mahogany, wawa, utile, sapele, makore and edium), and in 1980 the Timber Marketing Board imposed a ban on the export in log form of 14 main species in the hope of encouraging the marketing of less popular species. As in Côte d'Ivoire there has been severe depletion of forest resources and no adequate programme for conservation and regeneration. Between 1970 and 1982 log production fell from 1.5 million to 410 thousand cubic metres.

Plate 30 Palletized rice transport on Lake Volta, Yapei Port

Fishing

The up-welling of cool water off Ghana's coast provides valuable fishing grounds. Most coastal settlements have a fleet of fishing canoes. Many of the canoes are now powered by outboard motors, and at several places (e.g. Axim, Elmina), where there is more shelter, small motor vessels are used. Tema is the base for a deep-water fishing fleet and fish processing industry, but attempts to develop a locally owned fleet have not been very successful. Coastal fishing amounts to over 200,000 tonnes a year, and Lake Volta provides 20,000 tonnes of freshwater fish.

Industry

Industry accounted for 3.8 per cent of the GDP in 1960 and 18.0 per cent in 1982, its share of total employment rising from 9.1 to 12.1 per cent. About one-third of the manufacturing output is accounted for by the food, beverage and tobacco industries, with 18 per cent by textiles and 9 per cent by timber processing. The food processing industries are widely dispersed and largely based on local raw materials, and there is also a wide scattering of the informal sector textiles and woodworking. However, the formal sector, modern industries are much more heavily concentrated in the main towns – in particular at Accra–Tema, Takoradi–Sekondi and Kumasi – and in general a high proportion of their raw material input is imported.

During the 1960s there was considerable expansion of industry, much of it government controlled and including glass production, steel, cement, textiles, cocoa processing, canning (meat, fruit, vegetables, juices), vegetable oils, sugar, sacks, tyres, footwear, printing and ship repairs. In the private sector, textiles, vehicle assembly, paint, chemicals, plastics, metal working, aluminium products and electrical goods were some of the more significant industries. Many of the industries are marked by low efficiency and operate well below capacity. Vegetable, fruit and meat canning factories all existed before the local raw material supplies were assured, and a sack factory set up in 1965 to use local kenaf fibre has operated at only 15–20 per cent of capacity and mainly on imported jute despite attempts to stimulate local kenaf production. Over 62 per cent of industrial raw materials are imported, and even for industries supposedly based on local agricultural commodities the imported element is over 45 per cent. The textile industry operates at 60 per cent of capacity for lack of cotton.

The problems of industry have been exacerbated by lack of foreign exchange, import restrictions and resultant shortages of equipment, spares, raw materials and energy. While many of the industries have been logical in terms of the raw material base, they have not always been of the right scale, at the right time and properly managed. Ghana has failed to develop the linkages that are so necessary if industry is to be successful.

Development planning

Ghana's first 10-year development plan was initiated in 1919 by the far-sighted colonial governor, Sir Gordon Guggisberg. This gave

Ghana its first deep-water port (Takoradi), an improved road system, its first major hospital and Achimota College from which was to grow the present system of higher education. This emphasis on the economic and social infrastructure undoubtedly stimulated the extension of cash cropping, assisted mineral exploitation, helped develop human resources and paved the way for the sound economic base, budget surpluses and healthy reserves inherited at independence in 1957.

Ghanaian planning has continued to emphasize the provision of social and economic infrastructure, and this resulted in a second deep-water port at Tema, additional rail links, improved roads and airports, a massive increase in education and health services and improved urban fabric and services.

By 1965 the £200 million reserves, accumulated by paying the cocoa farmers less than the market price for their crop, had disappeared and large external debts had built up. The productive sector, poorly managed and inadequately capitalized, was unable to provide the revenue to finance development elsewhere. A succession of plans after 1951 that gave greater emphasis to industry than agriculture, were invariably abandoned as *coup* followed *coup*. They failed to produce real development or self-sustaining growth, and with time became more concerned with dealing with emergency financial conditions than with forward planning.

The Volta River Project (VRP). Since 1951 when Ghana first became self-governing, a main focus of development effort has been the Volta River Project. The idea of exploiting hydroelectric power to produce aluminium from Ghana's abundant bauxite was first suggested in 1915 and received intermittent attention until 1942 when bauxite mining started at Mpraeso and Awaso. During the 1950s plans for an integrated HEP scheme, resettlement programme, smelter and port were drawn up, and work on the dam at Akosombo, where the Volta river breaks through the Akwapim–Togo ranges, started in 1961. The dam is of the rock-fill type and uses local clay and rock for the core and armouring respectively (which reduced the need for imported cement) and is thought to provide a safer structure in an area subject to earth tremors.

The dam was completed in 1966 and by 1972 the six generators were producing 768 MW of power. Behind the dam a lake of 8500 km^2 penetrates over 400 km into the northern savanna interior (Figure 63) and necessitated the resettlement of 80,000 people. A population previously dispersed in over 700 small, isolated settlements lacking basic services and amenities was concentrated in 52 new townships, mostly more accessible and with improved water supplies, sanitation, markets, schools and in some cases industries (poultry and pig farming, textiles). Proposals for large-scale irrigation with lake water have yet to be implemented, but fishing developed rapidly and lake transport services were initiated – including roll-on/roll-off for palletized

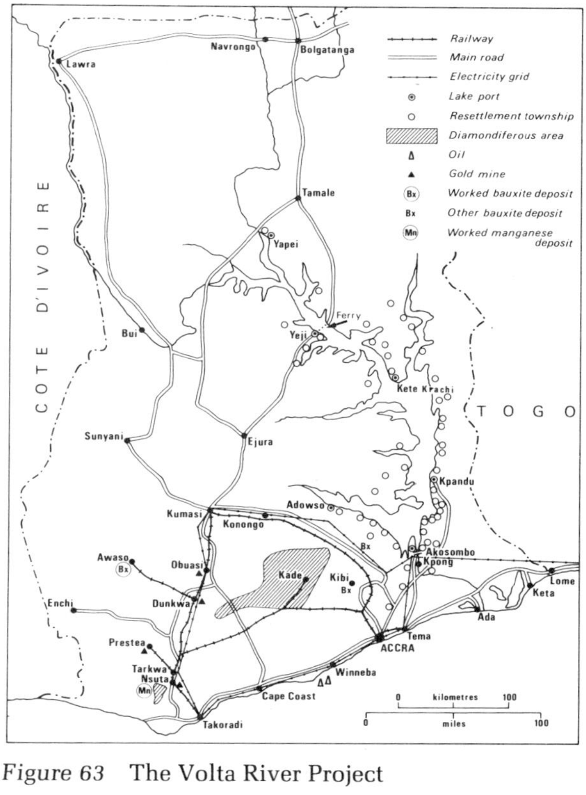

Figure 63 The Volta River Project

rice and cotton from the north.

An aluminium smelter was to be the financial lynch-pin of the scheme, and the guaranteed sale to the Volta Aluminium Company (VALCO) of two-thirds of the electricity produced provided the debt-servicing revenue. The 1962 master agreement wth VALCO can be severely criticized, particularly as it did not result in the use of Ghana's bauxite. Kaiser Aluminium, 90 per cent shareholders in VALCO, and connected with Kaiser Engineers who had acted as consultants to the dam project, wished to use alumina from their American plant. There is now the almost ludicrous situation in which Ghana exports its raw bauxite through Takoradi only to import alumina produced from Jamaican bauxite through Tema. It can also be argued that VALCO obtained its electricity far too cheaply and, despite several upward revisions, still pays less than most smelter companies. They were given a 10-year tax holiday and not required to pay tax in years when they made a loss; it was not until 1979 that they paid their first government taxes. It is, in effect, a good example of an 'island' economy with too few linkages and the multinational company seemingly the main beneficiary.

Yet on the credit side the dam is self-financing and the aluminium output, which expanded to a peak of 200,000 tonnes a year, has diversified the export base and brings in valuable foreign exchange. The 800 km grid has taken electricity to most of the larger mining and industrial centres of the south, and but for this HEP the 1970s escalation of oil prices would have been catastrophic for the economy. Ghana also exports electricity to Togo and Benin, but this also explains why Ghana has had to develop a smaller HEP plant on the Volta at Kpong and make plans for a larger dam at Bui on the Black Volta.

It is also reasonable to consider the port and new town of Tema as an integral part of the

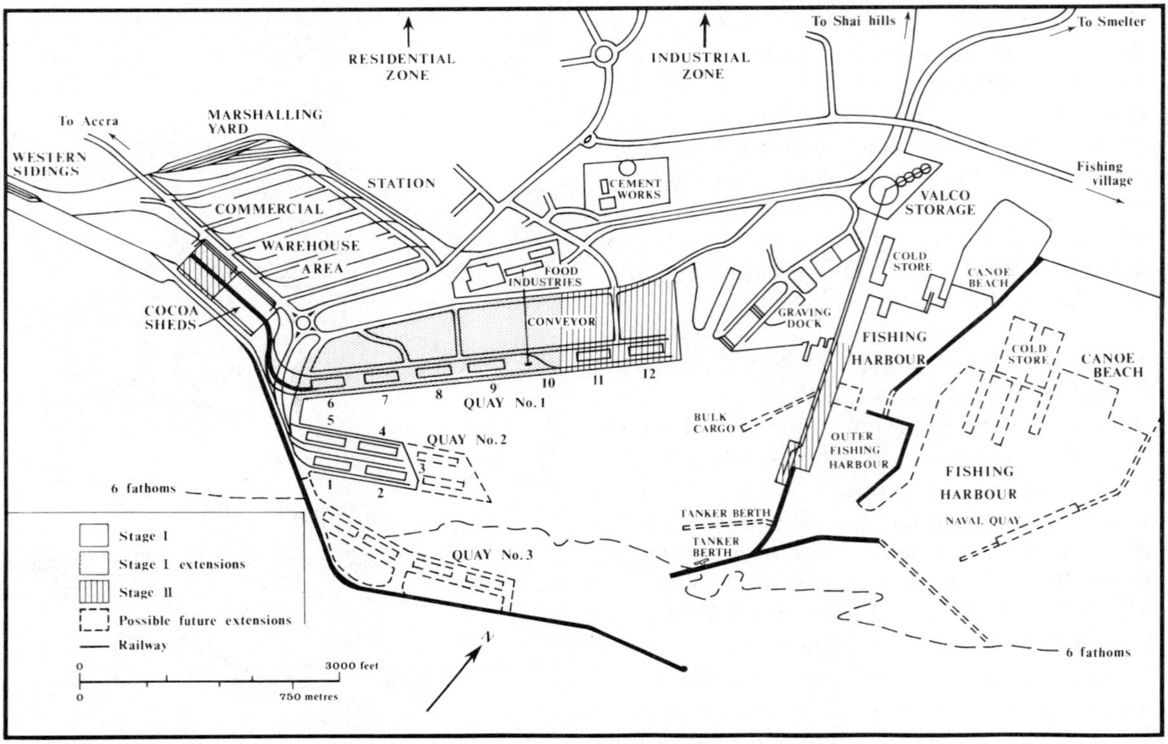

Figure 64 The port of Tema

VRP. Although Ghana needed the second deep-water port to serve Accra and the south-east, and had decided ahead of the VRP to start on construction, the port was necessary to handle all the construction material and equipment for the project. The decision to locate the smelter at the port rather than near the power plant links port and VRP even more closely, and VALCO has a private road link to its own berth at the port (Figure 64). Tema has an oil refinery based on imported crude oil but with hopes that an oilfield off Saltpond will supply increasing quantities of crude. Tema's 30,000 tonnes a year steel furnace, textile industry, cement works, ship-repair facility, vehicle assembly plant, flour mills, cocoa and chocolate processing, fish processing, cigarettes, plastics and foam rubber, electrical components and pharmaceuticals derive benefit from the new town's infrastructure. There is also an aluminium products industry, but it is only very recently that a rolling mill has been built so that local rather than imported aluminium can be used.

The Accra–Tema conurbation has been a powerful magnet, has grown to over one million inhabitants and is by far the largest concentration of industry in the country. That many of the industries have been less than successful may owe more to poor management than to the basic concept. Ghana has good natural and human resources, and with greater emphasis on agriculture, a stable investment climate and greater attention to sectoral linkages, economic growth and real development is still possible. It will, however, be necessary to redress the regional inequalities that derive from the distribution of resources and which have been exaggerated by the Volta River Project.

24
Togo and Benin

Togo, with an area of 56,000 km^2, is one of West Africa's smaller countries and Benin is just twice as large (113,000 km^2). Togo had its origins as a German colony. The agreed boundary with the British Gold Coast to the west was fixed in 1904 and cut through the tribal territories of four large groups – the Dagomba, Mamprusi, Gonja and Ewe. In 1919, parts of northern Togo reverted to the Gold Coast and the rest was given Trustee status, the southern part under Britain and a larger area in the north under France. In 1957 the British Trusteeship area was incorporated in the newly independent Ghana, and in 1960 the French-administered area became the independent republic of Togo. France consolidated its colonial control over Dahomey between 1851 and 1898 and the territory became independent in 1960 and assumed the name Benin in 1975.

From the point of view of their physical geography the two states may conveniently be considered together. The coastline from the Volta mouth in Ghana to Nigeria is smooth and lacks indentations, has heavy surf and is backed by a sand bar and lagoons. In places where they represent former river estuaries these lagoons broaden out into sizeable lakes (e.g. Lake Togo, Lake Nakoue). Inland from the lagoons (Figure 65) is a belt of Post-Eocene rocks, mainly sandstones, which give undulating country with elevations of 50–90 m and produce loamy clays of reasonable fertility. This zone is usually known as the **Terre de Barre**. There are several phosphate deposits and there is phosphate mining at Hahotoe, north of Lake Togo. There is limestone quarrying at Tokpli near the Benin Border, for cement production.

In Benin the Terre de Barre is bounded to the north by the lower-lying, seasonally flooded and marshy Lama depression, underlain by Eocene marine sedimentaries, and in the Abomey region is a higher, fragmented **plateau** area similar to the Terre de Barre. This in turn gives way to an extensive area of **plains** underlain by Pre-Cambrian crystalline rocks, with little relief except for occasional inselbergs with lateritic surfaces and an area of more mountainous relief, the Kabrai massif, north of Sokodé on the margins of the Togo–Atacora mountains. The soils of the plains are generally poor.

From just north of Accra in Ghana there is a narrow arc of mountainous terrain extending north-eastwards across Togo. This comprises much faulted Pre-Cambrian rocks, rising in places to over 800 m, sharply defined at its edges with deeply incised valleys and a discontinuous but pronounced longitudinal central depression. A depression in the Sokodé region separates these **Togo ranges** to the south from the Atacora mountains to the north. Soils tend to be thinner and poorer northwards, but everywhere there is the danger of soil erosion after removal of plant cover. Extending north-eastwards from Ghana's Volta basin is an arc of Palaeozoic sandstones, and these provide fairly level surfaces, thin soils, limited surface water and poorer natural vegetation cover in northern Togo and along Benin's north-western border. In the extreme north-west of Togo these sandstones are separated by a pronounced scarp from an area of granitic rocks; and towards the border with Niger these are overlain by more recent sandstones and there is extensive laterization.

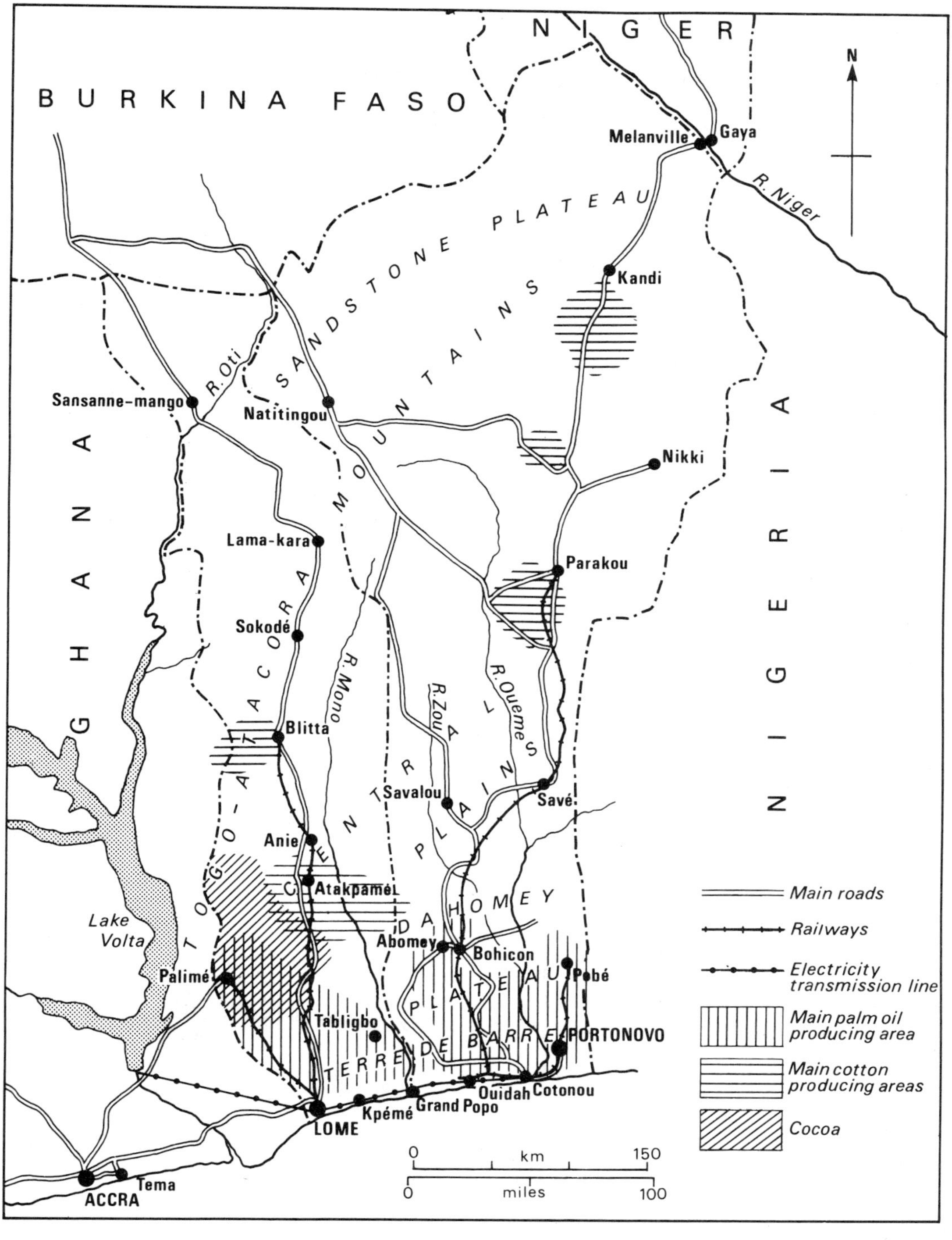

Figure 65 Togo and Benin

The anomalous low rainfall of the Togo–Benin coastal belt has already been remarked upon (Chapter 20). Lomé has an average 890 mm, but there is an increase along the coast to 1265 mm at Cotonou and also inland (Palimé has 1500 mm, the Atacora mountains 1400 mm). North of the Atacora the rainfall drops below 1000 mm. Thus, except in the limited mountain area, Togo and Benin are characterized by generally low rainfall and an overall moisture deficiency which will be reflected in agricultural potential.

TOGO

Based on a figure of 1.95 million in the 1970 census, Togo now has an estimated 2.85 million population and an average density of 50.1 people per km^2. Large parts of the drier central plains and sandstone plateau are relatively sparsely populated, and the highest concentrations are along the coast and in the valleys of the better-watered, areas such as the Kabrai massif.

In the southern part of the country cassava, maize and oil-palm are the main crops; northwards yams increase in importance. Guinea corn and millet predominate in the north, with some yams, groundnuts and rice of the dry upland variety except in a few valleys with more water. On the flanks of the Togo–Atacora range, cocoa and coffee are important cash crops, and cotton is grown in the region south of Atakpame. On the coast, sea and lagoon fishing are both important, but only at Lomé does the deep-water port provide facilities for larger, modern fishing vessels.

Table 22 *Togo: principal exports (percentage of total value)*

	1960	*1969*	*1978*	*1982*
Cocoa	38.5	35.5	29.3	9.6
Coffee	17.7	15.7	9.2	10.6
Palm produce	14.4	4.2	—	—
Cotton	11.4	1.3	—	8.6
Phosphate	—	29.3	39.2	44.0

Eighty per cent of Togo's population live off the land. Many are at or near subsistence level, with only small quantities of produce entering trade locally. In better-favoured areas there is a more substantial peasant production of cash crops such as cocoa, coffee, palm produce and cotton, and there are some foreign-owned plantations, in cases dating back to the period of German occupation. At the time of independence in 1960 agriculture provided the bulk of the exports (Table 22) and development planning concentrated on these. For example, under the Third National Plan (1975–80) an extensive replanting programme was initiated for cocoa and coffee as a result of which production increased, unfortunately at a time when world prices were low. The government has assisted in the provision of fertilizer, pesticides, and the introduction of animals for ploughing. A semi-state enterprise, Togo-Fruit, has planted citrus, mangos, avocados, bananas, pineapples and cashews. Sugar cultivation is being expanded at Anie and along the Mano river to supply a refinery at Anie, and a cotton ginnery and weaving factory have been established at Lama–Kara. Arguably, there has been too much emphasis on the cash-crop sector, although in Togo the food crop production has

Plate 31 Seasonal road flooding, southern Benin

kept in pace with population growth rather better than in neighbouring countries. Togo is virtually self-sufficient in millet and sorghum but has to import some other grains. The year 1975 was declared 'The Year of the Peasant' and in 1977 a Green Revolution was initiated. The Fourth Plan (1981–5) hoped to achieve food self-sufficiency, but the total rural investment programme is still small compared with that for industry. However, the plan does have a logical emphasis on small irrigation projects and water storage schemes, but also includes a major land-reclamation project at Mango and special attention to the National Ranch at Adele which it is hoped will provide all the country's beef needs.

Apart from the processing of agricultural products the industrial sector is not well developed. A one-million tonnes a year oil refinery using imported Nigerian crude operates well below capacity, and a joint Togo–Ghana–Côte d'Ivoire cement project at Tabligbo based on limestone from Takpli has been a financial failure. Togo has introduced an investment code which is attractive to foreign investors, but the local market is very small.

Open-cast mining of phosphates started at Hahotoe in 1960, the almost horizontal deposit being recovered after the removal of 7–30 m of over-burden. Compagnie Togolaise des Mines du Benin (CTMB) is now the country's largest employer (2500). Since the mid-1960s phosphates have in most years been the leading export (Table 22). The mine is about 50 km inland and is linked by rail to the enrichment plant and ship-loading terminal at Kpémé. Some of Togo's economic problems date back to a phosphates 'boom' of 1974–5 when revenue doubled and the over-ambitious Third Plan was initiated. Since that time the market has been depressed and revenue much reduced and production is well below the rated capacity of 3.5 million tonnes a year. However, there are still vast deposits to be worked and Togo is hoping to establish a fertilizer and phosphoric acid plant.

With 1400 km of the 2400 km of main road surfaced and a 500 km rail system, the internal transport is adequate in the southern part of the country. Until 1968, Togo's only general cargo port, at Lomé, the capital, consisted of a lighterage pier of very low capacity; but Lomé has now been provided with an artificial harbour where two finger quays provide a cargo-handling capacity of about 1 million tonnes a year. Attempts are being made to develop a 'free' industrial zone, and Lomé is trying to increase the transit traffic for Burkina Faso and Niger, small quantities of which it already handles by way of road links that have recently been up-graded.

Togo's balance of payments is adversely affected by the need to import crude oil and some electricity from Ghana's Akosombo hydroelectric power scheme. There is some export of refined petroleum products and a joint Togo–Benin HEP project is under construction on the Mano river. Large deposits of iron-ore have been discovered at Bengeli in the north and feasibility studies are being undertaken.

The relatively dry climate of the coastal zone, the scenic attraction of some of the mountain areas inland and the designation of wild-life reserves serve to encourage tourists, and there has been considerable expansion of hotel accommodation in Lomé (which has conference and convention facilities) and at small hotels, motels and holiday villages across the country. This is certainly an activity that could be expanded in the future, with the caution that this can result in considerable imported inputs and no great revenue generated locally.

Debt servicing is presenting problems, and with an average per capita GDP of $410, Togo is very much among the low income countries. Development is not helped by the small size of the domestic market, and in particular industry has been slow to expand. However, the country has a more varied resource base than some of its neighbours and the future could well depend on the extent to which this is harnessed.

BENIN

With an estimated 1982 population of 3.72 million, Benin has a much lower average population density than Togo, largely because it has a more extensive, sparsely peopled, semi-arid north. Over 70 per cent of the population is in the south. Benin's average per capita GDP ($300) is also lower than that of Togo, and the country is overwhelmingly dependent on agricultural production which accounts for 45 per cent of the GDP (in contrast with Togo's 25 per cent). In 1984, as a result of low rainfall, the government declared the whole country a 'disaster area' and had to appeal for food aid, drinking water supply units, livestock feed, livestock and electricity generators.

The subsistence agricultural base is much like that of Togo, with fairly intensive cultivation of cassava, maize, vegetables and cocoyams in the coastal zone with yams, millet, dry rice and beans more important northwards. Groundnuts are widely grown and shea nuts (crushed for their oil) are collected in the centre and north. The main export cash crops are palm produce (some from larger industrial plantations but still mainly from small-scale farmers and natural stands) from the coastal zone and from around Pobé and Abomey, cotton which is widely grown in the south and centre, groundnuts mainly from the Abomey and Natitingou areas of the centre, coffee from the south-west and cocoa from the south-east (or even possibly finding its way over the border from Nigeria). During the 1970s the production of these crops was either stagnant or declining, and exports likewise were showing no growth and therefore no capacity to support economic development (Table 23).

Table 23 *Benin: principal exports (percentage of total value)*

	1956–66	1977	1982
Palm kernel oil	37.9	23.7	30.7
Palm-oil	17.4		
Cotton	10.6	28.3	—
Groundnuts	4.4	1.0	—
Tobacco	3.9	—	—
Coffee	3.4	6.7	—
Copra	2.9	—	—
Cocoa	—	10.9	30.2

Since 1972 national planning has placed great emphasis on agriculture, and in the 1977–80 plan a 'campaign for national production' was launched. The 'socialist' approach favoured by the government has led to a network of cooperatives, collectivization and the creation of 'groupements révolutionnaires à vocation rurales' (GRVC), which it is hoped will lead to a modernization of agricultural production. The state support system for peasant cash crop production has not been very effective, and there is the suggestion of a switch from export to food crop production. Most investment has been directed towards capital-intensive developments such as the sugar project at Savé, the livestock ranch at Okpara, a cotton project in Borgou province in the north, a Niger valley rice project and oil-palm plantations (there are now over 29,000 ha of industrial plantations). It is doubtful if the bulk of the rural population, or indeed the country at large, has really benefited from these developments.

Industry is still at a rudimentary level but grew from a small base at 8 per cent of the GDP in 1960 to 12 per cent in 1979. Development has not progressed much beyond the primary processing of agricultural products. There are a number of palm-oil mills (at Porto Novo, Ouidah, Houin Agame and Bohicon), but processing capacity is three times that of output. There is a soap factory based on palm-oil and copra-oil and a number of cotton ginneries, the largest that at Parakou where there is an integrated textile mill. A wax printing works at Cotonou is largely dependent on imported raw materials. There is a groundnut-oil mill at Bohicon and a kenaf fibre mill. At Cotonou, the principal urban settlement, there are a number of import substitution industries (brewing, furniture, soft drinks, vehicle assembly). Industrialization is limited by the availability of energy, and Benin, like Togo, imports electricity from Ghana.

Mining is insignificant and is restricted to intermittent gold 'washing' near Natitingou. There has been geological evaluation of gold, chromite, phosphate, iron-ore, marble and oil deposits, but only in the case of oil has this resulted in production. A small offshore oil field (Seme) was brought on-stream in 1983, but the output is insufficient to justify the cost of local refining and the crude oil is exported. Prospecting continues in areas adjacent to Seme, and a new agreement of 1985 should see production expand to 25,000 barrels a day.

Porto Novo (with a 1984 population of 140,000) is Benin's capital, but much of the administrative, commercial and industrial activity is located at the country's only port of Cotonou. Here, the first deep-water berthage was provided in 1965, and this has since been expanded to accommodate traffic of 1–1.5 million tonnes a year. Cotonou has rail links east and west along the coast, and inland to Parakou an important railhead for transit traffic to land-locked Niger, Burkina Faso and Mali. It is this trade which Lomé has been trying to capture and it has also been reduced by the effect of the drought on agricultural production in the Sahel zone. The railway is a joint Benin–Niger enterprise, and the road from Parakou has been surfaced to Malanville where the Niger is now bridged. This route is certainly the most convenient one for the traffic of western Niger; but it is doubtful if the tonnage is sufficient to justify an extension of the railway, for which there have been plans for many years.

In general, there does not seem to be much evidence of effective, positive planning to deal with the stagnation and decline in the productive sector. A country which could be much richer than it is, even on the basis of its agricultural resources, has still shown little development progress.

25 Nigeria

The Federation of Nigeria is the largest member of the British Commonwealth in Africa and, with an area of 923,000 km^2 (almost four times as large as the United Kingdom), it is also one of the largest African countries. In common with many African countries there is uncertainty about the size of its population: census inaccuracies may have been severe and this makes any form of development planning difficult. A census of 1952/3 produced a total of 30.4 million and was thought to be an under-counting, whereas that of 1963 (55.7 million) was considered by many authorities to be inflated. The 1963 figure has continued to be the basis for planning purposes, although not officially accepted, and the 1973 total of 79.8 million has proved even less satisfactory. It has been suggested that the figures have been inflated in some areas in an attempt to gain greater political representation and larger shares of federal revenue. Calculations based on the 1963 census indicate that the population is very unevenly distributed, and three principal areas of higher population density can be identified (Table 24).

Table 24 *Nigeria: population within 1976 state boundaries*

	1952/3 (millions)	*1963* (millions)	*Population density* (per km^2)	*1973* (millions)
South	13.57	25.86		28.38
Lagos	0.50	1.44	403.6	2.47
Western	4.36	9.49	125.1	8.92
Mid-Western	1.49	2.54	65.6	3.24
Rivers	0.73	1.54	85.4	2.23
East Central	4.57	7.23	241.8	8.06
South Eastern	1.90	3.62	127.8	3.46
North	16.84	29.80		51.38
Benue/Plateau	2.30	4.01	39.8	5.17
Kwara	1.19	2.40	32.4	4.64
North Western	3.40	5.73	33.9	8.50
North Central	2.35	4.10	58.3	6.79
Kano	3.40	5.77	134.0	10.90
North Eastern	4.20	7.79	28.6	15.38
Total	30.41	55.66		79.76

In the south-west of the country is the predominantly Yoruba area centred on Ibadan, Abeokuta and Ife, where there existed a centralized political control and one of the few indigenous African cultures which could be described as urban. However, although some of the towns developed to considerable size, there was never a clear distinction in functional terms between urban and rural–agricultural.

The second region of higher population density is the east-central part of the country, the homeland of the Ibo people. They comprised a loose association of formerly nucleated villages with elements of communal cultivation, from which there has been dispersion to give a high-density rural population with intensive cultivation.

The third zone of markedly higher density, locally in excess of 400 per km^2, is centred on Kano in the savanna north of the country. This is the core area of the Hausa peoples whose culture dominates in the north-central and north-western parts of the country and finds its best expression in the 'close-settled zone' around Kano. This is unusual for a savanna area in that high rural densities, both nucleated and dispersed patterns, are sustained by perennial cultivation with little long-term fallow.

Table 24 shows that there is a middle belt, represented by Plateau, Kwara and southern parts of North Western State, with average densities as low as 30–40 per km^2. Historically, this has been a 'shatter-zone' of mainly small tribal groups, adversely affected by slave raiding from north and south, dry-season moisture deficits over porous sedimentary rocks, and a marginal location between the root-crop zone of the forest and the grain crop zone of the savanna. This more thinly populated 'middle belt' extends discontinuously across West Africa, is well marked in Ghana, and obviously has no simple explanation in either environmental or historical conditions.

THE POPULATION PROBLEM

There are three components of Nigeria's population problem: its ethno-cultural diversity, the absolute numbers and high growth rate, and rapid urbanization. Each has its influence on development in general.

The country's population includes nearly 400 ethno-linguistic groups of varying degrees of homogeneity and definition and diversity of physical type and culture. In detail the pattern is complex, arising as it does from the meeting and admixture of negroid peoples from southern Africa and Caucasoid peoples from the north, Bantu and Sudanic–Hamito–Semitic languages and Arabic–Islamic and European–Christian influences.

At independence in 1960, Nigeria became a federation of three states, Northern, Western and Eastern (Figure 66), based on the Hausa, Yoruba and Ibo homelands – these tribes respectively making up 21, 20 and 17 per cent of the total population in the 1963 census. In 1962 an additional Mid-West state was created between the Western and Eastern states, and in 1967 the country was divided into 12 states in order to protect minority interests and achieve balance. In 1976 this process was taken a stage further and 19 states emerged, even closer to the 24 provinces of the British colonial administration. The federal constitution allows for further states to be created, and in 1982 there were 50 proposals, 21 having been adopted in principle.

Each stage in this process of administrative fragmentation leads to more homogeneous ethno-linguistic political units, but it is clear that this sub-division cannot go on indefinitely. From the development viewpoint it does lead to a more even spread of modernization, each state wanting its own range of social and economic infrastructure and industrial base. However, it is costly in administrative terms and creates even more complex problems for the allocation of federal funds, a big part of which comes from oil produced in a few coastal states. Many of the new states have inadequate resource bases, and there is a continuing argument about the extent to which revenue allocations should be based on derivation (i.e. distributed according to proceeds derived from within state boundaries) or should be from a distributive pool, in which case population will be a main factor influencing state shares: hence the importance of accurate population figures and a possible reason why totals would appear to have been inflated in some regions.

The second element in the population problem is the overall size and rapid growth of the population. Whichever of the population estimates is accepted there must be concern for the size of the population in relation to resources, and any benefits from economic growth will be spread so thinly as to be virtually negligible. In a period of low economic growth it may well be that average per capita incomes will decline. If accepted, the census figures suggest a 3.6 per cent a year population growth rate from 1963 to 1973, although in the north this rises to over 7.0 per cent. A general figure of about 2.7–3.0 per cent seems more realistic; but this will give a total population

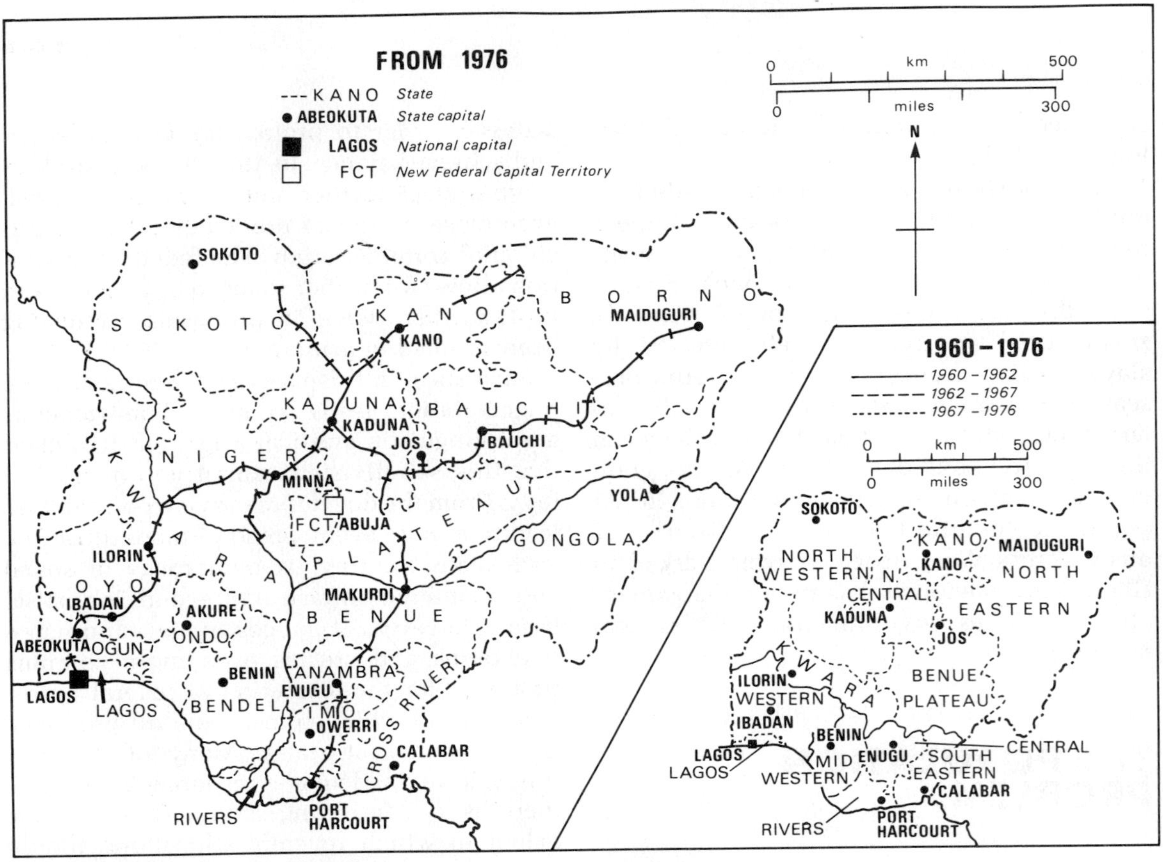

Figure 66 Nigeria: federal evolution

of over 200 million in 2010 and is certainly in excess of the growth rate in food production, with the result that food imports have been increasing and at mounting cost. In the 1970s the death rate was estimated at 22.7 per 1000 and the birth rate at 49.3 per 1000. There is therefore a youthful age structure and high dependency rate – some 45 per cent of the population is under 15 years of age. Thus, when in 1976 it was proposed to initiate universal primary education, the number of eligible children numbered 18 million and, not surprisingly, adequate physical and human resources have not been available for the full implementation of the proposals.

The increase in population also means a rapidly growing labour force with well over 30 million in the 15–55 years age range. While over 64 per cent of the gainful employment is accounted for by agriculture, this is not a sector that can absorb additional workers. Indeed, changing agricultural practices could reduce the demand for labour. If there is not to be mounting unemployment there has to be substantial growth of job opportunities in the service and industrial sectors. However, these jobs are likely to be in the urban areas and will contribute to regional disparity and rural–urban migration.

Indeed, rapid urbanization constitutes the third component of the population problem. In Nigeria 'urban' is technically defined as closely built-up, predominantly non-agricultural and with at least 20,000 population. On this basis the 1952/3 census identified 50 urban centres. In the next ten years the number increased to 66, and 36 of these experienced annual growth in excess of 6 per cent. Several towns grew at between 17 and 20 per cent a year (Ilesha, Ilorin and Ado Ekiti) and there are now 50 towns with a population over 50,000. Observation rather than census data suggests that the rate of urbanization increased during the 1970s as a result of faster migration from rural areas to towns, movement from smaller to larger towns and high levels of natural increase within towns. The creation of new states, each with its capital (e.g. Bauchi, Minna, Owerri, Yola) has meant additional urban growth points for administrative, commercial and industrial activities and associated population expansion.

It is impossible to be precise regarding the size of particular towns. However, Ibadan is thought to have a population well in excess of 1 million and estimates for the Lagos metropolitan area vary from 1.7 to 5.5 million. The larger Lagos State in 1983 registered 2.23 million voters, which suggests an overall population of around 5 million. A reasonable estimate for Lagos itself would be about 4 million. The result of this rapid, uncontrolled urban growth has meant unplanned urban sprawl, severe residential overcrowding and general urban congestion. Over 500,000 people have no regular habitation, the town has no central sewage system, and demand for water is already far in excess of that projected for the year 2000. The transport system is grossly inadequate and the traffic congestion severe – there was even an attempt to restrict cars by allowing access for vehicles with even and odd number plates on alternate days! The problems are compounded by the lagoon system which separates different parts of the urban area.

Both because of the problems of Lagos and the desire to have a more centrally located capital city, a decision was made in 1976 to create a new capital at Abuja in a sparsely populated area north of the Niger River. An 8000 km^2 Federal Capital Territory has been designated, a master plan for a city of 1.6 million inhabitants was approved in 1978, and work on the first phase developments has been progressing, albeit at a slower pace since 1983 with general economic depression and increased national indebtedness. The final move of capital functions from Lagos is scheduled, unrealistically, for 1991.

Some of the federal administrative functions have already been relocated at Abuja, but as the country's main entry point by sea and air Lagos seems likely to retain its advantages as a centre of commerce, distribution and industry. The cost of rehabilitating the urban fabric of Lagos would doubtless be vast, but much work will have to be undertaken anyway and the cost of this must be added to the estimated 9.7 billion Naira (£6.6 billion) for Abuja – all of which money could well have been spent on directly productive activities which might have been of more obvious benefit to the development of the country.

It is clear that with such a large population, policies are urgently needed to stem the flow of people to the towns and greater emphasis needs to be put on rural development and the creation of employment opportunities. The resource base for such development will now be considered.

THE RESOURCE BASE

The Niger–Benue trough and delta divides the country into the plateaux and high plains of the north, the south-western low plateaux and coastal zone, and the hill country of the east (Figure 67).

The northern high plains average over 600 m in altitude, and comprise crystalline basement schists, quartzites and granites in the central part, but towards the north-west and north-east in the Chad basin these are overlain by tertiary sedimentaries – clays and sandstones. Rising above the plains to over 1500 m is the Jos Plateau, an area of acid igneous and metamorphic rocks with important cassiterite deposits. Over large areas ferruginous tropical soils are found, but northwards lighter soils of former dunes predominate and provide ideal conditions for groundnut cultivation. The plains have numerous broad, shallow depressions, and these seasonally flooded 'fadama' lands with higher water tables are used for vegetables, sugar and other crops with small-scale, usually simple irrigation. More widely, quick-ripening millet is often followed by

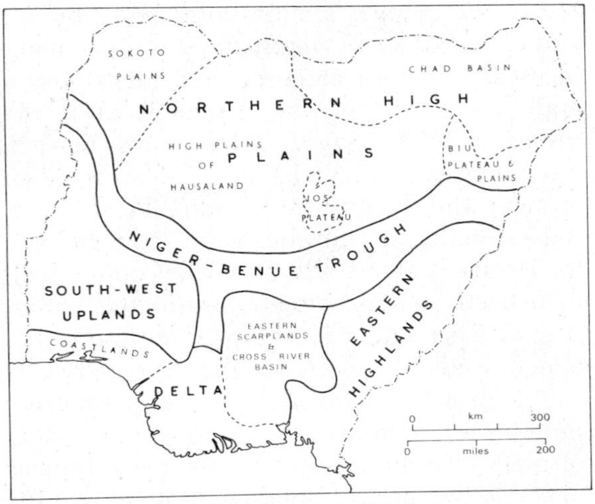

Figure 67 Nigeria: regional divisions

sorghum and long-season millet and multiple-cropping of groundnuts, cow peas and vegetables. This intensive cultivation supports the high population densities of the Kano 'close-settled zone', but there are large areas of low population density.

Further south the soils tend to be heavier and cotton more important than groundnuts. Useful trees such as shea nut, silk cotton, mango and neem are retained, even cultivated, in what has been described as a 'farmed parkland landscape'. Only a narrow zone in the north of the country is free from tsetse fly, and over much of the northern plains there is endemic animal sleeping sickness. Over 90 per cent of the cattle are found in the northern half of the country and their importance declines southwards. Cattle are mainly herded by Fulani people in places with arrangements whereby the manure is used on Hausa cultivated land, but nowhere is there a true mixed-farming system. In the Jos Plateau and Adamawa uplands there is limited dairying, but most of the cattle are traded as meat with the south – formerly 'on-the-hoof' but now increasingly by lorry.

Gold in small quantities is widely distributed in alluvial deposits deriving from the Pre-Cambrian rocks, and there is some mining in the Kano and Sokoto regions. More importantly, the volcanic rocks of the north, but particularly in the Jos Plateau, are a source of cassiterite, tin-ore, and associated by-product minerals such as columbite, tantalite and wolframite. Tin mining started on the Jos Plateau in 1906, was stimulated by the arrival of the railway in 1911, and production peaked at 14,000 tonnes in 1968, since when output has declined.

The Niger–Benue trough is mainly floored by Cretaceous sedimentaries. The Benue is very broad and level with the river often braided, but the Niger has some Pre-Cambrian rocks crossing the trough north of Jebba: these produced the Busa rapids, now submerged under Lake Kainji. Except near river crossing points the population densities tend to be low and typical of the Middle Belt.

The zone of alluvial soils is rather narrow. However, the ferralitic soils which characterize much of the area are not so deeply leached as in higher-rainfall areas to the south, and they are locally well-cultivated, notably in the Nupe area around Bida where sorghum, yams, millet and cotton are important and the Tiv area around Makurdi where yams, cassava, sorghum and beniseed are the main crops. The Nupe area is less densely populated than Tiv and is considered as a possible area for colonization – a settlement scheme at Mokwa in the early 1950s never realized its full potential, but the Shendam scheme in the Benue valley has been more successful.

Nigeria's first major hydroelectric power scheme was completed at Kainji in 1968, and 117 villages and two new towns were created to house the 40,000 people displaced by the lake. The dam has been provided with navigation locks, and the higher water levels above the dam improve navigation towards the border with Niger. Below the dam the regulated water flow has reduced seasonal flood cultivation but has increased the potential for systematic irrigation. The Niger–Benue and tributaries provide great scope for the extension of large-scale irrigation, especially for multiple cropping on long-growing crops such as sugar. There are important sugar schemes at Bacita, near Jebba, and at the confluence of the Gongola and Benue rivers. There are longer-term proposals for very large dams and storage reservoirs embracing the area of the Niger–Benue confluence and on the middle Benue.

In the regions of Yola and Makurdi there are extensive limestone deposits, and at Agbaga, Itakpe, Itobe and Shintake, just south of the Niger–Benue confluence, there are deposits of sedimentary iron-ore of relatively low grade (29–50 per cent Fe) and some poor coal. Nigeria's first integrated iron and steel industry is under construction at Ajaokuta on the Niger river, but initially it seems likely that higher-grade imported iron-ore and coal will be used, either entirely or for blending with that produced locally. An associated port is being built on the Niger, and the navigability of the lower Niger should reduce the transport problems of the new complex.

The south-western uplands. Exposed crystalline basement rocks give average altitudes of 300–600 m, undulating plains, and locally – where granites and quartzites outcrop – hill areas rising to 1000 m in the Niger watershed region. The northern parts are mainly grassland and savanna woodland, while to the south there is much modified forest vegetation.

This is essentially the Yoruba country, and the southern forested areas became important for cocoa and kola cultivation. Relative proximity to the coast, Lagos port and the early railway penetration line encouraged commercial activity. In the savanna northern part of the region cotton is important and formed the basis of a thriving traditional textile industry at places such as Akwete and Iseyin.

Eastern scarplands and Cross river basin. East of the lower Niger is an area of mainly Cretaceous sedimentaries with some well-developed scarp features alternating with broader plateaux surfaces. Eastwards, in the Cross river basin, average heights are lower and large areas subject to seasonal flooding. This is the core area of the east–west belt in which the oil-palm is the main tree crop, and

Plate 32 Oil work-over hoist, Niger delta

the area includes the high population dens of the Ibo lands and lower-density popula eastwards in the Cross river basin. In th areas, over-cultivation has led – espec areas of more marked relief – to ser erosion and considerable gullying slopes (e.g. the Awka Scarp).

Since independence, the low density of the Cross river has development of plantation c palm, rubber and cocoa. S tations are privately ow initiatives have been by

Approximating wit scarplands and del wards across the N

discontinuous belt of lignite which could be the basis for wax, resin and chemical production. More important at present are the subbituminous coalfields of the upper Cretaceous sedimentaries near Enugu. Mining started in the Udi Hills in 1915 when the area was connected by rail to the then new port at Port Harcourt. Unless blended, this coal is not suitable for coking, and its high sulphur content is a disadvantage in metallurgical processing. The main use is therefore for steam-raising, and in the cement industry (as at Nkalagu). Peak output of nearly 700,000 tonnes was achieved in 1960, production stopped during the civil war of 1967–9, and since that time production has been around 300,000 tonnes a year – but with hopes in 1986 that coal exports would resume.

Eastern Highlands. Forming the border with Cameroon, these crystalline highlands have widespread, almost horizontal, basaltic flows which give plateau surfaces at 1000 – 1500 m, the most extensive of which is the Mambilla Plateau. Elsewhere, greater dissection produces a more truly mountainous landscape rising in places to over 2000 m. Relatively isolated, the region supports some cultivation, especially in valleys; but more significantly the grasslands of the plateau provide the basis for considerable pastoral activity, mainly by Fulani peoples. There are areas of mountain and valley forest, and in the higher-rainfall southern part of the highlands forest reserves have been designated. There have been attempts to establish small-scale plantations of eucalyptus, coffee and tea.

Coastlands and delta. Nigeria's coastline is remarkably smooth, and in the west and east the low-lying coastal zone consists of sand dunes backed by lagoons. Lagoon outlets to he sea are often blocked by sand bars. At agos, the main port, access has been secured ith the construction of moles to direct scour d is maintained by considerable dredging. hese coastal zones the population density latively high.

e central coastal zone comprises the delta of the Niger, mud rather than sand predominates, and there are large negative areas of mangrove and low population density. Inland the mangrove is replaced by freshwater swamp and rain forest, and this has for long been the main source of export timber and a basis for local saw-milling and timber processing industries. Sapele has given its name to one well-known timber, is the location of a large plywood and veneer mill, and is an important timber exporting port that has recently been provided with additional deep-water berthage. Rubber is also an important crop and oil-palm cultivation is extensive.

In recent years the delta and adjacent offshore zone have been the scene of intensive oil exploration and have become the source of Nigeria's oil wealth. In the deltaic environment oil exploration and production is not easy, so that Nigeria's oil is expensive. Port Harcourt (originally a coal-exporting port) and Warri have become the main centres and service ports for the oil industry and the locations of two of Nigeria's oil refineries, but much of the crude oil is exported from offshore terminals linked by pipelines to the producing fields (Figure 68).

THE ECONOMY

Prior to 1860 Nigeria exported little apart from slaves, but during the mid-nineteenth century the palm-oil trade developed rapidly. Initially there was little systematic cultivation, the palm nuts were gathered from wild trees, and the waterways of the delta and eastern rivers provided easy access to the ports – indeed, this east-central area became known as the 'oil rivers'.

After the 1880s cocoa cultivation spread rapidly on the heavier, clay soils of the drier forest in the south-west, and on lighter soils the kola nut, a valued stimulant for West Africans, became important. Cultivation of these tree crops was encouraged by the gradual extension of the railway inland from Lagos after 1898, and Lagos developed as the primary port, city and economic centre – roles it

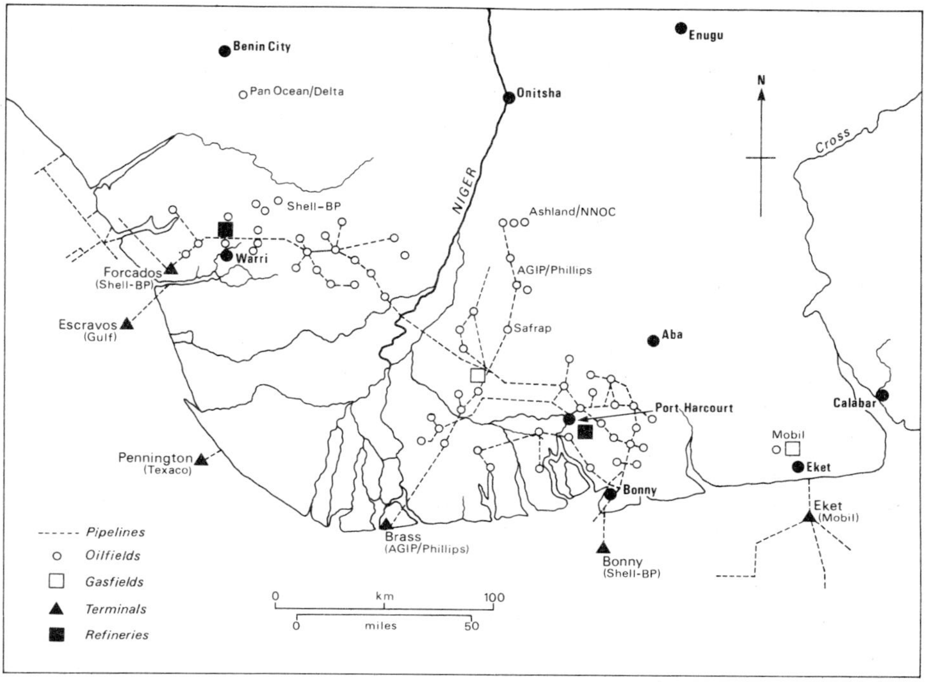

Figure 68 The Nigerian oil industry

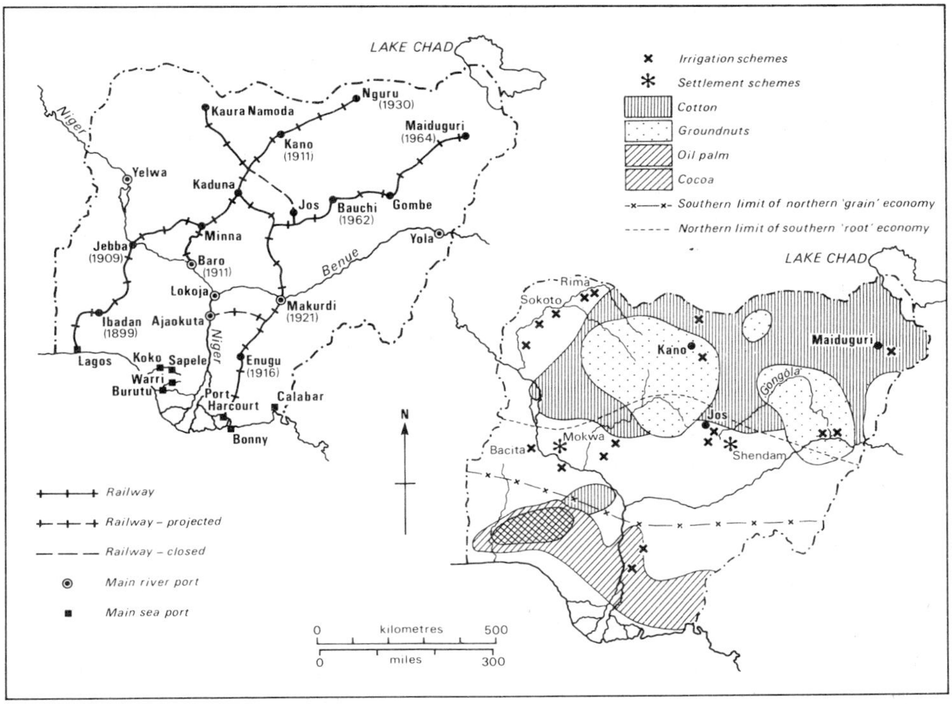

Figure 69 Nigeria: railways and agricultural development

still maintains. The railway reached Kano in the north in 1912, and the export of groundnuts, long grown for local use, increased from an average 450–500 tonnes a year to over 40,000 tonnes in ten years, and by 1960 reached over 500,000 tonnes. Cultivation has since been adversely affected by drought and by virus infection, and exports have virtually ceased.

There emerged distinct export regions – the palm-oil from the south-east, rubber and timber from the central-southern area, cocoa from the south-west and groundnuts from the north. These regions were closely related to the main areas of higher population density and the three dominant tribal groups. At independence in 1960, the economy was overwhelmingly dependent on these agricultural commodities (Table 25).

In 1960 industry accounted for only 5 per cent of the GDP and consisted mainly of small-scale traditional crafts (wood, textiles, leather, metal), food processing, first-phase processing of exports (vegetable oils, timber) and a limited import-substitution modern sector (tobacco, textiles, drinks). Clearly the economy has undergone considerable change since 1960, with agriculture declining absolutely and relatively and oil now overwhelmingly dominant.

Oil exploration first started in 1927, but the first significant finds were at Oloibiri near Port Harcourt in 1956. Onshore wells now account for 73 per cent of the total and offshore wells for 27 per cent. Proven reserves amount to 7 billion tonnes, but with large parts of the sedimentary basin still unexplored the total must be much higher. The oil is of high quality – a light crude with no sulphur – and has the advantage that it is near to the coast for export. Production increased from 275,000 tonnes in 1958 to 21 million in 1966, peaked at around 110 million tonnes in 1979, and dropped to 72 in 1985.

The oil industry has only a limited impact on employment and many key workers have to be imported. Nevertheless, oil has provided a vast increase in government revenue and an injection of purchasing power, official and private. Initially, it gave the economy a favourable balance of payments and opportunities for planned economic development with an assured income. The progress of planning can now be considered in more detail.

Table 25 *Nigeria: export trade*

	1959 (%)	*1969 (%)*	*1978 (%)*	*1982 (%)*
Cocoa	23	21	6	
Groundnuts	19	18		
Palm produce	24	5	0.3	
Rubber	7	3		
Cotton		1		
Timber		2		
Tin		5	0.2	
Petroleum		46	90.2	97.7
Total value (million Naira)	330	636	6063	

NIGERIAN DEVELOPMENT PLANNING

Development planning in Nigeria started in 1946 during the colonial period. The emphasis was very much on the provision of social infrastructure and funding derived from grants from the United Kingdom and, after the mid-1950s, from reserves accumulated as a result of high prices for agricultural exports. A new constitution of 1951 started the transfer of power from colonial to Nigerian hands and a new dynamism stimulated development strategies. There was a big increase in government spending, a greater emphasis on industrialization, and a transfer of responsibility for plan formulation and implementation for agriculture, industry, regional roads and education from the central to the regional administrations.

Between 1951 and 1964, manufacturing and public utilities grew from a low base at an average 30 per cent a year. There were tax-free

Plate 33 Improved infrastructure – the new Jebba road bridges, Nigeria

'holidays' for pioneer industries, relief from import duties, tariff protection and the creation of industrial estates at the main urban centres. Between 1951 and 1962 the road network was enlarged from 44,300 to 72,000 km and surfaced roads increased from 1000 to 12,800 km. The number of children in education at all levels increased threefold and the number of telephones fivefold.

Nigeria became fully independent in 1960 and launched the first of its comprehensive development plans in 1962. The principal objectives of the plans have been the modernization and diversification of the economy and a more equitable regional distribution of benefits. During the 1960s the money available for development funding was limited and there was an emphasis on directly productive activities rather than social provision. Despite setbacks resulting from the 1967–70 civil war, mining and manufacturing expanded rapidly between 1960 and 1972.

The second plan increased planned investment and placed rather greater emphasis on social and regional development. In any planning there is often a discrepancy between the planned targets and what is actually achieved – in many African countries the gap is so great as to make a mockery of the process of planning. In Nigeria's case the overall achievement has been about 70 per cent, but this has varied from only 42 per cent in the case of communications to 124 per cent in commerce and finance. The second plan put little emphasis on job creation in rural areas, and it did nothing to check the large-scale rural–urban migration – although an overall growth rate of 8.2 per cent a year was achieved.

The sudden oil price increases of 1973/4 gave Nigeria a massive injection of revenue, and the government and more fortunate individuals went on a spending spree. The immediate effect of this was a huge increase in imports of capital and consumer goods; and the transport system – the ports in particular – became heavily congested. At the port of Lagos a stage was reached in 1975 when over 400 ships were at anchor waiting to berth, over 250 of these with cement for construction projects. In 1974 manufacturing production rose by 22.5 per cent and turnover by 35.5 per cent, and in 1975 there were further increases of 34.0 and 52.6 per cent respectively. Investment expenditure increased by 10 and 39 per cent in 1974 and 1975, and in the same years construction companies experienced 22 and 73 per cent increases in their work. However, the big increase in money supply brought inflation of 25–30 per cent.

The increased revenue also allowed Nigeria to initiate a far more ambitious third plan, with investment up nearly tenfold. The aim of the third plan was to use the oil revenue to create infrastructure that would support self-sustaining growth – the proposed distribution of investment (Table 26) indicates the perceived priorities of the government.

The heavy emphasis on transport reflected the demonstrated inadequacy of the transport system to sustain high levels of economic growth. New projects included a 10-berth port complex at Tin Can Island, Lagos, additional port facilities at Warri, Sapele and Calabar, start on a new port at Onne near Port Harcourt, large-scale airport improvements (especially at Lagos), and a massive road-building programme.

Table 26 *Nigeria: third plan (1975/6–1980/1) proposed investments*

	Million Naira	*Percentage*
Economic	26,652	61.53
Transport	9,678	22.34
Manufacturing	5,486	12.66
Communications	3,529	8.14
Mining	2,646	6.1
Agriculture	1,681	3.9
Social	5,012	11.57
Education	3,222	7.43
Health	1,173	2.7
Regional	6,034	13.93
Housing	2,257	5.2
Town and country planning	1,589	3.7
Water	1,549	3.6
Administration	4,450	10.27

Source: Third Plan.

The second most important sector for investment was industry, with the object of making Nigeria self-sufficient in petroleum products (two new refineries at Warri and Kaduna), petrochemicals, paper and pulp, sugar and cement (three additional factories at Ashaka, Yandev and Shagamu).

There has been only slow progress on the country's first integrated iron and steel plant being built with Soviet assistance at Ajaokuta, but a direct-reduction steel mill at Warri now supplies rolling mills at Katsina, Oshogbo and Jos. There were plans for additional car assembly lines, a fertilizer plant, a liquefied petroleum gas plant (to use gas now flared off and wasted) and salt refining. The government encouraged foreign participation in industrial development: most of the consumer-goods industries are privately owned, with varying degrees of Nigerian involvement as decreed by government for different types of enterprise. The overall plan was for industry to grow at an average 10.3 per cent a year. In fact, recession was soon to restrict growth.

While the investment in agriculture increased greatly in absolute terms it still represented a minute proportion of investment, bearing in mind it provided the livelihood for the bulk of the population. The object was to counter the relative decline in agriculture's contribution to the GDP (70 per cent in 1960, 55 per cent in 1966 and 23 per cent in 1980), reduce the flow of people to the towns, provide more raw material for industry and, most importantly, reduce the growing burden of food imports (24 million Naira in 1960 and 354 million Naira in 1976). A 'Feed the Nation' programme was launched with an input package approach in which farmers could obtain credit, advice, equipment, machinery, fertilizers, pesticides, improved water supplies and better transport. There is no reason to think that all this was other than too little and too late. Like too many African governments, that of Nigeria placed far too little emphasis on the critical agricultural sector even when it had the money available.

The third plan also put renewed emphasis on social provision. A programme of free, universal primary education was initiated, with enrolment to rise from 5 to 11 million, secondary enrolments to be tripled to 1.5 million, and four additional universities to be funded. Malaria eradication was to be pressed forward, hospital bed numbers doubled to 93,000, and 122 new hospitals and 1400 health centres built.

Overall, about two-thirds of the planned investments were finalized; but at the end of the plan period industry still accounted for only 10 per cent of the GDP, many industries were still dependent on imported raw materials, and production was hindered by erratic electricity supplies. The education and health objectives were not fully implemented, and there was little evidence of improvement in agriculture. The greater success was in the provision of new port facilities and improving the road system. However, the cost of creating seven new state administrations and initial work on the new capital at Abuja greatly increased the administrative budget, at the expense of directly productive activities. The expected revenue from oil was not maintained as the demand for, and price of, oil fell on world markets.

It was to remedy some of the foregoing deficiencies that a fourth plan was initiated in 1981, with another big increase in the planned expenditure: this was certainly optimistic in view of the oil situation. The new plan claimed to give highest priority (13 per cent of the investment) to agricultural production and processing, with a 4 per cent growth target to reduce shortages of food and industrial raw materials. This was to be achieved by direct assistance to small farmers by way of the same input packages proposed in the third plan, and by large-scale agri-businesses.

In industry the idea was to move away from import substitution and place greater emphasis on the processing of local raw materials. In theory this has the advantage of decentralizing industry by placing it in the agricultural and mineral producing areas. However, there is already evidence of over-capacity in relation to raw material supplies in textiles, vegetable oil crushing and confectionery, but shortages in relation to demand for shoes, clothing (imports now banned), beer, soft drinks, ceramics, table ware and metal ware (domestic and industrial).

Industrialization has been the main theme of all the planning and there has undoubtedly been a great increase in the number of industrial enterprises. In absolute terms, Nigeria has a far better developed industrial sector than any of its West African neighbours, yet the overall range of industries is still small and the policy of concentrating on lighter industries with a significant proportion of imported inputs (raw materials, equipment, expertise) has led to an ever-increasing foreign exchange bill. In the 1980s, with declining oil revenue, imports have been cut and existing industry has suffered shortages of essential inputs. Clearly, to be effective the import-substitution industries have to move rapidly towards local supplies. The Ajaokuta iron and steel complex has been delayed and costs have escalated; and steel produced at the Aladja direct-reduction plant, using imported raw materials, is said to cost up to three times as much as imported steel.

The health of the economy now depends almost entirely on the demand for oil. After a peak export of about 110 million tonnes in 1979, Nigeria had to reduce production to satisfy quotas imposed by OPEC. Government revenue dropped sharply from $23,405 million in 1980 to $13,088 in 1982, and external debts, determined by high levels of borrowing on the strength of former oil revenue, rose from $1338 million in 1977 to $23,300 million in 1983. Such debts became increasingly difficult to service and had to be re-scheduled in 1985/6. General mismanagement of the economy and resource allocation was undoubtedly a contributory factor in the 1983 *coup* which led to a change of military government. After 1983 expenditure was cut, imports reduced and Nigeria became involved in counter-trade or barter, in which goods and services were paid for directly by oil. There is to be a resuscitation and streamlining of industries and the new capital city programme has been rescheduled over a longer time scale.

Despite all the planning and the oil revenue, development has been markedly concentrated in a few locations and the benefits in few hands, and there has been little 'trickle-down' effect. The lot of the average Nigerian has changed little, and with a per capita income of $160 in 1984 (to be treated cautiously in view of the inaccuracy of the population statistics) the world's seventh largest oil producer is far from being a rich country in any real sense of the term.

Very careful planning and management will be needed if the country's considerable resources are to be developed to satisfy the needs – let alone the aspirations – of the rapidly growing population. Political and social stability, lacking hitherto and very difficult to achieve in a country of such diversity, will be critical if 'the giant with a strained muscle' (a journalistic but still appropriate description) is to realize its considerable potential.

PART SIX: EQUATORIAL AFRICA

26
Cameroon, Equatorial Guinea and Gabon

Equatorial Africa includes the countries that comprise the Zaire basin – Zaire, Congo and the Central African Republic – together with their coastal neighbours – Cameroon, Equatorial Guinea and Gabon.

The Zaire basin is one of the most clearly defined drainage units in Africa. Although it is not the continent's longest river, the Zaire drains an area over most of which the rainfall is in excess of 1250 mm, and on reaching the sea has a discharge far greater than the other rivers. Drawing its tributaries from both hemispheres it also has a more uniform discharge throughout the year. The remoter parts of the basin were some of the last areas of Africa to be explored, and European penetration, settlement and economic activity dates back little more than 100 years.

In the coastal areas European influence dates back to the earliest Portuguese contacts. Although the northen parts of Cameroon have more in common with Nigeria and Chad, the highland border between western Cameroon and southern Nigeria does provide an effective geographical boundary. The Union Douanière et Economique de l'Afrique Centrale (UDEAC) unites Cameroon, the Central African Republic, Gabon and Congo, and there were suggestions in 1984 that Chad might rejoin after 16 years as an outsider. French provides a *lingua franca* for all the countries of the region with the exception of Equatorial Guinea, a former Spanish possession.

Taking the region as a whole, certain characteristics are distinctive. There is certainly great heterogeneity of landscape, but over large areas population densities are low and comparable with dry West Africa rather than the better-watered coastal areas with which there is more in common. Like population, economic activity is sparsely dispersed, with individual concentrations often separated by great distances. Extensive areas are still very isolated, negative and at a low level of economic development.

CAMEROON

After the 1884–5 Berlin Conference, Germany established a protectorate embracing most of what is now the Cameroon republic; the area was occupied by Britain and France during the First World War and later divided into two mandated territories. In 1946 the British- and French-controlled areas became United Nations Trusteeships, and in 1960 France granted independence to its part. In the following year a plebiscite in the British-controlled territory resulted in the northern part joining Nigeria and the southern part forming a federation with the former French Cameroon. Together these have an area of 475,000 km^2 with an estimated 1986 population of 10 million, which gives an average population density of 21 people per km^2 – much higher than the other countries of western Equatorial Africa.

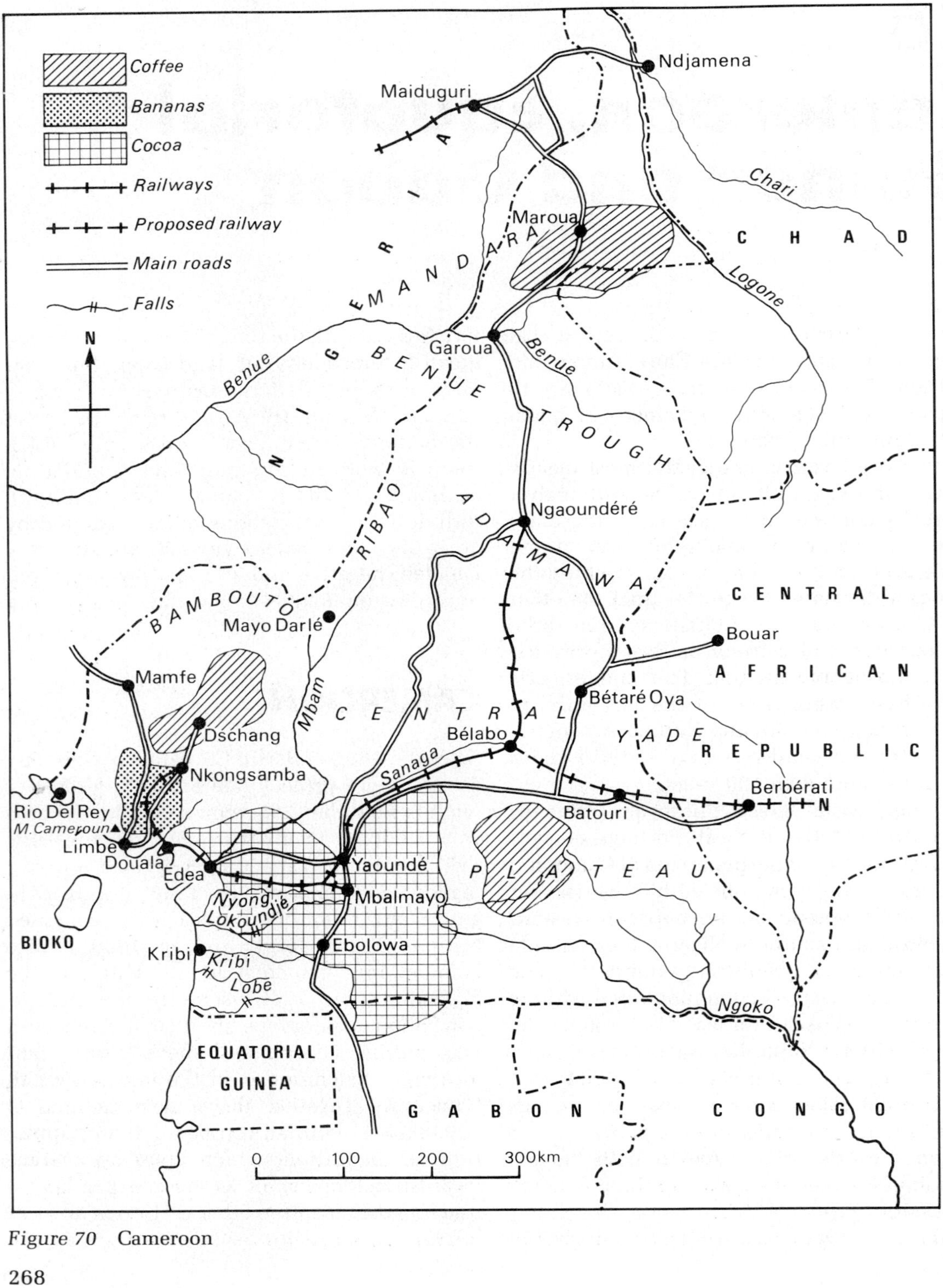

Figure 70 Cameroon

Extending from 2°N to 13°N over a distance of 1300 km from the Atlantic to Lake Chad and from sea level to 4000 m in altitude, Cameroon has diversity of terrain, climate and human response. Cameroon's place in the regional division of Africa has already been commented on, and its border characteristics are emphasized by its watershed role with drainage inland to Lake Chad, south-eastwards to Zaire, westwards through Nigeria and south-westwards to its own coast (Figure 70). It has a variety of population groups with ethno-cultural affinities with western, southern and northern Africa. Whilst in detail there is complexity, the broad outlines may be simplified.

There are only small parts of the country not underlain by Pre-Cambrian crystallines, and these include a small coastal zone of Cretaceous marine sedimentaries in the Douala basin and a narrow band of similar and more recent continental calcareous sedimentaries along the line of the Benue river and in the Logone–Chad basin of the north. A discontinuous arc of volcanic rocks stretches from Mount Cameroon in the south, through western Cameroon and the Nigerian border into the Adamawa massif. That this is a zone of active vulcanicity was demonstrated by the gas explosion at Lake Nios in 1986.

The coastal plain is of restricted width, especially in the south, and the shoreline is low-lying with extensive mangrove northwards of the Nyong river and more rocky to the south. The plain is crossed by numerous rivers such as the Lobé, Kribi, Nyong and Sanaga. Land rises quite abruptly to the plateau surface and there is a distinct fall line (e.g. Edea, Njock). Plateaux make up 80 per cent of the country; they average 600 m in the west but rise to over 1200 m in the Yadé plateau and northwards towards the Adamawa massif, where the terrain is more mountainous and individual peaks rise to over 1500 m. The Adamawa provides an effective boundary between the south and north of the country, and its northern margins provide an abrupt break of slope with the Benue depression. North of the Benue, the Mandara mountains provide a core of higher altitude, rising to 1450 m, from which the surface slopes gradually downwards to the Logone–Chad basin. Locally, especially northwards, the plateau surface is broken by inselbergs.

In western Cameroon and along the Nigerian border is an area of mountain country with complex relief. Mount Cameroon reaches 4070 m, but there are numerous other peaks over 2000 m in the Bambouto area. Northwards in the Ribao range the average altitude decreases.

Four principal climatic regions can be identified.

Cameroonian. This is the south-western coastal and mountain region with exceptionally high rainfall (Douala: 4015 mm) and only 2–3 months with less than 100 mm. The humidity is always high, the cloud cover often low and conditions oppressive.

Southern. Most of the south and centre of the country is characterized by rainfall in the range 1500 – 2000 mm, with some rain in all months but with two distinct peaks. The main rains peak in September–October and the 'small' rains in May. Yaoundé has only two months, December and January, with less than 100 mm.

Adamawa region. This is a transitional zone in which rainfall averages 1600 mm and rises to a single peak in August–September. Ngaoundéré has a longer 'dry' season with 5 months of less than 100 mm.

Northern region. Rainfall declines northwards from about 1000 to 500 mm and the dry season is extended to 8 months. The Harmattan, as in West Africa, is here a characteristic feature.

Cameroon has an associated diversity of natural vegetation. Some 37 per cent of the country, northwards to a line through Batouri and Yaoundé, has forest cover, but this tends to be richer in the west than in the east. Northwards the forest gives way to zones of derived savanna and gallery forest, savanna woodland, grassland and eventually scrub. The higher mountains of the west are characterized by montane vegetation with raffia palms and bamboo.

Agriculture

It follows from its physical diversity that Cameroon has a varied agricultural base. Cassava particularly, and maize to a lesser extent, are widely grown, with bananas, plantain and sweet potato in the forest zone and groundnuts, guinea corn, millet and livestock increasing in importance in the drier areas. Yams are important in the forest–savanna margins.

Cameroon is one of the few African countries in which food production has kept pace with the population growth. A government agency (MIDIVIV) promotes plantain production and has encouraged planting of new trees. Rice also has its state agency (SEMRY), with 6000 ha of rice cultivation in the north and production rising rapidly. In an attempt to reduce wheat imports another agency is coordinating a wheat cultivation programme. The country is virtually self-sufficient in the basic food crops, and animal and food imports account for less than 5 per cent of the import bill. With only 4 per cent of the total area under cultivation there is still considerable scope for the expansion of agriculture.

A former president of the country could claim that 'before petroleum there was agriculture and after petroleum there will be agriculture', a realistic approach all too rare in African countries. Agriculture employs 75 per cent of the workforce and accounts for 25 per cent of the GDP; and it is the basis for much of the country's industry. In the 1982–6 Development Plan agriculture receives 24 per cent of the planned investment, with subsidies being provided for fertilizers, pesticides and new planting.

Just prior to independence agricultural commodities accounted for over 90 per cent of the exports of both British (West) and French (East) Cameroon, and in the late 1960s made up 65 per cent of the republic's total exports

Table 27 *Cameroon: principal exports (percentages of total value)*

	1959		1967	1982
	East	West		
Cocoa	47.0	23.0	26.0	12.1
Coffee	25.0		28.0	15.6
Cotton	5.0		5.1	3.6
Bananas	4.6	55.0	1.6	
Rubber	3.0	7.3	1.3	
Palm produce	4.7	5.5	1.2	
Groundnuts	1.0		1.1	
Tobacco	—		0.8	
Timber	7.0	9.2	7.5	5.9
Aluminium			14.7	
Petroleum				46.8
Other	2.7	—	12.7	16.0

(Table 27). Most of the cash crops come from small-scale farms, although there are some plantations particularly in western Cameroon. The principal export crops are cocoa (almost entirely from peasant farms in the forest zone around Yaoundé and Kribi – see Figure 70), and coffee (mainly from the flanks of the highlands in the west around Dschang and from the Abong–M'Bang region of the south-east). The government has invested substantially in crop improvement schemes, and financial incentives for growers have resulted in expanded production, cocoa exports increasing from 71,000 tonnes in 1960 to 112,000 tonnes in 1982 and coffee increasing from 39,000 to 138,000 tonnes over the same period. Cotton is the principal cash crop of the north; production figures tend to reflect the considerable variability of rainfall from year to year, but the trend has been upwards and the 84,000 tonnes of 1982 was adequate to supply the country's textile plants and three oil mills, and to provide lint and oil for export. The loss of Commonwealth preference and problems of maintaining the quality have adversely affected the banana production of the Mungo region of the west, despite a gradual change from the Cavendish to the superior Gros Michel variety. Some of the banana plantations have been replanted with rubber, production of which reached a modest 17,000

Plate 34 Hanging sheet rubber on smoke-house trolleys, Mukonge, Cameroon

tonnes in 1982. The groundnut production of the centre and north of the country is mainly consumed locally, but in the same regions there have been attempts to improve animal husbandry by tsetse fly eradication and the initiation of extensive ranching of cattle.

In contrast with many other African countries, the Cameroon government has given the right priority to agriculture and has provided the necessary incentives and conditions for the development of a healthy agricultural base. It provides an example which Ghana, and others, could follow with advantage.

Forestry

The timber industry provides 5 per cent of the GDP and 7 per cent of modern sector employment, and with a 1980/1 production of 990,000 tonnes is a valuable export. The industry is 85 per cent controlled by European firms, but the government is encouraging local enterprises: in the 1982–6 plan period it was hoped to create 2000 additional jobs and to increase the accessible forest area from 9.4 to 15.0 per cent of the total. Large areas remain to be exploited, and the improvement of transport to, and at, the port of Kribi will open up parts of the south-west.

The oil revolution

Cameroon has a long-established but small-scale mining industry. Gold is obtained by simple 'artisanal' enterprises in the Betaré–Oya area of the east, and there is small-scale mining of cassiterite from alluvium in the Mayo–Darlé district. Although aluminium is an important export it is produced from imported alumina and processed with cheap hydroelectric power at Edea. There are large deposits of bauxite close to the railway at Ngaoundéré which may eventually provide a local raw material for this industry. In addition to bauxite, iron-ore, uranium and diamonds are known to exist but have yet to be systematically exploited.

As in other countries fortunate enough to possess it, oil can be a major influence in modifying the economy. Prospecting onshore started in the 1950s, but by 1963 the search was concentrated on offshore areas. Oil in commercial quantities was found in 1972 off Rio del Rey, close to the Nigerian border (Figure 70) and production started in 1977. In 1985, oil production amounted to 9 million tonnes and accounted for over 50 per cent of the value of exports. In 1981 an oil refinery came on stream at Limbe, with adverse results for the Gabon refinery industry from which Cameroon had previously imported its products. Plans for a natural gas plant at Kribi have been postponed pending further studies of gas reserves and in the hope of an increase in energy prices.

The impact of oil has been considerable. The relative – but fortunately not absolute – importance of agriculture has declined dramatically, and there is the suggestion that the significance of oil is purposely being underplayed officially so as not to create an oil-boom mentality from which Nigeria has clearly suffered. Government revenue from oil reputedly reached $469 million in 1982, and oil companies are strictly regulated and taxed. There has been a marked increase in capital investment, the capital growth in the 200 leading companies – which was 17.5 per cent from 1973 to 1980 – rising to 50 per cent between 1980 and 1982. This was largely a result of government shareholding in many industries. The once-dominant French influence has been greatly reduced, and American, German and British investment has been expanded. Urban areas now contain about 30 per cent of the population; but urban growth has accelerated rapidly and the drift to the towns could reduce the manpower available and so necessary for agricultural expansion. Oil revenue, as in Nigeria, has undoubtedly resulted in increased imports, and there is the danger that borrowing on the security of oil will produce a debt-servicing problem.

Industrialization

Even before the oil revenue became significant, Cameroon's industries accounted for 25 per cent of the GDP, and industrial development is now accelerating. The Edea HEP plant and aluminium smelter was completed in 1958, and there was already at independence a considerable industrial sector based on the processing of agricultural and forest products – saw-mills, oil-mills, meat, milk, coffee, cigarettes, soap, cotton ginneries and a textile mill.

In the years after independence there was some extension of the agro-based industries (rubber, cocoa, pineapple canning, sugar refining, paper-pulp) and the development of import-substitution industries – brewing, cement, textiles, footwear, chemicals, construction materials, utensils, furniture, steel frames, paint and motor vehicle assembly. During the 1982–6 plan there is a renewed emphasis on industries based on local raw materials, and there are plans for a second textile mill at Maroua, an inner-tube factory at Tiko, an asphalt plant adjacent to the Limbe oil refinery, brick works at Douala, Yaoundé and Garoua, sugar processing, a starch mill, a tomato paste factory, and a corn–soyabean complex at Foumbau. There is also a project for fish processing based on a larger, modern trawler fleet.

Infrastructure

Cameroon has maximized the potential for sectoral linkages; but there are several constraints on industrial development, the principal being energy and transport. Over 90 per cent of the available electricity is generated at HEP plants, Edea being the most important. Only 7 per cent of the population is supplied with electricity, and the coastal region accounts for 88 per cent of the consumption. The rest of the country either has no electricity or is served by small diesel generating plant. However, there are numerous potential HEP sites, and the availability of oil and gas should make it possible to increase electricity supplies to satisfy demand. There are known deposits of lignite and oil shale and a biomass energy study is in progress.

In 1974 the Cameroon railway was extended to Ngaoundéré so that the system now comprises 1143 km; but lack of proper maintenance has led to reduced capacity. On the Nkongsamba–Bonaberi line the deterioration of the service has been such that banana exporters have been forced to use road transport. The Douala–Yaoundé section is being rebuilt, and under the 1982–6 plan additional locomotives and rolling stock are being acquired to increase carrying capacity from 1.4 to 2.5 million tonnes a year. However, 58 per cent of the development plan's transport investment is for road improvement. Only 2500 km of the 60,000 km of roads is surfaced and of all-season quality, and even the main Douala (industrial–commercial capital) to Yaoundé (political–cultural capital) road is in poor condition. An additional 1000 km are to be surfaced and 4000 km of rural and strategic links are to be built or up-graded.

Douala is the main deep-water port, handling 90 per cent of the country's external trade – 3 million tonnes of imports and 1 million tonnes of exports in 1984. Extra berths were constructed in the late 1970s to bring the capacity up to 5 million tonnes a year, and there are proposals for further expansion. There have been improvements at Kribi for timber handling and Limbe has developed as a port to serve the offshore oil industry. There are plans to develop full deep-water facilities at Limbo, near Limbe.

These developments should go some way towards improving the infrastructure and make it possible for directly productive activities to be diversified and dispersed more widely. Cameroon has so far capitalized reasonably effectively on its geographical diversity. There are some problems arising from ethno-cultural diversity (English-speaking west and French-speaking east, north versus south); but if these can be overcome and political stability maintained, there are optimistic hopes that economic growth and further development will result.

EQUATORIAL GUINEA

Until 1963 Equatorial Guinea was a Spanish colony, and for ten years after independence it had a repressive, isolationist political regime which did nothing for national development. It remains one of the world's smallest (28,000 km^2, 400,000 inhabitants) and most backward states.

The country comprises two separate parts, mainland Rio Muni and the islands of Bioko (formerly Fernando Po) and Annobon. Rio Muni has an area of 26,018 km^2 and its low-cliffed coast has no natural harbours. The coast plain rises southwards and terminates abruptly inland against a number of spurs of the Crystal Mountains, which rise to over 1200 m. The territory is effectively bisected by the Rio Benito river. Apart from the normal food crops of the region (cassava, plantain) there is a small-scale production of coffee from the area bordering Cameroon. The main export of the mainland is timber from European-controlled concessions, and output peaked at about 300,000 tonnes in the late 1960s. General deterioration of the road system, the inadequacy of the roadstead, log-loading port at Bata and political uncertainty have created problems for the industry.

The island of Bioko has an area of 2036 km^2 and comprises three extinct volcanoes rising, in places very abruptly, to heights of over 3000 m. The only sheltered port is that at Malabo (formerly Santa Isabel). Level land is scarce, but the rich volcanic soils have led to the clearance of lower forested slopes and the establishment of plantations for cocoa, coffee and bananas and at higher levels for tobacco and cotton. Some 40,000 ha are under cocoa with over 1000 separate plantations, about 200 of them European owned and accounting for the bulk of the area. Production fell from 40,000 tonnes a year in the 1960s to 9000 tonnes in 1984, but is now recovering slowly; but the plantation industry in general is now very depressed. A large part of the labour force was traditionally 'on contract' from Nigeria or 'forced' from Rio Muni – the former have now been expelled and the latter repatriated. Many of the European farmers have left.

The small island of Annobon (17 km^2), south of São Tomé, produces small quantities of palm produce, coffee, cocoa and copra.

Apart from some saw-mills and palm-oil and coffee processing there is virtually no industry. There has been a recent attempt to reactivate the European plantations on the mainland and rehabilitate the timber, coffee and cocoa industries. Offshore, there has been exploration for oil but as yet no production. The country has the greatest difficulty feeding its 400,000 population, and health and social services are very poorly developed. There seem to be no developments in progress which could materially alter this dismal situation.

SÃO TOMÉ E PRÍNCIPE

The Republic of São Tomé é Príncipe comprises islands in the Bioko-Annobon chain about

200 km off the coast of Gabon and takes its name from the largest of the two islands. Independence was obtained in 1975 after over 450 years of Portuguese rule during the latter part of which there had been little in the way of development investment.

The archipelago totals 964km^2 with São Tomé itself accounting for 845 km^2 and over 90 per cent of the 102,000 population (1984). São Tomé rises to 2000 m with a rainfall of over 4000 mm on the south-western side and 1000 mm in the drier north-east. With monthly mean temperatures in the 23°C to 26°C range a variety of tropical crops can be grown and sugar, coffee, oil palm, coconut palm, bananas and cinchona are produced in small quantities. However cocoa became the principal cash crop and with 36,000 tonnes in 1913, São Tomé was the leading world producer. In 1975, Portuguese plantations, roças, accounted for 80 per cent of the total cultivated area and 11,000 tonnes of cocoa for export, but the Portuguese left the country in large numbers at independence and in 1976 cocoa exports amounted to only 4600 tonnes. In 1978 loans were obtained for the rehabilitation of the cocoa plantations and production had just started to increase when drought in 1982 and 1983 brought production back to the 1976 level.

In 1984 cocoa accounted for 90 per cent of the value of exports and the national economy demonstrates all the vulnerability that results from fluctuations in production locally and variations in world commodity prices. The position is the more critical because the country can produce only 10 per cent of its food requirements. The offshore zone is rich in fish, especially tuna, and the fishing industry is now being developed in the hope of improving on the 1984 production of 4000 tonnes. With São Tomé and Príncipe separated by 140 km even simple matters like fuel distribution creates problems and adds to costs.

GABON

Gabon has an area of 268,000 km^2 and a total population that is variably estimated between 0.56 and 1.5 million. Even if the higher figure is adopted the population density is only a low 6 people per km^2 – much lower than is found in comparable mainly forested regions of West Africa. It has been suggested, on no very firm evidence, that the population at one time must have been much higher and has been reduced by some subsistence crisis or disease. Whatever the cause, the low population total and density is undoubtedly a vital factor influencing the present level and potential for development.

Gabon is a reasonably well defined physical unit, comprising the entire drainage basin of the Ogooué river with the addition of the catchments of some smaller coastal rivers such as the Nyanga in the south and the Como in the north. South of Cap Lopez the coastline is relatively smooth, has fairly heavy surf and is backed by mangrove-fringed lagoons (e.g. N'Dogo, M'Gaze and N'Komi). North of Cap Lopez there are more indentations and less heavy surf. The coastal plain is narrow in the north but broadens considerably in the estuary regions of the Ogooué and Gabon rivers, where there is a flooring of oil-bearing, Cretaceous sedimentaries with a superficial covering of alluvium and sand.

Virtually the whole of the interior comprises highly mineralized Pre-Cambrian crystalline rocks eroded into a series of plateaux surfaces at heights from 460 to 600 m, with residuals rising to over 1000 m. These are divided by the river system into distinct physiographic regions such as the Crystal Mountains in the north and the Mayoumba Mountains and Moabi Uplands in the south, which provide the abrupt edge and 'fall-line' of the interior plateau. Inland, the Crystal Mountains give way to the Woleu M'Tem Plateau, and the Moabi Uplands are separated from the Chaillu massif by the N'Gounie depression which is etched out of less-resistant Palaeozoic sandstone. The Chaillu massif provides Gabon's highest point at Mount Ibongdjii (1574 m). In the south-east the Batéké Plateau provides the watershed between the Ogooué and Zaire rivers and an area of Cretaceous sedimentary rocks. There are certainly areas, such as the Chaillu massif, where the dissection is such that a basically plateau country takes on a mountainous appearance.

Gabon, situated astride the equator, experiences an equatorial climatic regime with uniformly high temperatures, high relative humidities and a rainfall of 1500–3050 mm with marked double peaking. The climatic conditions produce luxuriant rain-forest cover over 75 per cent of the country, and it is only on the sandier and lower-rainfall areas along the coast between Mayoumba and Cap Lopez, in restricted areas of the upper Nyanga and N'Gounie rivers and in the Batéké Plateau that savanna vegetation is found. There are also areas where forest exploitation has produced a forest-savanna mosaic. For long, the country's forest provided its main economic support.

Agriculture

In theory Gabon is able to produce the full range of forest and savanna crops, but in practice and in contrast with many African countries agriculture has contributed little to the export trade. Less than 1 per cent of the area is under cultivation, and agriculture accounts for less than 4 per cent of the GDP. This is to be explained in terms of the low overall population density, the impact of outward migration from rural areas, the relative inaccessibility of large parts of the country, and lack of labour. During the colonial period there were attempts by the French to concentrate population for administrative convenience at nodal points and along rivers.

About 75 per cent of the population is dependent on agriculture, but for many this is of a purely subsistence type and the country still imports 90 per cent of its food requirements. The only areas of more intensive agriculture do in fact coincide with the areas of relatively higher population density, principal of which is the Woleu N'Tem area of the north. This is the main area for the cash production of cocoa and coffee (Figure 71). The former was introduced after 1918 into Woleu N'Tem where the conditions are ideal, but there has since been a spread southwards into parts of Ogooué Ivindo and Ogooué Lolo where conditions of soil, climate and forest cover are more marginal. Coffee is probably better suited to Gabon, was introduced in 1941, but only spread after 1950 as a result of government encouragement and the provision of marketing and processing facilities. Exports of cocoa amount to only 4000–5000 tonnes a year and coffee 700 tonnes.

Palm-oil has for long been extracted from nuts collected from wild trees, but plantation cultivation has been developing slowly. Pioneered at Kango and M'Vili near Lambaréné, an oil extraction plant was established at Moabi and in 1983 a second palm-oil factory was opened at Lambaréné in the hope that the country would be self-sufficient by 1985 and exporting by the end of the decade.

A sugar refinery near Franceville is operating at only one-third of its 30,000 tonnes a year capacity. A 10,000 ha rubber scheme was started in 1982 but will not be in full production until well into the 1990s. At N'Dende there is a 500 ha paddy rice scheme, and cattle ranches have been established near Mounana and in the Nyanga and Haut Ogooué regions. Gabon still has to import most of its meat.

Government policy for agriculture is three-pronged. First, the main effort is clearly directed towards large, capital-intensive export-oriented agro-industrial projects, most of which are still in early stages of development. Given the low population density such projects probably make sense in Gabon, but they do rely heavily on costly imported expertise. The second approach has been the initiation of integrated rural development zones (e.g. for cocoa production in Woleu N'Tem), in which traditional crop cultivation will also be encouraged. These schemes involve regrouping population, the provision of feeder-roads and better extension services. The third approach has been to create favourable conditions for agricultural development by way

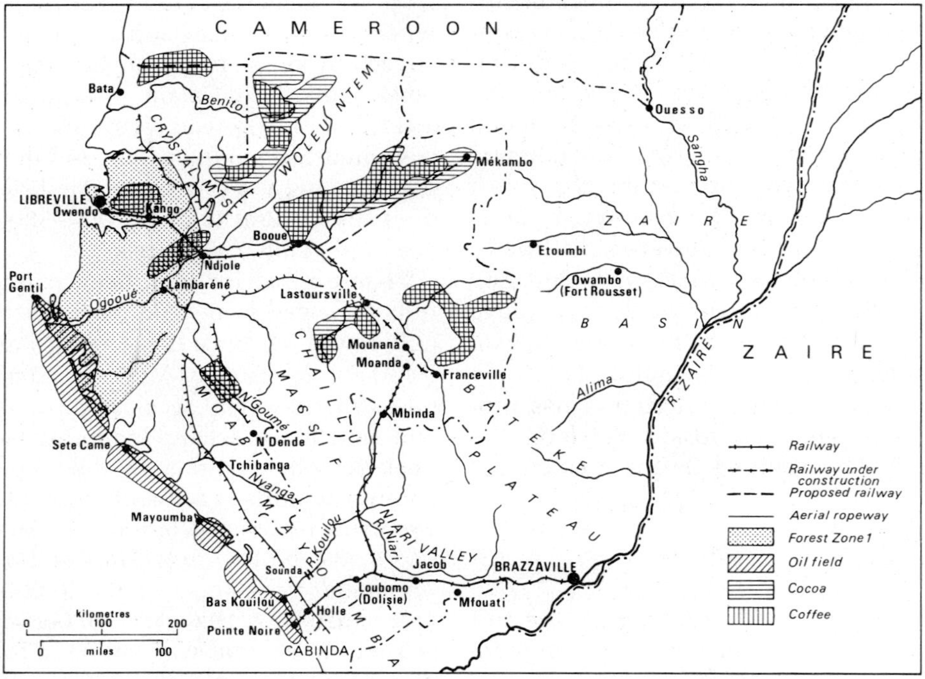

Figure 71 Gabon and Congo

of price support, marketing credit and technical services. It is too soon to say how effective these policies will be in stemming an active decline in agricultural production and stimulating new development. It is ironic that Gabon, with the second highest per capita GDP in Africa ($2742 in 1982) experiences chronic food shortages and is dependent on imports for over 60 per cent of its food requirements. Not without justification, agriculture has been called the 'Achilles heel' and the 'rural waste' of the national economy.

Forestry

Timber was for long the country's main export. Much of the forest is of a secondary nature in which a dominant species is *Aucoumea klaineana*, known more usually as okooumé or Gabon Mahogany. This is a pale pink, fine-grain wood of low density which peels, cuts and dries easily and is ideal for veneers and plywood. This wood is confined almost exclusively to Gabon and Equatorial Guinea, and in 1902 okooumé was already the leading export. In 1956 it accounted for 83 per cent of the value of exports and at independence in 1960 still made up 77 per cent; but it has since declined in relative importance (Table 28).

Characteristically, individual species are widely scattered in tropical forests and okooumé occurs at about 2 to 3 trees per hectare. In consequence, extraction is costly in terms of equipment, vehicles and routeway construction. Clearly, Gabon's low population density is an advantage and reduces land-use conflicts, but a high percentage of the workforce has had to be imported from other coun-

Plate 35 Log-lorry convoy on new forest access road, N' Djole, Gabon

tries – Nigeria is traditionally a main source. While there has been some Gabonese involvement in recent years, the nature of the operation is such that they are monopolized by a few large, mainly European-owned enterprises.

Much of the timber – about 80 per cent in terms of value – is still exported in log form. This has the advantage that rivers can be used for rafting and logs loaded to vessels directly from the water. There has been some associated industrial development, and at Port Gentil is one of the world's largest plywood factories. Saw-milling is more widely dispersed, and the most recent development has been a cellulose factory at Kango. Table 28 shows the dramatic decline in the significance of the timber exports in the period since independence in 1960.

The mining industry

Mining has brought about a transformation of the economy in the last two decades. For its size, Gabon must rank as one of Africa's richest zones of mineralization. Traditionally, gold and diamonds have been obtained in small quantities by simple mining methods, but in 1955, after 30 years of intermittent exploration, oil was found near Port Gentil and exploration was extended southwards along the coast, both onshore and offshore. The principal recent finds and main producing fields are now in the southern coastal area, and advanced recovery methods (such as water injection) are being used to keep production going in the older fields nearer Port Gentil.

Table 28 *Gabon: principal exports (percentages of total value)*

	1957	*1960*	*1973*	*1980*	*1982*
Timber and wood products	83.5	72.3	38.2	9.7	6.1
Minerals	—	—	17.6	10.4	11.4
Oil	7.7	20.8	40.8	78.9	81.5
Other (mainly agricultural)	8.8	6.4	3.4	1.0	1.0

It is likely that the Cretaceous basin has far more oil than has already been identified (in 1985 over 30 exploration wells were sunk), with the advantage that most of it is at shallow depths. However, in the coastal swamplands, exploration and production costs can be high; furthermore the profit per barrel produced, for oil companies and government, is less than for most other OPEC producers. Oil exporting started in 1957, and production increased from 750,000 tonnes in 1960 to a peak of over 11 million tonnes in 1976. However, although oil has continued to provide an increasing proportion of the value of exports, the recent decline in world demand and prices resulted in a drop in production (8 million tonnes in 1985), greatly reduced revenue for the Gabon government and the need for austerity budgets and problems of debt servicing. Oil companies are nevertheless required to reinvest in development projects in Gabon.

In 1967 an oil refinery was built at Port

Gentil to supply refined products to Gabon's partners in UDEAC (the Central African Customs and Economic Union), and in the early 1970s a second refinery was completed. Both refineries are of small capacity – about 2 million tonnes a year – and now meet severe competition from a refinery opened at Liumbe, Cameroon, in 1981. As a result the refineries are operating at only 50 per cent of capacity, since Gabon's own market for petroleum products is far too small to justify both refineries. Apart from a small quantity used in an electricity-generating station at Port Gentil, the gas is presently flared off and wasted and there are certainly gas fields that could be exploited. Future developments will depend on the world market for gas and oil both in terms of demand and price.

In 1962 Gabon started to export manganese-ore from Moanda, and with exports of about 2 million tonnes a year Gabon is now the world's fourth largest exporter. The ore body is one of the richest in the world, is 5 m in thickness and easily mined by open-cast methods. However, exploitation was made difficult by the remote location of the ore deposit in the south-east of the country and the need to evacuate the ore by way of a 76 km cableway, the world's longest, to the Congo border at M'Binda, from where a special rail link had to be constructed to the Congo Ocean Railway and port of Pointe Noire. When eventually completed, Gabon's new railway will allow the ore to be exported through a port being constructed at Owendo. As a result of the recession, exports dropped from 2.3 million tonnes in 1979 to 1.4 million in 1981, but there has since been a marginal increase. In the same region uranium is mined at Mounana and exports started in 1961.

Near Mekambo in the Belinga Massif in the extreme north-east of the country, Gabon has one of the world's largest iron-ore deposits. This amounts to over 500 million tonnes of low-phosphorus ore with an average 64 per cent iron content. The Trans-Gabon Railway project was originally justified as a means of opening up this area and allowing evacuation of iron-ore, but uncertainty in world iron-ore markets and a World Bank report which was critical of a railway designed largely to serve the one mining operation resulted in the diversion of the railway south-eastwards to serve the established mining industries of the Franceville region. World demand for iron-ore and prices will have to be much more favourable before Gabon can consider costly mining, either at Mekambo or at other known iron-ore deposits (e.g. in the Crystal Mountains and at Tchibanga).

Gabon is known to have considerable deposits of barytes (between Mayoumba and Tchibanga), talc (Tchibanga area), lead (Nyanga), molybdenum and copper. Gold exists, probably in small quantities, in numerous locations.

As a result of its minerals Gabon is blessed with a high per capita GDP, yet for the bulk of the population this still means little or nothing in terms of improved life-style. The benefits are confined to the urban areas, a very small number of Gabonese and a rather larger number of expatriate workers.

Infrastructure

With the broken terrain, forest cover and low population density provision of transport is difficult and costly. Yet any development in remoter areas, whether of agriculture or industry, depends on satisfactory transport services.

At independence Gabon had no deep-water port facilities and all trade was handled by lighters to ships at anchor. Logs could be floated alongside the ships. Gabon has only 6800 km of road and only 190 km of that, mainly in Libreville, the capital, and Port Gentil, is surfaced. Port Gentil, a main concentration of population and industry, is on an island and has no road connection with the rest of the country. The Ogooué is navigable for barges to N'Djolé, and this and other rivers are used for log rafting. At Owendo, just south of Libreville, an attempt to construct a deep-water port was abandoned in 1970 because of

Plate 36 Passenger train on the new Trans-Gabon railway

rapid siltation, but work restarted in 1972 on a modified design and was completed in 1974.

Owendo is the coast terminus of Gabon's, and possibly Africa's greatest transport project, the Trans-Gabon Railway. This is a costly, difficult and ambitious rail-building exercise but has become a focal point in Gabon's development strategy. World Bank refusal to provide finance left Gabon to find the capital on the open market. Work started in 1974, service roads had to be built, rock excavation was five times that estimated, weather and terrain created problems and even ballast has to be imported. The first section to N'Djolé was opened in 1978, that to Booué (330 km) in 1983, and the line was completed to Franceville in 1986. A new mineral-exporting terminal is being built at the port of Owendo and all traffic to and from the manganese and uranium mines will eventually move along the 673 km railway. The line is being built to the standard 1.435 m gauge; while this increases its capacity, it does make it difficult or impossible – should it be thought desirable – to link up with lines in Cameroon and Congo which are on the 1.0 m gauge.

The vast capital cost and debt servicing will place a heavy burden on the economy for a long time to come. However, freight traffic on the completed section reached 450,000 tonnes in 1984 and the line will provide access to vast forest and agricultural resources and allow the minerals of the Franceville area to be fully exploited. Should market conditions allow, a link could later be built to the Mekambo iron deposits, and this would greatly increase the accessible forest area. However, many feel that the railway is a political rather than economic project and that Gabon does not have the manpower to develop the resources that will now be accessible without greatly increasing the country's dependence on external inputs.

27
Congo and the Central African Republic

CONGO

While the western parts of the Congo Republic drain directly to the Atlantic, the bulk of the interior drains to the Zaire river. In part, Congo provides a southward continuation of some of the relief regions already identified in Gabon. The coastal plain is never more than 50 km in width and does not rise above 100 m. In the north there are lagoons backing the sand bar, but south of Kouilou the immediate coastlands become more swampy. As in Gabon, this coastal zone is underlain by oil-bearing marine sedimentary rocks.

Parallel with the coast and rising abruptly from the plain is the Pre-Cambrian Mayoumba Range, rising to over 800 m and creating problems of transport provision, but not really high enough to prevent the eastward penetration of modifying, maritime climatic influences. Westward-flowing rivers have cut gorges through this range, and at Sounda, on the Kouilou, one such site has been developed for hydroelectric power. A southward continuation of the Chaillu massif provides a region of higher elevation, and this gives way eastwards to the drier sandstone area of the Batéké plateau (Figure 71). This plateau averages 500 m in the west, but drops gradually to around 400 m on the margins of the Zaire basin. Much of the east and north of the country comprises Zaire riverine lands, with numerous water-courses and extensive seasonal inundation.

Both Pointe Noire (1200 mm rainfall) and Brazzaville (1470 mm) have 7 months with rainfall in excess of 100 mm during a main rain season from October to April. In the Batéké plateau there is a more extended dry season, with total rainfall of less than 1500 mm; but over much of the country 1600 mm is the average. Much of the rain falls as heavy convectional storms and thunderstorms are frequent.

Dense rain forest covers about 50 per cent of the country, including the Mayoumba ranges, the Chaillu massif and the country north of Fort Rousset. Swamp vegetation covers another 15 per cent; but on the coastal plain, in the Niari valley and Batéké plateau, savanna vegetation is more characteristic, with gallery forest along water-courses and some areas of natural oil-palm and rubber.

Agriculture

For most of the population in the rural areas subsistence farming based on bush fallowing is usual, with cassava and plantain as the main crops, and with maize and beans of secondary importance. Some 80 per cent of the cultivated areas is accounted for by traditional farming, and production of the main crops has increased more or less in line with the growth in population. However, yams have declined in importance, and maize production, insignificant in 1970, had increased to 9000 tonnes in 1980, with a target production of 27,000 tonnes for 1986. Nevertheless, Congo still has a food import bill of over $50 million a year.

Some of the farmers are involved in cash cropping of cocoa and coffee (in the Mayoumba region and Northern forest), oil-palms (Mayoumba, Chaillu margins and north), rubber (Chaillu and north) and groundnuts (Niari valley). During the 1960s, particular emphasis was given to the expansion of large-scale, modern agriculture in the Niari valley, both through government and private projects. One of the largest schemes was the Société Industrielle et Agricole du Niari (SIAN). The large areas of fairly level land, reasonable soils, natural grassland vegetation, possibilities for irrigation, higher population density and railway access, combined to favour this area. Cultivation of groundnuts, maize, vegetables, bananas, tobacco and rice has been extended, and at Jacob a large sugar refinery and associated plantations have been established. There was also an attempt to set up cattle ranches with tsetse-resistant N'dama cattle. The new farms ranged in size from peasant holdings through 'colonats' of 50–100 ha, individual European-owned farms of 500–1000 ha and industrial estates of 4000 ha.

There was an unfortunate phase of setting up state farms and nationalization: the former were highly inefficient and the latter resulted in a decline in sugar production at Jacob from 100,000 tonnes a year in the late 1960s to 5700 tonnes in 1978. From being a sugar exporter, Congo became an importer. Similar declines were recorded in cocoa and coffee production. There were three changes of government in the late 1970s, but the 1980s saw the adoption of more realistic policies. French management was restored at the sugar refinery and output has risen steadily, two new palm-oil mills have been built at Kunda and Etoumbi in the forested north, and there has been some attempt to rehabilitate cocoa, coffee and livestock production.

Agriculture's contribution to the GDP declined from 17 per cent in 1970 to 10 per cent in 1980, yet only 1 per cent of the total area is cultivated and the potential for agricultural development is considerable. However, the 1982–6 Development Plan devoted only 3.5 per cent of proposed investment to agriculture.

Forestry

Commercially exploitable forest covers 13 million hectares and the 300 species includes about 50 usable timbers. Production averages between 500,000 and 800,000 cubic metres a year and is largely controlled by a small number of European firms. The forest could sustain a yield of twice this amount; but more accessible areas have been over-cut and much of the forest is in remote areas, so exploitation must await considerable improvement to the now rudimentary transport network. There is some local saw-milling, but most of the timber is exported in log form. In the longer term there is great potential for expanding both log production and local processing, but this would certainly depend on an improvement in the world timber market.

Before independence in 1960 and through to 1972, timber provided the main export. However, its contribution to export earnings declined from 75 per cent in 1968 to 17.6 per cent in 1981. As in Gabon, this change in the relative importance of the timber industry was the result of increased activity in mining.

Mining

Since 1937 there has been small-scale mining of lead and zinc at Mfouati on the southern margins of the Niari valley, and some mining of tin and copper; but in 1969 minerals accounted for less than 5 per cent of export earnings. The exploitation of large potassium chloride deposits at Holle, on the foothills of the Mayoumba range inland from Pointe Noire, has been plagued by technical problems: production has fluctuated widely and has never reached expected levels.

In 1957 oil was discovered at Pointe Indienne, just north of Pointe Noire; but the reserves proved to be small, and after reaching 120,000 tonnes a year in the early 1960s, production declined. Continued exploration offshore produced better finds in the Emeraude field in the south and the Sendji–Youga and Loanga fields north of Pointe Noire. After 1972 production increased to 2.6 million tonnes in 1979 and 7.2 million tonnes in 1985 and, markets permitting, more could be produced. The Pointe Noire refinery came on-stream, seven years late, in 1982, with a capacity of 1.25 million tonnes a year. The initial increase in production in the early 1970s coincided with high world prices, but prices have since dropped and competition for markets has become fiercer. In 1982 it was decided that the gas reserves that had been discovered did not justify plans for a NG plant.

Small though Congo's oil industry is by world standards, it has had a profound impact on the national economy. Oil provided 89 per cent of the value of exports in 1982. The national budget increased five-fold between 1975 and 1983, although this has been paralelled by rapid increases in external borrowing and problems as the oil market slackened.

However, oil income can be cited as a possible factor leading to the neglect and decline of a once thriving agriculture, to the massive exodus from rural areas, and to Congo's exceptional level – by African standards – of urbanization (45 per cent). Brazzaville, the capital, grew at 7 per cent a year between 1960 and 1980, and two-thirds of the country's estimated 1.62 million people live in a 50 km strip either side of the Congo Ocean Railway from Brazzaville to Pointe Noire. The expatriate population has increased from 7000 to 12,000, with Pointe Noire the principal concentration. The 1982–6 development plan described the country away from the line of the railway as 'a human and economic desert' and colonization of this area has become a main feature of government policy.

Infrastructure and development

Any rehabilitation of existing economic activities or development of the rural areas presupposes a level of infrastructure provision that is now lacking. Only 600 km of the road system is surfaced and contact is difficult

Plate 37 Export terminal for manganese from Gabon, Pointe Noire, Congo

between different settlements and regions. The few roads, railway and rivers provide 'vertical' transport links, but not the necessary 'horizontal' feeder links. The mainly single-line 510 km Congo Ocean Railway is operating at full capacity, as is the river transport system on the Zaire, Oubangui, Alima and Sangha rivers and the seaport of Pointe Noire (where traffic increased from 3 million tonnes in 1978 to 3.7 million tonnes in 1980). The railway and port of Pointe Noire also handle Gabon's manganese traffic and trade from land-locked Central African Republic and Chad. Some relief, but also considerable loss of revenue, will follow the completion of the Trans-Gabon Railway line to Franceville. Further improvements to the Congo Ocean Railway are in progress and additional berths are to be built at Pointe Noire.

There are long-term plans for a main, north–south, all-weather road from Brazzaville to Ouesso. This would certainly assist in opening up the now inaccessible and undeveloped northern part of the country; but the road would be very expensive and the same effect could be achieved by the lower cost improvement of river transport and river ports.

Industrialization has not progressed beyond basic import substitutes, and what little industry there exists is concentrated mainly in Brazzaville and Pointe Noire. Undoubtedly, the Congo has the resources to attain a reasonable level of development, but progress may well be hindered by the small size of the local market and labour force and the problems of providing the necessary infrastructure in a country with a low overall population density of only 5 people per km^2 and extensive negative areas.

THE CENTRAL AFRICAN REPUBLIC

As a part of the former French Equatorial Africa, what is now the Central African Republic was known as Oubangui–Chari, a name which more satisfactorily described its location astride the ill-defined Zaire basin and Lake Chad watershed. For the most part the country consists of extensive, monotonous gently undulating terrain at an average elevation of 650 m, but dipping to around 400 m around Bangui and rising to over 1400 m in the Yadé plateau of the west and to similar heights in the Dar-el-Kouti in the east. Along the northern margin of the country, and along the Oubangui and some of its tributaries, there are extensive, seasonally inundated riverine zones.

Geologically, most of the country is underlain with Pre-Cambrian crystallines, and in the Bangassou-Bakouma region along the Oubangui there are rocks of the Katanga system with known deposits of uranium and numerous diamondiferous zones.

In Bangui and the south-west of the country is a zone with rainfall in excess of 1700 mm spread over a rain season of some 8 months (March to October). Northwards the length of the rain season decreases to about 5 months and the total to about 1000 mm. The better-watered Lobaye region of the south-west supports forest cover, but elsewhere, apart from swamp forest along water-courses, there is wooded savanna vegetation.

With its area of 623,000 km^2 and an estimated 1982 population of only 2.46 million, the country has a low average density of about 5 people per km^2. Thirty-five per cent of the population lives in the four prefectures of the forest zone, and large areas in the east and north of the country are very sparsely populated.

Agriculture

Agriculture accounts for over 50 per cent of the GDP and provides the economic support for 85 per cent of the population (Table 29). Nevertheless, it is possible that less than 2 per cent of the total area is actually cultivated. Cassava and sorghum are the main food crops, with maize, rice, groundnuts and sweet potatoes of secondary importance. Over large areas the farming is purely on a subsistence level, but in the better-watered areas there is a cash-crop element of some variety.

As in Chad, cotton was introduced compulsorily by the French in 1928–9, and it was not until 1946 that forced labour was abolished. A large number of farmers in a broad belt across the west of the country are now dependent on cotton (often rotated with groundnuts), and the industry is controlled by a government agency, the Union Cotonière Centrafricaine (UCCA). About 115,000 ha are now planted, but production has varied greatly from year to year – from 58,700 tonnes (1970) to 28,000 tonnes (1983). Farmers and village heads have been offered incentives to increase production.

Table 29 *Central African Republic: principal exports (percentages of total value)*

	1960	*1966*	*1972*	*1979*	*1982*
Coffee	98 (Coffee and Cotton combined)	24	23	30	27
Cotton		15	18	14	7
Timber			20	17	29
Diamonds		54	31	38	25

In more restricted areas, mainly near the Oubangui river in the vicinity of Bangui, Mobaye and Bangassou, coffee is important, with a declining proportion from European plantations and an increasing share from African farmers. As with cotton, and for reasons that are not clear, annual production is far from stable in the range from 6500 to 13,000 tonnes. Small though this is by world standards, it is a principal export. Cocoa, rubber, tobacco and sesame are also produced in small quantities.

Animal husbandry is restricted by tsetse fly, but there have been attempts to overcome the problems. As a result the cattle population increased five-fold to about 500,000 head between 1950 and 1970, at which figure it has remained. The principal cattle area is in the north, but the main abattoir has been located in Bangui.

Forest exploitation has been expanding in recent years but is hampered by problems of transport. Commercial production is almost entirely from the western Lobaye region, where concessions have been granted to firms prepared to provide local social and economic infrastructure. Production runs at about 500,000 m^3 a year, of which about one-third is exported. About 75 per cent of the exported timber is in log form and the rest is sawn.

Mining

The only significant mineral extraction is of diamonds from alluvial deposits, mainly in the western part of the country. Until about 1960 production was mainly by a few large companies, but the contribution of individuals gradually increased to 90 per cent of the total in 1969 when the government closed the mining companies. Some were later reopened, but production peaked at 638,000 carats in 1968 and by 1978 had dropped to 268,000 as a result of government intervention. It is clear that a properly organized diamond industry could be contributing far more to the economy, and in view of the generally feeble level of agricultural production this must be a priority area for rehabilitation.

Economic development

For 14 years the country was ruled by a megalomaniac president who eventually had himself crowned with great pageantry and at vast expense as Emperor Bokassa I; he brought about his own downfall. When he was overthrown in 1979, salaries comprised 85 per cent of the national budget, roads had deteriorated, river transport was almost non-operational and the country's few industries, mining and agriculture, were in collapse.

Since 1980 there has been a slow process of rehabilitation of roads, ferry and river services have been restarted, and there have been improvements in the supply of fuel. As a landlocked country, the Central African Republic has transport problems, and the main route to the sea by way of the rivers Oubangui and Zaire and the Brazzaville–Pointe Noire railway is 1800 km, is of low capacity and very costly. While some trade goes by road through Bouar to Cameroon, the condition of the road restricts the capacity of the route. There has for long been talk of a possible rail link with the Cameroon railway, but the CAR's traffic is insufficient to justify the construction of a 600 km route across difficult terrain, particularly in view of Gabon's problems of financing a railway for which there is a guaranteed, heavy mineral traffic. A link with this new Gabon railway would also be a possibility, but would also be costly.

A company was created in 1969 and reconstituted in 1975 to exploit uranium found in Eocene sediments at M'Patou, near Boukama, 480 km east of the capital, Bangui. The area in which the uranium is found is seasonally flooded and the ore will have to be obtained by a dredging method. The complicated river–road transport problems have yet to be solved and the slack state of the world uranium market has not encouraged rapid development. Nevertheless, were this project to become operational, it would mean great improvements in infrastructure, would provide employment and create a growth pole in a presently isolated and sparsely populated area.

Perhaps of greater importance, it would provide the government with a valuable source of revenue and allow other developments to take place. It therefore offers a slim hope that the CAR could increase its per capita annual income from the present $110 and lift itself from the ranks of the 'least developed'.

28 Zaire, Rwanda and Burundi

The Belgian Congo became independent in 1960 as the Republic of the Congo (Leopoldville). In 1970 the name Zaire was assumed; the capital, Leopoldville, became Kinshasa and many other names were 'Africanized'. There is still dispute whether or not the name Zaire should be applied to the Congo river, which is an international waterway.

It is a country with vast natural resources, but since independence has staggered from crisis to crisis. The first five years were marked by the attempted secession of Katanga province (now Shaba) and civil war, with United Nations intervention. There has been rebellion in the north-east and further revolt in Shaba. Since much of the infrastructure has been neglected, and there has been political uncertainty and a lack of positive development strategy, the productive sectors of the economy have stagnated or even declined. In the 1980s the Zaire economy has been the cause of international concern and debt rescheduling has been necessary.

With an area of 2.35 million km^2, Zaire is the third largest country in Africa and has the fourth largest population (26.4 million in 1982). Overall, the density is 11 people per km^2, which is well below the average (31.0) and median (20.0) for all African countries. It could be argued that, in the long term, the population in relation to the territory's size and resource endowment may well be too small, yet in the short term rapid growth (2.6 per cent a year), movement to towns and youthful age structure (40 per cent under 14) create serious problems.

The population is most unevenly dispersed, with the highest density in the Kinshasa area (Kinshasa, the capital, itself has 2.2 million people) and westwards towards the coast in the Mayoumba region, followed by other peripheral areas such as Bandundu (between Kinshasa and Ilebo) and the Kivu highland area of the east. Much of the heart of the country, the north-east and south are sparsely populated. About 33 per cent of the population lives in urban areas when only 20 years ago the figure was closer to 20 per cent. In particular, Kinshasa shows all the signs of too rapid growth and its associated problems of shanty development and pressure on urban services. The scattered nature of the population and its ethno-cultural diversity (there are 69 main tribal groups) does not encourage national unity, and this has been reinforced by the great distances between the fragmented pockets of economic activity and the concentration of a disproportionate share of wealth generation in the Shaba province.

THE PHYSICAL BACKGROUND

Although very large, the country has a certain compactness and simplicity deriving from the Zaire river itself and a vast depression in the continental interior upon which it is centred. The present middle-Zaire and Lualaba basin represents a former lake area. The average elevation of the central depression is 300–500 m, and the land tends to rise through a series of

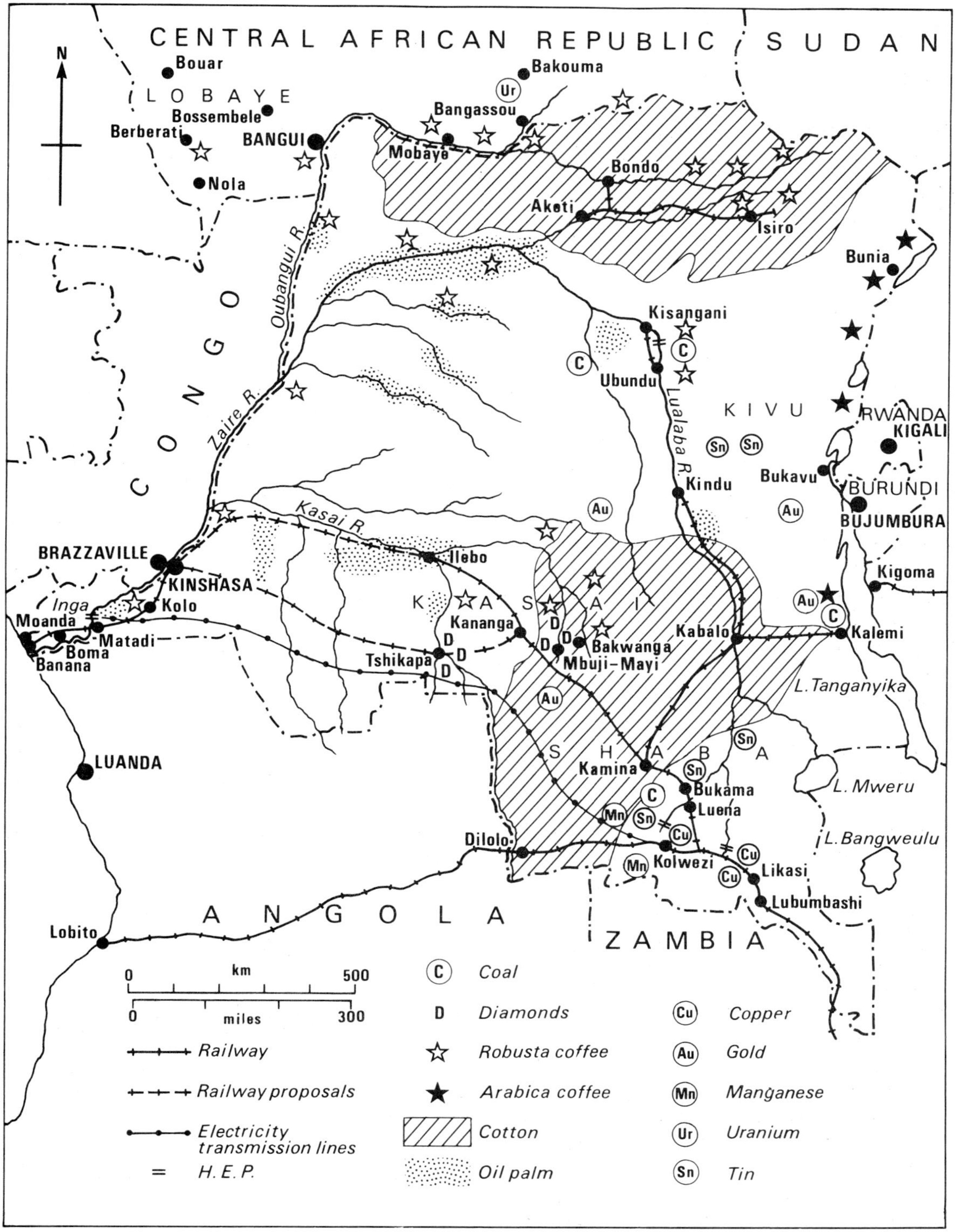

Figure 72 Zaire

plateau steps towards the margins, reaching elevations of 700 m in the north-east and 900–1200 m in Shaba and Kivu. In the latter area, on the faulted margins of the rift system, individual peaks of over 3000 m are found. In the south and south-east, including Shaba, there is an area of block faulting and fracturing with depressions marked by lakes Bangweulu and Mweru and the Lualaba river north of Bukama (see Figure 72).

To the west the Zaire river breaks through the continental upland rim in the Mayoumba mountains and produces the spectacular Inga rapids. The breaks of slope between the plateau surfaces and between the faulted blocks of the south-east interrupt the profiles of many of the rivers and have the disadvantage of impeding navigation and the advantage of providing potential sites for hydroelectric power.

The central depression is floored with the weak Lubilash lacustrine sedimentaries and recent alluvium. Surrounding this, almost as an aureole, there is a ring – wider in the south and east and narrower in the north and west – of continental sedimentaries of Cretaceous –Jurassic age, with some low-grade coal. The north-east, east, south-east and coastal Mayoumba region comprise Pre-Cambrian crystallines with high levels of mineralization. Gold and manganese are found in the oldest Pre-Cambrians, the Middle Pre-Cambrians of the east centre are associated with tin, tungsten and related minerals, and the Katanga series of the Upper Pre-Cambrian in Shaba province is a source of copper, cobalt, zinc, lead, silver, cadmium and nickel.

Zaire lies asymmetrically astride the equator, extending from 5°N to 13°S. The temperature regime is in places modified by altitude, and the diurnal and seasonal range will here be higher. In June and July the plateau of Shaba has what might even be termed a cool season. There are large areas along the equator where the rainfall exceeds 2000 mm, is fairly evenly distributed throughout the year and where convection is the main generator of the rainfall. Kisangani has no month with less than 50 mm and 9 months in excess of 100 mm.

This zone of equatorial type climate is bounded to the north by a narrow, and to the south by a much wider, belt with more marked double peaking and rather lower rainfall totals of 1500–1700 mm. In southern Shaba there is a well-defined dry season of 5–6 months and a single rainfall peak – January to March – and rainfall totals of less than 1250 mm. The much lower rainfall of the coastal region (about 750 mm) is largely the result of stabilized air over cooler off-shore waters associated with the Benguela current.

As much as 40 per cent of Zaire is forested with either swamp, lowland or montane varieties. The asymmetrical disposition about the equator means that there is gradual transition from this forest, both north and south, to forest–savanna mosaic, and to the south there is also a zone of wooded savanna and areas of grass steppe.

The best soils are flood plain alluviums along the numerous water-courses, the restricted volcanic soils of the Kivu highlands of the eastern margin and some soils derived from erosion in the Mayoumba and lower Zaire region. Over much of the country soils are severely leached, and there are considerable areas of laterization which support only sparse tufted grasses.

It will be clear from the foregoing that the best soils and mineral resources tend to be in peripheral areas, and this goes some way towards explaining the distribution of population already outlined and the problems of initiating and maintaining economic activity.

THE ECONOMY

Agriculture

Although there were strenuous efforts by Belgian colonial administrators to extend cash-crop farming, there is evidence to suggest that in the troubled time since independence there has been reversion to subsistence cultivation. This has been stimulated by rural depopulation, reduced spending power, inadequate transport and a general decline of the rural marketing system. Certainly, the government has neglected agriculture in favour of mining and manufacture.

Cassava is by far the most important food crop; but after 1970 yields were adversely affected by the rapid spread of blight in the eastern parts of the country and there has been little success in getting more resistant strains into the area. Plantain, maize and rice are the other main food crops, but there has been little or no effort put into the introduction of higher yielding varieties. There had been some attempt by the Belgians to concentrate settlement on cleared strips of land with a prescribed rotation of food and cash crops, but this never affected more than about 200,000 out of over 2 million families. Food products have been an increasing proportion of the import bill, and since the mid-1970s these have accounted for about 50 per cent of the value of consumer-good imports. The list is headed by fish, rice, wheat, maize, dairy products, beef, fruit and vegetables – most of which could be produced locally.

The country's main cash crops are coffee, rubber, palm produce, cotton, tea and cocoa, and these are produced in variable proportions by African farmers, large plantations and individual European farmers – but with a considerable reduction in the importance of the latter group since 1960. Coffee has been the main agricultural export in recent years (Table 30), being 85 per cent of the robusta variety used in the production of instant coffee and 15 per cent of the better-quality arabica. The arabica is almost entirely a European farm crop from the highland area of the east. Some soluble coffee is manufactured locally, but the bulk of the crop is exported as beans. The export quantity is limited by an International Coffee Agreement quota and the production capacity is thought to be under-utilized and not well-maintained. Transport problems add to the export price of the coffee.

The oil-palm is indigenous to tropical Africa and tolerant of a wide range of conditions; it is grown on about 200,000 ha, one-third of which is in the hands of African farmers. However, three-quarters of the output and the bulk of the exports derive from large European plantations. Unilever had 12 plantations and African producers tend to concentrate around the plantation to benefit from the infrastructure and processing facilities. There is industrial processing of palm-oil at Kinshasa, Kolo, Matadi, Boma and Lubumbashi. Production in 1982 was 160,000 tonnes; however, the government requires 50 per cent of the crop to be sold locally at controlled prices, and exports have declined. Much of the production is close to, and initial oil-pressing located along, the rivers which provide the main means of transport for this commodity. When one notes the importance of palm produce to the Malaysian economy, there can be no doubting that Zaire has neglected what could be a far more significant source of income.

Cotton was introduced in the early part of the First World War as a compulsory cash crop for African farmers, and it is still produced almost entirely by them in two zones, one to the north and the other to the south of the forest. Zaire therefore has the advantage of a twice-yearly harvest; but production was

Table 30 *Zaire: principal exports (percentages of total value)*

	1959	*1970*	*1980*
Coffee			8
Palm produce		5	1
Rubber		2	
All agriculture	40	14	12
Copper	32	69	46
Cobalt	6	7	21
Diamonds	7	5	4
Other minerals	15	5	7
Oil	—	—	10
All minerals	60	86	88

Source: UN Statistics, *Africa Research Bulletin*.

badly disrupted by the post-independence crisis and fell from 147,000 tonnes in 1956 to 41,000 in 1968. Until 1972 most of the crop was purchased on behalf of Belgian firms, but the government then established its own purchasing, collecting and ginning organization. Delays in the payment of farmers and disruptions to transport have resulted in stagnant or even declining production. A textile industry was first established in 1928 and was expanded in the 1960s. This has contributed to the decline in the export of raw cotton.

For long rubber was tapped from wild trees, but 90 per cent of the production is now from large plantations concentrated in the Mayoumba and middle Zaire river regions, again often close to the rivers for ease of transport. Rubber exports increased from 1000 tonnes in 1938 to 40,000 in 1959, but production in 1982 was reported to be only 28,000 tonnes. Cash crops of lesser importance include tea, cocoa, bananas, tobacco, sugar, cinchona (for quinine) and pyrethrum, and there is some processing industry related to these crops (e.g. cigarette factories at Kinshasa, Kisangani and Lubumbashi).

Zaire is seriously protein-deficient. Tsetse fly infection is endemic in the equatorial region, but on the highland margins cattle are kept by traditional herders and on European ranches in Kivu and the higher plateau of Kasai-Shaba. On balance, animal husbandry is not well developed, and over 50 per cent of meat requirements have to be met by imports. With its vast network of rivers and lakes supplemented by smaller fish ponds, fish production potential has been estimated at 260,000 tonnes a year. The actual catch is less than half this and fish products make up the largest food import in terms of value. With its diminutive coastline and few ports, there is only limited scope for extending sea fisheries; but that from inland waterways could receive much greater attention.

Perhaps surprisingly in view of the vast forested area, Zaire has never been a major timber producer. Indeed, the forest resources have never been fully evaluated. This must largely reflect the serious inadequacy of the transport system and the local absorption of the bulk of the 500,000 m^3 produced annually. There are a number of saw-mills and some production of plywood and veneer, but proposals for a cellulose and paper industry have yet to be implemented. Again, the forests represent a resource which is grossly underutilized and where there is considerable scope for integrated developments.

It emerges clearly that agriculture's relative contribution to exports has declined sharply over the 25 years since independence and, as already suggested, there are areas of agricultural production in which the decline has been absolute as well as relative.

Mining

The richness of Zaire's mineral resources has already been noted. Some mining started in Shaba (then Katanga) in 1906; but it was the extension of the railway northwards from Northern Rhodesia, now Zambia, in 1910 which really stimulated investment, principally by the joint Belgian–British combine, Union Minière du Haut Katanga. Copper has always been the principal mineral and presently accounts for 55 per cent of Zaire's exports. The mineralized zone is an extension of the Zambian 'copper belt', and mining is by the open-cast method for the oxidized ore (6 – 8 per cent copper) and underground for the 4 per cent copper sulphide ore. There are seven concentrating plants and electrolytic smelters at Lubumbashi, Shitwu, Luila and Kolwezi. A number of hydroelectric power generating stations have been built to serve the mines and mineral processing plant.

Union Minière was nationalized, and since 1967 the state-owned Gecamines has controlled the bulk of the mining. The other main producer is a Japanese consortium with 15 per cent Zairois interest. Copper output increased from 317,000 tonnes in 1966 to 417,000 in 1972 and with fluctuations reached 425,700 tonnes in 1982.

Zaire produces about 60 per cent of the

Plate 38 Rail–river integration is a necessary feature of the Zaire transport system

world's cobalt, and an export of about 15,000 tonnes a year accounts for over 20 per cent of the total value of exports. From Shaba there are also less significant quantities of zinc, lead and manganese, and some poor coal from Luena.

Zaire is the second world producer of industrial diamonds. The main source areas are alluvial deposits around Tshikapa on the Kasai river (mainly gem grade) and Bakwanga on the Bushimaie river (mainly industrial grade). In 1983 a new dredge started operations on the Mbujimayi alluvial flats. Annual production fluctuates around 10 million carats; but this is now well down on the peak of 18 million in 1961 as a consequence of high costs, inadequate maintenance of equipment, exhaustion of some deposits and a dramatic level of smuggling. At one kimberlite deposit at Mbujimayi there is an estimated 170 million carats waiting for the finance that will allow deep mining to commence.

Oil is now produced in modest quantities from offshore fields, and a refinery of 1.3 million tonnes capacity has been built at Moanda.

In addition there is bauxite mining in Mayoumba and a range of other minerals waiting to be exploited. However, low copper and other mineral prices in recent years, and vast increases in imports, have forced the economy into serious deficit and a series of 'rescue' operations have been mounted.

Industrial development

The vast distances, inconvenience of transhipment and high cost of transport encouraged the local initial processing of both agricultural and mineral products. Agro-industries include sugar refining, palm-oil mills, a margarine factory, flour mills, cotton textiles, canvas, sacks, cigarettes, soap, tyres, and drinks. Mining has led to copper refining, rolling and milling, castings in copper, bronze and brass. During the 1950s and 1960s a range of import-substitution industries were started, including matches, hoes and machettes, metal drums, paraffin stoves, shoes and cycle and vehicle assembly.

There was also an attempt to maximize local production of construction materials such as cement, asbestos cement, paint and varnish. Apart from the refining of metals, the mining industry encouraged production of sulphuric acid, oxygen, acetylene and explosives.

Zaire has always had a liberal investment code and has a wider range of industries than most African countries. Nevertheless, manufacturing provides employment for only 60,000 and contributes a mere 5 per cent of the GDP. The pace of industrialization has certainly slowed down as all the easy import substitution has taken place and the processing of local raw materials is now reasonably well advanced. The industry is heavily concentrated in the Shaba region and around Kinshasa, the capital, but with lesser concentration at centres such as Kisangani, Matadi and Kananga.

Economic infrastructure

Two main impediments to more rapid development have undoubtedly been shortage of energy and the serious inadequacy of the transport system.

Although not the region best suited to hydroelectric power development, Shaba's metal-refining industries required cheap electricity, and this has been provided mainly by modest-size HEP plant at Marinel and Delcommune on the Lualaba river and at Francqui and Bia on the Lufira. Shaba accounts for 75 per cent of the national electricity consumption. However, it has been estimated that Zaire has 10 per cent of the world HEP potential, and at one site – Inga betwen Kinshasa and Matadi on the Zaire river – a potential of 30,000 MW, or the equivalent of 40 per cent of the United Kingdom's installed capacity.

The first phase of a long-term project to harness the Inga rapids, to produce a 350 MW plant, was completed in 1973; but with the main demand located in Shaba it has been necessary to construct a 1820 km transmission line carried on 8500 pylons across difficult terrain at a cost of $240 million. Completion was delayed until 1980 by problems of finance, shortage of fuel, equipment and spare parts and the need to build access and service roads before construction could start. The transmission line does not even provide electricity to the regions through which it passes. It is certainly not the case that HEP is necessarily cheap electricity.

Zaire has small offshore oilfields and a refinery, but as with the electricity, it is more a question of distribution and the geographical matching of supply with demand. Plans to utilize electricity from Inga for aluminium smelting at Banana, near the mouth of the Zaire river, have yet to be implemented.

The explorer, H.M. Stanley, originally proposed sections of railway to link navigable sections of river, and the first link – that from Kinshasa to Matadi, by-passing Inga and other rapids on the lower Zaire – was completed in 1898 and eventually a river/rail route was opened from Shaba to the sea. The Rhodesian railway reached Lubumbashi (then Elizabethville) in 1910 and was extended to Bukama in 1919. The direct rail link from Shaba through Angola to the sea at Lobito, the Benguela Railway, was completed in 1931 and provides Shaba with its most direct link to the sea.

However, Shaba has several alternative routes. First, although the Benguela Railway is the shortest route and avoids transhipment, it was closed for most of the 1970s and is vulnerable to disruption as a result of Angolan domestic politics and conflict. Second, the Matadi routes have the advantage of being entirely within Zaire but involve river and rail transhipment, either by way of Kabalo and Kisangani or Kananga and Ilebo. Third, the Beira route does not involve transhipment but is subject to the political uncertainties which plague southern Africa. Finally, the Dar-es-Salaam route involves transhipment at Kalemi and Kigoma.

In 1981 the transit times were 30 days to Matadi, 29 days to East London, 49 days to Lobito and 96 days to Dar-es-Salaam, to which had to be added port waiting times averaging 54, 31, 83 and 62 days respectively. Goods in transit for such long periods are vulnerable to damage and theft and create cash-flow problems for the firms involved. For much of its external trade, Zaire is effectively a landlocked country, dependent on neighbours for transit of goods and disadvantaged by high transport costs.

Matadi, the country's principal port, is in a constricted site up-river from a large whirlpool, with little scope for real expansion of its present limited capacity and a poor operating record. For this reason new port facilities are being constructed at Banana on the north side of the Zaire river mouth, and in 1983 a bridge was completed across the river at Matadi to improve access to Banana. Initially this is for road traffic, but with the possibility of rail tracks on a lower deck so that the railway can eventually be extended to the new port.

Zaire has over 14,500 km of navigable waterway, and the importance of this as a factor influencing the location of agricultural production and processing has been noted. The system can be used by 800-tonne vessels over 2700 km (Kinshasa to Kisangani and

Ilebo) and a variety of push–tow and self-propelled craft are in use. There is the need for additional beacons to allow round-the-clock navigation, and river ports need improvement. While there is certainly scope for increasing the capacity of waterway transport, it is inevitably slow and involves costly trans-shipment.

Although the country has 145,000 km of roads, very few are surfaced and maintenance has been negligible, so that the usable system could be as little as 10,000 km. It is clear that the whole transport system needs urgent rehabilitation and then extension if the country's undoubtedly considerable development potential is to be realized. As it is, the transport network makes economic integration and even national unity impossible to achieve. Not without justice Zaire has been called a 'sleeping giant'. The sleep has been troubled with nightmares but there is always the hope that these may become dreams.

RWANDA AND BURUNDI

Formerly parts of German East Africa, Rwanda and Burundi were administered as mandated territories by Belgium after 1919 and until independence in 1962 were closely linked with the Belgian Congo, now Zaire. With areas of 26,338 km^2 and 28,000 km^2, Rwanda and Burundi are among Africa's smallest nations, but with populations of 5.7 and 4.5 million (1983 estimates) are more densely populated (216 and 161 people per km^2) than all other African countries.

Both countries may be divided into three physical regions, running from north to south. In the west there is the rift valley floor, containing lakes Kivu and Tanganyika, connected by the Ruzizi river valley. Rising sharply along the east of the rift are high mountains, reaching 2500–2750 m in many places and 4250 m in northern Rwanda, where there are volcanoes, two of them active. East of the mountain crest the land drops more gently towards Uganda and north-western Tanzania; there are extensive plateaux at 1500–1800 m, with rivers such as the Kagera draining to Lake Victoria. Although small, the countries have varied landscapes and attractive scenery.

As only about two-fifths of the land can be cropped, the amount of cultivated land works out at no more than 0.5 ha per person. In such overcrowded conditions it is not surprising that many areas are suffering severely from soil erosion and overgrazing. Most of the cultivation is undertaken by the Bahutu, and their main food crops are cassava, plantains, beans and sweet potatoes. The rich volcanic soils sustain the main cash crop of coffee, which occupies about 40,000 ha. Cotton and oil-palms are cultivated in the rift valley lowlands. Cattle are the main concern of the Watutsi, the tall pastoral people who invaded the area some four centuries ago. Cattle, reckoned as a form of wealth, are kept in large numbers, giving rise to serious overgrazing. Except in the rift valley lowlands there are practically no tsetse flies, but the cattle are of little commercial value and use land that could often better be devoted to crops.

In each territory the minority cattle-owning Watutsi group has assumed dominance over the much larger group of Bahutu cultivators, and both before and since independence there have been periods of serious conflict between the two. Because of the overcrowding on the land and lack of employment opportunities there has traditionally been out-migration, sometimes seasonal to neighbouring states (especially Uganda). With its own problems in recent years, Uganda has been less welcoming to such migrants.

It could be said of both countries that the main impediments to development are the high population densities, their distances from the sea and their land-locked locations.

Rwanda

The rugged, dissected terrain, steep slopes and generally poor soils – except where they are volcanic in origin – do not favour cultivation, and soil erosion is widespread. Arable land accounts for some 700,000 ha, with permanent crops totalling 250,000 ha. The main local food crops are plantains, sweet potatoes, cassava and maize, and the principal cash crops found largely on the better volcanic soils are coffee, tea, pyrethrum and cinchona. Coffee accounts for about 65 per cent of the value of exports and tea about 10 per cent.

Mining provides the second most important export, with tin and tungsten accounting for about 25 per cent of the exports. The country has a small tin foundry, and other industries are largely concerned with processing of agricultural commodities (coffee, tea, sugar) and some import substitutes in brewing, chemicals, plastics, engineering and textiles. An impediment to industrialization has undoubtedly been the lack of electricity, and to supplement a small hydroelectric plant at Ntaruka and Gisenyi about one-half of the electricity consumed was imported from Zaire. However, a recently completed HEP plant at Mukungwa should reduce this need to import.

About 90 per cent of the trade is through Tanzania to the port of Dar-es-Salaam, with smaller amounts through Uganda and Kenya to Mombasa and through Zaire to Matadi. The road links with Uganda and Tanzania are now surfaced, but the Uganda link has on occasions been closed by the Ugandan government. All these routes to the sea are lengthy and add greatly to the cost of imports.

A development plan (1977–81) aimed to reduce the drift of population to the towns (the capital, Kigali, is now 120,000) and regroup rural populations in more sparsely occupied areas in the east of the country and in marshy valley areas, where there was to be intensive sugar and rice cultivation. For the latter, Chinese technical assistance was obtained. In the Mutara region there were plans for collective ranching and a proposed dam and HEP station at Kitembi was to eliminate electricity imports.

As a member of the Economic Commission of Great Lakes Countries (Burundi is also a member), there are plans for the cooperative improvement of transport and the development of fisheries and natural gas resources.

Burundi

About 85 per cent of the population is supported by agriculture. For most this is not much beyond the subsistence level, and average per capita income is only $240 ($270 in Rwanda). The main food crops are cassava, sweet potatoes, bananas and beans, and the money economy is dominated by coffee, cotton and tea.

Coffee brings in about 85 per cent of the foreign exchange: in 1983 the crop amounted to 32,650 tonnes of higher grade arabica and 1365 tonnes of robusta. However, Burundi still failed to meet its international coffee agreement quota of 27,000 tonnes, largely as a consequence of problems in getting the crop to the ports in East Africa. Two recently built coffee-processing plants, at the capital Bujumbura and at Gitega, are able to process the whole crop, and this adds to the value for export.

Both the area devoted to cotton and the output have declined in recent years: in 1983 only 4737 tonnes was exported, about 6 per cent of the export earnings. The country is able to produce high-quality tea, but at around 2000 tonnes a year the quantity is small and there has been EEC aid for increasing the area under plantation cultivation at Teza, Rwegura and Muramvya.

In the five-year plan of 1978–82 an integrated rural development project was initiated on the Imbo plain, and this involved land reclamation for the cultivation of cotton and rice. An irrigated rice project was also started in the Mosso region. These were clearly responses to the drought that had adversely affected crop production and caused serious food shortages. Burundi embarked on a fourth 5-year plan in 1983, but the proposed emphasis on a restructuring of rural populations into villages on the lines of Tanzania's 'ujaama' pattern has not been favourably received by the overseas aid donors who are expected to provide 56 per cent of the planned investment.

Industry is poorly developed and consists mainly of first-phase processing of cotton, coffee and tea, vegetable-oil extraction, some saw-milling, cement, insecticides, footwear and clothing industries. Industry suffers from the remoteness of the country and the small local market. In the early 1970s a United Nations sponsored survey identified a very large nickel deposit at Musongati, but nothing has yet been done to exploit this, possibly because of the heavy investment that would be required. There is still hope of exploitable oil beneath the waters of Lake Tanganyika and the Ruzizi Plain.

The country has a dense road network, but only 200 km of the 6000 km of main route is surfaced – the roads from the capital, Bujumbura, to Gitega and Kayanga. Transport costs add greatly to costs. Coffee tends to be exported by the slow but cheaper route by way of lake Tanganyika to Kigoma and thence through Tanzania to Dar-es-Salaam. When open to it, the more perishable tea goes by way of the higher-cost but rather faster route through Rwanda, Uganda and Kenya to Mombasa. Some traffic crosses Lake Tanganyika into Zaire, another very slow route.

Population is increasing at 2.9 per cent a year whereas agricultural growth has been nearer 2.0 per cent. There is, therefore, an increasing food deficit and food shortages. There is no immediate prospect of the sort of income that would allow any real development to take place and the prospects for Burundi are not bright.

PART SEVEN: SOUTH-WESTERN AFRICA

29
The physical framework

Two major physiographic elements provide a basis for treating Angola, Namibia and Botswana as a regional entity – the Kalahari basin and the line of uplands extending southwards from Angola into Namibia. However, much of northern Angola falls strictly within the Zaire basin, while parts of the Kalahari are within the upper Zambezi catchment (Figure 85).

The belt of highland extending from the lower Orange river northwards through Angola largely comprises Pre-Cambrian granites and gneisses, with some later sedimentaries of Karroo age in eastern Namaqualand and north-eastern Angola. Eastwards the bedrock dips beneath the Kalahari sands, which have a depth of 90 m in places and probably derive from wind-distributed, weathered Karroo sandstone. The coastal zone is partially underlain with Cretaceous and Tertiary marine sediments which have a maximum width in the Lobito–Luanda area. A number of distinct regions can be identified.

PHYSICAL REGIONS

The coastlands

Lying mainly below 450 m, the coastlands are broadest in the north, 200 km at Luanda, but narrow southwards. Between the Orange and Cunene rivers is the extremely arid Namib desert with no permanent water-courses, while between the Cunene and Catumbula there are no perennial rivers of any size.

The subsiding mT air and stabilizing effect of the cool Benguela current means that in the Namib the rainfall is negligible, and in no coastal location south of Moçâmedes does it exceed 75 mm a year. Walvis Bay has a mere 7.5 mm average rainfall but more than 50 days of coastal fog. The cooling effect of the Benguela current decreases north of Moçâmedes, fog is less frequent and rainfall increases to 330 mm at Luanda and 680 mm at the mouth of the Zaire.

Most of the rain occurs between November and April but is highly variable as a consequence of the unpredictable distance of the inter-tropical convergence from the coast which it parallels.

In the drier coastal areas and on the lower foothills to the east a poor scrub vegetation is found, but southwards from Moçâmedes true desert conditions prevail with some acacias able to survive on moisture from mist and occasional drizzle or along intermittent watercourses.

The highlands

A belt of highland, bounded on its western margin by an often spectacular scarp feature, extends from southern Namibia to northern Angola (Figure 73) and comprises a series of mountains and plateaux.

In the south, gently dipping quartzite and limestone give extensive plateaux, but north of Windhoek the Khomas highlands rise to 2500 m in rugged terrain. Over large areas the elevation exceeds 1500 m, dropping eastwards to 900 m on the Kalahari margins. In the Otavi highlands, granite–gneiss produces a lower, more uniform surface with inselbergs which also drops more gradually westwards

Table 31 *South-western Africa: temperature and rainfall selected stations*

Station	*Altitude (m)*		*J*	F	M	A	M	*J*	*J*	A	S	O	N	D	*Year*
Luanda	58	T	25.5	26.8	26.8	26.8	25.0	22.2	20.5	19.9	21.6	23.9	25.0	25.5	24.4
		R	25	36	76	116	13	2	2	2	2	4	27	21	326
Moçâmedes	3	T	22.2	23.9	24.4	23.3	19.9	17.7	16.1	16.6	17.2	19.4	20.5	21.0	19.9
		R	7	10	17	13	2	2	2	2	2	2	2	2	63
Windhoek	1700	T	23.3	22.2	20.5	18.8	15.6	13.2	12.7	15.6	18.3	21.6	21.6	23.3	18.8
		R	76	74	78	40	9	2	2	2	2	11	23	49	268
Francistown	1080	T	24.4	23.9	22.8	21.0	17.2	13.8	14.3	16.6	21.0	24.4	25.0	24.4	20.5
		R	106	78	71	9	4	2	2	2	2	23	55	88	442

Notes: T = Temperature (°C); R = rainfall (mm).

to the Namib coastlands.

In southern Angola the Sierra de Chela, broken by the Cunene and Caroca valleys, continues the line of the Namibian highlands. The Pre-Cambrian quartzites of the Humpata plateau around Sã da Bandeira give heights of over 2250 m, and much of the Bié plateau lies between 1500 and 1800 m. The westward-facing scarp is still well marked, and to effect a crossing the Benguela Railway has to rise to 1851 m in its route from Lobito to southern Zaire. In northern Angola the Luanda uplands have a maximum elevation of 1493 m, over large areas average 450–1000 m, and are divided by numerous broad valleys. Here the escarpment has been virtually eliminated and the Atlantic–Zaire watershed pushed back some 480 km from the coast by rivers such as the Cuanza.

The highlands have better rainfall than the coastal zone, but there is the same general increase from south to north – Windhoek has 355 mm, the Bié plateau 1400 mm and Carmona 1850 mm. Temperatures are modified by the altitude so that the Bié plateau is cool considering it is only 13° from the equator. The annual range of temperature is higher in the south (Windhoek 11°C) than in the north (Caconda 6°C) (see Table 31).

There are limited areas of montane vegetation in the highest areas; but over much of the southern highlands savanna-grassland prevails, while in the Bié and Humpata uplands, open grassland with patches of woodland is characteristic. In northern Angola, especially on the western slopes of the upland and along valleys, the forest canopy thickens considerably and there are areas of true rain forest.

The Kalahari basin

Extending from the Orange river to the headstreams of the Zambezi, the Kalahari occupies the heart of southern Africa, and with an average elevation of 900 m it is best described as a plateau. The superficial sands which cover much of the basin are fixed by grass and scrub vegetation rather than being mobile. Much of the surface lacks drainage, but permanent streams with origins outside the area do traverse it – the Cunene in the north-west, the Cuando and upper Zambezi in the north-east, and the Orange. Three major interior drainage basins can be identified: the small Etoshi Pan in the north of Namibia, and the far more extensive Okavango–Makarikari in the north-east and the Molopo–Nossob system in the south. It would seem that the latter once drained into the Orange but under present climatic conditions with low rainfall is unable to do so. The Okavango basin draws water from areas with rainfall in excess of 1250 mm, but a flow of 13 thousand million cubic metres at the Botswana border is rapidly lost by high evaporation from the numerous reed-choked channels into which it divides in the 'swamp' area. Excess water now drains into Lake Dow, with flood overflow into the Makarikari depression. On Botswana's northern border is another marshy area along the line of the Linyanti river (the Cuando in Angola) which now drains into the Zambezi.

The rainfall averages 125 mm in the south but increases to over 500 mm in the north. The rainfall is highly variable and occurs mainly as thunderstorms in summer months. The effective moisture is low and drought often prolonged. The natural vegetation varies from poor grassland in the south, through an extensive area of mixed thorn forest and coarse grass with acacias, to open Mopani and Brachystegia woodland in the north. Smaller, variable areas around Okavango and Linyanti are occupied by swamp vegetation, and open grassland of moderate value for pastoral activity is found in depressions of Barotseland, Etosha and Makarikari.

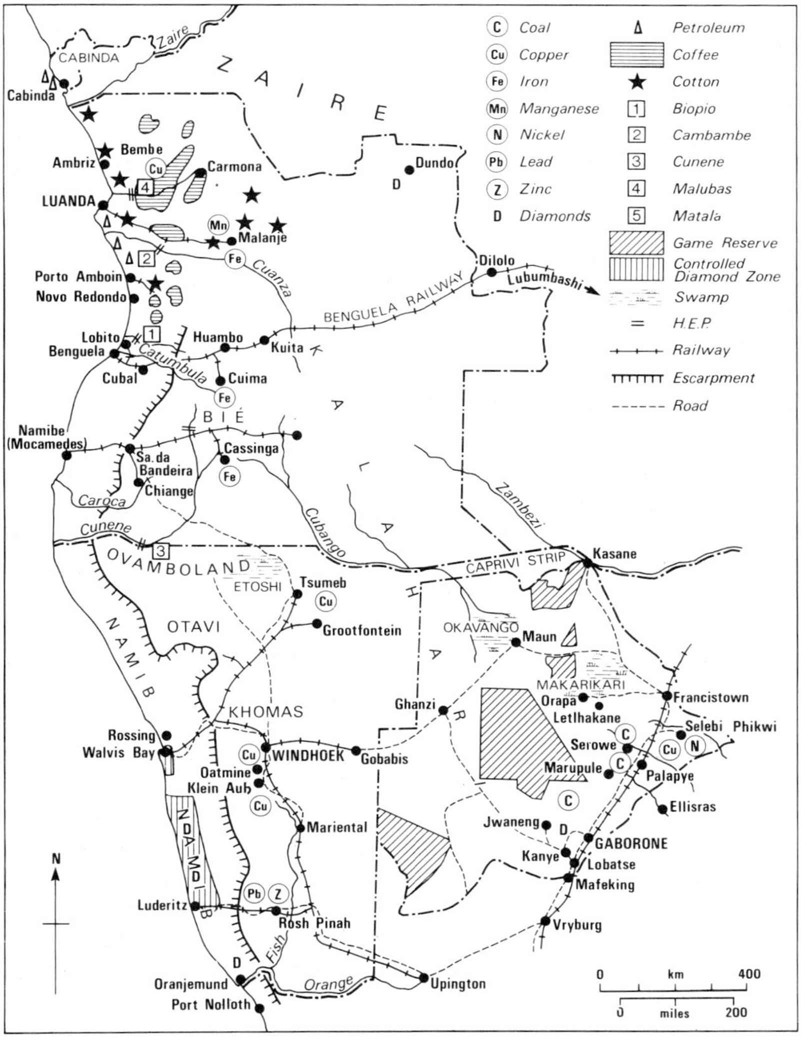

Figure 73 South-western Africa

30
Angola, Namibia and Botswana

ANGOLA

With an area of 1,247,000 km², Angola is Africa's sixth largest country; but its population density, while higher than that of the other south-west African states, is still only 6.6 people per km² and is modest in relation to the country's resource endowment.

The Angolan coastline was first explored by the Portuguese in 1482–3, and Luanda, which was to become the capital, was founded in 1575 and Benguela in 1615. The present low population density is to be explained in large part by over three centuries of intensive slave trading on this section of coast, Brazil being a principal destination. The Portuguese gradually consolidated their authority in the coastal areas by military conquest, obtained right of occupation after 1884–5, and the present boundaries were established in the 1890s. However, the interior was secured only by military pacification, which continued until the 1920s and led to the establishment of Portuguese settlements such as Nova Lisboa, Silva Porto and Sã da Bandeira, mainly on the Bié and Luanda uplands which provided the best conditions for Europeans.

To the Portuguese, Angola was not a 'colony' but an overseas province of Portugal itself, and about 300,000 whites, many of them poor farmers, were settled there. On the basis of education, blacks could achieve 'assimilado' and citizen status and theoretical equality with whites; but when independence was finally forced from Portugal in 1975 after many years of warfare, 85 per cent of the population was still illiterate and the remaining 15 per cent had little in the way of modern skills. For most of the time since independence the country has suffered from civil war between the Cuban-supported Marxist government party, the MPLA, and the South African-backed UNITA group. The actual development of the economy in relation to its potential must be understood against this background of centuries of military conflict and Portugal's own position as one of Europe's poorest nations.

Agriculture

Only 3 per cent of the possible arable land is under cultivation, and 80 per cent of the population is dependent essentially on subsistence agriculture. Cassava is the main food crop, followed by maize, a small surplus of which is exported. Although some Africans became involved in the production of cash crops their activity in this was marginal and often dependent upon European plantations, some on an industrial scale but many much smaller.

Coffee was introduced around Luanda in the 1830s and gradually spread into many parts of northern Angola where the rainfall is in excess of 1250 mm. Four-fifths of the production is from north of the Cuenza river, mainly from upland areas at altitudes between 300 and 900 m, but some plantations are at higher altitudes (Figure 73). Traditionally, about two-thirds of the coffee came from company plantations and small European farms and the rest from African smallholdings. After 1945 there was rapid expansion of production, which rose from an average of 49,000 tonnes a year for 1946–51 to over 200,000 tonnes in 1969. The bulk of the production is of good-grade robusta, but Angola has been required to restrict production to conform with quotas imposed by the International Coffee Agreement. Production was greatly disrupted by the revolt of the 1960s and by the abandonment of many Portuguese farms at independence. However, coffee played an important part in stimulating the development of the infrastructure (roads, and ports such as Ambriz, Ambrizete, Porto Amboin and Novo Redondo) and settlement growth (e.g. at Luanda and Carmona). In the late 1960s coffee provided one-third of the value of exports, but since that time has declined in relative importance.

Cotton, sisal and maize each provide about 2.5 per cent of the value of exports. Medium staple cotton was introduced by European concessionaires and taken up by about 60,000 African farmers for whom forced cultivation was only abolished in 1961, and they were largely dependent on the Europeans for seed, marketing, spinning and transport. The main areas of cultivation are along the coast in the north and along the line of the Luanda–Malanje railway. Cubal on the Benguela railway is the main centre of sisal production from European plantations, which at a peak amounted to 120,000 ha. Maize is essentially a crop from African farms, mainly along the line of the Benguela railway. Oil-palm is found in small plantations, especially in the northern coastal area, and sugar along the lower Dande and Cuanza valleys. Tobacco, groundnuts, sesame, wheat, beans, peas and arabica coffee are also grown in small quantities on the Benguela plateau.

South of the Benguela railway tsetse fly infection decreases and animal husbandry increases in importance, the most significant area being the south-west Angolan plateau from the railway to Vila Pereira d'Eca. Improved water supplies have been developed to encourage African involvement in animal husbandry, but this is not fully commercialized. Some European ranches provide cattle for abattoirs and meat processing plants at Sã da Bandeira and Moçâmedes. Of less importance is the area around Nova Lisboa where there is also an animal products factory.The industry suffers from the generally poor quality of the pastures.

Timber production has always been important in the Cabinda enclave, which in a geographical sense bears comparison with the Congo rather than the rest of Angola. Rainfall here exceeds 1500 mm and forest covers 84 per cent of the area. Extensive forest exploitation came only after 1945, and in the late 1960s timber accounted for about 3.5 per cent of Angola's exports. Some eucalyptus and cypress plantations have been developed in the Benguela region, both for fuel wood and as a basis for pulp and paper processing.

Fishing is important at many points along the coast. The cool Benguela current and fairly wide continental shelf favour the industry, but it is only since the 1960s that modern trawler fishing has been developed. Traditionally undertaken by the Portuguese, the fishing is mainly by unsophisticated methods and the catch is sun-dried or passed on to larger collecting and processing centres such as Moçâmedes, Benguela and Lobito. Fish meal and oil comprise over 75 per cent of the sales, the rest being canned and fresh fish.

Mining

Mineral resources have provided an increasingly important share of exports and some 30 commercial minerals are known to exist. Diamonds, both gem and industrial grades, have been mined at alluvial workings in the north-east at Dundo since 1917. The civil war and smuggling led to a dramatic decline in exports in the mid-1970s; but even with recent revival the 1 million carats of 1983 was only half that of 1974. The Lobito Mineral Company started mining iron-ore at Cuima in 1956 and in 1962 was linked by a 65 km branch line to the Benguela railway. During the 1960s iron-ore was exported from Cuima, Texeira da Silva and Andulo in the Huambo and Bié districts. In the late 1960s a much larger, higher-grade haematite deposit was opened up at Cassinga, 500 km from Moçâmedes, a branch line was built to the Moçâmedes–Serpa Pinto railway, and the ore exported from Moçâmedes. Peak production of over 5 million tonnes was attained in 1974. Manganese is mined in small quantities in the Malanje area and copper is mined and smelted at Bomba. Other minerals are present but exploitation depends upon the outcome of the current civil war.

Oil now seems to offer the best base for future development. First discovered on the coastal plain south of Luanda in the mid-1950s, there has been continuous exploitation in, and production from, this area and a small refinery was built at Luanda. Oil was first struck offshore from Cabinda in 1966, and this has since been the main focus of production, with about 65 per cent of the total. Output attained 12.7 million tonnes in 1985, making Angola the second largest producer in sub-Saharan Africa after Nigeria. Although not major by world standards, oil production is now by far the most important export (75 per cent in 1982).

For a long time metropolitan Portugal's hold on the economy restricted the development of manufacturing to the finishing of Portuguese semi-manufactures; but there was an increase in the rate of industrialization in the 1960s, and, by 1970, 12 per cent of the exports comprised processed products. The best-developed industries are those involved in food processing, but there has been some diversification into textiles, chemicals, glass, paper, tyres, cement and bicycle and vehicle assembly. This industry was almost entirely concentrated at Luanda but with minor developments at Lobito and Malanje.

Development planning

Until 1975 the development of Angola was very much a by-product of metropolitan Portugal's policies, and in particular the settlement of population from the home country. Two 6-year plans initiated in 1953 put emphasis on agricultural settlement schemes for poor Portuguese farmers, the principal location being at Cela, east of Novo Redondo and Matola on the Cunene river. The former was designed to provide farms of about 60 ha with a mixture of irrigated, non-irrigated and pasture land with machinery stations. Fewer than 500 families were attracted and poor management, inadequate road links to Luanda and a ban on using African labour limited success. Far more successful was the Matola scheme, where about the same number were settled but with an emphasis on irrigation. There were also several African settlement schemes, the most important being in the Loze valley, north-west of Carmona, and the '31 de Janeiro' scheme, south of Damba, in which prepared land was allocated to African farmers. Given the vast potential for irrigation and agricultural development, these schemes in fact contributed very little.

Another strand to development planning was the construction of a hydroelectric power plant to provide energy for industry. The plateau interior with its well-defined western edge provides a fall line with considerable HEP potential; sites were developed at Cambambe on the Cuanza river, for energy for Luanda and irrigation, at Biopio on the Catumbela for Lobito–Benguela, and at Matola on the Cunene for Sã da Bandeira and Moçâmedes. A joint Portuguese–South African scheme was also started on the Cunene river where it forms the boundary between Angola and Namibia. In 1984 plans were announced for a 520 MW HEP and irrigation scheme at Capanda on the Cuanza river to be built with Brazilian and Russian aid. There are numerous smaller HEP plants, and Angola probably has a power potential far in excess of its foreseeable needs. Plans to establish an aluminium smelter to capitalize on the energy potential have not yet been implemented.

Early this century the railway lines from

Moçâmedes to Vila Serpa Pinto and from Luanda to Malanje were constructed, and in 1928 the privately owned Benguela Railway was completed from Lobito to the then Katanga (now Shaba) province of the Belgian Congo. This latter served to stimulate development along its line, and Lobito developed as the second port after Luanda, the capital. The alignment of the Benguela Railway was improved in the 1960s, especially where it rises to the plateau in the Cubal area, and a link was provided to the Cuima iron-ore mine. At both Luanda and Lobito, natural harbours provided the basis for considerable port development in the 1950s and 1960s, and Moçâmedes was provided with its first deep-water berthage in the late 1950s and later extended to handle the iron-ore from Cassinga.

While the Portuguese presence undoubtedly distorted the economy, their hasty departure on Angolan independence in 1975 left large gaps which have never been filled. Only 30,000 of an estimated 300,000 Portuguese remained in the country, 80 per cent of the plantations were abandoned and 25,000 other Portuguese commercial enterprises closed. The vehicle stock was depleted, the best fishing vessels taken away, and 130 road bridges were destroyed in the fighting. In the period since independence the country has been in a state of civil war, with the anti-government UNITA group now controlling much of the south of the country. Over the last 10 years the Benguela Railway has frequently been sabotaged and has operated only intermittently. This has seriously affected production, including that of iron-ore, in the southern part of the country. Most of the coffee estate owners left the country and there has been considerable dislocation of population as a result of the liberation war and subsequent civil war. Coffee production had fallen to 30,000 tonnes in 1985, and storage, transport and marketing for even these small quantities was inadequate (and not all of it was sold).

Almost inevitably it was decided that the state should take over the larger abandoned units and hand over the rest to cooperatives and private individuals. Some units have been rehabilitated, and by 1980 overall national production had been restored to about 60 per cent of previous peaks, and 60 of the 130 bridges had been rebuilt. The wholesale and retail activity formerly controlled entirely by the Portuguese has yet to be adequately restored, especially in the rural areas. Rehabilitation of cultivation and livestock production has been far from successful, and from being a net exporter of food, Angola has become an importer. Lack of foreign exchange after 1981 reduced food imports. As a consequence of drought, local production declined, so that in 1983 an emergency economic plan was introduced which emphasized small-scale agriculture and increased food production.

Plate 39 Government textile factory, Textang II, Luanda

In 1983 Angola joined OPEC and there has been renewed oil exploration activity and increasing production. Oil now provides 90 per cent of export revenue, a dangerous over-dependence on a commodity that does not command the price that once it did. However, only a small part of the 46,000 km^2 continental shelf has yet been explored, and the coastal Benguela, Lobito and Moçâmedes basins are still untouched; oil could well be the mainstay of the economy for many years.

In the longer term more foreign investment will have to be encouraged if the large, as yet under-developed agricultural, mineral and energy resources are to be exploited. There will also be the need to develop Angola's human resources because there is a serious shortage of management, commercial and technical skills, the development of which has been largely neglected. Angola has been called an African El Dorado, but for its potential to be realized it will need peace and stability that has so far been completely lacking.

NAMIBIA

What is now Namibia came under German control in 1892 and was known as South-West Africa. Up to the Second World War the Germans were responsible for the first phase of economic development, with investment in ports, railways, mines and ranching. The Caprivi strip in the north-east was acquired in 1893 as an eastwards outlet to the Zambezi; but no use was made of it since the river here is of little practical use for navigation, and Rhodes blocked Germany's attempts to link up with her East African colonies. In 1915, South-West Africa was occupied by South African forces – in 1920 it became a mandated territory and later a trusteeship territory administered by South Africa for the United Nations.

In practice South-West Africa has been administered as a fifth province of South Africa, although in 1966 the United Nations revoked South Africa's trusteeship and in theory took over full responsibility. In the 1970s the South-West Africa Peoples Organisation (SWAPO) increased pressure for independence, and South Africa embarked on promoting an internal constitutional settlement that would lead to formal independence.

In the late nineteenth century a 1124 km^2 territory around Walvis Bay was annexed by Britain, and in 1922 it was decided that this should be administered as if it were part of the mandated territory. However, in 1977 the South African government effected the annexation of the Walvis Bay enclave. This could have profound implications for the development of Namibia (a name proclaimed in 1968 by the United Nations in accordance with the wishes of the African population) should it achieve full independence from South Africa, and is undoubtedly a factor influencing South Africa's reluctance to allow Namibian independence.

With an area of 824,000 km^2, two-thirds the size of South Africa itself, Namibia has a population of only 850,000 and a population density of just one person per km^2. The highest densities are found in the tribal area of the Ovambo people along the borders with Angola, and two-thirds of the black population is in the northern third of the country. The white population numbers about 90,000, of which Afrikaaners comprise over 60 per cent, and is heavily concentrated in either Windhoek or Walvis Bay. The Namib, ports and mining centres apart, and Kalahari are very sparsely populated.

For the purposes of administration the country has been divided into two distinct zones. The southern two-thirds is the 'Police Zone', which is the area of white settlement with segregated 'reserves' for blacks. The north and north-east are designated as tribal lands. The economy likewise displays a dualism. In the African reserves and tribal lands the agriculture is largely subsistence, and pastoralism based on cattle is dominant – but with increased cultivation of maize, groundnuts and millet in the north. Much of the income in the African areas derives from migrant labour employed in the white-controlled mining, agriculture, industry and commerce. At any time, 25 per cent of the Ovambo males will be away on contract work in the south and 65 per cent of the workers in farming and fishing derive from the north.

In contrast, the commercial sector of the economy – livestock, fishing and mining – is entirely white-controlled and the export economy is dependent on this primary production.

Agriculture

Given the low rainfall, sheep farming is the most practicable use of land over large areas of the south. Karakul sheep, introduced by the Germans, provide the so-called 'Persian lamb' pelts of which Namibia is the world's leading producer. As these pelts are taken from day-old lambs, the ewes do not have to support many young and can better survive the arid conditions. In the higher central areas around Windhoek with rainfall around 350 mm, cattle become more important for both beef and dairy produce. There are only limited areas of European cultivation based on spring waters around Tsumeb and Grootfontein and irrigation based on the Hardap dam on the seasonal Fish river near Mariental (Figure 73). In any year beef production provides about 55 per cent, dairy produce 5 per cent, pelts 32 per cent, wool 2.5 per cent and crops only 1 per cent of the value of agricultural production.

The cool Benguela current widens from about 160 km off the Orange river to 240 km north of Walvis Bay, and provides Namibia with fishing grounds rich in deep-water and pelagic fish. At a peak over 50 firms were involved in commercial fishing, with Walvis Bay the principal centre especially for pilchards and anchovies, and Luderitz for shellfish. Between 1947 and 1954 six large fish factories were built at Walvis Bay, and in peak years – from 1960 to 1976 – nine were operating: six for pilchard canning and meal/oil production, one for meal and white-fish processing, one reduction-only plant, and one pilchard freezing plant. There was a marked decline in catches after 1975, the pilchard virtually disappeared from coastal waters, and by 1981 all the fish processing plants had closed.

Mining

Minerals are now overwhelmingly the most important sector of the economy, accounting for 50 per cent of the GDP and 85 per cent of the value of exports. Discovered in 1908, the southern coastal Namib has extensive, rich, alluvial diamond deposits. Gemstones make up 80 per cent of the production and access to the main working areas is restricted. The Oranjemund operation of the De Beers Corporation employs over 5000 people on sea-bed and shore workings and accounts for the bulk of the production.

Particularly since 1945 there has been diversification within the mining sector. In 1946 former German copper mines at Tsumeb were re-opened by American interests and then greatly expanded, with on-site smelting of copper, lead and zinc from six separate mines in the area. Copper and silver are obtained from Oatmines and Klein Aub, south of Windhoek, lead/zinc from Rosh Pinah and tin from Vis. However, generally poor metal prices have created problems for the mines, and since 1978 there have been a number of closures: Berg Ankas (vanadium), Otjihase and Onganja (copper), and Krantzberg and Brondberg West (tungsten).

The main success story has been the Rossing uranium mine of Rio Tinto Zinc, which in 1981 accounted for 45 per cent of Namibia's mineral sales, with diamonds 33 per cent and copper 9 per cent. While Rossing's markets seem assured, the once predicted uranium bonanza has yet to materialize.

Problems for an independent Namibia

Should Namibia achieve independence in the near future there would be a severe shortage of skilled workers, especially as the country would probably wish to exert direct control over the mining industry. In the longer term, the uncertainty of mineral markets and the small employment generated (about 18,000 at present) might suggest that more emphasis should be placed on other sectors. However, the agricultural sector – which at the moment provides a livelihood at a relatively low level for the bulk of the population – offers no great potential for expansion, except possibly in the extreme north based on irrigation from the

Cunene scheme. There are indications that a Namibian government would wish to 'give land to the tillers', which would raise questions of inherited colonial land-rights over large areas of the south.

Much would clearly depend on the nature of the continuing relationship with South Africa. The present economy is very 'open' and largely dependent upon, and integrated with, that of South Africa. The spinal rail line following the highlands from Upington through Windhoek to Tsumeb, with links to Walvis Bay and Luderitz, are operated as a part of South African Railways, and it has been South African policy to channel trade by way of the railway and Walvis Bay which has become the main ore-exporting and general cargo port for the whole country. As an annexed territory of South Africa, Walvis Bay has been increasingly more closely integrated with the socio-political system of that country. An independent Namibia, assuming South Africa retained Walvis Bay, would therefore lose its principal port, would in effect become land-locked, and would also possibly lose access to railway maintenance facilities; railway rolling stock, and possibly road vehicles, could well be lost to South Africa.

While it is almost certainly a case of 'when' rather than 'if' Namibia becomes independent, the future of the country is likely to be determined by the precise nature of the arrangements that can be made with South Africa, and possibly with whatever government then controls Angola to the north.

BOTSWANA

Bechuanaland became a British protectorate in 1885, and ten years later the southern part, including the capital, Mafeking, was transferred to Cape Colony. The northern part was initially handed to Cecil Rhodes's British South Africa Company, which saw it as a necessary link in the grand Cape–Cairo rail plan. Company control was later restricted to the line of the railway from Mafeking north through Gaborone and Francistown to the then Southern Rhodesia. In 1966 Bechuanaland became independent as Botswana. With an area of 600,000 km^2, Botswana had a population of only one million in 1985 and an overall population density of 1.5 people per km^2. However, over 80 per cent of the population is in fact concentrated in a narrow zone along the line of the railway in the east of the country, where the highest rural densities are found and where the main towns are located – Gaborone (40,000) the capital, Lobatsi, Kanye and Francistown.

Southern and western Botswana is dominated by the Kalahari, but from almost true desert in the extreme south-west the rainfall increases to the north (550 mm) and east (450–500 mm), and vegetation improves from sparse thorn bush to dry woodland–savanna. The generally infertile sands of the Kalahari are replaced towards the north and east by relatively better soils developed on basement rocks.

Agriculture

Given the semi-arid nature of much of the country it is hardly surprising that the population density is so sparse and that European farmers have not been attracted in any number. There are a few along the Limpopo river, and in the Francistown and Lobatsi regions where they are engaged in ranching, dairy farming and limited cultivation based on small-scale irrigation.

Water shortages are clearly a limiting factor for agricultural development because of the low rainfall, high evaporation rates and relatively high porosity of much of the surface. Apart from the rivers Linyani in the north and Limpopo in the east, the only important source of surface water is in the Okavango basin and Lake Dow. A policy of sinking boreholes to tap sub-surface water commenced in the 1940s and has continued since. Nevertheless, it is estimated that Botswana has some 3.2 million hectares of cultivable land, a mere 5 per cent of which is actually used, and there is undoubtedly potential for increasing irrigation in the Okavango area – although possibly at great cost. The government's Arable Lands Development (ALDEP) Scheme had only marginal success before the drought of recent years demanded attention.

Traditionally, while there has been some cultivation of maize, millet and beans, animal husbandry has supplied the economic support for the bulk of the population, Africans owning 90 per cent of cattle. In years of average or better rainfall the pasture is satisfactory, and the overall carrying capacity is as low as one beast to 8 ha in better areas and one to 25 ha in drier parts. Over-grazing leads rapidly to grassland deterioration. Drought in the early 1960s and again in the 1980s seriously depleted the herds and demonstrated the vulnerability of an economy dependent on pastoral activity.

Plate 40 Plunge dipping of cattle on the Molopo Ranch, Botswana

At independence the economy was just that, with animal products providing over 90 per cent of the value of exports (carcass meat 42 per cent, hides and skins 18 per cent, meat extract 14 per cent, abattoir by-products 8 per cent, and live animals 5 per cent). Crops and minerals together accounted for only 6 per cent of the exports.

Mining

It has been written of Botswana that 'in the decolonisation of Africa there can seldom have been a more dramatic improvement in the post independence economic position of a country'.[1] The per capita GNP grew from $69 in 1966 to over $1000 in 1982, and during the 1970s growth averaged 13 per cent a year.

The improved economic performance resulted from mineral exploitation (Tables 32 and 33). Prior to independence there were two small South African-owned manganese mines (at Kwagwe Hill and Ramonstsa, both in the south-east) and one small asbestos mine at Ngwatketse. Large deposits of medium-grade coal and brine were known to exist and

Table 32 *Botswana: principal exports (percentages of total value)*

	1967	*1977*	*1984*
Animal products	93.0	27.0	10.6
Crops	5.2		
Manganese	0.3		
Diamonds		31.0	70.0
Cupro-nickel		26.0	8.9
Other	1.5	16.0	10.5

Source: ECA.

Table 33 *Botswana: mineral production*

	1969	*1971*	*1981*	*1984*
Manganese (1000 tonnes)	31	2,700		
Diamonds (1000 carats)		294	381	12,900
Coal (1000 tonnes)	31		47	480

preliminary studies had been undertaken with a view to mining. From only 5 per cent in 1973, mining increased its contribution to the GDP to 41 per cent in 1981.

Manganese extraction ceased in 1973, but the mining boom had started in 1971 with the opening of the Debswana diamond mine at Orapa and further mines were opened at Letlwakane (1979) and Jwaneng (1982). The mining is by open-cast methods in kimberlite pipes, 30 of which have been identified – that at Jwaneng thought to be the most important discovered anywhere since that at Kimberley in 1870. With 50 per cent of the stones of gem quality and a yield of about 79 carats per 100 tonnes, Jwaneng is the richest mine and like Orapa is thought to have a life of 25–30 years.

Coal mining started at Morupule in 1973 and Botswana has reserves of 17 billion tonnes. In 1983 production reached 395,000 tonnes, and in 1986 a 90 MW thermal power station near the mine started to use some of the coal. Preliminary studies of the Kgaswe coalfield near Palapye have indicated a possible 7.5 million tonnes a year mining capacity, and three possible mine sites are being considered.

A copper–nickel mine started operations at Selebi–Phikwe in 1974, and despite some operational and financial problems created by low world prices the copper–nickel matte output reached 48,000 tonnes in 1983. The matte is exported to the USA for refining. Employing over 5000 people, this mine is Botswana's largest private employer and has become the country's third largest town. Since 1982, four gold and silver mines have been started but production is still small. The output of precious stones amounts to about 13 tonnes a year.

Mineral exploitation has been kept at a high level and a variety of minerals are known to exist in the Kalahari region; but exploitation could be costly in view of the lack of roads and access, and problems of water and power supply. The Marupule coal mine was developed to provide power for the Selebi–Phikwe mining activity, and the Jwaneng diamond mine necessitated the construction of a 70 km link road from Kanye and a 125 km electricity transmission line. There are plans to exploit brine deposits at Makgadigadi to produce soda ash for export and salt for the home market, but plans to exploit the large coal deposits at Serowe could well depend on the construction of a rail link either to Gobadis and Walvis Bay or to Ellisras in South Africa.

Economic development

In the agricultural sector the government has adopted a general policy of letting commercial farmers fend for themselves, and much of the effort has been directed towards problems created by drought – providing animal and human food, distribution of seed, providing borehole equipment and machinery. Large-scale irrigation is seen as a longer-term strategy which will become more feasible as the infrastructure improves. An animal vaccine plant has been built at Gaborone mainly as a response to widespread foot-and-mouth disease in the late 1970s.

Since independence waged employment has trebled, but still only 20 per cent of the population is involved in formal sector activities. Manufacturing industry is still in its infancy, accounting for only 5 per cent of the GDP; but there is government assistance for small-scale industrial development. This has resulted in growth of about 8 per cent a year, mainly in clothing and construction materials industries; but the domestic market is small and there is a shortage of the raw materials for many industries. As a result of the drought, Kgalagadi Brewery, opened by the Development Corporation in 1976, asked people to restrict their use of water so that it would not have to reduce production!

The very remoteness of large parts of the country has meant the preservation of a rich wildlife. Game reserves have been designated and a tourism division created within the Botswana Development Corporation. The number of visitors rose from 171,000 in 1977 to 227,000 in 1981, and in 1983 about 30,000 arrived specially for 'game tracking'. Lodges and chalet camps are being developed in the Okavango and Chobe river regions, and Maun now has a scheduled air link with Gaborone. Tourism is still largely of the low-volume, high-price variety and it is perhaps best that it stays that way for environmental reasons. The Gaborone International Airport has been extended to handle direct international services and this, together with the gradual improvement of the road system, will encourage the steady growth of tourism.

Botswana is still very much within the economic orbit of South Africa through which it directs most of its exports and receives the bulk of its imports and the majority of its tourists. This is a natural reflection of the inherited transport links. Through its membership of the Southern African Development Coordination Conference (SADCC) Botswana has strong incentives to re-direct links with its northern neighbours; in 1983 the road from Francistown north to Kazangula was finally tarred, and there have been SADCC studies for a bridge to replace the present ferry across the Zambezi. In 1987 Botswana will have taken over control of the railway from the National Railways of Zimbabwe, by whom it has been controlled. Routes to the west through Namibia are unlikely to be developed greatly until the political problems of that territory have been solved.

The 1981 census enumerated over 900,000 people, about 10 per cent more than had been predicted from 1971 results. If correct, this suggests a 5 per cent annual growth rate. This could be accounted for by Botswana people returning home from South Africa, where they have traditionally sought employment but where restrictions on freedom have become increasingly unacceptable as living standards in Botswana itself have improved. The urban areas have been growing rapidly: Gaborone at 16 per cent a year, and the labour market at 15–20 thousand a year. Jobs have been increasing at only half this rate, and the shortfall will have to be accommodated by greater attention to agricultural development and diversification of industrial activity.

REFERENCES

1 Halpern, J., 'Botswana', *Africa South of Sahara*, Europa, 1971, p.153.

PART EIGHT: SOUTH AFRICA

31
The Republic: physical framework

South Africa is in many respects a unique part of Africa. First and foremost, it is the principal area of European settlement in the continent and more than half of the European population of Africa is found there. Settlement by Europeans has been continuous for more than 300 years and no other part of Africa possesses such an unbroken record of white settlement. Second, the government has always been in the hands of the whites in spite of the fact that they now account for only 18 per cent of the total population. Combined, these facts go a long way towards explaining the character and level of development, and why it is a country in which the spatial impress of central authority has been particularly marked.[1]

The Republic is also a country distinguished by a wealth of mineral resources, the exploitation of which has been a basis for higher levels of industrialization than anywhere else in the continent. South Africa accounts for over 40 per cent of the mineral output of Africa, yet manufacturing industry now contributes more to the national income than mining and agriculture combined. Nearly one-third of the income of the African continent is generated by this one country, while the per capita income is three times the average for sub-Saharan Africa.

For the purposes of this study, the so-called 'independent' African homelands are included in South Africa, although only time will tell whether or not this is realistic from both political and functional viewpoints. As in other parts of Africa, the political frontiers of the state do not coincide with natural boundaries. Although the frontier in part follows the lower Orange river in the west and the Limpopo in the east, these hardly constitute boundaries in any real geographical sense. The South African plateau is but the southern extremity of the continental shield and has no well-defined northern boundaries.

GEOLOGY AND STRUCTURE

As in the greater part of Africa, the south is underlain by a platform of ancient Archaean rocks. Over two-thirds of South Africa these are buried by later strata, of which three main groups are most significant.

The earliest group of rocks resting on the basement is Pre-Cambrian. At the base of the group lies the Dominion Reef System. Above it is the famed Witwatersrand System, consisting of quartzites, slates and the 'reefs' or gold-bearing conglomerates. In the Johannesburg area this system alone is no less than 7000 m thick. The geological sequence is continued by the Ventersdorp System, mainly volcanic, and then by the Transvaal System, with its extensive iron-ore deposits and limestones, providing two of the basic raw materials for the iron and steel industry. Finally, the Bushveld Igneous Complex, an immense intrusion of late Pre-Cambrian age, contains one of the world's most extraordinary assemblages of minerals, including platinum, chrome, gold, silver and asbestos. The lava and dolomites of the Ventersdorp and Transvaal Systems respectively are the most important water-bearing strata in South Africa, making a significant contribution to agricultural, industrial and domestic water needs in the southern and western Transvaal.

Second, in the south-west, a group of rocks of Silurian and Devonian age has been folded to form the Cape Ranges. At the base of the group the Table Mountain sandstone is up to 1500 m thick, and is most important physiographically, forming massive plateaux, or the hard cores of the Cape Ranges. The succeeding Bokkeveld Shales give rise to valleys or lowlands in the Cape. The third member of the group, only surviving in a few places, is the Witteberg Series of quartzites and shales.

Third, there is the Karroo System. Of mid-Carboniferous to lower Jurassic age, this has the most extensive outcrop of any formation in South Africa. It attains a maximum thickness of nearly 8000 m. At its base occurs an interesting series (the Dwyka) of glacial deposits and shales, which lie on the peneplained and glaciated sub-Karroo surface. Higher up in the Karroo System comes the Ecca Series, which contains vast coal reserves of inestimable value to South Africa.

RELIEF AND DRAINAGE

The essential physical framework of South Africa (Figure 74) consists of a plateau, depressed in the centre, and terminated by bold escarpments which overlook the coastal regions. More than half of South Africa lies more than 1200 m above the sea; in the east, parts of the plateau attain heights of 3000 m or

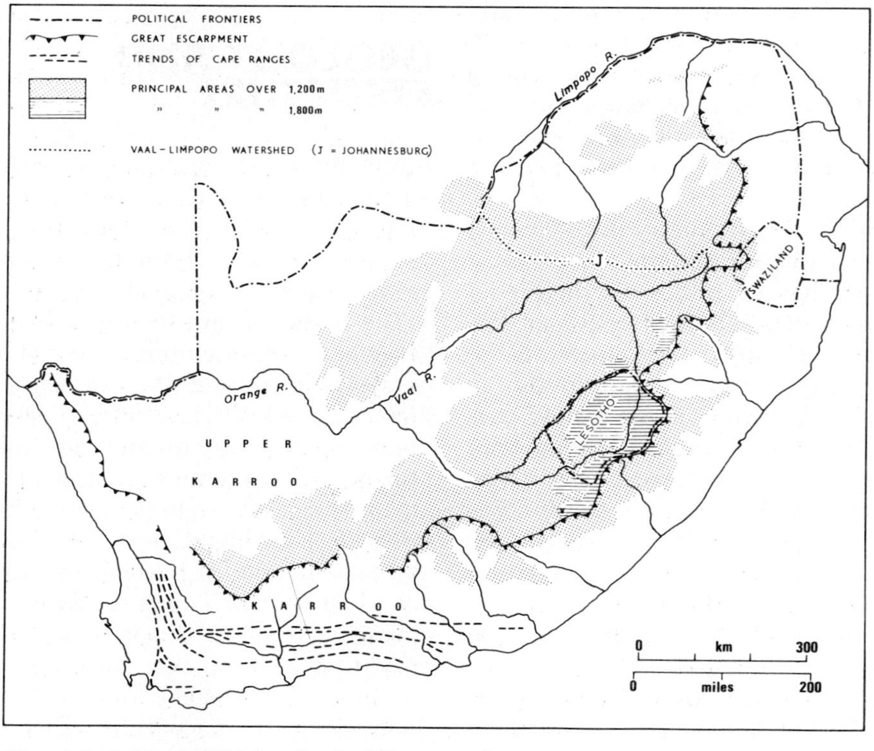

Figure 74 South Africa: physical framework

more. The plateau is drained principally to the west by the Orange–Vaal river system, though in the north a smaller portion feeds the Limpopo. The divide between the Limpopo and Vaal drainage runs approximately east–west through Johannesburg.

The escarpment edges of the plateau, overlooking the lower marginal or coastal zones, are collectively referred to as the **Great Escarpment.** Lying at distances of 55–240 km from the coast, the Great Escarpment has thus a variety of local names; in the east and south-east it is known as the Drakensberg, whose crest-line rises to over 3300 m; traced westwards through Cape Province, it is variously known as the Stormberg, Sneeuberg, Nuweveld Reeks, Roggeveld Berge and Langeberg. The crest-line in the western sections is not usually higher than 1500 m. Wellington[2] has described it as 'the most fundamentally important physical feature in the sub-continent'. Essentially, it is an erosion scarp, formed by the headward erosion of steeply graded rivers flowing down to the coast. It is formed of a great variety of rocks; but it is most impressive in areas where alternations of hard and soft beds are present, or where there is a resistant cap-rock formation. Examples of such resistant strata in the east are the Stormberg lavas (of upper Karroo age) and the quartzites of the Transvaal System. In areas of the Archaean granite or gneiss the escarpment is often less marked.

Inland from the Great Escarpment the country consists largely of extensive rolling plains dropping almost imperceptibly to 900 m in the centre of the sub-continent. These upland plains are of erosional origin, but the widespread presence of nearly horizontal strata has also contributed to the general evenness of the landscape. Only in Lesotho does mountainous and broken country form part of the interior, rising to 3482 m on the crest of the Drakensberg, the highest point in South Africa. The underlying rocks in Lesotho belong to the Karroo System, horizontally bedded, and include great thicknesses of lava. The numerous rivers have carved deeply into the lavas and sandstones, producing the most beautiful and spectacular scenery in South Africa. At the Maletsunyane Falls there is a sheer drop of 180 m. Nearly all the drainage of this high mountain country feeds into the Orange river, which escapes from the highlands in the south-west.

Surrounding Lesotho on the west and north is the plateau of the **High Veld**. The term 'veld' may be used in both a botanical and an altitudinal sense. Thus, 'High Veld' may refer simply to land over 1200 m (cf. 'Low Veld' for land below 600 m), or it may refer to an area of open grassland at about 1200 m. The term is usually applied to the eastern interior plateaux of the southern Transvaal and the Orange Free State, where grassland is the dominant vegetation and where the undulating land surface lies mostly between 1200 and 1800 m. The area is drained westwards by the Vaal, Caledon and Orange rivers. Its northern limit is represented by the Witwatersrand 'ridge' on which Johannesburg stands at 1800 m. There is no topographical boundary to provide a western limit to the High Veld – only gradually increasing aridity. Except in the north, where older Pre-Cambrian rocks are exposed, the region is underlain by Karroo strata, almost horizontally bedded.

North of the Witwatersrand lies an area usually known as the **Transvaal Bushveld.** The name 'Bushveld' refers to a type of dry savanna vegetation characterized by open grassland with scattered trees and bushes. The region lies inside the great bend of the Limpopo valley, and in elevation is much lower than the High Veld, parts falling below 600 m and the average being only 900 m. The topography is complex in detail, but broadly consists of a central basin, drained by the Olifants and Crocodile rivers, surrounded by a series of broken ranges. Geologically it is an area from which most of the Karroo rocks have been removed by erosion, exposing the Pre-Cambrian formations which here include the Bushveld Igneous Complex.

West of the High Veld extends a vast expanse of semi-arid plateau, sometimes known as the **Upper Karroo** or Cape Middle Veld, reaching to the Great Escarpment on the south and west. Across it flows the Orange river, entrenched in a gorge below the Aughrabies Falls. The relief on the whole is subdued, consisting either of surfaces planed across the Karroo strata, or of the stripped sub-Karroo surface bevelling of Pre-Cambrian rocks. The elevation drops steadily from the edge of the High Veld (at about 1200 m) and from the Great Escarpment crest in the south (at 1200–1500 m) to about 600 m in the region of the lower Orange river. Owing to the aridity, drainage apart from the Orange river is intermittent, flowing only after occasional torrential downpours in the summer. It has been said of this area that if you fall into a 'river', you brush the dust off and walk along the bed until you are able to climb up the bank. But after a rainstorm the river may come down in spate so rapidly that travellers by car or wagon have sometimes been overwhelmed and carried away.

On the seaward side of the Great Escarpment there is a much greater diversity of landscape and relief. First there is the **Karroo**. The term 'Karroo' is derived from a Hottentot word meaning 'waterless'. The term has been applied in a geological sense (the Karroo System of rocks), in a botanical sense (referring to scrub vegetation), and in the topographical sense used here. This region consists of the Great Karroo, lying immediately below the Great Escarpment, and the Little Karroo, separated from the Great Karroo by the Swartberge. The Great Karroo is underlain by Karroo sandstones and shales, generally horizontally bedded, except towards the Swartberge where the Cape folding commences. The altitude of the Great Karroo Plains is between 450 and 750 m. The Little Karroo is slightly lower; and it possesses some permanent rivers such as the Olifants and Gouritz, whereas on the Great Karroo intermittent stream flow is the rule.

Around the Karroo on the south and west stand the **Cape Ranges.** These are of folded structure, related to orogenic movements mainly in the Triassic, and built out of Silurian and Devonian rocks. The ranges fall into two sets. The first consists of the Cedarberg and Olifants Mountains, trending north-north-west to approach the west coast near the lower Olifants river; in the south this group of mountain ranges is cut off by the south coast around Cape Hangklip. The second set trends roughly east–west; it begins by crossing the first set around Worcester and the Hex River Mountains, producing an area of complex topography, and continues for nearly 650 km until cut off by the coast around Port Elizabeth. It includes the Swartberge (already mentioned) and the Langeberg (not to be confused with the Langeberg forming part of the Great Escarpment in western Cape Province). These east–west trending ranges consist of multiple anticlines, while the intervening lowland strips are generally synclinal. Most of the principal ranges are built out of Table Mountain sandstone; and parts rise to well over 2000 m. The transverse portions of the rivers which cut across the fold ranges appear to have been superimposed from Jurassic and Cretaceous sediments, which were worn off the original mountain ranges after uplift, filled in the synclines, and provided a surface on which the rivers were initiated. Later the rivers re-exposed the fold ranges and cut gaps (known as *poorts* or *kloofs*) across them; subsequent tributaries extended themselves along the softer sediments still remaining in the synclines, in some cases capturing other streams. Thus the present almost rectangular drainage pattern has emerged.

From the foot of the Drakensberg across to the east coast extends a belt of country most of which lies between 300 and 1200 m. Except in Zululand (north-east Natal), a true coastal plain is very narrow or entirely absent. Inland, the country has been greatly dissected by the rivers flowing steeply to the sea from the Drakensberg. But in spite of the broken character of the country, a series of steps or planation surfaces has been recognized, principally at 1400, 760 and 180 m. About two-thirds of the region is underlain by Karroo strata. The one area where the relief is relatively subdued is in the Low Veld of eastern Transvaal; here, rolling plains below 600 m are interrupted only by scattered granite inselberge.

Between the Atlantic coast and the Great Escarpment on the west there is a narrow belt of desert, a southwards continuation of the Namibian desert. The underlying rocks are of Archaean igneous and metamorphic formation, except next to the coast where Tertiary and Quaternary deposits occur. Behind part of the desert strip the Great Escarpment rises to 1700 m in the Langeberg, but elsewhere it is less prominent.

CLIMATE

General consideration of the position of South Africa (latitude 23°S to 35°S) suggests a subtropical climate; but closer examination shows considerable variations from the warm humid region along the east coast (e.g at Durban) to the cool conditions in the Lesotho highlands, where the highest parts support only a tundra-like vegetation. The temperature variations arise from differences of elevation rather than latitude, but there is a sharp contrast between the west coast affected by the cool offshore Benguela current (e.g. at Port Nolloth) and the east coast influenced by the warmer Indian Ocean waters (e.g. at Durban) – see Table 34.

Most of South Africa lies beyond the Tropic, and the relatively high elevation of many areas means that frost is likely to occur at times in most places. Light frosts may even occur occasionally in valley bottoms in the coastal areas; but inland, where frost is both more severe and also regular, it provides a definite limiting factor for crops such as sugar cane and citrus fruits.

Not only is there a close relationship between relief and temperature: the relationship between relief and rainfall is equally

Table 34 *Republic of South Africa: temperature and rainfall of selected stations*

Station	*Altitude (m)*		*J*	*F*	*M*	*A*	*M*	*J*	*J*	*A*	*S*	*O*	*N*	*D*	*Year*
Cape Town	12	T	22	22	21	18	16	14	13	14	14	17	19	21	17
		R	18	15	23	48	94	110	94	84	58	41	28	20	627
Port Nolloth	7	T	16	16	16	14	14	13	12	12	13	13	14	15	14
		R	3	3	5	5	8	8	8	8	5	3	3	3	58
Port Elizabeth	53	T	21	21	20	18	17	15	14	14	16	17	18	20	18
		R	30	33	46	46	61	46	48	51	58	56	56	43	601
Durban	5	T	24	24	23	22	19	17	17	17	19	20	22	23	21
		R	109	122	130	76	51	33	28	38	71	109	122	119	1008
Johannesburg	1665	T	20	19	18	16	12	10	11	13	16	18	19	19	16
		R	114	109	89	38	25	8	8	8	23	56	107	124	709
Kimberley	1116	T	25	24	22	18	13	11	16	13	16	20	22	24	18
		R	61	64	79	38	18	5	5	8	15	25	41	51	409

Notes: T = Temperature (°C); R = rainfall (mm).

apparent. Except for a very narrow coastal strip on the east, humid climates are coincident with the higher land. Generally, the most arid parts of South Africa are located in the north and west of Cape Province, where the land drops below 900 m. The wettest parts are to be found on the Drakensberg (annual averages up to 2000 mm) and on some of the Cape Ranges: the Drakenstein Mountains south of Worcester rise to 1500 m and record about 5000 mm a year. An annual rainfall of over 1000 mm is, however, rare in South Africa, and in fact 90 per cent of the whole country receives less than 750 mm per year. Roughly half of South Africa can be classed as arid or semi-arid. During the last 30 years South Africa has become increasingly aware of the limited nature of her water resources on which her agricultural and industrial development vitally depend. It has been calculated that the entire runoff from South African rivers for one year could be contained in the reservoir behind the Hoover Dam on the Colorado river in the United States, but only about one-tenth of South Africa's rainfall ever reaches her rivers. In only a small corner of South Africa can rain be expected in all months of the year – along part of the south coast. Elsewhere rainfall is markedly seasonal in its incidence – 85 per cent of South Africa has mainly summer rainfall.

The **western coastal strip** (Figure 75) is the driest region of South Africa, though a relatively cool one. Throughout the year it comes under the influence of mT air blowing off the Atlantic and over the cool Benguela current, the latter increasing the stability of the air (see Port Nolloth, Table 34). The distinctive feature of the **south-west Cape region** is the winter rainfall, brought by air masses of modified mP type. The rainfall is greatly accentuated on the mountain ranges, with corresponding rain-shadow effects in the intervening valleys and on the Little Karroo (see Cape Town, Table 34). The **southern coastal belt** is the only region of South Africa in which the rainfall is fairly equally distributed throughout the year. In winter it is brought by the mP air masses which move along the coast from the Cape at this time of the year. In summer the rain derives from mT air masses of Indian Ocean origin (see Port Elizabeth, Table 34). Along the **eastern coastal belt** rain falls in every month; but there is a pronounced concentration in the summer, brought by moist air masses from the Indian Ocean (see Durban, Table 34).

The rainfall over the interior plateau of South Africa varies from over 1000 mm in the Lesotho highlands to less than 75 mm around the lower Orange river. The rain is confined to the summer months, while the winter is a season of drought. The **western interior** comprises the vast semi-arid heart of the subcontinent, which climatically continues northwards as the Kalahari of Botswana. Complete drought prevails from May to September usually, when subsiding cT air is dominant. In the summer a weakening of the local anticyclonic conditions occasionally allows moist air to penetrate from the north and north-east. In the **central interior** aridity is less extreme (see Kimberley, Table 34).

The **High Veld and Lesotho highlands** lie east of the 500 mm isohyet. From this minimum rainfall increases eastwards to 750 mm around Maseru at the foot of the Lesotho highlands, and to 2000 mm at the crest of the Drakensberg. On the High Veld the winter drought period generally lasts through June, July and August, when the region is dominated by cT air; for the rest of the year rain in varying amounts is brought by disturbances of both tropical and mid-latitude origin. The barrier of the Drakensberg cuts off the South-East Trades; for most of the time the High Veld and Lesotho lie above the shallow layers of maritime air affecting the Natal margins. The seasonal summer rain of the High Veld is now known not to be a monsoon effect.

On the High Veld the rainfall is mainly associated with thunderstorms, due partly to the convectional instability of air masses passing over the hot land surface. This area is known to be one of the most thundery in the

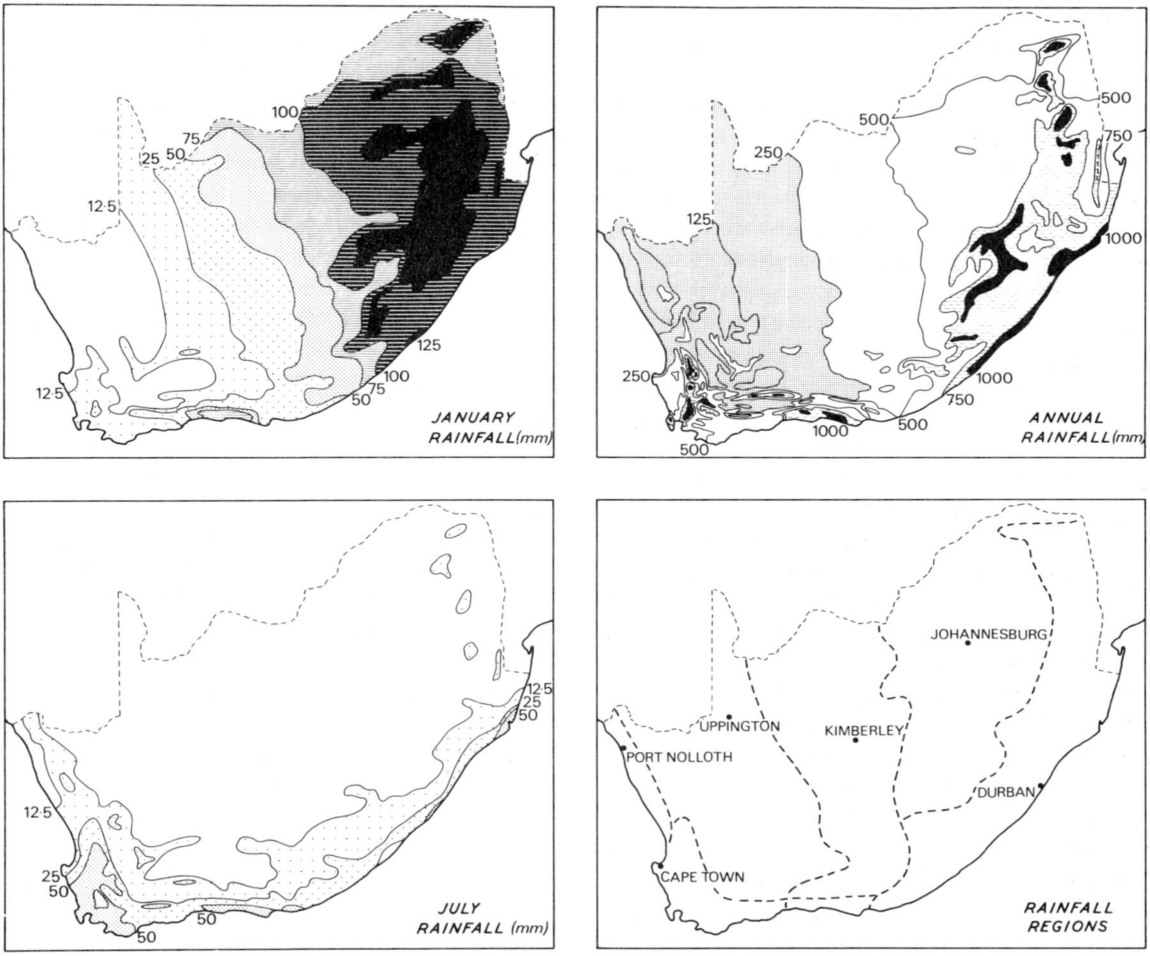

Figure 75 Rainfall in South Africa

world. One characteristic of the resultant rainfall is its intensity. On the Witwatersrand, for instance, about one-quarter of the rain falls in showers depositing more than 25 mm at a time. This characteristic also applies to the east-coast belt where the rain liberated by the mT air is also concentrated in short periods. In March 1940 Eshowe, the capital of Zululand, experienced no less than 580 mm in 36 hours, and though this is exceptional, it serves to emphasize that rainfall concentrated in this way can do much damage by flooding and soil erosion; it is also very wasteful of water. Another aspect of the rainfall of South Africa, especially important for agriculture, is its variability. In general it appears that the rainfall is most reliable in areas where it is heaviest, and conversely least reliable in the drier parts. This explains the necessity for irrigation over so much of South Africa, and it also shows how precarious farming can be in areas where rainfall amounts are marginal. There are, too, few parts of South Africa which never experience drought; the interior and parts of the High Veld seem to be most prone to this.

The effectiveness of the rainfall must also be considered. This is especially important in the summer rainfall zone, where temperatures – and therefore evaporation losses – are highest at the time of the rain. Figures for evaporation from an open water tank vary from about 1250 to 2750 mm a year in different parts of South Africa. Very few parts have the necessary rainfall to offset such potential losses; but, of course, the figures are misleading to some extent, since the natural ground surface is never continuously wet. Few measurements of evaporation losses from various types of ground surface have yet been made, and the same applies to transpiration losses from crops. Experiments at Pretoria showed that maize growing on a gentle slope there needed 635–900 mm of rain a year; of this about 50 per cent was used by the crop, and about 35 per cent lost by evaporation, most of the remaining 15 per cent being accounted for by runoff and percolation.

SOILS AND VEGETATION

There is a great variety of soils, arising from variations of relief and rainfall, and from the fact that temperatures in sub-tropical regions are often critical for certain soil-forming processes. Both podsolic and lateritic soils occur in South Africa. The strong relief associated with the various escarpments and the dissection of the coastal margins have given rise to many immature soils. In such areas parent rock type is often the principal determinant of soil character. Soils are also closely related to parent rock in the case of certain areas of volcanic and intrusive rocks – as in the Transvaal bushveld, or in the areas of upper Karroo basalts.

Few South African soils have an adequate humus content. This is mainly because of the limited vegetation cover over the western two-thirds of the country, including the Cape region, and the leaching in the wetter areas; but it is also the result of such practices as monoculture and over-grazing. In most areas under crops, fertilizers and some form of crop rotation are much needed to combat deficiencies in the soil.

Lateritic soils occur in areas with more than 500 mm of rain, and are better developed with more than 900 mm, combined with annual average temperatures of over 18°C. Under natural conditions these soils support grassland and occasional forest; cultivation succeeds well initially, but thereafter the soils become quickly exhausted and liable to erosion.

The High Veld is characterized by fairly acid podsolic soils, often low in humus content; but in certain areas of dolerite outcrops the soil improves to a black clay, which is excellent for maize. Black clays are also associated with the igneous rocks of the Bushveld Basin; in fact, accumulated minerals probably make them the most potentially fertile soils of South Africa, but unfortunately the rainfall is precariously low. Soils of the Cape region tend to be podsolic, generally immature and lacking in humus. Probably the best are the mildly acid loams associated with the Bokkeveld shales.

The soils of South Africa, like those of all other countries with seasonal rainfall occurring in heavy and spasmodic showers, are extremely vulnerable to erosion, and there are large areas with serious erosion problems. Numerous physical and economic factors contribute to this. Undulating or broken relief is characteristic of areas outside the Great Escarpment, and of those parts of the plateaux dissected by rivers; on the numerous steep slopes runoff is rapid and its erosive power considerable. Rain falling in torrential showers after dry periods when the soil hardens also encourages rapid runoff. In the drier parts vegetation is too sparse to have much binding effect on the soil. Man has contributed to the problem by many agricultural malpractices. In the pioneer days the European settlers thought little about such matters, with the result that pastures became dust-bowls, and arable land was gashed by gullying. The heavy rains washed away soil that in periods of drought had been laid bare by over-stocking or unsuccessful cultivation. Veld-burning was another injurious practice (not yet eliminated

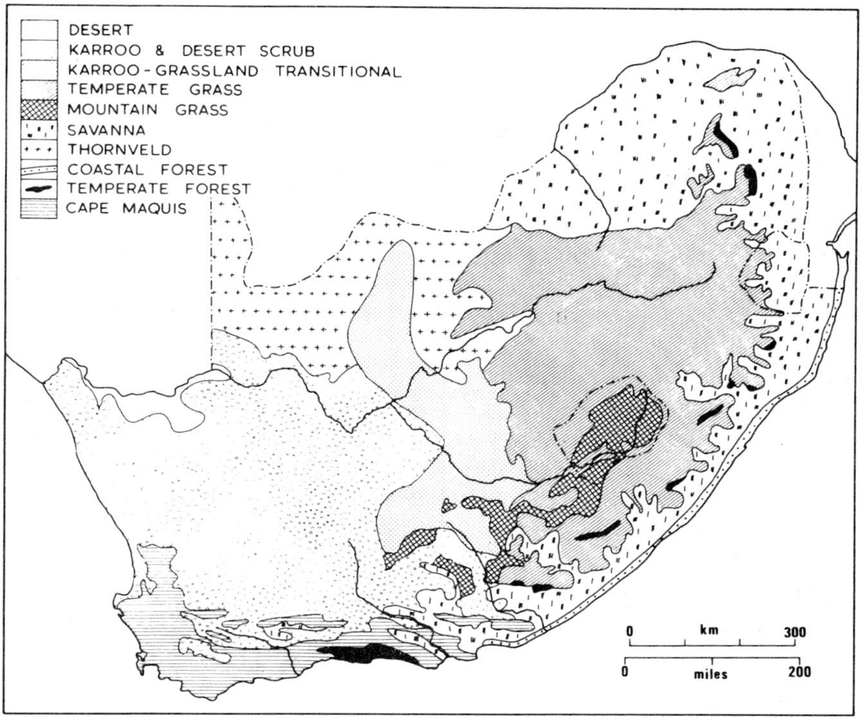

Figure 76 The vegetation of South Africa

in fact), while the spread of maize monoculture in the 1920s was a major factor in soil deterioration over large areas and the onset of appalling soil erosion in the 1930s. In the African areas over-stocking and uncontrolled grazing have always represented the greatest menace to the soils because these practices are so widespread; cultivated land is less extensive, but is often characterized by severe gully erosion, leaving steep ridges of bare red soil.

The principal vegetation zones stand out clearly on Figure 76; most extensive is the vegetation of the semi-arid zones – the Karroo and desert scrub. Second, and most important from the viewpoint of farming, there are the several grassland types, principally on the High Veld. Smaller areas are occupied by the maquis of the Cape, the savanna or tree veld of the east and north-east, and the various forest types. It should be emphasized that changes of vegetation between one zone and the next often occur very gradually: the grassland of the High Veld, for instance, grades imperceptibly west into the semi-desert. The extensive areas classed as semi-desert serve to emphasize how inadequate rainfall is over much of South Africa. It must also be remembered that the vegetation has been greatly modified by human interference: the temperate evergreen forest, which now occupies only a fraction of 1 per cent of the total area, was undoubtedly more widespread before the arrival of the Bantu or Europeans; the Cape maquis has been much thinned and impoverished by goats; and large areas of the veld are still subject to regular burning.

Grassland generally occupies the land over 1200 m with more than 350 mm of rain annually. Tree growth is restricted by the relatively low winter temperatures, for here the frost period may be 120–180 days. The principal species, occupying 60 per cent of the area, is the 'red grass', so called for its brownish colour as it dries out in autumn after the rains. According to the particular variety, it attains a height of 0.3–1.0 m, and it is recognized as one of the best pasture grasses in South Africa. The main problem for stock rearing on the

High Veld is the lack of rainfall outside the period October–March. Grass growth is limited to this period of summer rain, and grasses quickly lose their nutritional value in the winter. Provision of supplementary winter feed for animals is thus of vital importance for successful stock rearing. To encourage grass growth at the beginning of the rains, removal of dead grass is essential. To do this, farmers often resort to veld-burning, a practice which may be very injurious if the land is thereby laid bare to heavy rain showers.

The typical Karroo vegetation of western Cape Province consists of small scattered shrubs and bushes, varying in height from a few centimetres to about 1 m according to the degree of aridity, but all possessing great resistance to drought. A few coarse grasses may cover the spaces between them, but much bare land is apparent, and is in fact becoming more widespread with overgrazing. As a pastoral area the Karroo is only fit for sheep, and the maximum carrying capacity of good Karroo has been estimated at no more than 14 sheep per hectare.

Southwards the Karroo grades into the Cape maquis, also of limited pastoral value except for sheep and goats; and goats are exceedingly destructive. The maquis consists of drought-resisting evergreen shrubs, grasses only appearing on some of the wetter parts.

The savanna in South Africa is generally known as bushveld. It is found mostly in areas below 1200 m and with at least 350 mm of rain annually; again, a gradual transition is effected both to the higher grassland and to the Karroo and maquis in the south. The density and type of tree growth vary greatly. All varieties of savanna are represented, from open woodland at one extreme to grassland with only scattered trees at the other. Both evergreen and deciduous trees occur.

REFERENCES

1 Christopher, A. J., *South Africa*, London, 1982, p. xvii.

2 Wellington, J. H., *Southern Africa: a Geographical Study*, Cambridge, 1955, p. 39.

32
Population and settlement in the Republic

In South Africa some understanding of the population geography is fundamental to any discussion of economic activity and development processes. It is a country in which, far more than in any other, ethnic differences have provided a basis for government policies which influence the whole socio-economic fabric.

Before the arrival of the Bantu and white immigrants, the indigenous population of what is now South Africa comprised herders and hunter-gatherers (the Khoi-San – the Hottentots and Bushmen). Known for their rock art, these peoples either gradually retreated into remoter areas in the face of the advancing Bantus and whites or were incorporated into Bantu groups. Never large in number and sparsely dispersed, they were also reduced by European introduced diseases. To the extent that they survive in any pure form it is in Namibia and Botswana.

The Bantu peoples migrated southwards from East Africa and there emerged a number of groups with distinct ethno-linguistic characteristics. The largest group (Table 35) is the Nguni (including Zulu, Xhosa, Mdebele and Swazi) found mainly east of the Great Escarpment southwards to Algoa Bay. These better-watered lands provided the basis for animal husbandry and settled cultivation. The Sotho are widely dispersed, with a core area in the western Transvaal, a distribution reflecting a troubled history (some sought refuge in the highlands that became Lesotho), social disintegration and intrusion by other groups. On the drier plateau they were essentially pastoralists with seasonal migrations centred on larger settlements.

Table 35 *Republic of South Africa: population 1983*

Blacks		
Nguni		
Xhosa	2,533,000	
Zulu	6,200,000	
Swazi	932,000	
Ndebele	718,000	
Sotho		
Sotho	4,457,000	
Tswana	1,480,000	
Shangaan	1,095,000	
Venda	209,000	
Other	117,000	
Total	17,741,000	(67.9%)
Whites	4,748,000	(18.2%)
Coloureds	2,765,000	(10.6%)
Asians	870,000	(3.3%)
Total	26,124,000	

Source: Central Statistical Services of South Africa.

In the extreme north the Venda were probably late arrivals and have links with the Shona of Zimbabwe with whom they share mining skills. They are small in number and have remained a compact unit as a result of their inaccessibility from the main centres of

European advance. The Shangaan (Tsonga) are traditionally goat herders who overlap into Mozambique.

From their original settlement in Cape Town (1652) the Dutch, supplemented by Huguenot and German immigrants, gradually spread eastwards, engaged in extensive animal husbandry, introduced wheat, vines and citrus, and developed a distinct language, Afrikaans, and culture. They consider themselves Africans as no other European immigrants to the continent have done, and they comprise about 60 per cent of the present white population.

During the Napoleonic Wars Britain occupied the Cape Colony and English-language immigrants increased in numbers after 1820, mainly in the towns but to a lesser extent as farmers in eastern Cape and Natal. The land under white control increased steadily, and was to increase very rapidly after 1836 when the Boers ('farmers') started the 'Great Trek' northwards to avoid British colonial influence – which led to their establishment of independent republics in Natal, Orange Free State and Transvaal. Eventually, after a series of wars, the Union was created in 1910. At about the same time that the Dutch were extending their settlements eastwards and north-eastwards from the Cape, the Bantus migrated southwards from East Africa into the warmer and more humid areas of southern Africa and eventually as far as the area of the Great Kei river, where they first encountered the Dutch colonists. For this reason the Afrikaaners claim prior settlement of the southern and western parts of the Republic.

The effect of the European advance on the black population was dramatic. There was conflict over land and water, expropriation of vast areas of land for white use and gradual incorporation of blacks into the white economy. Initially this was as agricultural labourers, but with the start of mining increasingly as long-distance migrants on short-term contract in the growing mining townships. However, in these urban areas, where by 1911 they comprised 55 per cent of the population, the predominantly male blacks were housed in separate compounds – initially for security reasons on diamond mines, but eventually so that the labour could be controlled in the broadest sense of the term. This segregation was eventually to lead to the concept of separate development (apartheid).

MIGRANT LABOUR

Both on the land and in the mines, labour was not always available to meet demand without going outside the country. Between 1860 and 1896 about 120,000 contract labourers were imported from India, mainly for Natal's sugar plantations. Rather than return at the end of their contracts many accepted land grants, established their own plantations and spread into other employment, especially in urban areas (e.g. in the textile industry). Still mainly

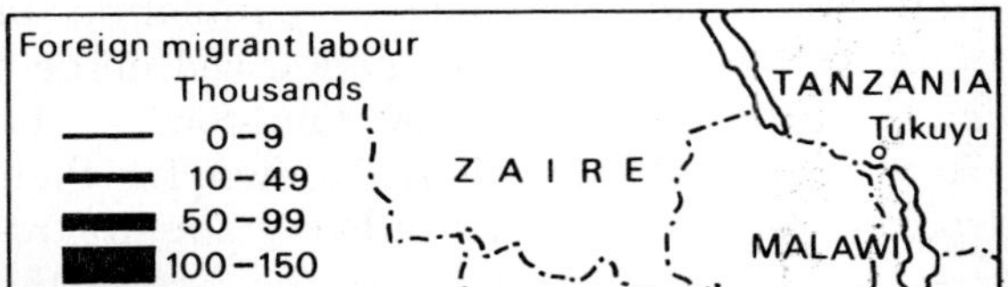

Figure 77 Migrant labour to the Republic of South Africa

concentrated in Natal, the Asian population now numbers 870,000 and provides a complicating dimension to the political problem. In the mines, labour was recruited from Mozambique, Botswana, Lesotho, Swaziland and Central Africa (particularly Malawi), and these countries are a continuing source of workers. In 1985 there were nearly 300,000 foreign workers in the mines, over 200,000 in gold and coal where they provide 40 per cent of the labour force. A threat to expel these workers (in July 1985) would have had severe repercussions not only for the mining industry but for the countries supplying the labour – the main sources being Lesotho (108,000) and Mozambique (51,000).

As a result of ethnic admixture, principally between Europeans and pre-Bantu and Asian peoples, there is now a group numbering about 2.75 million (1983) classed officially as 'Coloured'. This group is heavily concentrated in Cape Town and Cape Province.

POPULATION DISTRIBUTION

The total population now numbers over 26 million, which gives a low average density of about 22 people per km^2. The generalized distribution maps (Figure 78) show marked concentration of population along the eastern coastlands, where densities exceed 100 per

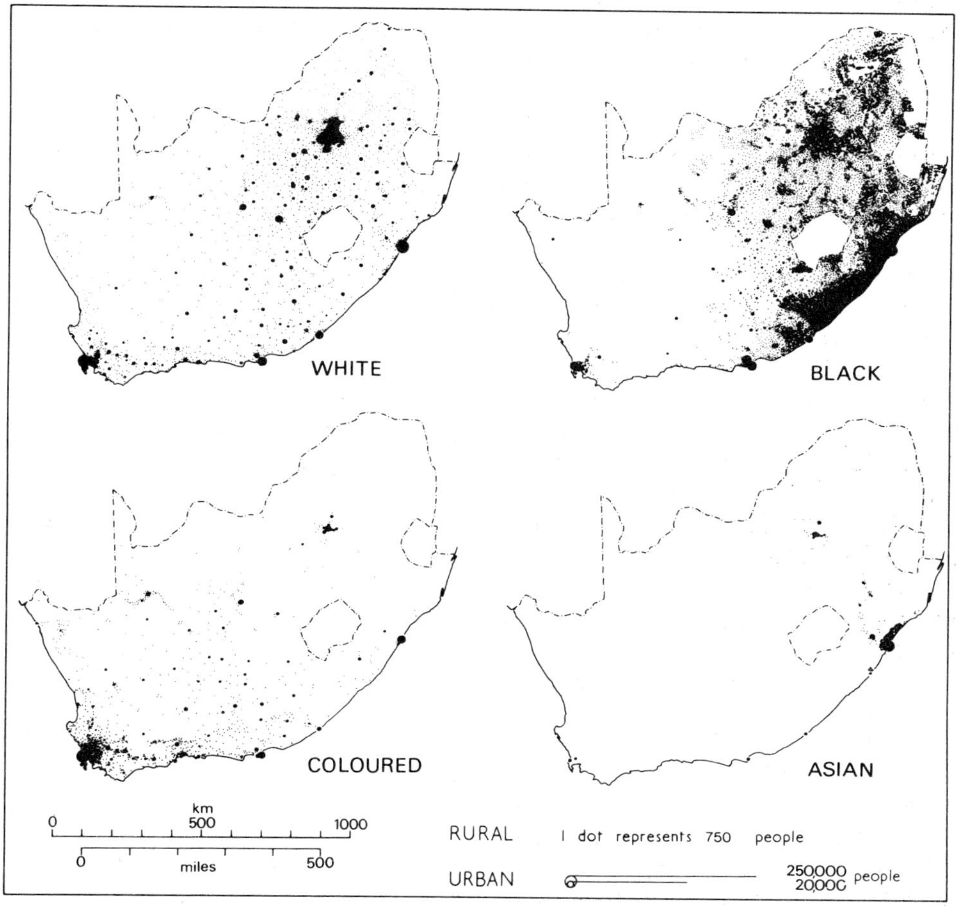

Figure 78 Distribution of the principal ethnic groups in the Republic of South Africa

km^2 in the Transvaal mining area and in the south-west Cape. Large parts of drier, northern and western Cape Province are very sparsely populated. There has been an overall shift in population from south to north, because the Cape Province share dropped from 46.6 per cent in 1904 to 23 per cent in 1980 whereas that of the Transvaal increased from 24.5 to 44.0 per cent. The overall average national growth rate is 2.26 per cent, but there are considerable variations between ethnic groups – Whites 0.83 per cent, Coloureds 1.84 per cent, Asians 1.9 per cent and Blacks 2.8 per cent. On this basis the population for the year 2000 is an estimated 40 million, with Blacks numbering 30 million.

Statistics show that South Africa has undergone rapid urbanization (Table 36). The Black urban population now numbers 6,480,000, of which 5,325,000 were in urban areas not located in the 'homelands' – this is a significant fact as will be discussed below. The principal urban areas are Johannesburg 1,726,000 (1 million Blacks), East Rand 848,000 (550,000 Blacks), Pretoria 740,000 (320,000 Blacks), West Rand 512,000 (309,000 Blacks), Vereeniging 480,000, Cape Peninsula 1,500,000 (820,000 Coloureds), Durban–Pinetown 960,000 (470,000 Asians), and Port Elizabeth–Uitenhage 585,000 (280,000 Blacks, 140,000 Coloureds). With over 4 million urban dwellers, the Pretoria–Johannesburg–Vereeniging (Vaal) region is an outstanding feature of the population geography. With less than 1 per cent of the national area it has 17 per cent of the total population.

Of fundamental importance is the way in which over time the government policy has regulated the ethnic segregation, industrial employment, residential characteristics and land-ownership patterns. Initially, the hope was to create fairly large, compact 'reserves' for the Black population, but this gradually gave way during the nineteenth century to smaller, controlled locations which reflected the highly fragmented nature of many of the tribal groups. The Natives Land Act of 1913 allocated 9.5 million hectares to the Blacks, and this was increased by another 6.6 million hectares in 1936. This amounted to about 13 per cent of the national area of which they were an integral part. Within these reserved areas the African social and traditional agricultural system persisted, with growing pressure as population increased. Already in 1923 the Natives (Urban Areas) Act excluded Blacks from freehold-land ownership in urban areas unless they were employed there, and this effected their physical and social isolation. However, with time there developed a landless group of Blacks in the reserves, and in the urban areas the Blacks outnumbered the Whites and in many cases their links with the reserves weakened.

Table 36 *Republic of South Africa: urban population of ethnic groups*

	Blacks (%)	Whites (%)	Coloured (%)	Asian (%)	All (%)
1921	14	60	52	60	28
1960	32	84	68	83	47
1980	38	89	79	91	53

Source: South African Yearbooks.

APARTHEID

Since 1948, Nationalist Party governments have created an elaborate legislative framework to control the movement, residence and employment of Blacks. The central pivot of the policy is that of apartheid – or separate development – in which the former reserves became 'homelands' (Bantustans) for the Black peoples and some of which eventually became 'independent' states – Bophuthatswana, Ciskei, Transkei and Venda. The 'independence' of these territories is not recognized internationally and probably means very little within South Africa. As the source of labour for South Africa's industry they are essential elements in the total economy; and, being highly fragmented (as many as 89 blocks – even in a proposed consolidated form Kwa Zulu would have 10 separate parts), they hardly provide an adequate resource base for an independent existence. This mutual dependence would seem to be a critical flaw in the idea of 'separate' development.

Within the urban areas in which the Blacks outnumber other peoples, the Group Areas Act (1950) defines the residential zone for each, these being separated by buffer zones. For the most part this has meant the removal (often forcibly) of all non-Whites from central areas and the construction of separate peripheral townships, which then become dormitory settlements. In the case of Soweto (South Western Township) the population may exceed in size Johannesburg which it serves. The housing is mainly uniform, low-cost and to rudimentary standards, and the townships are generally lacking in amenities. Only since 1978 has there been an attempt to give the townships some semblance of self-administration.

The lack of services provided in the townships clearly reflected the official view that the residents were temporary and had 'homes' elsewhere. It is increasingly difficult to justify this view, and there is therefore a demand – which may have to be satisfied eventually – for the development of more satisfactory urban living conditions for Blacks. With the difference that there is no way they can be assigned to a 'homeland', the Asian and Coloured people must be treated as permanent urban settlers and the conditions they enjoy are much superior to those of the Blacks.

Some critical contrasts between the ethnic groups are indicated in Table 37. In relation to their proportions of the total population the Blacks are under-represented in active employment and grossly lacking with respect to tertiary and technical education. In contrast the Whites are over-represented in each case, dramatically so in higher and technical education. In the case of the Coloureds and Asians the opportunities are much as would be expected in relation to their share of population. This lack of access to education will be reflected in job opportunities and possibilities for advancement, and lack of suitably trained personnel could act as a brake on expansion in industry.

It is the continued dependence of the South African economy on Blacks that is the weakness of apartheid and could eventually be the force for substantial change.

Table 37 *Republic of South Africa: education provision (percentages of totals)*

	Blacks	*Whites*	*Coloured*	*Asian*
Population	17,741,000	4,748,000	2,765,000	870,000
(per cent of total)	67.9	18.2	10.6	3.3
Economically active	63.1	22.6	11.0	3.2
Secondary education	51.6	29.6	12.8	6.0
Tertiary education	20.4	65.5	6.8	7.3
Technical education	3.8	85.5	8.4	3.1

Source: Central Statistical Services.

33 Farming, fishing and forestry in the Republic

Although classed as a 'developing country', South Africa stands in sharp contrast to all the other African countries. Its 1.2 million km^2 is a mere 3 per cent of the continental area, and its 26 million inhabitants account for 5 per cent of Africa's population; yet South Africa provides 45 per cent of the continent's mineral production, 40 per cent of its industrial output and 25 per cent of the total GNP. South Africa has two-thirds of the continent's railways, 46 per cent of the motor vehicles and consumes two-thirds of all the steel and electricity. South Africa is one of the few countries of the world that is a net food exporter. Impressive as South Africa's development has been, the aggregate figures undoubtedly conceal stark regional and ethnic contrasts in the distribution of resultant income, benefits and welfare.

AGRICULTURE

From the outline of the physical geography in Chapter 31 it will be clear that large parts of South Africa suffer from inadequacy or irregularity of rainfall, and nearly everywhere there is seasonal deficiency. The better-watered land is often hilly and liable to soil erosion, and the soils themselves are commonly poor. Underground water supplies are in places too saline, while the highly variable river regimes and unsuitable topography limit the opportunities for irrigation. Overall, good land is in short supply and only 12 per cent of the total area is cultivated. Yet South Africa has a variety of climatic conditions – sub-tropical, Mediterranean, semi-arid – and potential for a wide range of crops and animal husbandry.

Between 1960 and 1980 the value of agricultural output rose from R615 million to R4274 million and the volume of production doubled; yet agriculture's share of the GDP declined from 12.5 to 6.5 per cent over the same period, a reflection of the increasing relative importance of industry to the economy. Over the same time the number of farm units dropped from 106,000 to 70,000 and the agricultural area from 91.7 million to 85.0 million hectares. Increased production has therefore been achieved by better husbandry on smaller areas, expanded irrigation, more mechanization, greater inputs of fertilizer, feeds, sprays, dips and the introduction of higher yielding plant varieties and improved stock.

A distinction must, however, be made between the largely subsistence farming systems of the Blacks and the commercial farming mainly in the hands of the Whites. As elsewhere in Africa, traditional agriculture was based on land rotation, communal ownership and individual usufruct. White occupation led to widespread dispossession, the emergence of a large 'tenant' Black group and a growing impoverishment of traditional agriculture as the area over which it could be practised became more restricted by regulation – the 1913 Natives Land Act, the 1936 Natives Trust and Land Act, more recent delineation of African 'homelands' and 'independent' states. The problems of agriculture in these Black areas are increased by the small size and great fragmentation of some of the units; by the high population densities, and by selective out-migration to urban, industrial and other employment, leaving an ageing – often predominantly female – population to maintain the farming.

The 1955 Report of the Commission for the Socio-Economic Development of the Bantu Areas (Tomlinson Report) concluded that the homelands could support a farming population of 2.1 million – at present the population is at least five times that. Inevitably, over-cultivation, over-grazing, low yields and soil erosion are widespread and rural poverty and malnutrition endemic.[1] Indeed, it would seem that the general economic conditions in these peripheral Black areas are not too different from those prevailing in many other parts of Africa, despite the apparent relative prosperity of South Africa as a whole. The economic relief comes by way of remittances from migrant workers.

There have been attempts to improve agriculture in the Black areas. In different places this has taken the form of consolidation of arable land, redistribution of plots (e.g. Modjadji, northern Transvaal), and more generally the introduction of irrigation and specialized crop schemes. In some cases there has been transfer of land to Blacks, with continued cultivation of previous crops (e.g. pineapples, citrus). In other cases such transferred farm land has been sub-divided into a larger number of units. At Keiskammahoek in Transkei land has been divided into 4 ha plots for dairy farming based on irrigated grass and feed crops. There has also been the creation of some state farms for coffee growing (Venda government), tea (Transkei) and sugar (Kwa Zulu).

PASTORALISM

Commercial farming is largely controlled by the Whites. Although maize and sugar cane were introduced in the nineteenth century, the agricultural economy was largely dependent on pastoralism until 1900. Given the physical environment this was not perhaps surprising, and it has been estimated that 80 per cent of the country is suitable only for pastoralism. Even so, the carrying capacity is low and this was reflected in the large size of many early land-grant farms – in the most arid Kalahari area as large as 12,500 ha and widely in the 2500 ha–3500 ha size range.

Sheep-rearing is best adapted to semi-arid conditions. Merino sheep were introduced for their fine wool in 1789 and still account for two-thirds of the country's 27 million sheep. Other main breeds are the South African mutton Merino and the locally bred, non-wool mutton Dorper. In 1867, before mining became important, wool provided three-quarters of the exports. South Africa still has the fourth largest wool clip in the world, but wool now accounts for only 3 per cent of total export value, gold excluded. Sheep-rearing is found widely in the Great Karroo and Orange Free State High Veld and in the arid Namib margins. The Karakul sheep produce the famous 'Swakara' pelts. Goats are widespread, 60 per cent being Angoras producing mohair of which South Africa is the third world exporter.

Cattle number over 9 million head and, being less tolerant of arid conditions than are sheep, are found in greater numbers towards the east – except in parts of Zululand where there is tsetse fly infection. Beef cattle are found more widely than dairy cattle, but in drier areas the carrying capacities may be as little as one animal to 6–25 ha. South Africa's meat production now averages over 850,000 tonnes a year. There are over 50,000 dairy farms of varying size, their cattle amount to about one-quarter of the total, and they are concentrated in moister areas, except in the warmer, low-lying coastal areas of the east and in the north. With the exception of Durban, most of the larger towns have dairy farming in the hinterlands for fresh milk supplies, but away from the urban areas more of the milk goes to the production of cream, butter, butter fat and cheese. There has been a greater concentration of butter and cheese production in recent years and much higher output is being obtained from fewer, larger factories.

In recent years the animal husbandry has been improved by irrigated, intensively used grassland, more manufactured feedstuffs, better veterinary services and improved transport. There has also been a big increase in agri-factories for poultry and pigs.

CULTIVATION

Until about 1900 South Africa was primarily a pastoral country. During the nineteenth century maize and sugar-cane were introduced, and in this century the desirability of greater self-sufficiency in time of war and depression and the growth of the urban population stimulated a marked expansion of arable farming. South Africa is now the principal crop-producing country of southern Africa and an important source of foodstuffs for neighbouring states.

The poor physical conditions have already been noted. About 12 million hectares are cropped – about 10 per cent of the available land – but of this only about 4 million hectares can be classed as land of reasonable quality and this produces 40 per cent of the value of agricultural production.

The most important cereal grown is maize, the principal food crop of the Black farmers and also occupying about 45 per cent of the European arable land. It is found mainly in the summer rainfall areas of the east (Figure 79), with a marked concentration in the 'maize triangle' of the High Veld, and virtual absence from the drier west. The crop size is largely determined by rainfall and has varied from 4 million tonnes in 1983 to a record 14.6 million tonnes in 1980/1. Between 1968 and 1978, the introduction of higher-yielding varieties adapted to local conditions effectively doubled production and grain storage capacity had to be greatly increased.

Wheat cultivation was originally concentrated in the winter rainfall area of western Cape Province, but after 1930 there was rapid expansion in the eastern Orange Free State and southern Transvaal (Figure 79). Although the Cape's output has increased, its relative share has declined to about 35 per cent of the total production of 2.4 million tonnes.

Sugar was introduced into coastal northern

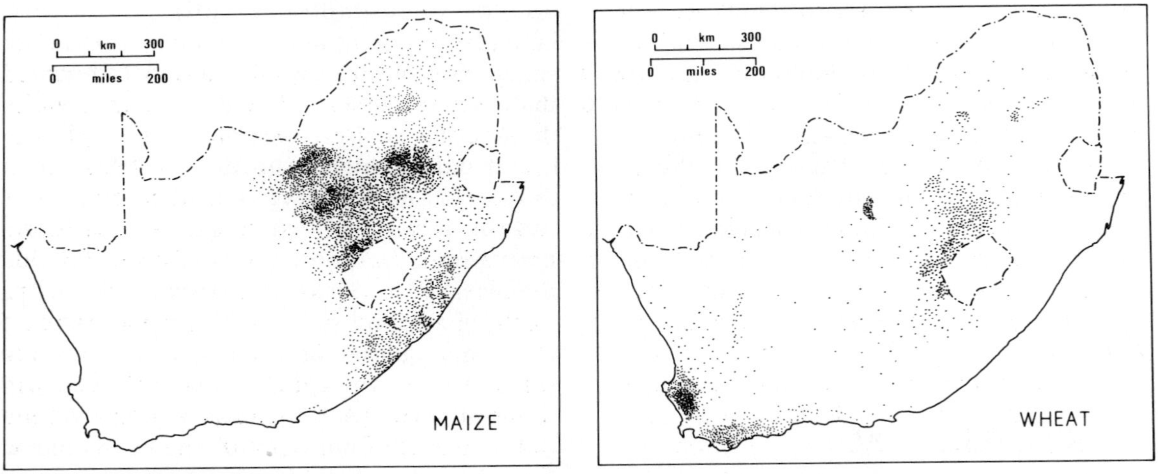

Figure 79 Generalized distribution of maize and wheat production in the Republic of South Africa

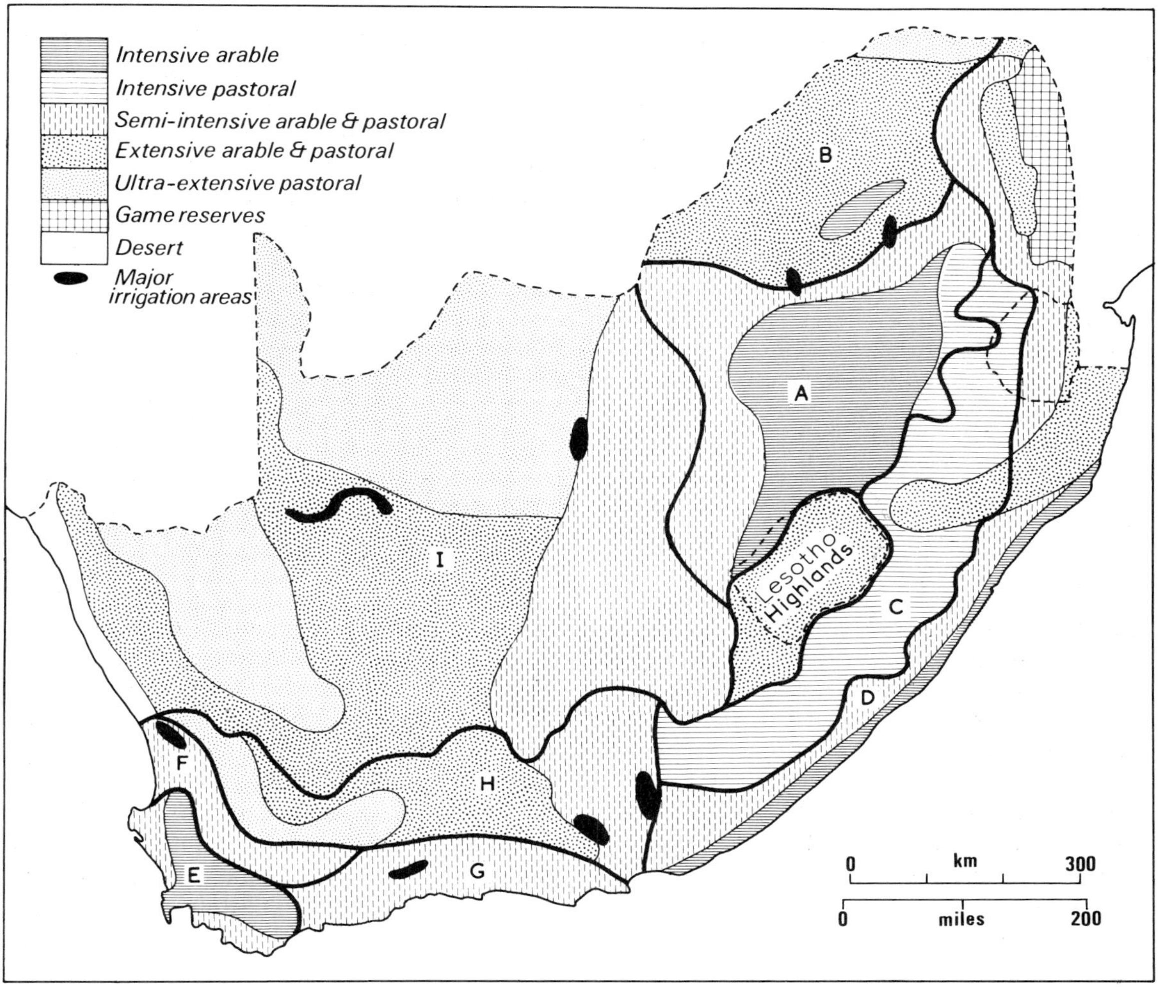

Figure 80 Major land-use regions of South Africa

Natal in the 1850s and spread progressively into southern Natal, Transvaal, Swaziland and most recently mid-Natal. The cultivated area now amounts to nearly 250,000 ha, and the peak annual production of cane has been as much as 19 million tonnes (in 1981). In these areas sugar makes up as much as two-thirds of the cropped area and is produced by large company estates, by smaller White farms, and by Indian farmers who were originally brought in during the late nineteenth century as indentured labourers on larger farms.

South Africa is suitable for a variety of orchard crops, and the most widespread are citrus fruits found in a broad arc from the south-western Cape to Transvaal. Output has trebled since 1950 and, with water availability a limiting factor, there has been growing dependence on irrigation. Deciduous fruits are much more markedly concentrated in the winter rain area of the south-west Cape, and particularly in basins such as Ceres and Elgin within the Cape fold mountains. A distinctive feature of agriculture in this same region is the vine which flourishes in the typically Mediterranean climatic conditions, with assistance in places from irrigation. About 90 per cent of the wine made is consumed locally, but exports have been expanding gradually in the face of competition from better-known European producers. Table grapes, raisins and sultanas also contribute to fruit exports, which now total about 4 per cent of the value of exports, gold excluded.

AGRICULTURAL REGIONS

The High Veld (Figure 80A) This is the most important area of White farming in South Africa. The land undulates gently between 1200 and 1800 m; rainfall is normally between 500 and 750 mm and long droughts are uncommon in the rainy season, though some irregularity is apparent. It is, however, an area of summer rainfall, and therefore subject to heavy evaporation losses. Most of the High Veld is in pasture, but it also contains over three-quarters of all the arable land in the Republic. The natural grasses provide excellent sheep pasture. Both beef and dairy cattle are also kept, with the emphasis on the latter; milk production for the cities of the Rand is important. The chief problem for stock-rearing on the High Veld is the supply of winter feed, and increasing attention is now being paid to fodder crops such as lucerne.

The outstanding crop of the High Veld is maize. It is concentrated in the so-called 'maize triangle', whose corners are approximately provided by Mafeking, Carolina and Ladybrand. This is a zone where a number of relatively favourable conditions for maize are combined, among them sufficient rainfall, flat land, and soils which are not highly fertile but above average for South Africa. Soil types range from black clays on dolerite outcrops to sandy loams. The maize triangle produces about two-thirds of the Republic's maize; the main collecting centres are Kroonstad and Bethlehem, and a considerable part of the maize crop is exported. Other cereals are less important. Wheat is grown as a winter crop – about 30 per cent of the Republic's wheat production; and oats and potatoes occupy small areas. On the western margins, where rainfall is less than 500 mm, sorghum is found.

Around the built-up area of the Witwatersrand there is a zone of intensive farming – market gardening, dairying, etc. Fresh vegetables for the Rand and other urban areas are also supplied from irrigated land in the Vaal valley to the south and in the Transvaal Bushveld Basin to the north.

The Transvaal Bushveld (Figure 80B). The complex topography of this area has already been noted, but there are also wide areas of flat land, such as the Springbok Flats. As regards climate, the relatively low elevation (average 900 m) and northerly location mean generally warm conditions and freedom from frost; rainfall is seasonal and low, many areas having less than 500 mm, much of which is in any case lost by evaporation. The drier parts are only really suited to extensive cattle grazing, and stock-rearing is the main aspect of farming in the region. Cultivation of crops generally depends on irrigation. Cotton, maize and tobacco are grown successfully in this way. The Transvaal is the largest producer of tobacco in the Republic, the best-quality leaf coming from the Rustenburg district. Citrus orchards are grouped in three main areas: (1) around and east of Rustenburg, using water from the Hartebeest-poort Dam on the River Crocodile, and from the River Hex; (2) south of Pietersburg, using tributaries of the River Olifants (the Zebediela Estates on the north-eastern Springbok Flats are probably the world's largest single citrus grove with 1 million trees planted); and (3) around Nelspruit, on the River Crocodile of the eastern Transvaal Low Veld.

There are possibilities of further extending cultivation of sub-tropical crops with irrigation in the northern Transvaal, but the water supply is definitely limited – the majority of streams are not perennial in flow.

The Eastern Uplands (Figure 80C). The parts of South Africa lying east of the Great Escarpment, between Swaziland in the north and the Great Fish river in the south, can be conveniently treated in two divisions: the Eastern Uplands lying above 600 m and the Coastal Region below 600 m. In the Eastern Uplands there are several physical limitations on agriculture. Much of the relief is dissected by the steeply graded rivers, the only reasonably flat areas being in the Midlands of Natal at 600–900 m north and south of Pietermaritzburg, and in some river basins (e.g. around Ladysmith). The rainfall is more reliable than in many other parts of South Africa, and generally 750 mm or more; but the winter drought period may be as much as four months in the interior. Soils are often leached and easily eroded. These limitations, singly or in combination, make large parts of this region unfavourable for arable farming; which, together with the poorer network of communications, explains why the area has less than one-tenth of the cropland of South Africa in spite of the relatively high rainfall. Beef and dairy cattle are important, utilizing the natural tall grasses; some very successful attempts have been made to improve the pasture by introducing new grasses. Maize and sorghum are the principal crops. A product peculiar to this area of South Africa is wattle bark, which is used for tanning. The wattle trees are grown either on plantations or on private farms, at elevations between 600 and 1200 m.

The eastern coastal region (Figure 80D). Subtropical temperatures prevail throughout the year, and the rainfall of some parts exceeds 1000 mm. There are, nevertheless, pockets of drier conditions where hill ranges cause rain-shadow effects, and the rainfall may also be erratic. The relief is more subdued than in the adjacent Eastern Uplands, but does not warrant the term 'coastal plain'. The main aspect of agriculture is the cultivation of tropical cash crops, sugar cane being the most important. Crops other than sugar occupy far smaller areas. Cotton growing is increasing in the northern parts, while citrus orchards are located chiefly in the Durban–Pietermaritzburg area and in the Mooi valley.

The Cape region (Figure 80E). The unique feature of this region is a winter rainfall (250–750 mm) sufficient for arable farming. The region lies outside the major Cape Ranges, extending from the mouth of the Great Berg river in the north to Cape Agulhas in the south, and inland to the foot of the Drakenstein Mountains, 50 km east of Cape Town. Most of the land consists of rolling hills below 300 m; apart from the Drakenstein Mountains themselves (which exceed 1500 m) there are few hills which exceed 900 m. This is the part of South Africa first settled by Europeans, the Dutch colonists in the seventeenth century establishing wheat farming and vineyards, and these have remained the principal features of the agriculture. More wheat is grown here than in any other part of South Africa, especially on the gently undulating areas of Swartland northwards from Cape Town to the Great Berg river, and the Ruens between Bredasdorp and Swellendam in the south. Yields are generally low and the wheat is usually grown in rotation with oats and other cereals. Sheep-farming is successfully practised, sometimes using stubble or fallow lands; the natural pasture is too poor for cattle. On the lowlands immediately north of Cape Town more intensive mixed farming is found, with dairy cattle based on old-established and improved pastures, and on fodder crops. Nearly half of Cape Town's milk is supplied within a radius of 30 km from the city.

In the early years vine growing was concentrated in the vicinity of Cape Town, especially in the Constantia valley. In the early eighteenth century it spread to the foot of the Drakenstein Mountains. Centres such as Stellenbosch, Paarl and Wellington came into being, and vineyards adorned the mountain slopes and valleys wherever rainfall was sufficient. Later viticulture moved over the mountains to the valley of the Breede river flowing past Worcester and Bonnievale, an area included under the next regional heading because of its greater aridity. Irrigation for vineyards becomes essential when the rainfall drops much below 500 mm.

A relatively new development in the Cape region is olive growing. The main olive-growing district today is found around Wellington, Paarl and Stellenbosch, well away from the sea, with at least 250 mm of rainfall. Although a species of wild olive is indigenous to South Africa, and climatic conditions in the south-west are broadly comparable with the main olive-growing regions of the Mediterranean, commercial olive growing dates only from 1935.

The dry south-west (Figure 80F). The rain-shadow effect of the mountains separating this region from the previous one means that most crops, including the vine, can only be grown with irrigation. Fortunately the region contains several large rivers which draw on groundwater in the dry season and are therefore perennial – the Olifants, Breede, Hex, the rivers draining the Ceres valley, and others. Owing to the need for irrigation, only the flat valley floors can be cultivated. Orchards and vineyards are most important, producing citrus and deciduous fruits, grapes, wine and brandy. Specialities include peaches from Elgin and Ceres, and pears from Ceres and the Hex valley. The Hex valley produces half the Republic's exports of table grapes. Some tobacco is grown, together with winter crops of oats and barley. The unirrigated land generally provides only poor sheep grazing, though some of the lower mountain slopes have been used for government forestry plantations. The several small towns in the region, including Clanwilliam, Worcester, Robertson and others already mentioned, are primarily concerned with fruit packing and drying, and the manufacture of wines and spirits. The region is well placed for export through Cape Town.

The southern coastal region (Figure 80G). From the Breede river in the west to Port Elizabeth in the east there is a narrow coastal strip lying south of the Langeberge and Outeniqua Mountains which receives rain all the year round, amounting to 500–650 mm in most parts, and up to 1250 mm on the southward-facing slopes of the mountains. In this region we can also include the lower Gamtoos valley which opens out between Port Elizabeth and Humansdorp. A great variety is apparent in the pattern of land-use; grass grows well in the relatively humid conditions, and both sheep and cattle are found. The main crops are oats and potatoes, followed by wheat; fruit orchards are deciduous (apples and pears particularly) and there are citrus trees on the rich alluvial floor of the Gamtoos valley. This valley is intensively cultivated and possesses the most valued land of the region.

The Karroo (Figure 80H). Under this heading are included the Great and Little Karroo, together with several of the Cape Ranges such as the Swartberge and Witteberge. The northern limit of the region is provided by the Great Escarpment; eastward the Great Fish river is a convenient boundary, though there is actually a gradual transition to the Eastern Uplands and the eastern coastal region. The climate is generally semi-arid: rainfall is less than 380 mm and in parts less than 250 mm; consequently, irrigation is essential for agriculture. Stream flow is generally intermittent, so that storage dams are required. In this way the waters of the Great Fish (with the Grassridge Dam), Sundays (with the Van Rynevelds Dam and Lake Mentz), Olifants, Dwyka, Gamka and Touws rivers have been used. The irrigated valley floors support citrus orchards in the case of the Great Fish and lower Sundays rivers; there are considerable problems here of rapid silting of the reservoirs. Other crops grown on the irrigated land include lucerne, tobacco and grapes. Oudtshoorn is the centre of intensive farming in the Olifants valley. Apart from the irrigable land, the Karroo is useful only as grazing for sheep and goats.

The dry plateau regions (Figure 80I). The Great Escarpment provides a physical boundary to the south and west; eastwards this region merges gradually into the High Veld. No rigid limit can therefore be drawn in this direction, though from the point of view of land-use the 500 mm isohyet provides a convenient dividing line, west of which agriculture is generally

Plate 41 Cape Province vineyards, Constantia

dependent on irrigation. Furthermore, the rainfall is unreliable, with long periods of drought, and some years of practically no rainfall at all in places. Most farms rely on bore-holes to provide water for domestic use and for their livestock. Extensive pastoralism is the characteristic form of land-use. Cattle find sparse grazing in the east, but elsewhere sheep are most numerous, and indeed represent the sole interest of some farmers.

Entering the region from the east, however, are several rivers of considerable size. The chief ones are the Orange and Vaal, which bring water from the wetter regions of the High Veld and the Lesotho highlands, and possess regimes that, with storage reservoirs, can provide for irrigation. The River Orange, even in its lower course, is a perennial stream, though its flow is greatly reduced by evaporation and relatively little reaches the Atlantic. Above Aughrabies Falls there are stretches of alluvium for about 240 km which provide suitable land for irrigation.

FORESTRY

Only about 1 per cent (1.26 million hectares) of South Africa is forest-covered, and of this only about 134,000 ha is indigenous forest – mainly in the mountains backing the coast where there is a government conservation programme. Pines and other softwoods make up one half of the area of introduced species, with fast-growing eucalyptus another 27 per cent and wattle 13 per cent. Mine-prop timber, one of the original reasons for extending commercial forestry, is available after 8–10 years growth and sawn timber after 30 years. Not surprisingly early plantations were near the mining settlements, but more recent expansion has been in Zululand, eastern Transvaal, Natal and southern Cape. South Africa now has over 230 timber processing plants, including pulping and paper.

FISHERIES

The fishing industry employs 10,000 people with nearly 6000 craft. It makes a vital contribution to South Africa's food supply, exports and agriculture by providing fishmeal, fertilizers and feedstuffs. About 600,000 tonnes are landed every year, more than 90 per cent from the cool waters off the west coast associated with the Benguela current. Pelagic shoal fish account for some 380,000 tonnes, with anchovy (81 per cent), pilchard (9 per cent) and herring (8 per cent) the principal species and the basis for meal, oil and canned fish industries. Much of the fishing industry of Namibia (Chapter 30) has been controlled by South African enterprises, but severe over-fishing along the whole of the west coast has resulted in declining yields. South Africa has imposed a 320 km controlled fishing zone and practises closed seasons, factory quotas and vessel controls in an attempt to conserve fish stocks.

REFERENCES

1 Best, A. G. G. and de Blij, H. J., *African Survey*, New York, 1977, p. 355.

34
The Republic: mining and manufacturing

South Africa is blessed with abundant mineral resources and can boast the world's largest known deposits of gold, chromium, platinum, vanadium, manganese, andalusite and fluorspar and considerable deposits of coal, uranium, diamonds, iron-ore, antimony, asbestos, nickel and phosphates. Mining accounts for 18 per cent of the GDP, gold alone provides 48 per cent of the value of exports and all minerals 65 per cent. There can be no doubting the importance of the mining industry in shaping the growth and character of the South African economy, and possibly in providing a model for the many other African countries which see mineral exploitation as their best path of development.

African peoples had traditionally worked a number of minerals and there were early small-scale European attempts to mine silver and copper. The big impetus to mining came in the mid nineteenth century, first with diamonds and then with gold.

MINING

Diamonds. The first finds were in alluvial deposits along the Orange river in 1867, followed by similar finds along the Vaal river, then a series of volcanic kimberlite pipes (Kimberley, 1870; Koffiefontein, 1875; Premier, 1902). In this century further large-scale alluvial deposits have been identified in marine terrace gravels along the Namib coast, mainly in Namibia but also south of the Orange river based on Alexander Bay (Figure 81).

Plate 42 Surface works and treatment plant at the new west coast Klenzie diamond mine

The excavation of the Kimberley pipe, which ceased in 1914, left the so-called 'Big Hole' – almost 1 km across and 400 m deep. Gradually the scale of mining went beyond the scope of the individual diggers and small companies that characterized early operations, and the mining became controlled by large companies such as De Beers with a large Black labour force housed in secure compounds.

Diamonds undoubtedly increased export income and provided security for capital

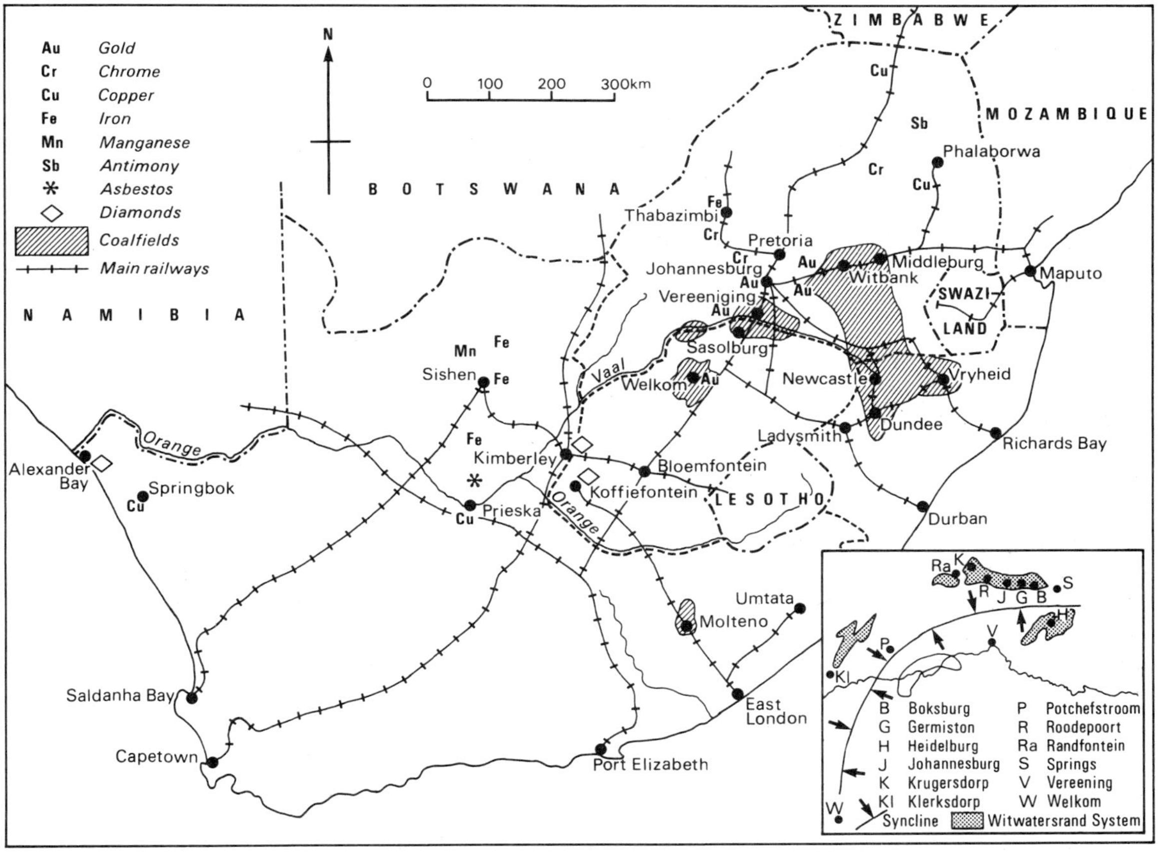

Figure 81 Mining in the Republic of South Africa

raised to build the infrastructure on which other developments would depend. In general, however, the diamond mining areas did not become the general industrial regions which were to typify gold mining. South Africa is still the world's largest producer of gem diamonds (14.4 million carats in 1983) and they account for 5 per cent of the total value of exports.

Gold. If diamonds provided the economy with its initial stimulus, it was to be gold that would transform it from rural and agricultural to urban and industrial. There was small-scale working of alluvial gold in the eastern Transvaal in the 1860s and 1870s, but rapid expansion followed the discovery of the gold-bearing conglomerate, 'banket', in the Witwatersrand in 1885. Mining was initially in shallow opencast workings but was rapidly replaced by the first adits (1888) and shaft mine (1892).

The gold-bearing Witwatersrand system is at the base of the Pre-Cambrian and outcrops on either side of a synclinal structure, which follows an arc from just south of Johannesburg to Welkom. Johannesburg was laid out as a 'planned' town in 1886 and the early mining was between Boksburg and Roodepoort on either side. Since the 1920s the production of the Central Rand area has declined and the principal mining area shifted first to the east (Springs–Heidelburg) in the 1920s, then later to the west around Randfontein, and in the 1950s to Klerksdorp and the Welkom area in Orange Free State. With time the mining has become deeper and at Western Deep Levels reaches 3800 m. The growing significance of uranium post-1945 has given many of the gold mines a new lease of life because the two minerals are often found together. Some of the mines now produce only uranium and for some others it is more important than gold. Since 1978 there has also been recovery of gold and uranium from mine dumps and 'slimes' dams, and there are now three such plants operating at Welkom, Brakpan and Klerksdorp.

In 1983 South Africa produced over 650 tonnes of gold valued at over R10,000 million (£3100 million). While gold prices have fluctuated over the years, the income generated has been the basis for the development of a sophisticated economic infrastructure, great commercial activity and considerable industrialization. Johannesburg is the country's largest metropolitan area, and the Pretoria–Witwatersrand–Vaal triangle is responsible for over 40 per cent of the country's generated wealth.

Coal. The essential energy base for South Africa's development has been provided by coal. The Karroo System contains proven reserves of 58 billion tonnes, some 97 per cent of the African total. Coal mining started at Molteno in the eastern Cape in 1864, and these low-grade deposits were linked to the Kimberley mines by rail. With improved rail transport the Natal coalfield (Newcastle, Dundee, Vryheid) was opened up rapidly in the 1890s and a start made on developing the Transvaal coalfields in the Witbank–Middleburg and Springs–Heidelburg–Vereeniging areas. There are now nearly 100 operational mines with a total production of over 130 million tonnes a year. Between 1983 and 1988, six new high-capacity mines are to be opened and total output is planned to reach 330 million tonnes by the year 2000.

There are the advantages that the coal seams are mainly quite thick (2–5 m), often nearly horizontal, at no great depth (60–220 m) and of coking and steam grades. A high proportion of the faces are machine-mined and the resultant coal is cheap. This means that it can be used economically for thermal production of electricity (about one-third of the coal produced) and, in the face of lack of domestic oil resources and an embargo on oil trade with South Africa, can be used as the raw material for petroleum products. Coal has become the second foreign exchange earner after gold, and the country has become the world's leading steam-coal exporter.

Other minerals. South Africa produces some 50 different minerals in all. Apart from the gold and diamond areas the most important zone of varied mineralization is the Bushveld Igneous Complex of the Transvaal. Here are found chrome, copper, nickel, vanadium, platinum, manganese, tin and silver, to mention just some. South Africa is in the top five world producers of antimony, asbestos, chrome, manganese, phosphate, uranium and vanadium. Clearly, some of these minerals have considerable strategic importance, and this goes some way towards explaining the reluctance of other nations to impose the rigid trade embargoes called for by some opponents of the country's apartheid policies.

South Africa has considerable deposits of iron-ore. Those at Thabazimbi (western Transvaal) and Sishen (northern Cape) were originally developed to serve the expanding domestic iron and steel industry. During the 1970s the output at Sishen was increased from 4 to 22 million tonnes a year, with three-quarters now exported by way of a new rail link to the coast at Saldanha Bay, north of Cape Town, where a new port has been built. At Richard's Bay on the Natal coast another new port has been built, with a main objective of providing coal exporting facilities.

Christopher has emphasized the importance of mining, not simply as the force behind the transformation of the economy, but also for its impact on the social geography of the country[1]. Many of the present towns had their origins as mining settlements. The need for tight control and security at the diamond mines resulted in the separation of the con-

Plate 43 Anti-pollution spray system at the Richard's Bay coal exporting terminal

tract Black workers in 'compounds', and this approach was also adopted at other mines even though the same security was not needed. This segregation was to become all-pervasive and the spatial dualism became enshrined in legislation in the apartheid system of 'separate development'. The now vast Black townships of Soweto and Sharpville are present-day expressions of the company compound. It can therefore be argued that much that is fundamental in the geography of South Africa – economic, social and political – has roots in the mining industry.

MANUFACTURING INDUSTRY

Most of the African states have placed emphasis on industrialization, but only South Africa has succeeded in creating the self-sustaining industrial activity that all seek. In this respect (but possibly only in this) South Africa provides an example to be followed, and the process of industrialization is worth examining.

The role of mining as a catalyst for economic change has already been noted. Initially it resulted in rapid urban growth at the mining centres and the demand for machinery, equipment and consumer goods which had to be imported. There was therefore growth at the ports, and the expanding railway network provided the vital links between ports and mines. Increasingly, local industries were established to provide import substitutes; but until well into this century manufacturing was very much a direct offshoot of the agriculture and mining it served and in 1911 still accounted for only 3.8 per cent of GDP.

After 1918 there was rapid expansion and diversification of industry, and two world wars encouraged the demand for greater self-sufficiency. By 1939 there were 10,000 manufacturing concerns of various sizes, and by 1948 (Table 38) manufacturing contributed 16.3 per cent of the GDP and now accounts for over one-quarter. South Africa is the only African state that can truly be classed as industrial.

Just as manufacturing now dominates the economy in production terms, so it does in employment. From 653,300 in 1960, the numbers employed more than doubled to 1,400,000 in 1983, nearly twice the number in mining. The importance of industry is reinforced by the somewhat precarious and limited potential for agricultural development and the vulnerable nature of an economy dependent on finite mineral resources, the demand for which is fluctuating and unpredictable and world prices generally unstable.

Table 38 *Republic of South Africa: sector contributions to GDP*

	1911 (%)	*1948 (%)*	*1960 (%)*	*1970 (%)*	*1983 (%)*
Agriculture	20.8	15.2	14.1	9.3	6.4
Mining	28.4	10.3	15.9	11.5	17.7
Manufacturing	3.8	16.3	23.5	26.6	26.3

Source: South Africa Central Statistical Services.

It has been suggested that three interrelated factors have been the basis for the country's substantial and sophisticated industrial base – state intervention, foreign capital and technology, and the exploitation of cheap labour, mainly Black, which is largely excluded from the benefits of industrial progress[2].

In South Africa the state has been involved both directly and indirectly in industrial development. During the 1920s and 1930s the government encouraged the channelling of domestic capital into industry, started the 'protection' of home industries, imposed import restrictions, adopted a policy of preferences for imported capital goods and material, and offered considerable tax incentives. Until the 1950s the main expansion was in light and labour-intensive industries such as textiles, clothing, food and engineering; but more recently the emphasis has been on strategic industries such as military equipment, vehicles, electronics, chemicals and equipment. If in other African countries the linkages have been neglected (for example, in Ghana), in South Africa they have been encouraged. Originally motor vehicles were assembled from imported components, but at least 66 per cent of the content must now be local in origin.

The involvement of government has been direct through the creation of state corporations, the earliest for iron and steel in the late 1920s and energy in the 1930s, and 30 per cent of the total industrial investment is by the state. Chief among state enterprises are SASOL (oil from coal), ISCOR (iron and steel), SENTRACHEM (chemical), NATREF (oil-refining), ESCOM (electricity) and ARMSCOR (military equipment).

Until 1945 industrial development was based mainly on local capital, but since that time there has been heavy overseas investment in a wide range of industries, including motor vehicles, chemicals, food processing and computers. The emphasis is on capital-intensive technology, although the country has a large reservoir of cheap labour.

This cheap labour has undoubtedly provided South African industry with considerable advantages. Much of the social cost associated with the labour is carried by the 'homelands'. Thus, the unemployed Black has no place to reside except his 'homeland' – he has no rights in the urban areas except that he has work there. In 1986 there was some sign of relaxation of this aspect of apartheid. South Africa has been fortunate in having the raw material and fuel for the creation of a substantial heavy industrial base.

Metal industries. The country's first blast furnace was built at Pretoria in 1917. In 1928 ISCOR was created to develop the industry, and in 1934, also in Pretoria, the first integrated iron and steel plant was opened. The iron-ore came from Thabazimbi, with coking coal from Witbank and Natal. A second integrated plant was opened at Vanderbijlpark, Vereeniging, in 1942, incorporating a long-established steel works based on scrap. There is now a third plant at Newcastle and a yearly total capacity of 6 million tonnes of liquid steel. In Johannesburg and Vereeniging there are steel mills based on scrap. With its range of non-ferrous minerals, South Africa has the raw materials for a variety of special steels – tungsten, chrome, vanadium – and for a range of other metal-processing industries – copper, zinc, tin and aluminium, for example.

Based on these, South Africa produces structural metal, sheet, pipe, rod and wire, and there are a range of engineering works. At the VECOR works at Vereeniging heavy machine parts are produced for cranes, turbines and mill machinery, and elsewhere there is the production of engines, agricultural machinery, machine tools, ship repairs and building, and vehicle and armaments manufacture. South Africa now has a high degree of self-sufficiency in the supply of industrial plant.

The large Sishen iron-ore deposit assures supplies for many years and there are unexploited deposits of many of the other minerals. Problems arise from the distance over which many of the materials have to be transported, and there are certainly areas, such as the Rand, where heavy water-consuming refining processes are at a disadvantage. However, many of the metal industries are located in the Pretoria–Witwatersrand–Vereeniging metropolitan area, where distance from the coast offers a degree of protection from imported products for which the transport costs are increased.

Chemical industry. Until the Second World War, explosives and fertilizers were the main chemical industries. There has been wide diversification into insecticides, plastics, man-made fibres, synthetic rubber and a range of chemicals based on coal, petroleum, salt, phosphate and pyrite. There is a considerable paint industry, and a sophisticated pharmaceuticals industry now produces serums, vaccines, antibiotics and drugs. Soaps, perfumes and toilet preparations are important. Much of the heavier chemical industry is located in the Johannesburg region, but the lighter types are more widely dispersed.

Textiles and clothing. South Africa now has more than 300 textile mills and 700 clothing factories employing over 230,000 people, or 8 per cent of the labour force (1982), chiefly drawn from the Coloured and Asian communities. Not surprisingly there is a longstanding woollen industry based on local raw materials, producing knitted goods and blankets for the home and export markets. Raw cotton is produced locally in only small quantities, but the last 30 years have seen the rapid expansion of the cotton and synthetic fibre industries which together now exceed the value of wool. Textiles still have to be imported in considerable quantities: there is scope for further expansion, and this is an industry that has the advantage of being relatively labour-intensive and particularly useful in South Africa's situation.

Food-processing. Food-processing industries now employ about 180,000 people, some 60 per cent of the output is exported, and together with fruit this accounts for 5 per cent of the value of exports. Domestic agriculture and fishing provide the raw-material base, and flour and grain milling, sugar refining, meat processing, dairy production, fish and fruit canning and wine making are important sectors. The location pattern derives from the geography of agricultural activity already described.

Plate 44 Sasol II – one of South Africa's vital oil from coal plants

INDUSTRIAL LOCATION

On the basis of the distribution of Gross Product the South African economy had early become dominated by the four main metropolitan regions (Table 39). The four metropolitan regions together account for over 86 per cent of the manufacturing, and the Pretoria–Witwatersrand–Vaal region alone accounts for over 50 per cent. Associated with this there are similar heavy concentrations of commerce, finance, transport and construction, and only the mining shows a more dispersed pattern – nearly 70 per cent being away from the metropolitan regions. The P–W–V region has as its base the gold, uranium and coal

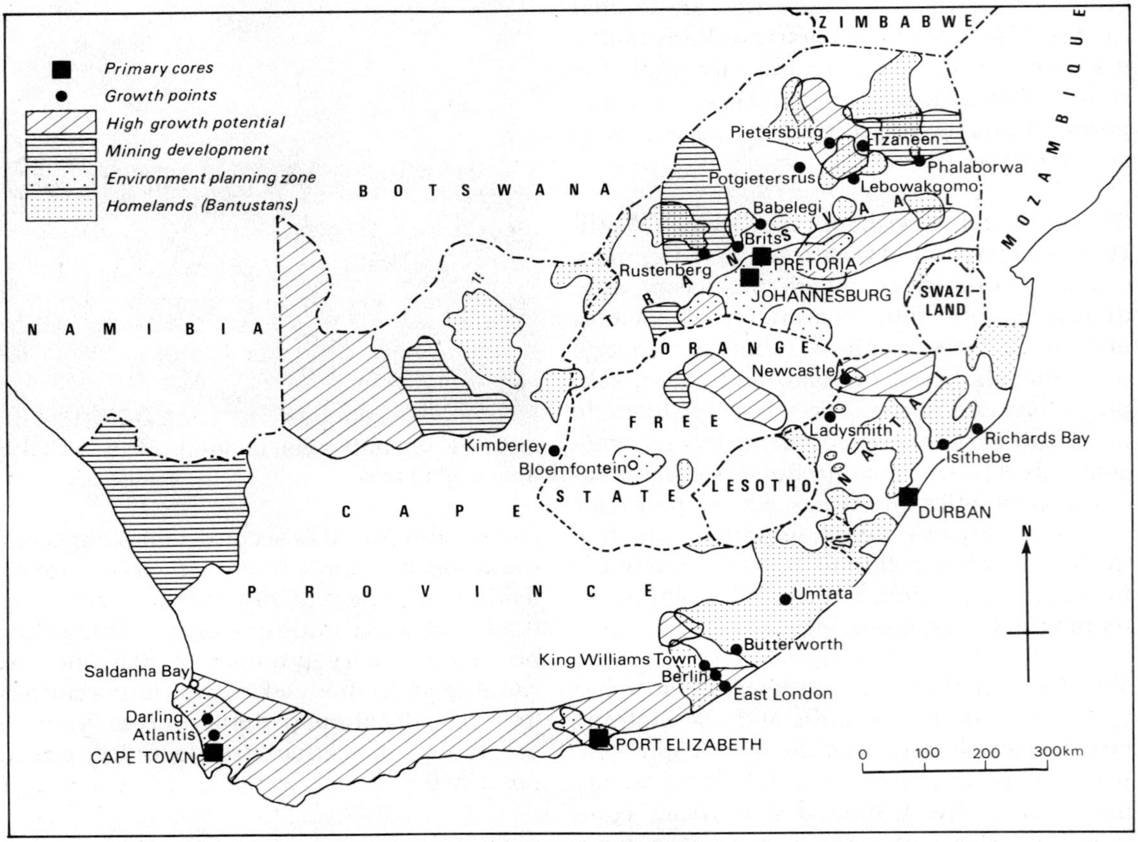

Figure 82 Economic planning zones of the Republic of South Africa
Source: After Wiese

Table 39 *South Africa: regional distribution of gross product in 1970 (percentages)*

	Durban–Pinetown	*Greater Cape Town*	*Port Elizabeth Uitenhage*	*P–W–V**	*Other regions*	*All*
Total gross product	14.14	12.24	3.91	42.07	27.64	100
Mining	0.29	0.36	0.15	29.85	69.35	100
Manufacturing	15.58	13.48	6.16	51.20	13.58	100
Electricity	10.72	12.72	2.99	32.92	40.65	100
Construction	14.33	12.26	2.80	52.65	17.96	100
Commerce	10.98	15.06	4.28	48.10	21.58	100
Transport	15.24	13.61	5.95	34.72	30.48	100
Finance	10.94	14.92	3.73	53.43	16.98	100

*Note:** Pretoria–Witwatersrand–Vaal.
Source: After Wiese (1984).

mining industries, the associated concentration of population and purchasing power, and a focal position in the network of transport that has evolved.

The other metropolitan regions have the advantages for industry of being ports, Durban with the additional benefit of being closest to the P–W–V region. Durban is the country's leading port (with 25 per cent of all traffic) and of the main industrial regions is the least disadvantaged by problems of water supply. It has attracted oil-refining, shipbuilding, rubber, chemicals, sugar-refining and synthetic fibres and has experienced particularly high growth rates in recent years. Cape Town, the second port, has declined relatively but is also an oil-refining centre and has wine, tobacco, food, textiles, clothing and vehicle assembly as main industries. Port Elizabeth also has vehicle assembly and tyres, footwear and textile industries.

The South African space economy is therefore markedly 'core–periphery' in structure, with the main manifestations of advanced development concentrated in a few urban areas and large parts of the Black homelands and White interior (e.g. the western and northern Cape) remaining underdeveloped. When this is combined with symptoms of over-concentration in the cores (increased commuting, traffic congestion, pollution, housing shortages, water supply problems, socio-political problems), there has, not surprisingly, been the demand for decentralization. However, since apartheid was formalized after 1948 it, too, has become a factor influencing the government's attempts to restructure industry. This arises because the system denies Blacks any residential rights in White areas unless they have employment in those areas, and because it is policy to keep to a minimum the number of Blacks in White areas. There is therefore a logic in locating industry in such a way that the Blacks can reside in their homelands. This can be done by locating industry either in or at the margins of the Black areas. The decentralization policy has passed through several distinct phases.

During the early 1960s the emphasis was on the development of small centres just beyond the margins of the existing primary areas (e.g. Hammarsdale outside Durban). In the mid-1960s second-tier urban centres such as East London and Pietermaritzburg became the focus of attention, and in the late 1960s centres rather more distant from existing concentrations – places such as Newcastle, Pietersburg and Ladysmith. The 1967 Environment Planning Act provided the statutory mechanism for steering industry into the homeland 'borders', especially the more peripheral ones to which industry had been reluctant to move of its own accord. The 1975 National Physical Development Plan and new regional incentives of 1982 have furthered the same policy. An initial policy not allowing White investment actually in the Black homelands was reversed in 1968.

The designated growth centres are indicated on Figure 82. Most successful of the homeland growth centres would seem to be Babelegi in Bophuthatswana, where 10,000 jobs have been created in about 100 enterprises; but a total of 30,000 new homeland jobs does little to detract from these areas as the source of labour for White core areas. In 1979 the Ciskei National Development Corporation started the Dimbaya Industrial Township scheme. Despite the Environment Planning Act there has been continued employment growth in core areas; and despite the growth centre incentives, an ALCOR aluminium wire, cable and fencing factory which opened at Richard's Bay in 1976, adjacent to an aluminium refinery, was closed only two years later when ALCOR decided to concentrate production at plant on the Rand – an indicator of the locational pull of the P–W–V area.

In total, job creation in the decentralized areas is between 7000 and 8000 a year, and the refusal of planning permission for a proportion of the new jobs proposed in the core areas only serves to reduce overall employment opportunities. The effect of the decentralization policy must be counted no better than modest and in certain respects counterproductive.[3]

ECONOMIC INFRASTRUCTURE

Many theorists have argued that the provision of infrastructure is a prerequisite for development. Certainly South Africa, as the most developed African country, has by far the best infrastructure – yet the Republic is perhaps a good example where the development of the road, rail and port system, and energy and water supplies, was closely related to established demand and was not provided in the mere hope that demand would be generated.

Transport

South Africa lacks navigable waterways and the versatile ox-wagon for long provided the main means of transport. South Africa's first railway was a short line inland from Durban (opened in 1860) and a line from Cape Town reached Wellington in 1863. Both were built on the 4′8½″ gauge but later modified to the 3′6″ (1065 mm) – which became the most widely adopted gauge, being cheaper to construct especially in the escarpment areas where there are particularly difficult engineering problems. By 1885 a line had linked Cape Town with Kimberley, and in the following year the first Natal coal reached Durban by rail. The growth of diamond and then gold mining stimulated the demand for rail transport, and by 1910 there were 12,000 km and today 24,000 km of route.

The emergence in the interior (in the Pretoria–Witwatersrand region) of the country's dominant concentration of economic activity and the importance of the mining industry generally places great demand on the rail system for bulk freight movement. Over 15,000 km – about 42 per cent of the total track – has been electrified, and this part of the system accounts for 85 per cent of all freight and passenger traffic. When completed, the Sentrarand computer-controlled marshalling yard to serve the P–W–V region, with its 62 marshalling tracks, 20 reception tracks and 32 despatch lines, will be one of the largest in the world. Railway freight rates have been set at levels to encourage use and assist industrial location policy, and from early in their history they have been government-controlled.

The ports are also controlled by South African Transport Services. Because it is the closest to the P–W–V area, Durban handles 25 per cent of the country's trade: its sheltered bay has dredged access of 12.8 m, allowing use by large container vessels. Traffic includes coal, manganese and sugar exports and oil imports. In terms of ship calls Cape Town is second port, but being largely concerned with general cargo (fruit, agricultural exports, consumer-good imports) its tonnage places it in fifth position. Port Elizabeth handles ores, fruit and wool exports. East London, a river port, suffers from silting, competition from Durban and Port Elizabeth, a relatively poorly developed hinterland, and questions regarding its longer-term relationship with the 'independent' Transkei and Ciskei.

South Africa also has two new ports. Richard's Bay, 190 km north of Durban, was commissioned in 1976 and is a designated growth centre. Built primarily for the export of Transvaal coal, it can accommodate 150,000-tonne vessels and its coal-handling capacity is being increased to 44 million tonnes a year. It also has a tanker berth and general cargo facilities and now handles over 35 per cent of the country's seaborne trade. There is mining for heavy minerals close by, an aluminium smelting industry, fertilizer and chemical plants, grain milling and electrical and mechanical engineering industries. The population had grown to 27,000 by 1979 and is planned to rise to 100,000. It is seen by the planners as a potential urban–industrial complex with fully developed port facilities.

Also opened in 1976, Saldanha Bay, 120 km north of Cape Town, was built as the export terminal for iron-ore from Sishen. Unlike Richard's Bay it is not a designated growth centre and suffers competition from nearby Atlantis, which is. World recession has led to the shelving of plans for iron and steel and ship-repair industries.

Because its railway system was well developed, South Africa paid little attention to a road network until the 1930s, when a National Road Act (1935) provided the planning and financial basis for road construction. However, by 1959 there were only 7055 km of 'national' roads, of which 6400 km were bitumen-surfaced. Since that time, as in most other countries, there has been increasing demand for road transport and the inter-urban networks ('national' and 'regional' control) now comprise 184,000 km, of which 48,000 km are surfaced. Between 1960 and 1983 the number of cars increased from 902,000 to 2,800,000 and commercial vehicles from 229,000 to 1,031,000. Reflecting the geography of economic activity, 52 per cent of the registered vehicles are in the Transvaal and 25 per cent in the Cape.

Freight haulage over larger distances tends to be controlled by SATS Road Services and in its pricing and operations is complementary to, rather than competitive with, the railway system. Over shorter distances road haulage predominates, being partly controlled by SATS and partly private.

Because much of the transport – rail, road and ports – has been government-controlled virtually since the Union was created in 1910, South Africa has a far better-integrated transport system than most countries. The government is able to use transport as a tool of policy (for example, by means of special rates for industrial development centres).

Energy

By the 1980s the republic had become a net exporter of energy and had achieved a high level of self-sufficiency. About 85 per cent of the primary energy derives from coal, 60 per cent of which is used in electricity generation, 17 per cent to produce synthetic fuels and 6 per cent for coking. The South African Coal, Oil and Gas Corporation (SASOL) produced its first synthetic petroleum at Sasolburg in 1955, and the oil crisis of the mid-1970s prompted the construction of two further plants, SASOL 2 and 3, at Secunda in the eastern Transvaal. These consume 32 million tonnes of coal a year and reduce the republic's dependence on imported crude oil.

The republic accounts for 60 per cent of the continent's generated electricity, well over 90 per cent coming from generating stations controlled by the government's Electricity Supply Commission (ESCOM). The total installed capacity amounts to nearly 25,000 MW. Not surprisingly 26 coal-fired stations provide the bulk of this, with six new stations having been completed in the 1980s, including the world's largest dry-cooled plant at Matimbra. There are plans to double the capacity. Much of this additional capacity will also be coal-fired, but in 1985 the republic opened its first nuclear power station at Koeburg, 30 km north of Cape Town. This has a capacity of 1800 MW and South Africa now has the ability to enrich uranium, which it produces in large quantities, for use in nuclear reactors.

Given the flow characteristics of South Africa's rivers they are not suitable for hydroelectric power generation, except with large storage reservoirs. On the Orange river the Hendrik Verwoerd and P.K. le Roux dams provide 320 and 220 MW respectively, and the Tugela–Vaal pumped-storage scheme in the Drakensburg provides 1000 MW to meet peak demands. On balance, it seems unlikely that HEP will provide any significant contribution to total energy demand, and South Africa could well be increasingly reluctant to buy from outside as she has done from Mozambique's Cabora Bassa HEP scheme.

The obvious weakness of the republic's energy situation is the lack of domestic oil reserves and the need to import oil in the face of sanctions imposed by some suppliers. While the SASOL coal-derived oil products go some way towards filling the gap, the country is still in a vulnerable position.

Plate 45 Hendrik Verwoerd Dam – South Africa's largest water storage scheme on the Orange river

Water supplies

If fuel is unlikely to be a constraint on further development, the supply of water for energy production, industry, agriculture and domestic use could be. Through its Directorate of Water Affairs the government has had to put great effort into ensuring water availability.

As already explained, South Africa is not a well-watered country: perennial rivers are found in only about one-third of the country and 18,000 million cubic metres is lost by evaporation and flooding. Groundwater yields about 1100 million cubic metres a year. The country's largest concentration of population, industry and mining in the P–W–V region is just where water supply creates special problems.

Irrigation schemes dating from the 1930s include the Buchuberg Dam near Prieske, and the Vaal–Hartz and Riet river schemes near Kimberley; but South Africa now has over 3000 storage dams of various sizes, with a total storage capacity of 24,000 million cubic metres. The Orange river has a flow of 7500 million cubic metres, and the Orange River Project initiated in the 1970s involves two main storage dams (Hendrik Verwoerd 6000 million cubic metres; P.K. le Roux 3000 million cubic metres), an 83 km water tunnel to take water from the Verwoerd reservoir to the Great Fish River, a tunnel and canal to take water from the Great Fish to the Sundays River and the Van der Kloof irrigation scheme. In the first phase 20,000 ha is to be irrigated, but the potential is 300,000 ha with 2200 million cubic metres for urban and industrial use.

The Tugela–Vaal project of 1974 involves the pumping of water from the eastward-flowing Tugela river to the Sterkfontein Dam in the Drakensburg, where evaporation losses are less than along the Vaal, and from where water can be made available to the P–W–V area. The scheme also incorporates the HEP project already mentioned. In the western Cape the Riviersonderend–Berg project of the 1980s involves several dams, diversion tunnels and a distribution system for agricultural, industrial and urban use. Water supplies for Durban and Pietermaritzburg are being improved by the construction of the Inanda Dam on the Umgeni river, which will increase the yield of the existing Midmer, Albert Falls and Nagle Dams from 380 to 526 million cubic metres. The Useta project (which is still in progress) involves the Jericho, Westoe and Morgenstond Dams, diversion of water, and supplementary pumping mainly to ensure water for several electricity generating stations and Sasol 2 and 3 at Secunda.

With demand for water increasing at over 3 per cent a year there is need for continuing attention to the supply problems. In the final analysis it may not be the quantity but the high cost of water that is critical.

SOUTH AFRICA – A DEVELOPING COUNTRY?

In contrast with other African countries, the republic's infrastructure has a level of sophistication and its economy a level of development that none can match. Yet a look at South Africa's trade (Table 40) suggests that it too is

Table 40 *Republic of South Africa: trade (million Rand)*

	1960	*1970*	*1983*
Exports			
Gold	536.0	837.1	9869.8
Agricultural products	267.8	382.2	1411.8
Diamonds	119.9	168.0	1157.8
Metal ores	41.4	94.7	543.7
Metal and metal products	85.5	261.4	1842.1
Chemicals	33.4	63.2	447.2
Other	334.0	567.0	5121.1
Imports			
Machinery	219.3	776.3	4391.1
Motor vehicles	134.9	354.3	1048.8
Textiles	139.4	162.0	594.6
Chemicals	78.1	199.1	1350.0
Metals and metal products	83.8	193.5	747.0
Other manufactures	249.5	466.0	3112.8
Other	1111.1	2547.2	3082.8

Source: Central Statistical Services (1984).

primarily an exporter of raw or basic commodities, while the imports consist largely of manufactured goods.

In terms of its trading structure it is still therefore comparable with many developing countries. With the big increase in iron-ore and coal exports this is a pattern that has been accentuated in recent years despite the significant development of its manufacturing industries. This is reflected at the ports which in 1985 handled 90 million tonnes – 73 million tonnes of exports and 17 million tonnes of imports. Richard's Bay (44 million tonnes) and Saldanha Bay (12 million tonnes) are first and third largest ports but concerned almost entirely with bulk exports. It might have been thought that this big increase in bulk exports would have encouraged South Africa's shipping industry but, as in many other developing countries, this has not happened. The explanation may well be the same in all cases, namely, that exports are mainly in the hands of mining companies which historically have left shipping to others and exported on an FOB (full-on-board) basis. Thus, Anglo-American, which controls 50 per cent of all the investments on the Johannesburg Stock Exchange, exports in this way.

It is estimated that over 90 per cent of the country's trade is controlled by a small number of large mining and financial houses. This too is a common feature of developing countries. Also like many other African countries, South Africa displays spatial and sectoral dualisms, a distinct core–periphery structure, and stark contrasts between the regions and people who 'have' and those who 'have not'.

While South African growth and development provides an example to other African countries – perhaps particularly with respect to the efficiency of organization and the sectoral linkages that have been developed – in the final analysis its main problem may be precisely the same: namely, there is the need to spread the benefits of growth more equitably, with the additional problems in South Africa which stem from the wealth being concentrated in the hands of an entrenched White minority. The future development of the republic could well depend on the way this problem is addressed.

REFERENCES

1 Christopher, A. J., *South Africa*, London, 1982, pp. 119–33.
2 Rogerson, C. M., 'Apartheid, decentralization and spatial industrial change', in Smith, S. M. (ed.). *Living Under Apartheid*, George Allen and Unwin, p.47.
3 Rogerson, C. M., op.cit. pp. 60–1.

35 Lesotho and Swaziland

The former British High Commission territories of Basutoland and Swaziland became independent in 1966 and 1968 respectively, Basutoland taking the name Lesotho. While having a political independence not shared by the 'homelands' within South Africa, they are nevertheless very much a part of the South African economic sphere of influence and are rendered the more vulnerable by being landlocked and of very small size – Lesotho is only 30,335 km^2 and Swaziland 17,400 km^2.

LESOTHO

Nearly all parts of the country exceed 1500 m in height, and in the east the mountains rise to over 3300 m, the greatest elevation in South Africa. The western parts are a continuation of the High Veld plateau surface of the Orange Free State, but eastwards as the ground rises the topography becomes more broken and eventually mountainous in character. The basal geological stratum is Karroo sandstone, which is overlain by a horizontally layered mass of Karroo lavas some 1200 m thick. Strong erosive action has sculptured this elevated country into a network of mountain ranges and ravines. Here are to be found the headstreams of the Orange river, and many of those of the Caledon, which explains the vital interest of the Republic of South Africa in this mountainous country. Rainfall is adequate for agriculture: 635 mm at Maseru rising to over 2000 mm on the crest of the Drakensberg. Better-watered Lesotho is therefore in contrast with the aridity of much of South Africa, but in 1983 it too suffered drought, there was a severe grain shortage and the need for food aid. Most of the rain falls in the summer months, often in torrential showers, but even in winter drought is not normally prolonged. On the higher ground there is widespread winter snow cover and temperatures are often below zero.

The basalt of the higher areas provides a rich, friable, black or brown soil, but the soils on the Karroo sedimentaries of the western lower land are poorer. Arable agriculture tends to be concentrated in the mountain valleys and lower areas of the west. The mountains provide the main grazing lands with sweet veld up to 2400 m and a less palatable sour veld at higher levels; above about 3000 m there is a tundra-type vegetation. Lesotho is free of mosquitoes and tsetse.

Despite lower rainfall and poorer soils, the western margins of the country – about 20 per cent of the total area – hold over 40 per cent of the population and have high rural densities. Pressure on the land has impoverished the soil and resulted in widespread erosion. The main crops are maize and millet, with some winter wheat especially along the Orange river valley. Here is located the country's capital, Maseru (pop. 48,000), and the best-developed transport network (Figure 83).

The centre of the country, of intermediate altitude, has generally better soils which are less eroded; but transport facilities are less well developed and pastoralism based on sheep, goats and cattle is the main agricultural activity except in valleys. The high eastern half of the country, with true mountain scenery in the Drakensberg, has thin soils, heavy

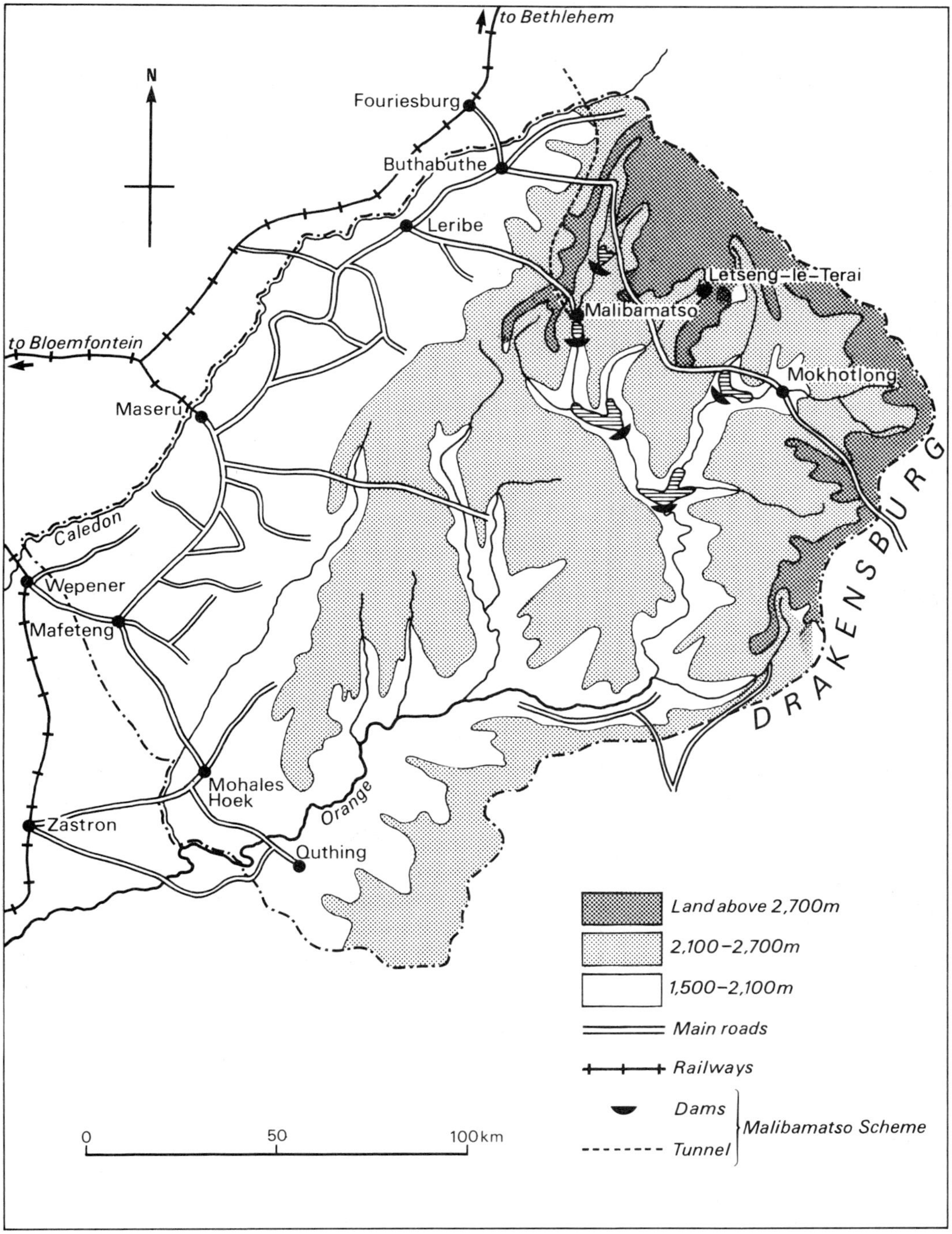

Figure 83 Lesotho

summer rainstorms, winter snow, a relatively short growing season and locally severe erosion. There is not a large population but there is considerable pressure on the available cultivable land.

A main problem for agriculture is the erosion that results from the combination of steep slopes, heavy rains and over-grazing and cultivation. Some attempts to control erosion were initiated in colonial days and there has been terracing in some areas, tree-planting, and water control. Altogether some 420,000 ha have been protected, but much remains to be done. With the population increasing at 2.5 per cent a year and terrain severely restricting the land available for farming, the pressure can only grow.

The economy

Poor as the agriculture is, it is the main support for the bulk of the population and provides the main exports – wool, mohair and live animals. There has been a small export of diamonds from a pipe at Letseng-le-Terai (Malibamatso) where a modern mine was opened in 1977 but ceased operations in 1982. Given the general inadequacy of the domestic resource base it is not surprising that the South African mines, industries and services have attracted workers from Lesotho. It is estimated that an average 45 per cent of the male and 6–10 per cent of the female labour force is employed in the Republic. About 18 per cent of the South African mine labour is from Lesotho and there are altogether between 150 and 200 thousand workers out of the country at any time. Their remittances are actually larger than the GDP and 60 per cent of the salaries goes directly to the Lesotho Bank from which it can then be drawn. In this sense it could be argued that people are the country's main export.

Development planning started in 1971 and there have since been three 5-year plans. Much of the country is accessible only by bridle paths, so the plans put emphasis on road improvement, especially in the mountain areas. Even now there are only just over 300 km of surfaced road and in 1983 over 900 km of 'food aid tracks' had to be built. There has also been an emphasis on agricultural improvement, and there have been a number of pilot schemes for large rural development projects with progressive farming methods, assistance with dryland farming, mechanization services, improved credit and marketing, storage and transport services. However, implementation is not helped by rigid social structures and communal land tenure. The Lesotho National Development Corporation (1967) has been creating the infrastructure for the development of industry. Industrial estates have been started at Maseru and Maputsoe. Grain milling, sugar packing (sugar for South Africa), wool and mohair processing, weaving, tanning, ice cream manufacture, fruit and vegetable canning, tyre retreading, and brewing, have added to the employment market; but the number of jobs created has been well below the planned targets and industry still accounts for only 5 per cent of the GDP.

Lesotho's rivers are not yet used for power generation nor for irrigation on any significant scale. The Malibamatso Project or Lesotho Highlands Water Scheme, formerly known as the Ox-Bow Lake Scheme, has been under discussion for over 20 years. As originally envisaged the scheme involved damming several of Lesotho's southward-flowing rivers and diverting the water by tunnel to Bethlehem and eventually the Johannesburg region of South Africa. If the Transvaal is to have this water available by the year 2000 when its present supplies become inadequate, construction needs to start in 1987; but it has proved difficult to reconcile Lesotho's desire for independence and full control of the water supply with South Africa's wish to have a guaranteed supply. If fully developed the scheme would be one of the largest in the world, with five dams (Figure 83), three HEP stations, 120 km of tunnel and 220 km of new road. There would also be possibilities for irrigation. South Africa needs the water as much as Lesotho needs the income and the infrastructure the scheme would bring, and it seems likely that they will eventually come to an agreement to proceed.

Lesotho has been attempting to attract tourists from South Africa by providing the organized gaming facilities which its neighbour forbids. At Maseru the Holiday Inn and Casino serve this purpose and there is also a new Hilton Hotel. The areas with scenic attractions and the possibilities for winter sports are often inaccessible, with poor roads either washed out by rain or snow-bound. The number of tourists increased from 4000 to 132,000 between 1968 and 1978 and there is clearly scope for extending this industry by providing the necessary infrastructure.

As yet Lesotho remains poor – the per capita GDP is about $450 – and overwhelmingly dependent on South Africa by which it is surrounded. Most of her trade is with, and the rest through, South Africa, which also supplies the bulk of the country's food deficit. The 1983 raid by South African troops on supposed sources of guerrilla activity located in Maseru, and January 1986 imposition of limited sanctions by South Africa, serve to emphasize the vulnerability of Lesotho and the problem it faces in developing an independent economy.

SWAZILAND

Africa's second smallest country after the Gambia, Swaziland, like Lesotho, suffers from being land-locked (but shares frontiers with both South Africa and Mozambique) and is overwhelmingly dependent on the republic. In contrast, it is well-watered, with considerable agricultural and some mineral resources and a population small enough (626,000) not to place too much pressure on the land. In 1907 a British-appointed commission allocated about 60 per cent of the territorial land to the Swazi people and on the rest there was a mixture of European-controlled activities. There was therefore an economic dualism between the largely traditional subsistence Swazi economy and the commercial activities of the Europeans.

The country can be divided into four north–south belts (Figure 84). The **High Veld** in the west lies above 1800 m. Rainfall is considerable here: from 1200 to 2000 mm a year (Mbabane: 1400 mm). The country is dissected, and many areas are unsuitable for cultivation. Soil erosion is a serious problem for arable farming; the main aspects of land-use are sheep grazing and forestry. The **Middle Veld**, between 400 and 800 m, is separated from the High Veld by a marked escarpment. It is an area of tall grassland, where there are considerable potentialities for the development of stock-rearing, and the cultivation of maize and various sub-tropical crops. Rainfall averages 750–1000 mm a year. The **Low Veld**, between 250 and 300 m, is a drier region (500–750 mm annually), so that successful cultivation of crops depends largely on irrigation. There is, however, much good cattle pasture here. The **Lebombo Range** in the east rises to 825 m.

The economy

The greater part of Swaziland is at present devoted to pastoral farming, with cattle rather more numerous than sheep or goats – though an important aspect is the wintering of sheep from the Transvaal. Where rainfall is sufficient crops of maize, sorghum, cotton and tobacco are grown. But there are considerable prospects for extending irrigation agriculture. Swaziland fortunately possesses several sizable perennial streams. The lower Usutu river, for instance, has an average annual discharge greater than that of the Vaal at Vaaldam in South Africa. So far the chief areas of irrigation are on the Usutu river at Big Bend and west of Bremersdorp, and around Eranchi and Hlume in the north-east using water from the Komati river. Crops of rice, citrus and other tropical fruits, and sugar-cane are grown.

Some sugar was introduced in 1958 and is

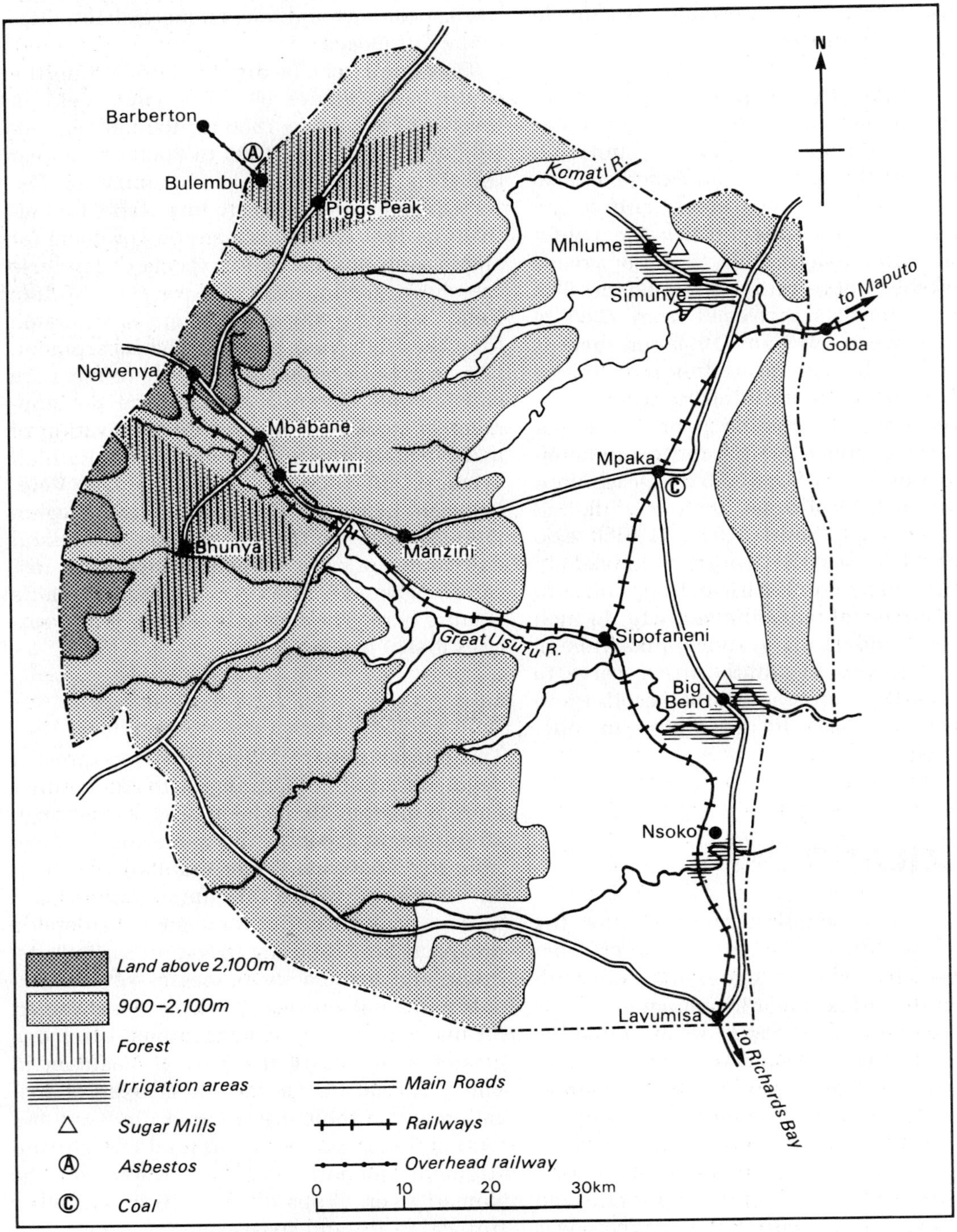

Figure 84 Swaziland

Table 41 *Swaziland: principal exports*

	1975 (%)	*1980* (%)	*1982* (%)
Sugar	55.6	48.8	32.7
Wood pulp	8.6	13.9	14.5
Iron ore	8.3	1.4	—
Asbestos	6.4	5.9	4.6
Citrus	3.0	2.9	4.8
Canned fruit	2.5	3.5	5.0
Meat	1.0	3.0	—
Other	15.2	20.6	—

Source: Economic Commission for Africa.

grown under irrigation in the low veld region of the east. The mills are foreign-owned and the cane mainly from plantations, but there has been an attempt to encourage Swazi farmers to supply the mills. This has been most successful on the Vulvulane Irrigated Farms project which supplies the Mhlume mill. Mills have been established at Mhlume (145,000 tonnes capacity), Suvunga/Big Bend (140,000 tonnes) and most recently at Simunye (126,000 tonnes). The last mill has been criticized for being capital-intensive, creating only 3000 new jobs and making Swaziland even more dependent on the fluctuating world sugar market. Production increased from 254,000 tonnes in 1979 to a current level of over 400,000 tonnes; altogether 13,000 are employed and over 80,000 dependent in whole or part on the sugar crop, and sugar exports now make about one-half of the export earnings (Table 41). Swaziland consumes only 20,000 tonnes a year and the EEC has taken about 120,000 tonnes a year at prices usually above those prevailing worldwide. The higher production now has to find markets elsewhere, and Swaziland's exports have been restricted by an International Sugar Organisation quota.

Other agricultural commodities make up about 10 per cent of the export value, with citrus, canned fruit and meat being the main items. There has been some air-freighting of meat to markets as distant as Gabon. Because

Plate 46 Orange packing station at Swaziland's Inyoni Yami irrigation scheme

the bulk of this export production comes from non-Swazi farms, the government has initiated Rural Development Area Programmes in which basic infrastructure (roads, water, clinics, schools) is provided to encourage agricultural production, with small-holders integrated with plantations and associated processing industries. Cotton and improved cattle feed crops have been introduced. The productivity of the low veld is thought to be only 4 per cent of its potential and 100,000 ha could be converted to high-yield farming by extending irrigation.

Wood pulp now occupies second place in the export list. This reflects comparatively recent expansion of the forest area with conifers and broad-leaved trees in the hill country around the Usutu river south of Mbabane, the capital, and in the north around Piggs Peak (Figure 84). With an emphasis on fast-growing varieties the 700 km^2 of forest is able to sustain a pulp industry (at Bhumya), the product of which is mainly exported, and pit props, industrial timber, veneer timber and fuel wood for domestic use. Employment is provided for 4000 people in the forests and 2500 in pulp and saw-mills.

Swaziland's mineral resources are mainly

associated with Pre-Cambrian granites which underlie much of the country; but minerals have been declining in relative economic importance. In 1970, iron-ore and asbestos made up 35 per cent of the exports, but this had dropped to 16 per cent in 1975 and by 1980 to only 7.3 per cent. In 1964 the country's first railway, a 225 km link to Maputo, allowed iron-ore mining to start at Ngwenya, and production peaked at just over 2 million tonnes a year in the early 1970s. The closing of the mine in 1979 demonstrated the vulnerability of an economy based on finite resources, the demand and price for which fluctuate with market conditions. Anzolite-asbestos is mined at Bulembu (Havelock) and averages between 35 and 40 thousand tonnes a year exported by way of a 20 km overhead cableway to Barberton in the Transvaal. Barytes and pyro-phyllite were produced in small quantities until the mid-1970s, and production of low-volatile, anthracite-type coal from the Mpaka mine provides for a small tonnage to be exported to Mozambique and Europe. The coal is deep and heavily faulted and is unlikely to be mined either cheaply or in very large quantities.

The government's industrial strategy has been to concentrate on the processing of Swaziland's own renewable resources: 85 per cent of the value added by industry now derives from agricultural commodities (sugar, citrus, meat, dairy produce, wool and timber). There has been recent diversification into fertilizers, bricks, cotton ginning and oil-seed crushing and woven carpets.

With a relatively limited array of developed resources, Swaziland has, like Lesotho, sought to expand the tourist industry and there was rapid growth in the 1970s. This growth was not maintained because rising fuel prices and oil rationing in South Africa reduced tourist numbers, and Swaziland received greater competition from Lesotho and 'Sun City', Bophuthatswana, which are nearer the main South African population centres. The main centre for tourists has been the Ezulwini valley between Mbabane, the capital, and Manzini, the main industrial centre. The valley has fine scenery and a wildlife sanctuary with varieties of big game. A second, larger, wildlife park has been developed at Hlane.

Economic planning

Swaziland demonstrates marked dualism. The bulk of the population is engaged in traditional agriculture, but the modern sector has grown rapidly and accounts for most of the GDP. The well-developed manufacturing sector contributes 22 per cent to the GDP, and in recent years the average annual growth rate of the economy has been about 5 per cent – creditable although less than the planned 7 per cent. The Third National Development Plan (1978–83) sought to create up to 4000 new jobs a year in the modern sector but has only attained about 2400 jobs a year in the face of 7000 annual school-leavers. This reflects the vagaries of world markets for primary products: the closing down of the iron-ore mine; the reduction in asbestos exports and a decline in numbers working in South Africa. There are now about 10,000 working there, a necessary link with the Republic. Swaziland is also dependent on South Africa for most of its electricity, the Swaziland currency is linked to the Rand, much of its trade is with the Republic and air transport and telecommunications are mainly routed through Johannesburg. Swaziland has also been conscious of its vulnerability as a land-locked state, and so a disproportionate share of investment has been in transport and communications projects. The dependence on the only rail link to Maputu and growing instability in Mozambique led to the opening in 1978 of another railway from Phuzomoya southwards to Golela and from there to Richard's Bay – thus, when Swaziland would ideally want to reduce its South African links, it has perforce to strengthen them. There are longer-term plans for a line northwards from Mpaka to Border Gate, Transvaal, and this would allow a more direct link between the Phalaborwa

Plate 47 Loading eucalyptus mining timber, Shiselmeni Forestry Company, Swaziland

mining regions of Transvaal and Richard's Bay – Swaziland would benefit from transit revenue. The Mnjoli hydroelectric power scheme in the Ezulwini valley reduces dependence on South African electricity.

In a country as small as Swaziland even relatively modest development projects may have a considerable impact on the job market and overall economic development. The building of the northern rail link, the Mnjoli HEP plant and Simunye sugar project are just such schemes, and development planning will be successful to the extent that well-integrated projects can be identified and the sectoral linkages created.

PART NINE: THE ZAMBEZI AND LIMPOPO LANDS

36 Physical geography

The basins of the Zambezi and Limpopo rivers are well-defined: in the north the watershed with the Zaire river, to the west the Kalahari, and to the south the rugged northern limbs of the Drakensberg. As in many other parts of Africa, physical and hydrographic boundaries here conflict seriously with political boundaries. The political entities within these basins are Zambia, Zimbabwe, Malawi and Mozambique.

GEOLOGY AND STRUCTURE

Except for the coastal plain of Mozambique, the greater part of the area is underlain by various rock groups of Pre-Cambrian age. Of these, the Archaean granites and gneisses are the most extensive. Of later Pre-Cambrian age are certain sedimentary formations; the Katanga System of Zambia (corresponding to part of the Transvaal System in South Africa) contains valuable mineral deposits, particularly of copper-ore. Zimbabwe is crossed by a major Pre-Cambrian intrusion known as the Great Dyke (an offshoot of the Bushveld Igneous Complex) which, appearing as a range of hills running north-north-east for 530 km, contains many important minerals. The most recent Pre-Cambrian rocks are the quartzitic sandstones of the Melsetter Highlands.

The Karroo System consists of continental-type sediments (sandstones, shales, etc.) laid down on the eroded surface of Pre-Cambrian rocks with, at the top of the system, great thicknesses of basalt lavas. Owing to later denudation it is now found mainly in down-faulted areas such as the middle Zambezi and Luangwa troughs. The Ecca beds of the Karroo System contain thick coal seams worked at Wankie; the upper Karroo basalts, equivalent in age to the Stormberg basalts of Lesotho, are well displayed in the gorges below Victoria Falls. The Cretaceous period saw extensive marine deposition in Mozambique – sandstones, shales and limestones – and this phase continued into the Tertiary. Searches for oil in these strata are in progress.

RELIEF AND DRAINAGE

Zambia and Zimbabwe are characterized by some of the most perfect planation surfaces in the world. Vast expanses of apparently level land at heights of 1200–1500 m dominate much of the territories. Cutting across these upland plains are the fault troughs occupied by the middle Zambezi and Luangwa rivers and, to the south, the Limpopo and Sabi rivers. The floors of the troughs may lie up to 1000 m below the surrounding plateau and are floored mainly by the Karroo strata. Structurally these features are part of the East African rift valley system. Both main rivers have winding middle courses, but their catchment areas and regimes differ. The Zambezi has a discharge fourteen times that of the Limpopo, which is reduced to a string of pools during the dry season. The **Zimbabwe uplands** consist of a broad zone along the watershed between the Zambezi and Limpopo–Sabi tributaries, bevelled at heights between

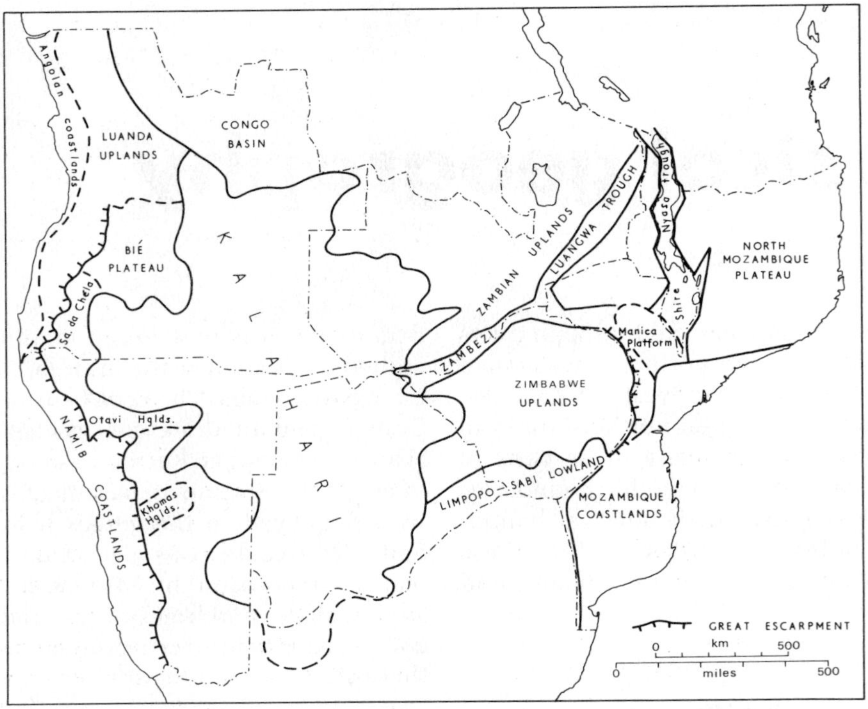

Figure 85 Physical regions of the Zambezi lands and south–western Africa

approximately 1200 and 1500 m. The exceptional evenness of the planation surfaces over large areas may be partly due to the fact that they are mostly cut in granite. Even the Great Dyke fails to form a major feature, rising in the Umvukwo Range no more than 450 m above the surrounding plateau (and usually less). River valleys are shallow, but usually well-defined. In the east the land surface stands at over 1500 m, where it ends in the Great Escarpment overlooking the lower country of Mozambique. Away from the central watershed zone, in the lower parts, the older (Tertiary) planation surfaces have been largely destroyed.

The Zambian Uplands are also cut by extensive planation surfaces varying in height (possibly as a result of later warpings) from 1000 m near Livingstone to over 1500 m in parts near the Zaire border. In detail the surfaces are even flatter and less well-drained than their counterparts in Zimbabwe. The main surface in the Copperbelt is the mid-Tertiary or African surface at about 1300 m; a few isolated hills rising to 1400 m are the last remnants of the older Gondwana surface. The planation surfaces of the uplands sink to 1000 m on the Kalahari border, and further west they disappear beneath a covering of Kalahari sand and other deposits. The surfaces are of great significance in the human geography of the Zambezi lands; their elevation has modified the climate and encouraged white settlement, while their level nature has greatly facilitated agriculture and the development of modern communications over large areas.

The Malawi–Shiré trough continues the East African rift valley system directly southwards. The rift containing Lake Malawi is deepest in the north between the Livingstone Mountains and the Nyika plateau. Here the lake is over 700 m deep and possesses virtually no bordering plain. Farther south, the lake has a fringe of flat land up to 50 km wide behind Kota Kota. The lake level averages 450 m; it is known to fluctuate by 7 m, largely because vegetation periodically blocks the shallow outlet. From the outlet downstream to Liwonde the Shire river falls only 2 m, but below this the river drops 425 m in the Murchison Rapids which are spread over 110 km. The Shire is navigable below Port Herald. Around Lake Malawi the highlands of Pre-Cambrian rock rise to 2650 m in the Nyika plateau. Isolated in the south, Mount Mlanje stands east of the Shire river and attains 3000 m.

Northern Mozambique consists of a platform built almost entirely of granite and metamorphic rocks, with a narrow coastal fringe of Cretaceous and Tertiary marine sediments. The surface slopes eastwards from heights of over 1800 m in the uplands near Lake Malawi, and from nearly 2500 m in the Namuli Mountains to about 300 m at the plateau edge. The coastline is probably a faulted one. The rivers drain east and north-east, the Ruvuma forming the border with Tanzania.

The Manica Platform in central Mozambique represents the work of river planation, producing a surface sloping from 900 m at the foot of the Great Escarpment (Umtali–Melsetter highlands) to 150 m near the coast. **The Mozambique coastal plain,** broad in the south, rises very gradually inland to about 150 m. The plain is underlain by Cretaceous and Tertiary limestones and sandstones. Coastal sand-dunes are of great size in places, blocking river exits. Inland, the river courses are often ill-defined, so that vast inundations may follow the rains.

The River Zambezi. The river rises in Zambia at about 1370 m. After passing through part of Angola, it enters the flat basin area of Barotseland, which floods in the summer. From Sioma to Victoria Falls the gradient steepens and rapids occur where the river encounters Karroo basalts. At Victoria Falls the river plunges over a drop of 108 m. One hundred kilometres below the falls there begins the lake impounded by the Kariba Dam (water level 490 m, almost the same as that of Lake Malawi). On the left bank below the dam the Kafue and Luangwa rivers enter. The Kebrabasa rapids in Mozambique and the Caboro Bassa Dam mark the limit of navigation on the lower Zambezi, about 620 m upstream from the delta. The great economic significance of the Zambezi lies not in the navigability of some stretches, however, but in the Kariba hydroelectric scheme, in the similar development at the Kebrabasa gorge in Mozambique and in the possibilities for irrigation in certain areas. The very size of the Zambezi, however, is an obstacle to communication: only two railways cross the river at present, at Livingstone and Sena. The bridge at Sena is no less than 3.5 km long. At Tete, the river is still nearly a kilometre wide. Between this point and Livingstone the only road crossing, apart from that at Kariba Dam, is at Chirundu, where the Great North Road on its way between Harare and Lusaka passes over the Otto Beit Bridge.

CLIMATE

Except for the south of Mozambique, the area lies within the tropics, reaching latitude 9°S in the Mbada highlands. Over most of the uplands temperatures are rarely excessive, owing to the modifying influence of altitude. Temperatures of 32°C are exceptional at 1500 m and the average temperatures of the warmest month at places over 1200 m are in the twenties. Mean monthly temperatures at Harare resemble those at Cape Town. On the other hand, in the Limpopo valley and the low-lying parts of Mozambique, maximum temperatures may reach 43°C. It will be seen that the annual range of temperature is relatively small – 6° only on the Mozambique coast, 8° on the uplands. Rainfall is a more important factor in the differentiation of the

Table 42 *Zambezi–Limpopo lands: temperature and rainfall of selected stations*

Station	*Altitude (m)*		*J*	*F*	*M*	*A*	*M*	*J*	*J*	*A*	*S*	*O*	*N*	*D*	*Year*
Harare	1450	T	20.4	20.4	19.9	18.8	16.1	13.7	13.7	15.6	18.8	21.0	21.0	20.4	18.2
		R	190	188	114	25	13	—	—	1	8	27	94	147	807
Bulawayo	1320	T	21.6	21.0	20.4	18.8	16.1	14.3	13.8	16.1	19.4	21.6	22.2	22.2	18.8
		R	140	126	114	20	15	—	—	—	5	15	78	125	638
Lusaka	1257	T	21.0	21.6	21.0	20.5	18.3	16.1	16.1	18.3	21.6	24.4	23.3	28.8	26.1
		R	240	185	130	24	18	20	7	—	4	21	70	140	860
Nkata Bay	480	T	25.0	24.4	25.0	23.9	22.2	19.9	20.5	20.4	23.3	25.0	26.8	25.5	23.3
(L. Malawi)		R	205	316	336	294	85	62	60	27	8	12	24	218	1647
Mozambique	15	T	27.7	27.7	27.3	26.8	24.4	22.8	22.2	22.2	23.9	25.5	27.7	28.3	25.5
		R	227	221	142	82	30	30	15	13	12	12	30	140	954

Notes: T = Temperature (°C); R = rainfall (mm).

seasons (Table 42).

The mean annual rainfall decreases to the south and south-west. Areas with more than 1200 mm are restricted to highlands (e.g. Umtali, Mlanje), and to parts of Mozambique. In the Limpopo valley the total rainfall is barely 380 mm and the fall is markedly seasonal; it also varies in amount from year to year, and its geographical distribution is not constant. As examples of these two last points, the recorded rainfall at Mazabuka on the railway south-west of Lusaka was 450 mm in 1923 and 1300 mm in 1924. Differences in rainfall between neighbouring farms in Zimbabwe of 300 mm in one year, with reversal of the amounts in the following year, have also been noted.

The rain is associated with mE air from the north, as the Inter Tropical Convergence (ITC) moves south across the territories. The first sporadic rains occur in September in the north and in November in the south, but precipitation is not at all reliable until a month or so later. Just before the rains break the air becomes hot and oppressive in the lower areas; then the rains arrive and for several months it may rain for short periods almost every day, turning the red dust into red mud. The rains fall in thundery showers, the rate sometimes reaching 150 mm an hour, so that much water fails to soak into the ground and the usefulness of the rainfall for plant growth is much reduced. Rainfall of this intensity is also highly conducive to soil erosion. Further, the rainy season begins generally in the warmest period of the year when evaporation losses are greatest. In between the downpours the clouds clear, and days with less than three hours' sunshine are infrequent.

The rains continue until March or April, and occasionally unreliable showers until May. The winter season (May to August), the most pleasant time of the year, is generally dry, with mild sunny days and frost on the higher parts at night. From the middle of August temperatures rise rapidly until the first thunderstorms of the rainy season break. This concentration of rainfall is repeated at most stations in this part of Africa. Beira, with 1400 mm a year, and Maputo, with 800 mm, both have more than 85 per cent of their rainfall in 6 months. The proportion at Livingstone on the Zambezi is 95 per cent, which indicates the reason for the great variation in flow of the river throughout the year. The average discharge of the Zambezi at Livingstone ranges from 100 million cubic metres in November to more than 9000 million in April.

SOILS AND VEGETATION

No comprehensive survey of the soils of the whole area is yet available. From the viewpoint of agriculture other factors, such as accessibility and climate, often take precedence over soil type. Granite, the most common rock, produces rather poor sandy soils, but these nevertheless have been widely cultivated in Zimbabwe in areas where transport facilities are reasonable. Some of the schists, gneisses and intrusions provide richer loams. The Karroo beds develop a variety of soils, of which those formed on limestone appear most valuable. In areas of relatively high rainfall and peneplained surface, strong lateritic tendencies are noticeable in soil formation, with reddish colouring in the upper horizon and iron-rich concretions. Generally speaking, the less highly laterized and more potentially fertile soils are found on the plateau margins where dissection is in progress and drainage better.

Various forms of savanna characterize much of the area. All types are to be found, from closely forested areas mainly in the valleys and on hill slopes, to open grassland with scattered trees on the level planation surfaces. According to the length of dry season and the amount of moisture available, trees may be evergreen or deciduous. One of the most widespread savanna forms is characterized by the tree species *Brachystegia*. It thrives on the plateau areas of 900–1500 m but is less common on the lowlands. In the drier warmer valleys of the interior the *Mopani* tree is dominant. Acacias and the baobab tree also favour drier areas. The savanna is useful for extensive grazing; in the early summer when the grasses have withered, before the rains, tree foliage can sometimes supply feed for animals and the trees themselves provide useful shade. On the higher lands of eastern Zimbabwe (Melsetter–Inyanga) and of Malawi, savanna is replaced by mountain forest on the wetter parts (generally around 1500 or 1800 m), including the magnificent cedar forests of Mlanje Mountain. Elsewhere in these highlands areas of grassland occur. Along the coast of Mozambique there extends a belt of tropical forest a few kilometres in width, where the short dry season and rainfall of up to 1200 mm encourages the growth of dense bush and evergreen forest, with palm trees, and occasional patches of mangrove swamp, as in the Zambezi delta.

THE HISTORICAL AND POLITICAL BACKGROUND

The occupation by white settlers of Southern Rhodesia, originally Mashonaland and Matabeleland, now Zimbabwe, began in the 1880s. Most of the settlers came from or through South Africa, as had many of the earlier explorers and mineral prospectors. In 1889 Rhodes founded the British South Africa Company to open up more of the territory (whose native population at the time was less than half a million), and the company in fact administered the Rhodesias until 1922. Following elections by the Whites in Southern Rhodesia, this country became a self-governing British colony in 1923 in preference to joining the Union of South Africa. Northern Rhodesia was taken over as a British protectorate in 1924. Nyasaland, first explored by Livingstone in the 1860s, became a British protectorate in 1891 after Sir Harry Johnston had negotiated a series of treaties with the African chiefs and suppressed the Arab slave trade.

In 1953, following long discussions and a referendum of the Whites in Southern Rhodesia, proposals to link the Rhodesias and Nyasaland in a federation were approved in the British parliament and a new major political unit was created in this part of Africa. During the ten years of its existence it became clear that there were many economic advantages to be derived from the union of the three territories, which together covered an entirely land-locked area approximately the size of the Republic of South Africa, and depended on Portuguese facilities for most of its overseas trade. However, Southern Rhodesia (now known as Zimbabwe), with its more advanced economy, benefited disproportionately. The secession of first Nyasaland and later Northern Rhodesia brought the federation to an end in 1963.

In 1964 both Zambia and Malawi attained total independence. The Rhodesian white minority government unilaterally declared independence from Britain in 1965; but neither Britain nor the United Nations recognized this state of independence, which terminated in 1980 after a long armed struggle. Mozambique (about twice the size of Zimbabwe) was a Portuguese overseas territory, where Portuguese settlement dates back to 1505. After a 10-year struggle the country became an independent republic in 1975.

In 1980 Rhodesia became fully independent on African majority rule and took the name Zimbabwe. Within Zimbabwe and Zambia (formerly Northern Rhodesia) there are more than 200,000 European settlers (70 per cent are in Zimbabwe), making this one of the chief areas of European settlement in tropical Africa. Of the white population, nearly half is of South African origin, though more English-speaking than Afrikaans. Malawi (formerly Nyasaland) has a few white people, but almost as many Africans as Zimbabwe.

37 Zambia

After many decades as a British protectorate Northern Rhodesia received its independence in 1964 and was renamed Zambia by the new African government. In contrast to Zimbabwe south of the Zambezi, the numbers of European settlers are relatively few, and more than half of them are concerned with mining in the Copperbelt. The total 1985 population of Zambia was 6 million, and it increases annually at the high rate of 3 per cent (a rate which could double the existing population in 24 years). The African population is slightly smaller than that of Zimbabwe, and since Zambia is a much larger country (753,000 km^2, approximately three times the size of Great Britain), one of the most striking features is its emptiness. Outside the Copperbelt the average population density is only 7 people per km^2. Yet Africans have lived in Zambia for centuries. Traces of ancient civilization dating back 1000 years before the advent of white settlers have recently been found in the Gwembe valley, south of Lusaka; evidence of gold and copper working, cotton spinning and weaving has come to light from old burial grounds here.

Zambia gives an impression of endlessly undulating plateau country, lying mostly between 900 and 1500 m. Driving north from Livingstone (the capital before 1935) along the main highway to the Copperbelt, the road passes first through about 100 km of dry sandy grassland, where trees are few and stunted. For the next 400 km the road becomes more hemmed in by trees, though after Kalomo, European tobacco farms and fairly extensive cattle ranches make their appearance. Termite mounds 3–6 m high are a regular feature of the landscape. In the midst of this European farming country lies Lusaka, the present capital. It stands on an open plateau at 1200 m; its history dates back to 1905 when a railway siding was built here. Since independence it has grown rapidly and with 650,000 population is almost the equal of Harare (formerly Salisbury), the capital of Zimbabwe. Its houses are mostly single-storeyed, and occupy large plots, giving the town a spacious appearance; but now at its edges are tawdry shanty towns of squatters.

North of Lusaka the bush becomes progressively denser; hill tops support *Brachystegia* and *Jubernardia* with sparse grass, while depressions contain tall grass and denser woodland. The tendency for tree cover to become denser over the plateau as one moves from south to north partly reflects the increasing rainfall. The low-lying floors of the middle Zambezi and Luangwa down-faulted troughs are relatively dry and very hot; many have less than 600 mm of rain, the effectiveness of which is much reduced by its arrival during the hot season. On the northern and higher parts of the plateau up to 1200 mm is experienced.

THE ECONOMY

Farming

There is great diversity of farming in Zambia, both of aims and methods. The agricultural sector only contributes about 12 per cent to the GDP, reflecting the inefficiency and low productivity of most of the farmers. Large-scale commercial farms dominate the sector; they produce half Zambia's beef, 30 per cent of its marketed maize and a high proportion of wheat, pork and poultry. Nearly all these farms continue to be worked by Europeans. African farming has been improving in recent years but the general picture is still one of subsistence cultivation which contrasts sharply with the farming of the European settlers. The more remote areas, particularly the northern plateau away from the railway, remain the stronghold of primitive shifting cultivation. In these areas methods of agriculture have changed little for centuries, and only the beginnings of a cash-crop economy can be seen. A shifting agricultural system is only suited to an area of low population density, for each family requires up to 100 ha for its subsistence. With villages moving every four or five years it becomes difficult to provide social services, including medicine and schools. Some Africans, particularly those who have gained experience by working on European farms, are now turning to cash-crop production and a number of government-aided schemes have begun.

In the upper Zambezi area of the west lies Barotseland, a kingdom of 500,000 inhabitants, and formerly a 'protectorate within a protectorate' – its special status deriving from early treaties with Queen Victoria. Here among the periodically inundated grasslands is the home of great cattle-owning tribes such as the Lozi, for the area is free of tsetse fly. A type of transhumance is practised, the people with their cattle moving to higher ground when the rivers flood in February or March, and returning once the floods have subsided to cultivate their maize and pasture their cattle.

Another area of regularly flooded ground in Zambia occurs in the north-east. Lake Bangweulu was discovered by Livingstone in 1868, five years before his death there. The lake is shallow and fed by the Chambeshi, which forms a great swampy delta, the home of some 10,000 Africans. The water level fluctuates seasonally: in the rainy season the people move to villages on higher mounds and cultivate cassava, while in the dry months the men live in fishing camps on the lake shore. However, there are also longer-term cycles of changing water level associated with temporary blockage of some channels with vegetation. In high-water cycles villages were flooded and crops ruined, whereas in low-water years the black swamp soils proved fertile. With recent dredging and channel cutting these fluctuations have been largely eliminated. The people trade the fish with surrounding Bemba tribes for maize, but they also sell quantities of dried fish to the Copperbelt where there is a large market for it.

European farming in Zambia is very restricted in extent compared with Zimbabwe. Many factors contribute to this. The presence of tsetse fly over approximately half the country, but more particularly in the Zambezi, Luangwa and upper Kafue valleys, severely restricts pastoral farming to which large areas might otherwise be suited. Rainfall on the plateau is not deficient in total amount, except possibly in the south-west, but it is more erratic in its incidence than in Zimbabwe, and strongly seasonal. Lateritic soils are extensive and possess the usual disadvantages for permanent cultivation. Land alienated to white settlers has been far less extensive than in Zimbabwe, consisting principally of areas along the railway and in the Copperbelt and amounting to only 6 per cent of the total area. For the European farmer the main consideration is accessibility; European farms are largely located near the railway, from about 50 km north of Lusaka south-west towards Kalomo. Lusaka is the commercial hub of this farming area, which concentrates on the combination of maize, tobacco, dairy farming and stock-rearing. Another important European farming area is at Mkushi, 250 km north of Lusaka. Mazabuka and Choma are smaller centres.

In the extreme east of the country around Chipata (formerly Fort Jameson), and in the north-east around Mbala (formerly Abercorn),

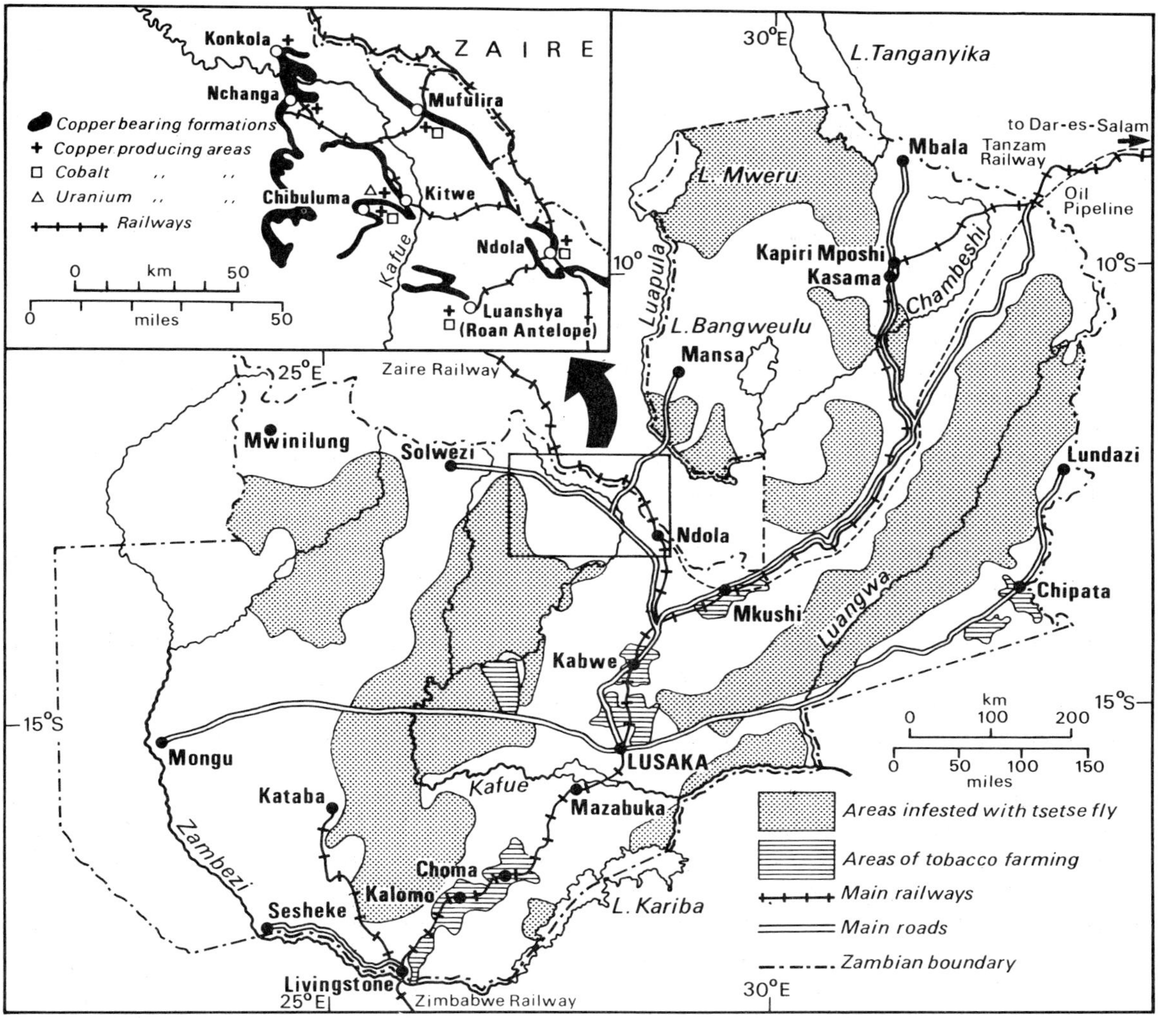

Figure 86 Zambia: tsetse fly distribution; tobacco farming and the Copperbelt

are much smaller areas of European farming, remote from railway and any large towns, which have declined considerably since their initial settlement. Before commercial farming can be further extended in Zambia, improvement of the transport system (and especially the roads) will be essential. Maize is the most extensive crop planted, occupying about two-thirds of the cultivated ground, and yielding about 7 million bags a year; tobacco, cotton and sugar are also grown.

There is thus a great diversity in farming in Zambia. Not only are there sharp contrasts between European farming and African subsistence agriculture, but – because of the variety of climate, soil and the distribution of tsetse fly – also great differences in the forms of agriculture on which the vast majority of the Africans depend for their livelihood.

Mining

In an area of less than 4200 km^2 on the Zaire–Zambezi watershed lies the Copperbelt (Figure 86), one of Africa's most valuable and highly mineralized zones, second only in importance to the Rand of South Africa. The production of copper is the key industry of Zambia, for copper is by far the most valuable export, accounting for 90 per cent of all export revenue. The mining sector as a whole accounts for 34 per cent of the GDP and is of paramount economic importance.

Zambia is one of the world's largest copper producers and has reserves that should last beyond the end of the century. However, a prolonged period of low copper prices has adversely affected the industry in recent years. Foreign exchange has become scarcer and this has caused difficulties in the maintenance and modernization of equipment. A project to extract copper from tailings at Nechanga began in 1985, and this may sustain production which has been falling since 1976. Rationalization is also being attempted by the merger of the two major copper companies and by more efficient use of processing and refining equipment.

The development of the Copperbelt has raised certain unique problems. The region is situated in the heart of the sub-continent of southern Africa, 1200 km in a direct line from the nearest coast. Harare, the nearest major town, is 560 km away (1700 km by rail). Before the 1930s the area of the Copperbelt, with its six producing mines, busy towns, highways and airfields, schools and theatres, shops and factories, was one of isolation. It was thinly populated and agriculturally unproductive, owing to a combination of poor soils, tsetse fly and primitive agricultural techniques. Roads were little more than tracks through the bush, rivers were crossed by rough ferries, malaria was an ever-present danger. It is estimated that there were fewer than 20,000 Africans in the region in 1931, compared with 300,000 in 1961 and 1 million in 1985 (Table 43).

British prospectors, attracted by reports of ancient copper workings, first discovered the copper-ores in the upper Pre-Cambrian rocks at about the turn of the century, and the region was tapped by rail, from the south, in 1909. Because of the low grade of the surface ores, mainly copper oxide, the area aroused little interest; but in 1925 copper-sulphide ores were located at depths of about 30 m below the surface. Invention of the flotation process in 1910 had solved the problem of refining low-grade (3.5 per cent) sulphide ores economically, and working of these began in 1928. In 1931 the area produced 3000 tonnes of blister copper (up to 99 per cent pure), production rising rapidly to 100,000 tonnes in 1933. Since the mid-1930s electrolytic copper (99.95 per cent Cu) has been produced in increasing quantities. By 1933 output had reached 220,000 tonnes; by 1958, 376,000 tonnes. In 1958 a new electrolytic refinery was opened at Ndola; production for 1968 reached 654,000 tonnes and 1985 (reflecting lower prices) 480,000 tonnes.

Table 43 *Zambia: growth of Copperbelt towns (population in thousands)*

	1939	*1961*	*1980*
Kitwe	21	90	341
Ndola	18	85	323
Chingola	6	44	192
Mufulira	18	68	187
Luanshya	24	57	164

Plate 48 Surface plant at Zambia's Nkana copper mine

Figure 87 Railways of the Zambezi–Limpopo lands

The chief mines are located at Nchanga, Nkana, Mufulira and Luanshya (Roan Antelope); newer ones are at Chibuluma, Bancroft, Chambishi and Chingola. The main settlements of the Copperbelt are based on the older mines. Ndola (pop. 320,000) has been the government administrative centre of the region since 1904, and its history as a settlement goes back much further; still to be seen in the town is the wild fig tree under which Arab and African slave-traders bartered human lives. The other principal town of the Copperbelt, Kitwe (pop. 350,000), is of more modern foundation (1928) and is today slightly larger than its rival Ndola.

These and other smaller towns of the Copperbelt contain well over half the European population of Zambia and one-fifth of the African population. Here, then, is a concentration of population which, apart from that of the southern Transvaal, has no equal anywhere else in southern Africa. The towns of the Copperbelt are linked to the rail-head at Ndola by branch railways, while there is also a good network of tarmac roads. Ndola is the principal airport. The mining companies have made full use of copper profits to provide housing, medical and recreational facilities for both Europeans and Africans. Newly grown mining communities are represented by neat rows of white houses shimmering in the heat haze.

Because of the situation of the Copperbelt – 1900 km by rail from the nearest port – it is necessary to refine the copper-ore in the mining area. In the past electricity was obtained from thermal power stations at each end of the Copperbelt operating on coal from Wankie, 900 km away in Zimbabwe. Some electricity was also bought from Zaire. The completion of the Kariba Dam temporarily solved the power problem, but worsening political relations with the white regime in Rhodesia persuaded Zambia to establish a powerhouse on its side of Kariba and to create its own hydro-electric scheme on the Kafue. In addition, small coalfields in the Zambezi valley west of Kariba reservoir were opened up and have made Zambia largely self-sufficient in coal.

Undoubtedly the principal problem the Copperbelt has to face, arising from its land-locked location, is that of transport. After refining, vast quantities of copper have to be sent by rail, and freight charges to the ports add one-third to the price of the copper. There is a choice of outlets – 1900 km to Lobito on the west coast, 2300 km to Beira on the east – together with other possible routes, now taking more copper traffic at present, such as that to Maputo (2300 km) and the Tanzam route to Dar-es-Salaam (1900 km). All the railways are single-track lines and at times become severely congested. The Benguela Railway across Angola has never taken the bulk of the copper despite the port being 4800 km nearer Europe than Beira. This was because at one time freight rates were lower on other routes and at another time strategic reasons were cited. It took increasing amounts after Rhodesia declared its illegal independence (see Chapter 36) and the more popular Beira route might then have been hazardous. This railway to Lobito has only been in sporadic use since 1975 owing to the Angola civil war. By good fortune that year saw the opening of the Chinese-built railway across Tanzania, from the Zambian Copperbelt to Dar-es-Salaam. Copper exports now share this route with that to Beira and Maputo. The Tanzam railway was lightly built and there have been maintenance problems, truck shortages and congestion since it was opened. This problem of transport affects not only the Copperbelt but all the Zambezi lands.

Plate 49 Zambia's Kariba North Bank HEP scheme

Other minerals worked in Zambia include cobalt, lead, zinc and coal. Cobalt is a by-product of copper mining and most comes from Nkana and Chibuluma. Lead and zinc are mined at the older Kabwe (formerly Broken Hill) mining area, where there are also deposits of vanadium and cadmium. Mining began in this area in 1906 with the coming of the railway from Livingstone.

INDUSTRY AND POWER

Industrial development in Zambia is far less advanced than that of Zimbabwe and faces far more difficulties in its growth. Manufacturing contributes barely 10 per cent of the GDP and employs no more than 13 per cent of the labour force. Industry concentrates in two areas, the Copperbelt and around the capital Lusaka. Its main areas of activity are food, beverages, tobacco, rubber, chemicals, plastics products, nickel products and textiles and clothing. The mines of the Copperbelt have provided the main stimulus in their demands for machinery and electrical equipment. Kitwe and Ndola have such manufactures in addition to making tyres, textiles, building materials and cars. Ndola has an oil refinery next to the terminal of the 1600 km oil pipeline from Dar-es-Salaam. Around Lusaka is grain milling, meat packing, a cotton ginnery and a cement plant. An expansion of the industrialized sector is highly desirable in view of the excessive reliance upon copper, but a variety of factors has prevented this occurring. Great distances, involving substantial freight costs, might seem to offer local manufacturing an element of protection against imported products; but this must be weighed against the shortage of skilled labour, the small home market, the generally stagnant economy and lack of foreign exchange which has had a serious effect upon a sector that relies heavily on imported raw materials, components and equipment. As a result Zambia's industrial sector is operating at well below capacity.

Power supplies to the Copperbelt and industry were once a pressing problem; at one time considerable quantities of electricity were imported from the Belgian Congo. The situation improved after 1959 with the damming of the Zambezi at the Kariba gorge. Here the river has cut through Karroo strata into the underlying Pre-Cambrian Basement: it narrows to 100 m and its sides rise abruptly 500 m above the river. The dam is 140 m high and the impounded water creates a lake stretching upstream for 280 km. The original powerhouse holding six 100 MW generators was built on the Rhodesian side, which after the unilateral declaration of independence placed Zambian supplies in potentially hostile hands. Zambia, with overseas help, then built a powerhouse (for 600 MW) on the north (Zambia) side of Kariba and another for 600 MW on the lower Kafue River, dammed where it flows through a deep gorge. Zambia now has more than enough hydroelectric power and she exports surplus power to Zaire

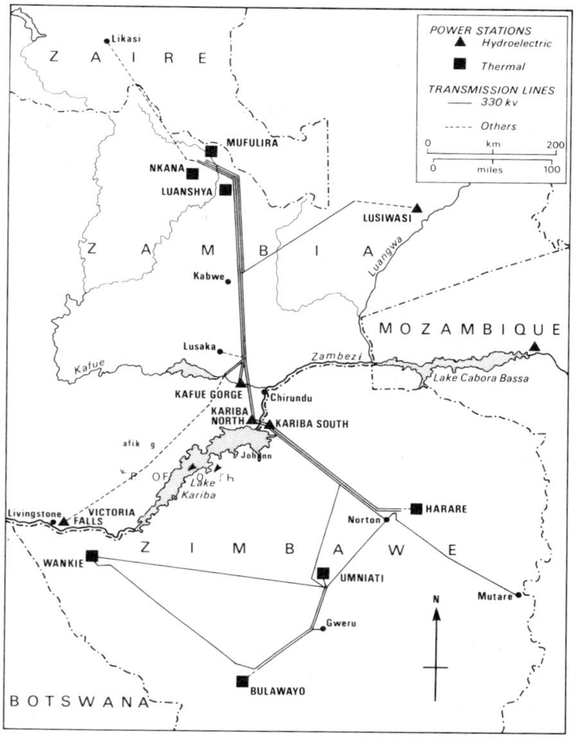

Figure 88 Zimbabwe and Zambia: power production and transmission

and Zimbabwe. Hydroelectricity now supplies two-thirds of Zambia's energy needs, oil imports have been reduced and now account for 16 per cent, coal supplies for the remainder.

DEVELOPMENT

It is unsound that the Zambian economy relies so much upon its mining industry, rendering it at the mercy of prices on the world metal markets. (For example, in 1973 copper was $2500 a tonne and in 1983 $350 a tonne.) Diversification of the economy is urgently needed; but, while this is recognized by the government, little has been attained. In the early years of independence various restrictions were placed upon non-Zambian farmers, such as limiting the repatriation of profits and exchange-control restriction on loans; but in an endeavour to revive a stagnant agriculture these were removed in 1977 as part of a number of measures to increase employment and rewards in rural areas, and so to reduce the disparity between urban and rural wages and thereby reverse the population drift to the towns. Zambia's early development plans following independence were badly coordinated, and failed as the 1970s saw a crisis compounded of world inflation, rocketing oil prices and economic disruption related to UDI and civil war in neighbouring Zimbabwe. The Third National Development Plan was launched in 1980 and, in an endeavour to diversify the economy, was aimed at strengthening agriculture and at rural rehabilitation. The rural–urban income gap has increased since independence – urban incomes are now four times those of the countryside. Conditions in the country remain primitive. Away from the spinal railway there are few all-weather roads, which limits farmers' access to markets. 'For many farmers, payment for produce delivered comes months late, and when payment is received, needed goods, whether farm inputs or consumer products, are rarely available. Farm-cooperative programmes, village reconstruction and tractor hire schemes have all failed'.[1]

Since independence state policies have resulted in farmers supplying the politically powerful urban population with cheap food, and the stagnation of the rural economy has nourished an exodus from the land to the towns. Heavy investment in basic infrastructure is an essential preliminary to strengthening the agricultural sector, and steps in this direction now under way include the drilling of bore-holes and the construction of small dams in the low-rainfall areas; attempts at some diversification of the rural economy; and encouraging the small farmers to produce marketable surpluses of basic foodstuffs. Zambia has much good farmland scarcely used owing to poor communications and poor marketing facilities. Except for areas in the east around Mbala and Chipata, it is the land along the line of the railway that is cultivated and away from this much good farmland is neglected. The government plan aims at changing this and even envisages greater participation by the state. The latter may prove a bureaucratic disaster, but rural industries are to be encouraged and self-supporting rural communities are ultimately envisaged. In reality a series of droughts have reduced rather than expanded the agricultural sector and the severe shortage of foreign exchange and skilled workers have kept manufacturing industry at a standstill. For several years austerity has been imposed, debts have had to be re-scheduled, inflation and unemployment have grown, and investment has been insufficient to break out of a stagnant situation.

REFERENCES

1 W. Smith, 'Crisis and response: *Agricultural development and Zambia's Third National Development Plan 1979–83*', *Geog.*, **66** (1981), p. 135.

38 Zimbabwe

Lying between the Zambezi and the Limpopo, this is one of Africa's smaller countries with an area (319,000 km^2) less than half that of Tanzania. Yet it has one of the largest white populations (180,000 in 1983) of any country between northern Africa and South Africa. The population contains over 7 million Africans whose chief tribes are the Ndebele (Matabele) and the Shona (Mashona). Two generations ago, when the white man first came to Rhodesia (as it was then called), the Africans probably numbered fewer than half a million; their society was then entirely tribal, existing by subsistence farming and cattle herding. The Shona of the moister northern areas were primarily cultivators, while the Ndebele, arriving somewhat later from the Transvaal and occupying the southern and western areas, were a more warlike people, primarily cattle folk, who obtained grain and other crops from the weaker Shona by raiding. With the advent of white settlers, and the pacification and sub-division of the country into white and African areas, the Ndebele cattle herders turned increasingly to cultivation. In the African areas the traditional economy and way of life have remained to some extent undisturbed, but elsewhere the more advanced economy of the white settlers has been superimposed.

THE ECONOMY

Farming

Although agriculture now contributes only 16 per cent of the GDP it is of great importance in the economy as a significant provider of exports, of raw materials for industry, and as the country's major employer of labour. Over 250,000 people are involved either in paid employment or, mainly, on a subsistence basis. The country is mainly self-sufficient in foodstuffs, but periodic droughts occasionally necessitate food imports. These droughts in the early 1980s prevented the restoring of the country's cattle herd to the former level of 6.7 million head. About one-half of the cattle belong to Africans, the animals mainly being of poor quality. To the African, wealth has for long been assessed in the numbers of cattle owned. Since villages are located near water, the cattle drink in the morning and are then driven out on to the common veld grazing. They are seldom driven far, and accordingly graze the same areas until these are bare. The denuded areas gradually extend until vast tracts of land are impoverished and become liable to erosion. Thus, together with the practice of shifting cultivation, deterioration of the land has been occurring over wide areas.

The African, living in his village within a tribal framework, cultivates his crops mainly (sometimes exclusively) for consumption within the family or village. With the simple techniques employed, the lack of crop rotation and the lack of fertilizers, the soils seldom permit more than three or four successive harvests from the same piece of land. Shifting cultivation and bush fallowing provided the traditional answer to this problem; only a few areas of richer alluvium in valley bottoms allowed more continuous cropping. Such methods of cultivation have proved extremely wasteful of land. The women are the main cultivators, for a large proportion of the younger adult male population is absent in the towns for long periods, working in factories or mines, or employed on European farms.

Prior to European occupation the landscape was characterized by a low density of villages or kraals, separated by wide stretches of open savanna which provided both grazing and firewood. But since then European settlers have taken over large tracts of the better land, especially along the higher and flatter parts of the uplands. In the 'native reserves' the African population grew steadily. Thus serious problems of congestion arose in the African areas, owing principally to the wasteful methods of farming employed and the rapid increase in population. In an effort to grapple with this state of affairs the Native Land Husbandry Act of 1951 was passed to control land-use and allocation, and thereby promote more efficient use of the land, particularly by limiting grazing per unit area and by arresting shifting cultivation. Since 1951 African farming has in many areas been completely revolutionized.

African farming is now improving in many areas under guidance from local administrators. Under the Native Land Husbandry Act land rights must be registered, land consolidation has begun and agrarian education is provided. Numbers of cattle are being controlled and even reduced, while overall crop production is definitely rising. About one-third of all the maize grown for sale in Zimbabwe is now produced by black African farmers. Finally, a start has been made in the Low Veld areas in introducing irrigation farming to African smallholders. Since 1977 all farming areas are open to ownership by Africans and a fund is in being to compensate European farmers if their land is expropriated for division among African smallholders. The application of these measures is restrained since it is the large commercial farms that supply the bulk of agricultural exports.

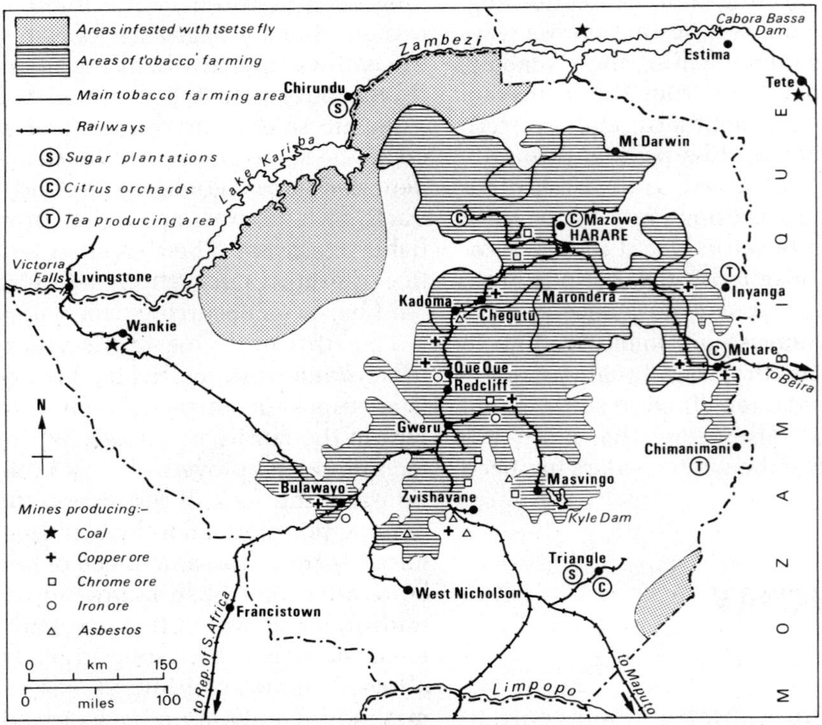

Figure 89 Zimbabwe: economic activities

European farmers have concerned themselves with large-scale commercial farming and until independence cultivated some 350,000 ha of the best land in the country. On the uplands above 1200 m there is plenty of relatively flat and undissected land, a pleasant climate with 600–900 mm of fairly reliable rainfall, and a shorter dry season than in many other parts of the Zambezi lands. But the uplands have not only their physical attractions for the European farmer but also economic advantages, for along the watershed zone runs the main railway, completed at about the turn of the century and linking the region now with the port of Beira, with the mining regions of Zambia, and with the Republic of South Africa. Costs of transport are vital in the development of commercial agriculture and, as in many other parts of Africa, distance from rail-head or main road plays its part in helping determine the type and pattern of land-use. The main crops – largely for export – are tobacco, cotton, tea, groundnuts, coffee and wheat. Today less land is allocated to tobacco and more to cotton and wheat. Tobacco planting by European farmers on a commercial scale dates from about 1910, since when Rhodesia rose to become one of the world's leading Virginia-type tobacco exporters. In 1945 tobacco surpassed gold as Southern Rhodesia's principal export and subsequently has been the mainstay of the country's economy.

The most important tobacco areas lie between 1200 and 1500 m with 800–900 mm of rainfall, though the actual limits are 900–1500 m with rainfall of not less than 700 mm. Within such areas the detailed distribution of tobacco farming is governed by the pattern of European-owned land, and access to railway. Expansion was particularly rapid after the Second World War. Some marginal districts increased their acreage fivefold, while the greatest absolute increase was in the Harare–Marendellas–Makoni districts. Of the 4800 European farms in Zimbabwe in 1983, about one-third counted tobacco as their principal crop. On an average tobacco farm tobacco occupies less than 5 per cent of the total farm acreage, yet may furnish three-quarters of the farm income. Fertilizers and crop rotation are essential to maintain good yields and high quality. The rotation nearly always includes maize, which is itself an important crop, grown for animal feed or for sale. Tracts of woodland are kept to supply timber for the tobacco smoke-curing process.

The main tobacco area in Zimbabwe extends from Umtali and Marendellas (Figure 89), past Harare and Hartley, to Darwin in the north and the Lomagundi–Urungwe districts in the north-west. Minor production comes from the Melsetter, Victoria and Gwelo districts. About two-thirds of the labour is supplied from outside Zimbabwe – indeed, many farms depend wholly on non-Zimbabwean migrant labour. About half of this migrant labour comes from Mozambique, one-third from Malawi and the remainder from Zambia.

Maize, often grown in rotation with tobacco, is the principal cereal crop. It is produced under a variety of conditions, but generally needs at least 650 mm of rain, and does best on the heavier red clays and loams. Yields are generally low compared with the United States or Argentina, since it is given little attention as a crop and rarely supplied with fertilizer. The most important maize-growing areas are in the Harare region. Production is rising, creating an exportable surplus; but high transport costs limit the sale to neighbouring countries which often so badly need it.

Other crops produced in Zimbabwe are of less importance. Sugar-cane is grown on irrigated plantations at Chirundu in the Zambezi valley, and the Triangle and Hippo valley estates in the Lundi valley. Those in the Lundi valley are irrigated from the new Kyle and Bangala Dams on the Mtilikwe river near Fort Victoria. In 1965 the Manjirenji Dam on the Chiredzi River was completed. Cotton is an associated crop. About 29,000 ha are now under irrigation. Citrus-fruit orchards have also been considerably extended in the Lundi valley. The Limpopo valley railway, opened

Plate 50 Tobacco provides Zimbabwe with a main export

in 1955 to Lourenco Marques (now Maputo) and its branch to Hippo valley (1964), are providing a new outlet for this part of Zimbabwe. Other fruit-growing areas include the British South Africa Company's citrus estates irrigated from the Mazoe Dam, and some deciduous fruit orchards in the Melsetter–Inyanga highlands. Finally, among the cash crops tea should be mentioned. It is, of course, restricted to the eastern areas of high rainfall. Although of far greater importance in Malawi, production in Zimbabwe is expanding, especially with the development of the new estates at Inyanga.

Stock-rearing by European farmers in Zimbabwe involves much greater areas than crop-growing. Many European farmers have been turning to livestock to reduce an over-dependence on maize–tobacco farming. Unlike Zambia, most parts of the Zimbabwean uplands are free of tsetse fly, while rinderpest, a great scourge since the earliest days of white settlement, has been brought under a measure of control. Large beef-cattle ranches are now a feature of the landscape; with exports of beef and skins in 1980 valued at £7 million, Zimbabwe is today the main meat producer of tropical Africa. Dairy farming is not far behind in importance, being well-established wherever there are railways to link with the urban centres and the major creameries at Bulawayo, Gweru and Harare.

Irrigation has enabled new areas for agriculture to be opened where drought, erratic rainfall or flooding have so far precluded it. Mention has already been made of the irrigated sugar-cane, cotton and citrus-fruit estates. In the Sabi valley an irrigation scheme for African farmers was begun as long ago as 1932. A survey in 1947 of this valley indicated that over 100,000 ha were potentially available, and the irrigated land has since been extended. The soils have proved very productive, and African farmers obtain good yields of maize, wheat, legumes and cotton grown in rotation on 1–2 ha plots. Further reservoirs are being built in the upper reaches of the Sabi. The Kariba scheme on the Zambezi has irrigated about 8000 ha below the dam. In all these irrigation projects the primary need is a storage reservoir that is able not only to supply water throughout the dry season in excess of evaporation losses but also is able to contain the floods in summer. On the Zambezi, for instance, the maximum flow at the Kafue confluence, before the Kariba Dam was constructed, was about forty times the minimum.

Mining

The mining sector is responsible for two-fifths of export earnings, mainly from gold, chrome and asbestos. Other important minerals worked include nickel, copper, coal, iron and silver. European gold mining dates from 1890. The main gold-bearing rocks are Pre-Cambrian and lie on either side of the Great Dyke, worked by many small and scattered mines. Recently interest has revived, and the larger mining companies are now taking a more active part in development. Kwe Kwe (Que Que: pop. 54,000) is the main centre. The Great Dyke contains valuable deposits of asbestos and chrome. Prior to independence Rhodesia's production of asbestos was second only to that of Canada, and of very high quality. The chief producing area is around Shabani, on the through-railway to Maputo. There are also extensive deposits of high-quality iron-ore, ample for the needs of the expanding iron and steel industry.

Zimbabwe is fortunate in possessing the second-largest worked coalfield in Africa at Wankie, first reached by the Bulawayo railway in 1904. The coal occurs in thick seams in the lower Karroo beds over considerable areas of territory (Figure 88), and reserves are put at 30 million tonnes. The Wankie coalfield, with that of Natal, is the only sizable deposit of good-quality coking coal in the whole of Africa. Output at present is about 3 million tonnes a year, and is in fact diminishing. Until 1960 Wankie coal was the main source of power for mining and industry in the Zambezi lands, and only limitations of railway capacity prevented expansion of coal output. Now electricity from Kariba is available, and Zambia is developing its own coalfields. The mining sector is beset by problems: since independence there has been a loss of key staff, costs have risen but metal prices have remained low. Output has declined since the peak year of 1976, and the creation by the government of a Minerals Marketing Corporation might be a preliminary to nationalization. Multinational corporations that might be affected include Anglo-American, Rio Tinto, Lonrho, Union Carbide, Turner and Newell.

Manufacturing

One of the most spectacular features in the economic development of Zimbabwe since the Second World War has been the growth of manufacturing industry. Several factors have contributed to this expansion. The mining industry has provided much of the capital, and the very considerable white immigration since the war has been extremely important. Rhodesia experienced the most rapid increase in white population in the history of the whole British Commonwealth, and many of the immigrants were industrialists. The Act of Federation, in 1953, by bringing together varied resources of minerals, agricultural produce and labour, also helped to encourage industrial investment. The completion of the Kariba Dam provided a new major source of electrical power for secondary industry, and the period of illegal independence when sanctions were imposed gave a fillip to local industry.

There is growing awareness of the potential markets for basic consumer goods in tropical Africa, and of the need to found the economy on a more substantial basis than that provided by tobacco and minerals. Already the several major towns along the railway in Zimbabwe from Bulawayo to Harare are forming the nuclei of an industrial region, second only in importance in southern Africa to that of the southern Transvaal. Although a quarter of the industrial output comes from food-processing industries, the iron and steel industry must receive first mention. At Redcliffe, 13 km from Kwe Kwe, is the large steel works opened by the Rhodesian Iron and Steel Commission (RISCO) in 1948 (now ZISCO). These works draw on local iron-ore and limestone, and purchase their coal and coke requirements from Wankie; new coke ovens on the site have recently been opened. Chrome-ore is available from the Great Dyke nearby. The Kwe Kwe area is now the focal point for heavy industry in Zimbabwe. Another iron and steel works developed by RISCO is sited at Bulawayo. South of Kwe Kwe on the railway lies Gweru (pop. 75,000), which has the advantage of being close to the new link with Maputo. Sited at Gweru are works producing ferro-chrome for stainless steel, asbestos works, and an important footwear industry. Kadoma (formerly Gatooma, pop. 45,000), north of Kwe Kwe, was originally concerned with gold mining, but has now become the centre of the Zimbabwean cotton-textile industry. The first experimental cotton mill was opened here during the Second World War. Cotton spinning and weaving is now one of the basic industries of Zimbabwe; about half the raw-cotton requirements are imported. Other works at Kadoma are concerned with engineering, and cement and brick manufacture.

At either end of the Zimbabwean 'Midlands' stand the major cities of Bulawayo (pop. 414,000) and Harare (pop. 650,000). Bulawayo is Zimbabwe's largest industrial town, with over 500 separate industrial establishments. Its proximity to the Wankie coalfield has been an advantage, and it is also a main railway junction. The range of industries is considerable: machinery, textiles, clothing, footwear, furniture and soap are produced, and there are grain and flour mills, sugar refineries, and other factories processing food. Harare has a similar range of industries, together with printing works, and tobacco factories and markets. It also possesses a large fertilizer factory, using apatite from mines in the Sabi valley. Rather separate from the main line of industrial towns from Bulawayo to Harare is Umtali (pop. 65,000). Its particular advantages for industry are its proximity to Beira, and a plentiful water supply. It has developed as a centre for industries processing agricultural products and has a motor assembly plant. More recently a paper mill has been located here based on local afforestation schemes in the eastern highlands – about 80,000 ha of conifers have now been planted. Nearby, at Feruka, an oil refinery with a capacity of 750,000 tonnes a year was built at the end of a pipeline from Beira.

Development problems

Zimbabwe became an independent republic in 1980 after 15 years of dislocation following the unilateral declaration of independence made by the Smith government in 1965. The guerrilla war and imposition of trade sanctions that followed the declaration brought the economy to a standstill. During the 1970s there was no real growth in the GDP and industrial productivity was reduced as capital equipment deteriorated and manpower was diverted to military service.

The early years of independence saw a marked upsurge in economic growth as trade picked up, equipment was renewed and grants and loans became available. This has slowed down with sluggish world demand for Zimbabwean mineral and agricultural exports. The main emphasis in the first development plan announced for 1982–5 was to further land redistribution and rural development (31 per cent of investment), to strengthen the infrastructure and social services; mining and manufacturing had low priority. The government repeatedly refers to increasing public participation and returning wealth to the people, for it faces a land-hungry peasantry many of whom are already squatting on commercial estates. Yet it knows that precipitate action of land expropriation for small-farm development could destroy the productivity of the white farming sector which has made Zimbabwe almost unique in black Africa in being able to feed itself and have a surplus for export. Nevertheless a slow shift in development emphasis and a redirection of resources to the rural areas is apparent. When available, purchases of large commercial farms provide land for the settlement of small farmers for whom credit facilities and advisory services are being established. It is realized that over time the small-scale sector must improve and participate in providing a larger share of food and raw materials for the nation.

In advancing manufacturing industry there are three main problems. First, the market represented by the African population is very limited in purchasing power, while that of the white population is small in size. Opportunities for the export of industrial goods appear limited, for there would be direct competition with the more highly developed South African industry, and several neighbouring territories in any case have their own plans for future industrial development. Second, labour needs to be more skilled, more efficient and productive. The third problem is that of attracting capital. A high rate of investment in the post-war years and, under federation, the high revenues from Zambian

Plate 51 Rail links provide a key to Zimbabwe's development

copper mining have been the basis of existing industrial development. The extent of future investment in Zimbabwe is difficult to assess.

The presence of a high level white population, which carried Rhodesia forward, is an asset independent Zimbabwe needs to continue to foster and utilize. Unpalatable though it may be, the development of the economy is likely to require for many years the services of white entrepreneurs, managers and technocrats who by their scarcity value command big rewards. Although this perpetuates an unequal society it seems to have become accepted by the Zimbabwean government.

39 Malawi

Malawi is a small and poor country, land-locked and possessing few natural resources. Its 118,500 km^2 lie in a narrow strip never more than 160 km wide, and the magnificent Lake Malawi covers one-fifth of the area. The country is mountainous and well-watered and is densely populated. Its African population of 6.3 million is larger than that of Zambia.

The dual nature of the farming economy, emphasized in Zimbabwe and Zambia, is again apparent in Malawi. The bulk of the population engages primarily in subsistence agriculture, growing crops of maize, cassava and millet, with rice appearing on the lake fringe (Figure 90). Along the shores of the lake the people supplement their diet by fishing from dug-out canoes. The commercial farming sector – a pattern of large estates – contributes two-thirds of all agricultural exports, particularly from the crops of tobacco, tea and sugar. Agriculture dominates the economy, contributing about 45 per cent of the GDP, 50 per cent of paid employment and 90 per cent of exports. Maize is the principal subsistence crop and since independence output has increased until the country is self-sufficient (except in a drought year).

The government encourages small farmers to grow cash crops, and its Agricultural Development and Marketing Corporation (ADMARC) now operates over 900 marketing outlets where small-holders can sell produce for cash and buy subsidized fertilizer and seed. Cotton and tobacco are the main cash crops thus grown. Tobacco is generally grown at altitudes of 500–1000 m, and particularly in the Shiré highlands around Blantyre (Kapeni) and Limbe, and on the Lilongwe highlands west of the lake. Production amounts to about 15 per cent of that of Zimbabwe. Cotton is grown mainly along the lower Shiré valley below 600 m. Sugar-cane growing is being developed in the south.

The large estates, while occupying less than one-fifth of farmland, produce half Malawi's total exports. Tea is the main crop of these farms; it was introduced in 1878, and reached its present position of importance in the southern areas of high rainfall – Mlanje and Cholo districts. Even in these areas the rainfall is not always reliable: at Chisunga, for instance, the total for 1960 (890 mm) was 530 mm below the average for the previous eight years, resulting in a considerably reduced crop. The Smallholder Tea Authority has, since 1978, been giving technical and conservation advice and a collecting and buying service, and each year the area under tea plantations shows a modest increase. In Africa Malawi's tea production is second to that of Kenya. Most of the large estates are in the hands of Europeans and the government now gives encouragement to wealthy Malawis to invest in plantation farming – a policy that sometimes clashes with finding land for the new small-producers' villages. Under this scheme, financed by the World Bank, villages are being established to serve about 80 small-holdings of 2 ha each. Health and social services are provided and productivity is raised by training in new techniques (irrigation, for example). About one-fifth of Malawi is officially classed as woodland or savanna–woodland, in spite of the fact that much of the natural forest has been destroyed. Remaining areas of forest are now carefully guarded,

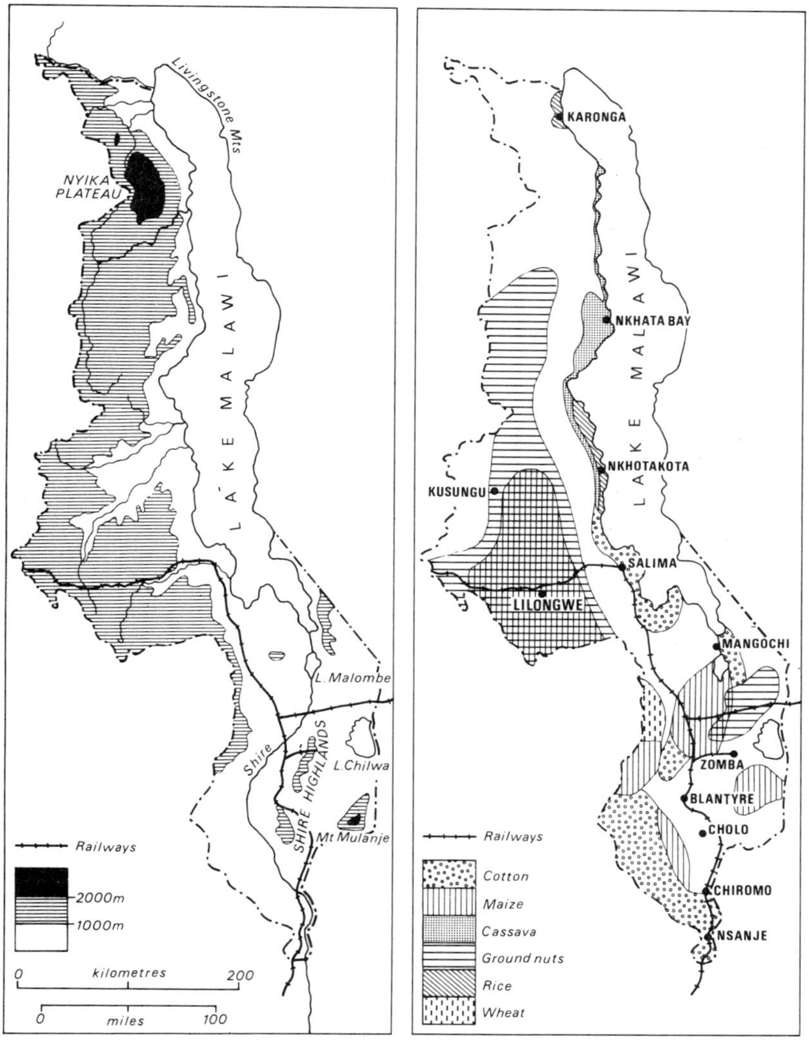

Figure 90 Malawi: relief and crop regions

especially the Mlanje forests. The Mlanje cedar grows only in Mlanje and the adjacent Mchese Mountains. It is really a form of cyprus, and as its wood is very durable and ant-resistant, it is highly valued. Afforestation schemes are now in progress in various parts of Malawi, using pines, eucalyptus and Mlanje cedar.

Malawi's industries are almost wholly concerned with the processing of the leading cash crops; cement manufacture is the principal exception. The Malawi Development Corporation, set up in 1964, has done much to stimulate industrial growth, so that output doubled during the 1970s. The main activities are cotton ginning, tea and tobacco processing, brickmaking, iron- and wood-working, clothing and footwear and soap-making. A recent addition to these industries has been an ethanol conversion plant which combines sugar by-products with petroleum to produce 'gasohol' for motor vehicles, reducing the cost of imported oil. A Small Enterprise Development Corporation was set up in 1982

Plate 52 Small-holder tea plantation sponsored by the Malawi Smallholder Tea Authority

supported by money from the European Development Fund, to establish industrial estates for training entrepreneurs.

More than two-thirds of Malawi's population lives in the Central and Southern regions. Population has been increasing substantially. Throughout the 1970s it was at the very high rate of 3.3 per cent (population doubling in 20 years), but by the middle 1980s it was down to 2.4 per cent. Overcrowding is becoming a problem in the southern provinces where shifting agriculture can no longer operate. The moving of the capital from Zomba in the south to Lilongwe in the more thinly populated centre has been one marked step to reduce the economic and political power of the south. The surplus labour in Malawi has over a long period migrated to work on farms in Zimbabwe, in the gold mines of the Rand and the copper mines of Zambia. Here the African can earn far more than he can by farming at home, and at any given time at least 200,000 young, able-bodied males are absent – a situation not relished by the government but accepted as a necessity.

After independence a major development scheme was the Shiré Valley hydroelectric project. By constructing a minor barrage at Liwonde the flow of the Shiré river below this point has been regulated, and power is generated at the Nkula Falls, north-west of Blantyre, where the river drops 55 m. This has enabled Malawi to reduce fuel imports and has encouraged light industry around Blantyre (pop. 230,000), the chief commercial town.

Land-locked Malawi relies upon rail routes to Mozambique ports for her foreign trade. The original and much-congested route went south from Salima via Blantyre to Beira. A second link that has eased pressure on the Beira line now runs due east from the busy Southern province to link with the Mozambique port of Nacala. Lilongwe, the new capital, is joined to this system by a spur from Salima. However, the Nacala line has been plagued with wear and tear and poor maintenance, and the other line to Beira has been repeatedly cut by guerrillas of the Mozambique National Resistance movement. Malawi's economic position is seriously threatened by these transport restrictions. She is heavily dependent upon the export of sugar, tea, tobacco and the import of fuel, fertilizers and manufactured goods, and in times of transport restriction has to send freight by the long and expensive road–rail route through Zambia and Botswana to ports of South Africa.

Dr Hastings Banda has been the country's President since independence and has from the first pressed that agricultural improvement should be the basis of economic development. He directs development spending towards the promotion of agricultural smallholdings, and the development of transport and public services. His liberal attitude to foreign investment and low-key step-by-step projects has attracted foreign capital and gained Malawi a reputation as an efficient user of development funds.

40 Mozambique

Four and a half centuries ago the Portuguese came to Mozambique, but it is only in the last 50 years that this territory of 783,000 km^2 emerged from a history of neglect and stagnation. In the early part of this century the country was in fact offered for sale to Britain at a price of £3 million, but the bargain was refused. Mozambique's period of modern growth stems from the construction of railways across the territory to link her western neighbours with the ports of Beira and Maputo (formerly Lourenço Marques). The greatest changes in the economic life of the country have come, however, since the Second World War. Portuguese investment increased steadily, especially with the Six-Year Development Plans (1953–8 and 1959–64), under which millions of pounds were spent on ports, transport, industry and irrigation. But many parts were not touched by these changes – towns such as Mozambique, the ancient capital of the north, or Quelimane, where Livingstone reached the sea after crossing the continent, have altered little through the centuries.

Portuguese interest and investment in the 'overseas province' came too late. An independence movement, Frelimo, began a liberation war in 1964 and in 1975 the Portuguese withdrew and independence was attained. Peace did not follow, however, for terrorists set up bases from which South Africa was attacked and strikes into Mozambique by South Africa followed. The guerrilla forces of the anti-government Mozambique National Resistance (MNR), better known as Renamo, also carried out sporadic campaigns of terrorism. The government's aim is to create a socialist state, but the magnitude of the changes and of the necessary technical expertise and finance soon led to an easing in the application of socialist principles and to closer relations with the aid-giving West.

The population numbered 13.2 million in 1983, of whom all but 100,000 or so were African (Bantu), though with a considerable admixture of Arab blood. About a million of the northern tribes adhere to Islam. At 2.6 per cent a year the rate of increase to the population is substantial and raises problems in the attempt to develop social services. The population is very unevenly distributed. The average density is 16 people per km^2, but for large areas such as the interior of the Northern plateau, the inner Zambezi valley and much of the coast plain between Beira and the Limpopo, the figure is under three. Many areas were denuded in the past by slave-raiding Arabs.

GEOGRAPHICAL REGIONS AND THEIR AGRICULTURE

(see Figure 91)

The northern plateau is essentially a southward continuation of the south-east plateau of Tanzania (see Chapter 44), bordered by Lake Malawi and the Malawi highlands in the west. The highest elevations are actually attained in the Namuli Mountains (2430 m); the eastward slope to the coastline is interrupted by minor steps. Only the higher parts are well-watered – over 1500 mm of rainfall on the Namuli Mountains and over 1100 mm on the Malawi highlands; in the valleys and towards the coast the rainfall is less than 890 mm. The

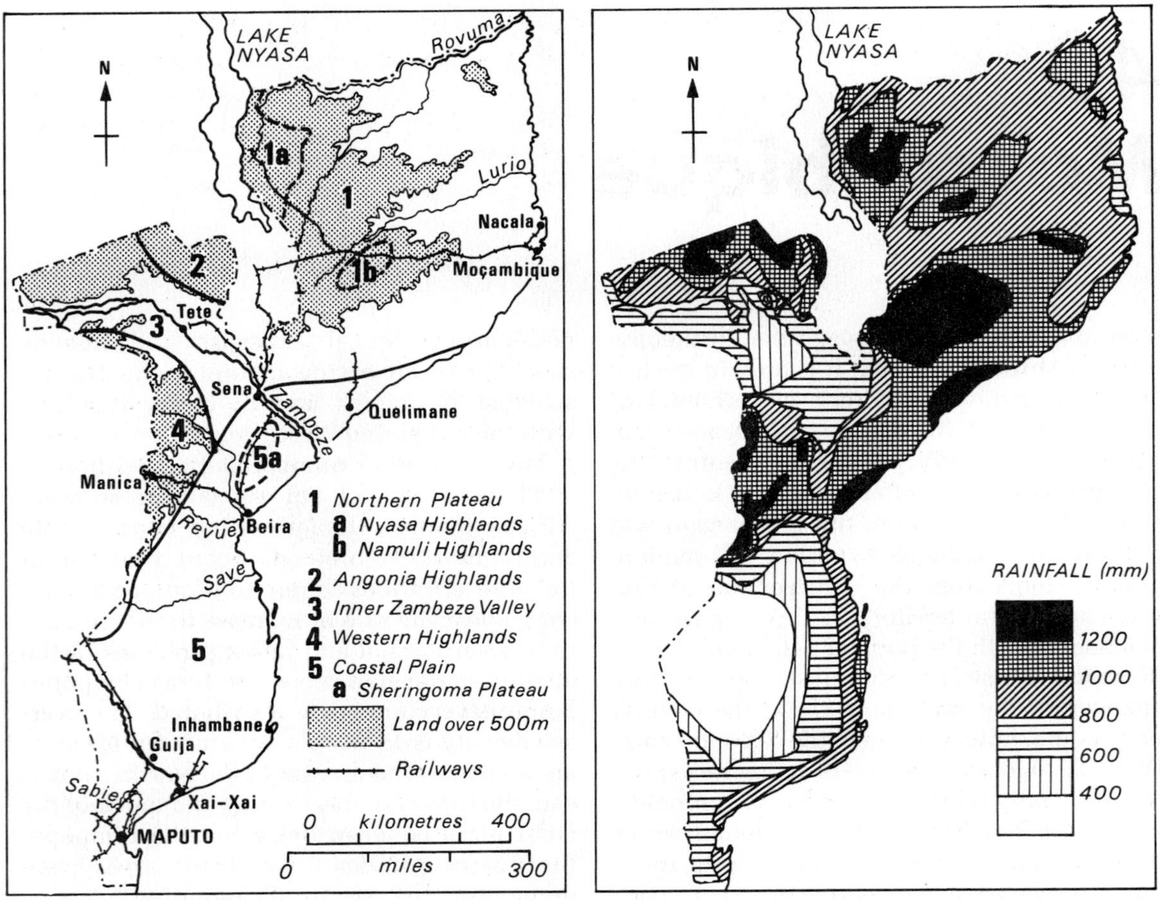

Figure 91 Mozambique: physical regions and rainfall

rain, moreover, is strongly seasonal and often erratic. Nevertheless, agriculturally this is an important region. Its eastern and south-eastern parts are relatively densely populated, though there is still enough land for shifting cultivation and bush-fallowing to remain common practices.

The main food crops are cassava and rice; maize becomes more usual in the interior. The outstanding cash crop is cotton. About three-quarters of all cotton produced in the territory comes from the north. Before cotton rose to its present position of importance, copra and sisal were the dominant products, coming mainly from plantations in coastal districts. Quelimane is reputed to have the world's largest coconut grove. On the wetter areas of the Namuli highlands tea is grown; it was introduced on a commercial scale in the 1930s and production is now about one-half that of Malawi. Tea accounts for about 5 per cent of Mozambique's exports.

The Angonia Highlands, isolated in the north-west, are the home mainly of Bantu cattle folk, cultivating a little maize and other food crops. Apart from the south and the Malawi highlands, this is one of the few areas in Mozambique free from tsetse fly.

The Inner Zambezi Valley is now changing its character with the completion of the great Cabora Bassa hydroelectric scheme and associated irrigation projects. Sugar-cane is a major crop in the newly irrigated areas, and there are older sugar estates at Sena where the great river enters the coastal lowlands.

The western highlands belong to the Zimbabwean uplands. The Great Escarpment rises sharply to heights of as much as 2400 m on the frontier; the Beira railway encounters it at Manica. There are a few European farms in this area, producing maize and tobacco.

The coastal plain is flat and often marshy; large areas are periodically inundated by the rivers. The alluvial soils of the river valleys are potentially highly fertile, but elsewhere there are vast tracts of poor sandy material. Agriculture and settlement have developed mainly south and south-west of Inhambane, as far as the Swaziland border, and to a lesser extent around Beira. Maize and rice are the principal food crops, sugar-cane the chief cash crop.

Development of agriculture on the coastal plain hinges on both drainage and irrigation works, paradoxical though that may seem. Even though considerable areas are flooded at one period of the year, in the dry season water is completely inadequate for crops such as rice and sugar-cane. Total rainfall diminishes rapidly inland – from 1000 mm at Inhambane to less than 400 mm within 150 km of the coast.

During the 1950s an important irrigation scheme was established based on the lower waters of the Limpopo river in an area of rather unreliable rainfall. The river was dammed at Guija, 110 km from its mouth, and nearly 40,000 ha, above Vilo de Joao Belo, are irrigated for rice, millet, lucerne, cotton and sugar-cane. The whole is operated by smallholders, both African and Portuguese. The former mosquito-ridden swamp is now a patchwork of fields divided up by roads, irrigation canals and dykes. The families live in three-roomed cottages grouped in hamlets. Each red-tiled cottage has a cow byre attached and is reminiscent of rural homes in Portugal. A larger irrigation scheme (100,000 ha eventually) is planned for the adjacent lower Incomati river, just north of Maputo. There will be two associated dams, one on the Sabie river near the Transvaal frontier and the other where the Limpopo valley railway crosses the Incomati.

MINING AND INDUSTRY

Mining is not important in Mozambique and is largely confined to small-scale coal working in the Zambezi valley at Moatize (near Tete), where the coal from Karroo beds is of good quality and plentiful. Most of the production, up to half a million tonnes a year, is used on the railways. Reserves are large and it is planned to mine up to 4 million tonnes a year by the end of the 1980s. Uranium-ore was discovered in the Tete area not long ago, and has been worked intermittently. A small quantity of bauxite is worked each year at Manica, and there are minor workings for gold, beryl and bismuth. A search for oil and gas in the Zambezi delta and adjacent coastlands is in progress; some oil has been located at Dondo near Beira and a large gas field is being tapped at Pande, near Inhambane.

The manufacturing sector is under-developed and supplies only about 12 per cent of the GDP. It is largely limited to factories processing agricultural products in the principal towns, especially Maputo (pop. about 1 million) and Beira. Cotton ginning, cotton spinning and weaving, sugar-refining, flour-milling and the manufacture of fertilizer, glass, paper, tyres, soap and cement are the major industries. This sector has lagged because agriculture is deemed to be of greater importance in the economy, and because there is a shortage of foreign exchange to spend on raw materials and spare parts. This shortage of finance has been a contributive factor in the lack of maintenance of plant and equipment, so that output has shown little growth.

The main source of power is now hydroelectricity from the great Cabora Bassa Dam on the Zambezi above Tete, at the downstream

Plate 53 Zambezi valley and Cabora Bassa dam, Mozambique

end of the Kebrabasa gorge. Work started in 1969 and the electricity from the first phase became available in 1976. This is the second largest project of its kind in Africa. The dam, higher than that at Kariba, has created a lake that stretches to the Zimbabwean border and the output of electricity is 3600 MW. The whole scheme is out of all proportion to Mozambique's requirements and capabilities and owes much of its development to South Africa, to whom it means a useful source of extra power. It was this aspect – the sale of electricity to South Africa – that enabled Portugal to obtain finance for the project. Malawi also is able to benefit from cheap power without having to make capital expenditure. To Mozambique it supplies power (distributed as far south as Maputo), and the opportunity to irrigate and develop a poor area into good agricultural land and, via the now navigable Zambezi and the new all-weather roads, to utilize the forests and develop known mineral resources in the Tete area.

DEVELOPMENT PROBLEMS

Until the last few decades Mozambique has been economically very backward. Considerable advances were made under Portugal's two Six-Year Plans before she relinquished her hold on the colony. These phases did much to strengthen the infrastructure, particularly transport. In the early years of this century the railway from South Africa was pushed north into Southern Rhodesia (now Zimbabwe) and terminated at the Mozambique port of Beira, which soon became established as a major outlet for the trade of the land-locked states of the interior. The first Six-Year Plan (1953–8) did much to improve Mozambique's railways. Growing traffic from the Rhodesias had led to rail and port congestion and a new line was laid from Rhodesia to Lourenço Marques (Maputo). Farther north Nacala, with its magnificent harbour, was modernized and its railway into the interior was extended to link with Malawi's railway north-west of Zomba. Beira and Lourenço Marques were linked by an all-weather road in 1965, and the Cabora Bassa works necessitated a similar road from Beira to Tete and the dam site. Nacala too has an all-weather road link with Beira.

Mozambique is fortunate in having some of the best harbours on the east coast of Africa and it has benefited as the transit state for the land-locked countries of southern Africa. The ports and railways serving this hinterland are Mozambique's biggest source of revenue. Maputo serves the Transvaal and Swaziland as well as Zimbabwe; Beira serves Zimbabwe and Zambia; Nacala now is becoming a major port for Malawi. Income from these services has helped to make up the financial gap between imports and Mozambique's mainly agricultural exports. However, it follows that dislocation of these railways harms the economy of Mozambique and of the inland states.

Beira and Maputo are by far the most important cities in Mozambique. The southerly location of Maputo is a disadvantage for administration as a capital. However, between them these two cities contain 60 per cent of all Europeans living in the territory, and both of them have a varied range of manufacturing industries. Other ports along the Mozambique coast, such as Mozambique itself, Quelimane or Inhambane, are of comparatively minor importance, dealing only with local traffic from the immediate hinterlands.

Upon independence the Frelimo government was committed to the establishment of a socialist state, initially through rural reconstruction that would create communal villages and cooperative farms. Later the public sector would reorganize industry and in the long term develop heavy industry. Not surprisingly at, and immediately after, independence these promises led to a large-scale withdrawal of Portuguese capital and skilled personnel. Mozambique lost most of its administrators, managers, technicians and artisans, and at the same time embraced schemes to industrialize on East European patterns. Operating factories on schedules laid down by a central authority soon proved a failure and industrial production has slumped. Equally, attempts to set up large mechanized state farms on former colonial plantations did not succeed. The required levels of management and technical skills were under-estimated and the peasantry showed little enthusiasm for such schemes. The early years of the new state therefore were hard. Some takeovers occurred: private banks were nationalized, insurance companies were taken over, a new state-owned company took over the oil-refinery and oil-distribution, coal and hydroelectric power came under state control. But by the middle 1980s (the tenth anniversary of independence) the country was weakened by war (the MNR controlling the greater part of Mozambique outside the main towns), the economy was in shreds, hunger and hardship stalked the countryside. The attacks by the Mozambique National Resistance (MNR) during the early 1980s severely reduced rail freight movements and closed the Beira line in 1983 and that to Nacala in 1984, disrupting the economies of both Mozambique and Halaun. Another serious effect of rebel activity was the rendering homeless of a million people and bringing starvation to an even greater number. By 1987 the United Nations reported a million internal refuges in Mozambique and another quarter of a million fled to neighbouring states.

The great dependence of the economy on the Republic of South Africa (there is a considerable migration there for work) has necessitated the continuance of political and commercial ties and, despite expanded relations with the Soviet Union, the economic situation has led to increasing links with the West. With economic prospects so bleak since 1983 there has been a marked shift of development policy. In 1983 a 3-year recovery programme was announced – the emphasis being on food production, small-scale industry projects and increased support for the private sector. Agricultural policy was switched from state farms to family farms which showed more scope for greater productivity. Aspirations for heavy industry were dropped (realistically), for even light industry remains in an embryonic stage. Droughts, floods, poor harvests and depressed prices led to acute deficits and foreign-exchange shortages. Debt servicing on earlier loans by 1984 was equivalent to 80 per cent of export income. Thus by the mid-1980s Mozambique was seeking debt re-scheduling, was re-structuring its tax system, attempting more austerity and giving more support to agriculture as the prime sector in the economy. It is doubtful whether these measures can stave off the eventual success of the anti-Marxist MNR, which offers a free market economy and espouses private enterprise.

PART TEN: EAST AFRICA AND THE ISLANDS

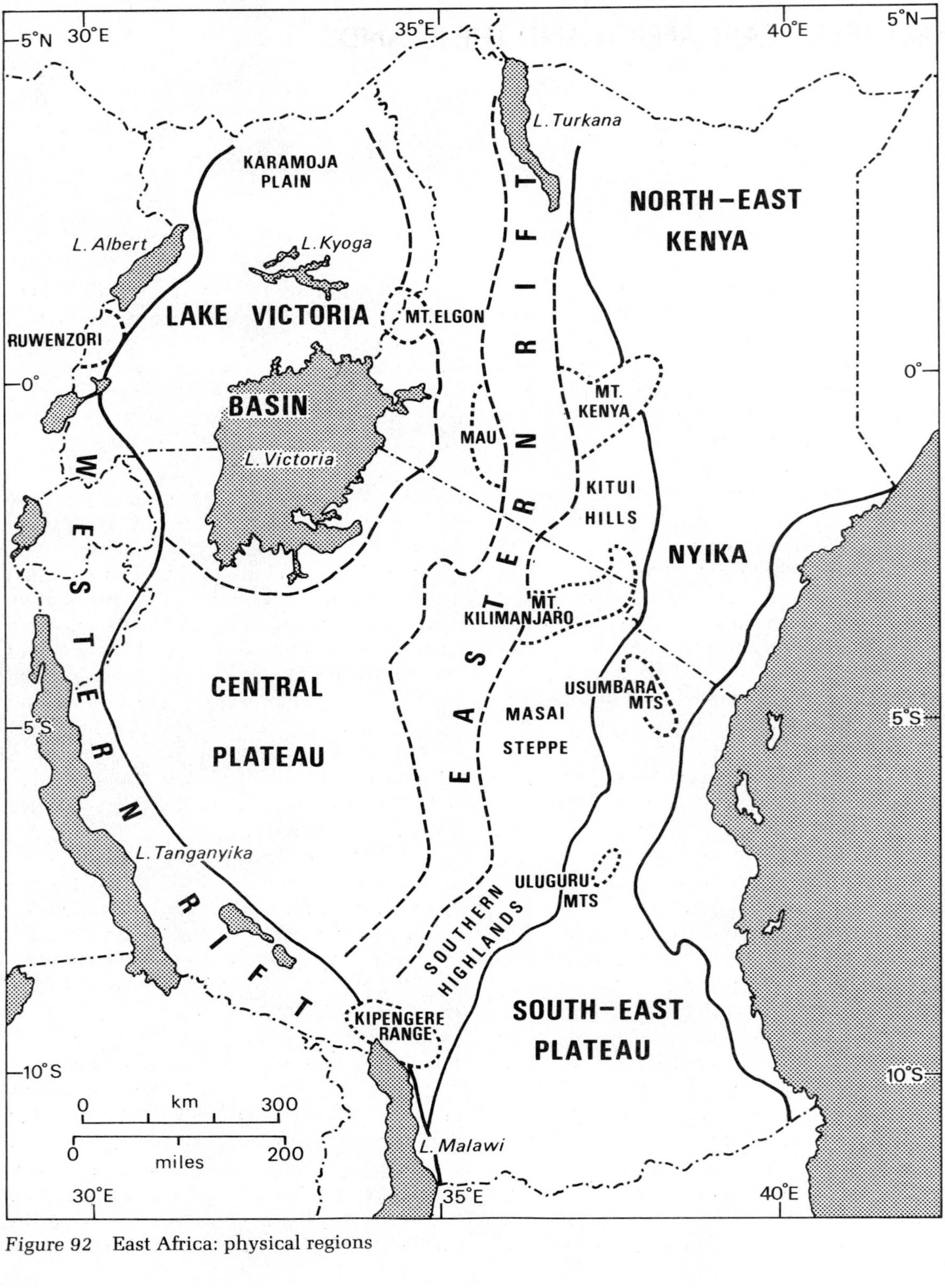

Figure 92 East Africa: physical regions

41 Physical geography

East Africa is an area of great physical landscapes ranging from desert to glaciers, from forest to immense open bush plains. It is the home of 50 million people disposed in over 200 tribes and varying in sophistication from primitive hunters to pin-striped office staff in the large cities, from pastoral nomads to wealthy cotton growers.

Now divided politically into three independent states, all were earlier territories administered by Britain, receiving their independence early in the 1960s. British commercial interests began trading in East Africa towards the close of the nineteenth century; subsequently the British Government assumed responsibility for agreements with the Africans and brought to a successful conclusion many years of attack on the Arab-organized slave trade. To develop Uganda and free her from slave traffic a rail link from the coast through Kenya was begun in 1895. The Africans were not attracted to such labour and the line was built by labourers brought over from India, many of whom remained in East Africa as the forbears of the present thriving Asian population. The railway reached Kisumu on Lake Victoria in 1901 and proved a vital factor in increasing economic development in both Uganda and Kenya. In 1885 Germany took Tanganyika from the Sultan of Zanzibar who claimed suzerainty over it. 'German East Africa' was conquered by Britain in the First World War.

East Africa is an ethnological mixing ground where three great ethnic groups are found. In northern Uganda are the southernmost of the pastoral *Nilotic* tribes; on the Kenya–Tanzania border are the *Half Hamites* of whom the Masai are the principal tribe; elsewhere the *Eastern Bantu* are the dominant peoples, divided into many tribes and attaining their highest level of development in Uganda. Arabs and Asians are most numerous in the coastal belt and in Zanzibar where Swahili is the *lingua franca*. Other Asians are spread widely in urban and commercial employment.

For many years before independence, under the East African Common Service Organization, certain services were administered in common. They included defence, a common customs service and the operating of a variety of social, research, scientific and economic services. Also, an East African Railways and Harbours Administration on a unified basis controlled the railways and chief ports and the operation of lake, river and some road services. Unfortunately after independence national aims and views began to conflict and by 1977 these joint services of the East African Community had ceased.

Much of the present-day East African topography owes its origin to the substantial earth-movements during the Tertiary period. In East Africa they resulted in a sequence of uplift and downwarp, the foundering of large areas to form a chain of rift valleys and the spewing out of much lava, which continued into the Quaternary period. Much of the region comprises Pre-Cambrian igneous and metamorphic rocks of the Basement Series which form the great plateau masses. The highest land (except for Ruwenzori) is formed by the later outpourings of volcanic materials. Sedimentary rocks are limited in area and sporadic in occurrence, being confined mainly to the coastal zone and the north-east of Kenya.

East Africa is really a country of plateaux representing a series of planation surfaces. They are dominated by some of Africa's highest mountains: Kilimanjaro (5895 m), Kenya (5199 m), Ruwenzori (5119 m). These mountains, related to the rifting, are all on or near the equator, yet they are snow-capped and possess glaciers. The rift valleys (see also Chapter 2) are aligned in one Main or Eastern Rift system which passes from Ethiopia and Lake Turkana (Rudolf) through the heart of Kenya and Tanzania, and a Western Rift branching off to form the deep trench now occupied by Lakes Albert, Edward, Kivu and Tanganyika. Lake Tanganyika is the world's second deepest lake, with a maximum depth of 1434 m.

PHYSICAL REGIONS

The coastal plain is low and narrow (15–60 km wide) and is composed of Quaternary sediments fringed with coral reefs. It is hot and, except in the extreme north, humid with mangrove swamps in the estuaries. Soils vary considerably from fertile alluvium of the river estuaries to extensive infertile spreads of coral shag. The plain is narrow throughout most of Kenya but broadens out behind Dar-es-Salaam to include the lower course of the Rufiji river. The western limit of the coastal plain is indicated by a series of minor escarpments or steps of successively older sedimentary rocks which lead on to the threshold of the massive plateaux that cover the greater part of East Africa.

The Nyika. Behind and above the coastal plain stretches the Nyika (Swahili – wilderness) of Kenya and northern Tanzania. It is a planation surface of end-Tertiary age rising gently inland and averaging 600 m in height. The surface is broken here and there by relict hill masses and inselbergs and dissected by a number of small rivers – including the Tana, Galana, Pangani and Rufiji – which empty into the Indian Ocean. This low plateau is nearly pinched out by the Pare–Usumbara Mountains, but farther south widens into the South-East Plateau of Tanzania. This is semi-arid countryside which becomes desert in the north-east of Kenya, where the annual rainfall is under 250 mm. In the west the Nyika is bordered by hills and ranges such as the Matthews Range and Kitui hills in Kenya and the Nguru Mountains and Southern Highlands of Tanzania. These introduce the true East African plateau.

The East African plateau. This great upland mass, comprising the greater part of Tanzania and Uganda and nearly half of Kenya, is composed mainly of the Basement rocks which attain heights of around 2150 m in Kenya and northern Tanzania. Here bevelled remnants and accordant summit levels are related to planation from the pre-Miocene period. Within this great plateau area a number of sub-divisions may be made. An outstanding feature occurring in this plateau is the **Eastern or Main Rift Valley.** This passes through these uplands south from Lake Turkana to Lake Malawi. Within southern Kenya it varies from 65 to 80 km in width and is flanked by mountain buttresses in places over 900 m high. The floor of the valley is quite high, ranging from about 400 m in the north to 1900 m at Lake Naivasha in the centre, and dropping to 600 m at Lake Manyara in Tanzania. Farther south the rift loses the trough-like character it exhibits in Kenya and becomes less of a topographical feature, the western boundary appearing as a cliff of varying height, the eastern face rarely prominent. Nevertheless, it guides the line of the upper Great Ruaha river within the Southern Highlands, where its floor rises to over 900 m. Within these highlands the Eastern and Western Rift systems unite. They pass beneath volcanic hills attaining over 2950 m – part of the Kipengere Range – cradle Lake Malawi, and direct the course of the Shiré river to the Zambezi and the sea.

Flanking the rift from Lake Turkana to Lake Manyara in northern Tanzania are higher masses and mountains composed of Tertiary to recent volcanoes and associated lava flows. These form extensive and massive bastions and peaks rising strongly above the general level of the plateau: notably Mount Kenya (5199 m), the Aberdares (to 4000 m) and the Mau uplands (to 3000 m), all in Kenya, and Kilimanjaro (5895 m) in Tanzania. The soils derived from the decomposition of volcanic rocks are here more fertile than those formed on the Basement Series. This fertility, coupled with the mitigation of the climate with greater altitude, made these areas favourable for white settlement – which led subsequently to the general term 'the White Highlands', now less appropriate since land ownership there is no longer restricted to Europeans.

The East African plateau bears in its centre the **Lake Victoria Basin.** All the planation surfaces in East Africa show evidence of warping, especially between the rifts where a great structural downwarp or sag contains the relatively shallow Lake Victoria and marshy Lake Kyoga to its north, both part of the Nile drainage system. This depression and a number of other downwarps in central Tanzania are conveniently called the Lake Victoria Basin. It includes much of Uganda, much of the Nyanza district of Kenya and part of the lake province of Tanzania. Most of this area is a little below 1200 m, and in the lower parts Pleistocene sediments have accumulated and mask the old crystalline rocks. South of the Lake Victoria Basin and including about half of Tanzania is the **Central Plateau.** Like the rest of the great plateau area it is composed of crystalline rocks of the Basement Series, but is at a rather lower elevation, averaging little more than 1200 m. The rather monotonous undulating landscape is brown and parched for much of the year.

The Western Rift Valley and highlands terminate the plateau in the west. The highlands flank the edge of the western branch of the rift valley, generally repeating the pattern already noted with the eastern branch. The rift extends in an arc from Lake Albert to Lake Tanganyika and contains within it Lakes Edward and Kivu. The floor of this rift is generally between 600 and 900 m, somewhat lower than its eastern counterpart. Again great peaks and masses tower above the Rift Valley in such mountains as Ruwenzori (5119 m), a great horst of Archaean rocks (the highest non-volcanic mountain in Africa), and the Mfumbiro chain of active volcanic peaks which crosses the rift from the Zaire to Rwanda and Burundi and forms the water-parting between drainage northwards to the Nile and that to Lake Kivu and the Zaire (Congo) system. Several of these peaks surpass 4500 m.

DRAINAGE

Most of the drainage of East Africa flows to the Mediterranean via the Nile system or to the southern Atlantic via the Zaire system. Drainage to the Indian Ocean is limited in amount, and in Kenya several rivers crossing the Nyika are seasonal, being reduced to a series of muddy pools during the dry season. The Tana and Galana are the only two perennial streams descending by falls from the plateau of the Basement rocks. Neither is navigable. Tanzania has few permanent rivers, for much of her Central Plateau has a dry season of 5–6 months when very little rain falls. The main rivers flowing into the Indian Ocean are the Pangani fed by the snows of Kilimanjaro, the Ruvu, the Rufiji, which receives many tributaries from the Southern Highlands, and the Ruvuma which forms Tanzania's southern boundary with Mozambique. Of these only the Rufiji is navigable for 100 km from its extensive delta. A number of other streams flow into Lake Victoria, Lake Tanganyika and Lake Malawi; thus Tanzania contains the divide separating the headstreams of the Nile, Zaire and Zambezi. A fourth division of the drainage is into inland basins. In Kenya there are a number of lakes in the floor of the rift such as Lake Turkana, Nakuru and Magadi, and in Tanzania Lake Natron, Manyara and Eyasi.

CLIMATE

The East African states extend between latitudes 4°N and 11°S and are therefore mainly equatorial. However, the compact mass of uplands and the great elevations attained locally are responsible for climates ranging from those of the tropical coastal belt (with temperatures around 27°C all the year and a high humidity), to temperate climates within the highlands where mean temperatures lie between 21°C and 10°C with diurnal ranges of as much as 20°C. Uganda with more uniform relief exhibits less marked climatic variation, mean temperatures generally being between 24°C and 21°C, with daily ranges nowhere greater than 15°C. Rainfall also shows a great range of variation, from 120 mm or less on the Somalia border to as much as 2500 mm in some of the mountainous areas (Table 44).

East African climates owe much to three factors: an equatorial location; the presence of so much high land; and, in particular, monsoonal influences. The character and direction of flow (tending to parallel the coast) of the major airstreams over East Africa account for the seasonality and the generally low rainfall experienced in an equatorial area, and give East African rainfall a considerable degree of variability from the norm.

During the southern summer in the period November to April, the Inter Tropical Convergence (ITC) moves far to the south, and behind it northerly and north-easterly airstreams flow over East Africa. In Kenya, Uganda and northern Tanzania these winds are of cT type and dry, arriving from Arabia and the continent of Asia. In southern and eastern Tanzania, additional influx of mT air from the Indian Ocean gives rise to sporadic rains. With the northwards movement of the ITC in the southern winter, mainly southerly airstreams blow over East Africa, including the mT air of the South-East Trades of the Indian Ocean, and mE air from an Atlantic source which passes over Zaire towards Ethiopia. The mT air loses much of its moisture over the Madagascan Republic and, like the northerly (winter) winds, does not deposit much rainfall over East Africa; while most of the precipitation from the south-west flow of mE air falls more to the north over the south-west Ethiopian highlands, East Africa experiences most rain in the transition months during the passages of the ITC. During these periods the winds become weak and variable, and the rainfall is small for an equatorial region. These rainy transition months are February to May and October to December. Most rain falls in the former period, known as the 'maize rains'; the lesser rains later in the year being called the 'millet rains'.

Table 44 *East Africa: temperature and rainfall of selected stations*

Station	*Altitude (m)*		*J*	*F*	*M*	*A*	*M*	*J*	*J*	*A*	*S*	*O*	*N*	*D*	*Year*
Mombasa	15	T	26.8	26.8	27.7	27.2	26.1	24.9	23.8	24.4	24.9	26.1	26.8	26.8	26.1
		R	20	18	64	203	320	102	89	58	51	85	107	51	1168
Dar-es-Salaam	13	T	27.7	27.2	27.2	25.5	24.4	23.3	23.3	23.3	23.8	24.9	26.1	25.5	25.5
		R	84	53	122	304	188	27	43	27	27	30	74	69	1023
Nairobi	1635	T	17.7	18.2	18.2	17.7	17.7	16.6	14.9	14.9	16.6	18.2	17.7	16.6	17.1
		R	49	91	107	226	142	56	23	27	29	59	135	71	1015
Entebbe	1160	T	21.5	21.5	21.5	21.0	21.0	21.0	20.5	20.5	21.0	21.0	21.0	21.0	21.0
		R	66	91	147	247	216	128	74	78	78	89	127	129	1470

Notes: T = Temperature (°C); R = rainfall (mm).

The coastal zone south of Mombasa experiences over 1000 mm and the higher plateau elevations surpass that figure. Much of the lower and middle plateau areas receive under 750 mm which, under conditions of equatorial heat, is inadequate for arable farming. It is in fact necessary to distinguish between rainfall and *effective* rainfall. Most rain is experienced on the south-facing mountain slopes and those relating to the Western Rift such as Ruwenzori.

Rainfall is of great economic significance, for the vast mass of the East African population depends on agriculture and pastoralism for a livelihood. Over considerable areas mean annual amounts of rain are marginal, and this situation is worsened by the unreliability of much of the rain. The year-to-year variation is large: many stations have recorded maximum annual rainfall more than four times the minimum and seasonal drought of 6 months or more affects nearly two-thirds of the area. Most of Tanzania experiences a southern-hemisphere regime, with one rainy season of 5–6 months and the rest of the year dry. Much of Kenya and Uganda, being nearer the equator, has a two-season rainfall, the longer of these periods lasting about 3 months. In the extreme north of Kenya and Uganda a northern-hemisphere regime of one wet season becomes apparent, but the amount of rain in northern Kenya is so reduced that desert conditions are experienced.

Typical equatorial temperatures, practically constant at around 27°C, are confined to the coastal plains near the equator where temperatures within one or two degrees of the mean annual of 25°C are recorded. These are not high temperatures; it is the high humidity that makes this climate very unpleasant and enervating. Away from the coast, altitude tempers the heat: above 1500 m is considered suitable for white settlement. Nairobi at 1660 m has a mean of 17°C, rather like that of an English summer month. However, the small annual range characteristic of equatorial latitudes persists; temperature throughout the year is pleasant but monotonous and the real variation is not seasonal but diurnal. Nights are cool with rapid radiation, and a difference of up to 15°C or more between daily maximum and minimum is common, giving support to the saying 'night is the winter of the tropics'. Frost is frequent above 2450 m, limiting agriculture, and snow occurs above 4300 m.

The marked influence of topography upon East African climate facilitates a division into climatic regions closely coincident with the physical regions already outlined, but modified according to latitude. The coastal belt, except in the extreme north, is hot and damp with rainfall of up to 1250 mm. From Mombasa south to Dar-es-Salaam is the strip exhibiting the nearest approach to equatorial conditions, although the annual total of rain (Mombasa: 1170 mm) is somewhat low. The temperature range is from 28°C (March) to 24°C (July), only 4°C. The Nyika and Jubaland on the Somali border are sparsely peopled, dusty brown, parched areas of desert and steppe. The annual rainfall, varying from 500 mm in the south probably to as little as 125 mm on the northern border with Ethiopia and Somalia, falls mainly on permeable rock.

Inland, with increasing altitude, temperatures become lower and rainfall increases. The most favoured regions of the middle and upper plateau stretch from central Kenya into Uganda. The greater rainfall is also more reliable and here is to be found the greater proportion of the population of the two countries. Whereas the highest area, flanking the Eastern Rift, receives well over 1250 mm, the Rift Valley itself (generally 600–900 mm lower) is in the rain-shadow of the plateau and around Lake Naivasha receives about 750 mm. This diminishes to about 250 mm at Lake Turkana in the north and to 500 mm over much of central Tanzania to the south. Thus the greater part of the Eastern Rift offers only poor grazing.

In south-eastern Uganda the proximity of the equator and presence of the vast water surface of Lake Victoria bring near-equatorial climatic conditions; Entebbe beside the lake at 1150 m has an annual temperature range of only 1°C and receives 1500 mm, with

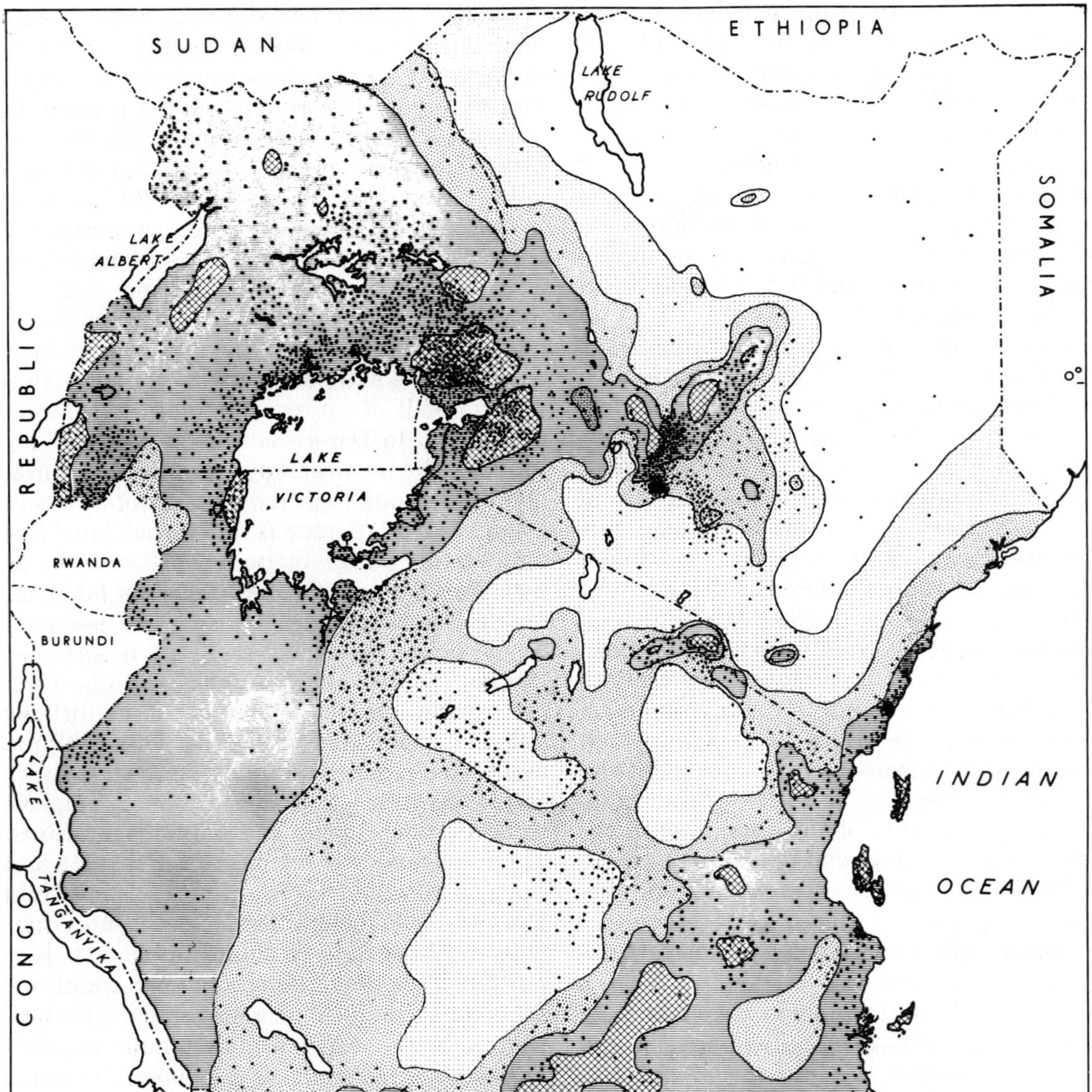

Figure 93 East Africa: rainfall probability and population distribution

rain every month and maxima in April and December. Humidity is high, and although malaria and other tropical diseases are coming under control, Uganda has never been attractive to Europeans.

THE SOILS

East Africa with its varied rock types, relief and climates has developed a considerable range of soils. Climate is the most important formative factor, since it affects the character and rate of the weathering and the growth of vegetation and bacteria. Both rainfall and temperature affect the rate of weathering, which becomes greater with higher temperatures; lateritic soils are widespread, and the occurrence of hard iron-pan layers often gives little depth of workable soil, even where higher rainfall and high temperatures might otherwise lead one to expect deep soils. Much of the parent rock in East Africa is crystalline, and the nature of the soils formed depends principally on the amount of quartz in the parent material. Sandy soils are derived from granites and sandstones, but parent rocks low in quartz – such as lavas – produce rather more fertile clayey soils.

Deep, mature, well-drained, fertile soils are limited in extent, mainly being confined to areas of rolling topography from 1250 to 3250 m, where rainfall is not less than 1000 mm, and where the parent rock is volcanic. Such soils can retain a high proportion of the seasonal rainfall for the use of crops and vegetation during the dry season. It will be deduced, then, that most East African soils are easily leached, lack humus and often show chemical deficiencies. The better soils are in the volcanic highlands of Kenya, where rainfall is also high and reliable. Most of the soils of Tanzania are sandy in character and the valleys become seasonally waterlogged ('mbugas'), mainly because of perched water tables where the gradient is very small during the rainy season, and in some cases because of iron-pan horizons – the only exceptions being the dark clays and clay-loams of the southern highlands. Uganda has useful clay and clay-loam areas on the north and west coasts of Lake Victoria, but in southern Uganda many valleys are permanently waterlogged and papyrus-filled. Farther north the waterlogging becomes more seasonal, and to the north-east soils become more sandy and arid.

VEGETATION

East African physical conditions engender a great range of vegetation. This variety and diversity depends primarily upon rainfall and altitude. The relatively low rainfall and the extensive area above 1200 m create conditions in striking contrast with those of the Zaire Basin to the west. Although astride the equator, equatorial forest is rare (it is found on the northern shores of Lake Victoria), and except for coastal and montane forests most of East Africa is clothed with varying forms of savanna. In the narrow coastal areas coconut palm and casuarina flourish, as do mangroves in the river estuaries and deltas. Inland, conditions become drier, and in the Kenya Nyika thorn woodland, the grotesque baobab and drought-resistant thorny scrub become dominant. Farther south in Tanzania, with slightly better rainfall, grasses improve. Over the whole area both domesticated and wild animals find sustenance, and the thorn-bush pastures of the north, although poorer, have the advantage of being free from the tsetse fly.

On the plateau proper of Kenya, Uganda and central Tanzania, where the annual rainfall averages 750 mm and exhibits a marked seasonal regime, open savanna prevails. The density of tree growth and height of grasses increase with the greater frequency and abundance of rain: from scattered trees with *Hyparrhenia* and other grasses 1–2 mm high, to savanna woodland with intermittent evergreen thickets and taller grass, such as elephant grass (*Pennisetum purpurem*) up to 4 m high. In Tanzania large areas of savanna woodland are called Miombo woodland, where *Brachystegia* canopy trees, evergreen thicket and tall grasses mingle. In Kenya, on the richer soils in the volcanic area between 1000 and 1500 m, the vegetation provides a valuable pastoral region, and Kikuyu grass (*Pennisetum clandestinum*) is a valuable grazing grass above 1900 m, thriving in rich, newly cleared forest soil. The mountains and the high plateau country demonstrate a vegetational zoning with altitude, reflecting the increasing and reliable precipitation and the lower temperatures. Above 1500 m evergreen trees predominate before merging into temperate rain-forests above 1900 m. Much of this woodland has been cleared for bush-fallowing type of agriculture or for coffee and tea plantations. Between 3000 and 3500 m on the moister mountains is a well-defined zone of mountain bamboo, *Arundinaria alpina*. This forms dense thicket growths with a height of 10–15 m, but above 3500 m it gives way to sub-Alpine and then Alpine vegetation. The sub-Alpine belt includes tree heathers, tussock grasses and patches of heathland, and merges into a zone of short Alpine grasses with a mingling of bulbous and leguminous plants. A few of the highest peaks surpass the snow-line, which is at about 4500 m.

AGRICULTURAL POTENTIAL

The wide range of conditions has been noted, but not all of them are beneficial to human settlement and means of livelihood. As with all communities relying upon farming for a living, rainfall and water supply are of paramount importance. In East Africa rainfall amount and reliability are decisive in affecting the type of farming undertaken. Experience has shown that there is little chance of successful cereal cultivation where the reliable rainfall is under 750 mm. Consequently the 750 mm rainfall reliability line serves to distinguish the pastoral from the arable lands and is also a useful guide in determining prospects for agricultural expansion.

Other factors also interact with rainfall reliability in restricting farming; they include environmental and physical obstacles, technical and organizational difficulties (among them are soils, tsetse fly, communications, manpower and level of skills). In most areas, however, it is the rainfall that is decisive. It is more than unfortunate that whereas climate and soil conspire to make part of Kenya and most of Tanzania into potentially great pastoral countries, the presence of the tsetse fly renders this impossible. Kenya has 10 per cent of its area subject to the fly, Tanzania 60 per cent and Uganda about 32 per cent. Not all the affected areas would be suited only to pastoral pursuits; much of that affected in Tanzania has a fair prospect of sufficient rain to support arable farming. Consequently much of the future economic development of East Africa hinges upon success in the battle with the fly and there are no prospects of any immediate triumph.

A series of techniques has been evolved that offers some success in the eradication of the insect and the diseases it transmits. Insecticides to kill the fly itself, bush-clearing to destroy its natural habitat, or the destruction of game whose trypanosome-infected blood forms the food supply of the fly, are three directions of attack. Research continues into methods of immunization for both men and cattle. Progress is slow and expensive, but so long as the fly is paramount, mixed farming will be impossible and agriculture will remain retarded over considerable areas.

An examination of the rainfall reliability map (Figure 93) and Table 45 reveals that approximately half of East Africa (including one-half of Tanzania and over four-fifths of Kenya) has little prospect of receiving a reliable 750 mm of rainfall each year, and therefore on this count must be classified primarily as pastoral. In fact, rather less than a quarter of East Africa enjoys a high reliability (nineteen years out of twenty) of a 750 mm rainfall

Table 45 *Rainfall probability in East Africa (percentage of land area receiving selected amounts of annual rainfall in four years out of five)*

Rainfall	*Kenya*	*Uganda*	*Tanzania*	*East Africa*
Less than				
500 mm	72	12	16	35
500–750 mm	13	10	33	20
750–1250 mm	12	72	47	41
Over 1250 mm	3	6	4	4

Source: *Natural Resources of East Africa* (Nairobi, 1962), p. 79.

(which generally makes arable farming possible) and most of this is already well-settled. It will be seen that Kenya has little of this land, Uganda much of it, and Tanzania lies between these extremes. Further, the limitations of the bulk of the pastoral zone must be recognized. Much of this land in northern Kenya and central Tanzania is too arid for satisfactory development and is likely to remain the home of hardy nomadic camel- and cattle-men who exist only with great difficulty. In the better savannas (such as the Masai and Kamba land units, the Mkata Plains, the grassy Southern Highlands of Tanzania, Karamoja and Ankole in Uganda) economic animal husbandry is possible – given fly eradication, the provision of water and education in animal and pasture management. These areas, however, are small and widely scattered and their development is likely to be slow. The undeveloped fertile land in south-west Tanzania will only become productive when the difficulties of communications, tsetse fly infestation and lack of capital for irrigation and other works are overcome.

In the north-western corner of the region artificial political boundaries carve into three unequal divisions the geographical and ecological unit of the Lake Victoria depression. This area is a single economic unit and constitutes a region of the greatest potential economic growth in East Africa. Unfortunately development by the three independent states, each differing in outlook and philosophy, has been uneven and mainly disappointing.

42 Kenya

Kenya was granted independence in 1963 after 68 years of British rule. It has an area of 583,000 km² and a population of 26 million. Since independence white numbers have fallen from 56,000 to 39,000 and Asians from 177,000 to 77,000, and Kenya now has the reputation of being a tolerant, multiracial society. Kenya's natural resources are very limited; her greatest is her soil, from which the livelihood of nearly all her people is obtained and most of her export revenue earned. The country exhibits such a variety of natural conditions – rising from sea-level to 5250 m, and ranging from desert to mangrove swamp – that practically any crop can be grown in some part of the country, from strawberries to coconuts, from potatoes to cassava. Nevertheless the productive area of Kenya is much restricted by a number of physical factors; the greatest of which (as we have seen) is the amount and reliability of rainfall. Two-thirds of the country is arid and serves to support a relatively few Hamitic and Nilo-Hamitic pastoralists; the greater part of the population is concentrated in the better-watered highlands of the south-western quadrant and the narrow coastal strip.

SETTLEMENT ON THE LAND

It was the construction of the railway from Mombasa to Kisumu that made possible the settlement and economic development of the Kenya highlands as well as of Uganda. Numerous branch lines were added, and in 1928 the railway was extended north of Lake Victoria to Kampala. When, in 1901, the railway had been pushed across the uplands to Lake Victoria, Sir Harry Johnston reported: 'Here we have a territory (now that the Uganda railway is built) admirably suited for a white man's country, and I can say this, with no thought of injustice to any native race, for the country in question is either utterly uninhabited for miles and miles or at most its inhabitants are wandering hunters who have no settled home . . .'[1]

The railway opened these apparently empty highlands to European penetration; the settled African peoples were in the high-rainfall area bordering Lake Victoria and on the slopes of Mount Kenya, the Aberdares and the hills of Ukambani. Between these well-watered fertile areas were extensive upland plains receiving rather less rainfall and grazed over by the pastoralist Masai. It was into these empty plains that white settlers moved and succeeded in obtaining good agricultural returns with their better techniques and equipment. In a series of enactments the Masai were restricted to definite areas and were finally allotted a large reserve on the border with Tanzania; intertribal struggle on the uplands thus came to an end. Later, objections were raised to the white settlement; in some cases tribal land that took its turn under shifting agriculture had been alienated, and in other cases Africans took advantage of the peaceful conditions to move into the land no longer supporting Masai herds, such as on the Mau hills. Here they met Europeans who had been allotted the land by the government. Similarly the early triangle of white settlement between Emali–Nairobi–Fort Hall was a no-man's-land between the Masai to the south, the Kamba on the better-watered Ithanga hills and the Kikuyu on the lower slopes of the Aberdares. In this way considerable areas of the highland above 1750 m became settled by Europeans who were allotted and sold land by the Crown which was not owned by the African tribes. By law African lands were made secure against white settlement, and in 1939 the white-settled areas were secured against African settlement. One result of British rule was a considerable increase of population, and in 1961 the status of the 'White Highlands' was changed and Africans were allowed to purchase land and farm in those areas. Loans and grants were made available to assist the better African farmers to do this. Less than one-fifth of the over-760 mm annual rainfall area was alienated to Europeans and Asians, but it is this land which before independence produced two-fifths of the gross agricultural production and no less than 85 per cent of the agricultural exports of the country.

FARM CONSOLIDATION

African farming output was poor owing to their system of land tenure and their unscientific farming. African land was normally held communally according to tribal law and custom, although gradually private tenure or ownership was becoming accepted. The indigenous system of tenure and inheritance had led to fragmentation and poor land-use, for on heavily fragmented land it is impossible to farm properly. 'It is, for instance, quite impracticable to make efficient use of 43 fragments aggregating 8 ha in extent and situated up to 11 km from the owner's homestead; but if consolidated this represents a holding capable of providing a full subsistence plus £200 per year or a net profit of £25 per acre; whereas fragmented the net profit would not exceed Shs. 30/– per annum at best'.[2]

Tribal lands are usually densely peopled and most males go out to work in towns and farms, leaving the bulk of the cultivation to the women. A tremendous potential of increased production was locked up in these lands, as land consolidation under the Swynnerton Plan showed. After the Second World War efforts to improve African farming became codified under the 'Swynnerton Plan (1954)'. The plan's aim was 'to intensify the development of African agriculture in Kenya', and it included the consolidation of farmland; the introduction of cash crops under scientific supervision; the introduction of improved livestock and mixed farming; the irrigation and reclamation of swamps; and the eradication of tsetse fly. The implementation of these programmes brought great changes to the landscape by introducing an enclosure system and private ownership of land. The consolidation of fragmented holdings and the registration of holdings set the seal on the private ownership as opposed to tribal ownership of land. White opposition was disregarded and the growing of cash crops under supervision was encouraged: coffee, tea, pyrethrum, pineapples, sugar-cane and tobacco were introduced. Thus began a transition from subsistence to commercial farming by large numbers of the peasantry. The White Highlands were open to farming by all races from 1960, and after independence (1963) the majority of white farmers were bought out and their land in various tenurial forms came to be farmed by black Africans.

Some large farms were split into 10 ha holdings for redistribution to Africans, a popular political move but soon revealing the loss of economies of scale (e.g. centralized watering places and cattle dips were lost, and the small farms needed most of their land for basic subsistence grains and little was available for animals). The high demand for land has also led to the rise of *minifundia*, with an average size of 1 ha sometimes granted in return for labour on an African-owned large farm and sometimes created by direct sales of divided 10 ha plots. Many European farms were acquired intact by well-off African Kenyans, while others were bought by the

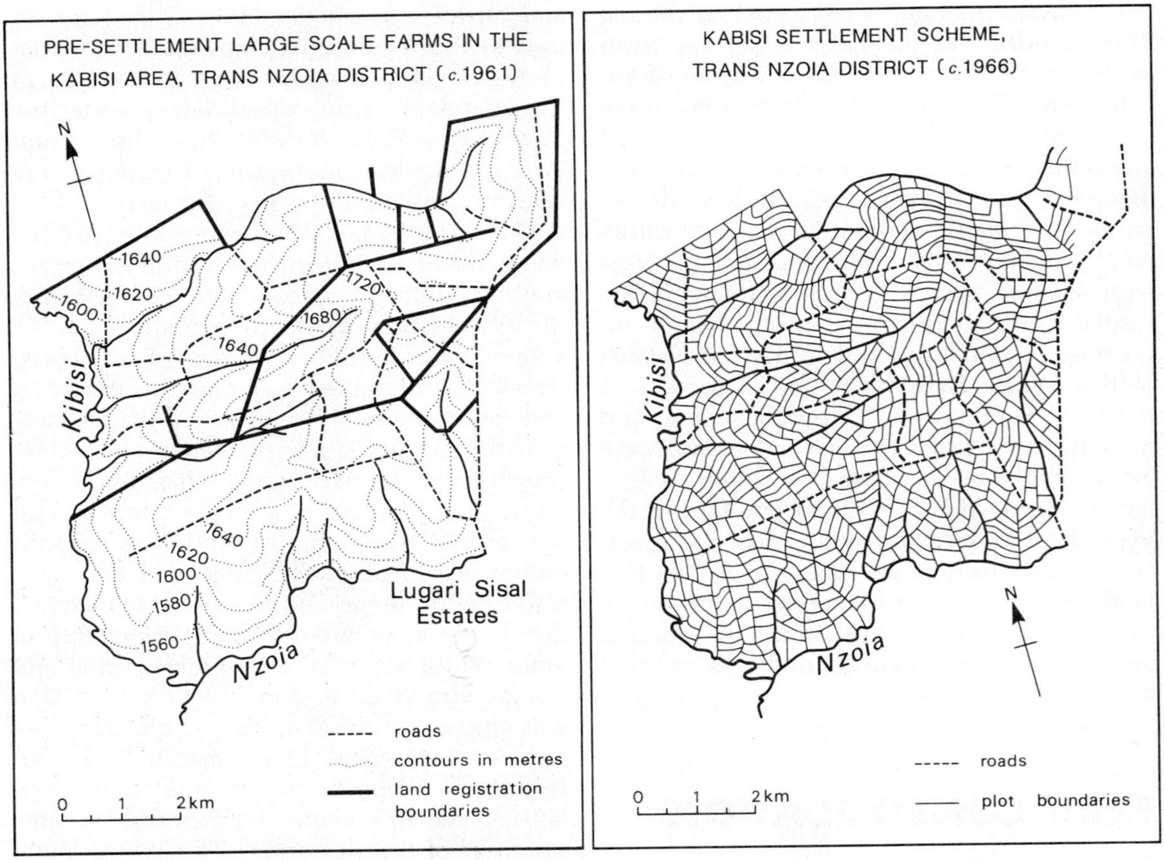

Figure 94 Kenya: the Trans Nzoia Settlement Scheme

government and were turned into state farms or cooperatives with the ownership shared by the workers. Here the advantages of large-scale operations have been retained. Thus some large farms remain under varied operating systems, and they include about 50 that remain in the hands of white Kenyans. They account for 2.8 million hectares and compare with about 4 million hectares farmed by small-holders with farm sizes averaging 2–3 ha. Pressure for land now shows itself in landless peasantry encroaching on marginal land assigned as cattle land to pastoralists such as the Masai. Kenya is one of the few newly independent African states that has not neglected investment in agriculture, and the standard of living of her farmers has been rising: average earnings in the major towns increased by 67 per cent between 1966 and 1975, compared with 108 per cent for the rest of Kenya. The subsistence farming sector is slowly shrinking: more than half of marketed agricultural production now comes from small farms.

A corollary to these resettlement operations has been the collecting of people into villages. These Bantu agricultural people were scattered in isolated family groups, their huts standing on their holdings. In the 1950s during anti-government guerrilla fighting in the Mau area, they were forcibly grouped into villages so that they could be better controlled. Unpopular at first, village life was found to have attractions; and although some farms are now set up on the larger newly consolidated holdings, small-holders and those with only garden plots remain in the villages, either

Plate 54 Weeding pyrethrum in the Chepsir Resettlement Area, Kericho, Kenya

finding work on a larger consolidated farm, or in the village, or even in Nairobi. The villages and small townships are a part of the new agricultural order and have become a permanent feature of the landscape, allowing health and educational measures to make greater and quicker impact.

AGRICULTURE

There are three important farming areas in Kenya: on parts of the coastal plain; on the highlands flanking the Rift Valley; and in Nyanza Province beside Lake Victoria.

The coastal plain. The well-watered southern part of the coastal plain is mainly under subsistence crops: maize, cassava, yams and rice in some river estuaries. Coconuts, sugar and cotton offer some commercial return, and there are a number of sisal plantations. Inland and to the north, the poor grass, scattered acacia trees and scrub of the Nyika are of little value except to Somali and Galla camel and cattle nomads. Farther inland on the plateau, first on the Basement Complex and then on the richer red-soiled volcanic rocks, where rainfall is assured, population density increases and agriculture is firmly established; although before British rule the virile and aggressive Masai pastoralists ranged widely over these grasslands, preventing their permanent occupation by agricultural tribes.

The Highlands. Within the Highlands are large areas of fertile, deep-red volcanic soils, annual rainfall of 1150 mm or more, and mild temperatures. Under a quarter of this land was held by Europeans and Asians until independence. Following the Second World War mixed farming patterns gave way to greater specialism on such commercial crops as coffee, tea and pyrethrum. Thus African production is no longer concerned solely with subsistence farming but, with the acquisition of much of the former European farmland, turns increasingly to cash-cropping. Cattle and sheep ranching takes place in the drier parts of the Central Rift. Most of Kenya's forested areas lie in the higher parts of the Central and Rift Valley provinces at between 2000 and 4000 m above sea-level. Their greatest contribution to the economy is water, for they protect the main water catchment areas of the country and only a small proportion of the forests is used commercially.

Nyanza. To the east of the Lake Victoria Basin is Kenya's third agricultural region, principally Nyanza Province. Here there has been little alienation of land to white settlers. This is a densely peopled region of thriving African agriculture. There are three major structural sub-divisions. (1) The first is a plateau north of the Kavirondo Gulf, rising to over 2100 m in the east and stretching up to Mount Elgon (4320 m) in the north. Much of this sloping up from the lake shore is part of the undulating Kavirondo peneplain on the Basement Complex; to the north this merges with the Tertiary volcanic rocks of Elgon. (2) In the centre is the Kavirondo Rift, a trough that trends 130 km east from the Kavirondo Gulf. (3) To the south are the Kisii highlands, a deeply dissected area of broad valleys and steep ridges reaching altitudes of more than 2000 m.

The soils north of the lake are sandy-brown on the granitic areas and richer and deep-red on the Elgon volcanics. Those of the Gulf lowland, mantling the nearly level rift floor, are black calcareous 'cotton' soils (although cotton cultivation is not restricted to these soils); and to the south and east, towards Kericho, there are extensive grassy areas on deep-red volcanic soils. The climatic influences of the equatorial location and of Lake Victoria are apparent in the distribution and amount of rainfall. A highly reliable rainfall varying from 750 mm in the Gulf to over 1500 mm on the uplands helps to make this a region of most productive agriculture. It has often been called the 'granary of Kenya', mainly because maize production, especially north of the Gulf, exceeds local needs and allows of export.

A great variety of crops is grown, matching the diversity of the physical conditions, though much of this is due to European influence and the introduction of new crops. Cotton was introduced with the arrival of the railway to Kisumu, for a commercial crop was needed to provide the line with freight. It was slow in becoming accepted. A ginnery was set up at Kisumu in 1908; at first most of its intake was from Uganda, but gradually cotton-growing spread throughout central and southern Nyanza. Coffee-growing on the Kisii highlands began in about 1935. In order to maintain quality, coffee in Kenya could only be grown under licence, and expansion of the coffee acreage here was slow until restrictions were eased after 1960. Rice was another crop introduced both as a famine-prevention measure and as a cash crop and, with bananas and sugar-cane, demonstrates the great variety of crops grown. Farther east the Kericho district is the major tea-growing area of Kenya, but most of these plantations still belong to Europeans.

Agriculture is the dominant sector of the economy. It accounts for one-third of the GNP, provides a livelihood for 80 per cent of the population, and employs 30 per cent of wage-earners. It is also responsible for 50 per cent of export earnings. Subsistence farming accounts for over half the output – mainly of maize, sorghum, cassava, bananas and sugar. There is no longer self-sufficiency in basic foods thanks to a massive weight of population growth, a series of droughts, poor storage facilities and the greater attraction of money-earning cash crops. The share of Africans in export crops continues to rise for, as with most of the African states who are heavily dependent on agriculture, these years are seeing great efforts to move the economy from subsistence to market agriculture, whereby higher income may accrue, and effective home demand for manufactured products be engendered, which in turn will support manufacturing industry and urban occupations. However, the government now pays much attention to supporting and aiding the poorer subsistence farmers to reduce the flow to the urban centres and to raise their living standards. Over the long term annual income per head has risen substantially in Kenya (from \$330 in 1978 to \$450 in 1985), but this is not evenly distributed and very little has reached the poorest people.

INDUSTRY

Industrial development in Kenya, while more advanced than amongst her neighbours, is still very small, contributing 20 percent of GDP in 1983. It is mainly confined to the processing of agricultural produce such as cotton-ginning, sugar-milling, drying and hulling of coffee and the pressing of oil from cotton-seed and groundnuts. There is some fruit and vegetable preservation, preparation of pyrethrum extract for insecticides and wattle extract for tanning. Lorry and bus bodies, cement, building materials of clay, wood and metal are made. Among consumer goods manufactured locally are beer, cigarettes, footwear, textiles and clothing, soaps and household metal products.

Industrial production has increased four-fold since independence, but much of this ex-

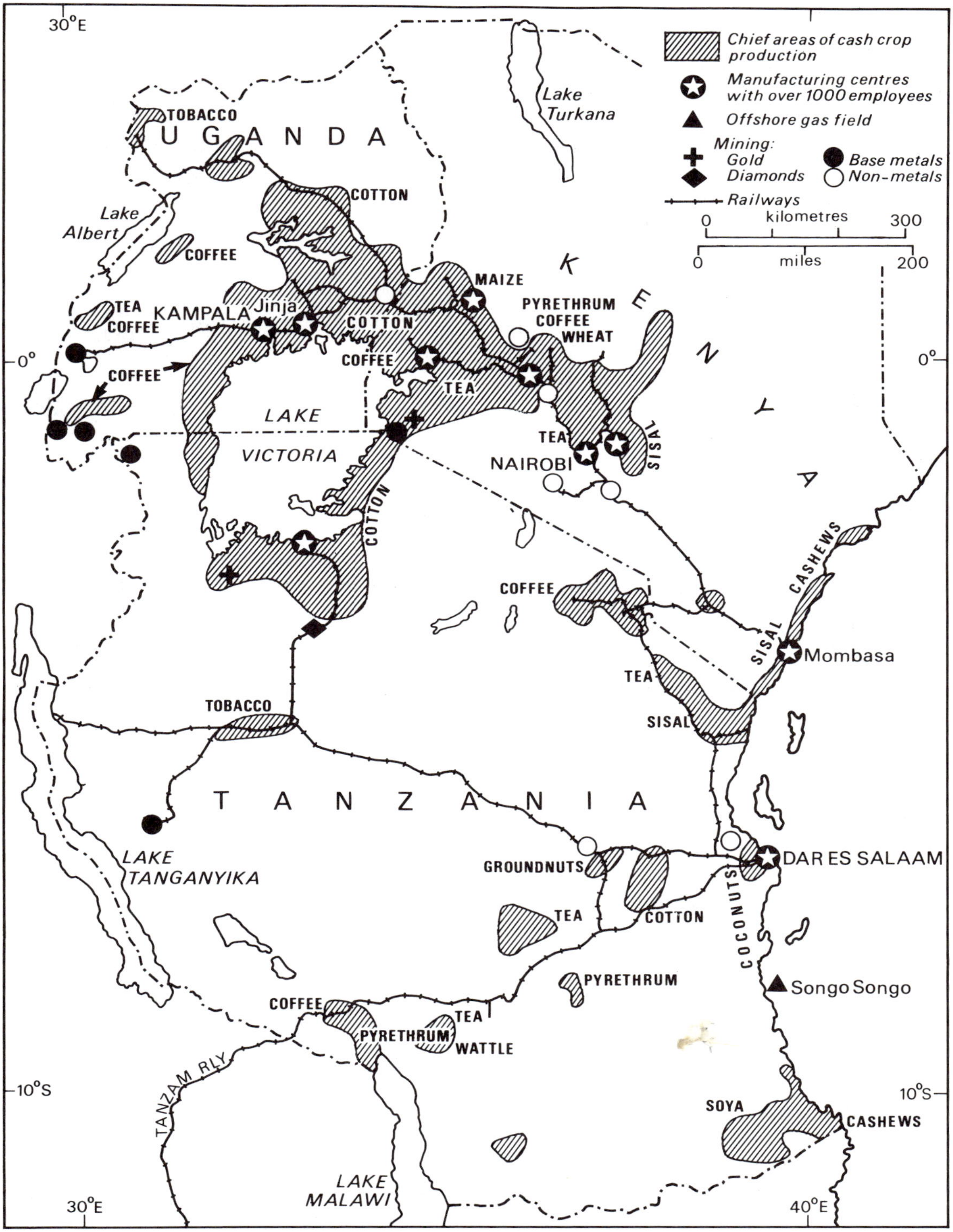

Figure 95 East Africa: economic development
Source: After T. J. D. Fair

pansion was in the earlier years when labour was cheap, raw material imports were paid for with over-valued currency and high tariffs gave strong protection. A general policy of import substitution industry has had little success, and in recent years progress has been erratic with import controls, foreign-exchange shortages, power shortages and rising costs. A major problem is the low purchasing power of the peasantry who constitute the bulk of the home market. Some export of aluminium hollow-ware, footwear and cigarettes to other parts of Africa has begun, but the real markets will be in Kenya with the raising of rural incomes.

The two major centres of manufacturing industry are at Nairobi and Mombasa, the two principal towns (the capital and chief port), where a sound infrastructure of public utilities and transport facilitates manufacturing, and a pool of labour and an effective market exist. Both towns have chemicals, glass, cement, and paint works and numerous small consumer-goods industries; in addition, Nairobi manufactures textiles, and there is an oil refinery at Mombasa. Many of the firms are subsidiaries of great industrial concerns like Unilever, ICI and Portland Cement. At Limuru, Bata have established a large footwear plant, and textiles are made at Nakuru. East Africa lacks coal and much industrial power is electrical, derived from hydroelectric sources or from thermal stations using imported fuels. Kenya is poor in hydroelectric potential but has small plants on the Maragua, Tana and Thika rivers. Some power is also obtained from the Owen Falls Dam in Uganda. Mombasa has thermal plants but obtains some hydroelectric power from the Pangani Falls in Tanzania. Except for cement, brewing and flour-milling, most of the industrial plants are small, making lighter demands on capital, managerial and organizational expertise, clerical and accounting personnel. However, lacking economies of scale, they are often high-cost producers.

In recent years Kenya's economic planning has been adversely affected by the vagaries of weather – reducing harvests – the raising of oil prices and the world recession. Although average earnings increased, purchasing power actually fell because of inflation. An economy based upon primary production is very much at the mercy of outside events and movements over which it may have no control. In the Four-Year Plans (1979–83 and 1984–8) industrial output increased moderately, but the main thrust of the planning has been on restructuring, to change the emphasis from unnecessary import-substitute industrialization in favour of processing local raw materials and export promotion. Expansion of the tourist industry is planned; it is the third largest foreign earner and in 1985 there were 450,000 visitors. Planning and investment provision is for 1 million visitors by 1988.

Plate 55 The Bamburi Portland Cement Company factory, Kenya

SETTLEMENT AND POPULATION

Kenya's sole great port is Mombasa, with its spacious harbour of Kilindini. From this port the trunk railway through Nairobi to Uganda was completed to Lake Victoria in 1901. A

Plate 56 Handling tea and maize for export at Mombasa

number of branches and extensions were made to it, sometimes in order to attract settlement and sometimes to serve existing settlements, such as white settlement in the Trans-Nzoia in 1921. The whole pattern of the white settlement and opening-up of Kenya devolves from the construction of this railway line by the British Government. It cost £5 million and took 5 years to build. It was very much a speculative venture, for there was no worthwhile freight to be carried to the coast at that time. The objects of the line were both strategic and humanitarian. British control of the interior in the face of German activity in Tanzania had to be made more effective and depended upon good communications; further, the construction of the railway obviated the carriage of goods by men and put an end to the lingering slave trade. The story of development can be measured in terms of freight and passengers: in 1902 the railway carried 13,000 tonnes of freight and 73,000 passengers; in 1979 the railway carried 3,900,000 tonnes of freight and 2,050,000 passengers.

The largest city in East Africa is **Nairobi** (at 1677 m), the capital of Kenya. It received a royal charter in 1950 and has a population of over 900,000. It dates from 1899, when the railway from the coast reached this spot on the great Athi Plain and a main workshop and depot were constructed. It began as a railway construction camp, but with a position in the midst of early 'empty' upland, attractive to white settlers, it soon grew in size and importance. It is now the transport focus of East Africa and the headquarters of many firms trading in East Africa. Its most important growth has been since 1945, in which time its population has quadrupled. One result has been the emergence of an ugly but lusty town sometimes reminiscent of the immature towns of America's Middle West.

Mombasa (pop. 320,000) is an old Arab centre, built on an island in a coastal inlet. Deep water on its western side forms the magnificent harbour of Kilindini, reckoned the finest on the east coast of Africa. It handles over 6 million tonnes of cargo annually – three times that of its nearest rival Dar-es-Salaam.

Kenya's 20 million population is concentrated in the three productive regions already discussed: the coastal zone centred upon Mombasa; the central province where Kikuyu, Meru and Embu Land Units cluster among the Aberdare and Mount Kenya foothills; and Nyanza Province (Figure 93). The rate of increase of Kenya's population is now put at 4.3 per cent, the highest rate in Africa and almost in the world. If this rate is unabated the population will double itself within 14 years. This frightening rate reflects the sharp success of the medical revolution in reducing death rates, set against an unchecked Third World birth rate. Belatedly, efforts are now being made to make family-planning measures acceptable.

Much has been achieved in the first 20 years of independence: tribal differences are still strong but government patronage is spread wide; privilege and corruption at higher levels is being contained if not reduced. An urban and detribalized black 'middle class' is now arising, indicating that the power of the tribe and associated patronage is weakening. Nuclear families are beginning to replace the traditional extended family. Colonial segregation of hospitals, schools and clubs has gone, and a growing peasant prosperity suggests some success in the orderly transfer of wealth and land to Africans.

REFERENCES

1 H. H. Johnson, *Report by His Majesty's Special Commission in the Protectorate of Uganda*, Cmd.671 (1901), p. 7.

2 L. H. Brown, *'Agriculture and land tenure in Kenya Colony'*, in E. W. Russell, *Natural resources in East Africa*, Nairobi, 1962, p. 105.

43 Uganda

The former British protectorate of Uganda became a fully independent member of the British Commonwealth in 1962. It was in 1894 that the British protectorate was declared over the Kingdom of Buganda and certain adjoining territories when Britain assumed the administrative responsibility of the British East Africa Company. Uganda consisted of a number of independent kingdoms, of which Buganda was the largest, now existing in a federal relationship. The Baganda, who inhabit Buganda, are among the most advanced African peoples. They had a well-developed political system of king, ministers and parliament and a flourishing agricultural economy when the Europeans first arrived. This was preserved under the British system of indirect rule. Since attaining independence and becoming a republic the country has been wracked by successive *coups*, notably a military one headed by Idi Amin (1971–9) under whose regime up to 300,000 people are alleged to have been murdered. Civilian rule was only restored after an invasion by Tanzanian troops; subsequently the military again took over.

Uganda has a total area of 236,000 km^2 (about the same as the British Isles), of which 15 per cent is water; this includes parts of Lake Victoria and Albert, the whole of Lake Kyoga and the Victoria and Albert branches of the River Nile. The 1980 population was 13 million and included 50,000 Asians, but only a few thousand Europeans – mostly administrators, educationalists and technicians. The average density of population, at over 80 people per km^2, is very high for Africa; in the most populous parts, around the shores of Lake Victoria, the density approaches 225 per km^2.

PHYSICAL BACKGROUND

The greater part of Uganda constitutes a shallow downwarp in the Basement Complex with upland around the edges: Lake Victoria fills the centre of the depression. Along the eastern frontier with Kenya, Mount Elgon attains 4370 m, and farther north the boundary is the watershed between Lake Turkana and the Nile drainage. Other mountains, including those in Karamoja, stand along the northern boundary with the Sudan. To the west is the extensive mountainous mass flanking the western Rift Valley, including parts of Toro, Ankole and Kigezi districts. The bulk of Uganda consists of a plateau between 1000 and 1400 m above sea-level. Near Lake Victoria the plateau (of the mid-Tertiary) is dissected into numerous tabular hills, with 150–260 m between hill top and valley bottom. Farther away the country is one of gentle undulations through which Nile waters slowly drain through a labyrinth of swamps that constitute Lake Kyoga. Navigable channels are maintained through the swamp vegetation, and the lake is used as a waterway by those farming the surrounding fertile countryside.

Although Uganda is on the equator, its climate avoids the full equatorial heat and rainfall, owing to the tempering effect of altitude and the considerable areas of lake water. In a sense the climate comes midway between that of the Zaire Basin and of the arid heat of eastern Kenya. Except in the extreme north-east, rainfall on the plateau varies from 760 to 1500 mm, the heaviest being experienced on the north shores of Lake Victoria, on the slopes of Mount Elgon and on the upland to the west and north-west. A less reliable and rather low rainfall is experienced in a discontinuous belt from the south-west to north-east. In the vicinity of Lake Victoria two maxima of rain are experienced, associated with the double transit of the Inter Tropical Convergence. The early maximum is usually the greater, but both play their part in making it possible to raise two crops from the same land in the year. In the north of the country, farther from the equator, a definite period of drought occurs which limits the productivity of the land. Along the north shore of Lake Victoria the probability of obtaining optimum water requirements for crops twice a year is as high as 74 per cent, whereas at Gulu, 320 km to the north, the probability is only 4 per cent.

Thus in the north the year divides into a warm, wet season and a hot, dry season, but near Lake Victoria the annual range of temperature is compressed almost to vanishing point. Elevation reduces temperatures; but the year-long humid heat so bountiful to plant growth is disliked by Europeans, and this helps to explain their small number, and an even smaller number of European settlers, in Uganda. The areas of reliable rainfall and general fertility favour plantation agriculture, and a few Europeans did settle before the First World War; but the enervating climate and the incidence of such insect-borne diseases as sleeping-sickness generally discouraged settlement.

The vegetation reflects the two main climatic zones, based on seasonality of rainfall, and it is climate also that has a paramount influence upon agriculture. Modified tropical forest is found in southern Buganda and Busoga near the lake shores, but much of it has been cleared and the prevailing vegetation is elephant grass (*Pennisetum purpureum*) with scattered trees. This gives way in the

Plate 57 Distribution of agricultural inputs to small-scale farmers, Atangala Cooperative, Uganda

drier area of west Masaka and north-east Mengo to short grass with scattered low trees.

AGRICULTURE

Climatic zones are reflected in distinctive crops and agricultural practices. There is a particular contrast between the high and low-rainfall regions, for in the former the food supply is mainly derived from planted crops – principally the plantain (or cooking banana), sweet potatoes and cassava – whereas in the remainder of Uganda sown crops predominate, notably finger millet, maize and pulses. This distinction is not absolute, for some seed-bearing crops are grown in the high-rainfall region, and some planted crops, notably sweet potatoes, are grown elsewhere. The low-rainfall (short-grass) zone is favourable for keeping cattle but not the wetter elephant-grass country, and although some cattle are kept they are grazed away from the cultivated areas and often herded by hired tribesmen from the drier cattle country. Tsetse flies, bringing human sleeping-sickness and ngana, still infest parts of the Lake Victoria northern

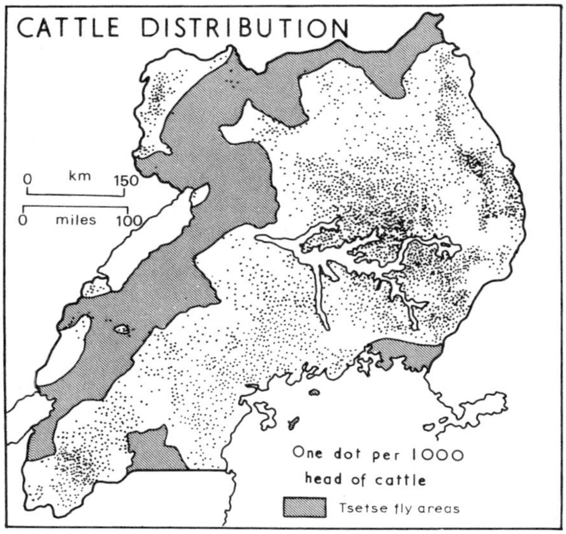

Figure 96 Uganda: distribution of cattle and tsetse fly

shores, especially in Busoga (Figure 96). Cultivation of the banana is easy and involves little toil; the plant sends out suckers so that a typical family grove contains about twenty stems in varying stages of maturity – enough to provide food all the year round. The foliage of the tree acts as an umbrella against the rain, excessive soil leaching is prevented, and the dead leaves form a useful mulch.

The main cash crops grown in the high-rainfall zone are cotton and robusta coffee. The introduction of cotton in 1904 resulted from a combination of circumstances and policies: the need to find freight to make viable the newly opened Kisumu–Mombasa railway, a movement in the United Kingdom to lessen Lancashire's dependence on cotton supplies from the USA, and the need to get the Africans to produce a cash crop in order to earn tax money upon which administration and development depended. The main response came from the Baganda, who already had a higher standard of living than their neighbours and who found that cash-crop production enabled them to satisfy their relatively sophisticated needs for good cloth, house utensils and paper. In 1905 cotton production was 241 bales worth £1089; in 1910, 13,378 bales worth £165,412, or more than half the total exports of the protectorate. Climatic conditions are not ideal for cotton, for there is an excessive production of foliage and the ripening season is not quite hot enough. Nevertheless conditions are such that the crop cannot fail: a sizable harvest is assured.

The success of cotton growing in Uganda has been particularly important in demonstrating the possibility of export-crop production by Africans on their own fields and without direct European supervision. Since the end of the Second World War coffee growing has increased to vie with cotton for first place, while a new crop, cocoa, has been successfully introduced. Both coffee and cocoa take several years to become established, but are then more than twice as profitable per hectare to the peasant than cotton and less demanding of labour. In this region also, particularly near the lake, sugar is grown and there are a number of tea estates.

In the 'short-grass' zone, where annual rainfall is usually below 1150 mm and more seasonal in distribution, farming is typical of much of Africa, being based on hoe cultivation of annual crops with livestock included in the farming in areas not invaded by tsetse fly. The main subsistence crops are finger millet, sorghum, beans, sweet potatoes and cassava. The most important cash crops are cotton and groundnuts. On the higher fringes of the zone arabica coffee is grown, and in parts of Ankole, Toro and West Nile districts it is the foremost cash crop. Government-sponsored tea estates are increasing. Cattle keeping is more general, although in places there is no great integration of crops and stock. In the drier areas of the Karamojo districts of the north, and the Ankole district west of Lake Victoria, keeping cattle is the major occupation and few crops are grown. In the higher mountain areas above 2000 m on Mount Elgon and in parts of the western province, where a number of Europeans have settled, more temperate crops can be grown, including pulses and the English potato. The cash crop, although not produced in large quantities, is arabica coffee.

The best cattle in Uganda are the big-horned animals from the high grasslands of Ankole. Generally cattle are of a poorer quality on the humid lowlands, where considerable areas are still subject to tsetse fly. The excessively starchy diet of Africans in the high-rainfall region leads to malnutrition, particularly protein malnutrition of young children (called Kwashiorkor). Goats, poultry and fish give some animal protein and variety, but beef and milk tend to be luxuries, and tribal taboos are a hindrance to progress in varying the diet.

MINERALS AND INDUSTRY

Uganda is not well-endowed with minerals in economic quantities, and mineral production is virtually confined to copper from the Kilembe Mine in the Ruwenzori Range. The mine was opened in 1956 following the completion of a 330 km western extension of the railway from Kampala, constructed for the purpose. It closed for a time during the Amin regime. Transport problems have undoubtedly hampered mineral development in Uganda; but that is not the sole reason, for much of the country has now been surveyed and no significant deposits have been located other than the copper of Kilembe, and phosphates in the Sukulu hills. In the volcanic and metamorphosed rocks of Mount Elgon–Nyanza, and flanking the Western Rift, a multitude of minerals has been discovered; but usually the deposits are small and scattered or larger and spread thinly, so that for the most part economic development is precluded. Much of Uganda is covered with red laterite which, while containing some iron-ore, has not sufficient concentration of bauxite to warrant commercial exploitation. The long distance to the coast (over 1200 km) adds considerably to the cost of any production.

A cement and asbestos–cement industry is now well-established at Tororo, based on the local limestone, hydroelectric power from Jinja (120 km to the west), and asbestos from Zimbabwe. Other minerals worked and exported in small quantities are wolfram, tin and cobalt.

Agriculture and livestock form the basis of Uganda's economy and occupy 90 per cent of the population. The industries that exist are mainly derived from the processing of agricultural produce: the main ones being cotton-ginning, sugar-milling, cigarette manufacture, vegetable-oil extraction, coffee and tea preparation. Most of these are located in the producing areas near Lake Victoria, especially in the Kampala–Jinja area. A wider spectrum of industry has been attracted to Uganda with the development of hydroelectricity at Jinja, where the Nile leaves Lake Victoria by the Owen Falls. The town's population is now 50,000 and it has become a focus of modern industries. The generating station, opened in 1954, has an installed capacity of 120 MW and a space has been left for two more turbines which will raise capacity to a maximum of 150 MW. A power grid has been built and this has allowed industrial expansion in Kampala and Tororo as well as at Jinja.

The largest electricity-user at Jinja is the copper smelter which refines Kilembe copper, and then the cotton-textile factory, set up in 1956. Also at Jinja brewing, vegetable-oil production, sugar-refining, cigarette and tobacco manufacture take place. A plywood factory, a flour mill and a commercial vehicle-assembly plant now operate.

Export-crop production and industrial development are concentrated mainly in Buganda and parts of the eastern region, areas widely accessible owing to road and rail facilities and directly profiting from the power station at the Owen Falls. This is creating a number of problems, for the growing opportunities and greater wealth in the south raise discontent elsewhere and act as a spur for population movement into the favoured areas.

ECONOMIC PROBLEMS

Uganda is a generally well-endowed country: normally its agricultural output is greater than either Kenya or Tanzania, but the value of its manufactures is much less than that of Kenya. It is favoured by climate and soil, but also suffers from its inland position and from tsetse fly infestation. Its people, however, are active and intelligent, and economic development since the first coming of the railway until the 1970s was spectacular. It is all the more unfortunate that its chaotic political situation throughout the decade of the 1970s reduced the country's wealth and productivity. Many businessmen and entrepreneurs left the country or were expelled, investment ceased, law and order became unenforced. Income per head of population, rising in the early years, decreased from $280 in 1977 to $220 in 1980. Programmes of rehabilitation supported by the International Monetary Fund were put in hand in 1981, and a recovery programme was introduced in 1982 designed to rehabilitate land and rescue the economy. This programme received funds from the World Bank, the African Development Bank and the European Economic Community. The total aid amounted to nearly $9 million. Industry was allotted 35 per cent, agriculture 27 per cent, the social infrastructure 20 per cent, transport and mining 4 per cent; and by the mid-1980s there were clear signs of an economic revival, the main thrust coming from increased exports of coffee, tea and cotton.

In the longer term Uganda faces a number of economic difficulties. The spread of cash-crop production together with the rapid rate of population growth makes for shorter periods of fallow. In the low-rainfall areas where rotation takes place this is not so serious, but in the high-rainfall regions where one or two plants are cropped regularly the land is beginning to deteriorate. There is, however, a heavy dependence upon two or three cash crops – notably coffee and cotton – that expose Uganda to the dangers of the considerable fluctuations in world prices for primary products.

Thus there is justification in current plans focusing on industrial revival. However, it must be expected that such industrial development will be modest: the fanciful talk at the time of the Owen Falls scheme of 'an African Detroit at Jinja' is no more. The hydroelectric plant at the Owen Falls (which also supplies some power to Kenya and Tanzania) is to be expanded as the major source of industrial energy. Uganda's transport system suffered from neglect during the years of turmoil but is now being rejuvenated. The road and rail systems are both being enlarged, and the railway extension to West Nile districts is completed. This should aid the opening up of a lightly populated area suitable for commercial farming and stock-rearing. Uganda's real wealth lies in her agriculture and much remains to be done to improve its productive capacity. There are physical problems of soil erosion and tsetse fly infestation to be overcome, and ways must be found to ease credit facilities to the small producer, to further the spread of agrarian education, to speed the diversification of crops, and to improve transport and marketing facilities.

44 Tanzania

Tanganyika became an independent state within the British Commonwealth in 1961 and adopted a republican form of government in 1962. In 1964 it entered into a political union with Zanzibar and the name Tanzania was adopted. The country is the largest but also the poorest of the three East African states. In 1891 this part of East Africa, nominally under the suzerainty of the Sultan of Zanzibar, was taken over as a protectorate by Germany. For many years the history of German rule was one of disturbance and bloodshed as tribes rebelled and were suppressed. The country was conquered in the First World War and subsequently divided as mandated territory between Belgium and Britain; the Belgians received Ruanda and Urundi (now Rwanda and Burundi) and Britain the rest. The area of the republic, 945,000 km^2, is larger than Kenya and Uganda together.

The greater part of Tanzania is plateau. Lower land flanks it on the coast and around Lake Victoria, while higher land is found in the Kilimanjaro–Pare–Usumbara Mountains of the north-east, the Southern Highlands and the mountains forming the western Rift Valley system. The eastern rift zone, although a geomorphological division throughout most of Tanzania, has little geographical significance.

FARMING REGIONS

The coastlands. Tanzania has about 800 km of coast and the plain bordering it for the most part varies between 15 and 60 km in width. It extends from the Kenya border at 5°S to Tanzania's southern border along the Ruvuma river at 11°S. All the coastal zone receives more than 750 mm of rainfall and from the Rufiji river north generally over 1000 mm. Mangrove swamps abound in the estuaries, usually backed by a belt of coconut palms. With the presence of cooler upland close behind the coast in the north, it is not surprising that the development of the north-east of the country should receive most attention from the Germans, who laid particular emphasis upon establishing plantations and settling Europeans. Some sugar, spices, rice and sisal are grown in the coastal zone. Sisal transplanted from the Yucatan, Mexico, in 1893 was the principal cash crop grown on the former European- or Indian-owned plantations. Once it accounted for one-third of Tanzania's total exports by value, but now it is of minor importance.

The north-east highlands. These include the mighty Kilimanjaro (5895 m), the highest mountain in Africa, Meru (4565 m) and the discontinuous upland appendage that trends to the south-east, including the Pare Mountains and culminating in the Usumbara Mountains (2569 m). Kilimanjaro and Meru are of volcanic origin and associated with the formation of the Rift Valley to their west; the rest of the uplands are up-tilted parts of the Crystalline Basement Complex. The upper parts of the Usumbara, Kilimanjaro and Meru receive 1500 mm of rain annually, but on their north-west side in the rain-shadow are areas which receive little more than 600 mm. On the whole, however, this upland region is more distinctive in its relief, its greater rainfall, more luxuriant vegetation and European influence than the surrounding plateau.

These highlands, especially at between 1600 and 2000 mm, were attractive to European settlement, and a variety of crops was tried on them, including rubber (at the lower levels), sisal and coffee. The Germans quickly started building a railway inland from Tanga, passing along the western side of the highlands. They had planned to build the railway across to open up reputedly rich lands around Lake Victoria; but when the British line from Mombasa reached the lake first they abandoned their plans and eventually, in 1911, made Moshi the western terminal (in 1929 extended to Arusha). They then turned their attention to the construction of a central line from Dar-es-Salaam across to Tabora and Kigoma on Lake Tanganyika (1914); a spur north to Mwanza on Lake Victoria was completed in 1928. These well-watered uplands nourish the greater part of Tanzania's forests, including valuable cabinet woods such as African mahogany and cedars. A great deal of this woodland was cleared for plantations early in the century. Coffee of the arabica variety has proved the most satisfactory crop of Kilimanjaro, but yields are poorer on the more siliceous soils of Usumbara. From 1923 further alienation of land to Europeans was forbidden and this has now become one of the more densely populated parts of the republic. The Kilimanjaro area is in the hands of the Chagga, who are now among the foremost and wealthiest African coffee producers.

The interior plateau comprises the greater part of Tanzania and includes the Masai steppe, the rift zone and the Central Plateau. The altitude varies between 1000 and 1500 m, and the topography is gently undulating, broken here and there by residual hills. This is an unfavoured area: pest-ridden, frequently drought-ridden and with poor soil. Much of the central part of this plateau receives little more than 500 mm of rain a year, while to the east and west rather more than 750 mm are enjoyed in an average year. Unfortunately there is a high variability of rainfall from year to year: in the centre it is very rare to receive 750 mm, in the better-watered east and west three years in ten may not produce that amount of rainfall. This makes arable agriculture hazardous and relegates most of the vast area to pastoral uses. For much of the year this is a brown country of dried-up open savanna; the heat is very great, the atmosphere dry; the rainless season becomes more definite and more prolonged as one moves south. The yellow–brown plateau soils hold little humus and in places are seasonally waterlogged, especially where an iron-pan has formed in the subsoil. Large areas of the plateau, particularly the south-west quadrant, are only lightly inhabited and scarcely utilized, for a combination of light, uncertain rainfall, poor soils, tsetse fly and remoteness militate against utilization whether by African or White.

Over large parts the semi-nomadic ranching of cattle, sheep and goats, often combined with rudimentary shifting agriculture, is almost the sole activity. Pastures are poor throughout the long, severe dry season and relatively abundant for the usually shorter rainy season. Tsetse fly infestation hinders the movement of stock in search of better grazing (Figure 97). The carrying capacity of the pastures is small but herds are often large; for example, it is often thought that the more stock one has, the more beasts are likely to survive the next drought.

Subsistence crops grown include millet, cassava, maize and groundnuts, but these are uncertain and poverty is widespread. Commercial production is small, but there are some sisal plantations, and cotton is grown around Kilosa and Morogoro in the central railway zone. Farther west Dodoma and Tabora, once ivory and slave-caravan centres, remain local market centres of some importance, being on the main route to Dar-es-Salaam. In 1972 Dodoma was designated to be the new capital of Tanzania by 1986, but the provision of infrastructure to raise a small, unflourishing town to a capital city is beyond

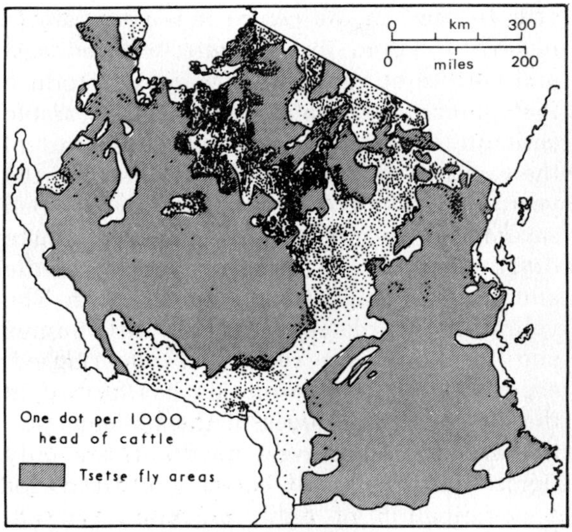

Figure 97 Tanzania: distribution of cattle and tsetse fly

Plate 58 Sisal drying in coastal Tanzania

local capability and finance and the project may be abandoned. Tabora is at the junction of the branch line north to Mwanza on Lake Victoria that taps this richer area after passing through the diamond field at Shinyanga.

The south-east plateau. A good deal of the southern part of the plateau between Lake Malawi and the coast is rather better-watered, although still lightly populated and subject to the tsetse fly. Local irrigation in the basin of the Rufiji river makes cotton growing successful and tobacco and cotton feature in the local crops, especially around Songea.

Although a failure, much was learnt from the ill-fated Groundnut Scheme soon after the Second World War. The scheme resulted from erroneous fears that the wartime shortage of edible fats and oils would be prolonged into the post-war years. A mission sent out to East Africa in 1947 made a hurried survey (much of it by air) lasting nine weeks, and recommended enthusiastically an enormous scheme of wholesale bush-clearing and large-scale groundnut and sunflower growing – both valuable oil-giving crops. Originally a total area of 1.3 million hectares was suggested, most in Tanzania but some in Northern Rhodesia and in Kenya. Farming units of 12,000 ha were envisaged – in other words, the creation of whole counties of continuous arable agriculture, particularly at Kongwa near the central railway line and Nachingwea in the slightly better-watered south. The whole scheme was based upon misplaced trust in capital: the view being that, given sufficient capital investment, human and physical difficulties can be overcome or avoided. Haste ruled the planning; no time could be spared for primary reconnaissance and survey, for soil investigation and mapping, for adequate investigation of meteorological data. No pilot schemes were undertaken. An outstanding collection of machinery (much second-hand) was assembled and put to work in clearing the matted, tangled vegetation and then ploughing the exposed soil. The machines were inadequate for the tasks since special machines to cope with those conditions had yet to be invented. The mass of vegetation at times was almost impenetrable; the hard-pan of iron or the lateritic soils rendered useless the first ploughs, and the machines, far from replacing man, needed his attention both for maintenance and operation.

The areas eventually cleared and cropped were ridiculously small compared with the initial plans. A series of dry years, the over-compacting of the sandy soil by the heavy machinery, lack of particular chemical constituents in the soils, made the harvests pathetically small. Further, such large-scale mechanized farming demands a considerable and highly expensive infrastructure of roads, railway, power stations, water supplies and, in the south, a port. In economically developed countries these costs do not fall on a single enterprise but are widely shared. Here they fell on a very limited range of crops and the costs were prodigious. In all £36 million was eventually written off by the British Government when the original scheme was abandoned in 1951. A continuing emphasis on big projects in many parts of Africa suggests that little has been learned.

In the south a huge area around Nachinwea, some 160 km inland, was marked for development. This meant the construction of a railway, of a pipeline for petrol and a deep-water port – the first between Mombasa and Durban. The port site was Mtwara, 60 km south-east of the established shallow port of Lindi. With the collapse of the 'groundnut scheme' the cleared area was taken over by the Tanganyika government and run as African small-holdings and experimental farms. The southern province is of high agricultural potential, but it is isolated. It produces the bulk of the cashew, cassava and sesame marketed in Tanzania and grows tobacco, coffee and sisal. However, the volume of freight never became enough to pay the cost of operating the railway; it was closed and the line lifted in 1962. Growing competition from road transport was another reason for its lack of success.

The southern highlands, trending north-east from Lake Malawi and reaching up to Kilosa, offer extensive rolling upland country 1000 m or more above the general level of the surrounding plateau. Rainfall is also well above 750 mm in most years, yet the area is very lightly settled. The two great drawbacks have been tsetse fly, a menace to both man and animals, and remoteness. There are few good roads, and until 1976 no railway to the rest of Tanzania and the coast. In that year the Chinese-built Tanzam railway was opened, linking the Zambian Copperbelt with the port of Dar-es-Salaam. The railway passes through the southern highlands and may well become a catalyst for the commercial development of agriculture. Coffee, tea, pyrethrum and tobacco are successfully grown on a number of large estates. African settlement is very sparse, perhaps as a result of the German suppression of rebellions early in the century. Around Njombe wattle-planting by Africans for tanning extract is being encouraged by the government; but such schemes are extremely limited while this area of great potentiality is so poorly served with communications.

The Lake Victoria lowlands of north-west Tanzania are densely settled and better-watered, although the rainfall is less than that of the Ugandan north coast of the lake. Most of the littoral enjoys 1000 mm and the coast-lands of Bukoba on the west of the lake have over 1500 mm. The main subsistence crops are millet, cassava and pulses, with cotton as the principal cash crop. In Bukoba coffee-growing is increasing at the expense of cattle-rearing, formerly a well-integrated feature of the farming that has helped to maintain soil fertility. With an increasing population and diminishing fertility of the land, the Tanzanian government here faces a problem of increasing seriousness.

Zanzibar and Pemba. In 1899 the islands of Zanzibar and Pemba were placed under British protection by the Sultan. In 1963 the islands resumed their independence within the British Commonwealth, becoming a republic and entering into a union with Tanganyika in 1964. They were keen to point out that they were not a British-created African nation: Zanzibar was independent when the English were fighting the Wars of the Roses. They have a proud sense of identity, of Arab roots and Islamic culture, and have a longer history than any African state except Ethiopia. However, times have changed. No longer does Zanzibar hold parts of the mainland, and no longer is the island the centre for trade (mainly in ivory and slaves) undertaken by Arabs across East Africa. With the development of the mainland economies and of the great ports of Mombasa and Dar-es-Salaam, Zanzibar's commercial functions have lessened; she is no longer the Venice of East Africa. Zanzibar Island (1660 km^2) is 35 km off the mainland and Pemba Island (980 km^2) 40 km to the north-east.

The climate is akin to that of the adjacent mainland coast but somewhat wetter, for the islands stand in the path of the saturated mT airstream originating as the south-east trade winds across the Indian Ocean. Most of Zanzibar Island receives 1500 mm and much of Pemba over 2000 mm. Some rain falls in most months of the year; but there are two rainy seasons, the first March–May and the second in November when the north-east winds blow from the Arabian Sea. High temperatures are experienced all through the year owing to the latitude (6°S) and low elevation. The marine effect may reduce temperatures by one or two degrees compared with Tanga and Mombasa. The range of temperature throughout the year is quite small. These conditions of humid heat for much of the year favour a growth of more luxuriant vegetation than on the mainland coast. The natural vegetation was dense forest, but over the centuries most has been cleared for agriculture and at the same time other tropical plants from India, Madagascar and the East Indies were introduced.

Cultivation in the islands is intensive and there is much concentration on the two cash crops, cloves and coconuts. Here is produced 60 per cent of the world's supply of cloves – actually the unopened buds of the clove tree which was introduced from the East Indies early in the nineteenth century. Disease during the post 1945 period cut back production in Zanzibar Island and there is now a greater concentration in Pemba. In all, the islands have about 3 million clove trees. There are about the same number of coconut-palms, and copra is an important export. These two commodities and derived products provide the base for almost the entire economy: much food has to be imported.

THE ECONOMY

Agriculture

Agriculture is the backbone of the economy. It supports 85 per cent of the population, accounts for over 50 per cent of the GDP and 80 per cent of export earnings. Nevertheless Tanzania is poorly endowed for agriculture; her water supplies are particularly deficient, for some 60 per cent of Tanzania is virtually waterless and consequently uninhabited. Only about 10 per cent can be regarded as well-watered, and this area holds over 60 per cent of the population. Tanzania has few rivers and even fewer suitable for irrigation schemes.

Whereas environmental hazards and shortcomings limit the scope for agriculture, over wide areas a more productive pastoral industry is possible. The map (Figure 97) shows the very uneven distribution of cattle in the republic, reflecting certain diseases (Trypanosomiasis and East Coast Fever carried by tsetse flies and ticks respectively), and lack of permanent water supplies. The areas with most cattle are the semi-arid parts of the country free from the chief pests and diseases but where water supplies are available. Cattle are concentrated in the northern half of the country and down the length of the southern highlands. Some of the pastoral tribes such as the Masai of the northern border are nomadic.

There is much scope for improvement. Communal land ownership – but with unrestricted grazing by large, individually owned herds – results in low productivity and deterioration of pasture, and the growth of man-made desert; for where the grazing is removed the soil washes away and erosion sets in, the water table is affected and springs dry up.

Mining and industry

Minerals played a small role in Tanzania's economy until relatively recent years. More than two-thirds of the republic's surface is composed of Archaean crystalline and metamorphic rocks favourable to mineral formation. Much detailed prospecting has yet to be done. Minerals now provide nearly 5 per cent of Tanzania's export earnings, most coming from diamonds. Small discoveries of diamonds have been known for many years; but in 1940 a major discovery was made at Mwadui by a Dr J. T. Williamson, and most of the country's output now comes from the Williamson Mine which the government controls. Production is worth about $15 million a year. Another important mineral is gold – from east of Lake Victoria (the Musoma gold field) and the Iramba plateau in Central Province. Other minerals produced in smaller amounts are lead, tin and mica.

In an endeavour to reduce reliance on imported oil, prospecting has been carried out for several years, without success. However, significant off-shore gas resources are now being developed at Songo Songo, 150 km south of Dar-es-Salaam. Industrial development is less advanced than in Kenya and Uganda and contributes only about 10 per cent of the GDP. It is mainly concerned with the processing of local commodities and with import substitution. The only significant centre of manufacturing is Dar-es-Salaam, where textiles are made and milling, brewing, soap manufacture, meat processing and packing and truck assembly also take place. There has been some attempt at expansion and diversification of manufacturing activities; but raw-material shortages, disruption of energy supplies, the small and contracting home market (as incomes have fallen), reduced exports, poor management and shortages of skilled labour and government interference lead to high cost production and have forced some plants to close down and most of those remaining are working at around 30 per cent of capacity utilization.

POPULATION AND TRADE

The estimated population of Tanzania in 1985 was 21,500,000, divided among over 120 tribes, most Bantu but some Hamitic and Nilo-Hamitic. The annual rate of increase to the population is 3 per cent, making it very youthful: 47 per cent of the population is under 15. Dar-es-Salaam, the capital and chief port, has a population approaching one million. Once a lighterage port, deep-water berths were constructed prior to independence and the port now handles 3 million tonnes a year. Much of the domestic hinterland of the port is unproductive and some of the produce from the richer Lake Victoria areas finds its way to Mombasa via the Kenya railways. Tanga, to the north, serves the coffee and sisal estates of the north-east highlands. The central railway and Dar-es-Salaam provide one of the outlets for Zaire and Burundi and Rwanda, and the Chinese-built Tanzam railway links that port with the Zambian Copperbelt and the southern highlands.

ECONOMIC PLANNING

Upon independence the World Bank gave advice and a first development plan was carried out in the period 1961–4. The emphasis was upon agriculture: to develop water resources and irrigation, to fight pests and diseases and to improve husbandry and stock-rearing. Three other 5-year plans followed, but for a variety of reasons there were many modifications and overall success was disappointing.

Ideology has played a part: following independence Tanzania was declared a socialist state and under President Nyerere a series of left-wing measures increasingly were applied.

The Arusha Declaration of 1967 committed Tanzania to economic independence via the twin goals of socialism and self-reliance, exemplified in the *Ujamaa* ('familyhood') programme. This involved wholesale regrouping of the scattered rural population into self-sufficient villages: the land would be worked on a communal basis, ensuring economies of scale, planned direction and facilitating health, education and social services. Individual peasant farming favoured personal acquisitiveness and this was deemed an obstacle to socialism. By 1980 over 13 million people were living in such villages. At first many had moved willingly, but subsequently when numbers moved became regarded as a measure of success forced resettlement took place, with little thought being given to practical implications. Little real planning was done for the new villages and sites were often too far from fields, lacked water systems or led to ecological deterioration.

From a grassroot movement *Ujamaa* was replaced by 'commandism' – enforced change directed and controlled from above. This collective system did not encourage personal

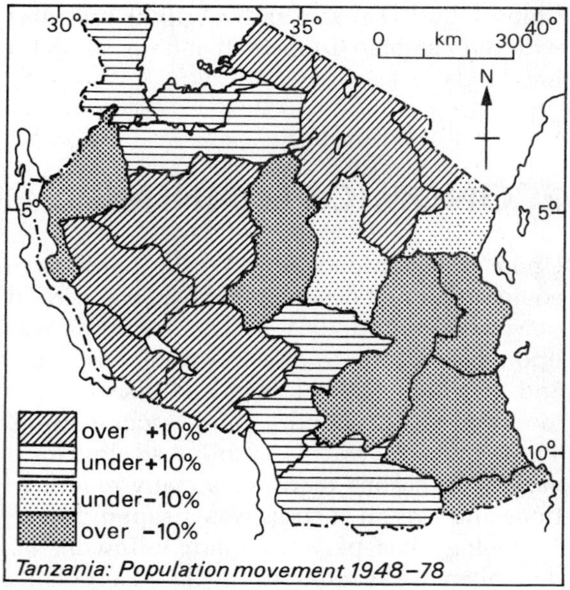

Figure 98 Tanzania: population movement 1948–78

initiative and crop prices set by the government were too low to give incentive. The result was peasant alienation and mistrust of such government measures and a contraction of Tanzania's agriculture, with increasing emphasis being put on subsistence-crop production with any small surplus vanishing on the black market. Export crops diminished (sisal, cashew nuts by 40 per cent), more and more food became imported for the urban population, foreign exchange dwindled away.

Not only the agricultural sector was blighted: practically the whole economy came under state control – banks, insurance, import and export businesses, large private firms, mining, wholesale trade, crop-marketing, commodity distribution all came under several hundred state corporations, who also have a say in transport, agriculture, plantations and housing. At independence Tanzania possessed fewer than 150 graduates, and it was clear that she lacked managers, accountants – even clerks – and simply did not have trained manpower to run such a multitude of bodies. The bureaucracy that burgeoned from this was incompetent, increasingly corrupt and catastrophic in its performance. The lack of engineers and mechanics reduced maintenance of roads, railways, lorries, buses and trains. Despite brave and costly plans the whole economy slowed up during the early 1980s. There had been droughts, the severe increase in the cost of oil, the heavy cost of war in Uganda and falling prices on world markets for Tanzania's agricultural products – all items that contribute to the country's difficulties. Nevertheless the core of the problem lies with the agricultural sector that supports 85 per cent of the population and supplies 80 per cent of foreign-exchange earnings. Imposed socialism has demoralized farmers and reduced their output. Now there is not enough exported to pay for imports nor to repay the mounting development loans. It is paradoxical that while this decline was occurring Tanzania was receiving more aid per head from the West than any other African country – aid that was being used to harry the private sector and to impose on it a calamitous state bureaucracy.

THE FUTURE

All the East African countries face serious difficulties in raising the standard of living of their peoples. Tanzania in many ways is even less well-endowed than her neighbours. It has been said that her 'trinity of priorities' consists of food, water and communications. Her communications problems are particularly severe. The main arteries upon which a transport network may grow are the railways. Tanzania has three separate lines running east–west from the coast to the interior. Between these lines are large stretches of territory unserved by railways and poorly served by roads.

Much of the railway system does not serve the best agricultural areas (over 750 mm rainfall reliability zones); for example, the great central line passes through hundreds of kilometres of arid bush and waste. The failure of the Mtwara–Nachingwea line in the south is a serious setback for those seeking investment for the opening up of southern Tanzania. Railways are costly to build and here there was no assured freight – only the hope that given a railway link to the coast, export-crop farming would expand. The Nachingwea line did not penetrate far enough inland to the better farming areas, so that much freight came by lorry to the railhead and subsequently, rather than break bulk there, went all the way by lorry to Mtwara or Lindi.

The three East African mainland countries face similar problems. A harshness of environment that so far has meant poverty and hardship for the mass of the population must still be overcome. To attain greater income per head requires capital investment for improving education, health, communications, water supplies, agricultural credit and so on. Since the annual income per head in East Africa is very low, especially in Tanzania and Uganda, there is little scope for saving or for generating the much-needed capital at home. These countries, like most of those of Africa, will depend for a long time upon grants, loans and investment by overseas countries.

The Royal Commission that investigated the economic and social problems of East Africa (1953–5) made a number of recommendations that are still very relevant. It emphasized that the road to better living was through specialization of production, the move away from subsistence agriculture and to the necessary expansion of markets. This in turn required improved communications. Individual land-tenure and ownership was a mechanism whereby credit might be made available and incentive to betterment could be inculcated. Again, this would be related to an expansion of education, particularly in its agrarian application. The real wealth of East Africa lies in its land, which so far is thoroughly under-developed. Industrial growth is never likely to be other than limited and related to the domestic market.

45
Madagascar and the Mascarene Islands

Separated from the African mainland by the 400 km-wide Mozambique Channel, Madagascar possesses characteristics that distinguish it from any other part of Africa – the language and culture of its native peoples, the widespread intensive cultivation of rice, and the absence of tsetse fly, for instance; yet physiographically it has definite links with the adjacent continent. The island measures nearly 1600 km from north to south, and with 587,000 km^2 exceeds France in area. Its size, mountainous character and isolated position were among the factors that delayed exploration of its interior until the 1860s, although the island was known to the Portuguese in the sixteenth century.

It is now generally thought that Madagascar was peopled originally by East Africans, who brought over a predominantly pastoral economy; much later Indonesians arrived, importing an Eastern-type culture and paddy-rice cultivation. Today there are some eighteen different tribes in the island, all of whom understand one basic language – Malgache. The first European colonists on the island in the seventeenth century were French. This eventually led to a rather vague French protectorate over the island in 1885. The formal annexation of Madagascar as a French colony under General Gallieni followed in 1896.

The existence of the magnificent harbour of Antseranana (Diego Suarez) was the reason for British invasion of the island in the Second World War, to prevent this strategically valuable base from falling into Japanese hands, for the local government of Madagascar sided with Vichy France. After the war the island returned to French rule; economic development progressed, and the varied resources of the island became better appreciated. In 1960 French rule came to an end, and the independent Malagasy Republic was born. It still, however, retains its links with the other African members of the French Community, and France is a major aid donor and takes a quarter of all exports.

The present population numbers 6 million, of whom 98 per cent are Malgache. Numbers of French have declined since 1960, when there were about 70,000, since many officials were replaced by Malgache. Few parts of the island are densely peopled. The principal areas of close settlement are some highland basins, and it is also in the highlands that the capital, and largest settlement, Tananarive, (pop. 400,000), is situated. The population is increasing rapidly, owing to improved health measures and disease control: malaria, for instance, has now been practically eliminated. The annual rate of population growth is about 2.6 per cent and there is a remarkably high proportion of young people: 40 per cent are under fifteen years of age.

RELIEF AND STRUCTURE

It is possible that Madagascar was joined to Africa as part of the former continent of

Gondwanaland until approximately Jurassic times. The eastern two-thirds of the island, including the highlands, consist of Pre-Cambrian igneous and metamorphic rocks, similar to the foundation rocks of the African continent. On the west is a series of sedimentary rocks, from upper Carboniferous to Tertiary and Quaternary in age, dipping gently towards the Mozambique Channel. The lower part of this series consists of the continental Karroo System, whose accumulation was brought to an end by the major marine transgression of the middle Jurassic period.

The highlands of Madagascar (Figure 99) are really a dissected plateau, whose flat-topped interfluves and hill summits fall most commonly in the range 1200–1500 m above sea-level – comparable with some major plateau surfaces in southern Africa. In places the mountains rise much higher, especially in the Tsaratanana massif of the north (up to 2835 m) and in the volcanic Ankarattra group (maximum 2600 m) south of Tananarive. As the coastline is near, dissection of the highlands by rivers has been rapid. Within the highlands there are a number of small alluvial basins, tapped by rivers, but in a few cases still containing lakes, such as Lake Alaotra.

In the east, the highlands end in escarpments overlooking the coastlands. Behind Tamatave there are two such escarpments, the lower one rising abruptly to 900 m and, behind a bench at this level, a further one rising to 1350 m. The eastern coastlands themselves are rarely more than 30 km wide, except locally behind Farafangana. They consist partly of a flat, sandy littoral, with a series of lagoons and swamps. West of the central highlands lies a series of plains and low plateaux, formed of the westward-dipping sedimentary

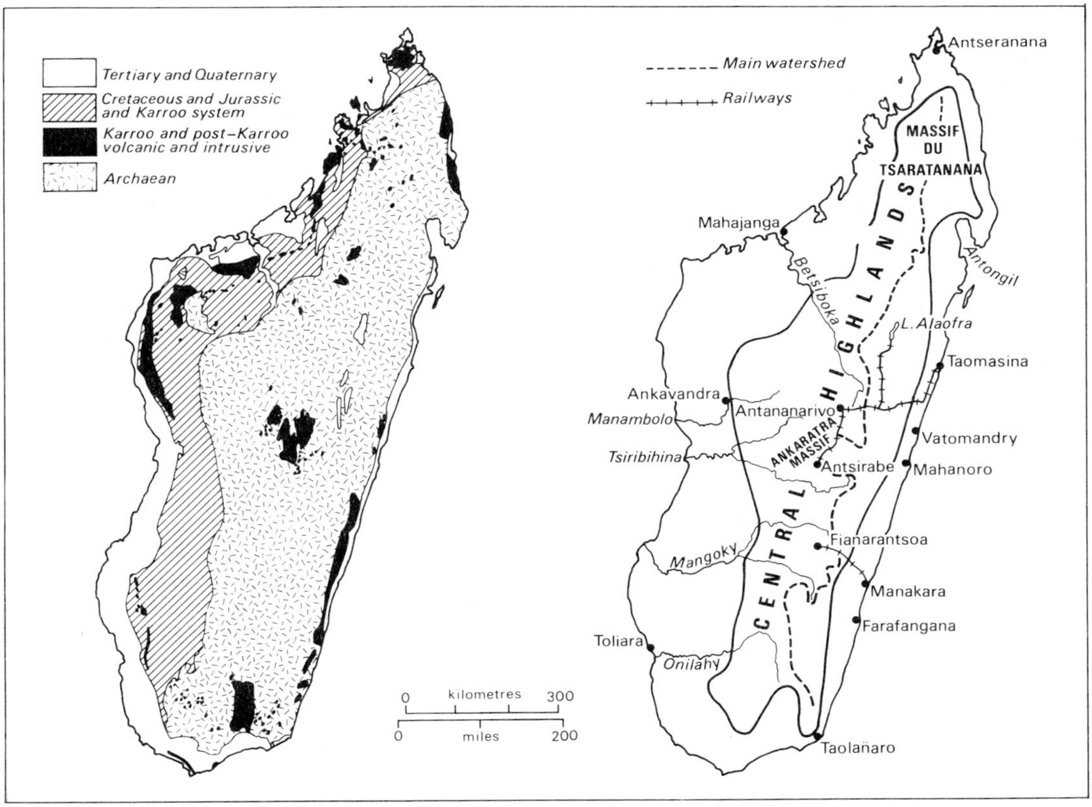

Figure 99: Madagascar: geology and relief regions

formations. Cuestas and strike vales are a characteristic feature, and there are broad, flat plains next to the west coast which consist of Tertiary and Quaternary sediments.

The coastline of Madagascar is for long stretches lacking in indentations, while most of those that do occur suffer from heavy silting by rivers draining into them, or else are exposed to the prevalent winds. Consequently, the island possesses few good natural harbours. Antseranana, the one exception to this, has its value greatly diminished by its location in the extreme north, away from areas of commercial importance.

The straightness of the east coast from Antongil Bay to Taolanaro is the result of faulting; the only modern port along this stretch is Tamatave (Taomasina), artificially constructed. The west coast, since it faces Africa, is less exposed, but all possible harbours are shallow and need constant dredging.

CLIMATE, VEGETATION AND SOILS

The climate ranges from humid tropical on the east coastlands to semi-arid tropical in the south-west. The most pleasant climate is in the highlands, where altitude mitigates the temperature and where there is also a pronounced division in the year between dry season and wet season (Table 46). In the past, malaria has been the curse of the coastlands and many other parts, but an intensive campaign of DDT spraying has now practically eliminated it.

In summer the Inter Tropical Convergence lies along the north of the island; the north coast is bombarded by the mE air from the north, and the eastern coast and highlands by equally moist and unstable air from the east or north-east together with regular tropical hurricanes which may do great damage on the coast. This is the season of heaviest rainfall in all parts of the island, with a great deal of thunder. In winter the whole island comes into the mT airstream of the south-east Trades, which have a long trajectory over the Indian Ocean and meet the highlands at right angles, giving the maximum orographic effect; thus, the east coast and eastern highlands receive further heavy rainfall, but the western half of the island lies in rain-shadow and is often under the influence of dry, easterly fohn-type winds.

Total rainfall varies from 3230 mm at Tamatave and over 2550 mm on the island of Nossi-Be in the north-west, to less than 380 mm in the south-west (where the dry season occupies 8–9 months of the year). Most of the central highlands receive 1000–2000 mm, with a dry season of 5–6 months. Temperatures on the coastlands are high in summer, the monthly mean reaching 27°C or

Table 46 *Madagascar: temperature and rainfall of selected stations*

Station	*Altitude (m)*		*J*	*F*	*M*	*A*	*M*	*J*	*J*	*A*	*S*	*O*	*N*	*D*	*Year*
Tamatave	6	T	26.8	26.8	26.1	24.9	23.3	21.6	21.0	21.0	21.6	23.3	24.9	26.1	23.8
(Taomasina)		R	366	376	452	400	265	282	277	203	132	99	116	262	3230
Tananarive	1350	T	21.0	20.4	20.4	19.4	17.1	15.6	15.0	14.3	16.6	19.4	19.9	21.0	18.2
		R	300	279	178	53	18	8	8	10	18	62	134	287	1355
Tuléar	6	T	27.7	26.8	26.1	24.4	22.2	21.6	20.4	20.4	22.2	23.9	25.5	27.3	21.0
		R	78	79	36	8	18	12	2	4	8	18	36	43	342

Notes: T = Temperature (°C); R = rainfall (mm).

more, and only a little cooler in 'winter'. On the highlands between 1200 and 1500 m, temperatures and conditions compare closely with the Zimbabwean uplands.

Forest formerly covered most of the central highlands, but burning for native agriculture and extension of grazing land left it occupying only one-tenth of the island. Mangroves fringe parts of the east and west coasts. In the central highlands savanna and steppe are now dominant, with only a few patches of woodland. As well as regular burning and grazing, the dry season helps to retard regeneration of the forest. In the south and south-west of the island, where conditions verge almost on semi-desert, scrubland is characteristic, with xerophytic types of plants including cacti.

The soils appear to be mainly lateritic and of limited fertility, except in some basins or coastal areas of recent deposition. There are also a few regions of richer volcanic soils, as around Lake Itasy and Antsirabe in the centre of the island. Soil erosion in the highlands is an acute and widespread problem, owing to the high rate of rainfall and the prevalence of steep slopes; deforestation and overgrazing are primarily responsible for the initiation of the process, leaving the red earth without sufficient protection from the intense thunder showers.

THE ECONOMY

A revolution in 1972, which put the military into power, dissolved the close links with France and expanded the public sector within the economy, nationalizing French interests. Economic growth faltered and fell, and throughout the 1970s the rate of increase in the GDP was less than the annual rate of population expansion (2.9 per cent). Living standards declined.

With the 1980s came political realignment and improvement of relations with France and the USA. However, the discouragement of private investment and initiative, the acute shortage of skilled and managerial staff, and the lack of capital made most difficult all attempts to improve the stagnant economy. Unsuccessful attempts to speed economic growth through industrialization were dropped and attention turned to agriculture, where disappointing performance lay at the root of the annual trade deficit. No longer was there surplus rice for export; instead large imports of the basic foodstuffs have been necessary. New efforts are being made to expand the rice acreage with a view to regaining self-sufficiency by 1988. The current emphasis is on agricultural improvement and export diversification.

Farming

Agriculture employs the bulk of the population and supplies about 80 per cent of exports by value. Farming ranges from shifting cultivation, which is found mainly in the east, to intensive production of rice, coffee and cloves. Rice is the major crop, occupying one-third of the cultivated area. Its cultivation as the primary food crop is one of the most distinctive features of Madagascar, sharply differentiating the island from any other part of Africa. Rice is found in most parts of the country except the south-west, although the alluvial highland basins, such as those of Lake Alaotra and around Tananarive, are the areas of most intensive production.

Hurricane damage in 1982 and 1984, and the demands of an increasing population, have stopped rice exports and are now necessitating imports. The expansion of rice acreage is now being encouraged: its cultivation is ideally adapted to help conserve the soil in hilly lands where terracing is practised. Other food crops include cassava, maize and groundnuts. Pastoral activities are very important for there are none of the restrictions which the tsetse fly imposes in many parts of tropical Africa. There are probably no fewer than 8 million cattle in the island – mainly African breeds and of poor quality. Their excessive numbers have given rise to overgrazing and problems of soil erosion in some areas. In the drier south-west a nomadic way of life is encountered.

Mining and manufacturing

The mineral resources of the island are not yet fully known but appear to be considerable, known deposits including graphite, chromite, mica, nickel, iron-ore, uranium and gold. Although Madagascar is one of the world's chief graphite producers, both graphite and mica – the two most important minerals obtained – account for a mere 2 per cent of the island's export trade. Graphite is mined on the east coast near Taomasina, and the island also possesses rich deposits of thorium sands around Behara in the south.

The only solid-fuel resources are represented by the small Sakoa coalfield in Tulear Province. Reserves probably amount to 3000 million tonnes, but the coal is ashy and of low carbon content. Petroleum, both onshore and offshore, was discovered in 1980 and the first wells have been drilled to tap the modest deposits off the west coast, thus easing the burden of high-cost oil imports. Small refineries operate at Taomasina and Bemolanga.

There is very little manufacturing industry in the island. Almost all that does exist is concerned with the processing of the local agricultural produce – the milling of rice, production of starch and tapioca from manioc, refining of sugar, meat-canning and rum distillation, for example. A textile works at Antsirabe relies on local cotton.

There are, however, two factors distinctly favourable for industrial development: the quite considerable potential for hydroelectric power, hardly yet touched. and the fact that the Malgache in general provide more efficient labour than do the African Bantu. Unfortunately, in common with so many other African countries, capital is scarce; nor will the remote position of the island and the limited market represented by its population encourage any rapid industrial development.

TRANSPORT AND TRADE

The rugged and mountainous nature of most of the island presents great difficulties for the construction of modern forms of surface communication: it is therefore not surprising to find that there are only two railway systems totalling no more than 800 km, and that there is only the same length of metalled road, but on the other hand, that there have been impressive developments since the Second World War in airfield construction. The island now boasts over 100 major airfields, with regular flights operating between all the chief towns. Railways carry a relatively small proportion of Madagascan trade – only one-fifth of all exports, for instance – since the centres of production are so widely scattered throughout the island. The first railway was completed in 1913 between the capital and the east coast; it has branches tapping the rich agricultural regions of Lake Alaotra and Antsirabe. The line from Fianarantsoa to the coast, opened in 1936, illustrates very clearly the problems of engineering involved in climbing from the eastern lowlands to the central highlands. In 160 km, it possesses forty-nine tunnels, and forty-seven bridges and viaducts. In the years following the war the French made great progress in railway modernization; the lines are now amongst the most efficiently run in Africa and use diesel or diesel–electric locomotives only.

Without doubt the finest natural harbour is that of **Antseranana**, a volcanic bay second only in size to Rio de Janeiro. Though important as a naval base, especially in the 1939–45 war, it provides an outlet for only the northern tip of the island, and possesses only a short deep-water quay. The only large modern port in the island is Taomasina (**Tamatave** pop. 59,000). Situated on the exposed and reef-girt east coast, the harbour is artificially enclosed; it is far from satisfactory, for during severe storms, unfortunately common in these parts, so much wave motion develops that ships have to put out to sea. Nevertheless, Taomasina is Madagascar's chief port, handling about half the total port traffic of the island. Majunga (pop. 52,000) on the north-west is the island's second port, handling about half the volume of Tamatave's traffic. It has a more sheltered harbour but lacks a deep-water quay. In spite of this many imports pass through it, for it is on the side of the island facing Africa and subject to less stormy weather than Taomasina. Furthermore, it possesses a good road connection to Tananarive, 600 km distant. The only other port of significance is **Tulear** (pop. 29,000) with some deep-water facilities, serving the south-west.

The general level of trade is low. The islands of Mauritius and Reunion together export as much as Madagascar. The five principal agricultural products – coffee, rice, vanilla, tobacco and cloves – account for two-thirds of the export trade. The island is still heavily dependent on France, which takes over one-half of all exports and provides nearly three-quarters of all imports. There is a considerable trade deficit, imports exceeding exports by as much as 30 per cent. The situation has deteriorated in recent years, as growing internal demand, partly resulting from a rising population, reduces the surplus available for export; at the same time, the republic is being forced to purchase more raw materials, capital goods and fuel in order to lay the foundations of a more modern economy, less heavily dependent on the sale of a few cash crops which are not always easy to market. The closing years of the 1980s will see government policies emphasizing a renewed commitment to agricultural development.

THE MASCARENE ISLANDS

Separated from Madagascar by a broad basin of the Indian Ocean, whose floor here lies at depths of 5000 m or more, is the Mascarene Ridge (Figure 100). Only its highest peaks break the ocean surface to form a number of islands, from the Seychelles in the north, to Mauritius and Reunion in the south.

The Seychelles

The ninety-two Seychelles Islands are mostly small and the majority uninhabited. They were visited by the Arabs in the twelfth century, later by the Portuguese, and first colonized by the French from 1756 onward. In the Napoleonic Wars a British force took over the islands, which became a British dependency in 1814. The population today is of both European and African descent, the Africans being brought over as plantation labourers until the abolition of slavery in 1824.

The present population numbers 66,000, of whom 80 per cent live on the largest island, Mahe (142 km^2). Mahe has granite peaks reaching nearly 900 m, but the other small islands are considerably lower and some are entirely of coral formation. The hills are clothed in forest, while coconut-palms fringe the shores.

The climate is maritime and equatorial, for the islands lie within 5° of the equator. Rainfall approaches 2300 mm a year. Temperatures are usually around 27°C with little seasonal variation. Unlike Mauritius and Reunion, hurricanes are very rare.

The islanders depend on the sale of copra (there are large coconut plantations), cinnamon bark and oil, guano and salted fish. There is a thriving and expanding tourist industry, for the islands offer beautiful scenery, a warm climate, fishing and bathing.

Mauritius

'The initial impression of Mauritius is of an island that is bizarre and slightly improbable. Grotesque pinnacled mountains rise up in groups around the dome-shaped central upland; going inland from Port Louis, one passes in a matter of miles from a coastland as dry as the Transvaal in winter to a mossy inland as green as Ireland and characteristically shrouded in cloud'.[1] The jagged peaks rising to 825 m are in fact all that

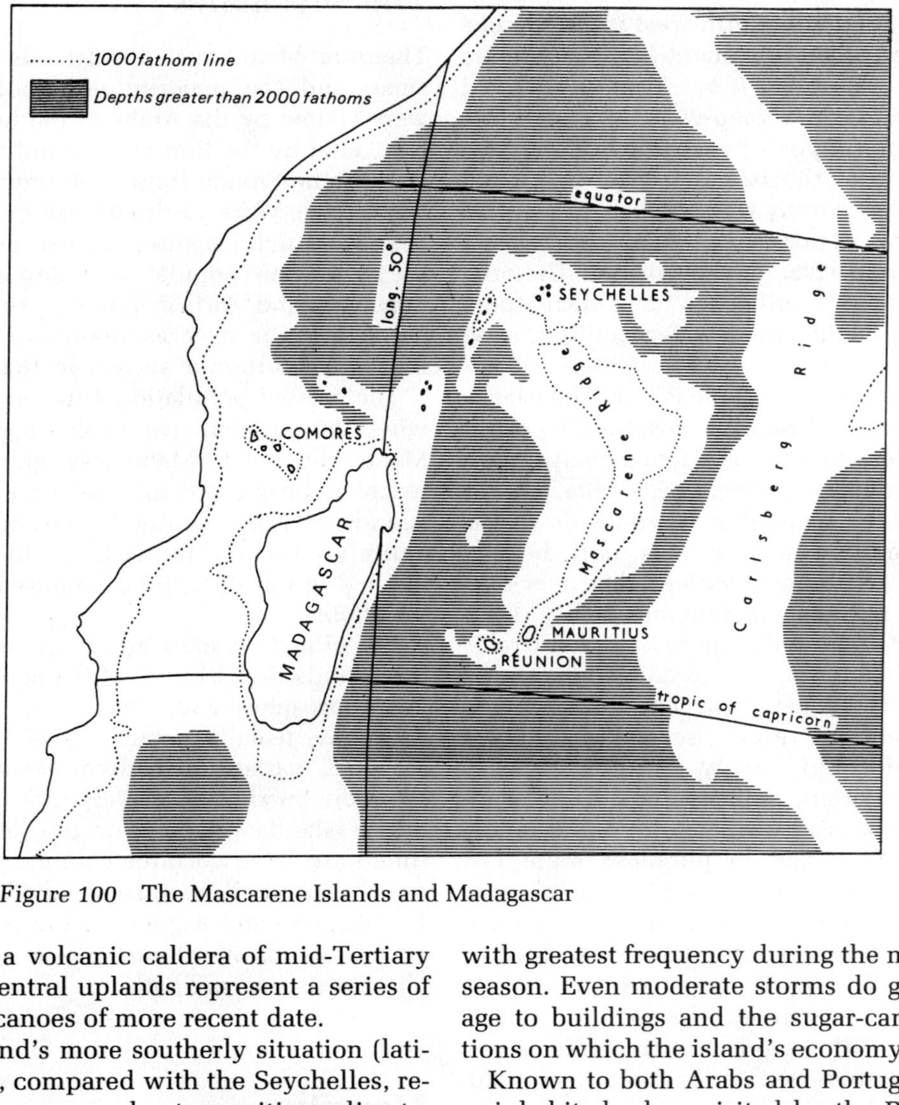

Figure 100 The Mascarene Islands and Madagascar

remain of a volcanic caldera of mid-Tertiary age. The central uplands represent a series of shield volcanoes of more recent date.

The island's more southerly situation (latitude 20°S), compared with the Seychelles, results in a more moderate maritime climate, mean monthly temperatures on the coast ranging from 20°C to 27°C. The climate is dominated by the south-east Trades, bringing nearly 5000 mm of rain to mountains on the east and centre; the north-west of the island is, however, in rain-shadow, with as little as 750 mm, and here are to be found all the main towns except Mahebourg. There are two rainy seasons, the principal one December to June, and a lesser one in August. Hurricanes are unfortunately a regular feature, occurring with greatest frequency during the main rainy season. Even moderate storms do great damage to buildings and the sugar-cane plantations on which the island's economy depends.

Known to both Arabs and Portuguese, and uninhabited when visited by the Portuguese in 1505, Mauritius was first settled by the Dutch in 1598. After the foundation of their more important Cape Colony in 1652, their interest in the island declined, and they abandoned it in 1710. The French were next on the scene, occupying the island until the arrival of a British force in 1810 during the Napoleonic Wars, for French pirates were preying too successfully on British traders returning from India. Mauritius was formally ceded to Britain in 1814.

The population now numbers 1 million and the density of population is very high. About two-thirds are of Indian extraction, Chinese account for about 4 per cent, about 20,000 are French-speaking, and the remainder mostly of mixed European–African blood. It would be hard to find a greater diversity of people on such a small area anywhere else in the world. When the slave trade was abolished the French planters on the island were left without a ready source of labour to work the sugar plantations, so like the planters in Natal, they brought over thousands of Indians (mainly from Madras) and Chinese. One-third of the population lives in the overcrowded towns such as the capital **Port Louis** (pop. 146,000), **Curepipe** (50,000) and **Mahebourg** (20,000). Port Louis has a sheltered harbour, though large vessels have to anchor offshore. Mahebourg borders a lagoon enclosed by a coral reef; the lagoon floor is exposed at low tide so that it is useless except for small pleasure-craft. A network of railways connects all the main towns.

The island's economy is dominated by sugar, which provides 70 per cent of export income and employs nearly 30 per cent of the workforce. Nearly one-half of the island's total area is under sugar-cane: there are 21 large estates, 450 medium-sized plantations and about 3000 small-scale producers. Low rainfall or the incidence of hurricanes can have devastating results, so annual outputs fluctuate considerably. Mauritius was a major beneficiary of the Lomé Convention sugar agreement under which the bulk of its crop is exported to the European Economic Community at preferential prices. Unfortunately the EEC now produces a surplus of sugar, so the Mauritian quota and the price paid were reduced in 1984. These pressures have also underlined the fact that there are too many sugar-mills and the equipment is outdated. A policy of rationalization and restructuring has been implemented with World Bank help, and 15 per cent of the sugar acreage has been converted to food crops and poultry-raising to give some diversification to the economy. Other crops are tea (some exported) and tobacco.

Reunion

Only slightly larger than Mauritius, this island is much more mountainous, with peaks reaching 2750 m and one – the Piton des Neiges – 3000 m. These highest points receive snow in winter, and there are signs of Pleistocene glaciation. The present climate is similar to that of Mauritius; both islands are menaced by hurricanes in the wet season.

The early history of European settlement and occupation followed much the same pattern as in Mauritius; but whereas the latter was confirmed in British hands in 1814, the island of Reunion was restored to France. The population (517,000) is largely African, or mixed European and African, with a minority of French officials and (in contrast to Mauritius) only a few Indians.

The density of population is not so high as in Mauritius, but there is nevertheless considerable pressure on the land. Most settlements are on the narrow coastlands, including the capital **St Denis** (pop. 104,000). The chief port is Pointe des Galets, or 'Le Port', on the north-west linked to St Denis by rail. Sugar-cane is, as on Mauritius, the principal crop. Most sugar plantations lie between 600 and 1200 m, above which the sharply rising slopes are covered with forest up to about 1800 m.

REPUBLIC OF THE COMOROS

North of Madagascar and 300 km off the northern Mozambique coast lies a small group of volcanic islands, the Comoros. Formerly administered by France, they are now (since 1975) an independent state. There are four main islands with a combined population of 370,000 and an area of 2240 km^2. The largest island, Njazidje (Grande Comore), consists mainly of the active volcano Karthala which attains 2400 m.

Ethnically the population is a mixture of Malgache, Malay, Persian, Arab and African peoples, but the culture is mainly Islamic. The population increases by 3.3 per cent a year, and pressure on the land is acute.

Vanilla and cloves are the main products, but the economy relies heavily upon foreign aid and upon remittances sent back by Comorans who emigrate to work in Malaya, East Africa and even France.

REFERENCES

1 H. C. Brookfield, *'Pluralism and geography in Mauritius'*, *Geog. Studies*, **5** [1958], pp. 3–19.

46

Conclusion: change and challenge in Africa

'Writing about modern Africa is like trying to sketch a galloping horse that is out of sight before you have sharpened your pencil.' With these words Elspeth Huxley drew attention to the dynamism of change in Africa in the period from the end of the Second World War to the mid-1960s. At that time it was a fair comment upon the changes that were taking place in African societies – politically, socially, economically and in terms of their landscapes. Doubtless, too, the view reflected the general euphoria and optimism in the newly independent countries themselves and amongst students of Africa in general.

Twenty years on it is more difficult to think of Africa in the same optimistic terms. The whole pace of change has slowed down – in many cases stopped – and Africa now seems to be the continent in which the problems of economic development are to be seen in their most acute forms.

Over the last three decades much has been accomplished to reveal the wealth, variety and personality of Africa to the rest of the world. This volume has shown repeatedly, however, the many disadvantages for development that the continent's geography displays. Physically, the greatest drawback is her lack of great alluvial plains; climatically, she suffers the penalties of the tropical environment – the poverty of widespread lateritic soils, fickle and unreliable rainfall over wide areas culminating in great deserts, the almost universal presence of predatory pests and debilitating diseases. In short, Africa has a harsh environment that is only now beginning to respond to the science, technology and capital brought in by the white man.

There is no doubt that the advance of Africa to the levels of living, education and wealth already attained in earlier developed continents depends fundamentally upon the successful conquest of the tropical environment. The greatest development that would alter the character of much of tropical Africa would be the eradication of the tsetse fly. Animals for draught purposes, improved agriculture with mixed farming, better diet and health for millions are the prizes for such an advance. The locust scourge, the worm diseases, malaria, and a multitude of endemic diseases have still to be conquered.

POLITICAL CHANGE

There is one significant area in which students of Africa still have trouble in keeping pace with events – the political instability. This in part reflects the artificiality of many of the state units inherited from the colonial era and the lack of coincidence between nation and state in the now independent territories. Many of the states are extremely small, in population and area; others are large but with relatively small populations; many have shapes that are administered with difficulty; while others find themselves land-locked and vulnerable. For many of them there are problems of ethnic diversity, lack of cohesion and problems of connecting constituent regions. No other continent is divided into so many separate states, with so many of the entities being politically weak and of doubtful economic viability.

As has been shown, a major weakness derives from the fact that the state apparatus is frequently dominated by a particular ethnic group, often intent upon maintaining its influence and therefore creating opposition from those who feel they are excluded from the decision-making processes or the distribution of benefits. For its part the government usually views such opposition as an undesirable expression of 'tribalism'. The one-party political organization, the charismatic leader and the prestige development projects which act as focal points for national aspirations have all been justified as means of providing a unity that is so obviously otherwise lacking.

It has been suggested that with independence many African states have suffered from a crisis of identity and legitimacy.[1] The new constitutions did not have any basis in the pre-colonial political structures, the colonial period itself was one of autocratic centralized control, and the result has been widespread adoption of various forms of 'personal rule' maintained by rigging of the electoral system (where that has been retained), patronage on a large scale, and force (sometimes with external support). The military provides the necessary support or, as has happened in over half of the countries concerned, has taken over complete control although invariably becoming a variant of the personal-rule theme.

Just as control by one ethnic group is likely to create conflicts, so too will personal rule, which has often resulted in disaffected groups attempting, and sometimes succeeding, in overthrowing the government. Frequent changes of government have become the norm and reflect the weakness of the political structures and the discontent and unrest generated among alienated groups and those dissatisfied with the pace of change. The established governments are rarely representative in any real sense, and it is partly for this reason that development planning has lacked proper direction, has often been based on wrong priorities, and has hardly anywhere resulted in maximum growth, more equitable distribution of wealth and benefit for the masses. It has also become clear that corruption has become endemic over much of Africa, and thus political power becomes associated with the means of enlarging personal wealth. This has arisen from the politicization of economic activity which principally dates from the closing years of colonial rule. Previously accustomed to handling modest sums, officials found vast sums of development capital (from loans, grants and aid) passing through their hands. Also, controls on entrepreneurial activity as in West Africa brought in restrictive licensing and gave yet more money-earning power to every tier in the swarming bureaucracy. Politicians and civil servants have a first loyalty to their families, tribe and political support. They are urbanites and rarely have sympathy with distant rural populations or with rather nebulous concepts of the public 'good'.[2] Millions of pounds have become deflected into private purses; many projects have limped because of inadequate local funding; an urban bias has seemed to prevail in most countries. The evidence of 30 years of development effort shows that over much of Africa the poor have remained poor or have actually got poorer. The élite of the African states have become markedly richer. Maldistribution of incomes has never been so severe.

ECONOMIC CHANGE

If political change has been all too frequent, in the economic field it is the sluggardly rate of change that now commands attention. However profound the impact of colonialism may have been, independence brought with it a new sense of urgency and the demand that political independence should rapidly be followed by economic independence. To translate this into reality, as we have seen, many of the new states embarked on 'planned' development and often adopted a 'socialist' approach which emphasized state participation in production – it was not thought adequate that government should merely provide an infrastructure and operate in a facilitating capacity. This was perhaps an inevitable reaction to capitalism and colonialism that had gone hand-in-hand before independence.

After examining the efforts that have gone into planned development by African states one realizes that growth of income has not only been low but in many cases less than the growth in population. The World Bank claims that fifteen African countries have registered negative growth during the 1970s. Even modest growth in income is all too quickly absorbed if population growth is not held in check, and most African countries have yet to embark on serious population-control programmes. In particular, food production has also fallen short of growth in population and rapid urbanization is increasing the mouths to be fed from an often declining agricultural sector. Sub-Saharan Africa is the only world region to show a decline in per capita food production between 1960 and 1980 and stands in sharp contrast to Asia, where food production in most countries has been expanding rapidly. Food deficits can of course be made good with imports, and between 1974 and 1983 commercial grain imports into Africa more than doubled while 'aid' cereal rose from 876,000 to 2,380,000 tonnes. Overall, there has been in Africa a serious neglect of farming, and in particular food production. But for a number of countries (Ghana and Nigeria provide obvious examples) even the basic export crop production has declined dramatically.

It can be argued that where the increasing cost of imported food can be covered adequately by income from exports there is no particular economic problem. However, most African countries have not been so blessed. Their income is in practically all cases derived from a limited range of primary exports, the terms of trade have steadily worsened over the last 20 years, and the income from their exports has bought ever less of the necessary imports – whether food, other consumer goods, industrial raw materials or capital goods. When world recession deepened in the 1970s the African countries were hit worse than most, and nearly all have suffered severe balance of payments problems. The oil producers have not been excluded from this.

It is necessary to distinguish between growth (increase in income, either national or personal), and development – by which is implied some structural change in the economy, the wider spread of benefits (medical, educational, housing) and an overall improvement in the way of life. While the two are related, it is possible to have growth without real development and it is possible to effect improvements in peoples' way of life without greatly increasing their incomes. If the growth record of African countries is poor, what of their development? Throughout the continent the dual character of the economies, inherited from the colonial era, has been shown to persist: the modern, or revenue-earning sector, based on a small minority of the population and the much larger element still largely subsistence in character. The only real change has been the replacement of a European, colonial élite by an African urban élite as the principal administrators and beneficiaries.

There has been little change in the overall structure of production in many of the countries: they are still for the most part what could be called 'colonial' in character, with a heavy dependence on a limited range of primary product exports (Table 47). In many cases there has been little change in the contribution of the different sectors to the GDP. In many of the countries much of the agriculture is not commercialized (and is therefore difficult to evaluate), but generally it provides the largest single sector of the economy. Oil producers such as Libya, Nigeria and Algeria and mineral producers such as Zambia are obvious exceptions. High industrial-sector contributions are invariably the result of mining activity, and manufacturing as such is rarely more than of minor significance.

In most of their early plans, African countries placed considerable emphasis on industrialization as a means of transforming their economies, but in most cases manufacturing has not progressed beyond infancy. The statistics may suggest impressive growth, but this has been from a very low base and manufacturing still provides little employment and contributes, on average, only 6–8 per cent of GDP. In global terms Africa's contribution to world-wide manufacturing is minimal – in fact, less than 1 per cent of world output. Value added in the manufacturing process in 1982 was less in real terms than it had been at the end of the 1960s. We have seen in a number of countries the limited success of much-vaunted and 'critical' policies of industrialization. South Africa is the only country which could reasonably be classed as industrial, and in a number of countries (Ghana, Nigeria and Zaire would be examples) the relative share of manufacturing has actually declined – in the case of Ghana and Zaire absolutely as well as relatively as economic and operational problems have reduced industrial production in existing plant. All too frequently, existing industrial enterprises operate well below their capacity and are adversely affected by import restrictions on raw materials (many of which could and should be produced locally), spare parts, equipment and energy. The scope for industrial development is restricted by the small size of many of the local markets, the lack of the right human resources, and an inadequate infrastructure which adds greatly to production costs. A further reason contributing to failure is the strategy, widely adopted, of concentrating upon import-substituting industry. The deficiencies already noted made for high-cost production, sustained by monopoly powers and soaring imports of machinery and raw materials.

The vast majority of Africans live in rural areas and derive their livelihood from agriculture; so it is perhaps the more surprising that

Table 47 *Structure of production in Africa*

Country	*GDP (US $ millions)*		*Contribution to gross domestic product (%)* Agriculture		*Industry*		*Services*	
	1965	*1983*	*1965*	*1983*	*1965*	*1983*	*1965*	*1983*
Ethiopia	1,180	4,270	58	48	14	16	28	36
Mali	370	980	49	46	13	11	38	43
Zaire	1,640	5,440	22	36	27	20	51	44
Burkina Faso	250	900	52	41	15	19	32	40
Tanzania	790	4,550	46	52	14	15	40	33
Togo	190	720	45	22	21	28	34	50
Ghana	1,330	3,720	41	53	19	7	41	40
Sierra Leone	320	950	34	32	28	20	38	48
Kenya	920	4,940	35	33	18	20	47	46
Lesotho	50	300	65	23	5	22	30	55
Zambia	1,040	3,350	14	14	54	38	32	48
Egypt	4,550	27,920	29	20	27	33	45	47
Morocco	2,950	13,300	23	17	28	32	49	51
Nigeria	4,190	64,570	53	26	19	34	29	40
Algeria	3,170	47,200	15	6	34	54	51	40

Source: World Development Report 1985 (New York, 1985).

this has been the neglected area in planning. Development effort has been overwhelmingly concentrated in the urban areas, and even where it has been directed to agriculture it has misguidedly emphasized large-scale mechanized and irrigated schemes and state-farming systems and ignored the peasant farmers. There is little doubt that greater attention to the peasant farmers would have produced far better results, and there has been a tendency to neglect the potential for innovation and spontaneous change which demonstrably exists in the rural areas and which, with incentives and encouragement, could lead to far higher production levels.[3]

SOCIAL CHANGE

Continuing high rates of population growth are undoubtedly placing great pressure on resources and amenities in urban and rural areas and often nullify the effect of what little economic growth there has been. In general the urban growth rate is roughly twice that of population growth. However, only in a small number of countries is the urban population yet the dominant element (Tunisia, South Africa, Congo and Libya), but the rural–urban migration which characterizes most Less Developed Countries has been exacerbated in Africa by the effect of drought and a strategic retreat from rural areas. This has been most marked in Mauritania, Mali, Niger, Chad, Sudan and Ethiopia; and while for some it may be no more than a temporary change, there is evidence in Mauritania that for many it may be permanent. In places (Lagos is the best example) the urban area has been overwhelmed by the influx, and water supply, sewage, transport and communications systems have been grossly inadequate. This has been one of the factors prompting the Nigerian government to embark on the construction of a new capital city on a 'greenfield' site up-country. If the scale is different, the problems are nevertheless present in many smaller towns.

Since independence more of the planned investment has gone on infrastructure, economic and social, than on any other developments. While the lot of the average African is unenviable by global standards, there have in fact been considerable improvements in some areas – medical services and education being significant in this respect. The proportion of children in primary education has almost universally shown great increases; and while the growth in secondary education is less spectacular, it has in a number of countries been considerable. Education is undoubtedly a critical area for investment if manpower with the appropriate range of skills is to be available for development, and not imported as now it often has to be. The benefits from such investment will be longer-term rather than immediate. Likewise, while health care is still often rudimentary, on a simple basis of persons per doctor, in many countries there have been marked improvements and this is a factor which contributes to the rapid growth of population – fewer children are dying in infancy and people are living to a greater age.

It is interesting to note that the best performance in the provision of educational and health services has been in those countries with the highest proportion of the population in urban areas. This in part reflects the urban bias in amenity provision and development planning, but also the practical consideration that the services are more readily and more cheaply provided where the population is concentrated in larger groups. It is also a factor making for the attraction of urban areas for rural people. The gap between the life styles of the peoples of the towns and country is still widening, and within the urban areas there is a sharp contrast between a small, relatively affluent, group and the much larger group which is poor, badly housed and on the fringe of the urban economy. Little has happened since independence to reduce the poverty of the mass of the population.

It is clear that the early expectations for growth and development have not materialized.

To some extent this is because the optimism was unrealistic and the problems were seriously under-estimated. To some extent the problems stem from the physical geography and resource endowment, the description of which has under-pinned the examination of development in individual countries in this book.

In many African countries a considerable proportion of investment has gone into economic infrastructure such as water supply, electricity generation and particularly transport; yet as one is constantly being reminded, their infrastructure is still in most cases woefully inadequate. The Band Aid assistance of 1985 went as much into the provision of transport as it did into food, medicine and equipment. A considerable proportion of Africa's population still lacks the accessibility and mobility that is essential for economic development. While this is manifestly true for the areas of sparse population, great distances and difficult terrain (the Sahel, Ethiopia, forest Zaire), it can also be a problem in more densely peopled, relatively well-developed areas. Farmers in Ghana's cocoa belt all too frequently have problems getting their cocoa crop to the purchasing centres and ports, and by continental standards Ghana's infrastructure is certainly better than average. Yet the provision of infrastructure is not in itself a sufficient condition for economic development, as Uganda's western railway, Nigeria's Bauchi line and Ghana's Accra–Tema motorway demonstrate. Rather it is the case that infrastructure ought to be part of a planned package of development inputs that could include water supplies, agricultural innovation, resettlement or new industries.

This brings one to the question of management. While we have certainly pointed to areas where the natural resources are restricting, for the most part they are still underutilized and badly managed. All too frequently we have drawn attention to productivity levels that are lower now than they have been in the past, to renewable resources such as forests and fisheries now being permanently depleted where they could be self-sustaining, and to industries which could well be based on local raw materials but instead depend on costly imports. Too frequently, inadequate attention has been given to the questions raised by the transfer of technology – *when* (is the time appropriate, the phasing correct?), *where* (is the best location selected?) and *what* (is the most appropriate scale and technology adopted?). Two further considerations might be *who* (are the right people making the decisions?) and *why* (are they being made for the right reasons?). Africa has unfortunately become littered with development projects that are badly timed (e.g. sugar and meat factories in Ghana built long before raw materials were assured), not in places where they will maximize the development impact (the Bauchi railway already mentioned), and of the wrong scale or technology. There are certainly too many examples of projects that have been pushed through with undue influence from external parties (contractor finance projects in many countries, 'tied aid' projects, projects developed as part of the global operations of multinational companies – e.g. Ghana's Volta River Project), and where decisions have been made for largely political or prestige reasons rather than in the best interests of economic development.

On past performance it would seem that the rise to a tolerable standard of living is beyond much of Africa's ability, given the economic situation and pattern up to the early 1980s. Frightening population growths that double populations within 20–25 years deflect more and more income into immediate consumption rather than into development investment. Domestic savings during the 1970s fell from 20 per cent of national incomes to no more than 5 per cent. There is now little domestic finance available for investment. This situation is worsened by the heavy burden of debt-servicing, sometimes taking a quarter to a half of the value of exports, with the capital amounts still to be repaid.

The problem of raising capital for development is heightened by the past record of ineffectual use and dissipation of international loans and grants. Here ideology bears some responsibility. Nearly all the independent states pledged themselves to various forms of socialism; in many this led to nationalization of major components of the economy and the furthering of communal living, cooperative farms and the creation of a new tier (generally urban-based) of officials and bureaucrats to oversee them. In country after country these projects, which have stifled individual initiative and entrepreneurship, have failed. Now, with the continent in travail, Africa is more receptive to the alternative ideas now firmly pushed by the United Nations and much of the developed world. Priorities have to be reordered: economies will have to be loosened from state control and a healthy private sector with freedom for the entrepreneur and support for private initiative must be tried. At the same time there is international pressure to turn African states from costly and unsuccessful industrial promotion in favour of a revival and rehabilitation of the agricultural sectors. Central control and management of development seems not to have been very successful, and the time has come to depend more on local and regional initiatives and replace the almost universal 'top down' with a 'bottom up' strategy.

There are now welcome signs that thinking amongst politicians in Africa is moving towards these possibly more fruitful approaches to development. There is need for greater cooperation and coordination of effort at the local and international levels, and the need to devise mechanisms whereby the grosser artificialities of the inherited political map can be overcome. Recent events have demonstrated that Africa continues to need aid and assistance of all kinds, but this must be channelled into self-sustaining projects related to locally established needs. Africa needs a measure of understanding that has possibly been lacking; and it is the hope that this book will contribute in some small way to the change of approach to development that allows us to entertain some optimism for the continent's future.

REFERENCES

1 Sandbrook, R. *The Politics of Africa's Economic Stagnation* (Cambridge University Press,1985).
2 Lord Bauer, *The Times*, 12 July 1984.
3 Richards, P. *Indigenous Agricultural Revolution* (Hutchinson, 1985).

Appendix

CONVERSION TABLES

1cm	=	0.394 inches	1 inch	=	25.4mm
1m	=	3.281 feet	1 foot	=	0.305m
1km	=	0.621 miles	1 mile	=	1.609km

1 hectare	=	2.471 acres	1 acre	=	0.405ha
$1km^2$	=	$0.386 miles^2$	$1 mile^2$	=	$2.59km^2$

Degrees Celsius	*Degrees Farenheit*
9	48.2
12	53.6
15	59.0
18	64.4
21	69.8
24	75.2
27	80.6
30	86.0
33	91.4
36	96.8
39	102.2
42	107.6

$$C = 5 \times \frac{(F - 32)}{9}$$

$$F = \frac{9 \times C}{5} + 32$$

Selected Bibliography

1 Introduction: geography and development

Kimble, G. H. T., *Tropical Africa*, New York, 1960.

Mountjoy, A. B., *Industrialization and Developing Countries*, Hutchinson, 1982.

O'Connor, A., *The geography of Tropical African development*, Pergamon, 1978.

Adedeji, A. (ed.), *Indigenization of African Economies*, Hutchinson, 1981.

Arnold, H. M., 'Africa and the new international economic order', Third World Quarterly, **2** (1980), pp. 215–304.

Grove, A. T. 'The state of Africa in the 1980s', *Geog. Jnl.*, **152** (1986), pp. 193–203.

Part One Physical Geography

2 Geology, structure and landforms

Best, A. C. G. and de Blij, H. J., *African Survey*, New York, Wiley, 1977.

Buckle, C., *Landforms in Africa*, Longman, 1978.

Choubert, G. (ed.), *Tectonics of Africa*, Paris: UNESCO, 1971.

Hayden, B., (*et al.*) *Classification of the coastal environments of the world: Part II, Africa*, Office of the Naval Research Geography Programs, Technical Report No. 3, 1973.

Pritchard, J. M., *Landform and landscape in Africa*, Arnold, 1979.

Baker, J., 'Oil and African development', *Jnl. Mod. Afr. Studies*, **15**(2) (1977), pp. 174–212.

Binns, J. A., 'The resources of rural Africa: a geographical perspective', *African Affairs*, **83**(330)(1984), pp. 33–40.

Dixey, F., 'African landscape', *Geog.Rev.*, **34** (1944), pp. 457–65.

Dixey, F., 'Erosion surfaces of Africa: some considerations of age and origin', *Trans. Geol. Soc. South Africa*, Marshalltown, South Africa, **59**(1956), pp. 1–16.

Hilling, D., 'Alternative energy sources for Africa: potential and prospects', *African Affairs*, **75**(300)(1976), pp. 359–71.

King, B. C., 'The geomorphology of Africa', *Science Progress*, **180**(1957), pp. 672–81, **181** (1958), pp. 97–107.

Klerkx, J. et al, 'Géologie africaine', *Rev. Geol. Dynamique et Geog. Phys.* Paris, **21**(5) (1979), pp. 317–427.

Thorpe, M. B., 'Geomorphology', in Clarke, J. E. (ed.), *An Advanced Geography of Africa*, Hulton, 1975, pp. 21–73.

White, H. P., 'The morphological development of West African seaports', in Hoyle, B. S. and Hilling, D. (eds.), *Seaports and Development in Tropical Africa*, Macmillan, 1970, pp. 11–26.

3 Climatology

Farmer, C. and Wigley, T. M. L., *Climatic trends in tropical Africa*, Climatic Res. Unit, University of East Anglia, 1985.

Thompson, B. W., *Climate of Africa*, Oxford University Press, 1965.

Trewartha, G. T., *An Introduction to Climate*, New York, McGraw Hill, 1956.

Trewartha, G. T., *The Earth's Problem Climates*, Methuen, 1962.

Bunting, A. H., 'Some problems of agricultural climatology in tropical Africa', *Geog.*, **46** (1961), pp. 283–94.

Kenworthy, J., 'Climatology', in Clarke, J. I. (ed.), *An Advanced Geography of Africa*, Hulton, 1975, pp. 74–116.

Laver, W. and Frankenberg, P., 'Eine Karte der hygrothermischen Klimatatypen Africas', Erdkunde, Bonn, **35**(4) (1981), pp. 245–8.

Tanaka, M., 'Recent African rainfall patterns', *Nature*, **225**, p.505.

4 Vegetation and soils

Moss, R. P., *The Soil Resources of Tropical Africa*, Cambridge University Press, 1968.

Phillips, J., *Agriculture and Ecology in Africa*, Faber and Faber, 1959.

Thomas, M. F. and Whittington, G. W. (eds.), *Environment and Land Use in Africa*, Methuen, 1969.

Cole, M. M., 'Vegetation nomenclature and classification with particular reference to the savannas', *S. Afr. Geog. Jour.*, Johannesburg, **45**(1963), pp. 3–14.

Stevens, J. H., 'Biogeography', in Clarke, J. I. (ed.), *An Advanced Geography of Africa*, Hulton, 1975, pp. 117–51.

Part Two Human Geography

5 Political Evolution

Fage, J. D., *An atlas of African history*, Arnold, 1978.
Perham, M. and Simmons, J., *African discovery: An anthology of exploration*, Evanston, 1963.

Barbour, K. M., 'A geographical analysis of boundaries in inter-tropical Africa', in Barbour, K. M. and Prothero, R. M. (eds.), *Essays on African population*, London, 1961.
Griffiths, I., 'The scramble for Africa: Inherited political boundaries', *Geog. Jnl.*, **152** (1986), pp. 204–16.
Hamdan, G., 'The political map of the new Africa', *Geog. Rev.*, **53** (1963), pp. 418–39.

6 Population and society

Clarke, J. I., Khogali, M. and Kosinski, L. (eds.), *Population and development projects in Africa*, Cambridge University Press, 1985.
United Nations, *Demographic Yearbook*, New York (annually).

Bryson, J. C. 'Women and agriculture in Sub-Saharan Africa', *Jnl. Dev. Studies*, **17** (1981), pp. 29–46.
Taylor, J., 'Some consequences of recent reproductions in mine labour recruitment in Botswana', *Geog.*, **71** (1986), pp. 34–46.

7 Settlement patterns, health and education

Abu-Lughod, J. and Hay, R. (eds.), *Third World urbanization*, New York, 1979.
Clarke, J. I. and Kosinski, L. (eds.), *Redistribution of population in Africa*, Heinemann, 1982.
Hill, A. G. (ed.), *Population, health and nutrition in the Sahel*, KPI/Routledge, 1985.
O'Connor, A., *The African City*, Hutchinson, 1983.

Birks, J., 'Overland pilgrimage, West Africa to Mecca', *Geog.*, **62**(1977), pp. 215–17.
Christopher, A. J., 'Continuity and change in African capitals', *Geog. Rev.*, **75**(1985), pp. 44–57.
Kloos, H. and Thompson, K., 'Schistosomiasis in Africa', *Jnl. Tropical Geog*, **48**(1979), pp. 31–46.
Peil, M., 'African squatter settlements', *Urban Studies*, **13**(1976), pp. 155–66.
Prothero, R. M., African Population mobility project, Working Papers, University of Liverpool, 1973–7.
Winters, C., 'Urban morphogenesis in Francophone Black Africa', *Geog. Rev*, **72**(1982), pp. 139–54.

8 Farming and industry

Allan, W., *The African husbandman*, Oliver and Boyd, 1965.
Manshard, W., *Tropical agriculture*, Longman, 1974.

Deshler, W., 'Cattle in Africa', *Geog. Rev.*, **53**(1963), pp. 52–8.
Mabogunje, A. L., 'Manufacturing and the geography of development in tropical Africa', *Econ. Geog.*, **49**(1973), pp. 1–20.
Wad, A., 'Science, technology and industrialization in Africa', *Third World Quarterly*, **6**(1984), pp. 327–50.

9 Minerals, power and transport

Arnold, G. and Weiss, R. *Strategic highways in Africa*, London, 1977.
Hoyle, B. and Hilling, D. (eds.), *Seaports and development in tropical Africa*, Macmillan, 1970.

Hilling, D., 'Alternative energy sources for Africa', *African Affairs*, **75**(1976), pp. 359–71.

Part Three North-West Africa and the Sahara

10 The physical background

Cambridge Atlas of the Middle East and North Africa, Cambridge University Press, 1986.
Despois, J., *L'Afrique du Nord*, Paris, 1964.

Abu-Lughod, J. L., 'Developments in North African urbanism: The process of decolonisation', in Berry, B. L. (ed.), *Urbanisation and counterurbanisation*, California, 1976.
Despois, J., 'Les paysages agraires du Maghreb et du Sahara', *Ann. de Geog.* (1964), pp. 17–32.
Lawless, R. I., 'Progress and problems in the development of Maghreb agriculture', *The Maghreb Rev.*, **1**(1979), pp. 6–11.

11 Morocco

International Bank, *The Economic Development of Morocco*, Baltimore, 1966.

Bouquerel,J., 'Le chemin de fer au Maroc et son role dans

le développement économique du pays', *Cahiers d'Outre-Mer*, **28**(1975), pp. 218–51.
Noin, D., 'Aspects du sous-dévéloppement au Maroc', *Ann. de Geog.*, **75**(1966), pp. 410–31.

12 Algeria

Brebner, P., 'Algeria: the transformation of a settlement system', *Third World Planning Rev.*, **3**(1981), pp. 43–56.
Nellis, J. R., 'Socialist management in Algeria', *Jnl. Mod. Af. Studies*, **15**(1977), pp. 529–54.
Sutton, K., 'Population growth in Algeria 1966–1977, with some comparisons from Tunisia', *The Maghreb Rev.*, **5**(1980), pp. 41–50.
Sutton, K., 'Algeria; Centre-Down development, State capitalism and Emergent decentralisation' (ch 14), in Wø Stöhr and D. Fraser, *Development from Above or Below*, Wiley, 1981, pp. 351–75.
Sutton, K., 'Industrialisation and regional development in a centrally-planned economy, the case of Algeria', *Tijd. v. Econ. en Soc. Geog.* (1976), pp. 83–94.
Sutton, K., 'The progress of Algeria's Agrarian Reform and its settlement implications', *The Maghreb Rev.*, **2**(1978), pp. 10–16.
Sutton, K., 'Natural gas in Algeria' *Geog.*, **64**(1979), pp. 115–19.
Sutton, K. and Lawless, R. I., 'Population regrouping in Algeria: Traumatic change and the rural settlement pattern', *Trans. Inst. Brit Geogrs.*, **3**(NS) (1978), pp. 331–50.

13 Tunisia

Despois, J., *La Tunisie, ses regions*, Paris, 1961.
Duwaji, G., *Economic development in Tunisia*, New York 1967.

Clarke, J. I., 'Population policies and dynamics in Tunisia', *The Jnl. Dev. Areas*, **4**(1969), pp. 45–58.

14 Libya

Allan, J., 'The Kufrah agricultural schemes', *Geog. Jnl.*, **142**(1976), pp. 48–56.
Grove, A. T., 'Geomorphology of the Tibesti region', *Geog. Jnl.*, **126**(1960), pp. 18–31.
Schliephake, K., 'Libyan agricultural: natural constraints and aspects of development', *The Maghreb Rev.*, **5**(1980), pp. 51–6.

15 The Sahara

Capot-Rey, R. *Le Sahara Français*, Paris, 1953.

Despois, J., 'Le Sahara et l'écologie humaine', *Ann. de Geog.*, **17**(1961), pp. 577–84.
Peel, R. F., 'Landscape in aridity', *Trans. Inst. Brit. Geogrs.*, 38 (1966), pp. 1–23.
Thorp, M. B., 'Some aspects of the geomorphology of the Air Mountains', *Trans Inst. Brit. Geogrs.*, **47**(1969), pp. 25–46.

Part Four The Nile Basin and Horn of Africa

16 Physical geography

Cambridge Atlas of the Middle East and North Africa, Cambridge University Press, 1986.
Abul-Haggag, Y., *Physiography of Northern Ethiopia*, London, 1961.
Hurst, H. E. *The Nile*, Constable, 1957.

17 Egypt

Mountjoy, A. B., *Industrialisation and Developing Countries* (ch. 10), Hutchinson, 1982.
Radwan, S. and Lee, E., *Agrarian change in Egypt: An anatomy of poverty*, Croom Helm, 1986.

Afifi, H., 'The Egyptian experience of Agrarian Reform', *E. Af. Jnl. Rural Dev.*, **5**(1972), pp. 193–200.
Allan, J. A., 'High Aswan Dam is a success story', *Geog. Mag.*, **LIII**(1981), pp. 393–5.
Barbour, K. M., 'The distribution of industry in Egypt', *Trans. Inst. Brit. Geogrs.*, **50**(1970), pp. 155–76.
El-Baz, F., 'Journey to the Gilf Kebir and Unweinat, south-west Egypt, 1978', *Geog. Jnl.*, **146**(1980), pp. 51-93.
Haynes, K. and Whittington, D., 'International management of the Nile: Stage three', *Geog. Rev.*, **71**(1981), pp. 17–32.
Mountjoy, A. B., 'The Suez Canal at mid-century', *Econ. Geog.*, **34**(1958), pp. 155–67.
Mountjoy, A. B., 'Egypt: Population and resources', in Clarke, J. I. and Fisher, W. B., *Populations of the Middle East and North Africa*, London, 1972.
Richards, A., 'The agricultural crisis in Egypt', *Jnl. Dev. Studies*, **16**(1980), pp. 303–21.

18 Sudan

Barbour, K. M., *The Republic of the Sudan*, University of London Press, 1961.
El-Bushra, El-S., *An Atlas of Khartoum conurbation, Khartoum, 1976.*

Adams, M. and Howell, J., 'Developing the traditional

sector in Sudan', *Econ. Dev. & Cult. Change*, **27**(1979), pp. 508–18.
El-Arifi, S. A., 'Pastoral nomadism in the Sudan', *E. Af. Geog. Rev.*, **13**(1975), pp. 89–103.
Berry, L. and Whiteman, A., 'The Nile in the Sudan', *Geog. Jnl.* , **134**(1968), pp. 1–37.
Briggs, J., 'Farmers' responses to planned agricultural development in the Sudan', *Trans. Inst. Brit. Geogrs.*, **3**(NS) (1978), pp. 464–75.
El-Bushra, El-S., 'Development of industry in Greater Khartoum', *E. Af. Geog. Rev.*, **10**(1972), pp. 27–50.
El-Bushra, El-S., 'Sudan's triple capital: Morphology and function', *Ekistics*, **233**(1975), pp. 246–50.
Howell, P., 'The impact of the Jonglei Canal in the Sudan', *Geog. Jnl.*, **149**(1983), pp. 286–300.
Khogali, M. M., 'The development and problems of Port Sudan', in Hoyle, B. S. and Hilling, D. (eds.), *Seaports in Tropical Africa*, London, 1970.
Mountjoy, A. B., 'Water policy unites the Sudan', *Geog. Mag.*, **XLIV**(1972), pp. 705–11.
Oliver, J., 'Problems of the arid lands: The Sudan', *Spec. Public. No. 1*, Inst. Brit. Geogrs., (1968), pp. 219–39.
Roden, D., 'Regional inequality and rebellion in the Sudan', *Geog. Rev.*, **64**(1974), pp. 498–516.

19 Ethiopia, Somalia and Djibouti

Forster J., 'The economy of the Gamu Highlands, Southern Ethiopia', *Geog. Mag.*, **XLI**(1969), pp. 429–37.
Jackson, R. T., 'Periodic markets in southern Ethiopia', *Trans. Inst. Brit. Geogrs.*,**53**(1971), pp. 31–42.
Roundy, R. W., 'Altitudinal mobility and disease hazards for Ethiopian population', *Econ. Geog.*, **52**(1976), pp. 103–15.
Wood, A., 'Regional development in Ethiopia', *E. Af. Geog. Rev.*, **15**(1977), pp. 89–106.
Wood, A., 'Rural development and national integration: The experience of post-revolution Ethiopia', *Geog.*, **66**(1981), pp. 131–3.

Pallister, J. W., 'The geomorphology of the Northern Region Somali Republic', *Geog. Jnl.*, **129**(1963), pp. 184–7.

Part Five West Africa

20 Human and physical geography

Catchpole, B. and Akinjogbin, I. A., *A History of West Africa in Maps*, Collins, 1984.
Dunn,J. (ed.), *West African States: Failure and Promise*, Cambridge University Press, 1978.
Ezenwe, U., *ECOWAS and the Economic Integration of West Africa*, Hurst, 1983.
Gugler, J. and Flannagan, W. G., *Urbanisation and social change in West Africa*, Cambridge University Press, 1978.
Harrison Church, R. J., *West Africa*, Longman, 8th edn, 1980.
Hart, K., *The Political Economy of West African Agriculture*, Cambridge University Press, 1982.
Hodder, B. W. and Ukwu, U. I., *Markets in West Africa*, Ibadan University Press, 1969.
Hopkins, A. G., *An Economic History of West Africa*, Longman, 1973.
Morgan, W. B. and Pugh, J., *West Africa*, Methuen, 1969.
Richards, P., *Indigenous Agricultural Revolution*, Hutchinson, 1985.
Udo, R. K., *A Comprehensive Geography of West Africa*, Ibadan: Heinemann, 1978.
White, H. P. and Gleave, M. B., *An Economic Geography of West Africa*, Bell, 1971.
White, H. P., 'The morphological development of West African seaports', in Hoyle B.S. and Hilling D. (eds.). *Seaports and Development in Tropical Africa*, Macmillan, 1970, pp. 11–25.

Hilling, D., 'The evolution of the major ports of West Africa', *Geog. Jnl.*, **135**(3) (1969), pp. 365–78.
Richards, P., 'Farming systems and agrarian change in West Africa', *Prog. in Human Geog.*, **7**(1) (1983), pp. 1–39.

Dalby, D., and Harrison Church, R. J. (eds.), *Drought in Africa*, London: School of Oriental and African Studies, 1973.
Ojo, O., *The Climates of West Africa*, Heinemann, 1977.
Rapp, A., *A Review of Desertification in Africa*, Stockholm: Secretariat for International Ecology, 1974.

Bunting, A. H. (*et al.*), 'Rainfall trend in the West African Sahel', *Q. Jnl. R. Met. Soc.*, **102**, 431 (1976), pp. 59–64.
Derrick, J., 'The great West African drought, 1972–74', *African Affairs*, **76**, 305 (1977), pp. 537–86.
Dalby, D., Harrison Church, R. J. and Beggaz, F. (eds.), *Drought in Africa*, International African Inst., 1977.
Derrick, J., 'West Africa's worst year of famine', *African Affairs*, **83**, 332 (1984), pp. 281–99.
Gallois, J., 'La situation de L'elevage bovin et la problème des eleveurs en Afrique occidentale et centrale', *Cahiers d'Outre-Mer* (Bordeaux), **32** (1979), pp. 113–38.
Gregory, S., 'A note on seasonal rains in the Sahel, 1931–60 and 1961–80', *Geog.*, **68**(1)(1983), pp. 31–6.
Grove, A. T. (*et al.*), 'Articles on drought', *African Affairs*, **73**, 291 (1974), pp. 137–77.
Grove, A. T., (ed.), 'Sahel Symposium', *Geog. Jnl.*, **144**(3) (1978), pp. 404–23.
Kamrany, N. M., 'The Sahel drought: major development issues', *Ekistics*, Athens, **43**, 258 (1977), pp. 314–19.
Mortimore, M. (*et al.*), 'Drought in Africa', *Savanna*, Zaria, **2**, 2 (1973), pp. 97–164.

21 The dry lands of West Africa

Diguimbaye, G. and Langue, R. (eds.), *L'essor du Tchad*, Paris: Paris University Press, 1969.

Gerteiny, A. G., *Mauritania*, Pall Mall, 1967.

Westebbe, R. M., *The Economy of Mauritania*, New York: Praeger, 1971.

Arnand, J., 'La Mauritanie decouvre son littoral', *Acta Geog.*, Paris, **43** (1980), pp. 23–45.

Bradley, P. N., 'Land without labour (Mauritania)', *Geog. Mag.*, **30**(3) (1977), pp. 167–8.

Hilling, D., 'Saharan iron ore oasis', *Geog. Mag.* Sept. 1969, pp. 908–17.

Pitte, J. R., 'La sécherresse en Mauritanie', *Ann. deGeog.*, Paris, **84** (1975), pp. 641–64.

Toupet, C., 'Nouadhibou and the economic development of Mauritania', in Hoyle, B. S. and Hilling, D. (eds.), *Seaports and Development in Tropical Africa*, Macmillan, 1970, pp. 27–40.

Vermeer, D. E., 'Collision of climate, cattle and culture in Mauritania during the 1970s', *Geog. Rev.*, New York, **71**(3) (1981), pp. 281–97.

Binns, J. A., 'After the drought: field observations for Mali and Burkina Faso', *Geog.*, **71**(3) (1986).

Hilling, D., 'Routes to the sea for land-locked states', *Geog. Mag.*, **44**(4) (1972), pp. 257–64.

Poulton, R., 'Cooperation against the drought (Mali)', *Geog. Mag.*, **55**(10) (1983), pp. 524–31.

Stryer, J. D., 'The Malian cattle industry: opportunity and dilemma', *Jnl. Mod. Afr. Studies*, **12**(3) (1974), pp. 41–57.

Courel, A. and Lardinois, R., 'La population du Haute Volta', *Cahiers d'outre-Mer*, Bordeaux, **32**, 125 (1979), pp. 39–65.

Ofari-Sarpong, E., 'The drought of 1970–77 in Upper Volta', *Sing. Jnl. Trop. Geog.*, Singapore, **4**(1) (1983), pp. 62– 72.

Songre, A., 'Mass emigration for Upper Volta', *Ekistics*, Athens (1974), pp. 26–7.

Agnew, C. T., 'Water availability and the development of rainfed agriculture in South West Niger', *Trans. Inst. Br. Geogrs.*, **7**(4) (1982), pp. 419–57.

Sidikou, A. H., 'Naimey', *Cahiers d'Outre-Mer*, Bordeaux, **28**, 111, (1975), pp. 201–17.

Decalo, S., 'Regionalism, political decay and civil strife in Chad', *Jnl. Mod. Afr. Studies*, **18**(1) (1980), pp. 23–56.

Sturzinger, U., 'Tchad: mise en valeur coton et dévéloppement', *Tiers-Monde*, Paris, July–Sept. 1983, pp. 643–52.

22 The western coastal states

Clarke, J. I. (ed.), *Sierra Leone in Maps*, London University Press, 1974.

Clower, R. W., Dalton, G., Horowitz, M. and Walters, A. A., *Growth without Development*, Evanston, 1966.

Dunsmore, J. R. (*et al.*), *The agricultural development of the Gambia*, Surbiton: Ministry of Overseas Development, Land Resources Division, 1976.

Peterec, R., *Dakar and West Africa Economic Development*, New York: Columbia University Press, 1967.

Riddell, J. B., *The Spatial Dynamics of Modernization in Sierra Leone*, Evanston, 1970.

Schulze, W., *A New Geography of Liberia*, Longman, 1973.

Baker, K. M., 'Structural change and managerial inefficiency in the development of rice cultivation in the Segenal river region', *African Affairs*, **81**, 325 (1982), pp. 499–510.

Crampton, P. D., 'The population geography of The Gambia', *Geog.*, **57** (1972), pp. 153–8.

De Jonge, K., 'Rural development and inequality in Casamance', *Tijd. Econ. Soc. Geog.*, Amsterdam, **69**, 1/2(1978), pp. 68–77.

Domingo, J., 'Deux experiences de dévéloppement de la pêche maritime au Senegal', *Cahiers d'Outre-Mer*, Bordeaux, **35**, 137 (1982), pp. 35–62.

Dubresson, A., 'Notes sur les activites industrielles en Senegal', *Inf. Geog.*, Paris, **42**(3) (1978), pp. 130–9.

Jarrett, J. R., 'The geographical regions of the Gambia', *Scot. Geog. Mag.*, **66** (1950), pp. 162–9.

Kirtley, M. A., 'Senegambia – a new and future nation', *Nat. Geog. Mag.*, **168**(2) (1985), pp. 224–51.

Lagalee, B., 'Le dévéloppement du tourisme au Senegal', *Inf. Geog.*, Paris, **42**(3) (1978), pp. 140–3.

Mitchell, P., 'Nation of villagers (Gambia)', *Geog. Mag.*, **47**(1) (1974), pp. 29–32.

Seck, A., 'The changing role of the port of Dakar', in Hoyle, B. S. and Hilling, D. (eds.), *Seaports and Development in Tropical Africa* Macmillan, 1970, pp. 41–56.

Denis, P. Y., 'Realisations récentes et perspectives de dévéloppement en Guinea', *Cahiers d'Outre-Mer*, Bordeaux, **29** (1976), pp. 321–47

O'Connor, M., 'Guinea and Ivory Coast – contrasts in economic development', *Jnl. Mod. Afr. Studies*, **10**(3) (1972), pp. 409–26.

Swindell, K., 'Industrialisation in Guinea', *Geog.*, **54**(4) (1969), pp. 456–8.

Airey, A., 'The role of feeder roads in promoting rural change in eastern Sierra Leone', *Tijd. v. Econ. Soc. Geog.*, Amsterdam, **76**(3) (1983), pp. 192–201.

Binns, J. A., 'Agricultural change in Sierra Leone', *Geog.*, **67**(2) (1982), pp. 113–25.

Gleave, M. B., 'Urban growth, urbanisation and development in Sierra Leone', *Malaysian Jnl. of Trop. Geog.*, Singapore, **3** (1981), pp. 7–17.

Gleave, M. B., 'Population redistribution in Sierra Leone', in Clarke, J. I. and Kosinski, L. A. (eds.), *Population Redistribution in Africa*, Heinemann, 1982, pp. 79–84.

Gleave, M. B., 'Assessing levels of agricultural development in Sierra Leone', *Singapore Jnl. of Trop. Geog.*, **3**(1) (1982), pp. 16–33.

Jedrej, M. C., 'The growth and decline of a mechanical agriculture scheme in West Africa (Sierra Leone)', *African Affairs*, **82**, 329 (1983), 541–58.
McKay, J., 'Physical potential and economic reality: the underdevelopment of the port of Freetown', in Hoyle, B. S. and Hilling, D. (eds.), *Seaports and Development in Tropical Africa*, Macmillan, 1970, pp. 57–73.
Riddell, J. B., 'Urban bias in underdevelopment: appropriation from the countryside in post-colonial Sierra Leone', *Tijd. v. Econ. Soc. Geog.*, Amsterdam, **76**(5) (1985), pp. 374–83.
Swindell, K., 'Sierra Leone mining migrants, their compositions and origins', *Trans. Inst. Brit. Geog.*, **61** (1974), pp. 47–64.
Swindell, K., 'Diamond mining in Sierra Leone', *Tijd. v. Econ. Soc. Geog.*, Amsterdam, **57** (1970), pp. 96–104.
Williams, Geoffrey, J., 'Sierra Leone stakes mineral claims', *Geog. Mag.*, **XLII**(6) (1970), pp. 398–401.
Williams, G. J., and Hayward, D. F., 'The changing land transportation pattern of Sierra Leone', *Scot. Geog. Mag.*, **89**(2) (1973), pp. 107–18.

Beleky, L., 'The development of Liberia', *Jnl. Mod. Afr. Studies*, **11**(1) (1973), pp. 43–66.
Ghoshal, A., 'The impact of the foreign rubber concessions on the Liberian economy', *Jnl. Mod. Afr. Studies*, **12**(4) (1974), pp. 589–99.
Hasselman, K. H., 'Liberia', in De Blij, H. and Martin, E. (eds.), *African Perspectives*, Methuen, 1981, pp. 137–72.
Harrison Church, R. J., 'The Firestone rubber plantation', *Geog.*, **54** (1969), pp. 430–37.
Joseph, W., 'Liberia', in Caldwell, J. (ed.), *Population growth and socioeconomic change in West Africa*, New York, 1971.
Schulze, W., 'The ports of Liberia: economic significance and development problems', in Hoyle, B. S. and Hilling, D. (eds.), *Seaports and Development in Tropical Africa*, Macmillan, 1970, pp. 76–101.
Stanley, W. R., 'Transport expansion in Liberia', *Geog. Reg.*, New York, **60** (1970), pp. 529–47.
Stanley, W. R., 'Changing export patterns of Liberia's seaports', in Hoyle, B. S. and Hilling, D. (eds.), *Seaport Systems and Spatial Change*, Wiley, 1984, pp. 435–59.
Swindell, K., 'Iron ore in Liberia', *Geog.*, **20**(1) (1965), pp. 75–8

23 Côte d'Ivoire and Ghana

Andrae, G., *Industry in Ghana*, Uppsala, Scand. Inst. of African Studies, 1981.
Chambers, R., *The Volta Resettlement Experience*, Pall Mall, 1970.
Dickson, K. B., *A Historical Geography of Ghana*, Cambridge University Press, 1971.
Hart, D., *The Volta River Project: a Case Study in Politics and Technology*, Edinburgh University Press, 1980.
Howard, R., *Colonialism and Underdevelopment in Ghana*, Croom Helm, 1978.
Moxon, J., *Volta Man's Greatest Lake*, Deutsch, revised 1984.
Wills, J. B. (ed.), *Agriculture and Land Use in Ghana*, Oxford University Press, 1962.

Ahiakpor, J. C. W., 'The success and failure of dependency theory: The experience of Ghana', *Int. Organ.*, Mass. Inst. Technology (Suummer 1985), pp. 535–52.
Asiama, S. U., 'The rich slum dweller: a problem of unequal access', *Int. Lab. Rev.*, Geneva (May/June 1985), pp. 353–62.
Benneh, G., 'The response of farmers in northern Ghana to the introduction of mixed farming', *Geog. Annaler*, Stockholm, **54(B)**, No.2 (1972), pp. 95–103.
Benneh, G., 'Population, disease and rural development programmes in the Upper East region of Ghana', in Clarke, J. I. *et al.* (eds.), *Population and Development in Africa*, Cambridge University Press, 1985, pp. 206–18.
Browne, H., 'Appropriate technology and the dynamics of village industry: a case of pottery in Ghana', *Trans. Inst. Brit. Geogrs.*, **6**(3) (1981), pp. 313–23.
Darkoh, M. B. K., 'The distribution of manufacturing in Ghana', *Scot. Geog. Mag.*, **87** (1971), pp. 38–58.
Darkoh, M. B. K., 'Industrial strategy and rural development in Africa with special reference to Ghana', *Geoforum*, **16**(1973).
Dickinson, H., 'The Volta dam: energy for industry', in Fransman, M. (ed.), *Industry and Accumulation in Africa*, Heinemann, 1982, pp.345–52.
Dickson, K. B., 'Background to the problem of economic development in Northern Ghana', *Ann. Assn. Ann. Geog.*, Washington, **58** (1968), pp. 685–98.
Hilling, D., 'Tema: the geography of a new port', *Geog.*, **51**(2) (1966) pp. 111–25.
Hilling, D., 'Ghana's aluminium industry: some locational considerations', *Tijd. Econ. Soc. Geog.*, Amsterdam, **33**(5) (1964), pp. 128–32.
Hilling, D., 'Port development and economic growth: the case of Ghana', in Hoyle, B. S. and Hilling, D. (eds.), *Seaports and Development in Tropical Africa*, Macmillan, 1970, pp. 125–45.
Hilling, D., 'Lakeland route through Ghana', *Geog. Mag.*, **49**(5) (1977), pp. 308–12.
Hilling, D., 'Ghana's tarnished anniversary', *Geog. Mag.*, **54**(3) (1982), pp. 131–4.
Nweke, F. I., 'Irrigation development in Ghana', *Oxford Agrarian Studies*, **7**(1978), pp. 38–53.

Alfthan, T., 'Industrialisation in the Ivory Coast', *Int. Labour Review*, Geneva, December 1982, pp. 761–74.
Armstrong, A., 'Ivory Coast: another new capital for Africa', *Geog.*, **70**(1) (1985), pp. 72–4.
Arnaud, J. C. and Sournia, G., 'Les fôrets de Côte D'Ivoire: une richesse en voie de disparition', *Cahiers d'Outre-Mer*, Bordeaux, **32**, 127 (1979), pp. 281–91.
Betts, D. C., 'The San Pedro project', *Geog,*, **56**(1) (1971), p. 47.
Bouthier, M., 'The development of the port of Abidjan

and the economic growth of the Ivory Coast', in Hoyle, B. S. and Hilling, D. (eds.), *Seaports and Development in Tropical Africa*, Macmillan, 1970, pp. 103–126.

Camara, C., 'Les cultures vivrieres en Republique de Côte d'Ivoire', *Ann. Geog.*, Paris, **93**(518) (1985), pp. 432–51.

Cotton, A. M. and Marguerat, Y., 'Deux riseaux urbains africains – Cameroun et Côte d'Ivoire', *Cahiers d'Outre-Mer*, Bordeaux, **29** (1976), pp. 348–85.

Due, J. M., 'Agricultural development in the Ivory Coast and Ghana', *Jnl. Mod. Afr. Studies*, **7**(4)(1969), pp. 637–60.

Hecht, R. M., 'The Ivory Coast economic miracle – what benefits for the peasant farmer?', *Jnl. Mod. Afr. Studies*, **21**(1) (1983), pp. 25–53.

Hilton, T., 'The changing Ivory Coast', *Geog.*, **50**(3) (1965), pp. 291–5.

Hinderink, J. and Templeman, G. J., 'Rural inequality and government policy: a case study of the river basin of the Bou in northern Ivory Coast', *Tijd. Econ. Soc. Geog.*, Amsterdam, **69**, 1/2 (1978), pp. 58–67.

Kirtley, M. A., 'The Ivory Coast: African success story', *Nat. Geog. Mag.*, Washington, **162**(1) (1982), pp. 94–125.

O'Connor, M., 'Guinea and Ivory Coast – contrasts in economic development', *Jnl. Mod. Afr. Studies*, **10**(3) (1972), pp. 409–26.

Penouil, M., 'Ivory Coast: an adaptive centre-down approach in transition', in W. B. Stöhr and D. R. Fraser Taylor (eds.), *Development from Above or Below*, Wiley, 1981, pp. 305–28.

Taylor, A., (*et al*)., 'Ivory Coast: political stability and economic growth', *Focus*, New York, **27**(5) (1977), pp. 1–14.

Teal, F., 'The foreign exchange regime and growth: comparison of Ghana and Ivory Coast', *Afr. Affairs*, **85**(339) (1986), pp. 267–82.

24 Togo and Benin

Hilling, D., 'Togoport – a new port of Lomé', *The Dock and Harbour Authority*, March 1969, pp. 43–4.

Nyassaogbo, K., 'L'urbanisation et son evolution au Togo', *Cahiers d'Outre-Mer*, Bordeaux, **37**, 146 (1984), pp. 135–58.

Roudié, P., 'Aspects du dévéloppement recent de l'economie Togolasse', *Cahiers d'Outre-Mer*, Bordeaux, **13**, 124 (1978), pp. 359–74.

Mondjannagni, A., 'Cotonou: some problems of port development in Dahamey', in Hoyle, B. S. and Hilling, D. (eds.), *Seaports and Development in Tropical Africa*, Macmillan, 1970, pp. 147–66.

White, H. P., 'Dahamey (Benin) – geographical basis of an African state', *Tijd. Econ. Soc. Geog.*, Amsterdam, **2** (1966).

25 Nigeria

Apeldoorn, G. J. van, *Perspectives on Drought and Famine in Nigeria*, George Allen and Unwin 1981.

Arnold, G., *Modern Nigeria*, Longman, 1977.

Barbour, M. (*et al.*) (eds.), *Nigeria in Maps*, Hodder and Stoughton, 1982.

Ekundare, R. O., *An Economic History of Nigeria, 1860–1960*, Methuen, 1973.

Kirk-Greene, A. and Rimmer, D., *Nigeria Since 1970*, Hodder and Stoughton, 1981.

Morgan, W. T. W., *Nigeria*, Longman, 1983.

Oguntoyinbo, J. S. (*et al.*) (eds.), *A Geography of Nigerian Development*, Ibadan: Heinemann, 1983.

Onoh, J. K., *The Nigerian Oil Economy*, Croom Helm, 1983.

Sada, P. O. and Oguntoyinbo, J. S. (eds.), *Urbanisation Processes and Problems in Nigeria*, Ibadan, University Press, 1978.

Schatzl, L. (ed.), *Industrialisation in Nigeria: a Spatial Analysis*, München, 1973.

Teriba, O. (*et al.*), *The Structure of Manufacturing Industry in Nigeria*, Ibadan, University Press, 1981.

Tims, W., *Nigeria: Options for Long Term Development*, Washington: Johns Hopkins University Press, 1974.

Abiodin, J. O., 'Aspects of the spatial impact of development efforts: a case study of Nigeria', *Tijd. Econ. Soc. Geog.*, Amsterdam, **72**(2) (1981), pp. 114–125.

Adams, W. M., 'Green revolution – by order', *Geog. Mag.*, **55**(8) (1983), pp. 405–9.

Adams, W. M., 'River basin planning in Nigeria', *Applied Geog.*, **5**(4) (1985), pp. 297–308.

Adams, W. M., 'Traditional agriculture and water use in the Sokoto valley, Nigeria', *Geog. Jnl.*, **152**(1) (1986), pp. 30–43.

Adeniyi, E. O., 'The Kainji dam: an exercise in regional development planning', *Reg. Studies*, **10**(2) (1976), pp. 233–44.

Adepoju, A., 'Development programmes and population redistribution in Nigeria', in Clarke, J. I. (*et al.*) (eds.), *Population and Development in Africa*, Cambridge University Press, 1985, pp. 194–205.

Ageni, B., 'Lagos', in Pacione, M. (ed.), *Problems and Planning in Third World Cities*, Croom Helm, 1981, pp. 127–55.

Brightmer, I., 'Kainji twenty years on', *Geog.*, **71**(1) (1986), pp. 71–73.

Dickinson, B., 'The development of the Nigerian ports system: crisis management in response to rapid economic change (1970 to 1980)', in Hoyle, B. S. and Hilling, D. (eds.), *Seaport Systems and Spatial Change*, Wiley, 1984, pp. 161–77.

Ebong, M. O., 'The planning implications of urban primacy, Lagos', *Mal. Jnl. of Tropical Geog.*, Singapore, **2**(1980), pp. 8–13.

Filani, M. O. and Onyemelukwe, J. O. C., 'Nigeria', in de Blij, H and Martin, E (eds.), *African Perspectives*, Methuen, 1981, pp.3–30.

Filani, M. O., 'The need to modify centre-down development planning', in Stöhr, W. B. and Fraser Taylor, D. R. (eds.), *Development from Above or Below*, Wiley, 1981, pp. 283–304.

Floyd, B. N., 'Agricultural planning in Nigeria', *Geog.*, **67**(4) (1982), pp. 345–7.

Forrest, T., 'Recent developments in Nigerian industrialisation', in Fransman, M. (ed.), *Industry and Accumulation in Africa*, Heinemann, 1982, pp. 324–344.
Frost, L. R., 'Recent trends in the foreign trade of Nigeria', *Geog.*, **66**(4) (1975), pp. 308–10.
Ijere, M. O., 'The impact of railways on agricultural development (Nigeria)', *Nig. Geog. Jnl.*, Ibadan, **16**(2) (1973), pp. 137–43.
Ledger, D. C., 'The Niger dams project of Nigeria', *Tijd. Econ. Soc. Geog.*, Amsterdam, **54** (1963), pp. 242–7.
Logan, M. I., 'The spatial system and planning strategies in developing countries (Nigeria)', *Geog. Rev.*, New York, **62**(2) (1972), pp. 229–44.
Melamid, A., 'The geography of the Nigerian petroleum industry', *Econ. Geog.*, Worcester, Clarke University, **44**(1) (1968), pp. 37–56.
Ogundana, B., 'Patterns and problems of seaport evolution in Nigeria', in B. S. Hoyle and D. Hilling (eds.), *Seaports and Development in Tropical Africa*, Macmillan, 1970, pp. 167–182.
Okafor, F. C., 'River basin management and food crisis in Nigeria', *Geoforum*, **16**(4) (1985), pp. 413–22.
Okpara, E. E., 'Rural urban migration and urban employment opportunities in Nigeria', *Trans. Inst. Brit. Geog.*, **11**(1) (1986), pp. 67–74.
Onyemelukwe, J. O. C., 'Industrial location policy as development strategy in Nigeria', *Nig. Geog. Jnl.*, Ibadan, **17**(2) (1974), pp. 151–63.
Oyebanji, J. O., 'Regional shifts in Nigerian manufacturing', *Urban Studies*, March 1982, pp. 361–75.
Prothero, R. Mansell, 'Nigeria loses count', *Geog. Mag.*, **47**(1) (1974), pp. 24–8.
Rogge, J., 'Balkanisation of Nigeria's federal system', *Jnl. of Geog.*, Chicago, **76**(4) (1978), pp. 135–9; **72**(2) (1978), pp. 44–5.
Sada, P. O., 'Urban growth and development in Nigeria', *Jnl. Trop. Geog.*, Singapore, **38** (1974), pp. 45–54.
Udo, R. K., 'Food deficit areas of Nigeria', *Geog. Rev.*, New York, **61**(3) (1971), pp. 415–30.
Weinard, H. C., 'Some spatial aspects of economic development in Nigeria', *Ekistics*, Athens, **36**, 214 (1973), pp. 182–8.

Part Six Equatorial Africa

26 Cameroon, Equatorial Guinea and Gabon

Cotton, A. M. and Marguerat, Y., 'Deux reseaux urbains africain – Cameroun et Côte d'Ivoire', *Cahiers d'Outre-Mer*, Bordeaux, **29** (1976), pp. 348–85.
Floyd, B. and Tandap, L., 'Intensification of agriculture in the Republique Unie du Cameronn', *Geog.*, **65**(4) (1980), pp. 324–7.
Gondolo, A., 'Evolution économique de la ville N'Gaoundéré (Cameroon)', *Cahiers d'Outre-Mer*, Bordeaux, **32**, 126 (1979), pp. 179–93.
Levrat, R., 'La place du coton dans la vie des paysans du Nord-Cameroun', *Cahiers d'Outre-Mer*, Bordeaux, **37**, 145 (1984), pp. 33–62.
Mainet, G., 'Douala: le port et la ville', *Cahiers d'Outre-Mer*, Bordeaux, **29** (113) (1976), p. 49.
Vincent, M., 'Urbanisation et dévéloppement au Cameroun', *Tiers Monde*, Paris, April–June 1984, pp. 427–36.

Liniger-Goumaz, M., 'La république de Guinée Equatoriale', *Acta. Geog.*, Paris, **43** (1980), pp. 1–22.

Bouet, C., 'Problèmes actuals de main d'oeuvre au Gabon', *Cahiers d'Outre-Mer*, Bordeaux, **31** (124) (1978), pp. 375–94.
Daverat, G., 'Un producteur africain de petrole: la Gabon', *Cahiers d'Outre-Mer*, (Bordeaux), **30**(117) (1977), pp. 31–56.
Hance, W. A., and Van Dongen, I. S., 'Gabon and its main gateways', *Tijd. Econ. Soc. Geog.*, Amsterdam, **1**(1961), pp. 286–95.
Hilling, D., 'The changing economy of Gabon', *Geog.*, **48** (1963), pp. 155–65.
Indomou, B., 'Les effets de l'urbanisation au Gabon', *Acta. Geog.*, Paris, **49**(1982), pp. 11–20.
Lebigue, J. M., 'Production vivrière et approvisionment urbain au Gabon', *Cahiers d'Outre-Mer*, Bordeaux, **33** (130) (1980), pp. 167–85.
Lotito, G., 'Le dévéloppement économique du Gabon', *Cahiers d'Outre-Mer*, Bordeaux, **23** (92) (1970), pp. 425–39.
Vennetier, P., 'Problems of port development in Gabon and Congo-Brazzaville', in Hoyle, B. S. and Hilling D. (eds.), *Seaports and Development in Tropical Africa*, Macmillan, 1970, pp. 183–201.

Daveau, S., 'L'ile de São Tomé', *Cahiers d'Outre-Mer*, Bordeaux, **15** (1962), pp. 92–5.

27 Congo and the Central African Republic

Hilling, D., 'Routes to the sea for land-locked states', *Geog. Mag.*, **44**(4) (1972), pp. 257–64.
Prioul, C. L., 'L'industrie et le commerce en République Centrafricaine', *Cahiers d'Outre-Mer*, Bordeaux, **22**(88) (1969), pp. 408–29.

Auger, A., 'Congo', in de Blij, H. and Martin, E. (eds.) *African Perspectives*, Methuen, 1981, pp. 193–225.
Denis, J., 'Pointe Noire', *Cahiers d'Outre-Mer*, Bordeaux, **8**(1955), pp. 350–68.
Vennetier, P., 'La navigation interieure en Afrique Noire: le reseau francais Congo-Dubangui', *Cahiers d'Outre-Mer*, Bordeaux, **12**(1959), pp. 321–48.
Vennetier, P., 'Population et économie du Congo-Brazzaville', *Cahiers d'Outre-Mer*, Bordeaux, **15**(1962), pp. 360–81.

Vennetier, P., 'La societé industrielle et agricole du Niari', *Cahiers d'Outre-Mer*, Bordeaux, **16**(1963), pp. 43–80.

Vennetier, P., 'Les transport dans le nord du Congo-Brazzaville', *Cahiers d'Outre-Mer*, Bordeaux, **16**(1963), pp. 126–32.

28 Zaire, Rwanda and Burundi

Gerster, G., 'River of sorrow, river of hope (Zaire)', *Nat. Geog. Mag.*, Washington, **148** (2) (1975), pp. 152–89.

Hance, W. A. and Van Dongen, I. S., 'Matadi, focus of Belgian African transport', *Ann. Assn. Am. Geog.*, Washington, **48**(1958), pp. 41–72.

Katzenellenbogen, S. E., *Railways and the copper mines of Katanga*, Oxford University Press, 1973.

Lerat, S., 'Une region industriélle au coeur de l'Afrique: la Katanga meridional', *Cahiers d'Outre-Mer*, Bordeaux, **14**(1961), pp. 435–42.

MacGaffey, J., 'How to survive and become rich amidst poverty. The second economy in Zaire', *African Affairs*, **82**(328) (1983), pp. 351–66.

Reemans, J. P. L., 'The social and economic development of Zaire since independence', *African Affairs*, **72**(295) (1975), pp. 148–79.

Charnock, A., 'Tiny Burundi has big plans for the future', *Geog. Mag.*, **55**(7) (1983), pp. 357–61.

Decondras, P. M., 'Burundi: le problème des voies d'approvisionment', *Cahiers d'Outre-Mer*, Bordeaux, **37**(141) (1984), pp. 205–34.

Bart, I., 'Le café dans l'agriculture rwandoise', *Cahiers d'Outre-Mer*, Bordeaux, **33**(132) (1980), pp. 301–17.

Gotanegre, J. F., 'La banane au Rwanda', *Cahiers d'Outre-Mer*, Bordeaux, **36**(144) (1983), pp. 311–42.

Rossi, G., 'Evolution des versants et mise en valeur agricole au Rwanda', *Ann. de Geog.*, Paris, **92**(515) (1984), pp. 23–43.

Vennetier, P., 'Une micro-realisation de dévéloppement agro-artisanal au Rwanda', *Cahiers d'Outre-Mer*, Bordeaux, **31**(123) (1978), pp. 209–24.

Part Seven South-Western Africa

30 Angola, Namibia and Botswana

Harvey, C. (ed.), *Papers on the Economy of Botswana*, Heinemann, 1981.

Moorsom, R., *Walvis Bay – Namibia's Port*, International Defence and Aid Fund, London, 1984.

Cooke, H. J., 'The Kalahari today: a case of conflict over resource use', *Geog. Jnl.*, **11** (1985), pp. 75–85.

Hance, W. A. and Van Dongen, I. S., 'The port of Lobito and the Benguela railway', *Geog. Rev.*, New York, **46** (1956), pp. 460–87.

Stone, P. B., 'New development in south Angola', *S. Afr. Geog. Jnl.*, Johannesburg, **39** (1957), pp. 55–60.

Van Dongen, I. S., 'Coffee trade, coffee regions and coffee ports in Angola', *Econ. Geog.*, **37** (1961), pp. 320–46.

Teixeira Pinto, L. M. and Martins dos Santos, R., 'Problems of economic development in Angola', in Robinson, E. A. G. (ed.), *Economic Development for Africa south of the Sahara*, London, 1964.

Van Dongen, I. S., 'La vie économique et les ports de l'enclave de Cabinda', *Cahiers d'Outre-Mer*, Bordeaux, **15**(1962), pp. 5–24.

Whittlesey, D. S., 'Geographic provinces of Angola', *Geog. Rev.*, New York, **14**(1924), pp. 113–26.

Whittington, G., 'Iron mining in Angola', *Geog.*, **49**(1964), pp. 418–19.

Best, A. C. C., 'Gaberone: problem and prospects of a new capital', *Geog. Rev.*, New York, **60**(1) (1970), pp. 1–14.

Parson, J., 'Cattle, class and state in rural Botswana', *Jnl. Southern African Studies*, **7** (1981), pp. 236–55.

Taylor, J., 'Some consequences of recent reductions in mine labour recruitment in Botswana', *Geog.*, **71**(1) (1986), pp. 34–46.

Logan, R. F., 'Namibia', in de Blij, H. and Martins, E. (eds.), *African Perspectives*, Methuen, 1981, pp. 173–92.

Simon, D., 'Recent trends in Namibian urbanisation', *Tijd. Econ. Soc. Geog.*, Amsterdam, **73**(4) (1982), pp. 200–212.

Simon, D., 'Independence and social transformation: urban planning problems and priorities for Namibia', *Third World Planning Review*, **7**(2) (1985), pp. 99–118.

Sparks, D. L., 'Namibia's coastal and marine development potential', *African Affairs*, **83** (333) (1984), pp. 477–98.

Weigend, G. G., 'German settlement patterns in Namibia', *Geog. Rev.*, New York, **75**(2) (1985), pp. 156–69.

Part Eight South Africa

31 Physical framework – 32 Population and settlement – 33 Farming, fishing and forestry – 34 Mining and manufacturing

Bell, T., *Industrial Decentralisation in South Africa*, Cape Town: Oxford University Press, 1973.

Cole, M. M., *South Africa*, Methuen, 1961.

Fair, T. J. D., *South Africa: Spatial Frameworks for Development*, Cape Town, 1982.

Jackson, S. P. and Tyson, P. D., *Aspects of Weather and Climate over Southern Africa*, Dept of Geography, University of Witwatersrand, 1971.

King, L. C., *South Africa Scenery*, Oliver and Boyd, 1963.

Lanning, G. and Mueller, M., *Africa Undermined*, Penguin, 1979.

Lemor, A., *Apartheid: a Geography of Separation*, Saxon House, 1976.

Natrass, J., *The South African Economy: its Growth and Change*, Cape Town, Oxford University Press, 1981.

Palmer, R. and Parsons, N. (eds.), *The Roots of Rural Poverty in Central and Southern Africa*, Heinemann, 1977.

Smith, D. M. (ed.), *Living Under Apartheid*, George Allen and Unwin, 1982.

Beavon, K. S. O. and Rogerson, C. M., 'Trekking on: recent trends in the human geography of Southern Africa', *Progress in Human Geography*, **5**(1981), pp. 159–89.

Beavon, K. S. O., 'Black townships in South Africa: terra incognita for urban geographers, *S. Afr. Geog. Jnl.*, Johannesburg, **64**(1) (1982).

Belcher, T., 'Industrial decentralisation and dynamics of forced labour in South Africa', *Jnl. Mod. Afr. Studies*, **17**(1979), pp. 677–86.

Best, A. C. G., 'South Africa's border industries: the Tswana example', *Ann. Assn. Amer. Geog.*, Washington, **61**(1971), pp. 329–44.

Best, A. C. G., and Young, B. S., 'Homeland consolidation: the case of Kwa Zulu', *South African Geographer*, Dennesig, South Africa, **4**(1972), pp. 63–74.

Board, C., Davies, R. J. and Fair, T. J. D., 'The structure of the South African space economy: an integrated approach', *Regional Studies*, **4**(1970), pp. 367–92.

Brookfield, H. C., 'Some geographical implications of the apartheid and partnership policies in southern Africa, *Trans. Inst. Brit. Geogrs.*, **23**(1957), pp. 225–47.

Browett, J. G., 'The application of a spatial model to South Africa's development regions', *South African Geog. Jnl.*, Johannesburg, **58** (1976), pp. 118–29.

Browett, J. G., 'Export base theory and the evolution of the South African space economy', *South African Geog. Jnl.*, Johannesburg, **59**(1977), pp. 18–29.

Browett, J. G., 'The evolution of unequal development within South Africa: an overview', in Smith, D. M. (ed.), *Living Under Apartheid*, George Allen and Unwin, 1982, pp. 10–23.

Christopher, A. J., 'Government land policies in Southern Africa', in Ironside, R. G. (ed.), *Frontier Settlement*, Dept of Geography, University of Alberta, 1974, pp. 208–25.

Christopher, A. J., 'The variability of the southern African standard farm', *South African Geog. Jnl.*, Johannesburg, **58**(1976), pp. 107–17.

Cowley, J. and Lemon, A., 'Bothuthatswana: dependent development in a Black "Homeland"', *Geog.*, **71**(3) (1986), pp. 252–55.

Davies, R. J., 'The South African urban hierachy', South African Geog. Jnl., Johannesburg, **49**(1967), pp. 9–19.

Phillips, E., 'State regulation and economic initiatives: the South African case', *Int. J. Afr. Hist. Studies*, Boston, Mass. **7**(1974), pp. 227–54.

Robinson, D. A., 'Agrarian crisis and change', *Geog. Mag.* **VLIII (8)** (1986), pp. 395–9.

Rogerson, C. M. and Letsoalo, E. M., 'Rural underdevelopment, poverty and apartheid: the closer settlements of Lebowa, South Africa'. *Tijd. Econ. Soc. Geog.*, Amsterdam, **72**(1981), pp. 347–61.

Rogerson, C. M. and Letsoala, E. M., 'Resettlement and underdevelopment in the black homelands of South Africa', in Clarke J. I. (*et al.*) (eds.), *Population and Development in Africa*, Cambridge University Press, 1975, pp. 176–93.

Rogerson, C. M. and Pirie, G. H., 'Apartheid, urbanisation and planning in South Africa', in Obudho, R. and El Shaklis, S. (eds.), *Development of Urban Systems in Africa*, New York, Praeger, 1979, pp. 323–44.

Smith, D. M., *Separation in South Africa: I People and politics; II Homelands and cities*, London, Queen Mary College, Dept of Geography, Occasional Papers Nos. 6 and 7, 1976.

Taylor, J., 'Changing patterns of labour supply to the South Africa gold mines', *Tidj. Econ. Soc. Geog.*, Amsterdam, **73**(1982), pp. 213–20.

Tyson, P. D., Dyer, T. G. J. and Mametse, M. M., 'Secular changes in South African rainfall 1880–1972', *Quart. J. R. Met. Soc.*, **101** (1975), pp. 817–33.

Wiese, B., 'The role of seaports in the industrial decentralisation process: the case of South Africa', in Hoyle, B. S. and Hilling, D. (eds.), *Seaport Systems and Spatial Change*, Chichester, Wiley, 1984, pp. 415–34.

Williams, D., 'South Africa', in de Blij, H. and Martin, E. (eds.), *African Perspectives*, Methuen, 1981, pp. 31–57.

Williams, Geoffrey J., 'The geopolitics of minerals', *Geog. Mag.* **LVIII(a)** (1986), pp. 450–6.

Wood, A., 'The human "mosaic"', *Geog. Mag.*, **LVIII(4)** (1986), pp. 171–6.

35 Lesotho and Swaziland

Perry, J. W. B., 'Lesotho', in de Blij, H. and Martin, E. (eds.), *African Perspectives*, Methuen, 1981, pp. 227–58.

Williams, J. C., 'Lesotho: economic implications of migrant labour', *S. Afr. J. Econ.*, Johannesburg, **39**(1971), pp. 149–78.

Fair, T. J. D. and Maasdorp, G. G., 'Swaziland', in de Blij, H. and Martin, E. (eds.), *African Perspectives*, Methuen, 1981, pp. 115–35.

Part Nine The Zambezi and Limpopo Lands

37 Zambia

Griffiths, I. L., Zambia coal: An example of strategic resource development', *Geog. Rev.*, **58**(1968), pp. 538–51.

Mihalyi, L. J., 'Electricity and electrification for Zambia', *Geog. Rev.*, **67**(1977), pp. 63–70.

38 Zimbabwe

Kay, G. and Smout, M., *Salisbury*, Hodder and Stoughton, 1977.

Kay, G., 'Zimbabwe's independence: Geographical problems and prospects', *Geog. Jnl.*, **147**(1981), pp. 179–87.

Stocking, M. and Elwell H., 'Rainfall erosivity over Rhodesia', *Trans. Inst. Brit. Geogrs.*, **1** (NS) (1976), pp. 231–45.

Williams, G. J., 'The changing electrical power industry in the middle Zambezi Valley', *Geog.*, **69**(1984), pp. 257–61.

Williams, O., 'Irrigation farming in the south-east Lowveld of Zimbabwe', *Geog.*, **66**(1981), pp. 228–32.

Zinyama, L. M., 'Post independence land resettlement in Zimbabwe', *Geog.*, **67**(1982), pp. 149–52.

Zinyama, L. M., 'Agricultural development policies in the African farming areas of Zimbabwe', *Geog.*, **71**(1986), pp. 105–15.

39 Malawi

Meliczek, H., 'Land settlement in Malawi', *Land Reform* (1977), pp. 55–68.

Perry, J., 'Malawi's new outlet to the sea', *Geog.*, **56**(1971), pp. 138–40.

40 Mozambique

Connell, J., 'Southern African power (Cabora Bassa)', *Geog. Mag.*, **XLIV**(1972), pp. 669–71.

Fitzpatrick, J., 'The economy of Mozambique: problems and prospects', *Third World Quarterly.*, **3** (1981), pp. 77–87.

Part Ten East Africa and the Islands

41 Physical geography

Atlases of Tanganyika, Kenya and Uganda, 1956, 1959, 1962.

Cook, A., 'Resource assessment in East Africa', *Geog.*, **64** (1979), pp. 96–103.

Hills, R. C., 'The organization of rainfall in East Africa', *Jnl. Tropical Geog.*, **47**(1978), pp.40–50.

Hills, R. C., 'East African rainfall and Inter-Tropical Convergence Zone structure', *Trans. Inst. Brit. Geogrs.*, **4** (NS) (1979), pp. 329–52.

Hirst, M. A., 'Tribal migration in East Africa', *Geografiska Annaler*, **52b**(1970), pp. 153–63.

Hoyle, B. S., 'Major seaports in East Africa', in Hoyle, B. S. and Hilling, D. (eds.), *Seaports and development in Tropical Africa*, London, 1970.

42 Kenya

International Bank, *Economic development of Kenya*, Baltimore, 1962.

Ogendo, R. B., *Industrial geography of Kenya*, Nairobi, 1972.

Campbell, D. J., 'The prospect for desertification in Kadjiado District, Kenya', *Geog. Jnl.*, **152** (1986), pp. 44–55.

Carey Jones, N. S., 'Decolonisation of the White Highlands of Kenya', *Geog. Jnl.*, **129** (1963), pp. 186–201.

Ferraro, G., 'Nairobi: Overview of an East African city', *African Urban Studies*, **3**(1978), pp. 1–13.

Freeman, D. and Norcliffe, G., 'National and regional patterns of rural non-farm employment in Kenya', *Geog.*, **69**(1984), pp. 221–33.

Jackson, R. T., 'Problems of tourist industry development on the Kenyan coast', *Geog.*, **58**(1973), pp. 62–5.

Morgan, W. T., 'Urbanisation in Kenya', *Trans Inst. Brit. Geogrs.*, **46**(1969), pp. 167–78.

43 Uganda

International Bank, *Economic development of Uganda*, Baltimore, 1962.

Hoyle, B. S., 'The economic expansion of Jinja, Uganda', in Dwyer, D. J. (ed.), *The City in the Third World*, Macmillan, 1974.

McMaster D., 'Uganda; Initiatives in agriculture 1886–1966, *Spec. Public. No. 1*, Inst. Brit. Geogrs. (1968), pp. 241–58.

Turner, B. J. and Randall, P. R., 'Tsetse control and livestock development. A case study from Uganda', *Geog.*, **53**(1968), pp. 249–59.

44 Tanzania

International Bank, *Economic development of Tanganyika*, Baltimore, 1961.

Darkoh, M. B., 'Desertification in Tanzania', *Geog.*, **67** (1982), pp. 320–1.

Hirst, M. A., 'A functional analysis of towns in Tanzania', *Tijd. v. Econ. en Soc Geog.*, **64** (1973), pp. 39–51.
Hirst, M., 'A recent villagization in Tanzania', *Geog.*, **63** (1978), pp. 122–5.
Hoyle, B. S., 'African politics and port expansion at Dar-es-Salaam', *Geog. Rev.*, **68** (1978), pp. 31–50.
Hoyle, B. S., 'African socialism and urban development: the relocation of the Tanzanian capital', *Tijd. v. Econ. en Soc. Geog.*, **70** (1979), pp. 207–16.
Perkins, F. C., 'Technology choice, Industrialisation and Development experiences in Tanzania', *Jnl. Dev. Studies*, **19**(1983), pp. 213–43.
Stren, R. E., 'Underdevelopment, urban squatter, and the state of bureaucracy: a case study of Tanzania', *Can. Jnl. Af. Studies*, **16**(1982), pp. 67–91.

45 Madagascar and the Mascarene Islands

Charpantier, J., 'Les Comores: économie agricole et transports', *Cahiers d'Outre-Mer* (1971), pp. 158–84.
Cracknell, C., 'La Réunion and Mauritius: Islands in the Indian Ocean', *Geog. Mag.*, **XLVI**(1974), pp. 641–6.
Earle, J., 'Mauritius diversifies for economic survival', *Geog. Mag.*, **XLIV**(1972), pp. 300–4.
Hance, W. A., 'Ports and economic integration in Madagascar', in Hoyle, B. S. and Hilling, D. (eds.), *Seaports and development in Tropical Africa*, Macmillan, 1970.

Index

Acknowledgements

The authors and publishers would like to thank the copyright holders below for the use of photographic illustrations.

Akwe Amosu, Plate 39; Anglo-American Corporation of South Africa, Plate 63; Bilfinger and Berger, Plates 10, 33, 36; O. Carr-Forster, Plate 41; J. Allan Cash Photolibrary, Plates 14, 58; M. Collins, Plate 13; The Commonwealth Development Corporation, Plates 34, 40, 46, 47, 49, 52, 55; D. Hilling, Plates 1, 3, 4, 5, 7, 11, 12, 25, 26, 27, 28, 29, 30, 31, 37; B. S. Hoyle, Plate 56; Hutchison Library, Plates 17, 38, 51; International Fund for Agricultural Development, Plate 57; T. Mahanadi, Plate 24; A. B. Mountjoy, Plates 6, 9, 19, 20, 22; Mozambique Information Office (Paul Fauvet), Plate 53; Oxfam (Bill Wise), Plate 23; Picturepoint, London, Plates 18, 50; Shell Photographic Library, Plate 32; K. Sutton, Plates 15, 16; South African Bureau of Information, Plates 42, 44; South African Department of Water Affairs, Plate 45; Sudan Government, Plate 21; World Bank, Plates 35, 54; UNICEF (Hewitt), Plate 8; UN (Isaac), Plate 2.